www.wadsworth.com

wadsworth.com is the World Wide Web site for Wadsworth and is your direct source to dozens of online resources.

At *wadsworth.com* you can find out about supplements, demonstration software, and student resources. You can also send email to many of our authors and preview new publications and exciting new technologies.

wadsworth.com
Changing the way the world learns®

Child, Family, School, Community

SOCIALIZATION AND SUPPORT

SIXTH EDITION

Roberta M. Berns

University of California, Irvine
Saddleback College (Emeritus)

THOMSON
WADSWORTH

Australia • Canada • Mexico • Singapore • Spain
United Kingdom • United States

THOMSON

WADSWORTH

Education Editor: *Dan Alpert*
Development Editor: *Tangelique Williams*
Editorial Assistant: *Heather Kazakoff*
Technology Project Manager: *Barry Connolly*
Marketing Manager: *Dory Schaeffer*
Marketing Assistant: *Neena Chandra*
Advertising Project Manager: *Shemika Britt*
Project Manager, Editorial Production: *Trudy Brown*
Print/Media Buyer: *Doreen Suruki*
Permissions Editor: *Beth Zuber*

Production Service: *Strawberry Field Publishing*
Text Designer: *Ellen Pettengell*
Photo Researcher: *Terri Wright*
Copy Editor: *Tom Briggs*
Cover Designer: *Laurie Anderson*
Cover Images: *Large photo: Mel Curtis, PhotoDisc. Small photos, top to bottom: Getty Images; Getty Images; David Young-Wolff/ PhotoEdit; Andersen Ross, PhotoDisc.*
Compositor: *Carlisle Communications, Ltd.*
Text and Cover Printer: *Phoenix Color Corp*

For more information about our products, contact us at:
Thomson Learning Academic Resource Center
1-800-423-0563
For permission to use material from this text, contact us by:
Phone: 1-800-730-2214
Fax: 1-800-730-2215
Web: http://www.thomsonrights.com

Library of Congress Control Number: 2002117701
ISBN 0-534-52519-9

Wadsworth/Thomson Learning
10 Davis Drive
Belmont, CA 94002-3098
USA

Asia
Thomson Learning
5 Shenton Way #01-01
UIC Building
Singapore 068808

Australia/New Zealand
Thomson Learning
102 Dodds Street
Southbank, Victoria 3006
Australia

Canada
Nelson
1120 Birchmount Road
Toronto, Ontario M1K 5G4
Canada

Europe/Middle East/Africa
Thomson Learning
High Holborn House
50/51 Bedford Row
London WC1R 4LR
United Kingdom

Latin America
Thomson Learning
Seneca, 53
Colonia Polanco
11560 Mexico D.F.
Mexico

Spain/Portugal
Paraninfo
Calle/Magallanes, 25
28015 Madrid, Spain

I dedicate this book to significant people in my life:

My Children—Gregory and Tamara (Their spouses—Kathleen and Alexander)

My Grandchildren—Helen and Madeline

My Family—husband, Michael, brother, parents, and grandparents

My School—Cornell University (Dr. Urie Bronfenbrenner), University of California, Irvine and Saddleback College (my colleagues and students)

My Community—New York (past) and California (present)

Contents

Preface xv

Chapter 1   **Ecology of the Child 1**

Prologue: Then and Now 2

Ecology, Change, and Children 3

Socialization and Child Development 3
    Socialization as a Unique Human Process 4
    Socialization as a Reciprocal Dynamic Process 4
    Socialization as an Intentional and Unintentional Process 7

Socialization, Change, and Challenge 8
    Parents, Children, and Social Change 8
    Change and the Concept of Childhood 10
    Change and Socialization 12

Examining Socialization in an Ecological Context 14
    Microsystems 15
    Mesosystems 16
    Exosystems 16
    Macrosystems 17

Interaction of Ecological Systems Over Time: The Chronosystem 19

Society, Change, and Consequences 23
    Change and Societal Trends 23
    Change and Consequences 26

Epilogue 28

Summary 29

Activity 30

Research Terms 30

Related Readings 30

Chapter 2   **Ecology of Socialization 32**

Prologue: Then and Now 33

Aims of Socialization 34
    Develop a Self-Concept 34
    Enable Self-Regulation 39
    Empower Achievement 39
    Acquire Appropriate Social Roles 40
    Implement Developmental Skills 40

Agents of Socialization 42
The Family 44
Schools and Child Care 47
Peers 48
Mass Media 49
The Community 50

Methods of Socialization 52
Affective Methods (Effect Emerges from Feeling) 52
Operant Methods (Effect Emerges from Acting) 54
Observational Methods (Effect Emerges from Imitating) 60
Cognitive Methods: Effect Emerges from Information Processing 61
Sociocultural Methods (Effect Emerges from Conforming) 64
Apprenticeship Methods (Effect Emerges from Guided Participation) 68

Outcomes of Socialization 69
Values 69
Attitudes 69
Motives and Attributes 69
Self-Esteem 70
Self-Regulation/Behavior 70
Morals 71
Gender Roles 72

Epilogue 72

Summary 73

Activity 74

Research Terms 74

Related Readings 74

Chapter 3

Ecology of the Family 76

Prologue: Then and Now 77

Family Systems 78
Basic Structures 79
Basic Functions 81

Family Transitions 82
Structural Changes 82
Functional Changes 96

Macrosystem Influences on Families, Socialization, and Children 101
Socioeconomic Status 101
Ethnic Orientation 108
Religious Orientation 111

Chronosystem Influences on Families, Socialization, and Children 113
Sociopolitical Changes 114
Economic Changes 114
Technological Changes 115

Meeting the Challenge of Change: Family Empowerment 116

Epilogue 118

Summary 118

Activity 119

Research Terms 120

Related Readings 120

 Chapter 4

Ecology of Parenting 121

Prologue: Then and Now 122

Parenting 123

Macrosystem Influences on Parenting 124
Political Ideology 125
Culture 126
Socioeconomic Status 129
Ethnicity/Religion 131

Chronosystem Influences on Parenting 138
Historical Trends 138
Family Dynamics 141

Parenting Styles 150
Microsystem Influences: Between Parent and Child 150
Mesosystem Influences: Between Parent and Others 156

Appropriate Parenting Practices 158
Developmental Appropriateness 159
Guidance and Discipline 159

Inappropriate Parenting Practices 159
Child Maltreatment: Abuse and Neglect 160
Correlates and Consequences of Child Maltreatment 163

Epilogue 167

Summary 167

Activity 169

Research Terms 169

Related Readings 169

Chapter 5

Ecology of Child Care 171

Prologue: Then and Now 172

Child Care 172
What Is Quality Care? 174
Macrosystem Influences on Child Care 178
Chronosystem Influences on Child Care 179

Correlates and Consequences of Child Care 181
Child Care and Psychological Development 181
Child Care and Social Development 184
Child Care and Cognitive Development 184

Mesosystem Influences on Child Care 186
Child Care and the School and Community 188

Child Care and the Government and Business 189

Child Care and Socialization 191
Socialization Effects of Different Preschool Programs 191
Socialization Effects of Child Care Ideologies 197

Developmentally Appropriate Caregiving 200
Collaborative Caregiving 200
Caregivers and Child Protection 202

Epilogue 206

Summary 206

Activity 208

Research Terms 208

Related Readings 208

Chapter 6

Ecology of the School 210

Prologue: Then and Now 211

The School's Function as a Socializing Agent 212

Macrosystem Influences on Schools 214
Factors in Educational Decisions 214
School Choice 216
Diversity and Equity: Gender, Ethnicity, Religion, and Special Needs 217

Chronosystem Influences on Schools 228
Adaptations to Social Change 229
Technology 231
Violence 232
Substance Use/Abuse 234

Mesosystem Influences 236
School-Child Linkages 236
School-Family Linkages 237
School-Peer Group Linkages 242
School-Media Linkages 243
School-Community Linkages 244

Epilogue 246

Summary 246

Activity 248

Research Terms 248

Related Readings 248

Chapter 7

Ecology of Teaching 249

Prologue: Then and Now 250

The Teacher's Role as a Socializing Agent 250

Teacher Characteristics and Student Learning 252
Teachers as Leaders 253
Teachers as Managers 255
Teacher Expectations 255

Student Characteristics and Teacher Interaction 257
  Gender 257
  Ethnicity 258
  Learning Styles 263
  Disability 266
  Children at Risk: Poverty, Substance Abuse, and Violence 270

Macrosystem and Chronosystem Influences on Teaching 276
  Philosophies of Teaching and Learning 277
  Socialization Outcomes of Different Classroom Contexts 279
  Accountability and Standardization 282

Mesosystem Influences on Teaching 282
  Families Empowering Student Success: Involvement in Learning 283
  Schools Empowering Student Success: Developmentally Appropriate Learning
    and Assessment 285

Epilogue 285

Summary 285

Activity 287

Research Terms 288

Related Readings 288

Ecology of the Peer Group 289

Prologue: Then and Now 290

The Peer Group as a Socializing Agent 291
  The Significance of Peers to Development 291
  Psychological Development: Emotions 297
  Social Development: Social Competence 297
  Cognitive Development: Social Cognition 299
  Peer Group Socializing Mechanisms 301

Macrosystem Influences on the Peer Group: Developmental Tasks 306
  Getting Along with Others 306
  Developing Morals and Values 307
  Learning Appropriate Sociocultural Roles 309
  Achieving Personal Independence and Identity 312

Chronosystem Influences on the Peer Group: Play/Activities 314
  The Significance and Development of Play 314
  Infant/Toddler Peer Activities (Birth to Age 2) 316
  Early Childhood Peer Activities (Age 2–5) 317
  Middle Childhood/Preadolescent Peer Activities (Age 6–12) 317
  Adolescent Peer Activities (Age 13 and Up) 319

Peer Group Interaction 319
  Development of Friendship 319
  Acceptance/Neglect/Rejection by Peers 321
  Peer Sociotherapy 323
  Peer Group Dynamics and Social Hierarchies 326
  Inclusion and Exclusion 326
  Bullies/Victims 327
  Gangs 328
  Peer Collaboration, Tutoring, and Counseling 329

Mesosystem Influences on the Peer Group 330
  Adult-Mediated Group Interaction 331
  Adult Leadership Styles 332
  Team Sports 333

Epilogue 334

Summary 335

Activity 337

Research Terms 338

Related Readings 338

Chapter 9

Ecology of the Mass Media 339

Prologue: Then and Now 340

Understanding Mass Media 342

Chronosystem Influences on Mass Media 345

Macrosystem Influences on Mass Media 346

Pictorial Media: Television and Movies 349
  Concerns About Television and Movies 350
  Mediating Influences on Socialization Outcomes 363
  Mesosystem Influences 366

Print Media: Books and Magazines 371
  The Power of Print Media: Literacy 371
  How Books and Magazines Socialize Children 372
  Concerns About Books and Magazines 374
  Books, Socialization, and Developmental Levels of Children 378

Sound Media: Popular Music 379

Interactive Media and Multimedia 382
  Computers and the Internet 382

Epilogue 385

Summary 385

Activity 387

Research Terms 387

Related Readings 388

Chapter 10

Ecology of the Community 389

Prologue: Then and Now 390

Community: Structure and Functions 391

The Community's Influence on Socialization 393
  Physical Factors 395
  Economic Factors 398
  Social and Personal Factors 399

The Community as a Learning Environment 403

The Community as a Support System 404

Chronosystem and Macrosystem Influences on Community Services 404
Preventive, Supportive, and Rehabilitative Services 405

Creating Caring Communities 412
Economic Assistance 413
Health Care 417
Support for Families 418
Special Child Care Services 421

Mesosystem Influences: Linking Community Services to Families and Schools 422

Involvement and Advocacy 425
Types of Advocacy Groups 425
Child Protection and Maltreatment 426

Epilogue 430

Summary 430

Activity 431

Research Terms 435

Related Readings 435

Chapter 11   Affective/Cognitive Socialization Outcomes 436

Prologue: Then and Now 437

Values 438
Values, Decisions, and Consequences 441

Attitudes 443
Development of Attitudes 443
Influences of Significant Socializing Agents on Attitude Development 445
Changing Attitudes About Diversity 450

Motives and Attributes 452
Achievement Motivation 453
Locus of Control 457
Learned Helplessness 461
Self-Efficacy 463

Self-Esteem 464
Development of Self-Esteem 466
Influences on the Development of Self-Esteem 468

Epilogue 474

Summary 475

Activity 476

Research Terms 478

Related Readings 478

Chapter 12   Social/Behavioral Socialization Outcomes 480

Prologue: Then and Now 481

Self-Regulation/Behavior 482

Antisocial Behavior: Aggression 485
Prosocial Behavior: Altruism 494

Morals 504
Development of a Moral Code 504
Influences on Moral Development 512

Gender Roles 522
Development of Gender Roles 522
Gender-Role Research 524
Influences on the Development of Gender Roles 525

Epilogue 534

Summary 534

Activity 536

Research Terms 536

Related Readings 537

Appendix A Developmental Tasks in Ten Categories of Behavior of the Individual from Birth to Death 538

Appendix B Basic Parenting Styles 542

Appendix C How to Choose a Good Early Childhood Program 543

Appendix D Teaching Strategies for Young Children Who Have Specific Disabilities* 547

Appendix E Teacher Observation Form for Identifying Preschool Children Who May Require Additional Services 551

Glossary 554

References 561

Photo Credits 601

Index 603

Preface

Purpose

I wrote *Child, Family, School, Community: Socialization and Support,* Sixth Edition, to reconfirm and document the most basic theory of relationships known to humankind—that people need people to survive. Children need supportive adults, as well as other children; adults need a supportive community, including other adults; and children are the core of society, nurtured by it and for it. The first edition of the text focused on the child socialization process. The second edition added information about how societal support can empower children and their families. The third edition featured ethnic diversity's influence in socialization. The fourth edition expanded the title and emphasized the role of school and child care as socializing agents in a changing society and embraced the concept of inclusion (that all children should have equal access to appropriate educational opportunities). The fifth edition emphasized the bidirectionality of interactions between children and various socialization agents, illustrating the

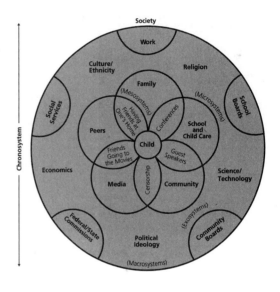

child's role in his or her own socialization. This sixth edition utilizes ecological systems theory as a model for organization and demonstrates the influence of the chronosystem (changes over time) on contexts in which children develop.

Audience

Child, Family, School, Community is for anyone who deals with children—parents, teachers, and professionals in human services, family and consumer studies, public health, psychology, and social work. It is an introductory text for the combination of disciplines that most affect children's development. It can be used for both lower- and upper-division courses, such as child and community relationships and child socialization. I have used it at both the community college and the university level by varying the type and depth of assignments.

Distinguishing Features

Child, Family, School, Community is distinctive because of its comprehensive coverage. It integrates the contexts in which children develop, the relationships of the people in those contexts, and the interactions that take place within and between contexts. It also addresses the need for parents and professionals who work with children to enable all children to adapt optimally to a changing world.

As the title of the book indicates, when one is concerned about children's development, one must also be concerned with the contexts in which children develop. For example, the teacher is concerned with children's families because when children come to school they bring with them their attitudes toward learning, experiences in dealing with others, and self-concepts, all of which germinated in the family. To enhance each child's development, the teacher must work with the child's family and communicate goals, be supportive of the family's values, and enlist the family's cooperation to provide optimal learning experiences.

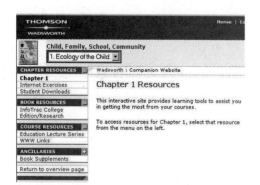

The professional is concerned with the child's family because when the child has a problem, whether it be emotional, intellectual, social, or physical, the professional must work with the family to determine the cause, develop a treatment plan, and evaluate the results.

Parents, teachers, and professionals are concerned with communities (including the peer group, media, and neighborhood) because communities make certain decisions that affect children. For example, a community shows its support for children in the way that it allocates its tax money for schools, services, libraries, and so on. A community also shows support for children via its business policies, such as maternal or paternal leave, flextime, and child care.

Ancillaries to the text include a student study guide, an instructor's manual, and a companion Web site.

Themes and Pedagogy

To provide an optimal environment for children's growth and development, parents need knowledge and skills, as well as support. To get or give support (psychological, financial, medical, or political), one must understand the roles of people and environments in the lives of children. Thus, I analyze the socialization influences of the family, child care, the school, the peer group, the mass media, and the community on children's development. I explain how the dynamic and reciprocal interactions of these agents, with children and with each other, contribute to the outcomes of socialization—values, attitudes, motives and attributes, self-esteem, self-regulation/behavior, morals, and gender roles. I also illustrate how children with special needs due to maltreatment, disability, and/or diverse family backgrounds, can be empowered via socialization supports.

I present both classic research and contemporary studies on children, families, schools, and communities, according to the ecological approach, to enable students to understand the many settings and interactions influencing development. The ecology of human development encompasses the disciplines of biology, psychology, sociology, anthropology, and education as they affect individuals in society.

Prologue | *Then and Now*

COLLABORATIVE CAREGIVING

THEN A classic fictional caregiving story, *Λ* Pamela Travers, tells of the adventures that Jane and Michael Banks. Jane and Michael

Whenever one analyzes something, one takes it apart and evaluates its components. Occasionally, in the process, one loses sight of the whole. I tried to avoid this by including a range of pedagogical features including:

- chapter outlines
- prologues as advance organizers (classic stories compared to modern ones with questions to stimulate critical thinking about the chapter)
- case studies
- examples
- "points to ponder" (open-ended questions to personalize bioecological concepts emphasizing bidirectionality)
- bold-faced glossary terms
- epilogues as conclusions to the prologues
- chapter summaries
- applications and activities in each chapter to enable the student to experience the relationship between theory and practice
- on-line research terms and book resources. The symbol (⚘) refers to the InfoTrac College Edition online library—a Thomson Learning exclusive. Access InfoTrac by following the instructions on the post card enclosed with every new copy of this textbook. Research terms can be entered into the powerful InfoTrac College Edition search engine. This world-class, online library offers full text articles from thousands of scholarly and popular publications.

Because our society is changing so rapidly, a major concern of parents, professionals, and politicians is how to socialize children for an unknown future. What skills can we impart? What knowledge should we teach? What traditions do we keep? The impact of historical changes on society is discussed to help us deal with future ones.

> **EXAMPLE** My mother wanted to learn how to use the word processing program on my computer. I demonstrated a few commands and let her practice, telling her to call me if she got stuck. When she felt she had mastered the basics, I showed her how to do more complicated things. With my assistance, my mother was able to learn more quickly than she would have on her own.

Points to Ponder

Perception is a biological construct that involves interpretation of stimuli by the brain. Factors such as maturation, attentiveness, past experiences, and emotions influence people's perception of things, events, and interactions. How did a teacher influence your perception of an event such as a Shakespeare play or the attack on the World Trade Center?

Activity

PURPOSE *To increase your awareness of television's impact.*

1. Monitor a child's (or your own) television viewing behavior for a week, using the accompanying as a model.
2. Note the total viewing hours for the week.
3. Keep track of the time spent on other leisure activities for a week.
4. Analyze your findings to determine what types of shows are viewed and what the impact of their content and commercial messages on viewers might be.

DAY AND TIME	NAME AND TYPE* OF SHOW	DESCRIPTION OF ACTION (CONFLICTS COOPERATION)	DESCRIPTION OF ROLE PORTRAYAL (ETHNIC, GENDER, OR OCCUPATIONAL)	NUMBER AND KIND† OF ADVERTISEMENTS

*Type—comedy, sports, news, drama, cartoon, musical, mystery, and so on.
†Kind—food, toy, beverage, medicine, public service, and so on.

Supportive Socialization Influences

The seeds for this book were sown over 40 years ago. I was a freshman in the College of Human Ecology at Cornell University taking a child development course taught by Dr. Urie Bronfenbrenner. Dr. Bronfenbrenner, distinguished professor of psychology, human development, and family studies, has stimulated much new research on children and families in various settings, as well as advocacy of government and business policies to support families.

To sum up Dr. Bronfrenbrenner's philosophy:

(1) A child needs the enduring, irrational involvement of one or more adults in care and joint activity with the child, and (2) for one or more adults to provide such care

and involvement, required are public policies and practices that provide opportunity, status, resources, encouragement, examples, and, above all, time for parenthood, primarily by parents, but also by other adults in the child's environment, both within and outside the home.

Dr. Bronfenbrenner's enthusiasm for children and families, his dynamic lecture style, and his probing questions regarding the current state of human development research and public policy provided me with an analytic perspective to examine whatever else I read or heard thereafter.

The seeds for this book could not have flowered had it not been for the care their host (the author) received in her growth and development. My family, my teachers, my friends, my neighborhood, and my experiences growing up all contributed to this book. Even as I move through adulthood, the seeds for this book are still being nurtured by others—my husband (Michael), my children (Gregory and Tamara) and their spouses (Kathleen and Alexander), my grandchildren (Helen and Madeline), my friends, my neighbors, my students, and my colleagues.

As flowers grow, to maintain their shape and stimulate new growth they must be pruned and fertilized. I would like to thank the reviewers of all editions, and my editors, for their valuable input in this process. Specific thanks to the reviewers of this edition: Robin Fox, University of Wisconsin, Whitewater; Barbara Goldenhersh, Harris Stowe State College; Gary Goodenough, Plymouth State College; Harriet Hartman, Rowan College; Christie Honeycutt, Stanley Community College; Randall Leite, Bowling Green State University; and Theodore Wagenaar, Miami University.

For the fruit of the harvest, this sixth edition, I would like to thank my editor, Dan Alpert, for plowing this version with me. Also, many thanks to the rest of the book team at Wadsworth: Tangelique Williams, associate development editor; Trudy Brown, project editor; Dory Schaeffer, marketing manager; and Heather Kazakoff, editorial assistant.

Roberta M. Berns

Child, Family, School, Community

SOCIALIZATION AND SUPPORT

SIXTH EDITION

Chapter 1

Hulton Getty/Getty Images

©Bob Daemmrich/Getty Images

Prologue: Then and Now

Ecology, Change, and Children

Socialization and Child Development
Socialization as a Unique Human Process
Socialization as a Reciprocal Dynamic Process
Socialization as an Intentional and Unintentional Process

Socialization, Change, and Challenge
Parents, Children, and Social Change
Change and the Concept of Childhood
Change and Socialization

Examining Socialization in an Ecological Context
Microsystems
Mesosystems
Exosystems
Macrosystems

Interaction of Ecological Systems over Time: The Chronosystem

Society, Change, and Consequences
Change and Societal Trends
Change and Consequences

Epilogue

Summary

Activity

Research Terms

Related Readings

Ecology of the Child

The more things change, the more they remain the same.

—ALPHONSE KARR

Prologue | *Then and Now*

CHILDHOOD CHALLENGES AND PARENTAL RESPONSIBILITY

THEN Times may change, but human nature endures. The dream to be able to fly is as old as humankind. In Greek mythology, a skillful inventor named Daedalus was summoned to the island of Crete by King Minos to trap the Minotaur, a half-man and half-bull-like creature. Daedalus brought his son, Icarus, to help him execute his design. To contain the beast, they built a labyrinth—a maze so confusing that when one entered he or she could not escape. So clever was the design that King Minos decided to retain Daedalus and Icarus so that he could use their talents in other ways. Wanting to return home, however, Daedalus began to plan an escape. He collected feathers and fastened them with twine and wax to some gently curving twigs. After observing how birds fly and practicing with the wings fastened to their shoulders, Daedalus and Icarus prepared for their flight home to Greece. When the weather was just right for their journey, Daedalus instructed his son "to fly a middle course"—warning him not to fly so low as to make the feathers heavy from the moisture of the sea, or so high as to cause the wax to melt from the heat of the sun.

The joy of flying completely captured the mind of Icarus; the temptation to reach heaven was too great for so immature a child. In spite of his father's shouts, Icarus soared higher and higher. Soon his feathers began to fall out, and realizing his mistake too late, he plummeted into the sea. After much searching, Daedalus found the body of his dead child and carried it back to Greece. He hung up his wings forever.

NOW Several years ago, a 7-year-old child from California, Jessica Dubroff, also tried to fulfill her dreams of flying. She wanted to be the youngest person to fly across the continental United States. Her father invested in flying lessons and rented a single-engine Cessna to "be her wings." Jessica's flight was closely followed by the media and so was witnessed by many via television. Jessica, her father, and the flight instructor exulted over the successful first leg of the journey. Unfortunately, excitement and overconfidence overtook reason and contributed to the decision to make the second leg of the journey even though weather conditions were not optimal. As the plane descended, the wind and rain proved too great to overcome, and the plane nosedived into a suburban highway.

Although the motives for Icarus's and Jessica's flights differed, his being escape and hers being fame, the cause of death was the same—self-exaltation; both were overconfident and overimpressed with their ability to fly. However, whereas Icarus had the voice of reason from his father to guide him away from such childhood fantasies (even though he ignored it), Jessica did not.

KEY QUESTIONS
- What is society's concept of "childhood" in terms of abilities, needs, and responsibilities?

- How do technology and media influence the concept of childhood?
- Should children be pushed to match adults' records of achievement?
- Should children be permitted to follow their dreams without adult guidance and limits? What is parental responsibility?

Ecology, Change, and Children

Ecology is the science of interrelationships between organisms and their environments; for humans, it involves the consequent biological, psychological, social, and cultural processes that develop over time (Bronfenbrenner & Morris, 1998). Environmental or societal change, influenced by such forces as demographics, economics, politics, and technology, presents challenges to human adaptation. The purpose of this book is to examine how growing up in a changing world affects the development of children via socialization. Children are socialized and supported by their families, schools, and communities. Children perpetuate the present into the future, thereby enabling continuation of society. Families, schools, communities, and society as a whole accept responsibility for ensuring children's well-being by providing a safe, healthy, nurturing environment in which to live and by investing in children's education.

Socialization and Child Development

Socialization is the process by which individuals acquire the knowledge, skills, and character traits that enable them to participate as effective members of groups and society (Brim, 1966). More specifically:

- Socialization is what every parent does: "Help your brother button his jacket," and "We use tissues, not our sleeves, to wipe our noses."
- Socialization is what every teacher does: "Study your spelling words tonight," and "In our country, we have the freedom to worship as we choose."
- Socialization is what friends do when they accept or reject you on the basis of whether you conform to their values and standards of behavior.
- Socialization is what every religion does: "Honor your father and mother," and "Do not steal."
- Socialization is what every employer does: "Part of your job is to open the store at eight o'clock and put the merchandise on the tables," and "Your request must be in writing."
- Socialization is what every community does through its laws and system of sanctions for violations.

The concept of socialization, including parenting or child rearing, social development, and education, really goes back in time as far as human life: "Train up a child in the way he should go: and when he is old, he will not depart from it" (Proverbs 22:6). As we shall see, many forces in society contribute to children's development—as do children themselves. Socialization takes place in the family, school, peer group, and community and via the media. While socialization enables a person to participate in social groups and society, it also enables the very existence of a society and its consequent social order. According to Elkin and Handel (1989, p. 27), socialization, in sum, (1) occurs over time, (2) through interaction with significant others, (3) by means of communication, (4) in emotionally significant contexts, (5) which are shaped by social groups of varying scopes.

SOCIALIZATION AS A UNIQUE HUMAN PROCESS

Most social scientists agree that socialization is unique to human beings. Over 70 years ago, George Mead (1934) wrote that it is language that sharply separates humans from other animals, that language makes ideas and communication of these ideas possible, and that language also makes it possible to replace action with thoughts and then use those thoughts to transform behavior. A little boy who breaks his mother's favorite vase and encounters her anger understands her threat the next day when she says, "If you don't hold your glass with both hands, it might fall and break, and then I will be very angry." The child now well understands what *break* and *angry* mean.

Language enables humans to develop *mind*—the ability to reason—and *self*—one's characteristic pattern of behavior. It is reason and behavior that enable us to internalize the attitudes of others. **Internalization** is the process by which externally controlled behavior shifts to internally, or self-controlled, behavior. The ability of humans to self-regulate behavior and emotions contributes to the development of a society in which people want others with whom they interact to behave as appropriately as they do. Thus emerges the motivation for social control.

> **EXAMPLE** Four-year-old Helen's thought one day was to try out Mom's makeup. In the process, the eye shadow got on her fingers, and she wiped it on her shorts. She then sat down on Mom's bed to look in the mirror, leaving a smudge of blue shadow on the bedding. She soon got bored with this activity; wiped her moist, red mouth on Mom's yellow towel; and went outside to play. Fifteen minutes later, tears were streaming down Helen's cheeks, indicating her feeling of remorse for her behavior. Mom pointed to the trail of evidence while scolding her for taking other people's things without permission (not to mention the mess that had to be cleaned).

Helen's thoughts led to behavior that caused her mother to vehemently express her feelings regarding taking other people's things without permission. Her mother's communication of values such as this to Helen will lead to Helen's internalization of self-control. If other children, too, learn to internalize behavioral control (for example, to respect each other's property), then a human society is possible.

SOCIALIZATION AS A RECIPROCAL DYNAMIC PROCESS

Socialization begins at birth and continues throughout life. It is a *reciprocal* process in that when two individuals interact a response in one usually elicits a response in the other. It is also a *dynamic* process in that interactions change over time, with individuals becoming both producers and products of responses (Collins, Maccoby, Steinberg, Hetherington, & Bornstein, 2002). These reciprocal dynamic processes become more complex throughout development and, as we will see, can influence children's competence, as well as serve as a buffer when children are at risk due to harmful events (Bronfenbrenner & Morris, 1998).

Newborns come into the world with certain needs, which change as they develop. They are given names, which indicates that they are members of society. They are clothed in a manner appropriate to the society into which they are born. For example, in the United States, they are diapered, dressed in stretch suits, and kept in cribs or cradles. In certain African societies, they are swaddled and put on their mothers' backs. The way their parents respond to their cries and to their needs, the way their parents communicate expectations, the people with whom their parents allow them to spend time (babysitter, relatives, and so on)—all contribute to infants' socialization and consequent development.

As children's development changes, so do parental expectations for behavior. Toddlers may need adult assistance when eating; preschoolers can eat independently using some utensils; schoolchildren are capable of taking some responsibility for meal preparation (such as making sandwiches, using a microwave, or cleaning utensils).

Throughout development, children play a role in their own socialization. As most parents will tell you, children sometimes instigate how others treat them. For instance, most children know that if they smile, they are more likely to get a smile back than if they frown. The way parents socialize children is often influenced by their children's reaction to them. For example, I needed only to look sternly at my son or speak in an assertive tone, and he would comply with what was asked of him. My daughter, in contrast, needed to experience consequences (usually several times)—being sent to her room, losing privileges, having to do extra chores—before she would comply with my rules. Thus, not only do children actively contribute to interactions, but, in so doing, they affect their own developmental outcomes, transforming themselves in the process and influencing how others reciprocate (Bugental & Goodenow, 1998) (see Figure 1.1).

Research supports what parents have known for centuries: Babies are born with different **temperaments** (Buss & Plomin, 1975; Chess & Thomas, 1987; Kagan, 1994; Thomas, Chess, & Birch, 1970). That is, they respond differently physiologically to various experiences. This becomes evident soon after birth in individual differences in activity level, distractibility, adaptability to new situations, mood, and so on (see Figure 1.2). Children's physiological responses fall into three broad temperamental categories—"easy," "slow to warm up," and "difficult." How caregivers respond to their children's temperaments influences the socialization process. If there is a "goodness of fit" between a child's temperament and his or her caregivers, then socialization is likely to proceed smoothly (Chess & Thomas, 1987). For example, if the child does not adapt easily to new situations (is a "slow-to-warm-up" child), and the caregivers understand this and are patient (not pushing the child, yet encouraging him or her to gradually get

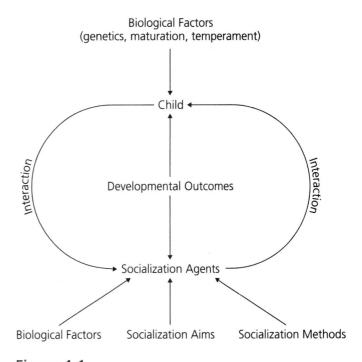

Figure 1.1

How Children Affect Their Own Developmental Outcomes

Figure 1.2

Temperament and Socialization
Source: Based on Chess and Thomas, 1987.

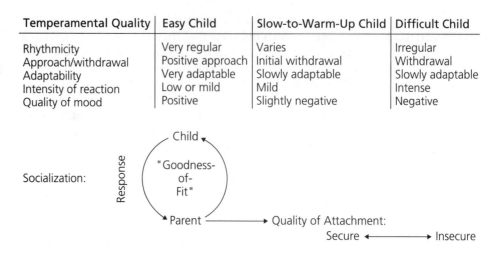

Temperamental Quality	Easy Child	Slow-to-Warm-Up Child	Difficult Child
Rhythmicity	Very regular	Varies	Irregular
Approach/withdrawal	Positive approach	Initial withdrawal	Withdrawal
Adaptability	Very adaptable	Slowly adaptable	Slowly adaptable
Intensity of reaction	Low or mild	Mild	Intense
Quality of mood	Positive	Slightly negative	Negative

used to new things), then socialization is likely to be smooth. In a longitudinal study on the socialization of "conscience," Kochanska (1995, 1997) found that the use of gentle parenting techniques such as persuasion ("Why don't you . . . because . . .") rather than harsh power assertion ("Do . . . or else . . .") was more effective in getting timid children than assertive children to comply.

If, however, the fit between the children's temperament and the caregivers' is poor, then socialization is likely to be rough. For example, if the child is very active, responds intensely to people and things, and is moody (a "difficult" child), and the caregivers force him or her to sit still, punish him or her for crying or being frightened, and demand a smile much of the time, then socialization may become a battle of wills. The impact of temperament on parenting styles is discussed in more detail in Chapter 4.

As infants become children, adolescents, and then adults, they interact with more people and have more experiences. In so doing, they acquire skills, knowledge, attitudes, values, motives, habits, beliefs, interests, morals, and ideals. For instance, they may learn to read from their first-grade teacher, learn to appreciate music from an uncle who takes them to concerts, and learn about sportsmanship from a coach and about love from the girl or boy down the street.

Thus, from the point of view of society, individuals are socialized to fit into an organized way of life (a *social* identity). And from a personal point of view, socialization has enabled them to discover themselves—their potentialities for personal growth and fulfillment (a *personal* identity). The environment also plays a part in the socialization process. The environment is that which children experience—the settings, roles, and interactions. For example, a child growing up in a large family on a farm has socialization experiences that differ from those of a child growing up in a single-parent family in the city. Over time, children choose and are exposed to many different environments that impact their development (Bronfenbrenner & Morris, 1998). By attending school, children not only gain knowledge but also find out what subjects they do best in. As members of peer groups, they not only learn to cooperate but also find out whether they are leaders or followers. Different children may discover that they like art, or dance, or sports. As these children are enabled to pursue their interests and their abilities are encouraged, they have different socialization experiences.

SOCIALIZATION AS AN INTENTIONAL AND UNINTENTIONAL PROCESS

Intentional Socialization

Much socialization is intentional. For example, when an adult tells a 6-year-old to share a toy with a 4-year-old sibling, that is *intentional* socialization. Or when an adult reminds a 10-year-old to write a thank-you note to Grandma, that, too, is intentional socialization. Thus, when adults have certain values that they consistently convey explicitly to children, and when they back these up with approval for compliance and negative consequences for noncompliance, intentional socialization takes place.

Unintentional Socialization

Much of socialization, however, takes place spontaneously during human interaction, without the deliberate intent to impart knowledge or values. *Unintentional* socialization may be the product of involvement in human interaction or observation of interaction. For example, suppose a 4-year-old approaches two teachers conversing and excitedly exclaims, "Miss Jones, Miss Jones, look!" One teacher says, "Sally, don't interrupt; we're talking." Later that morning, Sally and her friend Tanya are busily playing with Legos, with Sally explaining and demonstrating to Tanya how to fit the pieces together. Miss Jones comes to the housekeeping corner and interrupts with "Girls, please stop what you're doing and come see what Rene has brought to school." It is very likely that the message Sally receives from the morning's interactions is that it is *not* OK for children to interrupt adults but OK for adults to interrupt children.

Another example of unintentional socialization is the mother who has told her daughter that alcohol and drugs are damaging to her physical and mental health.

Sometimes parents are more eager for their child to participate in sports than is the child.

Yet when the daughter describes a party she went to where beer and drugs were available, and the mother indicates her fascination with the party's events by her attentive expression and her questions, what message is the daughter really receiving (especially if the mother herself uses alcohol or drugs, and her daughter sees this)?

In sum, children respond to and learn from experiences of emotion, body language, and other cues, as well as verbal statements. All this information is processed (constructed, interpreted, transformed, and recorded) in the brain to influence future behavior.

Socialization, Change, and Challenge

Children are socialized by many people in society—parents, siblings, grandparents, aunts, uncles, cousins, friends, peers, teachers, coaches, and characters on television, in the movies, and in books. These agents of socialization employ many techniques, which will be discussed in subsequent chapters, to influence children to behave, think, and feel according to what society considers worthy. What all these agents believe is worthy are outcomes of their own socialization—their values, morals, attitudes, and self-concepts.

PARENTS, CHILDREN, AND SOCIAL CHANGE

Socialization is a complex process indeed. The more technological and diverse the society, the more children have to learn in order to adapt effectively, the more socializing agents and experiences contribute to the socialization process, and the more time it takes. As society changes, more and more challenges are posed to socializing agents because there are more choices to be made. Should childhood be compressed to accommodate all the opportunities that exist, or should socializing agents evaluate and select what is to be learned? For example, as Asian, European, and Latin American countries increasingly compete with the United States in world trade, American children who learn languages other than English will have an advantage when they enter the business world. How involved in globalization should the United States be given the threat of terrorism in the world? How should the rights to freedom, privacy, and security be balanced?

When societal change occurs, such as rapid technological and scientific advances that result in economic fluctuations, socializing agents are affected. Adults are affected *directly* by the uncertainty that change produces, as well as by the new opportunities and challenges it may present. Economic fluctuations can affect job security and have a major negative impact on family finances. Family members might have to work longer hours, lose purchasing power, and even have to move. However, such stresses may also uncover positive strengths in family members—for example, spousal emotional support and children's assumption of more responsibility for household chores. How adults adapt to societal change *indirectly* affects children. For instance, two parents in the workforce usually require child care services, and family time becomes the "second shift" (Hochschild, 1990). Parents learn to adapt by performing several tasks simultaneously. New technology helps (talking on a speaker phone while folding clothes), but the efficiency gained in multitasking may contribute to diminished attentiveness to family members.

Points to Ponder

Adaptation is a biological mechanism enabling individuals to adjust to environmental change. A strategy I have used is to automate as many routine tasks as I can (washing clothes, purchasing groceries, and paying bills on a certain day every week, and performing new tasks in the same order until their execution becomes unconscious). Then, the rest of my time is available to do other activities. How do you adapt to the continuous changing nature of society?

One result of societal change can be seen in shifting goals of child rearing and education. Many psychologists (Elkind, 1994; Kluger & Park, 2001) see today's parents as being very concerned with developing the intellectual abilities of their children. This concern is evidenced by the growth of preschools and kindergartens with academic programs; the development of infant stimulation programs such as "Mommy and Me" classes; the availability of "how-to" books on teaching babies to read, do math, and be brighter; and the proliferation of computer software for children and of after-school activities. The concern is also evidenced by the pressure on elementary schools to emphasize formal instruction involving passive listening and memorization rather than a developmentally appropriate curriculum, which involves knowledge of children's normal growth patterns and individual differences, such as being exposed to active, hands-on, age-appropriate, and meaningful experiences. Developmental appropriateness is discussed in more detail in Chapter 5.

As a consequence of this parental concern with nourishing the intellect, children are under pressure to become intellectually independent and successful at an early age. This is measured by test scores, performance in various activities such as athletics and music, and acceptance into prestigious schools (even preschools!). Elkind (1988) cited an example of this push to raise superkids: A mother complained to her son's first-grade teacher, "How is he going to get into MIT if you only give him a 'satisfactory'!" Elkind believes that such a push for excellence is causing an increase in stress symptoms in children.

> **EXAMPLE** Carol's parents were very proud of their daughter. Considered a "gifted" student, she did well in school while juggling a full schedule that included ice skating, gymnastics, and piano lessons. At age 10, Carol won her elementary school's outstanding student award, placed first in an ice-skating competition, and gave a solo piano recital. At age 13, she was selected as a candidate for admission to a prestigious private girls' high school. Two days before the scheduled entrance exam, Carol took a fatal overdose of sleeping pills.
>
> Why did Carol choose suicide? Other adolescents face varying degrees of pressure and stress, yet develop coping strategies. Was it her family situation, friends, school, or community, or some combination of these complex relationships?

That children are pressured to know more than their parents is really not a new phenomenon; it is part of evolution or societal change. As new knowledge emerges, it is the children who learn it in school. For example, children in many schools use computers for learning tasks. There is likely to be tension in the parent–child relationship when children can figure things out more efficiently with computers than their parents can with traditional paper-and-pencil methods. As another example, children of immigrants are "Americanized" in school whereas their parents may cling to the traditional attitudes and behavior patterns learned in their countries of origin. Thus, societal change can produce family tensions; it can also present challenges. To reduce tension in the parent–child relationship resulting from an imbalance of knowledge, parents can strive to become knowledgeable in the very activities their children are pursuing. For example, parents can share activities; they can provide the opportunity for children to teach them; they can read books, talk to experts, and enroll in adult education courses (such as on how to use a computer); and they can volunteer to help in the classroom in order to learn along with their children. There needs to be a distinction between encouraging and motivating children to succeed and burdening them with inappropriate expectations. Schools can also be challenged to involve parents more in their children's developmentally appropriate learning. Parental involvement in school is discussed in detail in Chapter 6.

Another result of societal change, according to Elkind (1994), has been a shift in the value of the child's place in the family away from "child-centeredness." Traditionally, parents sacrificed for their children—their energy and resources went to their children. They may have saved money for their children's college education instead of buying a new car. Today, however, some parents see their needs and rights as being at least equal to their children's, rather than subordinate.

Elkind sees this trend evidenced in the pressure placed on children to attain emotional independence at an early age. For example, after school, many children return to homes devoid of adults, and they often are responsible for younger siblings as well. Even though they are independent for part of the day, many are fearful of staying alone. Some are resentful that they cannot play with their friends, because many such children are not permitted to let anyone into the home for safety reasons. Most spend their time watching television. What sorts of adults will these "independent" children become?

CHANGE AND THE CONCEPT OF CHILDHOOD

One of the challenges resulting from change is society's concept of childhood. We assume childhood to be a special period of time when we are cared for, taught, and protected because we are not mature enough to do these things for ourselves. Does the period of childhood change—lengthen or shorten—when society changes?

Prior to the Renaissance (fourteenth through sixteenth centuries), there was no concept of childhood; there was only infancy and adulthood. Children who lived beyond age 7 were treated like miniature adults (Aries, 1962). There was no distinction in the clothing worn by children and adults. Children were treated harshly, not lovingly; they were expected to work and participated in all adult activities, including drinking and partying. Seven-year-olds could even be punished the same way adults were (put in jail or hanged) for a crime such as pilfering.

With the development of the printing press in the middle of the fifteenth century came the attitude that one could not become an adult unless he or she could read (Postman, 1985, 1992). In the sixteenth century, this came to mean that schools were created so that children could be taught to read. Because the school was designed to produce literate adults, a concept of childhood emerged: Children came to be perceived not as "miniature adults" but as "unformed adults" (Postman, 1985). The concept of childhood as we know it evolved over the next three centuries. It came to be regarded as the bridge between infancy—total dependence—and adulthood—total independence.

Lewis Wickes Hine/© CORBIS

Children working in factories was a common sight prior to child labor laws prohibiting such practices.

As society became more complex, the need for an education preparatory to adulthood became more apparent. For example, one consequence of the Industrial Revolution (eighteenth to twentieth centuries) was the passage by many Western nations of compulsory education laws. Children *had* to attend school to prepare themselves to be functioning members of society.

The need to protect children from society's adult expectations also became more apparent. Another consequence of the changes that took place during the Industrial Revolution was the recognition of children's rights. Prior to the nineteenth century, children could be exploited to work in factories for long hours under harsh conditions. The nineteenth and twentieth centuries saw the passage of labor laws that limited the age at which children could be employed and the conditions under which they could work. Thus, from the Renaissance until today, the span of childhood has lengthened, and the special needs of children have come to be recognized.

Today, however, a common concern revolves around the supposed loss of childhood (Elkind, 1988, 1994; Garbarino, 1986; Kluger & Park, 2001; Weissbourd, 1996). Gone are many of the physical consequences of growing up in a changing society—toiling in the sweatshops, trekking 5 miles to school, dying from influenza—but in their place are psychological consequences: pressure to achieve, stress, substance abuse, violence, eating disorders, teen pregnancies, depression, and suicide (Children's Defense Fund, 2001; Elkind, 1994).

The childhood that evolved from the time of the Renaissance—a romanticized time of fantasy, play, lack of responsibility, and freedom to develop at one's own pace—has now been reframed as a time of reality, work, and rapid development to fit the pace of societal change. The time of childhood is once again shortening.

Children today must cope with a world in which both parents work, drugs are readily available, sex is as close as TV or the Internet, and violence is just around the corner (Children's Defense Fund, 2001; Elkind, 1994; Weissbourd, 1996).

Children are regarded as consumers. From the numerous ads for toys, video games, food, and clothing, one might think that children have major purchasing power. Sports are rarely played for amusement as they were a generation ago; learning specific skills and ways to compete have become goals. Soccer, football, and Little League games are now analyzed and even commercialized, just like professional sports. The video camera and computer enable games to be rehashed the next day and the next, instead of being tossed aside in the name of fun. Many businesses underwrite uniform, equipment, and travel expenses in return for advertising, potentially placing even more pressure on children to compete and win.

In sum, the age of protection for children has been undermined by societal pressures on parents. Today's children are increasingly expected to achieve independence and self-reliance before they have the requisite skills and abilities (Elkind, 1994; Garbarino, 1995a; Weissbourd, 1996). Consequences of this include the rise in psychosomatic ailments such as stomachaches, headaches, wheezing, dizziness, and chest pains among school-age children and the rise in emotional problems such as depression, substance abuse, eating disorders, and suicide among adolescents (Hewlett & West, 1998; Zill & Schoenbom, 1990). Even the law (for example, the Freedom of Information Act) has certain consequences for children. For 18-year-olds, the law grants certain privacy rights. This means that their parents are not entitled to get any information about them without their consent—whether about their grades, bank account, credit history, or health. Although some young people might consider this to be a positive, some parents who are helping their children make the transition to adulthood, perhaps by financing their education, might consider this application of the law to be counterproductive to their parenting role.

What can we do to cope with these consequences of change? Can we meet the challenges?

We need to understand the process of **socialization**—the process by which humans, beginning at birth, acquire the skills to function as social beings and participants in society. We also need to understand the impact of change on socialization. Finally, we need to be able to make choices that support and prepare today's children for tomorrow's challenges.

CHANGE AND SOCIALIZATION

Socialization is an elaborate process involving many variable and reciprocal experiences, interactions, and environments that affect children's development. Analyzing some of the variables in the process can help people adapt to change. For instance, understanding how the "input" of socialization—interactions in various settings and situations—affects the "output" of socialization—values, attitudes, attributes, motives, self-esteem, self-regulation, morals, and gender roles—may help enable us to manipulate that input to induce the desired output.

A simplified example of this kind of manipulation is described in a classic book, *Walden Two*, by psychologist B. F. Skinner (1948). Walden Two was a utopian community founded on behavioral principles. To teach self-control, young children (age 3–4) were given lollipops dipped in sugar at the beginning of the day, to be eaten later, provided that they had not been licked. In practice sessions, the children were urged to examine their own behavior in the following situations: when the lollipops were concealed, when the children were distracted from thinking about the candy by playing a game, and when the lollipops were in sight. Thus, when the children were given the lollipops again for a real exercise in self-control, they had at their disposal some adaptive behaviors to use (put them out of sight, keep busy) to help them avoid the temptation.

Another example of how input can be employed to affect output is Sherif's (1956) classic Robber's Cave experiment, in which manipulation of the environment was used first to bring about antisocial behavior (hostility) between two groups of young boys and then to reverse that pattern. How was this done? To produce friction, competitive tournaments were held—baseball, tug-of-war, touch football, and so on. Frustration led to name-calling, raids, and aggressive behavior. To eliminate this friction, counselors rigged a series of crises that forced the boys to work together in order to solve the problem. For instance, once, the water line was deliberately broken, and another time, the camp truck broke down just as it was going to town for food. In each case, antisocial behavior gave way to prosocial behavior when a compelling goal for all concerned had to be achieved. Anti- and prosocial behavior will be discussed in more detail later in the book.

The preceding examples are illustrations of intentional socialization, such that input affects desired output. In reality, we have unique biological characteristics and so come into the world with different "wiring," which causes each of us to perceive and interact with the world differently, resulting in a range of outputs. A muscular, coordinated child will tend to be attracted to sports, whereas a frail, timid child will tend to avoid competitive activities. Thus, children play a role in their own socialization (Scarr, 1992), which sometimes makes intentional socialization difficult. In contrast to the scientifically shaped utopian society described in *Walden Two* or the manipulated events in the Robber's Cave experiment, in real life, each human being is exposed to many different environments in which many different interactions and experiences, both intentional and unintentional, take place. Therefore, individuals reflect both their biological characteristics and their socialization experiences (Bugental & Goodenow, 1998; Collins et al., 2002). As children change, so must the process of socialization; socialization is not static, but rather is dynamic, transactional and bidirectional, or reciprocal (Sameroff, 1987). Ideally, as children develop, control over their behavior gradually shifts from adults to children. More specifically, infants and toddlers require much adult direction. Preschoolers are developmentally capable of directing some of their activities and exhibiting some self-control over their behavior. School-agers can direct most of their activities with some adult support and supervision. Adolescents who have been socialized by nurturant adults exhibit much self-control and self-directed behavior, even though they still need some adult guidance.

Some of the effects of various socialization experiences, interactions, and environments will be examined in later chapters when such questions as these are addressed: What are the effects of divorce on the child? What is the impact of both parents working outside the home? Is child care helpful or harmful? What type of schooling benefits the academic achievement of students? How influential are friends? Should children participate in organized sports? How do the media influence child development? Should children with disabilities be included in the mainstream? Should children from ethnically diverse groups be Americanized, or should societal institutions be modified to meet their special or unique needs? How can communities become more caring?

Examining Socialization in an Ecological Context

Developmental psychologist Urie Bronfenbrenner (1979, 1989, 1995; Bronfenbrenner & Morris, 1998) believes that the social context of individual interactions and experiences determines the degree to which individuals can develop their abilities and realize their potentials. His conceptual model (see Figure 1.3) placing humans in their various social environments—the ecology of human development—allows for a systematic study of interactions, including the child's role in his or her development over time, and serves as a guide for future research on the complex process of socialization.

Ecology, as noted at the beginning of the chapter, involves interrelationships between humans and their environments, including the consequent psychological, social, and cultural processes over time. According to Bronfenbrenner's bioecological theory, there are four basic structures—the microsystem, mesosystem, exosystem, and macrosystem—in which relationships and interactions take place to form patterns that affect human development. Such a conceptual framework enables us to study the child and his or her family, school, and community as dynamic evolving

Figure 1.3

An Ecological Model of Human Development
Source: "An Ecological Model of Human Development," based on concepts from U. Bronfenbrenner (1989, JAI Press). Ecological systems theory in R. Vasta (Ed.) Annals of Child Development Vol. 6.

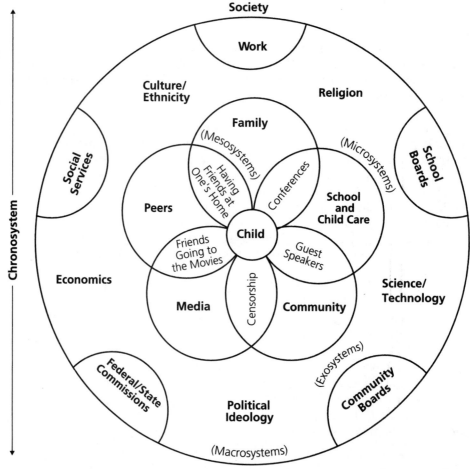

systems influenced by change (the chronosystem), as in economics, politics, and technology. A computer analogy might be hypertext and links on the Internet. Web sites are always changing, new links via hypertext are always forming, and the information you glean from one site affects the information you can obtain from another.

MICROSYSTEMS

The first basic structure, the **microsystem** (*micro* meaning "small"), refers to the activities and relationships with significant others experienced by children in a particular small setting such as family, school, peer group, or community.

The family is the setting that provides nurturance, affection, and a variety of opportunities. It is the primary socializer of children in that it has the most significant impact on their development. According to Garbarino (1992), children who are not adequately nurtured or loved, such as those who grow up in abrasive or dysfunctional families, may have developmental problems. Also, children who do not have sufficient opportunities to manipulate objects, model desirable behaviors, initiate activities, or be exposed to a language-rich environment will be at a disadvantage when they reach school. This early disadvantage will persist and even worsen as these children progress through school, unless intervention, such as that provided by some child care programs, modify the opportunities at home and in school.

The school is the microsystem in which children formally learn about their society. Schools teach reading, writing, arithmetic, history, science, and so on. Teachers encourage the development of various skills and behaviors by acting as role models and by providing motivation for children to succeed in learning.

The peer group is the setting in which children are generally unsupervised by adults, thereby gaining experience in independence. In peer groups, children get a sense of who they are and what they can do by comparing themselves with others. Peers provide companionship and support, as well as sources of learning experiences in cooperation and role taking.

The community, or neighborhood on a smaller scale, is the main microsystem in which children learn by doing. The facilities available to children determine what real experiences they will have. Is there a library? Are there stores and workplaces nearby where children can observe people at work? Are the people with whom children interact in the community similar or diverse? Do the people in the community act as advocates for children? These questions relate to the significance of the community as a socializer.

The media, exemplified by television, movies, videos, books, magazines, music, and computers, are not regarded as a microsystem by Bronfenbrenner because they do not represent a small, interactive setting for reciprocal interaction. However, I consider the media to be as significant a socializer as the microsystems just described because they present settings in which children can view the whole world—past, present, and future; places and things; roles and relationships; attitudes and values; behaviors to emulate. Many TVs have interactive capabilities. In addition, because computers are interactive and can be combined with any media, they provide potentials for relationships (e-mail, chat groups, cell phones, and so on).

Children's development is affected in each of the aforementioned settings not only by their relationships with others in the family, school, peer group, or community but also by interactions between members of the particular microsystem. For example, the father's relationship with the mother affects her treatment of the child. If the father is emotionally supportive of the mother, she tends to be more involved and to have more positive interactions with the child (Cox, Owen,

Henderson, & Margand, 1992). For another example, a child's classroom performance varies as a function of whether the teacher taught the child's older sibling and how well that sibling performed (Seaver, 1973). A teacher who taught a high-achieving older sibling tends to have high expectations for the younger sibling. The younger sibling, in turn, is more likely to perform as expected.

MESOSYSTEMS

The second basic structure, the **mesosystem** (*meso* meaning "intermediate"), consists of linkages and interrelationships between two or more of children's microsystems, such as the family and the school, or the family and the peer group.

The impact of mesosystems on children depends on the number and quality of interrelationships. Bronfenbrenner (1979) uses the example of the child who goes to school alone on the first day. This means that there is only a single link between home and school—the child. Where there is little linkage between home and school in terms of socialization values, expectations, and experiences, there also tends to be little academic achievement by the child. In contrast, where all these links are strong, there is likely to be academic competence. To illustrate, in a longitudinal study following adolescents from their last year of middle school through their first year of high school, researchers found a relationship between academic performance and the joint effects of family and school (Epstein, 1983). When the style of family interaction was similar to the school's, in that both settings encouraged children's participation, academic performance was enhanced (Ginsberg & Bronstein, 1993). Thus, the more numerous the qualitative links or interrelationships between children's microsystems, the more impact they have on socialization. Mesosystems, then, provide support for activities in microsystems. For example, when parents invite a child's friends to their home, or when parents encourage their child to join a certain club, team, or youth group, the socialization impact of the peers is enhanced through parental approval.

Another example of the impact of mesosystems involves community censorship of movies that can be shown in local theaters; the impact of the media as a socializing agent is then reduced because of lack of sponsorship. However, censorship may actually motivate some individuals to see a movie, thereby increasing its influence.

EXOSYSTEMS

The third basic structure, the **exosystem** (*exo* meaning "outside"), refers to settings in which children are not active participants, but that affect them in one of their microsystems—for example, parents' jobs, the city council, or parental social support networks. The effects of exosystems on children are indirect via the microsystems. To illustrate, when parents work in settings that demand conformity rather than self-direction, they reflect this orientation in their parenting styles in that they tend to be more controlling than democratic. Thus, their children's socialization is impacted. When the city planning commission approves a freeway through a neighborhood or an air traffic pattern over a school, children's socialization is impacted in that the noise interferes with learning. Studies have shown that parental income and employment setting affect child development outcomes. For example, low-income parents involved in work-based antipoverty programs (ones that provide sufficient family income, child care, health insurance, and support services) have been shown to enhance the school performance and social behavior of their children (Huston et al., 2001). In contrast, high-income parents living in upwardly mobile suburban communities have been shown to have children who exhibit a relatively high rate of lower-than-expected school performance and negative social behavior (anxiety, depression, substance abuse) as a reaction to achievement pressure (Luthar & Becker, 2002).

MACROSYSTEMS

The fourth basic structure, the **macrosystem** (*macro* meaning "large"), consists of the society and subculture to which children belong, with particular reference to belief systems, lifestyles, patterns of social interaction, and life changes. Examples of macrosystems include the United States, the middle or lower class, Hispanic or Asian ancestry, Catholicism or Judaism, and urban or rural areas. Macrosystems are viewed as patterns, or sets of instructions, for exosystems, mesosystems, and microsystems. For instance, democracy is the basic belief system of the United States and so is considered a macrosystem. Democratic ideology affects the world of work, an exosystem—for example, employers cannot discriminate in hiring. Democratic ideology affects how schools communicate with families; school–family interaction is a mesosystem—for example, schools must inform parents of policies, and parents have the right to question those policies. Democratic ideology also affects what is taught in schools, a microsystem—for example, children must learn the principles upon which the United States was founded.

Although individuals may live in the United States and subscribe to its basic belief system of democracy, and so be influenced by that macrosystem, they may also be part of other macrosystems such as their ethnic group. **Ethnicity** refers to an attribute of membership in a group in which members identify themselves by national origin, culture, race, or religion. Because the United States is becoming more and more ethnically diverse, we need to understand some basic effects of various macrosystems. Specific ethnic groups are discussed throughout the book.

According to cultural anthropologist Edward T. Hall (1964, 1966, 1976), people from different macrosystems, or cultures, view the world differently, unaware or indifferent to the fact that there are alternative ways of perceiving, believing,

Low-context cultures value cultivating the land whereas high-context cultures value living in harmony with it.

Table 1.1

Low- Versus High-Context Macrosystems

	LOW-CONTEXT MACROSYSTEMS	HIGH-CONTEXT MACROSYSTEMS
GENERAL CHARACTERISTICS	Rationality Practicality Competition Individuality Progress	Intuitiveness Emotionality Cooperation Group identity Tradition
SIGNIFICANT VALUES	Emphasis on concrete evidence and facts Efficient use of time Achievement Personal freedom Humans able to control nature and influence the future Change good	Emphasis on feelings Establishment of solid relationships through human interaction Character Group welfare Nature and the future governed by a power higher than human Stability good

- *What if these views represented two individuals wanting to marry?*
- *What if one view represented a teacher's and the other a student's?*
- *What if one view represented an employer's and the other an employee's?*

behaving, and judging. Particularly significant are the unconscious assumptions people make about personal space, time, interpersonal relations, and ways of knowing. These assumptions can interfere with communication, a point upon which Hall focuses to illustrate differences as well as similarities among cultures.

Hall classifies macrosystems as being low or high context. Generally, **low-context macrosystems** are characterized by rationality, practicality, competition, individuality, and progress; **high-context macrosystems** are characterized by intuitiveness, emotionality, cooperation, group identity, and tradition (see Table 1.1).

In a low-context macrosystem, such as the Euro-American, suburban middle class, meaning from communication is gleaned from the verbal message itself—a spoken explanation, written letter, or computer printout. *What* is said is often more important than *who* said it. For example, employees in government, business, or education routinely communicate by phone or memorandum without ever meeting the other individuals involved. In contrast, in a high-context macrosystem, such as Native American, Hispanic American, Asian American, or rural Euro-American, meaning from communication is gleaned from the setting in which the communication takes place. For example, a Spanish-speaking person can communicate familiarity by whether he or she uses the formal or informal word for "you." A person raised in traditional Japanese culture can communicate degree of respect by how deeply he or she bows.

In general, people in low-context macrosystems tend to try to control nature (for example, irrigating desert areas) and have more fragmented social relations in that they may behave one way toward friends, another way toward business colleagues, and yet another way toward neighbors. People in high-context macrosystems tend to live in harmony with nature and with other humans who are part of their social network. Whereas individuals in low-context macrosystems usually develop an identity based on their personal efforts and achievements, people in high-context macrosystems tend to gain their identity through group associations (lineage, place of work, organizations). Members of low-context cultures expect personal freedom, openness, and individual choice. Members of high-context cultures are less open to strangers, distinguish between insiders and outsiders, and are more likely to follow traditional role expectations.

Both low- and high-context macrosystems illustrate the importance of adaptiveness for human survival: Low-context cultures provide ways of adapting, changing, and applying new knowledge to benefit society, and high-context cultures provide strong human support networks that help guard against the alienation of a technological society.

EXAMPLE Different parenting styles influence children's degree of dependence on others and desire to explore new things. On a recent day-long cruise to see the glaciers in Alaska, I had the opportunity to observe the contrast in parenting styles in a high- and a low-context family. The high-context family consisted of a mother and father, a baby (about 10 months old), and a grandmother and grandfather. The baby was continually held and played with by one of the adults. She was kissed and jiggled and spoken to. There were no toys to amuse her. When it was lunchtime, the mother, after distributing the food she had brought to the adults, took some food from her plate, mashed it between her fingers, and put it in the baby's mouth. After lunch, the grandmother and grandfather took turns rocking the baby to sleep. The baby never cried the whole day. The care she received fostered a sense of interdependence.

In contrast, the low-context family, consisting of a mother, father, and baby (about 15 months old), had brought a sack of toys for the baby to play with while the parents enjoyed the sites through a nearby window. After a while, the baby began to fuss; the father picked him up and brought him to the boat's window, pointing out seals and birds and glaciers. Later, when the baby tired of his toys, the mother held his hand and walked him around the deck. The baby was given crackers and a bottle to soothe him when he cried. The care he received fostered a sense of independence.

Interaction of Ecological Systems Over Time: The Chronosystem

The **chronosystem** involves temporal changes in ecological systems or within individuals as they develop that produce new conditions affecting children's development. For example, changes in computer software technology may result in our having to purchase new equipment or learn different passwords for Internet access and security. For another example, significant societal events can produce a variety of effects on children. The school shootings in Columbine, Colorado, affected many schools' on-campus security procedures, resulting in the installation of metal detectors, the hiring of guards, and the implementation of "zero-tolerance" policies wherein aggressive students are expelled for one offense. Certainly, safety concerns in schools have increased. As a final example, consider how physical changes individuals experience during puberty can affect their self-esteem, depending on how their developing body compares to their friends', as well as to the cultural ideal body type.

Thus, changes in a macrosystem can result in changes in exosystems, mesosystems, and microsystems. A very thorough, longitudinal study of 167 California children born in 1920–1929 illustrating the effects of such changes was conducted by sociologist Glen Elder (1974, 1979, 1998) and his colleagues (Elder & Hareven, 1993; Elder, Van Nguyen, & Casper, 1985). They compared the life course development of children whose families had experienced a change in their socioeconomic status due to the Great Depression and those who had not. The immediate exosystem effect was loss of a job. This, in turn, caused emotional distress, which was experienced in the home and affected the children (effect on a microsystem). There were also secondary exosystem effects: In families hit by the Depression, the father lost status in the eyes of the children while the mother increasd in importance. The affected father's parenting behavior became more rejecting, especially toward adolescent girls. Children, especially boys, from affected families expressed a stronger identification with the peer group. Children from affected families also participated more in domestic roles and outside jobs, with girls being more likely to do the former and boys the latter.

The fact that longitudinal data were available over a period of more than 60 years enabled Elder to assess the impact of childhood experiences, within and outside the family, on behavior in later life (effects of the chronosystem). He found that the long-term consequences of the Depression varied according to the age of the child at the time. On the one hand, children who were preadolescents when their families suffered economic loss, compared with those of the same socioeconomic status from families that did not suffer economically, did less well in school, showed less stable and less successful work histories, and exhibited more emotional and social difficulties, even in adulthood. Such adverse effects have later been explained (Conger et al., 1994) as due to the impact of economic hardship on the quality of parenting, and hence the psychological well-being of children. On the other hand, those who were teenagers when the Depression hit their families did better in school, were more likely to go to college, had happier marriages, exhibited more successful work careers, and in general were more satisfied with life than youngsters of the same socioeconomic status who were not affected by the Depression. These favorable outcomes were more pronounced for teenagers from middle-socioeconomic-status backgrounds but were also evident among their lower-status counterparts.

Interestingly, adults whose families escaped economic ruin turned out to be less successful, both educationally and vocationally, than those whose families were deprived. Why was this so? According to Elder (1974),

> It seems that a childhood which shelters the young from the hardships of life consequently fails to develop or test adaptive capacities which are called upon in life crises. To engage and manage real-life (though not excessive) problems in childhood and adolescence is to participate in a sort of apprenticeship for adult life. Preparedness has been identified repeatedly as a key factor in the adaptive potential and psychological health of persons in novel situations. (pp. 249–250)

Thus, a major consequence of the Depression was that economic loss changed the relation of children to the family and the adult world by involving them in work that was necessary for the welfare of others. This early involvement contributed to deprived children's socialization for adulthood. Elder hypothesized that the loss of economic security forced the family to mobilize its human resources. Everyone had to take on new responsibilities.

With regard to the effect of today's abundance on the socialization of youths, Elder (1974) expressed the following concern:

> Since the Depression and especially World War II various developments have conspired to isolate the young from challenging situations in which they could make valuable contributions to family and community welfare. Prosperity, population, concentration, industrial growth with its capital-intensive formula, and educational upgrading have led to an extension of the dependency years and increasing segregation of the young from the routine experiences of adults. In this consumption-oriented society, urban middle-class families have little use for the productive hands of offspring, and the same applies to community institutions. . . .
>
> This society of abundance can and even must support "a large quota of nonproductive members," as it is presently organized, but should it tolerate the costs, especially among the young; the costs of not feeling needed, of being denied the challenge and rewards which come from meaningful contributions to a common endeavor? (pp. 291–293)

Elder's challenge is to bring adults back into the lives of children and children back into the lives of adults.

Elder's study showed how ecological change over time can have varying impacts on a child's socialization depending on other variables, such as the age and gender of the child, the existing family relationships, and the socioeconomic status of the family prior to the change. In this way, a multiplicity of variables interact to affect socialization.

Because socialization must pass on the cultural heritage to the next generation while also enabling members of that generation to become competent adults in society, every socializing agent engages in preparing children, paradoxically, for both stability and change. Training for stability, which entails passing on the cultural heritage and the status quo to children, involves making children's behavior somewhat predictable and conforming; preparation for change, which includes enabling children to act competent in some future society, very likely involves disrupting some stable patterns and encouraging new ways of thinking and behaving. The challenge, then, of successful socialization in today's society is to rear children to maintain certain values, morals, attitudes, behaviors, and roles while being adaptable to change, so that they become responsible, caring, competent adults.

What is it that makes some people responsible for their actions and others not? Does the answer lie in the way they were socialized—did the responsible individuals become that way because their parents were loving, and these individuals grew up wanting to please them? Or were these individuals punished from a very early age when they did not behave responsibly (for example, did not call to say they would be home late)? Or were they trusted to take on tasks involving responsibility, such as babysitting, gardening, or money management, at an early age and expected to accept the consequences for their mistakes (not being hired again as a sitter or a gardener), as well as the rewards for their successes (more jobs, higher pay)? Did they have responsible adults to emulate, or did they spend most of their time with friends or in front of the TV? Did their teachers have certain standards and demand that they assume responsibility for their actions (for example, homework turned in on time or not accepted), or were the standards and evaluation procedures vague?

EXAMPLE Julie, an attractive young lady about 20 years of age, came to me with tears in her eyes after the semester was over, requesting to take my child development course again. When asked why, she broke down and sobbed, "I got an F. . . . I got Bs on all the exams, but I didn't do the observations. I guess I didn't organize my time responsibly." I could understand her tears. She was an attentive student who contributed to class discussions and, judging by her test scores, studied the material. What I couldn't understand was why she didn't take the time to do the required observations, which represented 40 percent of her grade, when she very well knew the consequences. (My grading policy is written on the course syllabus, which everyone is given, and it is discussed several times.)

As a college professor who interacts with hundreds of students each year, I am continually plagued with the question of why some students responsibly prepare for examinations, complete their assignments, and turn in papers on time while other students do not. Those in the latter group are generally nice people who are usually attentive in class, yet when they get their final grades, they show astonishment and come to me to request a reprieve, a chance to repeat the course with the promise of completing the required work.

The dilemma exemplified in the box relates to influences of microsystems and mesosystems on socialization. What about influences of exosystems and macrosystems?

We live in a society in which the lines of responsibility are often vague. Years ago, if I got sick, I was responsible for paying the doctor. Today, it is primarily my insurance company's responsibility (my employee benefits include health coverage). Years ago, when a carpenter was hired to build some cabinets, that person assumed responsibility for the quality of materials and work. Today, because of diversification and specialization, it is rare for one person to be responsible for a whole job—there is the bank that may loan money for the materials, the lumberyard that supplies the materials, and the delivery trucks that bring the materials to the lumberyard and to the customer. If a job is not completed on time, perhaps it is due to the bank taking longer than expected to approve the loan, or the lumberyard ordering the wrong materials, or the delivery trucks not operating because of a union strike. Who is really responsible?

Similarly, years ago, if you did not pay your bills on time, you had to face people—people at the bank or the store or the telephone company, for example. Because face-to-face encounters usually cause some embarrassment, most people try to avoid them. Thus, a motivating factor causing people to pay their bills on time was the avoidance of shame-producing situations. Today, a computer handles the billing; generally, those to whom people owe money are not even aware of it. People do not have to face computers, however, and worry about their reputations in town if they should default on a payment.

Do technological advances in society, then, lessen responsibility? How are children affected by such advances? Children experience toys that do not work as advertised, textbooks that do not arrive on time, and adults who abdicate responsibility (do not pay child support, become substance abusers, or simply do not care). Thus, children reared to be responsible—by their families, their religion, their culture, and their school—may still be exposed to many situations in which irresponsibility exists. Some situations even seem to reward irresponsibility. For example, people who default on their debts may be able to get a loan to pay them, as well as being able to deduct from their taxes the interest on certain loans.

In sum, the outcomes of socialization influenced by microsystems and mesosystems are extremely complicated, and they become even more so when the effects of change on children's exosystems and macrosystems are also considered.

Society, Change, and Consequences

With change comes consequences, some affecting many people and others affecting few. As Mahatma Gandhi said, "The future will depend on what we do with the present." To understand the world our children will inhabit in the twenty-first century, significant worldwide changes impacting children's development are mentioned here. For optimal development of children to occur, the various ecological systems must create caring communities, a theme that will recur throughout the book via real, ideal, and research examples.

CHANGE AND SOCIETAL TRENDS

Societal trends (Kaplan, 2002; Naisbitt & Aburdene, 1990) that impact children and families include the following:

- *Biotechnology.* Manipulating nature to increase food supplies (through fish farms, disease-resistant plants, artificial insemination of cows, and so on) has been an accepted practice for years. However, applying similar principles to humans raises concerns. For one thing, genetic engineering can potentially cure inherited diseases by substituting normal genes for defective ones; but what about using such techniques to increase intelligence? For another, assisted reproductive techniques (sperm donation, egg donation, in-vitro fertilization, frozen embryos, surrogacy) enable adults with fertility problems to become parents; but what about medical, legal, and ethical risks? (To exemplify: If a male and a female contribute sperm and egg for conception to take place in a dish, several resulting embryos are frozen, one or two are implanted in a surrogate who is paid to carry through with the pregnancy, and the biological parents die, to whom do the babies and embryos belong?) Finally, viruses for biological warfare have been manufactured with government approval; but who will decide on the appropriate uses?
- *Reconceptualization of societal and individual responsibilities.* Political ideology is shifting from "paternalistic" policies (the strong authority takes care of less-able citizens) to "empowerment" policies (any individual can learn to care for him- or herself). Government is moving from providing public housing to needy families to supporting programs enabling homeownership. Government regulation of private enterprise is yielding to free-market economic mechanisms. Government welfare support is waning while "workfare" is waxing. And government funding for Social Security plans is diminishing in the fall of private insurance and investment programs.
- *Mobile technology.* Wireless networks (the combination of cell phones and cable modems) allow users to work, play, and shop anytime, anyplace. For businesses, operations can be streamlined and efficiency increased as

As technology increases, humans compensate by finding ways to interact, as exemplified by beepers and cell phones.

workers make plans, decisions, sales, and reports without going to the office. For consumers, mobile commerce enables them to shop for tickets, books, pizza, and so on while waiting on line or at the doctor's office. They can also download music, videos, and games on their hand-held devices. And goods and services increasingly are available worldwide. Will this mean even more advertising and more distractions? Will this connect us more to loved ones or come between us.

- *Globalism/nationalism.* Economic conditions have caused corporations to pressure governments to favor trade agreements between nations for both production of goods (hiring labor) and consumption of goods (profiting from sales). Telecommunications and transportation facilitate a global economy. At the same time, "When people are buffeted by change, the need for spiritual belief intensifies" (Naisbitt & Aburdene, 1990, p. 272). Cultural nationalism increases as well. As people throughout the world are exposed to more homogeneity via travel, media, and telecommunications, they may cling to their religious/and ethnic traditions for identity. In *Jihad vs. McWorld* (Barber, 1996), the author classifies "McWorld" as the "universe of manufactured needs, mass consumption, and mass infotainment." It is motivated by profits and consumer preferences; this is known as "self-determination." "Jihad" (holy war) is shorthand for the "fundamentalist politics of religious, tribal, and other zealots." It is motivated by faith in a spirit that governs all aspects of life; this is known as "spirit-determinism." The terrorist attacks in the United States on September 11, 2001, were an extreme example of the fanatical belief in spiritual determinism versus self-determination.
- *Information intermediaries.* One way the business world has capitalized on today's information glut is by offering endorsements (celebrity), gimmicks (rewards), and services (consulting) to help consumers make decisions.

© David Young-Wolff/Getty Images

Today's consumers have many choices.

When you buy a book, isn't it easier to choose one from the *New York Times* best-seller list or Oprah Winfrey's Book Club than to read the jackets? Do you choose an airline because of its rewards program or the convenience of its schedules and destinations? Do you need to hire a wedding planner or an investment counselor? In the same vein, when I began writing in the 1980s, I relied on journal articles that contained peer-reviewed research. Not only are there more journals today, but books and Internet sources have proliferated as well. As the amount of available information increases and people's time and areas of expertise decrease, they are likely to rely on intermediaries to "predigest" material not readily understood or to narrow the choices available. For my part, I am looking more to peer-reviewed *reviews* of the research as an intermediary to enable me to incorporate new knowledge. Thus, not only will children have to learn more adaptive critical skills as information takes on new forms (Alexander & Tate, 1999), but they will also have to apply these skills to information intermediaries. Schools will have to add information literacy to their curriculums.

Consequences of scientific, technological, economic, and political changes for children depend on how traditional power structures in health care, schools, banks, businesses, governments, and so on deal with the new realities in science, medicine, education, economics, communications, media, transportation, security, privacy, and ecology. Futurists Alvin Toffler (1990) and John Naisbitt (1994) describe a world plugged into information via telecommunications; power is directly linked to knowledge, and knowledge has become central to economic development. Thus, the control of knowledge has the potential for changing traditional power structures. For example, on a global level, access to information gave terrorists the power to coordinate horrific destructive acts, and as a result, travel security measures and privacy rights have changed dramatically. For another example, in the United States, access to knowledge has altered the doctor–patient relationship. Power has shifted from the doctors (who possess most of the medical knowledge) to the patients and the insurance companies; doctors practicing inappropriately are likely to be sued by their patients, and what doctors may be paid for their services is often determined by what insurance companies deem equitable (managed care). A third example involves changes in the traditional power structure between politicians and constituents. People no longer have to depend on their representatives to propose a law; now, if they gather enough voter signatures, they can have an initiative put on the ballot. A fourth example is the changed relationship between educators and the public. Not only do parents serve on school boards that make decisions regarding schools, but educators are accountable for children's learning. Thus, the more knowledgeable more and more people become, the less likely it is for power to remain in the hands of the few, and the less likely it is that traditional power structures will remain constant over time.

A challenge resulting from the shift in power structures of social institutions is the need to create caring communities that teach children to think: to apply, analyze, synthesize, and evaluate information, and not simply regurgitate facts (Fiske, 1992). The ability to think and to apply knowledge becomes critical in a world plugged into machines and bombarded with information and choices (Postman, 1992). Children will have to learn to solve problems not previously encountered. They will have to extrapolate from previous experiences. Who will teach them?

CHANGE AND CONSEQUENCES

As has been discussed, the future is shaped by the present. Specifically, social trends over time (the chronosystem) affect macrosystems and exosystems, which, in turn, affect microsystems and mesosystems. Accompanying these trends are positive and negative consequences—some of which are dangerous to children's development, such as terrorism. The following ecological trends challenge families, schools, and communities' commitment to children's needs (Children's Defense Fund, 2001; Federal Interagency Forum, 2001):

- Family size is shrinking.
- The United States is a highly mobile society, and few children spend their entire childhood in one residence.
- The proportion of children with mothers in the labor force has grown dramatically.
- The number of families with children that are homeless has increased.
- The proportion of children living with both biological parents has declined while the proportion living with single-parent families has grown. The number of children who experience divorce and remarriage has risen as well.
- The number of children who are abused or neglected has increased.
- Children are more likely than members of other age groups to live in poverty, with children under age 6 living in a female-householder family particularly at risk. Children who are poor are more likely to have health problems and physical or mental disabilities.
- The number of children who have no health insurance has increased.
- The suicide rate for adolescents is increasing.
- Poverty, intolerance, drugs, and family violence are contributors.

Violence in the community is a reality many children face.

- Children with disabilities increasingly are included in programs for all children.
- More children are attending early childhood education programs.

To monitor the effects of change on children, the federal government has developed some measures. *America's Children: Key National Indicators of Well-Being, 2001* (Federal Interagency Forum, 2001) reports on the overall status of the nation's children. Indicators measured include the following:

- *Economic security.* These document poverty rates and household income among children, and the availability of basic necessities such as housing, food, and health care.
- *Health.* These document the physical health and well-being of children, including immunizations, and the probability, at varying ages, of dying.
- *Behavior and social environment indicators.* These document the number of youths engaged in illegal, dangerous, or high-risk behaviors such as smoking, drinking alcohol, using drugs, or committing violent crimes.
- *Education indicators.* These document success in educating the nation's children, including preschool attendance, reading proficiency, overall achievement, and completion of high school and college.

James Garbarino, professor and author of *Raising Children in a Socially Toxic Environment* (1995), believes that violence, drugs, uncaring communities, poverty, abusive families and custody battles are poisoning children's lives and are responsible for the less-than-optimal well-being of America's children. Just as pollution poisons our physical environment, our social environment is being poisoned by the breakdown of family and community support systems resulting in anger, alienation, depression, and/or paranoia.

Garbarino (1995) argues that society must redefine childhood as "the social space in which to lay the foundation for the best that human development has to offer" (p. 12). All children should "be shielded from the direct demands of adult economic, political, and sexual forces" (p. 8). Children have a right to be protected from poverty. They have a right to be protected from excessive consumerism and commercial advertising that preys on their immaturity. They have a right to be protected legally from situations deemed harmful.

Garbarino discusses what can be done to strengthen children's "social space":

- Children need stability; government and business must therefore promote policies supportive of families, such as personal leaves.
- Children need security; law enforcement policies must therefore ensure that their physical and social environments are safe from violence.
- Children need affirmation and acceptance; they must therefore have opportunities to spend time with caring adults who enable them to be part of the larger community and who give them a sense of values and spirituality.

Joy Osofsky (1997), a professor of pediatrics and psychology, agrees, citing "evidence that many adolescents and young adults who first become delinquent and later develop into criminals were exposed earlier in their lives to much violence, disorganized families, poor education, and limited opportunities" (p. 5). She asserts the need to make a commitment to changing media values communicated to children, providing economic opportunities and other options for youths, and applying stricter gun control measures.

That growing up today is more difficult than it was a generation ago is documented by economist Sylvia Ann Hewlett and educator Cornel West in their book *The War Against Parents* (1998). Hewlett and West show how government, business, and media have waged a silent war against parents. Families' functions of commitment and care have been negatively impacted by taxes and government housing policies, corporate greed, and media values. Parents need support from the macrosystem and exosystems to do their job, which is to create a caring community for children. Hewlett and West call for parents to advocate a Parents' Bill of Rights (pp. 231–232). Specifically, parents are entitled to (1) time for their children (paid parenting leave), (2) economic security (a living wage, job opportunities, tax relief), (3) a profamily electoral and legal system, (4) a supportive external environment (violence- and drug-free neighborhoods, quality child care, family health benefits), and (5) honor and dignity (an index of family well-being, parents afforded certain privileges, like those granted to senior citizens).

Epilogue

Child socialization outcomes are dependent on contexts of development, with a change in one context affecting changes in other contexts. A change over time (the chronosystem) is society's concept of childhood. This concept is influenced by macrosystems such as history, politics, economics, culture, and technology. Seven-year-old Jessica Dubroff could fly a plane because the technology was available at that time in history. There were no laws limiting her aeronautical activities. Her parents could afford her flying lessons. Her culture encouraged achievement, competition, and winning. The media reported on her quest. And her parents believed love meant supporting their child's dreams without constraints.

Summary

Ecology involves studying humans in their physical, social, and cultural environments, all of which are affected by societal change. The purpose of this book is to examine how growing up in a changing world affects the development of children via socialization—the process by which individuals acquire the knowledge, skills, and character traits that enable them to participate as more or less effective members of groups and society.

Socialization is unique to humans due to our capacity for language. Language enables us to communicate ideas and replace actions with thoughts, and then use thought to transform behavior. Self-regulation/control comes from the internalization of thoughts.

Socialization begins at birth and continues throughout life. It occurs through human interaction and so is reciprocal, or bidirectional, with children playing a role in their own socialization resulting in transformations in the individual. Thus, it is also dynamic, changing as children change. Socialization may be intentional or unintentional.

One of the challenges brought upon by change is society's concept of childhood. The period of protection for children has gone from being short during the Renaissance to long during the Industrial Revolution. As societal pressures increase, many fear that the concept of childhood will be compressed.

When societal change occurs, the agents who socialize children are affected, and children bear the consequences. The agents of socialization are the family, the school, the peer group, the media, and the community. These agents employ different socialization techniques. Children play a transactional role in their own socialization, too, eliciting different techniques as they develop. However, generally, the "output" of socialization (values, attitudes, attributes, motives, self-regulation/behavior, morals, gender roles, self-esteem) is affected by the "input."

Socialization can be thought of as occurring in an ecological context. Bronfenbrenner's model of human ecology consists of the child's development in the microsystem, mesosystem, exosystem, and macrosystem in which relationships and interactions take place over time (the chronosystem).

The microsystem is the immediate setting children occupy at a particular time. The mesosystem consists of the interrelationships between two or more microsystems. The exosystem refers to external settings in which children do not actually participate, but which affect them in one of their microsystems. The macrosystem refers to the larger society in which children grow up and its accompanying ideology. Macrosystems can be classified as high or low context, with each type having different influences on people's perspectives on the world. The chronosystem refers to changes in ecological systems and in individuals resulting in new conditions that affect development.

Effects of change in the macrosystem on exosystems, mesosystems, and microsystems are exemplified by Elder's study comparing families who were economically deprived during the Depression and those who were not. A major influence for children growing up in deprived families was their involvement in the adult world of work, which was necessary for the welfare of others. The long-term consequences of the Depression were found to depend on the gender and age of the child, the existing family relationships, and the socioeconomic status of the family at the time when economic hardship hit.

The interaction of micro-, meso-, exo-, and macrosystems over time makes socialization very complex. The challenge is to pass on the cultural heritage to the next generation while also enabling that generation to adapt to change.

Societal trends impacting children include biotechnology, reconceptualization of societal and individual responsibility, mobile technology, globalism/rationalism, and information intermediaries. Accompanying societal change are consequences such as children being exposed to an increasingly socially toxic environment. For parents and other adults to fulfill their commitment and caring roles, they need support from government and business.

Activity

PURPOSE *To understand the impact of change (chronosystem) on microsystems and mesosystems.*

1. Describe one to three changes you observed in the following contexts:
   a. In your family as you grew up
   b. In your school
   c. In your peer group
   d. In the media—television or books
   e. In your community
2. Pick one change for each microsystem and discuss the following:
   a. Why you think it occurred
   b. How it impacted you
   c. What impact it had on the other microsystems (mesosystem), if any

Research Terms

Adaptation
Child socialization
Child well-being
Human ecology
Societal trends
Temperament

Related Readings

Aries, P. (1962). *Centuries of childhood: A social history of family life.* New York: Knopf.
Bronfenbrenner, U. (1979). *The ecology of human development.* Cambridge, MA: Harvard University Press.
Chess, S., & Thomas, A. (1987). *Know your child.* New York: Basic Books.

Cleverly, J., & Philips, D. C. (1986). *Visions of childhood: Influential models from Locke to Spock.* New York: Teachers College Press.

DeGraaf, J., Wann, D., & Naylor, T. H. (2001). *Affluenza: The all-consuming epidemic.* San Francisco: Berrett-Koehler.

Elkind, D. (1998). *Reinventing childhood.* Rosemont, NJ: Modern Learning Press.

Garbarino, J. (1995). *Raising children in a socially toxic environment.* San Francisco: Jossey-Bass.

Moen, P., Elder, G. H., Jr., & Luscher, K. (Eds.). (1995). *Examining lives in context: Perspectives on the ecology of human development.* Washington, DC: American Psychological Association.

Naisbitt, J., & Aburdene, P. (1990). *Megatrends 2000.* New York: William Morrison.

Postman, N. (1992). *Technopoly: The surrender of culture to technology.* New York: Vintage.

Rogoff, B. (2003). *The cultural nature of human development.* New York: Oxford University Press.

Skinner, B. F. (1948). *Walden two.* New York: Macmillan.

Chapter 2

Prologue: Then and Now

Aims of Socialization
Develop a Self-Concept
Enable Self-Regulation
Empower Achievement
Acquire Appropriate Social
    Roles
Implement Developmental
    Skills

Agents of Socialization
The Family
Schools and Child Care
Peers
Mass Media
The Community

Methods of Socialization
Affective Methods: Effect
    Emerges from Feeling
Operant Methods: Effect
    Emerges from Acting
Observational Methods:
    Effect Emerges from
    Imitating
Cognitive Methods: Effect
    Emerges from
    Information Processing
Sociocultural Methods:
    Effect Emerges from
    Conforming
Apprenticeship Methods:
    Effect Emerges from
    Guided Participation

Outcomes of Socialization
Values
Attitudes
Motives and Attributes
Self-Esteem
Self-Regulation/Behavior
Morals
Gender Roles

Epilogue

Summary

Activity

Research Terms

Related Readings

Four by Five/Superstock

Ecology of Socialization

The childhood shows the man, as morning shows the day.

—JOHN MILTON

WHAT IT MEANS TO BE HUMAN

THEN *The Adventures of Pinocchio*, by Carlo Collodi (1972[1882]), is a classic story illustrating the trials and tribulations of a little boy growing up and the agents who contribute to his socialization. Gepetto, a woodcarver, wants a son very much, so he carves a little boy out of a block of wood and names him Pinocchio. While Gepetto sleeps, the Blue Fairy appears and gives the wooden boy life.

The Blue Fairy tells Pinocchio that if he wants to become a real boy, he must prove himself to be brave, truthful, and unselfish: "Be a good son to Gepetto—make him proud of you! Then, some day, you will wake up and find yourself a real boy."

However, the Blue Fairy warns Pinocchio that the world is full of temptations and that he must learn to choose between right and wrong in order to become human. Pinocchio asks how he will know the difference. The Blue Fairy explains that he must rely on his own conscience to tell him. Pinocchio, who does not know what a conscience is, remains perplexed. Fortunately, a little cricket, Jiminy Cricket, who had been observing the whole scene, volunteers to serve as Pinocchio's conscience. The Blue Fairy leaves Pinocchio in Jiminy Cricket's hands, asking him to give Pinocchio the benefit of his advice and experience.

Unfortunately, Pinocchio is unable to resist temptation. One time he starts off to school but sells his books in order to go to a marionette show. Another time he wanders off and meets with thieves, who steal his money and try to kill him. He is saved by the Blue Fairy, who then puts a spell on him that makes his nose grow long every time he tells a lie—which is supposed to remind Pinocchio not to do wrong. Eventually, however, Pinocchio succumbs to the temptation of Playland, where boys can be lazy and play all day. There he finds out that laziness can last for just so long. Good-for-nothing boys end up making jackasses of themselves. Without Jiminy Cricket, who helps him escape from Playland before it is too late, Pinocchio would have turned completely into a jackass.

Full of remorse, Pinocchio searches for Gepetto, only to find out that the woodcarver has been swallowed by a whale, so he goes to sea to save him. Pinocchio vows to work hard at his studies to become someone of whom Gepetto can be proud. Because Pinocchio has risked his life, thereby demonstrating braveness and unselfishness, the Blue Fairy turns him into a real boy. And so Pinocchio finally becomes socialized into the human race.

NOW Like the story of Pinocchio, which is about socializing agents and their influence on a marionette, the movie *E.T.* (2002[1982]) is about the reciprocal and dynamic relationship between an extraterrestrial and a 10-year-old boy named Elliot, influencing the socialization of both.

E.T. is accidentally left behind on Earth when his spaceship hastily leaves. Elliot finds him and takes him home to hide him. The two learn to communicate with each other and become friends. Elliot and his family care for E.T. in secret because they fear his discovery might cause the government, or someone else, to kill him. E.T. and Elliot learn to read each other's emotions. Thus, E.T. knows Elliot wants him to stay, and Elliot knows E.T. misses his home. However, when E.T. becomes ill, Elliot's true friendship is tested; he has to put E.T.'s needs before his own desires. He helps E.T. build a device to send a message to E.T.'s parents to come to Earth and take him home.

KEY QUESTIONS

- Why did Pinocchio and Elliot put other's desires before their own (Pinocchio giving up the pleasures and freedom of play for the hard work and responsibilities of school, and Elliot giving up a cherished friend and playmate)?
- Was the change in Pinocchio's behavior motivated by his love for Gepetto? The fear of punishment? The desire to be rewarded by the Blue Fairy? Did he learn from his experiences?
- Was Elliot's decision to send E.T. home motivated by friendship or fear of punishment, or both?

Aims of Socialization

The story of Pinocchio's struggle to become a real boy parallels any child's struggle to become socialized—hence its timelessness. The Blue Fairy's warnings are like those of a parent. Jiminy Cricket's advice is like that of a teacher. Pinocchio's adventures with the lazy boys are like those with one's peer group. Finally, Pinocchio's discovery of the difference between good and evil represents a most significant outcome of socialization—a conscience. The story of E.T. illustrates the meaning of care and sacrifice. When one forms a close attachment to another, one learns to share and puts the other's needs first when required. E.T. also represents a significant outcome of socialization—prosocial behavior (kindness, caring, helpfulness, loyalty). This chapter explores the process of socialization, including its aims or goals, its agents and their methods, and its outcomes. Figure 2.1 shows an ecological model of the systems involved in the process. Because socialization outcomes characterize the adult, they will be discussed more specifically in the concluding chapters.

Socialization enables children to learn what they need to know in order to be integrated into the society in which they live. It also enables them to develop their potentialities and form satisfying relationships. Through socialization, children develop a self-concept, learn self-regulation, empower achievement, acquire appropriate social roles, and implement developmental skills.

DEVELOP A SELF-CONCEPT

Self-concept is an individual's perception of his or her identity as distinct from that of others. It emerges from experiences of separateness from others. The value one places on that identity, **self-esteem,** is discussed later in the chapter under outcomes of socialization.

When you were born, your parents named you and may have sent out announcements to relatives and friends that a new individual had entered the world. While everyone else treated you as a separate being, you still were unaware of where your environment ended and "you" began.

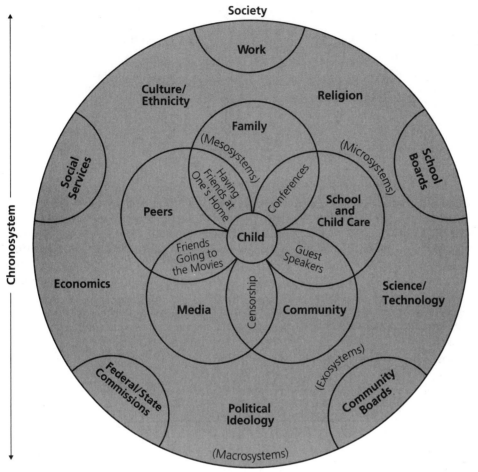

Figure 2.1
An Ecological Model of Human Development
Socialization involves bi-directional interactions between the child and significant others in microsystems, mesosystem, exosystems, macrosystems, and the chronosystem.

As the months passed and you had some experiences using your senses, you noticed that when you touched your own hand you felt something in your fingers and your hand, whereas when you touched your mother's hand, you felt a sensation only in your fingers.

Gradually, as people met your needs, you came to realize that they existed even when you could not see them. And as you developed language, you learned that objects have names (as did you) and that each had an independent existence. Language enabled you to describe and compare. Sometime around age 15 to 18 months, you put things together and understood that you are you. You could recognize yourself in a mirror. You could assert your wants ("Me do it!"), especially when you perceived that someone else was controlling you.

As you got older, your concept of self—your identity, your understanding of who you are—was influenced by significant others. If your needs were met consistently and you were given opportunities to discover things on your own, you developed a sense of autonomy, or self-regulation and self-control. If, however, your needs were not met consistently and you did not get to explore your environment, you developed a sense of doubt. The significant others in your life also acted like a mirror. Your parents, teachers, and friends provided constant feedback on your achievements and failures. Thus, in developing a self-concept, or identity, you also develop self-esteem.

As you entered adolescence, your self-concept included how you related to others. Being a member of a group was important to your identity. In later adolescence, your self-concept expanded to include how you related to the larger community. Self-concept involves not only "Who am I?" but "Where am I going?" and "How will I get there?"

Charles Horton Cooley (1964), one of the founders of sociology, observed that through the experiences of interacting with others children begin to distinguish themselves from others. Children call themselves "I" or "me"—"I hungry" and "Me go." As they begin to act independently, they become aware that others are evaluating them, saying "Good boy/girl" or "No, don't do that." Thus, their behavior is judged according to certain rules and standards, which must be learned and understood before individuals are capable of self-evaluation. As children learn these criteria, they develop a self-concept; this concept reflects the attitudes of others and is termed "the looking-glass self." Mead (1934) referred to this gradually maturing way of looking at the self as "the generalized other." When children refer to themselves as "shy" or "hardworking," they have incorporated the standards of others into this self-description.

Thus, people's self-concept develops when the attitudes and expectations of significant others with whom they interact are incorporated into their personality, making it possible to regulate their behavior accordingly. Individuals' perceived competence in self-regulation/control is part of their self-esteem. Harter (1998, 1999) studied various types of competence involved in self-esteem—namely, behavioral, academic, physical, and social. Self-esteem is discussed in more detail in Chapter 11.

Psychologist Erik Erikson (1963, 1980) explained the personality development of individuals as the outcome of their interactions in their social environment. He identified eight critical stages of psychosocial development in a person's life that impact the self-concept: (1) trust versus mistrust, (2) autonomy versus shame and doubt, (3) initiative versus guilt, (4) industry versus inferiority, (5) identity versus identity diffusion, (6) intimacy versus isolation, (7) generativity versus self-absorption, and (8) integrity versus despair (see Table 2.1).

Infancy: Trust Versus Mistrust (Birth to Age 1)

The first "task" of infants is to develop the cornerstone of a healthy personality, a basic sense of trust in themselves and the people in their environment. The quality and consistency of care infants receive determine the outcome of this stage. The child whose basic needs for nourishment and physical contact are met will develop a sense of trust, which lays a foundation for positive self-esteem. The child whose care is negligent or inconsistent will develop a sense of mistrust, which may persist throughout life and result in negative self-esteem. Some mistrust, however is healthy in that it can protect individuals from danger and manipulation. Contemporary research shows a positive relationship between parental nurturance and self-worth (Harter, 1998, 1999; Hopkins & Klein, 1994). Elliot's nurturing care of E.T. led to a trusting bond between them.

Early Childhood: Autonomy Versus Shame and Doubt (Age 2–3)

Physical and cognitive maturation enables children to behave autonomously—to walk without help, feed themselves, get things off the shelf, assert themselves verbally, and so on. If children are allowed to be self-sufficient according to ability lev-

Note that an individual's development can be described as being at any point on a dimension rather than at one extreme or the other. The importance of interactions with one's social environment in the development of a self-concept is indicated by the socializing agents that are most significant at various stages.

Table 2.1

Erikson's Eight Stages of Psychosocial Development

1. INFANCY	Trust					Mistrust
			Family			
2. EARLY CHILDHOOD	Autonomy					Shame/
			Family			doubt
3. PLAY AGE	Initiative					Guilt
		Family	School (child care)			
4. SCHOOL AGE	Industry					Inferiority
		Family	Peers	School	Community	
5. ADOLESCENCE	Identity					Identity
		Family	Peers	School	Community	diffusion
6. YOUNG ADULTHOOD	Intimacy					Isolation
		Family	Peers	Community		
7. ADULTHOOD	Generativity					Self-
		Family	Peers	Community		absorption
8. SENESCENCE	Integrity					Despair
		Family	Peers			

els, the outcome of this stage will be feelings of autonomy. If children are deprived of the opportunity to develop a will, if they are continually being corrected or reprimanded, they may come to feel shame when being assertive and self-doubt when being independent. However, some shame is healthy in that it can prevent certain socially unacceptable behaviors such as picking one's nose in public.

Play Age: Initiative Versus Guilt (Age 3–5)

Children's increasing ability to communicate and to imagine leads them to initiate many activities. If they are allowed to create their own games and fantasies, to ask questions, and to use certain objects (a hammer, nails, and wood, for example) with supervision, then the outcome of this stage will be sense of initiative. If they are made to feel that they are "bad" for trying new things and "pests" for asking questions, they may carry a sense of guilt throughout life. Probably the reason *Pinocchio* has remained a favorite story is that, like all children, Pinocchio was continually learning which activities he initiated were OK and which ones were not. Thus, some guilt is healthy in that it can control misbehavior.

School Age: Industry Versus Inferiority (Age 6 to Puberty)

During school age, while learning to accept instruction and to gain recognition by showing effort and producing "things," children are developing the capacity to enjoy work. The outcome of this stage for children who do not receive recognition for their efforts, or who do not experience any success, may be feelings of incompetency and inferiority. Children who are praised for their efforts will be motivated to achieve; children who are ignored or rebuked may give up and exhibit helplessness. Yet,

Children develop a sense of initiative by having opportunities to produce things.

some feelings of inferiority are healthy in that they can prevent children from feeling invincible and taking dangerous risks.

Adolescence: Identity Versus Identity Diffusion (Puberty to Age 18+)

With rapid growth and sexual maturation, adolescents begin to question people, things, values, and attitudes previously relied on and to struggle through the crises of earlier stages all over again. The developmental task during adolescence, then, is to integrate earlier childhood identifications with current biological and social changes. The danger in this stage is that while young people are trying out many roles, which is a normal process, they may be unable to choose an identity or make a commitment, and so will not know who they are or what they may become (identity diffusion). Because adolescence is a time for exploration, some diffusion is healthy in that it allows individuals to learn what is suitable behavior and what is not.

Young Adulthood: Intimacy Versus Isolation (Age 18+ to Middle Adulthood)

Individuals who have established an identity are now able to achieve intimacy with themselves and with others, in both friendship and love. The danger here is that those who fear losing their identity in an intimate relationship with another may develop a sense of isolation. Some isolation is healthy, however, in that it can enable people to learn about themselves and provide time for individual pursuits.

Adulthood: Generativity Versus Self-Absorption (Middle Adulthood to Late Adulthood)

From the development of intimate relationships comes **generativity,** the interest in establishing and guiding the next generation. This interest can be manifested by becoming a parent or by being involved with the development of young people through teaching, church, Scouts, and so on, as well as being productive and creative in one's work. There is the possibility in this stage that the lack of generativity may result in self-absorption, which may be manifested as depression, hypochon-dria, substance abuse, or promiscuity. Yet, some self-absorption is healthy in that it can lead to creativity and the pursuit of hobbies.

Senescence: Integrity Versus Despair (Late Adulthood to Death)

Individuals who have achieved an identity, developed satisfying intimacy with oth-ers, and adapted to the joys and frustrations of guiding the next generation reach the end of life with a certain ego integrity or positive self-esteem. They accept responsibility for what their own life is and was and where it fits in the continuum of life. For those who have not achieved that integrity, this stage may be character-ized by despair or extremely low self-esteem. Despairing individuals tend to be in ill health, abuse drugs and/or alcohol, and even commit suicide. They may become burdens to their families physically, financially, and/or psychologically. In contrast, individuals with a sense of integrity are likely to have friends, be active (physically and mentally), and look at life positively even though they know that death is imminent. The concept of a sense of integrity can be summed up in what Rose Kennedy, who lived to be 104, said before she died: "I find it interesting to reflect on what has made my life, even with its moments of pain, an essentially happy one; I have come to the conclusion that the most important element in human life is faith" (quoted in Goldman, 1994, p. 20). Probably the only despair that is healthy is that which leads to change or greater appreciation of life.

ENABLE SELF-REGULATION

Self-regulation involves the process of bringing one's emotions, thoughts, and behavior under control. This can be interpreted as routing our feelings through our brains before acting on them according to the situation. Regulated behavior often involves postponing or modifying immediate gratification for the sake of some future goal. This implies an ability to tolerate frustration. For example, you curb your urge to spank a child who has just thrown a bowl of food on the floor in a tantrum because you want to set an example of how to deal with frustration. When you are trying to maintain your weight, you postpone satisfying those hunger pangs until mealtime. You postpone sexual intercourse until marriage because of your religious or personal goals. Even though you hate to wake up early, you set your alarm in order to be at work on time because your supervisor depends on you and you need the money.

Early relationships, especially attachment to parents, play a significant role in the development of emotional regulation (Bridges & Golnick, 1995) and "emotional intelligence" (Goleman, 1995). As children progress from infancy to childhood, emotional and behavioral regulation gradually shifts from external socializing agents to internal, self-induced mechanisms (Eisenberg, 1998). Caregivers provide children with information (body language, facial expressions, verbal instructions and explanations) to help them deal with situations. As children develop cogni-tively and have more experiences, they learn how to interpret events, how to express emotions appropriately, how to cope with disappointment, frustration, rejection, anger, and so on. Self-regulation/control is related to moral development, an outcome of socialization discussed in detail in Chapter 12.

EMPOWER ACHIEVEMENT

Socialization furnishes goals for what individuals are going to be when they grow up—for example, a teacher, police officer, or business executive. These goals provide

This child is having difficulty controlling his temper.

Niyati Reeve/Getty Images

the rationale for going to school, getting along with others, following rules, and so on. In other words, socialization gives meaning or purpose to adulthood and to the long process children have to go through to get there. In order for Pinocchio to become a real boy, he had to go to school, as well as learn right from wrong.

Significant adults and peers influence children's motivation to succeed. For example, adults who understand child development provide appropriate challenges at the "right" time with the "right" amount of support to produce highly competent and motivated children (Eccles, Wigfield, & Schiefele, 1998). The motivation to achieve and the attributes of achievement, such as explanations for success and failure, are socialization outcomes. They are discussed in more detail in Chapter 11.

ACQUIRE APPROPRIATE SOCIAL ROLES

To be part of a group, individuals must have a function that complements the group. For example, in a group of employees, the supervisor's function or role is to lead the employees; in a family group, the parents' role is to nurture the child; in a peer group, the role of friends is to provide emotional support. We have many social roles throughout life, some of which occur simultaneously, and we must assume the appropriate behavior for each at the appropriate time. For instance, I am a wife, a parent, a daughter, a teacher, and a friend—all at the same time. As a wife, I am a confidante; as a parent, I am nurturant; as a daughter, I am submissive; as a teacher, I am a facilitator; as a friend, I am emotionally supportive. Elliot and E.T. learned the meaning of friendship.

Gender is a social role, too, in that boys and girls learn gender-appropriate behavior from significant members of their society (Ruble & Martin, 1998). What is appropriate (Maccoby, 2000) is affected by culture, ethnicity, and religion (macrosystem influences), as well as time (chronosystem influence).

IMPLEMENT DEVELOPMENTAL SKILLS

Through socialization, children acquire social, emotional, and cognitive skills so that they can function in society. Acquiring social skills may involve learning how to obtain information from other people, use the telephone, conduct business negotiations, and the like. Acquiring emotional skills may involve controlling aggressive impulses, learning to deal with frustration by substituting another goal for one that is blocked, or being able to compensate for mistakes. Acquiring cognitive skills may involve reading, mathematics, writing, problem solving, geography, history, and science.

Psychologist Robert Havighurst (1972) examined how society's expectations with regard to certain behavioral skills change according to the maturation of the individual (chronosystem influence), using the term **developmental task** to explain this aspect of socialization. According to Havighurst, a developmental task is midway between an individual need and a societal demand. The developmental tasks of life are those things we must learn if we are to get along well in society (macrosystem influence). As we grow, we develop physically, intellectually, and socially. Our physical development enables us to walk, control our bladders, and use a pencil. Our intellectual development enables us to learn to read, do arithmetic, and solve problems. Our social development enables us to cooperate, empathize, and interact with others. And our emotional development enables us to regulate our impulses and express our feelings. Developmental tasks categorized according to societal demands for certain behaviors are listed below; the ways in which they change for individuals from birth to death are outlined in Appendix A.

- Achieving an appropriate dependence/independence pattern
- Achieving an appropriate giving–receiving pattern of affection
- Relating to changing social groups
- Developing a conscience
- Learning one's "psychosociobiological" role
- Accepting and adjusting to a changing body
- Managing a changing body and learning new behavioral patterns
- Learning to understand and control the physical world
- Developing an appropriate symbol system and conceptual abilities
- Relating oneself to the cosmos

As we develop in these dimensions, we face new expectations from significant socializing agents in the society. We are expected to learn to walk, talk, use the toilet, and dress ourselves. We are expected to read, write, add, and subtract. We are expected to share, develop a conscience, and fill an appropriate gender role. We are expected to love other people and be responsible for our own actions.

Thus, developmental tasks arise from societal pressures on individuals according to their development: "If the task is not achieved at the proper time, it will not be achieved well, and failure in this task will cause partial or complete failure in the achievement of other tasks yet to come" (Havighurst, 1972, p. 3). If children do not have experiences in language, such as being spoken to and making sounds during the critical stage of language development (first year), their ability to communicate will be handicapped for the remainder of their lives. The child who is not socialized to develop a conscience may engage in delinquent behavior in adolescence. The child who is not socialized to receive and give affection may not succeed in a marital or family relationship.

Those who do not succeed in a developmental task risk the disapproval of others because they have not behaved as expected. As a reminder of the Blue Fairy's disapproval, Pinocchio's nose grew long whenever he did not tell the truth. Even though E.T. tried to be human emotionally, physically he could not and became ill.

Developmental tasks differ from society to society, and each group in a given society has its own developmental definitions and expectations. For example, a common developmental milestone for Euro-American, middle-class infants is to sleep through the night. This expectation is usually fulfilled by about age 4–6 months and is often facilitated by parents' feeding the baby just before they go to sleep and/or by playing with the baby and putting him or her down for the night as late as possible. However, for many other ethnic groups, in which the infant sleeps with the mother and nurses on demand, sleeping through the night is not valued as a developmental milestone.

Differences in developmental definitions and expectations may account for some of the social adjustment problems in school among children from diverse ethnic or cultural groups. For example, the developmental task for achieving an appropriate dependence/independence pattern may be interpreted differently by various groups. Most middle-class American mothers, as well as American teachers, tend to expect children to be independent of adults by the time they reach school age in that they can take care of personal needs and learn on their own with some direction. Japanese mothers, in contrast, tend to expect some of their children's dependency needs to be transferred to teachers when their children go to school, and Japanese mothers generally remain very involved in their children's learning throughout school. Hispanic and Hawaiian mothers tend to expect their children's dependency needs to be transferred to older siblings, and interdependence, rather than independence, is encouraged. Thus, Japanese, Hispanic, and Hawaiian children, and children from other high-context cultures, may experience conflicts between developmental skills taught by their families and those taught in American schools (Bennett, 2003).

Every individual in a society (along with his or her genetic traits) represents the outcome of the process of socialization. The success of this outcome in terms of society's expectations depends on a series of interactions with significant socializing agents, such as parents, teachers, peers, and media, that constitute the community in which this individual lives (Collins, Maccoby, Steinberg, Hetherington, & Bornstein, 2000) (see Figure 2.2).

Agents of Socialization

The generalized community comprises many groups that play a part in socializing individuals. These groups or agents of socialization exert their influence in different ways and at different times.

In the early years, the family assumes the primary role of nurturing the child. As the child grows older, the peer group becomes a primary source of support. In primitive societies, training for competency occurs in the family in the form of learning to hunt or to build a shelter, whereas in industrial societies, it occurs in the school in the form of learning to read, write, compute, master science or geography, and so forth.

Figure 2.2
Socialization Processes and Outcomes

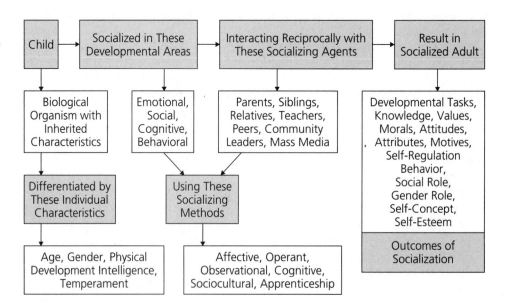

Each agent has its own functions in socialization. Sometimes the agents complement each other; other times they contradict each other. The value of getting along with others is usually taught in the family, the school, the church, the peer group, and perhaps the media, with the agents complementing each other. The value of academic achievement, however, may be supported by some families and the school but scorned by the peer group—an example of contradiction among the agents of socialization. The media and the peer group may support sexual experimentation while the family and church condemn it.

Socializing Agents and Their Messages: The Reality

Typical American children start the day with some instructions and expectations from their parents about finishing breakfast, setting an after-school schedule, cleaning their rooms, and so on. A few additional remarks may be forthcoming from older siblings regarding the condition of the bathroom when they went to use it.

On the way to school, the bus driver may prohibit loud talking or changing seats once the bus has begun moving. At school, one teacher may stress independence and competition, and another may emphasize cooperation and dependence on the group. After school, teachers may assume different roles, perhaps as coaches or club leaders. The team or the club members may value the best athlete or the one who sells the most raffle tickets, but in the classroom setting, peers may dislike the person who gets the best grades or reads the most books.

Back at home, television sends messages via the various programs. One day a child may watch *Sesame Street* and feel empathic and altruistic. Another day the child may watch *Spiderman* and come away feeling aggressive. Nintendo and other video or computer games provide for the interactive expression of emotions without adult involvement.

In reality, children receive many demands from socializing agents, as well as conflicting messages. As discussed in Chapter 1, the process of socialization is reciprocal and dynamic, with children playing a role in their own socialization. Children's **temperament**—the innate characteristics that determine individuals' sensitivity to various experiences and responsiveness to patterns of social interaction—can elicit different reactions in caregivers. For example, a relaxed, happy baby tends to elicit smiles, and a tense, crying baby tends to elicit concern or anxiety. As children develop and change, so, too, do other's reactions to them.

Points to Ponder

Temperament is characterized by inborn ways of responding to stimuli, based on such factors as activity level, irritability, fearfulness, and sociability. My son and I have similar temperaments, which made the management of socialization goals and methods easier than for my daughter, whose temperament is different from mine. What role do you think your temperament played in the bidirectionality of socialization interactions in your family?

THE FAMILY

The **family** is the child's introduction to society and, therefore, bears the major responsibility for socializing the child. The family into which a child is born places the child in a community and in a society; newborns begin their social lives by acquiring the status their families have, which influences their opportunities. For example, children in low-income families not only have fewer material things but also have fewer opportunities to develop their abilities. Because they cannot compete with others of their age who have more things and more opportunities, children from low-income families tend to believe they have little control over the future and so try less hard in school and accomplish less. Characteristics of families and possible outcomes for children are discussed in detail in Chapter 3.

The family also passes on its socioeconomic status through its ability to afford higher education for its children. Children from middle- and upper-income families are more likely to go to college after high school, whereas children from low-income families are more likely to go to work. And those who have not achieved in high school, perhaps due to a lack of motivation, have fewer job opportunities. Educational level, then, is a strong determinant of future occupation and income.

In addition, the family exposes children to certain cultural experiences available in the society—perhaps religious instruction, Scouts, music lessons, Little League, or soccer. Parents buy certain toys for their children and arrange activities such as games, outings, and vacations—all of which depend to a large extent on socioeconomic status.

The family functions as a system of interaction, and the way in which it conducts personal relationships has a powerful effect on the psychosocial development of children. Through various interactions with family members, such as siblings, grandparents, and other relatives, children develop patterns for establishing relationships with others. These patterns are expressed and further developed in relationships with peers, authority figures, co-workers, and ultimately a spouse and children.

EXAMPLE Marie, the oldest of three children, was responsible for helping her mother care for her younger siblings. She often had to play a game with her little sister while her mother nursed the baby or had to watch the baby while her mother drove her sister to preschool. In her relations with her friends, Marie was the one always saying, "Let's play this" or "Let's play that" or "This is the way you're supposed to draw a house (or dog or cat)." In school, she was often appointed to be a monitor. As an adult, Marie rose to a managerial position in her office.

"The family into which a child is born is the child's first reference group, the first group whose values, norms, and practices one refers to in evaluating one's behavior" (Elkin & Handel, 1989, p. 143). For example, there is now evidence that marital conflict and distress are related to spouses' difficulties with peers as children (Rubin, Bukowski, & Parker, 1998). For another example, research has revealed that children of employed mothers from kindergarten age through adulthood have less restricted views of gender roles (Ellis, 1994). In passing on values, expectations, and practices, families also pass on to children certain behavior patterns, which tend to vary by culture and ethnicity (Greenfield & Suzuki, 1998; Rotherdam & Phinney, 1987). Parenting styles will be examined in Chapter 4.

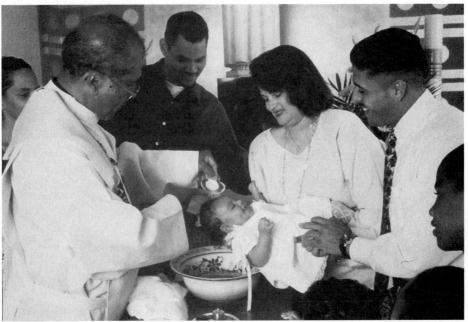

Babies are born into a culture and learn appropriate social roles.

Dimensions of Ethnic Behavior Patterns

The extreme examples of dimensions of ethnic behavior patterns are presented here for purposes of illustration; individual members of groups can vary accordingly (Trumbull, Rothstein-Fisch, Greenfield, & Quiroz, 2001).

- *Orientation: From collectivistic to individualistic.* At one extreme of this dimension is collectivism (orientation toward the group), as commonly exhibited by families representing such ethnic groups as Japanese, Hawaiian, Mexican, and Middle Eastern. These groups tend to emphasize affiliation, cooperation, and interpersonal relations. At the other extreme of this dimension is individualism (orientation toward the individual), which is commonly exhibited by many families representing middle-class Euro-Americans. They tend to focus more on individual accomplishment, competition, and independence from the group. One's orientation on this dimension becomes significant in situations in which one has to choose between obligation to one's family or to one's personal ambitions, such as keeping a job to remain geographically close to kin rather than relocating to earn more money or prestige. One's orientation on this dimension also influences risk taking and innovation versus conservatism and conformity in entrepreneurship (Hayton, George, & Zahra, 2002).

- *Coping style: From active to passive.* An active coping style is associated with "doing" and "getting things done" rather than on "being" or "becoming," which is characteristic of a passive coping style. An active coping style also involves a future time orientation in which time moves quickly and a perception that one can control and change the environment; a passive coping style reflects the belief that all events are determined by fate and so are inevitable. Generally, those from Hispanic backgrounds are less active in coping style than are those from Euro-American backgrounds (Bennett, 2003). One's coping style on this dimension becomes significant in motivating families to seek social services, such as psychological, when problems occur (McGoldrick, Giordano, Pearse, & Giordano, 1996).

- *Attitude toward authority: From submissive to egalitarian.* At one end of this dimension, children regard their parents and teachers as clear authority figures whom they respect and obey without question; at the other end, children see them as more nearly equal figures with whom they may disagree. Young children from Hispanic or Asian backgrounds have been found to be more obedient, respectful, and accepting of authority than are children from Euro-American backgrounds (Bennett, 2003). One's attitude toward authority on this dimension becomes significant in such situations as workplaces that reward assertiveness (Hofstede, 1991).

- *Communication style: From open/expressive to restrained/private.* Generally, children with an African heritage have been found to be more openly and freely expressive, both positively and negatively, in a wide variety of situations (Bennett, 2003) than children with a Euro-American heritage. These latter children, in turn, are more direct and open in social interactions than are children with an Asian heritage, who tend to be more polite and ritualistic (Bennett, 2003). One's communication style on this dimension becomes significant in relating to those whose way of interacting differs.

In Chapter 1, socialization outcomes of different worldviews were discussed. Likewise, these examples of behavior patterns from diverse ethnic groups passed on by families are important, as will be seen throughout the book, especially when they differ from the standards promoted by the schools.

According to extensive cross-cultural research done by Kagicibasi (1996), family behavioral patterns and consequent socialization practices can be categorized as interdependent (emphasis on family loyalty, intergenerational dependency, control, and obedience) and independent (emphasis on individual achievement, separateness of generations, egalitarianism, and consensus). A child brought up with interdependent values would *give* his or her parent money if needed; a child brought up with independent values might *lend* the parent money, perhaps even charging interest.

Many immigrants have brought their cultural behavior patterns to the United States. The following is an excerpt from a family analysis done by a college student from a Persian Jewish family in Los Angeles (cited in Greenfield & Suzuki, 1998):

EXAMPLE Being a first generation immigrant I have had to deal with . . . adjusting a collectivistic upbringing to an environment of individualism. In my home my parents and family coming from a country and culture . . . [with] beliefs of family as the central and dominant unit in life, endeavored to instill in us a sense of family in the collectivistic sense.

We were brought up in a home where the "we" consciousness was stressed, rather than the "I" consciousness. We were taught that our behavior not only had implications for . . . ourselves but also for the rest of the family; for example, if I stayed out late at night, not only would I be taking the chance of getting robbed, raped, and/or murdered (implications of that experience for me), but also my younger brother and sister who looked up to me would . . . be jeopardized (implications of my actions for others). . . .

We were also taught to be responsible not only for ourselves, but also responsible for every other family member; thereby sharing the responsibility for both good and bad outcomes and playing a major part in each other's lives. For example, if my brother did bad in school, I was also responsible because as his older sister I was responsible to help him and take care of him and teach him right from wrong. I was, to an extent, as responsible for his actions as he, and my parents were. . . . (p. 108)

SCHOOLS AND CHILD CARE

The school acts as an agent of society in that it is organized to perpetuate society's knowledge, skills, customs, and beliefs. The school's part in the transmission of culture is continually under debate because the growth of knowledge and technology make it impossible to convey *all* information. Thus, difficult choices must be made as to what is most important—with consequent conflicting opinions. All education springs from some image of the future.

Socializing children for a society of rapid change is a continual challenge. In such changing conditions, when educators are unsure of what the next generation should learn in order to be adequately prepared for the future, the trend becomes education for adaptability. What is education for adaptability? Does it involve teaching basic skills or problem solving? Is it an individual or group enterprise? Computers can enable individualized learning, and cooperative activities can enable group learning; schools must choose how to balance the two approaches. Schools must encourage the creative capacities of the young to adapt to a changing physical and social environment, but they still have the task of maintaining the status quo and ensuring cultural continuity. Ideally, the school acts as an agent to foster respect and adherence to the existing social order of society, but in reality, this is not necessarily the case.

Education professor John Goodlad (1984) studied documents related to the purposes of schooling spanning 300 years of U.S. history. He found four broad categories of goals: (1) academic (reading, writing, arithmetic), (2) vocational (preparation for world of work), (3) social and civic (preparation to participate in a democracy), and (4) personal (development of individual talent and self-expression). Schooling goals and outcomes are discussed in Chapter 6.

The social order of society is communicated to children primarily in the classroom. In this setting, they are evaluated by teachers' comments, report cards, marks on papers, charts, classmates' judgments, and self-judgments—"Who can help Sally with that problem?" "Who has read the most books?" "Only papers with the best handwriting will be displayed for parents' night." Evaluation contributes to socialization in that the norms and standards of society are learned via the criteria of the evaluation. The self-concept emerges from how well children meet the expectations of others, the evaluators (Brophy, 1986; Harter, 1998).

The political ideology of society is communicated to children via textbooks and the way subjects are taught. How is the classroom setting organized? Do students compete with one another to participate in discussion? Do they pursue activities independently, or do they collaborate and help each other on projects?

Socialization outcomes in teacher-centered and learner-centered classrooms are different (Linney & Seidman, 1989). Teacher- and learner-centered classrooms are discussed in more detail in Chapter 7. Teachers also contribute to the socialization process by serving as models for children to imitate. Teachers who are involved in their subject matter tend to have active, curious students who want to learn (Brophy, 1992).

Child care has become an important socialization agent due to societal changes. The specific effects of care from someone other than a parent are controversial due to many variables (Belsky & Rovine, 1988; Clarke-Stewart, 1987), such as the child's temperament, the type of care, and the level of parental involvement. Specifics are discussed in Chapter 5.

PEERS

The peer group comprises individuals who are of approximately the same age and social status and who have common interests. Experiences in child care facilities can expose children to peer relations months after birth. However, reciprocal interactions in the peer group don't usually begin until about age 3, when children start to understand the views of others and, therefore, are able to cooperate, share, and take turns. Cognitively, they are beginning to move away from **egocentrism**— the characteristic of being able to look at the world only from one's own point of view. As children mature and develop new interests, their peer groups change. Some may be based on proximity, such as the kids in the neighborhood or the classroom, or others on interest, such as the soccer team or Scouts. According to Elkin and Handel (1989),

> The peer group gives children experience in egalitarian types of relationships. In this group they engage in a process of give-and-take not ordinarily possible in their relationships with adults. . . . In the peer group they gain their first substantial experience of equality. Children entering a peer group are interested in the companionship, attention, and good will of the group (particularly of the members of the group who are significant for them), and the group is in a position to satisfy this interest. For behaving in the appropriate or valued manner, the group rewards its members by bestowing attention, approval, or leadership or by giving permission to participate or to employ certain symbols. For behaving otherwise, the peer group punishes by disdain, ostracism, or other expressions of disapproval. (p. 184)

Thus, children come to look at themselves from the point of view of the group. The peer group rewards sociability, or getting along, and rejects deviations such as eccentricity, aggression, and showing off (Kindermann, 1998). Children learn to obey the "rules of the game" and to assume the various roles required in the game, such as batter, pitcher, catcher, and fielder. The peer group exerts control by refusing to include those who do not conform to its values or rules.

EXAMPLE An example of the power of peer group pressure is the classic children's story by Hans Christian Andersen, "The Emperor's New Clothes." The emperor, who was very vain about his clothes, bought some cloth that—according to the merchants who sold it—was visible only to those not worthy of their positions in life. He proudly wore his new outfit made of this unique cloth in a parade before the entire town. No one dared admit to others that the emperor really hadn't any clothes on, for fear of being judged unworthy. It took the astonished cry of an innocent child to make everyone realize the truth.

The peer group functions as a socializing agent in that it provides information about the world and about its members from a perspective other than that of each member's own family (Hartup, 1983; Rubin, Bukowski, & Parker, 1998). It is a source of social comparison. From the peer group, children receive feedback about their abilities. Through interaction with their equals, people find out whether they are better than, the same as, or worse than their friends in sports, dating, school-work, and so on. Within the peer group, children can experiment with various roles—leader, follower, clown, troublemaker, or peacemaker—and discover how the others react.

Peers also serve as a support group for the expression of values and attitudes (Hartup, 1983). Members often discuss situations with parents, siblings, and teachers. Beyond that, friends may offer sympathy and/or advice in handling problems. That children are spending increasing amounts of time with their peers was illustrated in a study of children age 2–12 (Ellis, Rogoff, & Cromer, 1981). The researchers observed that, by age 8, children were interacting with other children more than six times as much as with adults. Internet and cell phone capabilities for instant messaging offer infinite opportunities to connect to peers. Such technology provides a means for school-agers and adolescents to relate to one another virtually any time and any place, and anonymously if they so choose. The peer group, then, as an agent of socialization exerts a strong influence on children's ideas and behavior, especially those who seek social approval and fear rejection. The quality of the parent–child relationship is the most important factor impacting peer group influences (Collins et al., 2000). Peer group influences are examined in Chapter 8.

MASS MEDIA

Mass media include newspapers, magazines, books, radio, television, videos, movies, computers, and other means of communication that reach large audiences via an impersonal medium between sender and receiver. Unlike other agents of socialization, the mass media do not ordinarily directly involve personal interactions; the interactions are of a more technical nature. The mass media must, however, be considered socializing agents, because they reveal many aspects of the society and elicit cognitive processes in children that affect their understanding of the world (Harris, 1999; Huston & Wright, 1998; Perse, 2001). Newspapers report on such things as baseball games and government policy; magazines illustrate the latest fashions or suggest things to do with free time in the summer; radio stations play popular songs; books discuss such issues as sex and drugs; television gives glimpses of hospitals, courtrooms, and domestic situations. Television, videos, and movies also show relationships between people in various settings, providing children with models of how to behave or interact in similar situations.

Television, movies, books, and computers (via the Internet) convey information about society. Through them, we come to learn about parts of the world we might not otherwise encounter or experience. We are taken under the sea, to outer space, to the jungles, to other times, and to other countries. The media also provide role models—the hero, the villain, the detective, the doctor, the lawyer, the mother, and the father. In addition, the media reflect social attitudes—beliefs about political issues such as war or taxes, and social issues such as abortion or child abuse.

Children, because of cognitive immaturity, are of special concern with regard to media influences (Huston, Zillman, & Bryant, 1994; Perse, 2001). They process the content they see and hear and transform it into something meaningful to them, which may or may not be accurate or desirable. One concern is that young children may come to think of all people in a given group as having the same characteristics as the people in that group presented on TV or in books, and this may influence their attitudes. For example, on the majority of TV shows and in most movies, the white male is portrayed as dominant, brave, powerful, and competent (Comstock & Paik, 1991; Huston & Wright, 1998; Isaacs, 1999). This applies in textbooks as well. This is especially true for children who do not have the real experience to evaluate the attitude portrayed.

Another concern is children's susceptibility to advertising (Condry, 1989; Huston & Wright, 1998). Many children ask parents to buy products and toys shown on TV. Children often imitate well-known media characters, especially active, powerful ones. They role-play the characters, they bring the toys to school, and they wear clothing decorated with the characters. The problem with media-related toys, clothing, and supplies is not only the materialistic and competitive values they foster but also the aggressive acting-out behavior they inspire in children's play (Levin, 1998). Commercialism abounds in children's sports and schools, as well as on TV.

With the introduction of new technology to the mass media, such as modems connecting to the Internet and cell phones connecting to friends, children now play a greater role in their own socialization. They can, for example, access any information that is on the Internet (unless access to a site is blocked). They also have more opportunities to interact with media independent from adult mediation, given that many households have more than one TV, and cell phones, pagers, and e-mail provide opportunities for instant communication. Various media influences are discussed in Chapter 9.

THE COMMUNITY

The term *community* is derived from the Latin word for "fellowship." **Community** refers to the affective relationships expected among closely knit groups of people with common interests; it also refers to people living in a particular geographical area who are bound together politically and economically. The function of the community, then, is to provide a sense of belonging, a source of friendship, and socialization of children (Etzioni, 1993). Many sociologists and psychologists are concerned with the supposed erosion of community ties (Garbarino, 1992; Schorr, 1997). Chronosystem and macrosystem influences contributing to this erosion, such as fear of violence, technology, and "busyness," as well as support to enable coping strategies, are discussed in Chapter 10. A survey by the National League of Cities cited five characteristics that make a city "family-friendly": (1) education (accessible quality school programs), (2) recreation, (3) community safety, (4) citizen involvement, and (5) physical environment (Meyers & Kyle, 1998).

The size, population, and mobility pattern of a community determine the pattern of human interaction. In a town with a small and stable population of a few thousand, most people know each other, in contrast to a large, more impersonal town of many thousands. Small-town interaction involves more knowledge of intimate details of people's lives than does large-town interaction. In a small town, people see each other in many settings—at the store, school, movie theater, and church. In a large town, relationships are more fragmented—it is unlikely that one would just happen to see a friend at a restaurant, simply because there are so many restaurants available to dine at in a large town. Similarly, a large town provides more activities than does a small town. Thus, one's interactions focus on the community groups to which one belongs—Scouts, Little League, the Y, the church, and so on.

One function of such community groups is to give children different perspectives on life—to broaden their range of experience and give them new statuses or roles. In this respect, community agencies and organizations contribute to the socialization of children. In Scouts, for example, children learn about various occupational roles through a badge program. The Scouts might be supervised by a designated community "sponsor,"—such as a veterinarian, in performing various tasks such as caring for animals. A church youth group might participate in a program in which members visit people in a home for the elderly on a regular basis. Community libraries open the world of reading to children; museums open the worlds of art, science, geography, zoology, and so on.

Neighborhoods are often stratified by economic status (Levine & Levine, 1996)—with the lower-economic-status families living in less desirable sections and upper-economic-status families living in large homes surrounded by green lawns or in posh apartment buildings with doormen. The location of these neighborhoods in the larger community influences interaction patterns. If children from different neighborhoods attend the same school or share community services such as a recreation center and a library, they all have an opportunity to interact with many diverse individuals. If, however, the neighborhoods are segregated, each having its own school and recreational facilities, the children generally interact with others like themselves.

The adults and older children in the neighborhood are the ones with whom young children interact and "probably stand second only to parents in terms of their power to influence the child's behavior" (Bronfenbrenner, 1979, p. 161; Schorr, 1997). The adults in the neighborhood are role models. They may be carpenters, engineers, entrepreneurs, teachers, or recreation leaders. The older children are models of behavior and interaction. Children often learn games and cues about getting along with people from older children: "Mrs. Grady is an old grouch; she won't give your ball back if it goes in her yard."

A community can have an informal social support system—relatives, friends, and neighbors who can be counted on to help in a crisis. For example, when Mrs. Cooper goes into the hospital, her mother-in-law might come to care for the children while the neighbors take turns cooking meals and running errands for the family. A community can also have a more formal social support system, such as institutionalized child care, Big Brothers/Big Sisters, Meals on Wheels, and Parents Without Partners. These formal support systems can be funded by tax dollars, donations, or membership fees.

Formal support systems in a community usually emerge through the process of advocacy. **Advocacy** means speaking or writing in support of something—for example, setting goals on behalf of children and seeing that politicians or governmental agencies implement them. It is a long and arduous process, however, to go from goals to laws. Thus, if community members want to improve opportunities for their children, they must get involved in politics. Politics begins locally, in one's own community. Thus, community members want their children to have the right to full opportunities for play and recreation, they can communicate this desire to their city council members and follow through by examining how their local tax dollars are being spent. For example, one city doubled the money previously budgeted for programs such as child care, youth activities, senior citizens' food, and a shelter for victims of domestic violence. Most of the money had previously been allocated to street repairs. The most effective community services supporting children and families are those that empower informal and formal networks working collaboratively (Epps & Jackson, 2000).

Methods of Socialization

Given that socialization is the process by which people learn the ways of a given society so that they can function effectively within it, the next issue is how these methods are transmitted to children (see Table 2.2).

AFFECTIVE METHODS (EFFECT EMERGES FROM FEELING)

Affective refers to feelings or emotions such as love, anger, fear, and disgust. Affective mechanisms include responses to others, feelings about oneself, feelings about others, and expressions of emotions. Affect emerges from person-to-person interaction, which leads to attachment. The socialization of children, whether intentional or unintentional, is accomplished through person-to-person interaction. When people are attached to one another, they interact often; thus, attachment and interaction are bidirectional (Thompson, 1998).

Attachment is an "affectional tie that one person forms to another specific person, binding them together in space and enduring over time" (Ainsworth, 1973, p. 1). Socialization begins with personal attachment (Elkin & Handel, 1989; Collins et al., 2000). Humans are born helpless, requiring care from others to survive. In the process of caring for infants, parents or caregivers hold, play with, and talk to them. These caregivers respond to the feelings evoked in them by the infants. This sensitive, responsive caregiving forms the foundation for social interaction, and it is

Table 2.2

Methods of Socialization

METHOD	TECHNIQUES
AFFECTIVE (effect emerges from feeling)	Attachment
OPERANT (effect emerges from acting)	Reinforcement Extinction Punishment Feedback Learning by doing
OBSERVATIONAL (effect emerges from imitating)	Modeling
COGNITIVE (effect emerges from information processing)	Instruction Standard setting Reasoning
SOCIOCULTURAL (effect emerges from conforming)	Group pressure Tradition Rituals and routines Symbols
APPRENTICESHIP (effect emerges from guided participation)	Structuring Collaborating Transferring

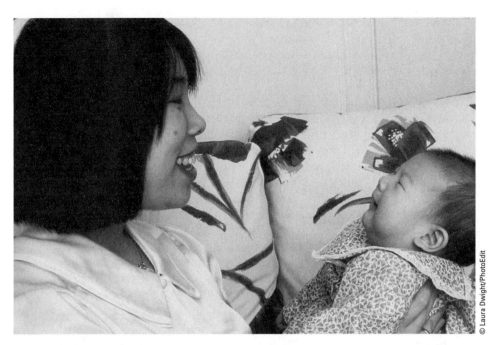

Mother–child interaction is the basis for attachment and a sense of trust.

this interaction that contributes to many socialization outcomes for children (Bowlby, 1988; Thompson, 1998).

Infants who are responded to when they cry, who are fed, held, and spoken to, develop a secure attachment to and a sense of trust in the world. Infants who receive minimal or inconsistent care develop an insecure attachment and a sense of mistrust (Erikson, 1963). Our first human relationship, then, provides the basis for our subsequent expectations regarding other relationships.

An outcome of attachment, other than feelings of trust or mistrust for future social interactions, is the feeling of competence. Paradoxically, the more securely attached children are to a nurturing adult, the safer they feel to explore their environment. In contrast, the more insecurely attached they are, the less likely they are to leave their caregivers and try out new things (Ainsworth, 1973). Follow-up observations in preschools showed that infants who were judged to be securely attached at age 18 months were more enthusiastic, sympathetic to others, cooperative, independent, and competent than those who displayed insecure attachment at that age (Sroufe, 1978). Several studies have reported that insecurely attached children exhibit disruptive, hostile, or aggressive behavior in preschool (Sroufe, 1996; Waters, Posada, Crowell, & Kengsling, 1993). Attachment to the primary caregiver is the first of many important emotional relationships with significant others that children form; these significant others may include relatives, teachers, friends, and coaches. Because each of these people is unique and because each situation in which children encounter these others is unique, each will contribute in a different way to children's socialization.

Elkind (1981b, pp. 20–24) discusses the importance of attachment in determining how children learn: "In children's early years, adults predigest experience for them much as mothers predigest food to provide milk [nourishment] for their babies." Adults, then, communicate to children their own learning experiences. The adults are mediators. Elkind cites an example of a teacher who always had children around her when she used various art materials. She showed them different ways paper could be folded and brushes could be used, and she joyfully produced new colors when she mixed the paints. The children acquired both the ability to fold paper, make brush strokes, and mix paint and an attitude of enjoyment of and appreciation, and respect for art materials. This kind of learning is referred to by Elkind as the "acquisition of mediating structures." Personal attachment to adults enables children to abstract mediating structures from them.

An example of mediating structures is described by Feurstein (1980). In comparing children who immigrated to Israel from Yemen and from Morocco, Feurstein found that, even though both groups of children attended school in Israel, the Yemenite children were better learners than the Moroccan children. Case histories of the children revealed that as part of their religious training the Yemenite children had studied with their fathers. Feurstein called this kind of interaction a "mediated learning experience," in which adults provide the mechanisms for the acquisition of learning and instill in the children a positive attitude toward future learning.

When the child is attached to the caregiver, socialization takes place in many ways. Some of these result from the child's action (an operant method), some from the child's imitating (an observational method), some from the child's information processing (a cognitive method), some from the child's cultural traditions (a sociocultural method), and some from guided participation (an apprenticeship method).

OPERANT METHODS (EFFECT EMERGES FROM ACTING)

Operant refers to producing an effect. When some behavior is followed by a favorable outcome (reinforcement), the probability of that behavior occurring again is increased. When the behavior has no favorable outcome (for example, it does not get attention or is ignored) or has an unfavorable outcome (it results in punishment), the probability of that behavior occurring again is decreased. Operant methods take into account the participatory role of individuals in their own socialization.

Several socialization techniques can be used to increase desired behavior including positive reinforcement, negative reinforcement, and shaping.

Reinforcement

Reinforcement is an object or event that is presented following a behavior and that serves to increase the likelihood that the behavior will occur again. **Positive reinforcement** is a reward given for desired behavior—for example, food, physical contact, or praise. **Negative reinforcement** is the termination of an unpleasant condition following a desired response—for example, allowing a child to come out of her room when she stops a temper tantrum, or restoring a child's privileges when he apologizes.

When we want to reinforce a complex behavior involving many steps, such as writing the alphabet, shaping can be used. **Shaping** is the systematic, immediate reinforcement of successive approximations of the desired behavior until that behavior occurs and is maintained. Writing the alphabet involves holding a pencil and copying lines, circles, and so on in a specific way on a piece of paper. The lines and circles must be a certain size and a certain distance from one another. At a child's first attempt, the teacher may reward a line of any size that resembles the letter. Then the teacher may reward only straight lines, then straight lines of a certain size, and so on, until the child reaches the desired level of performance. Shaping is an effective socializing mechanism to teach various skills.

The following is a summary of conditions under which reinforcement can be effective as a socializing technique (Martin & Pear, 1996):

- The desired behavior must first be exhibited before it can be reinforced. In training children to defecate in the toilet, the caregiver must put them on the seat and wait for the behavior to occur before reinforcing it. The main unresolved question accompanying the technique of positive reinforcement is: How do you get children to make the desired response in the first place so that they can be rewarded?

- The desired behavior must be reinforced immediately after it first occurs. If you want children to verbalize their requests rather than point to or grunt for desired objects, you must reward them when they say, for example, "Juice."

- Initially, the desired behavior must be reinforced each time it is exhibited. Every time children verbalize their requests, they should get what they ask for. Every time children defecate in the toilet, they should be rewarded.

- When the newly acquired behavior is being performed relatively frequently, reinforcement can then become intermittent. A reward or praise can be given every few times the behavior is performed, or it can be given every few days instead of every time ("I'm glad you're asking for what you want" or "I'm proud you're using the toilet now").

- Because the long-range goal is self-reward, subjective reinforcers such as privileges and praise should be used in conjunction with objective reinforcers such as food, toys, or money.

There are several problems in using reinforcement as a socializing technique, other than having to wait for the desired behavior to occur. First, individuals respond differently to reinforcers. For some children a toy is an effective reinforcer; for others, adult approval is more effective. And it is sometimes difficult to find the best reinforcer. Second, children may become bored with the reinforcer, so that its effectiveness diminishes. Third, being human, it is difficult for adults to constantly reward children's desired behavior, even during the initial stages. If parents want to train a child to urinate in the toilet, they must both be present and be ready to put the child on the toilet at appropriate intervals. They also must wait patiently for the desired behavior to occur. Fourth, adults sometimes unintentionally reinforce the very behaviors they want to eliminate. When children who have been toilet trained begin to wet their pants again, perhaps because they see their baby brother or sister doing it, and their mother says, "I thought you were a big boy (girl)," it is highly likely that the undesired behavior will occur again

Behavior, such as using the toilet, that is reinforced will likely be repeated.

© Elizabeth Crews

because negative attention is better than no attention. Finally, although the goal is for children to internally regulate their behavior, reinforcement is externally regulated and may reduce the motivation for self-control.

There are also socialization techniques that can decrease or eliminate undesired behavior, such as extinction, punishment, feedback, and learning by doing.

Extinction

If reinforcement increases the likelihood of a response occurring again, then the removal of the reinforcement should eventually eliminate, or extinguish, the response. **Extinction** is the gradual disappearance of a learned behavior due to the removal of the reinforcement. Basically, it involves ignoring undesirable responses. For example, to extinguish the habit of nail biting, a father may decide to ignore his daughter every time she bites her nails, instead of nagging her to stop, as he used to do. In this way, he removes the previous reinforcement of attention. When she does not bite her nails for a 10-minute stretch, however, he praises her. Gradually, the interval between nail-biting episodes becomes longer and longer, with the father giving her praise every half-hour for not nail biting but still ignoring his daughter when she does bite her nails.

Extinction must be used in conjunction with reinforcement to be effective as a socializing method. Annoying behaviors such as tantrums, dawdling, and tattling respond well, but more complex or deep-seated behaviors such as aggression, stealing, and overeating do not.

"Time-out" is a type of extinction in which all reinforcement is removed. Usually, the child spends a specified amount of time in his or her room, or in a corner, or in any place where behavior can be ignored. Time-out can give a child time and space to better manage emotions and behavior. Reasons for the time-out should be given so the child can employ them for self-control in the future.

Punishment

According to Ausubel (1957), it is impossible to guide behavior effectively using only positive reinforcement and extinction; children cannot learn what is not approved or tolerated simply by making a reverse generalization from the approval they receive for acceptable behavior. Children have to be taught to process what they are *not* supposed to do, as well as what they *are*. Thus, punishment that is not hostile and provides constructive feedback designed to correct misbehavior can have an informative effect.

Punishment consists of physically or psychologically painful stimuli or the temporary withdrawal of pleasant stimuli when undesirable behavior occurs. A physically painful stimulus might be a spanking; a psychologically painful stimulus might be a scolding or harsh criticism; withdrawal of a pleasant stimulus might be removing a privilege such as TV. Punishment has been used as an intervention technique to discourage undesirable behavior. It is probably most valuable when some behavior must be stopped quickly for safety reasons. Thus, a 2-year-old who runs out into the street is more likely to be stopped from doing so in the future by a quick swat on the rear than by a reward for staying on the sidewalk. A 2-year-old also can't really understand the logical reasons for not running into the street, so a more concrete physical reminder may be necessary.

For punishment to be effective as a socializing technique, the following elements must be considered (Martin & Pear, 1996):

- *Timing.* The closer the punishment is to the behavior, the more effective it will be.
- *Reasoning.* Punishment accompanied by an explanation is more effective than punishment alone: "We do not play in the street because cars might hurt us."
- *Consistency.* If children are consistently punished for repeating a behavior, they are more likely to stop it than if they are sometimes punished, sometimes ignored, and sometimes rewarded. Aggression is an example of a behavior sometimes handled inconsistently. It may be punished at home or at school when the child is caught, yet be rewarded in the peer group.
- *Attachment to the person doing the punishing.* The more nurturant the relationship between punisher and punishee, the more effective the punishment. A child whose parent denies a privilege for undesired behavior, such as coming home late, is less likely to repeat that behavior than if an acquaintance, such as a babysitter, administers the punishment.

The use of punishment as a technique for modifying behavior has been criticized for the following reasons (Martin & Pear, 1996):

- Punishment may stop the undesirable behavior immediately but, by itself, not indicate appropriate or desired behavior.
- Punishment may merely slow the rate at which the undesirable behavior is emitted, rather than eliminate it entirely. Or it may change the form of the undesirable behavior. For instance, people who stop smoking often report that they begin eating more. Children who are punished for physical aggression may engage in verbal aggression: "I hate you" or "You big doody head."
- Punishment by an adult may have an undesirable modeling effect on the child. Parents who abuse their children are likely to have been abused by their parents.
- The emotional side effects of punishment (fear, embarrassment, shame, low self-esteem, tenseness) may be psychologically more damaging than the original behavior.

In sum, punishment can function as a socializing technique when used appropriately (Martin & Pear, 1996). It can provide an opportunity to reestablish attachment or affection following emotional release; it can promote vicarious learning through observation of others being punished; it can reduce guilt by providing an opportunity to correct the misbehavior; and, when combined with reasoning, it can enable the internalization of moral standards. Thus, when using punishment, be aware of the negative, as well as the positive, consequences for children.

EXAMPLE When a group of 10-year-old boys wrote on the wall of their camp cabin, their counselor required them to spend the afternoon scrubbing walls instead of going swimming. This type of punishment is referred to as a "logical consequence"— one that is arranged by the parent or other adult and that is logically related to the misbehavior (Dreikurs & Grey, 1968). For a logical consequence to be effective, however, it must make sense to the child. For example, Todd continually left his clothes around his room after repeatedly being told to put them in the hamper. His mother finally said, "Clothes that do not get picked up do not get washed." Todd still did not pick up his clothes. Finally, when Todd wanted to wear his favorite shirt and realized it was not washed because he had not put it in the hamper, the consequence became effective—he picked up his clothes.

Table 2.3

Basic Behavioral Modification Methods

TYPE	DEFINITION	EFFECT
Positive reinforcement	Present stimulus (give attention)	Increases desirable response
Negative reinforcement	Remove aversive stimulus (stop scolding)	Increases desirable response
Extinction	Remove pleasant stimulus (stop giving attention)	Decreases undesirable response
Punishment	Present aversive stimulus (start scolding)	Decreases undesirable response

Table 2.3 summarizes basic behavioral modification methods.

Feedback

Feedback is evaluative information, both positive and negative, about individual behavior. It can take the form of an approving nod, a questioning look, a comment, further instructions, or a reminder. Feedback provides knowledge of results and ways to improve them, which has been shown to be important to learning (Bangert-Drowns, Kulik, Kulik, & Morgan, 1991).

An example of a classic feedback experiment illustrates the value of knowing the results while learning a simple skill (Baker & Young, 1960). The task to be learned was to reproduce on paper the length of a 4-inch piece of wood. The subjects were blindfolded, but they could still feel the piece of wood. One group of subjects was told after each performance whether they were within 1/5 inch of the correct length; the other group received no feedback. When both groups were tested, the group receiving feedback consistently improved, whereas the group receiving no knowledge of results made no consistent progress. And when the feedback was halted, the first group's accuracy dropped abruptly.

This experiment demonstrated that, in order to increase accuracy of performance, individuals must change incorrect responses. In this case, unless the individuals were made fully aware of their incorrect behavior, change was unlikely to occur.

The effects of feedback on performance can be summarized as follows (Good & Brophy, 1986):

- Feedback generally increases motivation.
- Feedback usually improves subsequent performance.
- Generally, the more specific the knowledge of performance, the more rapidly performance improves.
- Feedback given punctually is usually more effective than that given long after a task has been completed.
- Noticeable decreases in feedback often result in a marked decline in performance.
- When knowledge of results is not provided, individuals tend to develop substitutes. For example, they may compare their performance with that of peers to determine whether it is better or worse.

Feedback, then, is an important socializing mechanism. It provides children with information on how they are measuring up to standards of behavior and performance: "Susie, your letters need to go on the line; I've circled your best one; make five more just like it," or "Jack, that frown on your face is most unpleasant; what is your problem?" or "Garth, next time you have a friend over, say 'Thank you for coming,'" or "Terry, that outfit looks very good on you."

Learning by Doing

Sometimes socialization occurs through experiencing and interacting. As an ancient Chinese proverb says, "I hear and I forget, I see and I remember, I do and I understand." Psychologist Jean Piaget (1952), known for his developmental theory of cognitive development, states that children learn through their own activity. Likewise, psychologist Jerome Bruner (1981) believes children learn through discovery. Learning is a slow process of construction and transformation of experience into meaning, sometimes referred to as "constructivism." Learning to ride a bicycle is an example of learning by doing. It involves experimenting and discovering how to shift your weight while pedaling, holding on, and watching where you are going, all at the same time. Psychologist Albert Bandura (2000) relates learning by doing to the attribute of **self-efficacy**—the belief that one can master a situation and produce positive effects. For example, children who are encouraged and given opportunities to become competent (as in learning to cook, putting a puzzle together, or creating artwork) tend to be motivated to achieve on other tasks.

Offering developmentally appropriate choices—meaningful activities that create opportunities for children to succeed—enables them to learn by doing because they can experience what works and what doesn't. For example, evidence from studies on children supports the relationship between learning by doing and successful problem solving. In one study (Smith & Dutton, 1979), a group of children was given the opportunity to play with materials involved in a problem. Another group received instruction on how to solve the problem but was not given the opportunity to play with the materials. The group that played with the materials ended up solving the problem as easily as the children who had instruction. And on a more complex problem requiring innovative thinking, the group that had the opportunity to play with the materials did better in solving the problem than the group that received instruction. Thus, as Piaget and Bruner assert, experience leads to discovering ways to tackle problems. Learning by doing, then, transforms individuals in some way, affecting future development.

The computer is an interactive tool that provides opportunities for experiential learning—problem solving, simulations, and personal tutoring (Lepper & Gurtner, 1989). It also is capable of supporting many different learning styles while enabling users to learn how to learn (Papert, 1993). Every time I get new software for my computer, I learn how to use it by doing it, seeing what works and what doesn't.

Problem solving can involve interacting with others. In fact, most interactional skills are learned by doing. Thus, when you smile and say "Hi," you usually get a positive response. When you sulk after losing a game, you may not be invited to play again—another example of constructivism.

When children play, they are learning by doing (Hughes, 1998). They are being socialized in that they are practicing physical, intellectual, and social skills: physical skills such as climbing, jumping, writing, and cutting; intellectual skills such as remembering, reasoning, making decisions, and solving problems; and social skills such as communicating, sharing, cooperating, competing, and empathizing. For example, as children experiment with different behaviors and social roles, they find out what it feels like to be Mom or baby brother; they experience what it is like to

This child learns to roller blade by doing it.

wash the car or to play doctor; they feel the joy of approval and the despair of disapproval. They are constructing views of the world that will influence future thinking and behavior.

OBSERVATIONAL METHODS (EFFECT EMERGES FROM IMITATING)

> **EXAMPLE** Six-year-old Vicky went on her first boat ride in her uncle's new boat. She watched the waves ripple on the lake as her uncle joyfully demonstrated his boat's power to her parents. When they docked, Vicky's uncle tied up the boat. Vicky could not wait to go for another ride. The next day, while motoring around the lake, she besieged her uncle with questions, and when they pulled up to the dock, to her uncle's amazement, Vicky jumped out, grabbed the rope, and tied up the boat.

Vicky's behavior, her attitude about boating, and her performance in tying up the boat illustrate socialization via observational learning, or modeling.

Modeling

Modeling is a form of imitative learning that occurs by observing another person (the model) perform a behavior and experience its consequences. It enables us to learn appropriate social behavior, attitudes, and emotions vicariously or second-hand. The models can be parents, siblings, relatives, friends, teachers, coaches, or TV and movie characters. Kagan (1971) explained how children assume complex patterns of behavior through identification with models:

> Identification is, in fact, the belief of a person that some attributes of a model (for example, parents, siblings, relatives, peers, and fictional figures) are also possessed by the person. A boy who realizes that he and his father share the same name, notes that they have similar facial features, and is told by relatives that they both have lively tempers, develops a belief that he is similar to his father. When this belief in similarity is accompanied by vicarious emotional experiences in the child that are appropriate to the model, we say that the child has an identification with the model. (p. 57)

Modeling is a significant socializing method. As children mature, they acquire a wide range of behaviors through modeling from parents, siblings, teachers, and friends, which become part of their repertoire for future interactions.

Modeling involves the ability to abstract information from what is observed, store it in memory, make generalizations and rules about behavior, retrieve the appropriate information, and act it out at the appropriate time. Thus, modeling enables individuals to develop new ways of behaving in situations not previously experienced. Vicky, for example, "knew" how to tie up the boat without having previously done so or been instructed on how to do it. However, the probability that children will imitate a model is a function of their (1) attention, (2) level of cognitive development, (3) retention, (4) interest in the activity being observed, (5) motivation, (6) ability to reproduce the behavior, and (7) repertoire of alternative behaviors (Bandura, 1989; Bandura, Ross, & Ross, 1963).

Many ethnic groups, especially those from high-context cultures such as Native Americans, emphasize observation and modeling as socialization methods. These methods enable children to participate in chores alongside adults or older siblings according to their developmental abilities. For example, in some African tribes, girls as young as age 3 are given their own hoes to work in the gardens with their mothers and older sisters (Whiting & Edwards, 1988).

Various factors affect the extent to which children imitate modeled behavior. Models who are perceived as similar (physically and/or psychologically) to the observer are likely to be identified with and imitated: "I have yellow hair, just like Mommy," or "You have a strong will just like your grandfather." Models who are perceived as nurturant are more likely to be identified with and imitated: "My daddy always brings me presents when he comes back from a trip," or "My coach always has time to listen to me." Models who are perceived as powerful or prestigious are more likely to be identified with and imitated (Bandura, Ross, & Ross, 1963): "My grandmother won first prize in the fair for her chocolate cake!" or "My teacher is the smartest person in the whole world!"

Children's behavior is also influenced by whether the model with whom they identify is punished or reinforced. It has been demonstrated that children who see a model being punished for aggressive behavior are less likely to imitate that behavior than children who see a model being rewarded or experiencing no consequences (Bandura, 1965).

Television provides an excellent example of a context in which observational learning and consequent modeling take place. There is much evidence that children learn both prosocial and antisocial behavior by watching TV (Comstock & Paik, 1991; Pearl, 1982; Perse, 2001). For example, children who watched an episode of *Lassie* in which the master risked his life to rescue Lassie's puppy were more helpful in a task following the show (Sprafkin, Liebert, & Poulos, 1975). For another example, studies of preschool children showed that there was a relationship between violent television viewing and aggressive behavior during free play (Levin & Carlsson-Paige, 1995; Singer & Singer, 1976).

The reason for the likelihood of televised behavior being modeled, whether it be prosocial or antisocial, is that children observe someone being rewarded for an act. Prosocial behavior on TV is generally reinforced by the person getting lots of attention or becoming a hero. Antisocial behavior is generally reinforced by the person "getting away with it" or obtaining a desired object.

COGNITIVE METHODS: EFFECT EMERGES FROM INFORMATION PROCESSING

Socialization techniques using **cognitive** methods involve those that specifically focus on how individuals process information or abstract meaning from experiences. Strategies used by socialization agents are instruction, standard setting, and reasoning.

Instruction

Instruction provides knowledge and information and is a useful socializing mechanism. For instruction to be effective, however, children must be able to understand the language used and to remember what was said. In other words, instruction must provide specific information at an appropriate level. "Bring me your shoes" would be appropriate for a 2-year-old; "Get your jacket out of the closet, turn out the pockets, and bring it to me" would not. Even a 2-year-old who knows what a jacket is will probably forget the second part of the instruction ("turn out the pockets") because a child at that age simply cannot remember to do three things at once.

"Instructions" conjures up the image of the booklet in the box containing dozens of bicycle parts. Instructions usually communicate how to do something, but they also communicate directions or orders: "Don't sit on the coffee table, sit on the chair."

EXAMPLE "Greg [age 9], please clean up your room," said Mom.
An hour later, Mom went into Greg's room and observed that his bedspread was rumpled, his desk covered with books, and his model airplanes are strewn among his shoes on the floor of his closet.
Mom yelled, "I told you to clean up your room!"
Greg replied, "But I did; I put all my books and toys away."
And that he had.

The problem here is that the instructions were not specific enough for Greg. (If the instructions for putting the bicycle together were as vague as Mom's, the parts would still be in the box.) Mom probably has an image of a clean room that includes an unrumpled bed, books on the bookshelf, and toys on the appropriate closet shelf. Greg's image of a clean room, in contrast, may simply involve space to walk and lie down. Thus, Mom's instructions, to be effective, must be phrased this way: "Greg, please clean your room—straighten your bedspread, place your books on the shelf, and put your toys in your closet on the shelf." If Greg were younger—for example, age 4—he might answer, "But I don't know how to straighten my bed." Then Mom would know what parts of the instructions could and could not be followed independently. Thus, for instructions to be effective, they must be understood. And for instructions to be understood, the instructor must be willing to rephrase, to demonstrate, and to repeat. Coaching techniques involving instruction, explanations, practice, and feedback were employed successfully with preschool and school-age children to enable them to make friends (Mize & Ladd, 1990; Oden & Asher, 1977).

Standard Setting

A **standard** is a level of attainment or degree of excellence regarded as a goal or measure of adequacy. When parents set standards for children, they are telling children what they should do: "You are three years old now; I want you to dress yourself," or "I expect only A's and B's on your report card." Setting standards provides children with advance notice of what is expected or not expected of them, thus helping them become socialized. The laws of a country, the licensing requirements for driving, and the zoning rules in a city are all examples of standards. A contract, or written agreement, specifying goals for learning or behavioral expectations can be a vehicle by which standards are communicated.

Standards are set by many socializing agents. In *Are You There, God? It's Me, Margaret* by Judy Blume (1970), to be a member of the secret sixth-grade club, girls had to wear a bra, tell when they got their period, and keep a Boy Book (a list of boys they liked)—standards set by a peer group. Standards are also set by teachers. Some accept only good handwriting and perfect spelling on papers; others may set standards regarding content and creativity. Good and Brophy (1991) noted that teachers demand better performances from high-achieving students—for example, teachers are less likely to accept an inadequate answer from them than from low-achieving students. Standards are set by coaches: "You will do a hundred sit-ups every day, get eight hours of sleep a night, and eat a balanced diet." Thus, setting standards is a recurring method of socialization throughout life.

Reasoning

Reasoning involves giving explanations or causes for an act. The purpose of giving reasons in the process of socialization is to enable children to draw conclusions when encountering similar situations, thereby internalizing self-regulatory mechanisms. For instance, when a teacher says to a preschool child who has just spit on another child, "Keep your spit in your mouth; spitting spreads germs and is rude. How would you like that?" that teacher is using reasoning to influence the child's behavior.

The problem with giving reasons is that children may not understand the words used (for example, "spreads germs" or "is rude") and/or may not be able to generalize a reason to another situation. According to Piaget (1974), children under age 3 are generally **egocentric,** lacking the cognitive ability to take another's point of view and consequently believing that everyone looks at things the same way they do. The child in the spitting example can't mentally take the view of the child who has been spat upon and so doesn't relate to the teacher's reasons.

Some children under age 3 do react to others' emotions with altruistic behavior. **Altruism** refers to actions that are intended to aid or benefit another person or group of people without the actor's anticipation of external rewards. Such actions often entail some cost, self-sacrifice, or risk on the part of the actor. A team of researchers (Radke-Yarrow & Zahn-Waxler, 1986; Radke-Yarrow, Zahn-Waxler, & Chapman, 1983; Zahn-Waxler, Radke-Yarrow, & King, 1979) interviewed mothers of 15- and 20-month-old children. The mothers were trained to observe and report on incidents of their children's altruism when other children were distressed, such as attempting to provide reparations when someone was hurt, trying to comfort a victim, offering a toy, or going to find someone else to help. The researchers found that the way the mother interacted with her child when someone else was in distress was clearly related to her child's degree of altruism. The mothers of highly altruistic children did not simply offer reasons for the other's distress; they reacted emotionally, sometimes quite strongly, and stated forcefully that socially responsible behavior was expected—for example, "You made Shawna cry; you must never bite." Consequently, for children under age 3, if reasoning is to be used as a socializing technique, it must be combined with other methods, such as an emotional reaction, to be effective.

Children age 4–7, who are moving away from egocentrism and toward **sociocentrism**—the ability to understand and relate to views and perspectives of others—may be able to understand how other people feel or view things but not be able to generalize the reasons to another situation. This is because at this age a child's ability to reason is **transductive** (connecting one particular idea to another particular idea based on appearance rather than logic) as opposed to **inductive** (connecting a specific idea to a more general idea based on similarities) or **deductive** (connecting a general idea to a particular idea based on similarities and differences). The following are illustrations of the different types of reasoning:

- *Transductive reasoning:* "Kyle has red hair and hits me; therefore, all boys with red hair hit."
- *Inductive reasoning:* "I can't hit Kyle; therefore, I can't hit any other children."
- *Deductive reasoning:* "I can't hit other children; therefore, I can't hit Kyle."

Around age 7, children begin to think less intuitively and more concretely (Piaget, 1952); that is, they can understand reasons if they are associated with real events, objects, or people. Thus, the 7-year-old understands when told "You must not hit people with blocks because it hurts very much; look at how Kyle is crying," because 7-year-olds can *see* that hitting Kyle with a block caused Kyle to cry. Children who think concretely, however, cannot yet reason in terms of abstract principles; they cannot yet understand that "the law punishes people who hit." Because they cannot visualize it, the law is an abstraction that these children do not grasp.

Around age 11 or 12, children begin to think less concretely and more abstractly. They are able to perform formal, or logical, operations (like those involved in science), and they are capable of rational thought (Inhelder & Piaget, 1958). They can think in terms of past, present, and future, and can deal with hypothetical problems: "If everyone went around hitting everyone else whenever angry, then the world would end up in a war."

Reasoning as a socializing mechanism is most effective when children exhibit the ability to think logically and flexibly. This occurs after age 11 or 12, as children enter adolescence. At this stage, reasoning ability allows for adaptation to whatever problem is presented, thus enabling adolescents to benefit and learn from concepts imparted to them as young children. Reasoning is used more often as a socializing method in ethnic groups that value verbal skills, abstract thought, assertiveness, and self-reliance (Kagan et al., 1986).

Baumrind (1971a,b, 1989) distinguishes parents who are willing to offer reasons for their directives (**authoritative** parents) from parents who offer no directives and rely on manipulation to obtain compliance (**permissive** parents) and from those who expect children to accept their word as right and final without any verbal give-and-take (**authoritarian** parents). According to Baumrind, the authoritative approach may best enable children to conform to social standards with minimal jeopardy to "individual autonomy or self-assertiveness." In one study, preschool children from authoritative homes were consistently and significantly more competent than other children (Baumrind, 1989). In another study (Elder, 1963), it was shown that seventh- to twelfth-graders were more likely to model themselves after their parents if their parents explained the reasons behind their decisions and restrictions.

Thus, even though reasoning as a socializing mechanism is not as effective for young children as it is for adolescents, the continual use of reasoning by the parents is habit-forming. Children who are habitually given reasons for directives benefit more and more from reasoning as they mature in terms of being increasingly able to rationalize and guide their own behavior (Hoffman, 1988).

SOCIOCULTURAL METHODS (EFFECT EMERGES FROM CONFORMING)

Culture involves learned behavior, including knowledge, beliefs, morals, law, customs, and traditions, that is characteristic of the social environment in which individuals grow up. The sociocultural expectations of people around these individuals continually influence their behavior and ensure conformity to established precedents. Some of the socializing techniques by which sociocultural expectations influence behavior are group pressure, tradition, rituals and routines, and symbols.

Group Pressure

Group pressure is a sociocultural method of socialization because it involves conforming to certain group norms. Communities comprise social groups—families, neighborhoods, churches, peers, clubs, and schools. The groups to which one belongs influence one's behavior. Because humans have a need to affiliate with other humans and because social approval determines whether one is accepted by the group, they tend to conform to the group's expectations (group pressure).

In a classic study by Asch (1958), male subjects were asked to judge the length of lines. In each experimental session, there was only one actual subject; the other participants had been previously coached to express certain opinions. Thus, the real subject often faced a situation in which his eyes told him that one line was the longest, but the others in the group insisted that another line was the longest. Several of the subjects consistently yielded to the pressure of the group, even though the group's opinion was erroneous. In subsequent interviews, those who conformed to the majority opinion explained that they thought something was wrong with their eyesight and that the majority was probably correct.

In a similar experiment by other researchers (Hamm & Hoving, 1969), children age 7, 10, and 13 were asked to judge how far a light moved—a perceptually ambiguous task. Before the subjects made their decisions, however, two other children gave their answers. Just as Asch discovered, many of the subjects patterned their answers on the group estimates.

Group pressure was one of the factors involved in the South Central Los Angeles riots in 1992, both in the vandalism and in the rebuilding. People who believed "a black man has no rights," or "the police can get away with anything" (because the officers who beat up Rodney King were not punished), responded by looting and arson. When the damage was done, other groups joined forces to regain control of their community and rebuild.

Individuals are influenced by group pressure because they desire social identity, social approval, and/or because they believe the group's opinions are probably correct (Bugental & Goodenow, 1998). The influence of the social group varies according to several factors (Hartup, 1983):

- *Attraction to the group.* The more people want to belong to a group, the more likely they are to conform to group pressure. In elementary and junior high school, attraction to the group becomes very important. Children of this age may have the same hairstyles, wear the same kind of shoes, and even talk alike.
- *Acceptance by the group.* The role or status a person has—leader versus follower—in a group affects the degree of influence. A follower is more subject to group pressure than is a leader. For example, in one study, boys who were anxious, dependent, and not sure where they stood in the group were more susceptible to group influence (Harrison, Serafica, & McAdoo, 1984).
- *Type of group.* The degree of influence a group has depends on the affective relationships between members. Groups in which the ties are close, such as family or friends, exert a stronger influence than groups in which the affective ties are more distant, such as Scouts or Little League.

When individuals are influenced by group pressure because they believe that the group's opinions are probably correct, it is usually because they lack confidence in their own judgment. For example, if you like a movie but find out that everyone

Traditions, such as holiday celebrations, help remind us of socialized values, like being thankful.

else dislikes it, or if you have a certain political opinion but find out that the rest of the group believes differently, you might begin to question your own judgment.

Children generally lacking the experience and knowledge to have faith in their own judgment are more likely to succumb to group pressure, especially if group members are older, because they are more likely to trust the group's opinion.

Certain ethnic groups, such as Japanese, who value a sense of dependence on the group and community, emphasize group pressure ("What will other people think?") as a socializing technique to control nonconforming behavior and foster achievement (Stevenson & Lee, 1990).

Tradition

Tradition is the handing down of customs, stories, beliefs, and so on from generation to generation. In an ethnic group, tradition refers to all the knowledge, beliefs, customs, and skills that are part of that group's heritage. In religion, tradition refers to the unwritten religious codes handed down from Moses, Jesus and the Apostles, or Muhammad. In the family, tradition is implemented in the way it celebrates holidays and tells stories. The stories that families tell represent perspectives on events and relationships that are passed on from one generation to the next; these stories give meaning to the family (Fiese et al., 1999).

Because tradition represents humans' solutions to past problems, through socialization, members of each new generation receive a "design for living" from their ancestors—how to obtain shelter, get along with one another, dress, feed themselves, and so on. Traditional beliefs, attitudes, and values are also transmitted from one generation to another—the belief in God, the attitude that children should be protected, the value of hard work, and the like.

Tradition is a sociocultural method of socialization in that it sets the pattern for the way individuals satisfy basic biological needs—eating, sleeping, elimination, or sexual behavior. Some ethnic groups traditionally eat with chopsticks; others use forks and knives. Some ethnic groups sleep on the ground; others prefer beds. Some cultures eliminate outdoors; others have enclosed toilets. Some ethnic groups have premarital sexual taboos; others do not.

Tradition also sets the patterns by which people interact with one another. Social interaction refers to who does what in the society (roles) and how (behavior). In some ethnic groups, women traditionally do the cooking; in other ethnic groups, men do it. In some ethnic groups, the elderly are considered fonts of wisdom and are revered; in other ethnic groups, they are viewed as obsolete and useless. In some ethnic groups, a price is fixed in advance for an exchange in the marketplace; in other ethnic groups the exchange is accomplished by an agreed-upon price only after a certain amount of haggling has occurred. In some ethnic groups, people greet one another by surnames; in other ethnic groups, first names are used.

Traditions become unquestioned ways of doing things that stay with us even though we may forget the reasons behind them. Consider the following:

EXAMPLE   A bride served baked ham, and her husband asked why she cut the ends off. "Well, that's the way Mother always did it," she replied.

The next time his mother-in-law stopped by, he asked her why she cut the ends off the ham. "That's the way my mother did it," she replied.

And when Grandma visited, she too was asked why she sliced the ends off. She said, "That's the only way I could get it into the pan." (James & Jongeward, 1971, p. 97)

Rituals and Routines

Rituals connect us with our past, define our present, and give us a future direction (Black & Roberts, 1992). A **ritual** is a set form or system, a ceremonial observance of a prescribed rule or custom. The symbols or symbolic actions associated with rituals embrace meaning that cannot always be easily expressed in words. Some familiar examples of rituals are the baptism or naming ceremony; the communion, signifying acceptance of the church's beliefs; the bar or bas mitzvah, signifying the age of responsibility; graduation, signifying an accomplishment; and the Navajo ritual called *Blessing Way,* signifying "for good hope." Rituals serve not only a socialization function but also a protective one for children, because they provide stability, something they can "count on" in spite of change (Parke & Buriel, 1998).

The ritualization of behavior is a way of creating respect for traditions, of evoking appropriate feelings. For instance, the ritual of saying the Pledge of Allegiance evokes feelings of loyalty and reaffirms national identity. The ritual of saying grace evokes feelings of humility and thankfulness. The ritual of marriage signifies faithfulness and procreation.

Rituals also function to signify changes in people's status as they move through the cycle of life. These rituals are called **rites of passage.** The most common rite of passage occurs at puberty, acknowledging passage from childhood to adulthood and celebrating the transformation. Some rites involve a circumcision ceremony, as in some African or Australian tribes; some involve parties, such as a debutante ball; some involve the recitation of knowledge, as in the bar or bas mitzvah. Graduation from high school is a familiar rite of passage. This ritual serves as a mechanism of socialization in that it announces to the rest of society that a certain individual has a new position and will fill a new role in the society, and it makes the individual aware of the new status and its accompanying responsibilities.

Routines are repetitious acts or established procedures. In families, they can include bedtime, mealtime, and anything else done on a regular basis. They play a part in socialization in that children come to know what to expect, giving them a sense of security and a chance to practice appropriate behaviors.

Symbols

Symbols are acts or objects that have come to be generally accepted as standing for or representing something else (Vander Zanden, 1993), especially something abstract. For instance, the dove is a symbol of peace, the cross a symbol of Christ's death, and the circle a symbol of the never-ending (such as a wedding ring).

Symbols are a powerful code or shorthand for representing and dealing with aspects of the world (Hewitt, 1994). The significance of symbols as socializing mechanisms lies in the images and attitudes they conjure up and the accompanying behaviors they stimulate. For example, a crown conjures up the image of authority, and the associated behavior is respect and obedience. A country's flag conjures up feelings of patriotism, and a salute might be the socialized behavior. Certain ways of dressing may serve as symbols of status and roles in society, with a uniform indicating a police officer, a BMW symbolizing wealth, and a sarong symbolizing virginity. Symbols, then, as socializing mechanisms, serve as cues to behavior.

According to anthropology professor Leslie White (1960),

> All culture (civilization) depends upon the symbol. It was the exercise of the symbolic faculty that brought culture into existence and it is the use of symbols that makes the perpetuation of culture possible. Without the symbol there would be no culture, and man would be merely an animal, not a human being. (p. 73)

The symbol to which White is referring is language. Language makes it possible to replace behavior with ideas and to communicate these ideas to the next generation.

APPRENTICESHIP METHODS: EFFECT EMERGES FROM GUIDED PARTICIPATION

According to Rogoff (1990; 2003), all the methods of socialization discussed thus far are imparted in the child's macrosystem via various apprenticeships. In other words, the child, or novice, is guided to participate in various social activities and to master tasks by someone who has more expertise—a parent, sibling, relative, teacher, peer, coach, and so forth.

To illustrate how apprenticeship as a socializing method works, think about how children learn to feed themselves. First, the child is totally dependent on his or her mother for nourishment. As the child matures physically and cognitively, he or she observes others feeding themselves and wants to try the activity independently. The mother, or caregiver, *structures* the feeding activities according to the capability of the child, at first providing food the child can grasp with his or her fingers, such as fruit or crackers. Then the caregiver might give the child a utensil such as a spoon or pair of chopsticks, at first guiding it into the child's mouth until the child can do it him- or herself. Thus, the caregiver and the child participate or *collaborate* in the activity together. When the child exhibits appropriate mastery, the caregiver *transfers* the responsibility for independent feeding to the child.

In sum, apprenticeship as a method of socialization progresses from the expert structuring activities for the novice according to ability, to collaborating in joint activities with support provided when needed, to transferring responsibility for the management of the activity when the activity is appropriately mastered.

The ages at which these progressions in apprenticeship take place vary according to the macrosystem in which the child grows up. For example, in some Euro-American groups, self-feeding (drinking from a cup and using a spoon or fork) is expected by age 2, whereas in some Asian American groups, the child is breast-fed until age 2 (and in some groups, age 4), thereby extending the apprenticeship progression from dependence to independence.

Outcomes of Socialization

A brief overview of major socialization outcomes follows. Each is discussed in more detail in Chapter 11 (affective/cognitive outcomes—values, attitudes, motives and attributes, self-esteem) and Chapter 12 (social/behavioral outcomes—self-regulation/behavior, morals, gender roles).

VALUES

Values are qualities or beliefs seen as desirable or important. Socializing agents in microsystems influence the internalization of values. For example, what message did your parents give you about "money," or "work," or "spirituality"? What message did your teachers or coaches give you about "succeeding"? What message did your friends give you about "being liked"?

Significant societal events (chronosystem and macrosystem influences) also impact values. For example, (as we discussed) the Depression in the 1930s made people aware of the need to be thrifty. World War II in the 1940s evoked feelings of patriotism. The prosperous 1950s brought forth the value of materialism. The social upheaval of the 1960s stimulated people to critically evaluate traditional systems. And recent acts of violence and terror caused people to reexamine the value for privacy versus security.

ATTITUDES

Attitudes are tendencies to respond positively or negatively to certain persons, objects, or situations. Like values, attitudes are learned from socializing agents. Attitudes may be acquired via instructions (DeShava is not allowed to play with Sam because he doesn't attend the same church), modeling (the teacher shows concern when Juan says his father is sick), and direct experience (Leslie plays with Helena, who has cerebral palsy).

The macrosystem influences attitudes, too. During World War II, Japan was an enemy of the United States, and Japanese American citizens were interned. Now Japan is a political and economic ally. What groups are currently being racially profiled, and why?

MOTIVES AND ATTRIBUTES

Motives are needs or emotions that cause people to act in certain ways, such as the need for achievement. **Attributes** are explanations for their performance, such as "I failed the test because there were trick questions" (*external* attribute), or "I failed because I didn't study" (*internal* attribute).

Most developmental psychologists agree that humans have an inborn desire to explore, understand, and control their environment (Mayes & Zigler, 1992; White, 1959), known as **mastery motivation.** Some children are also motivated to achieve mastery of challenging goals; this is known as **achievement motivation** (McClelland, Atkinson, Clark, & Lowell, 1953).

The motive to achieve, however, is not necessarily a reliable predictor of subsequent performance. Atkinson (1964) found that successful performers pursued challenging tasks because the desire to master them was greater than the fear of or embarrassment of not doing so (motive to avoid failure). Thus, expectancies of success or failure influence achievement.

Weiner (1992) explains the role of attributions in achievement expectancies—and hence motivation. Specifically, people interpret past successes and failures in terms of whether they think they can control the outcomes of performance: Was success/failure due to personal ability or lack thereof, the amount of effort expended, the level of difficulty or easiness of a task, or the influence of good or bad luck?

SELF-ESTEEM

Recall that self-esteem is the value individuals place on their identity. Why do some children come to view themselves as competent and worthy, while others view themselves as incompetent and unworthy?

As pointed out earlier in this chapter, Cooley's "looking-glass self" (1964) and Mead's "generalized other" (1934) reflect the process of evaluating oneself in terms of one's ability to perceive the opinion of significant others. Interactions with parents, peers, and significant adults who communicate approval, validation, and support influence self-esteem.

Until recently, self-esteem was viewed as a unitary, global construct. But Harter (1999) has examined more specific domains related to physical competence, academic competence, behavioral competence, and social acceptance.

It is generally agreed that self-esteem begins to develop with a secure attachment to a caregiver who is sensitive and responsive to the infant's needs. Parenting styles that are warm and supportive, and that set clear standards for behavior with discussions of reasons, are also influential. Peer acceptance and generally favorable social comparisons ("I can run faster than you even though you're better at math") have an impact on both global self-esteem and its specific domains. Finally, the influence of significant adults (relatives, teachers, coaches) who are accepting plays a role as well.

SELF-REGULATION/BEHAVIOR

Self-regulation is the process of bringing emotions, thoughts, and/or behavior under one's control. **Behavior** consists of what one does or how one acts in response to a stimulus.

Self-regulation in infancy consists mostly of biological reflexes (sucking to get nourishment, defecating to rid the body of waste). But as children mature physically and cognitively, they become more capable of directing external behavior and internal thought processes (eating at regular intervals rather than on demand, using the toilet instead of diapers). There are various theories explaining the influence of socialization on the development of self-regulation (Bronson, 2000):

- *Psychoanalytic theory.* Freud (1938) suggested that the ego (decision maker) develops as a result of self-regulatory capacities of trying to meet the demands of the id (biological needs and instincts) and the standards of the superego (conscience, or societal ideals).

- *Behavioral learning theory.* Skinner (1948) viewed self-regulation as the learned ability to delay gratification. Self-regulation is the response resulting from having been reinforced for waiting for an appropriate time and place to express a need, desire, or emotion. For instance, children who are praised for waiting their turn on the swing will more easily adapt to waiting their turn at bat in a ball game.
- *Social cognitive theory.* Bandura (1986) explained self-regulation as the result of internalizing observed standards of models who were reinforced for such behavior and the consequent self-reinforcement for imitating those standards.
- *Cognitive developmental theory.* Piaget (1952) considered self-regulation to be adaptive behavior. As children mature and interact with their environments, they assimilate and accommodate standards of behavior, adding them to existing cognitive structures and modifying the structures as their understanding changes.
- *Vygotskian theory.* Vygotsky (1978) focused on the role of social and cultural factors in the development of self-regulation and behavior. He believed that language enables children to learn social rules and cultural roles. The language of others ("social speech") becomes internalized ("private speech") and enables children to think and regulate behavior accordingly.

A socialization goal of self-regulation is the development of prosocial, or helpful, behavior rather than antisocial, or aggressive, behavior (Bronson, 2000). Socialization methods associated with the development of prosocial behavior are attachment (warmth), instruction (clear rules), reasoning (discussion of standards), modeling, and learning by doing (participation in activities that involve helping and cooperating) (Eisenberg & Fabes, 1998). Socialization methods associated with antisocial behavior are rejection, punishment, and group pressure (Patterson, DeBaryshe, & Ramsey, 1989).

MORALS

Morals are an individual's evaluation of what is right and wrong. Morals involve acceptance of rules and govern one's behavior toward others.

Theories of moral development have (1) an affective, or emotional, component (moral feelings such as guilt, shame, and empathy), (2) a cognitive component (moral reasoning such as conceptualization of right and wrong and related decision making), and (3) a behavioral component (moral action encompassing how one responds to temptations regarding violated moral rules such as lying, cheating, and stealing).

Turiel (1983) distinguishes between rules governing moral behavior that focus on the welfare and rights of others (moral rules—no hitting, stealing, or lying) and those that focus on conduct in social situations (social-conventional rules—raising a hand before talking or saying thank you). General moral reasoning is linked with cognitive development (Kohlberg, 1984; Piaget, 1965); specific perspectives on rules differ according to age, gender, and culture. For example, children as young as age 2½–3 consider moral rule misbehavior to deserve more punishment than those social-conventional misbehavior (Smetona, 1985).

Some theorist believe that individuals' different cultural and social experiences while growing up contribute to different moral perspectives. For example, according to Triandis (1995), in individualistic cultures, morality generally is oriented toward "justice" (principles of equality, fairness, and rights); and in collectivistic cultures, morality generally is oriented toward "care" (principles of welfare, compassion, and relationships).

Cultural values regarding right and wrong influence children's moral perspectives. For example, a study compared children age 5–13 in the United States with children in India (Shweder, Mahapatra, & Miller, 1987) on responses to 39 moral transgressions. The Indian children, who were Hindu, believed that it was worse morally for the eldest son in a family to eat chicken and get a haircut the day after his father died (thereby showing disrespect) than it was for a husband to beat his wife for going to a movie without his permission after having been warned not to do so (thereby fulfilling his duty as head of the family). Hindus believe that respect for father and husband is a universal moral rule, not an arbitrary social convention.

Thus, differences in socialization contribute to moral development—specifically, parents' affect and attachment, their use of reasoning (Laible & Thompson, 2000), the modeling of appropriate behavior, the use of reinforcement, peer interaction, and experiences in school and community, with diverse viewpoints necessitating discussion and compromise.

GENDER ROLES

Gender roles are qualities that individuals understand and that characterize males and females in their culture. The term *gender* usually refers to psychological attributes, whereas the term *sex* usually refers to biological ones.

Males and females differ in their chromosomes (male—XY; female—XX), their hormones, and their physiologies. They also differ in the social roles they assume based on societal expectations. The female's biological capacity to bear children is associated with many societies' expectation that she will assume a nurturing, cooperative role. The male's hormones (testosterone) and his muscular physique are associated with many societies' expectation that he will assume an assertive, dominant role.

Theories of gender-role development explaining how children are socialized to assume behaviors, values, and attitudes considered appropriate for their sex are discussed in more detail in Chapter 12. Psychoanalytic theory focuses on how one learns to *feel* like a male or female based on identification with the same-sex parent. Behavior learning theory focuses on how one learns to *act* like a male or female based on reinforcement of expected gender-appropriate behavior. Social cognitive theory focuses on how one learns to *imitate* gender-role models. Gender schema theory focuses on how one *processes* gender-related information and *selects* what is appropriate and worthy for him or her.

Epilogue

To be human is to be caring and to have a conscience. Socialization of the child into a "human being" is a multifaceted and reciprocal process. Socialization methods vary in effectiveness according to the people implementing them, the situation, and the children to whom they are directed.

Pinocchio was influenced by Gepetto, Jiminy Cricket, the Blue Fairy, and others. Gepetto provided love and acceptance; Jiminy Cricket provided instructions, feedback, support, and encouragement; the Blue Fairy provided standards and rewards; and the others provided experiences for learning by doing. After experiencing many consequences, both positive and negative, Pinocchio adopts Gepetto's "good" values and is rewarded by turning into a "real boy."

E.T. and Elliot illustrated reciprocal socialization, bringing out "human" characteristics in each. They became attached to one another, growing sensitive to each other's needs. They also learned the meaning of "sacrifice," discovering that to keep the friendship in spirit they had to give it up physically.

Summary

Socialization involves aims, agents, methods, and outcomes. It is a reciprocal, dynamic process, with children playing a role in their own socialization.

One goal of socialization is to develop a self-concept. Erikson's eight stages of psychosocial development are important here: trust versus mistrust, autonomy versus shame and doubt, initiative versus guilt, industry versus inferiority, identity versus identity diffusion, intimacy versus isolation, generativity versus self-absorption, and integrity versus despair. Socialization also aims to enable self-regulation and empower achievement. It teaches appropriate social roles and developmental skills (social, emotional, cognitive). A developmental task falls somewhere between an individual need and a societal demand. Developmental tasks differ from society to society.

Every individual in society is the outcome of the socialization process. The success of this outcome in terms of society's expectations depends on a series of interactions with significant socializing agents that are components of the community in which the individual lives. Significant agents of socialization include the family, the school, the peer group, the mass media, and the community.

The family is the child's introduction to society and has, therefore, borne major responsibility for socializing children. The family is a system of interaction. The relationships have a powerful effect on the psychosocial development of children. The family is the child's first reference group for values.

The school acts as an agent of society in that it is organized to perpetuate that society's knowledge, skills, customs, and beliefs. It also acts as an agent to foster respect for and adherence to the existing social order while educating for adaptability.

Child care has become an important socialization agent due to societal changes, as seen in amount of time children now spend being cared for by individuals outside the family.

The peer group gives children experience in egalitarian types of relationships. Children learn to look at themselves from the group's point of view. Peers also serve as a support group for the expression of values and attitudes. They exert a strong influence on individuals who seek a social identity and social approval.

The mass media, unlike other agents of socialization, do not directly involve personal interaction. The media are also considered to be socializers, however, because they teach many of the ways of the society. Children process media information, constructing meaning and transforming it to behavior.

The community provides a sense of belonging and friendship. The population distribution of a community affects the interactions children have. The types of agencies, such as the Scouts, the "Y," and Little League, that a community provides affects the experiences children have while growing up. The services a community provides, such as libraries, museums, and cultural events, affect which parts of society are open to children. Communities can be support systems for families; advocacy is the process by which this occurs.

Socialization is the process by which individuals learn the ways of a given society so that they can function effectively within it. Methods by which these ways are transmitted include the following: affective (attachment), operant (reinforcement, extinction, punishment, feedback, learning by doing), observational (modeling), cognitive (instruction, standard setting, reasoning), sociocultural (group pressure, tradition, rituals and routines, symbols), and apprenticeship (structuring, collaborating, transferring).

The outcomes of socialization are affective/cognitive—values, attitudes, motives and attributes, and self-esteem—and social/behavioral—self-regulation/behavior, morals, and gender roles.

Activity

PURPOSE *To understand the impact of agents of socialization on development.*

1. Name the three most important things you learned from your parents while growing up.
2. Name three people other than your parents who had a major influence on you as a child or adolescent.
3. Describe each one's influence, using specific examples.
4. What methods of socialization did your parents and the significant others in your life use?
5. Whom are you influencing in ways similar to the ones you have described?
6. What are your aims and methods of socialization?

 Research Terms

Apprenticeship
Attachment
Developmental appropriateness
Information processing
Observational learning
Rites of passage

Related Readings

Ambert, A. (1992). *The effect of children on parents.* Binghampton, NY: Haworth Press.
Bandura, A. (1986). *Social foundations of thought and action: A social cognitive theory.* Englewood Cliffs, NJ: Prentice-Hall.

Bowlby, J. (1988). *A secure base: Parent–child attachment and healthy human development.* New York: Basic Books.

Brazelton, T. B. (1984). *To listen to a child.* Reading, MA: Perseus Books.

Erikson, E. (1963). *Childhood and society.* New York: Norton.

Golding, W. (1954). *Lord of the flies.* New York: Putnam.

Goleman, D. (1995). *Emotional intelligence.* New York: Bantam Books.

Pleck, E. H. (2000). *Celebrating the family: Ethnicity, consumer culture, and family rituals.* Cambridge, MA: Harvard University Press.

Rogoff, B. (1990). *Apprenticeship in thinking: Cognitive development in social context.* New York: Oxford University Press.

Chapter 3

Prologue: Then and Now

Family Systems
    Basic Structures
    Basic Functions

Family Transitions
    Structural Changes
    Functional Changes

Macrosystem Influences on Families, Socialization, and Children
    Socioeconomic Status
    Ethnic Orientation
    Religious Orientation

Chronosystem Influences on Families, Socialization, and Children
    Sociopolitical Changes
    Economic Changes
    Technological Changes

Meeting the Challenge of Change: Family Empowerment

Epilogue

Summary

Activity

Research Terms

Related Readings

© Jose Carrillo/PhotoEdit

Ecology of the Family

My soul knows that I am part of the human race, . . . as my spirit is part of my nation. In my very own self, I am part of my family.

—D. H. LAWRENCE

TIES THAT BIND, TWINE, AND UNWIND

THEN The Bible tells of the beginning of the human race and the ways in which people coped with living in groups and surviving on Earth. A main theme is procreation and family obligations and alliances. Adam and Eve are told by God to "be fruitful and multiply." After many years of infertility, Abraham and Sarah are promised a son in return for a covenant with God. Their son, Isaac, then becomes the destined ancestor of many future generations. To assure that the family line will continue as agreed, Abraham selects his son's future wife from another land, sending gifts to the betrothed's family. Rebekah, the bride-to-be, leaves her family and homeland to live with Isaac and his family and to bear his children. In this way, the pattern of traditional family formation was borne—a patriarchal family based on kinship and community ties, with members having certain rights and obligations. The goal was security and continuance; "happiness" was secondary.

NOW For a half-century, television has been depicting families as if they reflected the current reality. The 1950s gave us *Father Knows Best*, a show about the "normal" problems in a family consisting of a husband and wife and their children, ultimately solved by the sage father. The 1960s gave us *The Brady Bunch,* a blended family (a widow and her three daughters married to a widower and his three sons) who work out their sibling relationships just fine. The 1970s gave us *One Day at a Time*, a show about a divorced mother raising two teenage girls. The 1980s gave us *Full House*, a show about two males (a widower father and his brother-in-law) parenting three daughters. The 1990s gave us *Once and Again,* the story of a divorced father of two and his stormy relationship with a newly separated mother of two. The 2000s gave us *Friends,* a group of 20- or 30-somethings who share intimacies, even conceiving a child, out of wedlock. And so we have been exposed to all kinds of families. These TV families represent a broad range of family values, presenting the family as an institution whose purpose is to foster personal happiness, or obligation to the self, rather than family duty, or obligation to others.

KEY QUESTIONS

- What are the personal and family consequences (positive and negative) of subscribing to a value of obligation to oneself on one end of the spectrum and obligation to others on the other end of the spectrum?
- Who has the most at stake in the marriage or family union—adults or children?
- How are one's views on societal change and the socialization of children related to the family system (structure, functions, relationships)?

Family Systems

This chapter focuses on what families are and do, how different families adapt to change, and how they cope with external forces. Figure 3.1 shows an ecological model of the systems involved in the process. Family systems' theory views the family as a whole, in terms of its structure and organizational patterns, and at the individual level, in terms of how members interact with one another (Parke & Buriel, 1998).

In Chapters 1 and 2, the aims, methods, and outcomes of socialization were discussed, and the agents of socialization identified. Here, the family, the primary agent of socialization, is explored. A family is a microsystem. The classic (structural-functional) definition of a family, according to sociologist George Murdock (1962, p. 19), is "a social group characterized by common residence, economic cooperation, and reproduction. It includes adults of both sexes, at least two of whom maintain a socially approved sexual relationship, and one or more children, own or adopted, of the sexually cohabitating adults." The biblical families cited in the prologue are examples.

How many people do you know who fit into the classic definition of a family? Today, there are more relationships that do *not* conform to Murdock's definition

Figure 3.1

An Ecological Model of Human Development

The family is a primary influence on children's development.

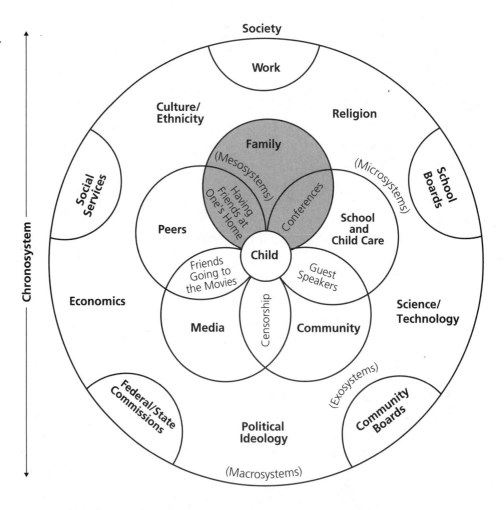

than do, illustrating the impact of societal change on the family system's form and function. The TV families cited in the prologue are examples.

To accommodate changes in family patterns, the U.S. Bureau of the Census defines a **family** as "two or more persons related by birth, marriage, or adoption, who reside together." Thus, a family can be two or more adult siblings living together, a parent and child or children, or two adults who are related by marriage, but have no children, in addition to adults who adopt a child.

Some states (Vermont, for example) and cities have legally recognized certain unrelated people in caring relationships who live together in a household as a "family." These laws pertaining to "domestic partnerships," "reciprocal partnerships," or "civil unions" are intended to provide gay couples, foster parents, related pairs (mother and daughter, two brothers), and stepfamilies with rights and privileges related to health insurance policies, medical and educational decisions, employment leave policies, employment benefits, and annuities and pensions.

It is important to understand the changes in the concept of family structure because these changes affect the functions that families perform, the roles its members play, and the relationships its members have with one another, thereby affecting the socialization of children.

Points to Ponder

Reproduction is a basic instinct. Because sex can occur without any subsequent commitment to care for any children born, families evolved to ensure their protection. However, families can exist without biological children, without any children, and so without any child care. What is your concept of a family?

BASIC STRUCTURES

Families are organized in different ways around the world. A family consisting of a husband and wife and their children is called a **nuclear family.** For the children, this is the **family of orientation**—the family into which one is born. For the parents, the nuclear family is the **family of procreation,** that which develops when one marries and has children (see Figure 3.2). In the nuclear family, the wife and husband depend on each other for companionship, and the children depend on their parents for affection and socialization.

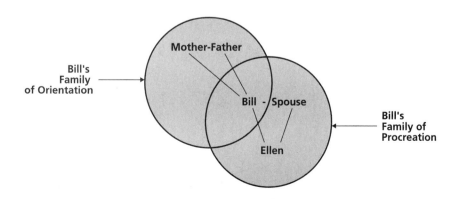

Figure 3.2

The Nuclear Family

Figure 3.3
The Extended Family

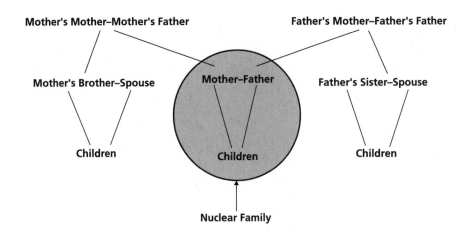

The significance of the nuclear family structure is that it is the main source of children and so provides for the perpetuation of society. Most societies assign responsibility for the care and socialization of children to the partners who produce or adopt them, and sanction the sexual union of a male and a female by law or tradition—in our society, by legal marriage. The institution of marriage, then, serves not only to legalize sexual unions but also to fix the obligation toward children who result from those sexual unions.

The **extended family** includes relatives of the nuclear family who are economically and emotionally dependent on each other. They may or may not live nearby (see Figure 3.3).

In some cultures or ethnic groups, such as Native Americans, Asian Americans, and Italian Americans, the emphasis is placed on the extended family, with obligation to the family superseding obligation to the self. In these groups, tradition dictates certain obligations and responsibilities to various members of the extended family. For example, who socializes the children? Who decides how family resources are allocated? Who cares for needy family members? Some cultures emphasize the mother's side of the family as having the responsibility for the socialization of children, the weeding of authority, and resources allocation. These families are known as **matriarchal.** A contemporary example is the royal family in Great Britain headed by Queen Elizabeth II. Other cultures emphasize the father's relatives as having the responsibility for the care of family members, the wielding of authority, and resources allocation. These families are known as **patriarchal.** This organizational pattern is much more common in the world than is the matriarchal. Examples of patriarchal families can be found in the Bible and in the popular television series *The Sopranos.*

In the United States, both sides of the extended family are generally regarded as equal, or **egalitarian.** Thus, your mother's parents have as much legal authority and responsibility over you as do your father's parents. That is, if something happened to your parents and they could no longer care for you, both sets of grandparents would have equal claim to your custody.

Because we live in an egalitarian society, whose parents' house you visit on holidays after you are married sometimes has to be negotiated. In traditional societies, the rules are set; in modern ones like ours, the rules are ever changing (Silverstein & Auerbach, 2001).

Regardless of whether your extended family is matriarchal, patriarchal, or egalitarian, its main function is support—relatives are the people you turn to when you

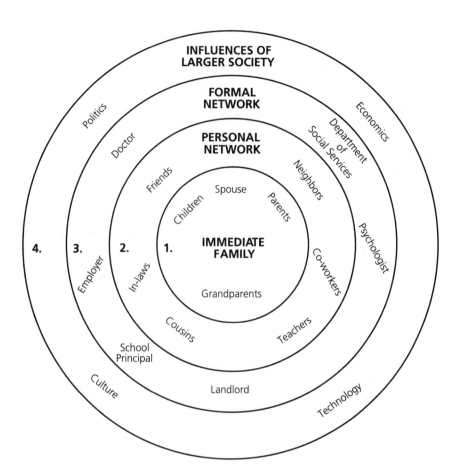

Figure 3.4

Sources of Family Support
Source: Adapted from Dean, 1984.

need help or when you have joys to share. However, because many families today do not have an extended family for support (for a variety of reasons including relocation, divorce, remarriage, and death), the people they turn to for help might be friends, neighbors, co-workers, or children's teachers. These people assume some of the traditional support functions of the extended family and become an individual's personal network (Dean, 1984). It has been shown that people who have no such personal network have to rely on the formal network of society—professionals or government agencies—for support (Garbarino, 1992). Support services provided by the formal network are influenced by politics, economics, culture, and technology. For example, the federally funded preschool program Head Start, launched by the Democrats in the 1960s, saw its funding later reduced by the Republicans. The American cultural norm of working for a living influenced the change in financial support for needy families—from welfare to workfare. Technology such as cell phones and computers can influence family members' time together (see Figure 3.4).

BASIC FUNCTIONS

To understand the significance of the family, we need to look at the basic functions it performs. In general, the family performs certain functions that enable society to survive generation after generation, although these functions may vary widely. Family functioning can be viewed on a continuum with "healthy," or functional, on one end and "unhealthy," or dysfunctional, at the other (keeping in mind that no family is "healthy" all the time). Economic, health, and social stresses can upset some or all of the following family functions:

- *Reproduction.* The family ensures that society's population will be maintained—that is, that a sufficient number of children will be born and cared for to replace the members who die.
- *Socialization/education.* The family ensures that the society's values, beliefs, attitudes, knowledge, skills, and techniques will be transmitted to the young.
- *Assignment of social roles.* The family provides an identity for its offspring (racial, ethnic, religious, socioeconomic, and gender roles). An identity involves behavior and obligations. For example, a Jew may not eat pork and may feel obliged to give to charity. A Chinese American may eat with chopsticks and defer to the authority of his or her elders. A person born into a high socioeconomic status may feel pressured to choose a spouse from a similar background. In some families, girls are socialized to do housework and be caregivers, and boys are socialized to be breadwinners.
- *Economic support.* The family provides shelter, nourishment, and protection. In some families, all members except very young children contribute to the economic well-being by producing goods. In other families, one or both parents earn the money that pays for goods the entire family consumes.
- *Nurturance/emotional support.* The family provides children's first experience in social interaction. This interaction is intimate, nurturing, and enduring, thus providing emotional security for children. The family also cares for its members when they are ill, hurting, or aging.

Family Transitions

Throughout history, family structure has altered to accommodate economic, social, political, and technological influences (the chronosystem). Examples include the Industrial Revolution, no-fault divorce, welfare reform, and birth control.

STRUCTURAL CHANGES

Structural family changes can include the addition of family members to the household due to birth, adoption, remarriage, or relatives moving in, and the removal of family members due to death, divorce, or children becoming adults and moving out.

Family Ties

Although families are always in a process of transition (marriage, childbirth, aging, death), certain events affect the socialization of children more than do others. These include divorce, single parenting, and stepparenting.

Changes in family ties are reflected in the increase in divorce and in the proportion of children living with only one parent. According to the U.S. Bureau of the Census (2000) and the National Center for Health Statistics (2000), the divorce rate was 25 percent in 1966, 53 percent in 1979, and 47 percent in 1990. One in two children live with one parent (divorced or never married) at some point in childhood.

Library of Congress

Early American farm life required everyone's participation for family survival.

Parental divorce is not a singular event but rather represents a series of stressful experiences for the entire family that begins with marital conflict, ends in the actual termination, and includes many adjustments both during and after. Families must often cope with "the diminution of family resources, assumption of new roles and responsibilities, establishment of new patterns of interaction, reorganization of routines . . . , and the introduction of new relationships into the existing family" (Hetherington & Camara, 1984, p. 398). More specifically, parents in conflicted marriages are less able to help their children regulate emotions and behavior, as well as self-soothe their own stress (Kelly, 2000; Wilson & Gottman, 1995).

Even as the divorce rates rose in the 1990s, so did the rate of the remarriage (U.S. Bureau of the Census, 2000). Married adults now comprise more than half of all American adults. When a divorced person remarries, the children gain a stepparent, and with the stepparent come additional kinship relationships. This means that new roles and obligations not dependent on custom and tradition have to be adopted or faced.

Divorce and the Family. The fragmentation of the family, its diminished functions, unrealistic expectations, role changes, the economic state of society, stress, and changes in the law—all have been blamed for divorce.

Formerly, the law permitted divorce only if one spouse committed serious marital misconduct such as adultery, cruelty, or desertion. Traditional divorce proceedings involved the determination of who was guilty and who was innocent. Child custody arrangements and financial settlements were intended to reward the innocent party and punish the guilty one. Divorce cases were often costly financially and emotionally—for both parents and children. Criticisms of existing laws led to the passage of no-fault divorce laws. These laws do away with assigning blame and allow divorce on the basis of "irreconcilable differences" or "marital breakdown." However, the framers of the new laws, who were preoccupied with the defects in the traditional ones, apparently failed to consider that the old laws did offer protection to women and children. For example, a woman, deemed to be the innocent party, did not have to agree to a divorce unless her husband, deemed to be the guilty party, provided adequate financial support for her and the children. Furthermore, judges often divided property in accordance with family need, with the mother and children retaining the family home and enough support to avoid sudden poverty (Skolnick, 1987).

Today, in most states, the family's assets are divided equally between divorcing spouses. Often the family home must be sold in order to divide the couple's tangible assets. The husband and wife usually each retain their intangible and tangible assets such as education, career, future earning power, pension(s), and insurance (Weitzman, 1985). Thus, today's divorce laws have had a tremendous influence on families' adjustment to the inevitable changes accompanying dissolution of a marriage.

Divorce has certain consequences for family functioning and the socialization of children. For example, barring external social support, the effect of divorce on the custodial parent is that the responsibilities double. The single parent is responsible for financial support, child care, and home maintenance. And because the parent is usually under great stress, parenting is likely to diminish (Emery, 1988; Goodman, Emery, & Haugaard, 1998). The children may have to assume increased responsibility for themselves, as well as having less time available to spend with the parent and receiving less love and experiencing less security. Some states are enacting statutes mandating waiting periods, mediation, and marital counseling before granting applications for divorce (American Bar Association, 1996).

To assess the effect of divorce, we must examine how the various members of the family deal with the transition, reestablish their role obligations to one another, and perform such functions as the following (Hetherington & Clingempeel, 1992; Hetherington, Stanley-Hagan, & Anderson, 1989):

- *Socialization/education.* Child rearing must continue, with behavior monitored, and values and morals imparted.
- *Assignment of social roles/authority.* Power for decision making within the family must be allocated, and responsibilities for tasks assigned.
- *Economic support/domestic responsibilities.* The family must obtain enough money to support its members. The physical well-being of the children must be provided for, and the residence must be maintained in a safe and healthy manner.
- *Nurturance/emotional support.* Caring for and involvement with family members must occur to provide for the emotional well-being necessary for family survival.

The ability of the family going through a divorce to carry on its former functions is affected not only by the coping skills of its members but also by macrosystem forces. These forces include economic disparity for females, societal attitudes idealizing the two-parent family, and available informal or formal support services (Coontz, 1997; Hetherington, 1989).

Regardless of their marital status, women do not earn income on the same scale as men. Although men are legally required to support their children following divorce, and in some cases their wives as well, the majority of men do not continue to provide support even though the courts order them to do so (Children's Defense

Fund, 2001). Sometimes a woman who heads a family must turn to her own family of orientation or to the public welfare system for economic assistance. Children who live in mother-only families have almost a 1 in 2 chance of being in poverty, in contrast to less than a 1 in 10 chance for children living with two parents (U.S. Bureau of the Census, 2000).

The change in the economic status of the family resulting from divorce means not only a change in family consumption habits but often a change in housing (Weitzman, 1985). Moving in itself is a source of stress to the family. For one thing, former neighborhood supports are no longer available; for another, maintaining two households is costly when a parent lives in one but must contribute to the other.

Divorce affects the distribution of authority within the family. Prior to the divorce, the father may have had more authority because, traditionally, fathers were regarded as the primary breadwinner, or authority may have been shared by both parents. After the divorce, however, the custodial parent assumes day-to-day authority over the children, and the noncustodial parent's authority is restricted to areas spelled out in the divorce agreement. Hetherington and Clingempeel (1992) found that both fathers' and mothers' authority over children, as indicated by their parenting practices, tended to deteriorate in the first two years following the divorce. There was less consistency, control, and affection.

Divorce affects the distribution of the domestic functions of the family. Prior to the divorce, both parents perform chores related to family functioning. If the mother was not employed outside the home, she probably was primarily responsible for household duties and child care while the father was earning the money. After the divorce, the mother is more likely to have custody of the children (Hetherington & Clingempeel, 1992). Generally, she has to find work outside the home because of the father's reduced economic contribution to her and the children. In addition, she has to find someone to care for the children. For his part, the father has to assume the domestic duties associated with his separate household or else hire someone to clean, cook, shop, do laundry, and so on. And if the mother was employed outside the home prior to the divorce, the father may have shared domestic responsibilities with her. This means that after the divorce she has to assume his chores as well.

Hetherington, Cox, and Cox (1982) found that the families of divorced mothers who had custody of their children were less likely to eat dinner together or play together than intact families. Divorced mothers were less likely to read aloud to their children when putting them to bed, and their children had more erratic bedtimes. Also, the households of divorced mothers and fathers were more disorganized than were nondivorced households.

The isolation of the nuclear family from relatives adds to the burdens thrust upon the single-parent family—relatives cannot be called on for help with child care or household duties or for emotional support. Because emotional support is one of the functions of the family, and divorce removes one adult from the picture, the remaining adult no longer has someone with whom to share the burdens (and joys) of child rearing. Neither is there someone with whom to share the daily decision making and to provide needed psychological support.

Effects of Divorce on Children. According to the National Center for Health Statistics (2000), almost one out of two marriages ends in divorce. Most divorces occur within the first 10 years for both first marriages and remarriages. Children in divorced families experience a deep sense of loss, develop divided loyalties, and feel helpless in the face of forces beyond their control. In a review of recent research on the effects of divorce, Kelly (2000) found that, although children of divorced parents, as a group, have more adjustment problems than do children of never-divorced parents, the divorce per se is not necessarily the major cause of these problems. Rather, the negative effects of conflict in troubled marriages can be observed in children years before the divorce takes place.

Parental divorce involves a series of stressful interactions between children and their environment as the family restructures. However, not all children react to divorce in the same way (Sandler, Tein, & West, 1994). Children's reactions depend on the personalities involved, on their own coping skills, and on their relations with their parents (Cowan, Powell, & Cowan, 1998). Reactions also depend on such factors as children's age and gender, the level of family disharmony prior to the divorce, and the availability of other people for emotional support (Hetherington, Stanley-Hagan, & Anderson, 1989). Studies by Hetherington (1988, 1989) have shown that during and after parental divorce children often exhibit marked changes in behavior, such as acting out, particularly in school. An analysis of academic achievement of high school students showed that those from divorced families had significantly lower achievement levels than those from intact families (Cherian, 1989).

Wallerstein and Kelly (1996) found that divorce affected the self-concepts of preschoolers. In particular, the children's views of the dependability and predictability of relationships were disrupted. Some children blamed themselves for the breakup. For example, one 5-year-old child said, "If only I didn't whine like Daddy said, he wouldn't have left me." Even a year later, in a follow-up study, almost half of the children in the sample still displayed heightened anxiety and aggression. These authors also found that school-age children responded to divorce with sadness, fear, feelings of deprivation, and some anger (Wallerstein, Corbin, & Lewis, 1988; Wallerstein & Kelly, 1996). They, like the preschool children, were still struggling, after a year, with the changes in their lives. School-age children had difficulty focusing their attention on school-related tasks.

In various studies done by Hetherington and Clingempeel (1992), young children of divorce were found to be more dependent, aggressive, whiny, demanding, unaffectionate, and disobedient than children from intact families. They feared abandonment, loss of love, and even bodily harm. The behavior and fears expressed were, in part, due to the parents' preoccupation with their own needs, as well as the ensuing role conflicts. When compared with parents of intact families, divorced parents of preschoolers were less consistent in their discipline and less nurturant. Also, communication was not as effective, and fewer demands for mature behavior were made of the children.

Adolescents, unlike younger children, feel little sense of blame for the separation of their parents, but they do feel resentment. They are often pawns as each parent bids for loyalty: "She tells me terrible things about my dad; when I'm with him, he tells me terrible things about her." They are also still burdened by the painful memories of the divorce 10 years later (Wallerstein, Corbin, & Lewis, 1988, pp. 90–91).

Gender influences the impact of the divorce, with research showing that boys are harder hit. Hetherington (1988), and her colleagues (1989), in attempting to explain this, suggested that boys receive less support from their mothers, teachers, and peers than do girls. Girls tend to cry and whine to vent their sadness—and this gets them help—whereas boys tend to bully other children and cry only when hit back.

According to Lamb (1997), the father's role in the socialization of children is very important. He models and teaches not only gender roles but also other values and morals. As children grow, each parent interprets society for them. Children from single-parent families lack the live-in, gender-role model of the parent, usually the father, who has left. Single parents can, however, provide children with opposite-sex role models via relatives, teachers, coaches, and community service workers.

Children involved in custody battles are the most torn by divorce (Kelly, 2000). To avoid this situation, some parents assume joint custody, sharing responsibility for their children. The effects of various custody arrangements are discussed shortly.

Although divorce is upsetting to everyone involved, it is probably worse for children living in embattled households. For parents, divorce is a highly stressful time, and feelings of depression, loss of self-esteem, and helplessness interfere with parenting abilities. These parents must find support outside the family to bolster their confidence in themselves and their ability to parent. They must tell their children that, even though they are divorcing each other, they are not divorcing the children.

A serious long-range effect of divorce is the removal of marriage models, leading to unrealistic expectations for future mates. Children may grow up idealizing the absent parent. Unfortunately, ideals are wishes for perfection, untempered by reality. For example, a child growing up in a two-parent home may experience the father's illnesses (Daddy needs to be cared for, too), parental disagreements (which may or may not be worked out), and physical affection in terms of input from both parents. In contrast, the child growing up in a single-parent home may fantasize situations and relationships regarding the missing parent; reality, inevitably, brings disappointment.

Single-Parent Custody. In the United States, the percentage of children living in single-parent households has more than doubled since 1970. Single mothers raising children now outnumber single fathers raising children by two to one (U.S. Bureau of the Census, 2000).

Single parenthood can occur through death, divorce, desertion, births outside marriage, adoption without marriage, or even artificial insemination. Some people believe that having a husband is no longer a prerequisite for raising children. However, "children in female-headed homes are often deprived of two types of resources a father might provide—economic and socioemotional" (McLanahan & Carlson, 2002, p. 151). Apparently, motherhood is not a prerequisite for raising a child, either. The Uniform Parentage Act, a law in about 20 percent of the states, awards custody based on care considerations, rather than biology, when appropriate.

Female heads of households often have to work outside the home in addition to caring for the children and maintaining the household. They are likely to depend on other caregivers. Frequently, female-headed families are poor, or at least experience a drop in the standard of living occurs if the woman was previously married. Thus, single-parent mothers experience economic as well as emotional and physical strain (Hetherington & Clingempeel, 1989).

Generally, preadolescent boys show more deep-seated and enduring problems in response to their parents' divorce than do girls. Two years after the divorce, many boys have trouble concentrating and so do poorly on intelligence tests and have difficulty with math. Also, they interact aggressively with their mothers, and teachers and with boys their own age. Monitoring of boys was lower in divorced nonremarried households, and these boys engaged in more antisocial behavior (Hetherington, 1993; Hetherington & Clingempeel, 1992). Although preadolescent girls seem to adjust to the divorce within a few years, evidence has accumulated showing problems related to female gender-role development during adolescence. Problems include difficult heterosexual relationships, precocious sexual activity, and confrontational exchanges with the mother (Hetherington, 1993; Hetherington & Clingempeel, 1992).

If the father is absent and, consequently, the father–daughter relationship is halted, then two possible patterns of difficulties in heterosexual relationships can occur. One is passiveness toward, withdrawal from, and shyness with males. The other is aggressiveness, overt sexual activity, and flirtatiousness (Hetherington, 1972). During the teen years, daughters of divorce may exhibit increased conflict with their mothers, increased noncompliance, and problematic sexual behavior, including pregnancy (Chase-Lansdale & Hetherington, 1990). Studies (Coontz, 1997; Miller, Forehand, & Kotchick, 1999) that control for family process (monitoring, communication) have found that single parenthood is *not* related to early teen sexual behavior but that *rules* about dating are; ethnicity was not influential. Apparently, it is harder to establish and enforce such rules when one parents alone, without support.

In sum, the effect of the father's absence on boys and girls depends on the age of the child at the time of separation from the father, the length of the father's absence, the quality of the mother–father relationship prior to the separation, the availability of appropriate substitute male models, and the emotional state of the mother during and after the separation (Biller, 1993; Kelly, 2000; Wallerstein & Kelly, 1996).

Because children under age 18 are much more likely to be living with their mothers than with their fathers, little research has been done on children being raised by single-parent fathers, and most such studies have involved school-age children. Until recently, custody of the children of divorcing parents was usually automatically awarded to the mother. Now, however, many courts are taking into consideration the actual needs of the children involved when custody is awarded, and more fathers are gaining custody.

Another reason little research has been done on children being raised by single-parent fathers is that fathers with custody, more than mothers, tend to use additional caregivers, such as babysitters, friends, relatives, and day care workers. Thus, children growing up in single-father homes are likely to have opportunities to interact with female role models, which makes it more difficult to research the effects on children of the absence of their mothers. Father-custody children have more contact with their mothers than mother-custody children have with their fathers (Parke & Buriel, 1998; Santrock & Warshak, 1979).

Studies done by Santrock and Warshak (1979) and by Santrock, Warshak, and Eliot (1982) compared families in which the mother was awarded custody, families in which the father was awarded custody, and two-parent families. They found that girls who live with their fathers and boys who live with their mothers tend to be less well adjusted than those who live with the same-sex parent. Boys who live with their fathers tend to be less demanding, and more mature, independent, and sociable, and they tend to have higher self-esteem than girls in father-custody situations. Likewise, girls who live with their mothers tend to be less demanding, and more mature, independent, and sociable, and they tend to have higher self-esteem than boys in mother-custody situations. However, another study (Downey & Powell, 1993) of 400 eighth-grade boys and girls failed to find any evidence that boys and girls benefit significantly from living with their same-sex parent.

Problems for fathers raising children are similar to those of mothers. In general, fathers find it difficult to obtain child care help (day care, after-school care, housekeepers). Sometimes day care centers' hours do not coincide with their own work hours, and the cost of a housekeeper or nanny can be prohibitive. There is also role overload in having to work, care for children, and maintain the house. Social life suffers.

A common problem among these fathers is that they tend to be unprepared for homemaking and parenting responsibilities. Buying groceries, mending, and ironing clothes, doing dishes, and keeping the house clean are difficult adjustments. Many fathers also have little knowledge regarding the normal developmental stages of children or parenting (Biller, 1993). Although fathers' *economic* responsibility for their children has been the focus of public policy and consequent legislation, fathers' *emotional* responsibility has been ignored until recently (Amato, 1998). Fathers are now being included in prenatal exercises as well as in preschool and elementary school programs.

Recommendations for Community Support of Single Parents

1. Extend availability of day care facilities to evening hours.
2. Form babysitting cooperatives in neighborhoods or workplaces.
3. Make transportation available for children to and from day care to the parent's home or work.
4. Provide classes on single parenthood and opportunities for support groups.
5. Provide "Big Sister" programs for girls from mother-absent homes and "Big Brother" programs for boys from father-absent homes.

Joint Custody. Joint custody is a modern-day solution to the quandary facing many judges: Which adult claimant should be given custody of the children? It also provides the rationale for father–mother involvement in child rearing that enables children to relate to both male and female role models (Biller, 1993). A concern expressed by Mary Ann Mason (1998) in her book *Custody Wars* is that the legal shift to "equal treatment" of men and women has translated into parents' rights taking precedence over children's needs.

Joint legal custody divides decision-making authority over children between the divorced parents. Typical areas requiring decisions include discipline, education, medical care, and religious upbringing. Sometimes physical custody is divided as well. For example, a child may spend weekdays with one parent and weekends and holidays with the other, or 6 months with one and 6 months with the other.

As the number of divorces has increased, so has the number of states giving legal sanction to some form of joint custody. As a result, some nuclear families split by divorce are evolving into a new form, called the **binuclear family,** in which the children are part of two homes and two family groups. Binuclear families are not limited to joint custody cases, but parents without custody tend to become less involved in their children's lives.

Joint custody has as many negatives as positives, depending on the individuals and situations involved. The main advantage is that it requires that the parents' top priority be the child. Parents have to set aside their differences and make decisions based on the child's welfare, not their own (Bowman & Ahrons, 1985). Joint custody is more apt to encourage continued child support payments and mutual sharing of parental responsibilities (Steinman, Zemmelman, & Knoblauch, 1985). An analysis of studies on children in joint physical or legal custody showed they were better adjusted than children in sole-custody settings and no different from those in intact families (Bauserman, 2002).

The practical disadvantage, however, to joint custody is that usually the parents are divorcing because they can no longer communicate or cooperate with each other. What may happen, then, is that parents divide authority, and the joint-custody child, instead of having two decision-making parents, ends up with none because the parents can't agree. A lack of consensus, as well as inconsistency, is confusing to children and may undermine discipline.

If the divorce was bitter, then the increased communication between the parents, as required by joint custody, is likely to become more hostile, thereby exposing children to even more conflict and psychological damage (Johnston, Kline, & Tschann, 1989). Another problem occurs when parents use the children to communicate messages between them (Furstenburg & Cherlin, 1991)—"Tell your father to send the check, or he won't get to see you next weekend"—and to inform each parent of the other's activities (Parke & Buriel, 1998).

Although joint custody gives children access to both parents, thereby reducing feelings of being abandoned by the noncustodial parent, some children, especially younger ones, are actually harmed by the inevitable continual separation and reattachment. Preschool children have a very difficult time understanding why everyone can't live in the same house, asking "Why, if Mommy loves me and Daddy loves me, don't they love each other anymore?" School-age children express confusion and anxiety over their schedules, anxiety that spills over into school performance and relationships with friends (Francke, 1983). For example, a 6-year-old became obsessed with carrying his backpack everywhere because he was afraid of leaving his homework at one parent's house while he was staying at the other's. For another example, an 11-year-old girl felt that she could never be anyone's "best" friend because she didn't stay in one house long enough. To her, being a best friend meant being around all the time.

Among the unreanswered questions about joint custody is, What happens over time? Children grow and change, and some parents remarry, take new jobs, and/or relocate. What works today may not work tomorrow.

Kin Custody. An increasing number of children are being raised by relatives (kin) other than parents, the most common being grandparents raising grandchildren. Some of these families have informal arrangements (without legal custody or guardianship), and others are part of the formal foster care system (Children's Defense Fund, 2001). Family relationships beyond the nuclear family are becoming increasingly important in American society (Bengston, 2001). Extended family members help care for children and provide emotional support.

About 6 percent of children under age 18 are cared for by their grandparents, a 76 percent increase from 1970 (U.S. Bureau of the Census, 2000). Some reasons are that the child's parents are deceased, the child was abandoned, or the court granted legal custody to the grandparent(s) because the parents were deemed unfit due to substance abuse, age, divorce, physical or mental illness, abuse, neglect, and incarceration (U.S. Bureau of the Census, 2000). Many custodial grandparents do not fit the stereotype of senior citizens enjoying retirement activities (Smith, Dannison, & Vach-Hasse, 1998). Their median age is 53, and some have to care for their own parents in addition to their grandchildren. Many of these grandparents are physically, emotionally, and financially drained—challenged by changes in relationships with their spouse and other family members, financial stress, a sense of uncertainty

© Robert E. Daemmrich/Getty Images

Many grandparents today are raising their grandchildren. This grandfather shares his love of fishing with his granddaughter.

or isolation, feelings of anger or grief or fear, and worries about health or death (deToledo & Brown, 1995; Minkler & Roe, 1993).

A key challenge faced by children being raised by grandparents is developing a sense of belonging and stability amid the transition from their own homes. Common feelings are grief, fear, anger, guilt, and embarrassment. Sometimes these feelings are exhibited in such "acting-out" behaviors as physical or verbal aggression, regression to immature behavior (crying, whining, bed-wetting), manipulation, withdrawal, and hyperactivity (deToledo & Brown, 1995; Minkler & Roe, 1993).

Stepfamilies. Due to the changing nature of families, as well as to budgetary constraints, the U.S. Bureau of the Census no longer provides statistics on the number of children residing in stepfamilies. However, according to projections based on earlier data, one out of three Americans is now a stepparent, a stepchild, a stepsibling, or a cohabitating member of a stepfamily (Larson, 1992; Stepfamily Association of America, 2000).

Because of the increase in the number of stepfamilies, the concept of family needs reexamining, according to the Stepfamily Association of America: "All kinds of institutions from schools to hospitals to the courts will have to adapt to the special needs of stepfamilies" (quoted in Kantrowitz & Wingert, 1990, p. 77). Most such institutions have policies geared toward intact families. Although stepparents may act as full-time parents to their spouses' kids, in many cases they have no legal rights. For example, if a child needs emergency surgery, hospitals almost always require the consent of a biological parent or legal guardian.

In addition to legal issues, psychosocial issues represent special problems for the stepfamily. Each family member has experienced the trauma of divorce or death or separation from a parent or spouse. When a new family is formed, new problems are likely to arise. The impact of remarriage on the family is second only to the crisis of divorce (Hetherington & Clingempeel, 1992).

The interactions in stepfamilies are similar to those in any other family, which means they are sometimes tainted with anger, jealousy, value conflicts, guilt, and unrealistic expectations. One of the most common unrealistic expectations is for instant love. Stepparents must often assume parenting roles before emotional ties with stepchildren have had a chance to develop, whereas the parenting role of biological parents evolves as their children grow.

Children in a stepfamily may feel abandoned by a parent with whom they have formed a close bond after the divorce. Having to live with new rules and values, while still trying to deal with the old rules and values from both parents, places an enormous burden on them. Also, the stepfamily often adds more children to the household, which entails adjustments in relating to new siblings. Thus, when families blend, the members are very much affected. In the early months of remarriage, there is likely to be less family cohesion, more poorly defined family roles and relationships, diminished family communication, less effective problem resolution, less consistency in setting rules, less effective disciplining, and reduced emotional responsiveness. Both stepmothers and stepfathers take a considerably less active role in parenting than do custodial parents (Bray, 1988). Even after 2 years, disengagement is the most common parenting style (Hetherington, Stanley-Hagan, & Anderson, 1989). Stepfamilies also may suffer from a lack of external support, fueled by media myths such as the "wicked stepmother," and the "molesting stepfather" (Rutter, 1994).

In general, families in which the custodial father remarries and a stepmother joins the family experience more resistance and poorer adjustment for children than do families in which the custodial mother remarries and a stepfather joins the family (Hetherington, Stanley-Hagan, & Anderson, 1989). The introduction of a stepparent may also strain the child's relationship with the noncustodial parent. Remarriage often presents children with loyalty dilemmas that they are too inexperienced to solve (Francke, 1983). If they like the stepparent, is that disloyal to their noncustodial parent? Or worse, will they lose the love of their biological parent? Does the noncustodial parent compete with the stepparent for the child's loyalty by buying the child things or by "putting the stepparent down"? Does the child view the stepparent as usurping the biological parent's role? ("She wants us to call her 'Mother,' but won't," said a 10-year-old girl; "He can't tell me what to do; he's not my real father," said a 7-year-old boy.)

Families in which both parents bring children from a previous marriage tend to be associated with the highest level of behavior problems (Santrock & Sitterle, 1987). The addition of "instant" siblings to the family constellation is both bewildering to and taxing for children (Francke, 1983; Rutter, 1994). For example, overnight the birth order hierarchy may shift: The child who has been the oldest may inherit an older brother, or the child who has been the youngest may inherit a baby sister. Children often compete for attention, especially with the biological parent. Children who have differing histories of upbringing must now live under the same roof with new sets of rules. For example, a child who previously was given choices at mealtime must now adapt to having to eat whatever is on his plate, or "no dessert." A child who has had to make her bed and clean her room now has to share a room with a child who has never had those responsibilities.

At least half of children living in stepfamilies are likely to face an additional strain—the birth of a half-sibling to their biological parent and the new spouse (Kantrowitz & Wingert, 1990). Not only is there yet another threat to securing parental love, but common sibling rivalry is intensified by half- versus full-blooded relationships (Francke, 1983; Rutter, 1994).

The complications in roles and relationships faced by stepparents are evidenced by the increased risk of divorce among remarriages, especially those with children from a previous marriage (Emery, 1988). Whereas about 50 percent of first marriages end in divorce, for second marriages the estimated divorce rate is 60 percent (Kantrowitz & Wingert, 1990). Divorce is most likely to occur in remarried families during the first 5 years, the time in which the new stepfamily is trying to restructure and "refunctionalize" (Parke & Buriel, 1998). After 5 years, however, stepfamilies are as stable as intact families of the same duration (Rutter, 1994).

Of course, not all stepchildren have behavioral or emotional problems. Studies have indicated that younger children and older adolescents are most likely to accept a stepparent, whereas preadolescent and early adolescent children age 9–15 do the poorest (Hetherington & Clingempeel, 1992; Hetherington, Stanley-Hagan, & Anderson, 1989). In the first 2 years following remarriage, conflict between mothers and daughters was found to be high. Hostility, coercion, and demandingness were exhibited toward both mother and stepfather. Interestingly, although boys tended to exhibit more antisocial behavior following divorce, 2 years after remarriage their behavior was no different from that of boys from nondivorced families (Hetherington, 1989). It may be that for girls a stepfather is an intrusion on the relationship with the mother, whereas for boys the stepfather provides support and acts as a role model. The 6-year follow-up to one ongoing study of stepfamilies found that, where the stepparent was firm but warm and where the children's biological parents maintained close relationships with them, the children were functioning better than those in either single-parent families or conflict-ridden intact families (Hetherington, 1989).

In sum, the effect of remarriage on the child depends on several factors (Hetherington & Clingempeel, 1992; Hetherington, Stanley-Hagan, & Anderson, 1989; Stinnett & Birdsong, 1978):

- The presence of additional stressors (moving, finances, stepsiblings)
- The age, developmental status, and sex of the child
- The quality of the child's relationship with both biological parents (custodial and noncustodial)
- The quality of the child's relationship with the stepparent and siblings
- The temperament, personality, and emotional stability of the child and the parents
- The availability of parent substitutes or other social supports for the child
- The parenting styles of biological parents and stepparents

A majority of divorced adults remarry within a few years to form a stepfamily (Stepfamily Association of America, 1999). A positive consequence for children who have seen the disruption of adult relationships, through either death or divorce, is the opportunity to observe a couple working together in a constructive way. Communicating and allowing feelings to be vented, perhaps in family meetings or in private discussions with each parent, can help blended-family members adjust to one another and form positive relationships. Knowing what the pitfalls are can help stepparents deal with them as they arise. Counseling and/or self-help support groups, such as the Stepfamily Association of America, can be very beneficial.

Families of Unmarried Parents. Marriage is a legal contract with certain rights and obligations. It is society's institution for founding and maintaining families.

Families of unmarried parents include heterosexual adults who choose to live together without legal sanction and homosexual adults who live together unwed because society declines to legalize their relationship. Such unconventional families, which are increasing (Kantrowitz & Wingert, 2001), are discussed here because of their impact on children.

These unconventional families can give children love and stability, but it is more difficult because of the general absence of community support. What makes things more challenging for these families is the fact that traditional rights and obligations are not necessarily either expected or implemented. For example, financial support of children under age 18 is not a legal obligation for the cohabitating partner. And the cohabitating partner is not automatically included in the child's school or social functions.

Most research on children growing up without a married mother and father reports a higher incidence of poverty, poor academic performance, emotional or behavioral problems, and substance abuse (Department of Health & Human Services, 2000). However, there are numerous factors involved in the circumstances under which children are born to unmarried parents that affect developmental outcomes. These factors include socioeconomic status, the relationship of the biological parents to each other and to the children, the relationship of cohabitating adults (if not biologically related) to the children, the children's characteristics (age, temperament, cognitive development), the mother's and father's characteristics (age, temperament, education, parenting style, substance abuse, domestic violence, and/or child abuse), the relationships with other children in the household or family, extended family relationships, and neighborhood characteristics (safety, supports, services) (Vosler & Robertson, 1998). What makes these factors more salient in nonmarried households with children is the lack of legal sanctions that accompany the marriage contract to ensure protection of children.

Families with homosexual parents are becoming more visible in society (Goodman, Emery, & Haugaard, 1998). Most common are two lesbian women living together and raising children from one or both of their previous relationships with men. There are also lesbian relationships in which one of the women was artificially inseminated or adopted a child, as well as two gay men living together with custody of their own or adopted children.

Attitudes toward homosexuality generally stem from people's personal feelings about their own sexuality. These attitudes include fear, disgust, indifference, and acceptance (Brown & Zimmer, 1986). Because of widespread negative attitudes, many homosexuals, especially those raising children, hide their relationships (Kantrowitz, 1996). Children whose homosexual parents are open about their relationship face being teased by other children (Gollnick & Chinn, 2002): "Why do you have two mommies?" or "Your dad is a ——— !"

Many issues faced by homosexual families are similar to those faced by divorced, stepparent, or other families. Overriding these, however, is the stigmatization of the homosexual family by society, which does not legally sanction homosexual marriages or families. Some cities and businesses, however, have implemented policies for domestic partners or members of civil unions related to housing, insurance benefits, emergency room visits, and school permission forms to include the cohabitating partner.

The initial reactions of children of gay and lesbian parents to their parents' homosexuality are confusion, lack of understanding, worry, shame, disbelief, anger, and guilt (Harris & Turner, 1986). Children in homosexual homes may be afraid to bring friends home or to become involved in school activities because contact with others threatens exposure (Ross, 1988).

Homosexual parents may also attempt to cope by being secretive or by pretending to be heterosexual. Being open about their homosexuality renders them vulnerable to discrimination and ostracism. However, being secretive, although arguably adaptive, is accompanied by feelings of self-betrayal and disconnectedness from social support (Ross, 1988). New associations must be continually monitored regarding the safety of disclosure. Many homosexual parents fear they will lose custody of their children if their sexual preferences become known (Kantrowitz, 1996).

Research on children living with homosexual parents and their partners has focused on three fearful attitudes society in general possesses: (1) that the children will become homosexual, (2) that they will be sexually molested, or (3) that there will be psychological damage due to the stigma of being raised by homosexuals. According to research by Goodman, Emery, and Haugaard (1998), there is no higher incidence of homosexuality among children raised by homosexuals than among those raised by heterosexuals; neither have there been any reported incidences of sexual abuse. Furthermore, children reared by homosexuals are not necessarily more psychologically troubled than children reared by heterosexuals.

However, as children approach adolescence and become concerned about their identities and sexual orientation, any family deviations from the norm can be magnified in importance. The normal developmental changes that occur during adolescence, coupled with the problem of having to cope with a stigmatized parent, can multiply the potential problems facing the adolescent and his or her family (Ross, 1988).

Variables affecting the adolescent's perception of the situation include his or her relationship with the biological parents, the partner, and friends; the amount of acceptance in the community; and his or her level of self-confidence. The adolescent who is struggling to develop an identity and sexual orientation may feel the need to prove that he or she is not homosexual by engaging in sexual acts with members of the opposite sex. He or she may become panicked by his or her own homosexual feelings, which are common in adolescence, yet potentially more threatening to one being raised by homosexuals (Ross, 1988).

Families of Adopted Children. There are many reasons families adopt children, such as the inability to conceive, the desire to care for a child without the sanction of marriage or to care for a child with special needs (one who has been abused or neglected, has disabilities, or comes from another country), or the wish to make a foster care arrangement permanent. Regardless of the reason, the American Academy of Child and Adolescent Psychiatry (AACAP) (1999) recommends that the child be told about the adoption by the adoptive parent(s) in terms the child can understand based on age and maturity. This helps the child to view the adoption as wanted by the family and as a positive experience.

Adoptive parents need to be prepared for new, and perhaps damaging, interpretations of the adoption even years after the situation was explained (AACAP, 1999). The child may create fantasies about the birth parents and may even deny the reality of the adoption (Pavao, 1999). Or the child may believe that he or she did something bad and was sent away. Some children even believe they were kidnapped by the adoptive parent(s). In adolescence, when identity formation is a normal challenge, the adopted child faces more complex issues, such as whether to tell her or his friends, whether to contact the birth parent(s), what medical history is relevant, and whom to be loyal to. The identity issues are even greater in transracial adoptions. Other potential issues include fear of abandonment, painful reminders of identity at birthdays, a need to grieve for what is perceived to be lost, and the need to deal with the unknown (Eldridge, 1999).

FUNCTIONAL CHANGES

Throughout history, families have changed the ways they execute their various functions, including reproduction, socialization/education, assignment of social roles, economic support, and nurturance/emotional support. Such changes in family functioning are adaptations to macrosystem influences such as economics, political ideology, and technology.

Reproduction

Technological changes such as birth control and reproductive assistance (donation of egg and sperm, in-vitro fertilization, embryo transfer, surrogacy) have impacted family size. Economics, too, has played a role. Many young people choose to postpone childbearing until they achieve financial stability. However, delaying conception until the late 30s impacts fertility. This is why couples who have difficulty conceiving turn to technology for assistance or choose to adopt. In any case, however, family size has decreased over the past century, unlike in the past, when families had many children in the hope that some would survive to reproduce the next generation (National Center for Health Statistics, 2000).

Socialization/Education

The socialization/education domain of the family has decreased over the past century. Until the nineteenth century, children were educated at home. Education consisted of religious teachings and training to work on the farm, in the family business, in the household. The Industrial Revolution provided work outside the home and farm for women and children, as well as for men. Thus, families could no longer be totally responsible for their children's education and training for the adult world. Gradually, schools took over this function.

The public, or "common," school emerged in the middle of the nineteenth century under the leadership of Horace Mann. The main rationale for compulsory, free public education was that families could no longer socialize their children for a productive role in the increasingly complex U.S. economy. Schools were expected to teach good work habits and basic reading, writing, and arithmetic skills, as well as to mold good character. Today, many states require that, in addition to the basics, schools teach such topics as sex education, substance abuse prevention, and anger management, subjects previously assumed to be the domain of the family.

Assignment of Social Roles

Social roles within the family are defined by which members perform what jobs and how authority is distributed. Changes in family roles, as discussed here, illustrate chronosystem influences.

Wife/Mother. When the family was agrarian and self-sufficient, the wife's role consisted of preparing food, making clothes, caring for children, managing the house, caring for the animals, and cultivating the gardens. But her husband wielded the authority in the family. When the economy began to change from agriculture to industry, and farms started to sell produce and animal products, men took over the responsibilities of making contacts for sales and transporting the goods; women's roles diminished.

Industrialization provided an opportunity for the expansion of women's roles, but few jobs were open to women initially. In the nineteenth and early twentieth centuries in the United States, women were usually employed only as seamstresses, laundresses, maids, cooks, housekeepers, governesses, teachers, and nurses. Not until World War I did this pattern change. Today, over half of mothers with children under age 18 are employed outside the home, occupying work roles similar to those of men.

Husband/Father. Traditionally, the man was responsible for economically supporting his wife and children, and the woman was responsible for maintaining the household. This division of labor between husband and wife affected their parental roles (Mintz, 1998). In colonial times, children learned appropriate gender roles from both father and mother, because there was no sharp split between work and home. In nineteenth-century families, however, mothers assumed more child-rearing tasks as fathers increasingly worked outside of the home in factories.

Today, the role of father is being redefined by technological and ideological changes in our society. In many families, men are assuming more household and child care responsibilities (Parke, 1995; Tamis-LeMonda & Cabrera, 1999). This is especially true in families in which the mother is employed. It is also true for divorced families in which the father has full or partial custody, of the children. Today many fathers are active participants in the socialization of their children.

Children. In preindustrial times, children contributed to the family's economic well-being by helping adults on the farm, in the shop or business, and in the home. Today most adult family members work for pay outside the home, and children rarely work at all. Work and family life are separate entities. Families have become consumption units rather than production units. Children used to be an economic asset in that they contributed to the family by doing chores or contributing wages earned outside the family. Now they have become an economic liability in that they not only have to be sheltered, clothed, and fed until age 18 but have to be educated as well. In dual-earner families, the cost of child care must be added to the economic burden. Not only are children expensive to raise, most cannot be counted on to provide economic support when their parents reach old age.

Authority Patterns. Authority patterns in the family can be traced back through history. The biblical family pattern is described as patriarchal and extended. Thus, Abraham, Isaac, and Jacob had several wives who, along with their children, constituted their families. In ancient Rome, absolute authority (*patria potestas* [paternal power]) was given to the father over his children. The father was guardian over his sons as long as he lived, and he even had the right to kill them. When the sons married, they lived with their families in the father's household, forming an extended family. To continue their lineage, families arranged marriages for their sons with women of equal status. The bride-to-be often came with a dowry that was negotiated between her family and her husband-to-be's family; the dowry signified her worth. Marriage was monogamous—the commitment was to one person at a time (usually for life). The marital union really constituted a binding tie between extended families, rather than only the couple. This arrangement still applies in many cultures around the world today.

In the United States, similar patterns were evident during colonial times. Families were patriarchal and extended, with the father responsible not only for the economic survival of the family but for the socialization of the children as well. It wasn't until the twentieth century that mothers gained status as family providers, due to political events, specifically, their help was needed in the workforce during World War II while many men were engaged in the war effort (Coontz, 1997). However, not until implementation of the Civil Rights Act of 1964, which outlawed ethnic and gender discrimination, did women gain more equal authority in the workplace and, consequently, at home. Now authority patterns in many families approach an egalitarian pattern, or some sort of collaborative one negotiated between the parents, with the father being responsible for some tasks and the mother for others (Kaslow, 2001).

Economic Support

Although a major function of the family remains economic support of its members, the scope of responsibility has changed, as have family members' contributions to the family's economy. Until the eighteenth century, most American families were extended. They owned and occupied farms and plantations that were self-sufficient, producing most of what the families needed. They built their own houses, grew their own food, and made their own furniture and clothing. Things they needed but did not produce were usually obtained through barter.

These early American families were economic units in which all members, young and old, played productive roles. Thus, children were essential to the prosperity of the family. The boys helped cultivate the land and harvest crops, while the girls helped to cook, sew, weave, and care for domestic animals and younger children.

During the nineteenth century, farm families began raising crops to sell and using the proceeds to buy goods produced by others. Thus, families gradually became less and less self-sufficient. As industry developed in America, family members began to work for wages in factories and businesses. Money, then, became the link between work and family. The nuclear family became more common as homes decreased in size and family providers increasingly relocated to where the work was (Coontz, 1997).

Today most families require the economic contributions of both parents in order to afford food, clothing, shelter, services, and other goods needed for themselves and their children.

Dual-Earner Families. Ideology in the United States has been influenced by a deep-seated view that the woman's role is in the home (Brazelton, 1989; Hochschild, 1989), that if she is not there for her children they will suffer in some way. This biased attitude has contributed to society's reluctance to give employed women the support they need, especially in the area of child care, including parental leave and services.

About two-thirds of mothers with children younger than age 6 now work outside the home. Labor force participation rates for these women have increased about 50 percent since 1975 (Children's Defense Fund, 2001).

Mothers' employment almost always improves the economic well-being of families with children, and often it is the difference between whether or not they can make ends meet. To the extent that mothers' working keeps children out of poverty and ensures that their basic material needs are met, it has important benefits (National Commission on Children, 1991). Other benefits of dual-earner families besides increased family income include personal stimulation for the mother (if she enjoys her job), a closer relationship between father and children (due to his increased participation in family matters), and a greater sense of responsibility for the children.

The main socialization effect of dual-earner families is the potentially reduced quality of care for the children. Other dual-earner family liabilities include "role overload" resulting from the increased responsibilities of the parents and the sacrifice of social relationships. Most employed mothers have less time to spend with their children. They also no longer have time to visit relatives and friends, or to participate in community and school organizations.

Hoffman's (1989) review of the research on maternal employment reveals that a variety of effects, depending on individual factors, result when the mother is employed outside the home. In general, Hoffman concludes that such mothers provide different role models than mothers who remain at home. She also reports that employment affects the mother's emotional state—sometimes providing satisfaction, sometimes role strain, and sometimes guilt—and this, in turn, influences mother–child interactions. When the mother is satisfied with her career and does not feel guilty about working, her relations with her children are similar to those of nonemployed mothers who are content with their homemaking role.

Factors influencing the impact of mothers' employment include the age, gender, and temperament of children; the socioeconomic status of the family; the quality of the marriage; the mother's satisfaction with her job; the father's satisfaction with his job; and the father's involvement with the children and support of the mother.

One common finding in various studies is that children of mothers employed outside the home have less stereotypic views of gender roles (Parke & Buriel, 1998). This is influenced by the mother's discussion of her work and by the father's participation in household tasks and child care.

Some evidence suggests that mothers employed outside the home use different child-rearing practices than do mothers not so employed. Generally, employed mothers are more authoritative, or democratic, in that there is more discussion about expectations and responsibilities (Greenberger & Goldberg, 1989). This parenting style is discussed in more detail in Chapter 4.

Preschool boys have been found to be more sensitive to the type of care they receive, apparently needing a caregiver who is "tuned in" to their needs (Baydar & Brooks-Gunn, 1991). Therefore, boys exhibit more negative behavior such as crying, noncompliance, and aggressiveness when their mothers are employed, especially full-time.

School-age and adolescent children of mothers employed outside the home have been found to be better adjusted socially, to get along better with their families and friends, and to feel better about themselves than do school-age and adolescent children of mothers who stay at home (Hoffman, 1989). Perhaps this is because employed mothers, out of necessity, are likely to grant their children greater independence when they exhibit readiness, in addition to giving them more household responsibilities (Hoffman, 1989). Adolescent daughters of working women have been found to be more outgoing, independent, and motivated, and they score higher academically than do daughters of homemakers (Hoffman, 1989)—perhaps due to the role model presented by the employed mother and the encouragement to achieve.

Longitudinal studies on intact, white, middle-class families have found, however, that maternal employment in the first year of children's lives is negatively related to their cognitive and behavioral development, persisting to age 7 or 8 in some children but not others (Han, Waldfogel, & Brooks-Gunn, 2001).

The trend today is toward dual-earner families. The impact of this trend on the family ultimately depends on the adaptive and coping strategies of the particular family: What are the parents' attitudes toward each other's jobs, as well as their own? How are work and family life coordinated? Who cares for the children, and what kinds of care are they receiving? Who does the household chores? How are unexpected problems (machine breakdowns, illnesses) handled? How flexible is each parent's work schedule?

All the changes, and the consequences of change on families and children, are influenced by macrosystems such as socioeconomic status, ethnic orientation, and religious orientation.

Coping Strategies for Parents in Dual-Earner Families

1. Think of themselves as household managers who delegate and supervise rather than do.
2. Determine what their priorities are and what is really essential—for example, clothes ironed or a game played with the children.
3. Set aside routine "quality" time for each other and the children. For each other, uninterrupted time away from household and child care duties will do. For children, any activity that raises children's self-esteem is quality time—for example, talking about their day, reading to them, or playing a game with them.
4. Establish traditions and rituals to which they and their children can regularly look forward.
5. Schedule time alone to pursue interests and recharge their batteries.
6. Learn to say "no" sometimes. When invited somewhere or asked to help on a committee, they might respond, "Let me check and get back to you." This response gives them time to evaluate the invitation and see if it conflicts with other commitments to family members.
7. Advocate for family-responsive corporate policies such as leaves, flexible work hours, job sharing, child care support, and seminars dealing with work/family issues.

Nurturance/Emotional Support

Although the nurturing and emotional support function of families for the young (and sometimes the old) has remained fairly stable, the range of caregiving has diminished. For example, as medicine advanced, the family turned to doctors and nurses to provide health care. In the nineteenth century, health care as we know it today did not exist. There were no preventive inoculations (except for smallpox in the latter part of the century), no clinics, few hospitals, and few medications, and doctors were few and far between. The sick were cared for by their families, as were the elderly. Today, we have insurance plans to cover costs of long-term care in residential facilities; we have disability plans; we have hospices to care for the dying. Because of the expense of caregiving outside the family, the importance of multigenerational bonds and links to extended kin needs to be reassessed (Bengston, 2001).

Macrosystem Influences on Families, Socialization, and Children

Specific effects of macrosystems (socioeconomic status, ethnic orientation, religious orientation) and the ways in which they influence socialization are examined to provide insight into how larger contexts can impact family systems.

SOCIOECONOMIC STATUS

All societies have their own ways of ranking people and their own criteria for placing people in certain classes or statuses. Some societies stratify members by **ascribed status;** that is, family lineage, gender, birth order, or skin color determines a person's class. For example, in the British royal family, marriage partners must be members of the nobility, and the first-born son is automatically heir to the throne.

Other societies stratify members according to **achieved status;** that is, education, occupation, income, and/or place of residence determine an individual's class. The United States exemplifies a society in which status can be attained by achievement— for instance, Abraham Lincoln, the sixteenth president of the United States, was the son of a farmer. Academic achievement, business skills, musical ability, and athletic talent enable some lower-class youths to attain high status.

© Myrleen Ferguson Cate/PhotoEdit

This child learns the traditional skill of weaving as her mother supervises and provides help when necessary.

Traditional societies, which rely on customs handed down from past generations as guides to behavior, tend toward ascribed status for stratification; **modern societies,** which look to the present for guides to behavior and are thus responsive to change, tend toward achievement status. Stratification is based on the importance of individuals' contributions to a particular society's ability to function. Suppose one person makes jewelry, another sells shoes, and another is a doctor. Jewelry may be important to those who can afford it; shoes may be necessary for everyone in cold climates; a doctor contributes to the well-being of everyone in the society. Thus, people in societies are not equally dependent on one another; rather, some people are more important to society than others and so are ranked higher in terms of social class or status. How a society stratifies or ranks people in social classes depends on income earned and prestige acquired. In the United States, doctors rank high and salespeople rank low.

It is more difficult for people to change their rank, or social class, in societies using ascribed criteria than in societies using achievement criteria. In societies using ascribed criteria, however, it is possible for achievements to change individuals' rankings. For example, a person born into a lower-class family can become a soldier or priest and thereby attain higher status. In contrast, in societies using achievement criteria, individuals' ascribed criteria (conditions of birth) affect their status. For example, the person born into the upper class receives a head start on achievement due to the family's ability to educate him or her, live in certain neighborhoods, and buy certain material things.

When statuses are ascribed, the roles are set in tradition. In other words, when children are born into a certain status, they are socialized primarily by modeling their elders and being instructed in the traditional ways. When statuses are achieved, however, as is the case in modern societies undergoing change, "the established system for assigning individuals to recognized statuses may break down. Wholly new statuses may come into existence" (Inkeles, 1969, p. 616). Thus, in societies that stratify by achievement, members may find themselves inadequately socialized to play the roles of the statuses they seek or have been assigned. For example, farmers who want to be competitive and profitable have to seek more technical knowledge than that which they learned from their parents. Society, then, has to compensate for this inadequate socialization by the family and rely on other institutions such as the school or business to prepare individuals for their new roles. Farmers may take such courses as plant pathology, genetics, animal husbandry, and economics.

According to sociologist William Goode (1982), it is the family, and not merely the individual, that is ranked in society's class structure. This is an illustration of the macrosystem's influence on children's development in that the social class and status of the family help determine individuals' opportunities for education and occupation, as well as for social interaction. The members of the community in which the family lives, the children's friends, and the guests invited to the home generally come from the same social class. Even though Americans play down the existence of social classes, social scientists recognize that different groups in our society possess unequal amounts of money, prestige, influence, and "life chances" (Levine & Levine, 1996). Despite its egalitarian principles, in the United States, the gap between the rich and the poor has been widening (Children's Defense Fund, 2001).

Social class membership begins exerting its influence before birth and continues until death. For example, the incidence of birth defects is higher in the lower classes than in the middle and upper classes. Economic pressures and a lack of opportunities affect the mental health of lower-class families, as well as determining socialization practices (Parke & Buriel, 1998). Lower-socioeconomic-status parents have been found to be more dominant, controlling, and punitive than higher-socioeconomic-status parents, who tend to be more verbal and democratic and to use various parenting techniques. Economics, or lack of money, prevents lower-class parents from using an allowance as a reward. Children from lower-class families generally cannot be sent to their rooms as punishment, because there is no room they can call their own to which they can be sent. Neither can such children have privileges removed for noncompliance, such as going to the movies, because they do not have those opportunities anyway. Thus, lower-class families frequently use physical punishment as a socializing technique, whereas middle- and upper-class families have more options available (Hart & Risley, 1995).

Socioeconomic classes can be described in terms of averages; that is, they differ, *on average,* by income, occupation, housing, education, social interaction, and values. It is these defining criteria that influence socialization. Sociologists vary, however, in the way they see the social structure in the United States. Some sociologists believe that, although differences in rank exist, true class lines cannot be drawn, because the United States is an open society that permits upward and downward mobility and numerous informal social interactions.

Class Descriptions

The following descriptions apply to the majority of people in a given socioeconomic class, but not to every person in the class (Levine & Levine, 1996) (see Figure 3.5).

Upper Class. In general, upper-class families have inherited their wealth and have a family tradition of social prominence that extends back several generations. Much emphasis is placed on the extended family, which can be either patriarchal or matriarchal.

Many upper-class families believe that proper rearing is more important in order to fulfill adult roles than is formal schooling. If children do go to school to

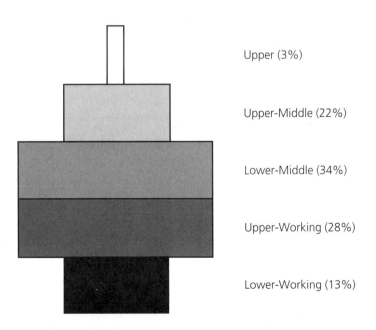

Upper (3%)

Upper-Middle (22%)

Lower-Middle (34%)

Upper-Working (28%)

Lower-Working (13%)

Figure 3.5

Social Class Structure in the United States
Source: From Donald U. Levine, Rayna F. Levine, *Society and Education,* 9e. Published by Allyn & Bacon, Boston, MA. Copyright © 1990 by Pearson Education. Reprinted by the permission of the publisher.

train for an occupation, it must be a high-status one such as medicine, law, or business. Upper-class children generally attend private schools and prestigious private colleges.

Middle Class. In general, middle-class families have earned their status by achievement (education and/or hard work): "It is not who you are, but what you are." Much emphasis is placed on the nuclear family even though ties are still maintained, often loosely, to the extended family. These families tend to be egalitarian.

A high value is placed on achievement, respectability, and harmonious interpersonal relationships within the family. Education and the ability to get along with others are considered essential to adult success.

The upper-middle class generally includes business executives and professional people. The lower-middle class generally includes salespeople, small business owners, contractors, craftspeople, and farmers.

Lower Class. In general, lower-class families are composed of semiskilled and unskilled workers. Much emphasis is placed on the extended family, and close ties with relatives are maintained. Patriarchal patterns are more common (except where the father is absent), as is the distinction between male and female roles.

Many lower-class families emphasize respect for elders and the importance of survival. These families are most affected by economic fluctuations. Many experience being in debt, being laid off, and/or being on welfare. Often, children must help the family rather than further their own education, and some don't complete high school.

Historically, the lower class has included the newest immigrants to the United States, who are willing to work at menial jobs while learning the ways of American society.

Underclass. In recent years, many social scientists have begun to identify another class: the underclass. This class differs from the others in its degree of hopelessness to achieve upward mobility. People in the underclass are stuck at the bottom of the social structure and perceive themselves as having little chance of ever escaping from a poverty-ridden environment (Wilson, 1987). The underclass has many faces: female-headed families; homeless alcoholics, drug users, and the mentally ill who have been "deinstitutionalized"; the destitute elderly, illegal aliens, and rural families from economically depressed areas; and any other group who, for whatever reason, cannot obtain adequate schooling, employment, or housing. The underclass, in essence, represents a contradiction to the concept that social mobility is available to anyone in America who is willing to work hard enough for it. Unfortunately, because of the virtual impossibility of escaping such extreme poverty, the underclass has become a culture of illegitimacy, drugs, and crime, as well as joblessness. How the underclass developed and what should be done about it remain hotly debated issues among social scientists and policy makers. The problems for underclass children include exposure to drugs and AIDS, child abuse, poor housing or homelessness, crime victimization, insufficient health care, inferior education, insufficient child care programs and other community services, and economic dependency on government (Children's Defense Fund, 2001). The federal government's response since 1996 has been to provide Temporary Assistance to Needy Families (TANF) while the parent(s) get job training and learn coping skills to become self-sufficient.

Families that have many responsibilities without adequate resources negatively impact the present and future opportunities for their children.

The Influence of Socioeconomic Status on Socialization

Children from lower-class families are often identified in school as slow learners, aggressors, and truants. Studies comparing the relative intelligence of children from high- and low-socioeconomic-status families have shown that those from high-status homes score higher on IQ tests and achievement tests than do children from low-status homes (Patterson, Kupersmidt, & Vaden, 1990). The differences in intelligence are more marked in later childhood and adolescence than in infancy (Levine & Levine, 1996; Tozer, Violas, & Senese, 2002).

Various theories have been advanced to explain this contrast in intelligence. One theory has to do with heredity—intelligence is inherited, and brighter persons achieve higher statuses (Jensen, 1969, 1988). Another stresses environment—the limited resources of lower-status families prevent them from providing intellectual stimulation, especially verbal, for their children. According to recent brain research, the influence of environmental stimulation and stressors during infancy is significant and has long-lasting effects on cognitive development (Young, 1994). Evidence has shown that if special schooling is provided, especially in the preschool years, the IQ scores of children from lower-status families improve (Bereiter & Engelmann, 1966; Spitz, 1992). A third theory is that of the self-fulfilling prophecy. The argument is that IQ tests are biased toward the middle class, so children from lower-class families, which have a different set of experiences, do not score as well. Their scores cause teachers to have low expectations: "Because Johnny has a low IQ, I won't give him as many math pages as the others." Thus, Johnny does not learn as much as the others, and his intellectual potential decreases (Brophy & Good, 1986).

The belief that improving the environment of children from lower-class families could reduce the difference in achievement levels between the classes led to the

War on Poverty in the 1960s. Under the leadership of President Lyndon Johnson, many governmental programs were instituted. For instance, compensatory programs provided for the education hiring remedial reading specialists, counselors, and truant officers. Project Head Start was launched to provide preschool children considered to be disadvantaged with various learning experiences to enable them to be more successful when they entered elementary school. Program components included language experiences and abstract thinking activities in response to significant social class differences in the use of language and concept development (Levine & Levine, 1996; Tozer, Violas, & Senese, 2002).

The structure and syntax of language used by the upper-middle class is far more complex than that used by the lower class (Bernstein, 1961). Use of complex language indicates a more abstract, as opposed to concrete, perception of reality. Bernstein (1961) offers the following example to illustrate this concept: "I'd rather you made less noise, dear" might be what a mother from the middle class would say to her boisterous child, whereas "Shut up!" might be what a mother from the lower class would say. Thus, the child from the middle-class family learns the abstract meanings of words like *rather* and *less;* the child from the lower-class family receives a simple, concrete message.

Other experiences provided for Head Start children are opportunities to be successful and to be rewarded for this success. It has been shown that the socializing technique of reinforcement or reward for desired behavior given by significant people in children's lives is very effective in motivating them to repeat the behavior. Parents from the middle class usually reward children, especially sons, for ambition, high-level aspirations, and long-range goals. To achieve one's ambitions and long-range goals, one must defer gratification. Generally, children from middle-class families learn from their parents to defer gratification ("Save for a rainy day," and "Study hard now so you'll be able to get a good job in the future"), whereas children from lower-class families do not.

Parents from the middle class generally train their children to be achievement oriented. Self-discipline, initiative, responsibility, academic achievement, and restraint of aggression are encouraged. Parents from the lower class, in contrast, generally focus on the behavior rather than the attitudes or motivation of children. Perhaps this is because they tend to view the world in terms of concrete events and practical outcomes. Faced with the realities of substandard housing, overcrowded neighborhoods, and inadequate public services, the lower classes' apparent lack of achievement motivation reflects a profound lack of trust in a social system that traditionally has excluded them from its benefits (Wilson, 1987).

Various studies (Dodge, Petit, & Bates, 1994; Levine & Levine, 1996) have examined the relationship between lower-class socialization and achievement, as well as behavior. Levels of achievement depend on what people believe can be attained. More important than achievement to those struggling to survive is security. Toughness in boys is admired as an ability to get ahead of other people; intellectualism is regarded as "unmasculine." Students grouped according to their abilities tend to reinforce each other's attitudes and behavior. Living for the present is the norm, perhaps because opportunities to "live it up" are so rare. Skills in budgeting time and money tend to be lacking.

In upper-class families, children are generally regarded as the carrier of the family's name, heritage, and status. The family is able to bear the maximum costs of child rearing (material goods, private schools, business or career opportunities). Children are expected to meet family standards for behavior and for educational and vocational attainment. Socializing children in upper-class families to be responsible and to achieve is a challenge when such children already "have everything." Pressures to conform to family standards come not only from the nuclear family, but from the extended family (even the dead relatives) as well: "What would Grandfather Smith say?"

Whereas relatives play a large role in the socialization of children from upper-class families to conform to family standards, children from middle-class families are reared more by their families of orientation; relatives are expected not to interfere. For their part, lower-class children and their parents tend to rely on their kin for support, mostly emotional, rather than for the intentional purpose of socialization, even though much unintentional socialization does take place through social interactions among relatives. The purpose of this networking is to reduce insecurity and to develop defenses against criticism from society. Besides relying on relatives, lower-class families tend to adapt to their lifestyle by relying on fate and luck; belief in such factors as causes of their destiny helps to relieve their feelings of responsibility for their poverty (Elkin & Handel, 1989).

Lower-class families, in rearing their children, put emphasis on children's not being a nuisance to other people, especially adults. Physical punishment is the form of discipline most likely to be used. Children must be trained to adjust to the conditions of many people occupying the same small space. They are also usually taught early to assume responsibility for doing chores around the home, caring for smaller children, and running errands. Middle-class families are more likely to use reasoning and nonphysical forms of discipline (Maccoby, 1980; Parke & Buriel, 1998). They emphasize conformity to "what people will say" or "how it will look." Children are usually taught early to look toward the future: "Eat your vegetables so you'll grow big and strong," or "When you can use the potty, you'll be able to wear big-boy pants like Daddy instead of diapers."

Lower-class families are so burdened with survival concerns in the present that they tend to have difficulty socializing their children to delay gratification or be oriented to the future, as our society's education system is structured. They have inadequate resources, such as income, education, and good jobs, to meet their needs in life. They are often plagued with sickness, injuries, and entanglements with the law, and lack the money, knowledge, and access to support services to cope with these problems. The pessimistic view that "things will turn out as badly as they generally have in the past" often pervades their lives. Their relatively low level of skill makes them easily replaceable in the workplace. And because they have previously experienced little success in shaping their lives, they tend to expect nothing more in the future (Levine & Levine, 1996).

However, generalizations about the influence of socioeconomic status on socialization do *not* always apply. In her book *Common Purpose*, Lisbeth Schorr (1997) describes support programs that have strengthened families and neighborhoods in the United States. For example, a program called Youth Build, begun in Harlem, New York, recruits adolescents from poor families to build and renovate low-cost housing. The youths are trained by journeymen in construction skills and the personal habits and qualities that contractors seek in entry-level workers. They also attend school and are trained in leadership skills that, together with job skills, helps them rebuild their lives and gain hope of moving out of the lower class. What makes Youth Build successful is the caring support and commitment of its staff, as well as the sense of family and community among its members. Building something tangible and useful in their own neighborhoods provides program participants with a sense of pride and respect, which, in turn, leads to a sense of personal responsibility for life's outcomes.

Implications of Socioeconomic Status for Professionals: The Challenge

Professionals whose experiences have been typically middle class must understand the differences in various social class behavior and motivations if they are to work effectively with children from all socioeconomic statuses.

The ability to delay gratification is a middle-class value; immediate gratification is the norm among the lower class. Professionals can provide children with feedback on their behavior through cues or specific instructions and through tangible, immediate rewards such as small tokens (stickers, toys), rather than giving hypothetical reasons—for example, "You must do well in school so that you'll get a good job," or "You must take turns on the slide so the others will be your friends."

When a teacher tells a 5-year-old child not to hit "because it hurts" and the 5-year-old replies, "That's why I hit him," the teacher needs to learn that lower-class values include "Stand up for yourself," "Fight for your territory," and "Don't ask for help." That teacher cannot rely on reasoning in this case to modify the child's aggressive behavior. A more effective socializing technique might be setting standards and providing reinforcement for compliance and consequences for noncompliance. In other words, the teacher tells all the children the standard or expectations in advance, as well as the consequences for deviation: "We use our words to tell someone our angry feelings," and "When I hear words, I will give you a sticker," and "We do not hit anyone. If you hit someone, you get a warning; if you hit someone again, you will have to sit in the hall outside the room for five minutes."

For professionals who work with groups outside their own class experience, the challenge is not to convert everyone into upper- or middle-class people, but rather to downplay those aspects of class socialization that hamper personality development (limited language, experiences, and cognitive stimulation) and enhance those aspects of class socialization that make the individual a unique, contributing member of society (helpfulness of kin, responsibilities given to children, ability to cope with adversity).

ETHNIC ORIENTATION

Ethnicity, as discussed previously, is an attribute of membership in a group in which members continue to identify themselves by national origin, race, or religion. Ethnic distinction can be based on physical and/or cultural attributes. Physical attributes include such things as skin color, body build, and facial features. Cultural attributes include a shared history, language, traditions, rituals, customs, beliefs, attitudes, and values. Ethnic orientation, then, constitutes a macrosystem.

Ethnic groups differ in the way they deal with basic issues of living (Harrison, Wilson, Pine, Chan, & Buriel, 1990). The need to eat is universal, but the kind of food one eats and the way one eats it are determined by the ethnic group to which one belongs. The need for clothing and shelter is also universal, but the types of dress and housing depend on the particular culture. Ethnic groups also differ in child-rearing practices—in their methods of socialization of children. Another variable introduced into families ecologies is their immigration history—which family members emigrated to the United States, and when? Which have adopted American values for child rearing, which maintain those of their culture, and which are bicultural (Parke & Buriel, 1998)?

Because children are socialized by various methods of communication and interaction, examining differences in the way parents relate to children can provide insight into general socialization outcomes according to ethnic orientation (Greenfield & Suzuki, 1998). For example, a study that compared Euro-American and Japanese mother–infant interaction found that the Euro-American mothers interacted more vocally with their infants, whereas the Japanese mothers exhibited more body contact with their infants and, in so doing, soothed them into quiescence. The Euro-American infants tended to be more vocal, active, and explorative of their environments than the Japanese infants, who tended to be more passive (Caudill, 1988).

Parents socialize children to encourage the development of those qualities and attributes required for their expected adult roles in their particular society or according to their specific ethnic orientation. To illustrate, in a classic study, Barry, Child, and Bacon (1959) evaluated 104 societies to find out whether the child-rearing practices of parents in industrialized societies, such as the United States, differed from those of parents in agricultural societies, such as India. They found that parents in industrialized societies socialized children for achievement and independence, whereas parents in agricultural societies socialized children for obedience and responsibility. In a study examining attitudes toward family obligations, the researchers found that Asian-American and Latin American adolescents possessed stronger values and greater expectations regarding their duty to respect and assist their families than their peers with European backgrounds. These differences were substantial and consistent across socioeconomic status and gender (Fuligni, Tseng, & Lam, 1999).

Another socialization outcome affected by ethnic orientation is the way in which children learn to adapt to their environment. One way of adapting is to be actively independent in struggling to master problems and overcome challenges; another is to be passively obedient, cooperating with others and accepting environmental stresses rather than trying to change them. Socialization outcomes for children are implemented through sleeping arrangements, feeding practices, parenting styles, and peer, school, and community experiences—all of which vary by culture (Greenfield & Suzuki, 1998). For example, an important socialization outcome generally valued by American parents involves guiding children to learn to make their own decisions and establish separate existences. Children are taught to assert themselves and stand up for their own rights; they are encouraged to verbalize their needs and disagree even with elders. In contrast, Japanese parents generally value self-control, compliance with adult authority, and cooperation. Children are taught to depend on parents, defer to elders, and sacrifice personal goals for those of the family. They also are encouraged to keep their feelings to themselves and not cause others embarrassment by disagreeing.

There are many ethnic groups in the United States, and not all have the same status and power as the majority group (white Anglo-Saxon Protestant, or Euro-American), even though equality is a dominant cultural value. These other ethnic groups are commonly referred to as "minorities" even though, in reality, these groups are beginning to outnumber Euro-Americans. Being socialized in a family of a different orientation from that of the school, which represents the majority orientation, can be problematic for minority children (Trumbull, Rothstein-Fisch, Greenfield, & Quiroz, 2001). Table 3.1 outlines some areas of diverse socialization patterns; keep in mind that there is variation within groups.

Table 3.1

Diverse Socialization Patterns in the United States
Sources: Kluckhohn, 1961; Maehr, 1974; and Thiederman, 1991.

SOCIALIZATION AREA	MAJORITY ETHNIC ORIENTATION	MINORITY ETHNIC ORIENTATION
INTERPERSONAL RELATIONS	Competition and individual accomplishment, risk taking, active learning style	Cooperation and group accomplishment, face saving, passive learning style
ORIENTATION TOWARD TIME	Focus on working now and saving for a better future; efficiency, punctuality, idea that time should not be "wasted"	Focus on the present, belief that the future will be provided for; units of time undifferentiated; the past, tradition, and ancestors highly valued
VALUED PERSONS	Busy, materialistic, practical, assertive	Relaxed, spiritual, emotional, quiet
RELATIONSHIP OF HUMANITY TO NATURE	Control of nature, use of science and technology to "improve" nature	One with nature, respect for and harmony with nature, belief in fate
CHERISHED VALUES	Independence, individual freedom, achievement	Dependence, loyalty to the group and tradition

Ethnic Norms/Values

Part of people's ethnic orientation involves **norms**—the rules, patterns, or standards that express cultural values and reflect how individuals are supposed to behave. Some dimensions of differing ethnic behavioral patterns were introduced in Chapter 2. The focus here is on ethnic or cultural norms from the perspective of variations in ways of surviving. In the 1960s, Florence Kluckhohn (1961; Kluckhohn & Strodbeck, 1961), in analyzing the seemingly limitless variety of cultural lifestyles, suggested that there are certain basic questions that humans in all places and circumstances must answer, questions that greatly help our understanding of ethnic diversity and socialization:

- *How do humans relate to each other?* Do relationships have an individualistic orientation, with emphasis placed on individual accomplishments and on personal rights and freedom? Or is the emphasis on belonging to some group, such as family, peers, or community (a collectivistic orientation)? The Euro-American norm, as exemplified by the Bill of Rights, is personal freedom, whereas the Japanese norm, as exemplified by family loyalty, is commitment to the group.
- *What is the significant time dimension?* Is it the past, present, or future? Some cultures associate time with religious beliefs; for example, some Hispanics live each day as it comes, believing that God will provide for the future. Other cultures, such as Euro-American and German, generally associate time with progress and therefore prefer to plan for the future even though doing so may require sacrifices in the present. Still others view the concept of time as subordinate to activities and interactions instead of dominating them. For example, some African Americans and Latin Americans may approximate when an event will start or end (the party takes place when everyone gets there), whereas Anglos tend to put events on a precise schedule (the party takes place from 8:00 to 12:00).

- *What is the valued personality type?* Is it simply "being"? Is it "being in becoming"? Or is it "doing"? Asians generally believe that a person "is being in becoming" in that one's deeds in this life determine the quality of one's next life. Anglos generally stress "doing" to enhance the quality of one's present life.

- *What is the relationship of humans to nature?* Are humans subjugated to nature? Are humans seen as existing in nature? Do humans have power over nature? Western cultures generally assume that nature can be controlled. Examples are our use of pesticides, irrigation, and various technologies that make farming more efficient. Other cultures, such as Native American, however, view the land as something to be cared for and shared, not carved up and exploited.

- *What are the innate predispositions of humans?* Are they evil? Neither good nor bad? Innately good? Those who believe that humans are essentially bad and assume that children's will must be broken tend to use punitive and controlling measures to socialize children—as was done by Calvinist and Puritan parents, for example. Those who believe that humans are neither good nor bad assumes that children can be molded and shaped by experiences provided by adults. This philosophy was advocated by British philosopher John Locke (1632–1704). Those who believe that humans are essentially good assumes that children will seek out appropriate experiences and develop accordingly. Jean-Jacques Rousseau (1712–1778), a French philosopher, advocated such a belief.

RELIGIOUS ORIENTATION

Religion is a "unified system of beliefs and practices relative to sacred things, uniting into a single moral community all those who adhere to those beliefs and practices" (Durkheim, 1947, p. 47). Understanding some basic purposes of religion also helps us be more sensitive to diversity.

About 85 percent of the population in the United States and Canada identify with one of five major Judeo-Christian faiths: Protestant (58 percent), Catholic (25 percent), Jewish (2 percent), Latter-Day Saints (Mormons) (2 percent), and Orthodox (1 percent) (U.S. Bureau of the Census, 2000). Although these religious groups share the same Old Testament heritage, their interpretations and beliefs differ. Other major world religions found in the United States include Islam, Buddhism, and Hinduism.

Religion is a macrosystem in that it influences gender roles, sexual behavior, patterns of marriage and divorce, birthrates, morals, attitudes, and child-rearing practices. It also may affect people's dress, dietary habits including alcohol consumption, health care, and social interactions including ethics (Gollnick & Chinn, 2002).

If the family subscribes to an organized religion, newborns are often inducted into it via a public naming ceremony. The family's religious beliefs determine what is selected from the environment to transmit to the child. The family also interprets and evaluates what is transmitted. For example, Roman Catholics value strict obedience to authority and do not believe in divorce or birth control. Thus, children from Roman Catholic families are brought up to obey their parents and the church. They are also reared to believe in the sanctity of marriage and the idea that sex is for procreation, not pleasure.

Not only does religion influence families and their socialization of children, it affects the community as well, in terms of values and behavior. The most dominant

Participants in a bar mitzvah celebrate this 13-year-old boy's studies in Jewish history, culture, and prayer.

religious group in the United States (Protestants) has undoubtedly influenced the political and economic foundations of our country (Weber, 1930). The **Protestant ethic** is a religiously derived value system that defines the ideal person as individualistic, thrifty, self-sacrificing, efficient in the use of time, strong in personal responsibility, and committed to productivity. By following this value system, believers can reach salvation. An example of the Protestant ethic's influence on politics is welfare reform—laws passed requiring welfare recipients to work (be self-sufficient) after a certain amount of time receiving government assistance. Religious beliefs can impact communities when religious groups get members elected to political offices and school boards and influence policies related to abortion, school prayer, the curriculum (evolution versus creation), and so on.

Functions of Religion

Generally, religion provides people with "a way of facing the problems of ultimate and unavoidable frustration, of 'evil,' and the generalized problem of meaning in some nonempirical sense, of finding some ultimate why" (Williams, 1960b, p. 327). Religion, its followers, and its influence on nonreligious dimensions of human life will likely continue as a significant force in American society (Greely, 2001).

Every religion includes some beliefs that are shared by all its adherents. For example, Judaism teaches that a "good life" can be led only in a community; good Jews must always view their actions in terms of their effect on others, accepting responsibility for others and regarding charity as a virtue. Muslims give a percentage of their annual income to the poor. The ultimate goal of Buddhism is to be fully "in the world" and to relate compassionately to others.

Most religions provide an ideology that enables adherents to comprehend events that happen to them; death, illness, financial crises, and injustice all make sense if viewed as part of a divine plan. Religion helps fill the gap between scientific and technical knowledge and the unknown.

Religious beliefs and practices help individuals accept and cope with crises without suffering overwhelming psychological costs. For example, prayer helps a person feel that she or he is "doing something" to meet the crisis. If the crisis is resolved, the individual's faith in prayer is confirmed. If the crisis is not resolved, the individual can explain the outcome as part of God's plan, thereby avoiding the feeling that life's catastrophes are senseless.

Most religions have beliefs about death. Some preach damnation for those who transgress in life on Earth and salvation for those who lead a good life. The prospect of a blissful immortality makes the death of a loved one more tolerable and the thought of one's own death less terrifying.

Many religious activities help people establish identities and give meaning to their lives. Religious rituals symbolize faith, honor God, or serve to remind members of the group of their religious responsibilities. Rituals may include observing holidays, saying prayers, tithing, handling sacred objects, wearing certain clothing, and eating certain food (or fasting). For example, Holy Communion commemorates the climactic meal of Jesus' life and his sacrifice for humankind. In partaking of the holy bread and wine, the communicant partakes of Christ.

Carl Jung (1938) wrote that religion provides individuals who have a strong commitment to traditional norms and values with moral strength and behavioral stability. In other words, religious people are more likely to comply with societal norms, especially if they believe that those norms are divinely sanctioned. They look upon social deviance as a form of religious deviance. This assertion was confirmed via research (Gorsuch, 1976; Hassett, 1981) showing that moral behavior was consistently related to religious commitment.

Chronosystem Influences on Families, Socialization, and Children

"Families are not static but dynamic and are continuously confronted by challenges, changes, and opportunities" (Parke & Buriel, 1998, p. 511). Some families develop coping styles to adapt to changes and remain healthy and functional. Others become victims of the consequences of change, experiencing stress, dissolution, or an unanticipated lifestyle. Thus, they are at risk for becoming unhealthy, or dysfunctional. Chronosystem influences impacting the health of families include political changes, such as changes in the law (for example, welfare to workfare); economic changes, such as certain jobs becoming obsolete (for example, telephone operators); and technological changes, such as computers completing tasks faster, enabling more work to be done and increasing performance standards.

The general chronosystem effect of change on families is stress. Change, in itself, is neither good nor bad; rather, our reaction to it determines its worth. Stress is a concept from physics that refers to physical forces and the ability to withstand strain. Dr. Hans Seyle applied the concept to refer to the human ability to adjust to danger signals. He was interested in the biochemical changes that occur when individuals react to stress. He defined **stress** as "the nonspecific response of the body to any demand" (Seyle, 1956, p. 54). Others have expanded the definition to include any demand that exceeds the person's ability to cope (Honig, 1986). There are *physical* stressors such as disease, overexertion, allergies, and abuse. There are *sociocultural* stressors such as crowding, traffic, noise, bureaucracies, and crime. And there are *psychological* stressors such as personal reactions to real or imagined threats and to real or imagined pressure to achieve (Kuczen, 1987).

Stress is not new. In hunting-and-gathering societies, the fear of not finding food or shelter was a stressor. In agricultural societies, the unpredictability of the weather was a stressor. In industrial societies, the need or demand to work long hours was, and still is, a stressor. In information societies, information overload and excessive choice are stressors; people must make decisions in areas in which they have little or no expertise and facts and opinion may be blurred. Children today face many of the same stressors of growing up that children a generation ago faced: separation anxiety, sibling rivalry, school, peer pressure, and dependence versus independence.

However, children today also face stressors that were practically nonexistent a generation ago (Elkind, 1994; Hewlett & West, 1998)—For example, violence in families and communities, global terrorism, and consumerism into homes, schools, and extracurricular activities, as well as in the media. Another stressor is the fragmentation of family life, with people increasingly pressured by occupational and community demands for their time. Pagers, cell phones, and e-mail have all contributed to merging the boundaries between family and other commitments. Thus, time for the family is jeopardized.

SOCIOPOLITICAL CHANGES

Sociopolitical changes influencing family functioning include foreign policy regarding immigration and war, and domestic policy regarding security and privacy issues, and social services. Newcomers to this country usually occupy lower-income jobs, require English-language training, and may need housing assistance, health care, and other services until they adapt to American life. Children of immigrants have to accommodate to the culture of their parents as well as that of their new country.

War obviously affects the functioning of military families when one parent is called to duty. War and terrorism also affect the functioning of society as a whole. For example, terrorism has impacted travel rules and communication procedures and led to an increase in racial profiling. Flexibility in travel has diminished, thereby impacting family visits and vacations. Mail is subject to inspection due to fear of biological contaminants (anthrax, for example). Families from ethnic backgrounds similar to those of known terrorists are subjected to more searches and interrogation in public places, and their children have been ostracized and treated cruelly.

Children victimized by war or terrorism who have experienced loss of a loved one may react with emotional detachment or a seeming lack of feeling, by exhibiting regressive or immature behavior, by acting out or exploding, and/or by continually asking the same questions because they cannot understand what happened (National Association of School Psychologists, 2001). All of us are affected in some way by the current geopolitical uncertainty. In response, there have been documented increases in substance abuse, people seeking therapy, and individuals turning to spirituality for comfort (Kaslow, 2001).

Social services, such as government financial assistance, have decreased. Welfare reform has brought changes in family structure and functions. Recognizing that most poor families are headed by single parents, law makers in 1996 emphasized the responsibility of both parents to support their children. In addition to strengthening the child support enforcement system, the welfare reform law included provisions designed to decrease childbearing outside of marriage and to promote two-parent families (McLanahan & Carlson, 2002). But the long-term consequences for parents, children, community support services, and society in general of these new welfare regulations are unclear.

ECONOMIC CHANGES

Economic changes influencing family functioning may involve job uncertainty due to corporate maneuvering (company buyouts, downsizing, and layoffs), the cost of living increasing (requiring both parents to be employed), and the erosion of employee benefits (Gallay & Flanagan, 2000).

Reduced levels of economic well-being have been found to increase parental stress, resulting in less affection toward children and less effective disciplinary interactions. Children in such families are more likely to be reported by teachers as having behavior problems and negative social relations with peers (Mistry, Vanderwater, Huston, & McLoyd, 2002).

When both parents are employed, family life may be at risk for fragmentation. The father works, the mother works, and the children go to child care or school—all of which requires coordination. If working hours are staggered, the family may not eat together. Household tasks have to be done after work. If children have after-school activities, they have to be coordinated with the parents' already busy schedules. Then there are meetings—school, work, and community. With hardly any time left for family communication or shared leisure, stress levels can soar. Children may feel rushed, or tense, or ignored, or out of control. And what happens when one parent is transferred to another city or state and the other parent's job doesn't allow for similar mobility? For single parents, the risk of fragmentation may be greater unless there is another supportive adult to assist with family functioning and buffer stress. Support and buffering have been shown to enable single parents to perform multiple roles that can contribute to their emotional well-being (Barnett & Hyde, 2001).

TECHNOLOGICAL CHANGES

Technological changes influencing family functioning include designed obsolescence—things having to be replaced because the parts are no longer available or are not compatible with newer objects. Obsolescence leads to added expenses for families and can influence people's jobs. For example, although machines increasingly are taking over repetitive tasks, enabling people to use more cognitive skills in performing their jobs, ironically more decisions are being programmed into computers, leaving people with fewer opportunities to use their higher cognitive functions.

Technological changes also include things that enable "multitasking" and "instantaneousness." Generation Y—the nearly 60 million children born after 1979—are the first to grow up in a world saturated with networks of information, digital devices, and the promise of perpetual connectivity" (Montgomery, 2000). Individuals perform multiple tasks when they are shopping while talking on their cell phones, or eating while driving, or working on the computer while watching TV. There is so much to do that we feel we have to maximize our time. Businesses have changed to help us adapt. We have superstores with "one-stop" shopping; we have fast foods; we have fast lanes. Because we hurry through experiences so quickly that we need additional ways to spend our time, we have mega-theaters with mega-movie choices; we have cable or satellite TV with hundreds of channels; we have new sports added to the old ones every year with their accompanying new equipment for sale.

Some parents react to the time bind by "overscheduling" their children's activities. Does "busyness" cause family members and friends, to say nothing of children, to get the short shrift of our attention? Some phone and Internet servers have capitalized on this concern by offering free or low-cost services such as call-waiting, caller ID (you talk only to those you choose), unlimited calls to preselected individuals, and instant e-mail messaging.

What is the effect of constantly being "turned-on" and "tuned-in"? Does our "fast-forward" world with multiple, simultaneous activities (for example, several screen images or messages on one's TV or computer screen) make people talk faster, interrupt more, become bored more easily, and continually seek novelty or stimulation? What is the effect of constantly being exposed to the *virtual* reality provided by the media on individuals' perception of reality and their ability to cope with it?

Meeting the Challenge of Change: Family Empowerment

As we have discussed, change can produce stress. The family is a dynamic social system that has structure, functions, roles, and authority patterns. The way the system operates and adapts to change affects the relationships within it. Family stress affects all members of the family. Stressors other than death, illness, divorce, and relocation that have been found to cause significant problems in family functioning include the following (Curran, 1985):

- Economics
- Children's behavior
- Insufficient couple time
- Lack of shared responsibility in the family
- Communication problems with children
- Insufficient "me" time
- Guilt for not accomplishing more
- Spousal relationships
- Insufficient family play time
- Overscheduled family calendars

The challenge to families of adapting to the impact of societal changes can probably best be met by looking at the characteristics of functional or successful families as models to emulate, rather than clinging to some family pattern that worked in

The physical closeness between father and child is important to foster attachment and interdependence.

the past (Coontz, 1997). How families cope with stress can be assessed in terms of their problem solving, communication, and adaptation to change; their social supports, spiritual beliefs, self-esteem, and personal adjustment; and their levels of pathology, deviance, and drug use (Curran, 1985; Stinnett & Defrain, 1985). Studies have shown that functional families that are resilient to stress are more likely to exhibit certain key characteristics—behaviors and values—than are families that are at risk for dysfunction when stressed. The strength of each characteristic and the combination of characteristics, as well as how they are demonstrated, may vary from one family to another and may be influenced by ethnic orientation. But, in general, the total picture of functional families is as follows:

- *Display of love and acceptance.* Family members show their love and appreciation for one another. This acceptance and warmth is expressed spontaneously—physically (smile, touch, hug) or verbally ("I love you," or "You're a good son/daughter"). Family members cooperate rather than compete with one another.
- *Communicativeness.* Family members are spontaneous, honest, open, and receptive to one another. This means expressing negative as well as positive feelings. Conflicts are faced and handled, rather than repressed and allowed to fester. However, some ethnic groups such as the Japanese believe it is better not to express negative feelings in order to avoid conflicts.
- *Cohesiveness.* Family members enjoy spending time together. Sharing chores, resources, and recreational activities is important to them. There is also respect, however, for individual differences, autonomy, and independence. It is common in Anglo families for members to engage in both individual and family pursuits; but this is not necessarily the pattern among other ethnic groups.
- *Communication of values and standards.* Parents have definite and clear values, which they make known to their children. These values and standards are discussed and practiced. There is also tolerance and respect for individual differences. Parents are models as well as teachers.
- *Ability to cope effectively with problems.* Stress and crises are faced optimistically, with the goal of finding solutions. Alternatives are explored, and family members are mutually supportive.

How can families develop resilience to stress? **Empowerment** involves enabling individuals to gain control over resources affecting them. Enabling families to gain access to knowledge and skills that enhance their ability to influence their personal lives and the community in which they live is the first step toward resiliency (Vanderslice, 1984). Empowerment is a process that evolves from analyzing one's own strengths and resources, becoming educated in skills one is lacking, and participating in the community. Empowerment is part of the current social policy. For example, government funding to families is tied to their becoming self-reliant instead of dependent. Rather than viewing families with problems as helpless, the government offers various programs to help people help themselves, such as financial aid for a college education, vocational rehabilitation, and child and health care services. Public and private community agencies that help empower families are discussed further in Chapter 10.

Epilogue

Family structure and function are affected by historical changes as evidenced by biblical families versus the contemporary ones portrayed on television. Family systems vary and are influenced by larger contexts, or macrosystems, including culture, politics, economics, and technology. Macrosystem values, such as obligations to oneself or others, affect family functions. Values affect child developmental outcomes. Security and continuance of family values provide stability for children, while personal happiness family values may result in uncertainty for children.

Summary

The family is a system affected by external and internal factors. The concept of family has changed from "a social group characterized by common residence, economic cooperation, and reproduction including adults of both sexes, at least two of whom maintain a socially approved sexual relationship and one or more children, biological or adopted, of the sexually cohabiting adults" (Murdock, 1962) to "any two or more related persons by birth, marriage, or adoption who reside together" (U.S. Bureau of the Census, 2000).

The basic structures of the family are nuclear and extended. A nuclear family consists of husband, wife, and children. An extended family consists of kin related to the nuclear family who are emotionally, and perhaps economically, dependent on each other. Extended families can be matriarchal, patriarchal, or egalitarian.

In general, the family's basic functions are reproduction, socialization/education, assignment of social roles, economic support, and nurturance/emotional support. Functional families maintain resilience and adaptability; dysfunctional families are at risk for breakup or problems. The scope of specific family functions has changed.

Family transitions have affected family structure and functions. Divorcing parents affect children. All children do not react to divorce the same way—personalities involved, coping skills, parents' relations with their children, the age and gender of children, and availability of others for support are all variables. Divorce affects the custodial parent, too, in that responsibilities double and stress increases. Joint-custody arrangements may give the children access to both parents but may also cause confusion.

Stepfamilies and remarried families are stressful for children. Children in a stepfamily have to form new relationships and accept new rules and new values while still having to deal with the old relationships, rules, and values. Reestablishing an effective functioning family system is a challenge. Kin custody, usually the grandparents, is another arrangement affecting children, especially in regard to their sense of belonging and stability. Community support is beneficial. Families with unmarried parents by choice may affect children's stability, depending on variables such as economics and relationships within the family. Families with homosexual parents, on the increase, can influence children if they become concerned about their sexual identities. How the community responds is also a factor in these children's development. Families of adopted children vary according to the reasons parents choose to adopt. Adopted children may have misunderstandings about their adoption, fears of abandonment, and identity issues.

Functional changes related to family transitions include the roles family members engage in. In dual-earner families, work, household responsibilities, child care, and leisure time pursuits must be coordinated. The effects of maternal employment outside the home depend on the age, gender, and temperament of the children, the socioeconomic status of the family, the quality of the parental marriage, the mother's satisfaction with her job, the father's satisfaction with his job, and the father's involvement with the children, as well as availability of quality child care.

Macrosystem influences on families, socialization, and children include socioeconomic status, ethnic orientation, and religious orientation. Socioeconomic status involves stratification. In traditional societies, status is usually ascribed; in modern societies, status is usually achieved. People's status or social class influences how they are socialized. The different socioeconomic classes rear children differently, which affects academic performance and behavior.

Ethnicity involves identification with a group based on national origin, race, or religion. Ethnic attributes can be physical, cultural, or both. Members of an ethnic group share a history, language, and set of traditions, rituals, customs, beliefs, attitudes, and values. People of different ethnic orientations differ in how they deal with basic questions of living, which affects socialization and consequent behavior patterns.

Religion is a unified system of beliefs and practices relative to sacred things, uniting into a single moral community all those who adhere to those beliefs and practices. Families that practice an organized religion usually induct their children into it. The family's religious beliefs influences its socialization practices. Religion provides an ideology that enables individuals to comprehend events that happen to them and gives them an identity and a support system for traditional norms and values.

Chronosystem influences on families, socialization, and children include sociopolitical changes such as war, economic changes such as job security, and technological changes such as computers and cell phones.

Activity

PURPOSE *To understand the influence of certain family characteristics on socialization and development.*

1. What was the socioeconomic status of your family of orientation? Upon what criteria did you base your answer?
2. List the values, beliefs, or attitudes supported by your ethnic group.
3. List the values, beliefs, or attitudes supported by your religion.
4. What were some stresses your family of orientation experienced, and how did it adapt?
5. What were three socialization goals communicated by your family of orientation? (Were they successful or unsuccessful?)
6. List three goals you have for yourself.
7. List three goals you have for your family of procreation.
8. Is there any connection between your family of orientation's socialization goals and your goals for your family of procreation?

Research Terms

Adoption
Binuclear
Child well-being
Custody
Empowerment
Matriarchy
Patriarchy

Related Readings

Barnett, R. C., & Rivers, C. (1996). *She works; he works.* Cambridge, MA: Harvard University Press.

Blankenhorn, D. (1995). *Fatherless America.* New York: Basic Books.

Bria, G. (1998). *The art of family: Rituals, imagination, and everyday spirituality.* New York: Dell.

Coleman, M., & Ganong, L. (1994). *Remarried family relationships.* Newbury Park, CA: Sage.

Coontz, S. (1997). *The way we really are: Coming to terms with America's changing families.* New York: Basic Books.

Cummings, E. M., & Davies, P. (1994). *Children and marital conflict: The impact of family dispute and resolution.* New York: Guilford Press.

Elkind, D. (1994). *Ties that stress: The new family imbalance.* Cambridge, MA: Harvard University Press.

Gilbert, D., & Kahn, J. A. (1987). *The American class structure: A new synthesis* (3rd ed.). Chicago: Dorsey Press.

Hareven, T. (1999). *Families, history, and social change: Life course and cross-cultural perspectives.* Boulder, CO: Westview Press.

Hetherington, E. M. (Ed.). (1999). *Coping with divorce, single parenting, and remarriage: A risk and resiliency perspective.* Mahwah, NJ: Erlbaum.

Kornhaber, K., & Forsythe, K. (1995). *Grandparent power: How to strengthen the vital connection among grandparents, parents, and children.* New York: Crown.

Lerner, J. (1994). *Working women and their families.* Newbury Park, CA: Sage.

Martin, A. (1993). *Lesbian and gay parenting handbook: Creating and raising our families.* New York: HarperCollins.

Mason, M. A. (1998). *The custody wars: Why children are losing the legal battle—and what we can do about it.* New York: Basic Books.

McAdoo, H. P. (Ed.). (1993). *Family ethnicity: Strength in diversity.* Newbury Park, CA: Sage.

Pavao, J. M. (1999). *The family of adoption.* Boston, MA: Beacon Press.

Stinnett, N., & Defrain, J. (1985). *Secrets of strong families.* Boston: Little, Brown.

Wallerstein, J. S., & Kelly, J. B. (1996). *Surviving the breakup.* New York: Basic Books.

Wilson, J. (1978). *Religion in American society: The effective presence.* Englewood Cliffs, NJ: Prentice-Hall.

Chapter 4

© Myrleen Ferguson Cate/Getty Images

Ecology of Parenting

You are the bows from which your children as living arrows are sent forth.

—KAHLIL GIBRAN

Prologue: Then and Now

Parenting

Macrosystem Influences on Parenting
Political Ideology
Culture
Socioeconomic Status
Ethnicity/Religion

Chronosystem Influences on Parenting
Historical Trends
Family Dynamics

Parenting Styles
Microsystem Influences: Between Parent and Child
Mesosystem Influences: Between Parent and Others

Appropriate Parenting Practices
Developmental Appropriateness
Guidance and Discipline

Inappropriate Parenting Practices
Child Maltreatment: Abuse and Neglect
Correlates and Consequences of Child Maltreatment

Epilogue

Summary

Activity

Research Terms

Related Readings

Prologue | *Then and Now*

MATERIALISTIC MAYHEM

THEN An ancient Greek myth tells of a wealthy king named Midas. He was fonder of gold than of anything else in the world except, perhaps, his young, golden-haired daughter Marygold. As a parent, he thought the best thing he could do for his beloved child would be to bequeath her the largest pile of glistening coins that had ever been heaped together since time began. Whenever he saw the gold-tinted clouds of a sunset, or yellow dandelions in the fields, or orange roses growing in his garden, he wished they would turn into gold coins.

He became so obsessed with his desire to possess gold that he forgot his original reason for wanting it so badly—to show his love for his daughter concretely. One day while he was in his treasure room admiring his gold collection, a stranger dressed all in white appeared.

"You are indeed a wealthy man, King Midas," observed the stranger.

"Yes," said the king, "but think how much more gold is out there in the world."

"Are you not satisfied?" asked the stranger.

"No, of course not. I often lie awake at night planning new ways to get more gold. Sometimes I even wish that everything I touched would turn to gold."

"Do you really wish that, King Midas?"

"Yes, nothing would make me happier."

"Then you shall have your wish. Tomorrow when the sun rises, you shall have the golden touch," proclaimed the stranger. And with that, he vanished.

Midas thought he had dreamed the whole encounter, but he went to sleep that night hoping it was true. When he awoke the next morning and touched his slippers, they turned to gold! Excitedly, he began touching things in his room; they all turned to gold.

He looked out the window at the garden where his daughter Marygold loved to play and run outside to touch all the flowers. "Won't Marygold be happy," he thought. But when Marygold saw the garden, she cried. "I won't be able to smell the flowers anymore; I won't be able to play in the garden, either!"

Not knowing how to comfort her, King Midas ordered breakfast served. However, as soon as Midas's lips touched the food, it turned to gold. He sputtered and spat. Marygold, thinking her father had burned his mouth, went to hug him, but alas, as her arms went about his chest, she, too, turned to gold.

King Midas began to sob; his beloved daughter was now a statue who couldn't laugh, or play, or kiss him. He had robbed her of her essence.

The stranger appeared again and asked, "Are you happy now, King Midas?"

"How can I be happy? I am miserable. I can't eat, I can't smell, I can't touch my daughter . . ."

"But you have the Golden Touch . . ."

"Please give me back my little Marygold and I'll give up all the gold I have. I've lost all that was worth having."

"You have become wise," said the stranger. "Go plunge in the river and take from it water to sprinkle on whatever you wish to transform."

Midas learned that being the best parent to his daughter did not mean giving her all the gold in the world. Such materialism only served to turn her into a material being herself; and statues have no spirit.

NOW   Centuries later, other parents thought they were doing the best for their daughter by encouraging her to compete for materialistic things. As Midas collected gold for his daughter, John and Patricia Ramsey collected competitive opportunities for theirs. Jon Benet Ramsey, age 6, was a beauty pageant star. The parenting style of her parents came to the attention of the media in 1996 when their daughter was found murdered in their Colorado home on Christmas morning.

Photos of Jon Benet in her beauty pageant attire and makeup led the public to believe her parents had created a seductress, but did her parents kill her? If so, why? If not, who did? That Jon Benet was part of the adult world of vanity, competition, and consumerism leads one to suspect some malicious motive.

Even if the Ramseys did not kill their child, many say they killed her childhood. Did they push on her their values of fame and fortune, much as King Midas did to Marygold? Was their parenting style pressured by a society that values appearances and material wealth? Unfortunately, unlike Midas, they did not get the chance to reevaluate.

KEY QUESTIONS

- Where do we get our values and information about how we should parent?
- What is a "good" parent—in terms of society, children, and oneself?

Parenting

As a complement to Chapter 3, this chapter explores a major task of families, which is the protection, nurturance, and socialization of children—commonly referred to as parenting. Parenting is a relationship that unfolds over time (Bornstein, 1995) and is affected by children themselves, as we will see.

Parenting means implementing a series of decisions about the socialization of one's children (Kagan, 1975)—what one does to enable them to become responsible, contributing members of society, as well as what one does when they cry, are aggressive, lie, or do poorly in school. Parents sometimes find these decisions overwhelming. One of the reasons parenting can be confusing is that there is little consensus in the United States today as to what children should be like when they grow up or what parents should do to get them there. Another reason parenting is confusing is that it is bidirectional and dynamic—an adult's behavior

Figure 4.1

*An Ecological Model
of Human Development*
*Parenting is the means by
which the family socializes
children.*

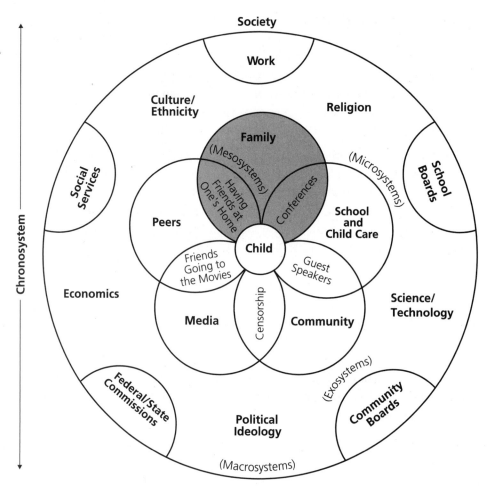

toward a child is often a reaction to that child's behavior, changing with time as
the child develops (Lerner, 1998). Thus, by influencing adults, children influence
their own development as well. In this sense, causes for behavior are viewed from
a circular rather than a linear perspective (Cowan, Powell, & Cowan, 1998). The
concept of the bidirectionality of parenting is exemplified throughout the chapter.

Whereas parenthood is universal, parenting is highly variable among different
cultures and groups within societies. This chapter examines macrosystem influences on parenting styles, such as political ideology, culture, socioeconomic status,
ethnicity, and religion, and chronosystem influences such as historical trends and
family dynamics.

Figure 4.1 shows an ecological model of the systems involved in the process.

Macrosystem Influences on Parenting

Examining the macrosystem influences on parenting provides insight into the political, cultural, economic, and social values or practices that contribute to children's
socialization and development.

POLITICAL IDEOLOGY

Political ideology refers to theories pertaining to government. It influences parenting styles in that children must be raised to function as citizens in society. Most traditional societies subscribe to an aristocratic political ideology, or government by the highest-ranking class of individuals. Traditional examples are tribes in Africa, New Zealand, and Australia; modern examples include the United Kingdom, Japan, and Spain, which have hereditary monarchs as heads of state. In an **autocracy,** such as Iraq or Cuba, one person has unlimited power over others. However, many modern societies, such as the United States, subscribe to a democratic political ideology. In a **democracy,** those ruled, at least in theory, have power equal to those who rule; the principle is equality of rights. In an autocracy, relationships between people are understood in terms of a pecking order. The traditional autocratic family system follows the order: The father has power over the mother and children, who have few rights. In a democracy, relationships between people are based on consensus and compromise. The modern democratic family system considers the rights of all members.

Fifty years ago, parenting decisions were easier to make because it was assumed that people's main purpose in life was to serve God by being faithful and following the teachings of their religion. Thus, children were constantly exhorted to overcome their supposed base natures in order to please God (Spock, 1968). This concept still holds true today as preached by some of the fundamentalist sects of religions around the world.

Historically in some countries, people's purpose in life was held to be to serve their country—for example, in France under Napoleon Bonaparte and in Germany under Hitler. This still holds true today in China, where parents and teachers are expected to agree with the country's leaders about what values and attitudes to instill in children.

In other parts of the world, it is assumed that children are born and raised to serve the purposes of the family. For example, in rural India, children are trained to work at jobs considered of value to their family, and they defer to their elders. In addition, marriages are often arranged for the benefit of the family.

In the United States, few children are brought up to believe that their principal destiny is to serve their family, their country, or God. Rather, Euro-American children generally are free to set their own goals in life. However, other ethnic groups in the United States, subscribe to the value of interdependence and so instill in their children a sense of obligation to their families (Fuligni, Tseng, & Lam, 1999; Trumbull, Rothstein-Fisch, Greenfield, & Quiroz, 2001). Some examples are Mexican Americans and Asian Americans.

As U.S. society underwent social and economic changes, people began to question the inadequate implementation of democratic ideals written in the Constitution, particularly those regarding equality. In the 1960s, people were especially concerned with the lack of opportunities for ethnic minorities and women. As a result, the Civil Rights Act of 1964 was passed, which required that these groups be treated equally in housing, education, and employment. Similar legislation was extended to individuals with disabilities in 1990. Such legislation has had beneficial economic effects in terms of opportunities to earn a living, as well as beneficial psychological effects on minorities' self-concept.

The notion that unlimited authority is no longer appropriate in U.S. society, because it is incongruent with democratic ideals, has filtered down to children.

Parents today find it difficult to raise children by the "do it because I said so" method. Also, children learn democratic ideals in school and from the media, and as a result are not willing to be ruled autocratically. Appropriate child rearing in a democratic society thus represents a challenge, especially for parents who were raised autocratically.

CULTURE

Culture includes the knowledge, beliefs, art, morals, law, customs, and traditions acquired by members of a society. Culture encompasses the way people have learned how to adapt to their environment, their assumptions about the way the world is, and their beliefs about the way people should act (Triandis, 1994). The culture in which individuals grow up has indirect effects on their parenting attitudes and consequent parenting styles (Parke & Buriel, 1998). To illustrate, Garcia-Coll (1990) reviewed the literature on cultural beliefs and caregiving practices and concluded that parenting goals and techniques depend to some extent on the tasks adults are expected to perform or the competencies they are supposed to possess in a given population. For example, in the United States, adults are expected to read, write, and be economically self-sufficient. American children are thus expected to achieve in school, are given an allowance to learn the value of money, and are pressured to get a job at least by the time they finish their schooling. In the Fiji Islands, in contrast, adults are expected to farm, fish, and send profits to relatives on other South Pacific islands (West, 1988). Fijian children are thus expected to relate to others in the community, to help adults work, and to share resources.

LeVine (1977, 1988) proposes that there are universal parenting goals that involve (1) ensuring physical health and survival, (2) developing behavioral capacities for economic self-maintenance, and (3) instilling behavioral capacities for maximizing cultural values such as morality, prestige, and achievement. However, cultures vary in the emphasis they place on these goals, as well as in how they implement them. Also, if one goal is threatened, it becomes the foremost concern and overrides the need to implement the others. For example, if a society has a high rate of infant mortality, parents will concentrate more on the goal of physical health and survival; the pursuit of learning to participate economically and to acquire cultural values will be postponed until a later age, when children's survival is relatively certain. Societies with limited resources for subsistence place emphasis on training children in skills that will be economically advantageous in adulthood, thereby reducing survival risks. Once society has tested and adopted various methods for survival, these methods become part of the culture and are passed on to children.

How various cultures prioritize these universal parenting goals may explain differences in maternal behavior toward infants (Richman, LeVine, New, & Howrigan, 1988). For example, the Gusii of Kenya prioritize the parenting goal of physical health and survival. They interpret holding the child as a form of protection from physical hazards such as cooking fires and domestic animals, and have no alternatives like cradle boards, playpens, or infant seats. Gusii mothers also soothe their infants through immediate physical comforting when they cry. This close physical contact enables the mother to know when her baby is becoming sick, as opposed to merely being hungry or temporarily distressed, because a sick baby will not be comforted by physical contact or food.

For another example, American mothers prioritize the parenting goal of developing their children's capacities for economic self-maintenance. They verbalize with and gaze at their infants more frequently than do the Gusii. This reflects the belief that infants can communicate socially. After American infants learn to walk, holding declines rapidly; infant seats, playpens, and high chairs are used to protect the locomotive youngster from harm. This reduction in human physical contact reflects the value Americans put on individuality and independence.

Culture, Economics, and Children's Behavior

Economics involves the production, distribution, and consumption of goods and services. Cultural anthropologists Beatrice Whiting and John Whiting (1975) investigated the relationship between socioeconomic systems, family structures, and parenting styles. Did the way a society governed and supported itself to survive relate to the way its children were reared?

The Whitings classified socioeconomic systems as either simple or complex. *Simple* societies had economies based on subsistence gardening. Roles for men, women, and children were clearly defined, and emphasis was placed on cooperation in order to survive. *Complex* societies had economies based on occupational specialization. There was a class system and centralized government, and competition was emphasized. The Whitings classified family structures as extended or nuclear, depending on whether there were specified relations with kin or whether the family was free to do "its own thing."

The Whitings observed the behavior of 134 children between the ages of 3 and 11 in Kenya, the Philippines, Mexico—representing simple socioeconomic systems—and Okinawa, India, and the United States—representing complex socioeconomic systems. The categories of social behavior found in children from all six cultures, in varying degrees, included nurturance, responsibility, dependence, dominance, sociability, intimacy, authoritarianism, and aggressiveness. Because some of these behaviors consistently occurred together in the various cultures, the Whitings organized them according to two dimensions, in order to determine the effects of culture on the social behavior of children. One dimension of behavioral categories was nurturant-responsible (offered help, offered support, suggested responsibility) versus dependent-dominant (sought help, sought attention, sought dominance). The other dimension was sociable-intimate (acted sociably, teased sociably, touched) versus authoritarian-aggressive (reprimanded, assaulted).

The societies having a relatively simple socioeconomic structure—with little or no occupational specialization, no class or caste system, a localized and kin-based political structure, and no professional priesthood—had children who were more nurturant-responsible and less dependent-dominant. The societies having a more complex socioeconomic structure—characterized by occupational specialization, social stratification, a central government, and an organized priesthood—had children who scored low on nurturance-responsibility but high on dependence-dominance.

The children in societies whose family structure was nuclear and egalitarian scored high on sociability-intimacy and low on authoritarianism-aggressiveness. The children in societies whose family structure was based on the extended family and was patriarchal scored high on authoritarianism-aggressiveness and low on sociability-intimacy (see Figure 4.2).

In societies having a patrilineal, extended family structure, the male head of the family exercises authority over family members. He must be able to express aggression when necessary, a skill learned in reprimanding younger siblings during childhood. In societies having a nuclear, neolocal (newlyweds set up a new place of residence) family system, authoritarianism and aggressiveness are not as necessary as sociability and intimacy.

Figure 4.2

Relationship Between Sociocultural Characteristics and Socialized Behavior

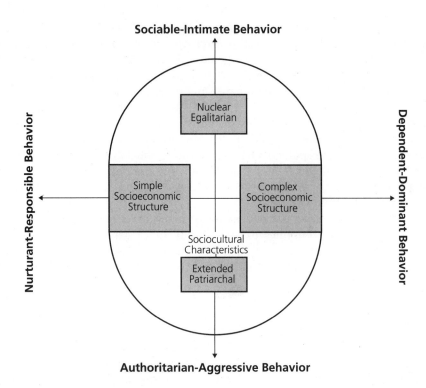

The Whitings (1975) concluded:

> Formulas for appropriate adult social behavior dictated by the socioeconomic and family system are embedded in the value system of the culture. Nurturance and responsibility, success, authority, and casual intimacy are types of behavior that are differentially preferred by different cultures. These values are apparently transmitted to the children before the age of six. (pp. 178–179)

In another study, Whiting and Edwards (1988) examined the ideologies of six cultures with regard to expectations for children according to age and gender. They focused on the social behavior of girls and boys age 2–10 who lived in communities in India, Japan, the Philippines, Mexico, Kenya, and the United States. With whom did the children interact? Did they go to school? Did they have responsibilities at home? What activities occupied their time—caring for siblings, doing errands, or playing?

They discovered that different societies varied their expectations of behavior according to age. In some societies, 6-year-olds were expected to learn the ways of their ideology by taking on household responsibilities and caring for younger siblings, whereas in others, 6-year-olds were expected to go to school. Different societies also varied their expectations of behavior according to gender. Some societies had different ideologies for boys and girls, and assigned children to settings or activities accordingly. Boys were allowed more autonomy and expected to exhibit more dominant behavior with others; girls were kept in close proximity and expected to engage in more nurturing activities with younger siblings.

Thus, the social behavior of the children from each culture was found to be compatible with the adult role requirements of the society. In societies based on a simple socioeconomic structure, reciprocity among kin and neighbors is essential.

People offer help and support to one another, dominance and attention seeking are frowned upon. Children take on helping responsibilities early on. In societies based on a more complex socioeconomic structure, dominance and attention seeking are behaviors that may enhance a person's social status; the help and support of others are regarded as counterproductive. Children's autonomous behavior is encouraged.

SOCIOECONOMIC STATUS

A family's **socioeconomic status** is its rank or position within society based on social and economic factors such as income, occupation, and education of the parents. In general, parents with high socioeconomic status have high incomes and highly respected occupations, and are well educated; parents with low socioeconomic status have low incomes, work at unskilled or semiskilled jobs, and are poorly educated; parents with middle socioeconomic status have medium incomes, work in business or professional occupations, and a decent education. However, not all families can be classified according to the criteria discussed here; some parents are very well educated and have very low incomes (graduate students, for example), and some parents have very high incomes and are not well educated (some businesspersons, for example). Also, there is as much variation within socioeconomic status groups as between them. For example, in a study of lower-class, blue-collar families, LeMasters (1988) found that fathers had different ideas about raising their children, especially their sons, than did the mothers. According to the blue-collar fathers in the study, to become a "man" a boy has to learn to fight, to defend himself, and to give back at least as much punishment as he takes. If he doesn't learn this, he will be weak and tend to be "victimized" all his life, by men and women. The blue-collar mothers in the study, in contrast, were trying to raise their boys to fill family roles—to be more sensitive and cooperative rather than "macho."

The following descriptive (not evaluative) generalizations are based on many research studies that compare the parenting styles of families from high- and low-socioeconomic statuses (Hart & Risley, 1995; Parke & Buriel, 1998); keep in mind that variations exist within each class:

- Parents from low-socioeconomic statuses are more likely to emphasize obedience, respect, neatness, cleanliness, and avoidance of trouble; parents from high-socioeconomic statuses are more likely to emphasize happiness, creativity, ambition, independence, curiosity, and self-control.
- Parents from low-socioeconomic statuses are more likely to be controlling, authoritarian, and arbitrary in their discipline and to use physical punishment; parents from high-socioeconomic statuses are more likely to be democratic, using reason with their children and being receptive to their children's opinions.
- Parents from high-socioeconomic statuses are more likely to show warmth and affection toward their children than are parents from low-socioeconomic statuses.
- Parents from high-socioeconomic statuses are more likely to talk to their children more, reason with them more, and use more complex language than are parents from low-socioeconomic statuses.

A major reason parenting styles differ according to socioeconomic status is that families tend to adapt their interactional patterns to the level of stress they are experiencing. Both high- and low-socioeconomic families experience stress due to work problems, health problems, relationship problems, and so on. However, low income and other stressors related to poverty (low-equality housing, unsafe neighborhoods, job turnover) influence parents' well-being, the tone of their marriage, and the quality of their relationship with their children (Cowan, Powell, & Cowan, 1998). According to several studies (Dodge, Petit, & Bates, 1994; McLoyd, 1990, 1998), economic hardship experienced by lower-class families is associated with anxiety, depression, and irritability. Emotional stress, in turn, increases the tendency of parents to be punitive, inconsistent, authoritarian, and generally nonsupportive of their children. The emotional strain encourages parents to adopt parenting techniques, such as physical punishment and commands without explanation, that require less time and effort than other methods, such as reasoning and negotiating. Expecting unquestioning obedience from children is more efficient than trying to meet the desires of all family members when one is experiencing stress.

Parental Occupations and Children's Behavior

So far we have discussed macrosystem influences such as political ideology, culture, and socioeconomic systems on parenting styles. Now we examine an exosystem influence—the parents' work. Complex societies in which there are many roles to perform have complex stratification systems, or many criteria upon which status is based, such as income, occupation, education, and place of residence. The more complex the society and the more roles that exist, the more complex the task of socialization becomes. When someone performs a role, he or she takes on the behavioral expectations of that role through the process of socialization. For example, army officers behave in an authoritarian manner, giving commands, whereas lawyers use logic, reason, and explanation in performing their roles. Do the socialized role behaviors performed in people's occupations (the exosystem) carry over into parenting styles?

To find out, Miller and Swanson (1958) examined the child-rearing practices of American parents in different occupational roles, which they classified as bureaucratic versus entrepreneurial. *Bureaucratic* occupations were characterized by a straight salary and relatively high job security—for example, civil service employees, public school teachers, military personnel, and some corporate employees. *Entrepreneurial* occupations were classified as those in which individuals were self-employed or worked on the basis of commissions—for example, physicians, business owners, and certain salespeople such as real estate agents. Miller and Swanson found that bureaucratic families tend to stress egalitarian practices and to emphasize social adjustment or "getting along"; entrepreneurial families tend to emphasize independence training, competence, and self-reliance. The entrepreneurial parents also tend to depend heavily on psychological techniques of discipline: "You've disappointed me with your behavior," rather than "No television tonight for you."

Sociologist Melvin Kohn (1977) analyzed the ways in which middle-class occupations in general differ from lower-class occupations. Middle-class occupations typically require workers to handle ideas and symbols, as well as be skilled in interpersonal relations, whereas lower-class occu-

People who work in bureaucratic jobs, like those in an office, tend to incorporate the value of following the rules in their parenting styles.

© Sanna Lindberg/Getty Images

pations typically involve physical objects rather than symbols and do not require as many interpersonal skills. Also, middle-class jobs often demand more self-direction in the prioritizing of job activities and the selection of methods to get the job done than do lower-class jobs, which are more often routinized and subject to stricter supervision.

Kohn's (Kohn, 1977; Kohn Naoi, Schoenbach, Schooler, & Slomczynski, 1990) subsequent research on differences in parent–child relationships in middle and lower classes indicated that lower-class parents are likely to judge their children's behavior in terms of its immediate consequences and its external characteristics, whereas middle-class parents are more concerned with their children's motives and the attitudes their behavior seemed to express. Kohn explained these differences as due to the different characteristics required in middle- and lower-class occupations.

Kohn (1977; Kohn et al., 1990) demonstrated that middle-class parents are more likely than lower-class parents to want their children to be considerate of others, intellectually curious, responsible, and self-controlled; lower-class parents are more likely to want their children to have good manners, to do well in school, and to be obedient. Thus, middle-class parents tend to emphasize self-direction in children, whereas the lower-class parents tend to emphasize conformity. Kohn also demonstrated that fathers whose jobs entail self-direction, who work with ideas instead of things, who are not closely supervised, and who face complexity on the job value self-direction in their children, whereas those whose work requires them to work under close supervision and conform to a highly structured work situation are more likely to want their children to conform. Similarly, Bronfenbrenner (1979) and Crouter (Bronfenbrenner & Crouter, 1982; Crouter & McHale, 1993) suggest that parents' workplaces affect their perceptions of life and the ways in which they interact with family members. Therefore, parenting styles tend to be extensions of the modes of behavior that are functional for parents. In dual-earner families, so prevalent today, it is possible for mothers and fathers, due to the nature of their jobs, to come to favor different parenting practices, and these, in turn, may further vary according to their children's age and gender (Crouter, Bumpus, Maguire, & McHale, 1999; Crouter & McHale, 1993; Greenberger, O'Neil, & Nagel, 1994).

In sum, the differences in socialization practices related to various socioeconomic statuses are due to both variations in physical resources and the types of adult models available to children for patterning behaviors, the breadth and quality of learning experiences provided for children, and the kinds of child-rearing practices implemented by the parents as influenced by their occupations.

ETHNICITY/RELIGION

Ethnicity refers to an attribute of membership in a group in which members identify themselves by national origin, culture, language, race, or religion. **Religion** refers to a unified system of beliefs and practices relative to sacred things. Ethnicity and religion impact people's values, perceptions, attitudes, and behavior. Here we examine some aspects of ethnic and religious influences on child-rearing goals and practices. The purpose is not to stereotype by the examples provided, but rather to highlight the power and pervasiveness of traditional beliefs and practices that originally were developed as adaptive survival strategies and were passed from generation to generation. As various ethnic and religious groups become part of the mainstream, their values may change, as may those of the mainstream. This is evident in generational differences between grandparents, parents, and children (Parke & Buriel, 1998).

To begin to understand differences in group values, we examine the work of Ferdinand Tonnies (1957), a German sociologist who saw the reasons for this diversity as being tied to how societies adapt to political, social, and economic changes The social order is largely based on the customs and traditions of groups sharing the same ethnicity or religion. He classified groups according to *"gemeinschaft"* characteristics on one end of the spectrum and *"gesellschaft"* on the other. In **gemeinschaft** groups, interpersonal relationships tend to be communal, cooperative, intimate, and informal. Social sanctions and political control are based on an established hierarchy, with ascribed rights and obligations. Personal opinions and beliefs are private, and the customs of the community are adhered to and respected. In **gesellschaft** groups, interpersonal relationships tend to be associative, practical, objective and formal. Social sanctions and political control are achieved through public discussions and consensus, emphasizing fairness and equal rights. The concepts of *gemeinschaft* and *gesellschaft* community relations are discussed further in Chapter 10.

Because families are embedded in larger social groups such as ethnic or religious groups, they can be similarly categorized, albeit generally, as cooperative/interdependent (collectivism) on one end of the spectrum (more likely found in *gemeinschaft* societies) and competitive/independent (individualism) on the other end (more likely found in *gesellschaft* societies). **Collectivism** emphasizes interdependent relations, social responsibilities, and the well-being of the group (fitting in); **individualism** emphasizes individual fulfillment and choice (standing out) (Trumbull et al., 2001). Collectivism reflects a "we" consciousness, group solidarity, the sharing of duties and obligations, group decision making and particularism or partiality toward group members; individualism reflects an "I" consciousness, autonomy, individual initiative, the right to privacy, pleasure seeking, and universalism or impartiality toward group members (Hofstede, 1991). About 70 percent of the world cultures can be described as collectivistic (Trumbull et al., 2001).

Collectivistic and individualistic orientations are exhibited by diverse parenting values and child-rearing practices in families—specifically, in the authority roles, the communication that takes place, the way emotion is displayed, the way children are disciplined and guided, and the skills that are emphasized. Children socialized in a collective context are amused by people—by being held, teased, and *shown* how to do something; children socialized in an individual context are amused by things—by being given space and toys and *told* how to do something (Trumbull et al., 2001). For example, at our fall picnic to welcome faculty and graduate students in our department, I observed an Israeli parent trying to keep her 2½-year-old child occupied and away from the cooking area by continually talking to him. He was quite verbally adept for his age, and the attentive conversation seemed to distract him from the barbeque. In contrast, the preschool children of the parents from the United States were given toys to play with while their parents talked and cooked.

Some generalizations on ethnic/religious patterns of parenting follow, organized according to collective and individualistic orientations, and to specific family dynamics regarding (1) authority roles, (2) communication, (3) displays of emotion, (4) discipline/guidance of children, and (5) skills emphasized (Garcia-Coll, Meyer, & Britton, 1995; Parke & Buriel, 1998; Theiderman, 1991). Affecting the homogeneity or heterogeneity within the generalizations is the degree of assimilation into, and adoption of, mainstream ways. For example, Euro-Americans tend to be more oriented toward individualism than collectivism; Native Americans tend to be more oriented toward collectivism than individualism; and African Americans tend to be more oriented toward collectivism than are Euro-Americans but more oriented toward individualism than are Native Americans (Trumbull et al., 2001).

The Cooperative/Interdependent (Collective) Orientation

Authority Roles. Generally, authority roles in groups with collective orientations are hierarchical. Thus, children are taught to respect age and status. Appropriate behavior is ascribed in social roles—mothers do certain things, as do grandparents, and teachers, and so on. Different treatment of individuals according to rank and/or situation is known as particularism. Authority figures are expected to have more rights and privileges than other group members because they have more obligations and responsibilities to protect and care for these members.

Asian American family structure and roles are based upon Confucian principles of order, hierarchical relationships, and harmony. Typically, Asian American families are patriarchal, and members place family needs above individual needs. Children show obedience and loyalty to parents and are expected to take care of elderly parents (Bugental & Goodnow, 1998).

Native American families "may be characterized as a collective cooperative social network that extends from the mother and father union to the extended family and ultimately the community and tribe" (Bugental & Goodnow, 1998, p. 504). Children are socialized by the extended, as well as the nuclear, family, and there are strong bonds of affection between family members. Traditionally, it is the old people who pass on the cultural heritage to the younger ones. Children are not expected to communicate their opinions to older people, but rather are taught to respect their elders (age is a "badge of honor"—if you have grown old, you have done the right things). Respect is taught by example and by instruction.

Hispanic American parents encourage their children to identify with the family and community. Children are close to members of the extended, as well as the nuclear, family, which fosters a sense of obligation to the family. The religious principles of Catholicism, are commonly followed, and respect for parents is emphasized, as is obedience and respect for authority. Typically, age and gender are important determinants of roles and status. Hierarchical relationships tend to assure that people assume appropriate roles and behave accordingly. Older children are given responsibility for socialization of younger ones. The family is viewed as the main source of individuals' sense of self, and its honor in the community is highly valued. To set up a life separate from the family is considered irresponsible; in adulthood, offspring owe allegiance and support to parents and extended family members.

Some African Americans derive a sense of community and identity from an organized religion rather than from race or national origin. Authority roles in the family follow those of the religious group. For example, Muslim immigrants and their families who follow the practices of Islam believe that all things belong to God and that wealth held by men is held in trust. Islam, like other religions, requires that a portion of people's accumulated wealth be given to those in need.

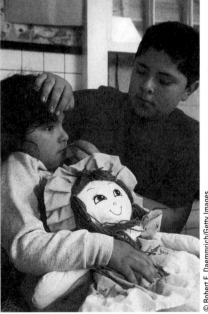

In some cultures, children are given important responsibilities that contribute to the welfare of the family.

© Robert E. Daemmrich/Getty Images

Communication. Communication patterns vary among collective groups although they tend to rely on nonverbal communication (body language, gestures, touch, facial expression, eye contact) more than do individualistic groups.

Compared to Euro-Americans, Asian Americans use relatively restrained verbal communication, preferring nonverbal means such as facial expressions and body language.

Some groups value silence and pauses in communication, while others value interruptions. For example, Asian Americans and Native Americans pause during conversations to contemplate what was said and to think about how to respond. Middle Eastern Americans, Italian Americans, and Hawaiians tend to interrupt as a means of getting involved (Theiderman, 1991).

African Americans tend to encourage body contact (embraces in greeting or thanks). Mothers are physically close to their infants, often sleeping with them. They feed their babies on demand rather than on a schedule and become involved early on in toilet training. Nonverbal communication with babies is common, such as caressing them and rubbing their feet (Hale, 1994).

In observing communication styles in low-income African American families, Heath (1989) found that adults asked children different types of questions than typically are heard in middle-class Euro-American families. Euro-American parents tend to ask "knowledge-training" questions such as "What is this story about?" The African-American parents in Heath's sample asked only "real" questions—those to which they did not know the answer, such as "What's in that box?" Often conversations were acted out with body language and contained a lot of teasing. African Americans may also coin words if doing so enhances and furthers communication. For them, it's not so much what is said, but how it is said, that is important (Hale, 1994). Eye contact is important, too. When speaking, many Euro-Americans look away from their "listeners," glancing at them from time to time; yet when they listen, they look directly at the speaker. African Americans, in contrast, generally do the opposite: When they speak, they tend to stare at the listener, and when they listen, they mostly look away (Dresser, 1996).

Sometimes a word is a symbol for several concepts. For example, the Hebrew word *shalom* means both "hello" and "peace be with you." In the Hawaiian word *aloha*, each letter stands for something: *a* is short for *akahai*, meaning "to be kind"; *l*, short for *lokahi*, means "to be inclusive"; *o*, short for *olu'ola*, means "to be agreeable"; *h*, short for *ha'aha'a*, means "to be humble"; and the second *a*, short for *ahonui*, refers to "patience." Combining the letters, *alo* means "space" and *ha* means "breath." Thus, when you say, "Aloha," you are saying, "Hello, share my space and my breath."

Displays of Emotion. Some groups display their emotions outwardly, and others do so inwardly. Emotions kept inside can be expressed through change in personal distance (the African American who steps backwards while engaged in a loud conversation), shunning (the Native American who ignores and avoids his friend for boasting), or deviations in performing routines (the Japanese American husband who knows his wife is angry because she fills his teacup only halfway with lukewarm tea).

Generally, African Americans show emotions outwardly, through facial expressions, sound, and body movement (Theiderman, 1991), whereas, Native Americans and Japanese Americans rarely show their feelings publicly (Triandis, 1994). In Japan, a smile can disguise embarrassment, mask bereavement, and conceal rage, and a straight face can hide happiness (Stewart & Bennett, 1991).

Discipline/Guidance of Children. Hierarchical groups consider age to be of high status in that age is equated with knowledge. Children, who are of low status in such groups, are not asked their desires, nor are they expected to communicate their opinions to older people. Instead, they are expected to be guided by the wisdom of adults, to obey and imitate. Even when children in such collectivistic groups play, an adult or older sibling is nearby to guide as needed.

Asian American children are closely nurtured in their early years by the mother. Parenting of these infants can be described as responsive—they are seldom allowed to cry for prolonged periods before they are picked up; they are fed on demand; they are weaned at a later age than Euro-Americans; they are allowed to sleep with their parents; and they are toilet trained gradually. Thus, Asian American children become dependent on the mother to satisfy their needs. This dependency, as well as the physical closeness, fosters in children a sense of obligation, which is continually reinforced as they grow older. Consequently, mothers are able to use shame and guilt to control behavior by appealing to this sense of duty when children deviate from their expectations. The power of shame is expressed in a Chinese proverb: "If you disregard the question of face, life is pointless." Avoiding shame, or "saving face," is part of the desire to maintain harmony and balance in the group—no one should be caused embarrassment. Related socialized behaviors to avoid shame and save face include reluctance to admit lack of understanding or ask questions, to take the initiative or do something a new way, to confront or disagree with someone. As a Japanese proverb states, "The nail that sticks out gets hammered down."

Asian American parents are generally not overtly affectionate with children, but show their love in indirect ways, such as by sacrificing their own needs for their children's. As children reach school age, they are subjected to stricter discipline and taught that their actions reflect not only on themselves but on their families. Fathers usually assume the role of disciplinarian.

Native American adults indicate approval through a smile, a pleasant tone of voice, or a friendly pat. Children are typically corrected by the adult lowering his or her voice. Generally, there is no physical punishment, nor is there verbal praise. Frowning, ignoring, withdrawal of affection, and shaming are forms of social control, as is group pressure. Criticism of others is traditionally communicated indirectly through another family member, rather than directly.

Hispanic American children tend to be encouraged to learn by observing, by doing, and by monitoring the reactions of others. Perhaps this is due to the traditional practice of including children in many adult activities. Self-regulation occurs through the building of new behaviors onto old ones. Feedback is used to help children improve. Like other collectivistic groups, Hispanic Americans frown on overpraising performance because it may make one person feel more important than others (Trumbull et al., 2001).

African American parents use a variety of discipline techniques. Those living in poor neighborhoods tend to demand strict obedience from their children and to use physical punishment as a consequence for noncompliance because, knowing the dangers of ghetto life, they want to protect their children (Ogbu, 1994; Pinderhughes, Dodge, Bates, Pettit, & Zelli, 2000).

Skills Emphasis. Different groups place different emphasis on skills they believe are important for children to learn to get along in the group and to become contributing adults.

Native American children are generally taught such values as brotherhood, sharing, and personal integrity, as well as spirituality (via rites and rituals). They readily share personal items because the boundaries of property ownership tend to be permeable. Cooperation is highly valued—generally, there is no competition within the group, nor is there majority rule; rather, consensus is sought based on the needs of the group overriding the needs of the individual. Modesty and moderation are stressed—don't talk for the sake of talking, don't boast when one achieves, and don't show emotions. Children are not expected to be perfect, but only to do what they are capable of at a given age. Therefore, failure is not a concept. The goal is simply to improve on past performance.

Hispanic American children are not usually encouraged to exhibit curiosity or independence; rather, cooperation and helpfulness are emphasized. Children are socialized to be sensitive to the feelings and needs of others.

African American families generally value close family ties and a strong sense of familial obligation. Children relate to many people of all ages in the household. Commonly, there is more emphasis on interaction with people than with things.

Competitive/Independent (Individualistic) Orientation

Authority Roles. Individualistic groups tend to value *achieved* authority, unlike collectivistic groups, which tend to value *ascribed* authority. For example, in an equal-opportunity work environment, employees recognize that authority is usually achieved by hard work and so is respected; in a hierarchical work environment, employees recognize that authority is usually related to one's privileged status, and so obedience and respect are required (Theiderman, 1991). In individualistic and equal-opportunity settings, the rules are assumed to be universal, or the same for everyone; in collectivistic and hierarchical settings, the rules are assumed to be particular, or flexible according to individuals' status and the situation. The particularistic approach, wherein rules are malleable, impacts parenting styles and children's socialization. To illustrate, I have some students who never question the policies and procedures set forth in the course syllabus because they accept that the standards are universal. But I have other students who are quite creative in their attempts to bend the requirements to fit their particular situation.

Communication. Communication of messages can be direct and independent of context (as in a memorandum), or it can be indirect and dependent on context (as in a face-to-face meeting).

Compared to other groups, Euro-Americans tend to use direct communication. Due to their pragmatic style, they are specific and come to the point quickly. They are comfortable with written and electronic messages because what is stated is the message; the context in which it is said is not important. Other groups, such Middle Eastern Americans or Japanese Americans, tend to be more indirect. They might first inquire about family members, health, or other matters seemingly unrelated to the purpose of the conversation. However, such questions are necessary for assessing the choice of language to be used and the degree of familiarity with which certain topics can be discussed (Stewart & Bennett, 1991).

Some groups, such as Native Americans, who tend to rely on the context to fully understand the communication (including nonverbal behavior and relational cues), may not be comfortable with written or electronic messages.

Displays of Emotion. Some groups of individuals openly express their feelings to others; some hide their feelings from others; and still others are open with those people with whom they are intimate and closed with others. This display of emotions (open or closed) is likely an adaptive strategy developed and passed on regarding how to best get along with others—share one's feelings with all, hide one's feelings from all, or be selective.

EXAMPLE An example of how people differ in their display of emotions comes from a story in the business section of the *Los Angeles Times* (Pham, 2002). Two engineers, Hinton and Marr, paired up for a project to design a computer chip that performed multiple tasks. Hinton was loquacious, constantly throwing out ideas, and talking to everyone he met in the hall about the project. Marr was quiet, focused, and methodical, recruiting her allies in advance of crucial meetings, and analyzing how the meetings would turn out before they began. Marr came to believe in Hinton's ideas, and Hinton respected Marr's ability to get things done. Both styles were necessary to design the chip and to convince the many engineers working on the project to implement every step and every mathematical algorithm.

African Americans generally are openly expressive, as are Hispanic Americans and Middle Eastern Americans. Asian Americans tend to be more closed, and Euro-Americans typically fall in between, being warm to relatives and close friends and neutral to casual acquaintances.

Discipline/Guidance of Children. Among individualistic groups, children are socialized to solve problems they encounter. Some groups guide children by instruction or modeling; others expect children to learn by doing and by asking questions. Providing reasons to children for desirable behavior so that they will internalize them and be self-directive is a common practice.

Euro-Americans believe there is a rational order in the world, and they see themselves as individual agents of action ("Take the bull by the horn"). They assume that problems and solutions are the nature of reality. The emphasis is on taking action in the present to avoid problems in the future ("A stitch in time saves nine"). For example, in the area of health, children get vaccinated so they won't succumb to certain illnesses. Children also get a lot of socialization to avoid risks (Stewart & Bennett, 1991). However, they are encouraged to engage in trial and error ("If at first you don't succeed, try, try again").

Native Americans tend to learn all the ramifications of a problem before attempting to solve it, if it is deemed solvable. Children are therefore taught to think before they act (Trumbull et al., 2001).

Chinese Americans who subscribe to the Confucian values of strict discipline, respect for elders, and socially desirable behavior expect children to achieve academic and social competence to make their families proud (Chao, 1994).

Skills Emphasis. Skills emphasized with children from individualistic groups can come from religious beliefs, traditional beliefs, or beliefs in self-determination. Many Euro-Americans believe that the self is "located solely within the individual and the individual is definitely separate from others. From a very young age, children are encouraged to make their own decisions" (Lustig & Koester, 1999, p. 95). They are also expected to maintain clear boundaries between the self and others. Emphasis is placed on individual achievement, self-expression, and personal choice. A tenet of Judaism is personal choice: If one chooses to live a good life, being kind to others and sharing with those less fortunate, one will experience self-reward.

Judaism is one of the world's oldest religions and the first to teach the existence of one God, giving birth to both Christianity and Islam.

Euro-Americans tend to judge achievement in terms of comparisons with the self and others: "You swam faster today than you did yesterday," or "You got the highest grade in the class on the math test." Praise is given generously, not only to reward achievement but to enhance self-esteem (Trumbull et al., 2001). Competition between groups promotes performance and "team spirit"; competition within the group promotes creativity and productivity ("The early bird catches the worm").

Euro-American parents generally teach children to accept personal responsibility for their own learning, behavior, and possessions. A sense of personal responsibility for success or failure is ingrained, as the old saying "The buck stops here" suggests (Theiderman, 1991).

A significant religious influence on the individualistic orientation and the inherent socialized skills comes from Protestantism. Recall that the Protestant ethic is the belief that salvation is achieved through hard work, thriftiness, and self-discipline: "Where there is a will, there is a way," and "God helps those who help themselves."

Chronosystem Influences on Parenting

Parents today must address questions that previous generations seldom had to face: Should we have children, and if so, how many and how far apart? Should we terminate the unexpected pregnancy or the imperfect fetus? Should we be strict or permissive? Should we stress competitiveness or cooperation? What activities should we encourage? Because society is changing so rapidly and because of new advancements in science and technology, people cannot look to experience for answers as their parents could.

Several social scientists (Bronfenbrenner, 1989; Hewlett & West, 1998) are concerned that a number of developments—many themselves beneficent—have conspired to isolate the family and to reduce drastically the number of relatives, neighbors, and other caring adults participating in the socialization of American children. Among the most significant forces are occupational mobility, the breakdown of neighborhoods, the separation of residential from business areas, consolidated school districts, separate patterns of social life for members of different age groups, and the delegation of child care to outside institutions. What today's parents lack is a support system.

In today's rapidly changing society, parents spend less time with their children. A majority of mothers hold jobs outside the home. Fathers often must travel in connection with their work and can be away for days or even weeks at a time. Parents may have meetings in the evenings and social engagements on the weekends. Various studies have found that lack of time together is perceived as the greatest threat to the family (Hochschild, 1997; Leach, 1994).

Due to the changing nature of society and its pressures on the ability of the family to function optimally, parenting today has become a "journey without a road map."

HISTORICAL TRENDS

Prior to the eighteenth century, it was not uncommon for children to be considered significant only if they contributed to their elders' welfare; no thought was given to their individual needs. If parents could not afford to care for them, they could be abandoned. Thus, parenting was adult-centered.

In colonial America, the father was the primary authority. Children were to be seen and not heard; immediate obedience was expected. Discipline was strict and children who disobeyed were believed to be wicked and sinful and so were severely punished. Tradition and religion influenced child-rearing practices: "He that spareth his rod, hateth his son: but he that loveth him chasteneth him betimes" (Proverbs 13:24), and "Train up a child in the way he should go: and when he is old, he will not depart from it" (Proverbs 22:6). There was also much emphasis on manners and courtesy (Berger, 1995). Colonial Americans viewed early childhood "as a negative period of life, a sort of necessary evil full of idle deviltry and cantankerous mischief; the child survived it and his parents endured it as best they could until late adolescence, when life hesitatingly began" (Bossard & Boll, 1954, p. 526). Childhood was regarded as a foundation period of great importance, a period of bending the twig to affect the shape of the future tree.

Beginning in the eighteenth century, there was some improvement in the way children were treated. Contributing to this reform was a reexamination of the writings of Locke, Rousseau, and Pestalozzi, who all advocated **humanism,** a system of beliefs concerned with the interests and ideals of humans rather than those of the natural or spiritual world (Berger, 1995). Specifically, the British philosopher John Locke (1632–1704) argued that the newborn's mind is a blank slate (**tabula rasa**) and that all thought develops from experience. Children are neither innately good nor innately bad. The influence of this concept on contemporary parenting has been to encourage parents and teachers to mold children's minds by providing them with optimal experiences.

Parenting was also influenced by the French philosopher Jean-Jacques Rousseau (1712–1778), who believed that children are innately good and need freedom to grow because insensitive caregivers might otherwise corrupt them. Rousseau's writings influenced Johann Pestalozzi (1746–1827), who emphasized the importance of the mother as the child's first teacher. The mother, he suggested, was more likely than other adults to be sensitive to her child's needs. That the mother was most important in the upbringing of the child was corroborated by Sunley's (1955) analysis of nineteenth-century magazines, books, and journals on child rearing.

Another influence on contemporary attitudes toward child development and parenting was psychologist G. Stanley Hall (1846–1924), who, like Rousseau, believed that young children are innately good and will grow naturally to be self-controlled adults, if not overdirected (Berger, 1995). Parenting was becoming child-centered. Thus, by the end of the nineteenth century, the parenting literature was espousing love and affection for children in order to mold their characters. Around the turn of the century, however, the discipline method, based on rewards and punishments, was advocated to mold character. *Infant Care*, published in 1914 by the Children's Bureau, recommended strict child rearing. For example, thumb sucking and masturbation were believed to damage children permanently (Wolfenstein, 1953). Thus, at the beginning of the twentieth century, the parenting literature advocated rigid scheduling for infants. Mothers were instructed to expect obedience, ignore temper tantrums, and restrict physical handling of their children (Stendler, 1950).

In the 1920s, John B. Watson's theory of **behaviorism,** which holds that only observable behavior is valid data for psychology, and Sigmund Freud's theory of personality development, which dealt with nonobservable (unconscious) forces in the mind, began to gain influence. Watson defined learning as a change in the way individuals respond to a particular situation; he argued that behavior that is reinforced or rewarded will be repeated, whereas behavior that is not reinforced will be extinguished or eliminated. Both Watson and Freud believed in the importance of the early years in setting the stage for later development. Watson advocated parental firmness early in children's lives, because behavior is conditioned by specific stimuli; if parents "give in" to bad behavior, then that behavior will persist. Thus, good habits must be conditioned from the beginning. Freud believed that harmful early experiences can harm children's development (especially when these are buried in the unconscious mind); that **fixations,** or arrested development, can occur at any time in life; and that children's growing personalities must therefore not be repressed, or else children will be inevitably emotionally scarred as adults. The scientific methods described by Watson gave credibility to behaviorism. Freud's writings regarding the need to express, rather than repress, emotions were also extremely influential.

In the 1940s, mothers were told that children should be fed when hungry and be toilet trained when they developed physical control—a significant departure from the rigid scheduling of feeding and toilet training formerly advocated. Even children's handling of their own genitals was considered natural, whereas previously parents had been warned to take every precaution to prevent it (Wolfenstein, 1953). Dr. Benjamin Spock, in his landmark 1946 publication *The Common Sense Book of Baby and Child Care,* advised parents to enjoy their children and their roles as parents. He also advocated self-regulation by children rather than strict scheduling by parents. Spock encouraged parents to develop a greater understanding of children and to be more flexible in directing their upbringing. He based his recommendations on the writings of educators such as John Dewey (who believed that children should learn by doing) and psychoanalysts such as Freud (who believed that children's psychological development occurs in natural stages and that healthy outcomes are influenced by parents).

Bigner (1979) analyzed articles on child rearing in several women's magazines from 1950 to 1970. He found that in the early 1950s physical punishment (spanking) was condoned, but that by the end of the decade it was discouraged on the grounds that physical punishment only showed children that parents could hit. Most articles encouraged self-regulation by children. Parents were advised to hold, love, and enjoy their children and to emphasize to children that they were loved. Parents were also urged to recognize individual differences and to realize that development occurs naturally, that maturation cannot be pushed. The psychologist and pediatrician Arnold Gesell's (Gesell & Ilg, 1943) extensive work influenced this view. He published norms, or average standards, of child development based on observations of children of all ages and concluded that the patterns for healthy growth were biologically programmed within children and that if the parents would relax growth would occur naturally.

Toward the end of the 1950s, after the Soviet Union's successful launching of the first satellite into space, the concern for intellectual development in children became urgent. The Swiss psychologist Jean Piaget's theories on cognitive development were of interest to professionals working with children. Piaget emphasized that knowledge comes from acting in one's environment. Thus, the importance of giving children a stimulating environment and many experiences was reinforced.

The movement from a parent-centered approach to child rearing, with its strict discipline, to a more child-centered approach, with more flexibility, is partially the result of the mass media's publicizing scientific and humanitarian views on child rearing. Interestingly, Dr. Spock revised the 1946 edition of his book on child care, which advocated a child-centered approach, to reflect a change in his attitude. The 1957 edition read, "Nowadays there seems to be more chance of a conscientious parent's getting into trouble with permissiveness than with strictness" (Spock, 1957). Spock recognized the consequences of parents focusing exclusively on what children need from them, rather than what the community will need from children when they grow up. Even though Spock maintained his belief that children's needs should be attended to, subsequent editions of his book addressed the rights of parents—children need to feel loved, yet parents have the right to demand certain standards of behavior (Spock, 1968, 1985). Other contemporary parenting views concur (Parke & Buriel, 1998).

In sum, the trend in parenting attitudes in the United States over time has swung from parent-centeredness to child-centeredness to more of a balanced approach.

FAMILY DYNAMICS

Parenting involves a continuous process of reciprocal interaction that affects both parents and children. When individuals become parents, they rediscover some of their own experiences from childhood and adolescence—for example, making snowmen, playing hopscotch, playing hide-and-seek, and running through the sprinklers on a hot day. When they become parents, their experience is expanded. Not only do children have unique ways of looking at the world (for example, they believe that the moon follows them at night when they go for a ride in the car, that dreams come through the window when they are sleeping, and that people can walk on clouds), they also open new doors for parents. My son became interested in astronomy and opened up a world of telescopes, stars, planets, and galaxies to our family. My daughter became interested in running and opened up a world of track and field to us. When children bring their work home from school, new information, ideas, and values are shared with their parents.

Like a game involving strategies and counterstrategies, parenting requires continual adaptation to children's changing capacities. As children grow, parents need to adapt to the increased amount of time they are awake. As children learn to walk, parents need to set limits for their safety. When children go to school, parents have to make decisions about achievement, friends, television, activities outside of school, and so on. When children approach adolescence, parenting involves determining which decisions are to remain the parents' and which are to be assumed by the adolescent.

Parenting is time consuming and difficult; it is also joyful and satisfying. Children are loving, open, and curious. What could be more gratifying than the first handmade card your child gives you that says "I luv u," or the first time your grown-up child asks for your advice?

Although parenting styles influence children, and children influence parenting styles, both parents and children interact in a dynamic family system that has certain influential characteristics of its own.

Children's Characteristics

Characteristics of children that influence family dynamics and parenting styles in a bidirectional way include age, temperament, gender, and the special needs, such as a disability.

Age. As children get older, parent–child interactions change. During infancy, parenting tasks are primarily feeding, changing, bathing, and comforting. As young children stay awake more, play is added to the repertoire of activities. During the second year of life, physical and verbal restraint must be introduced for children's safety. That is, they must be prevented from going into the street, eating poisonous materials, handling sharp objects, and so on.

During the preschool years, parenting techniques may expand to include reasoning, instruction, isolation ("time-out"), withdrawal of privileges (negative consequences), and reinforcement or rewards (positive consequences). As children mature during the early school years, parents may encourage them to become more responsible for their behavior by allowing them to make certain decisions and to experience both the positive and the negative consequences. For example, if a child requests a pet fish for her birthday, then the parents should allow her to be responsible for feeding it. If a child chooses to bounce a ball off the side of the house and breaks a window accidentally, then he should be responsible for paying for the damage.

As children enter adolescence, parents may deal with potential conflicts by discussion, collaborative problem solving, and compromise. For example, my son neglected to clean his room, calling it "a waste of time" to make his bed and put his things away because he would just be using them again. Because I like order and neatness, his behavior caused me to nag. After discussing his reasons for not complying with my standards and my reasons for wanting him to do so, we agreed on a compromise: The day I cleaned house, he was to tidy his room; other days, he could keep the door closed but not locked.

Researchers (McNally, Eisenberg, & Harris, 1991; Parke & Buriel, 1998) have found that, although specific parenting practices change according to children's age, basic parenting styles remain stable over time. For example, a parent might isolate a preschooler who is hitting a younger sibling until some self-control is established. The same parent might use reasoning and/or withdrawal of privileges for a school-ager who fights. Parenting practices may also change according to the situation. For example, a parent who usually gives a child instruction on how to behave in advance may resort to yelling when rushed or hurried. Thus, even though the methods may change, parents' goal of enabling children to control their own behavior and emotions remains stable.

Parenting and the Prevention of Adolescent Problem Behavior

Studies have shown that adolescents whose parents are warm, affectionate, and communicative, and who have certain standards for behavior, are less likely to abuse drugs or engage in delinquent acts or join gangs than children who do not have good parental relationships (Baumrind, 1991; Greenberger & Chen, 1996; Grotevant, 1998; Steinberg & Morris, 2001).

Adolescence is a time when parent–child relations are tested. Many of the everyday demands of family life—doing one's assigned chores, being considerate of other members, communicating, adhering to standards (coming home on time, keeping appointments, writing thank-you notes, doing homework)—can become areas of conflict.

Psychiatrist Judith Brook (Brook & Cohen, 1990) has proposed a developmental model of adolescent substance abuse. She believes that the seeds for adolescent problem behavior can be sown during early childhood if parents don't provide adequate nurturance and families are conflict-ridden. Children growing up in such families fail to identify with parental attitudes, values, and behavior. As these children approach adolescence, they lack self-control and turn to peers for immediate gratification. They thus become susceptible to drug and alcohol abuse, especially if their friends do drugs and/or drink alcohol.

When parents react negatively to adolescents' push for autonomy and become overly strict or overly permissive, the adolescents are more likely to rebel by exhibiting problem behavior (Patterson, DeBaryshe, & Ramsey, 1989).

The research also suggests that the effect of conflict between a child and one parent can be offset by a positive relationship with the other parent. Positive parent–child relationships can also negate the influence of a peer group that abuses drugs or alcohol and engages in delinquent behavior. Thus, parenting styles established in childhood impact adolescent problem behavior.

Temperament. Temperament is the combination of innate characteristics that determine individuals' sensitivity to various experiences and responsiveness to patterns of social interaction. It is a central aspect of each person's personality and has been shown to be stable over time. For example, Kagan and his colleagues (Kagan, Reznick, & Gibbons, 1989) have studied shyness and sociability. Children who were classified as shy, or inhibited, at age 21 months due to their timidness with unfamiliar people and their cautiousness in strange surroundings exhibited similar behavior when they were examined at age 7½. Children who were rated as sociable, or uninhibited, as toddlers were talkative and outgoing with strange adults and peers in unfamiliar settings at age 7½.

Temperament influences how infants respond to their caregivers and how caregivers respond to children, thereby illustrating the concept of bidirectionality. Thus, certain parenting styles may be elicited by children's temperament (Sameroff, 1994). For example, a very active child may have to be told more than once to sit still at the table or have to be removed from the table to eat alone, whereas a less active child may only have to be told, "Sit still at the dinner table so the food won't spill off the plate." Some methods of child rearing may have to be modified to suit the individual child's temperament. For example, a child who has irregular patterns of hunger is better suited to a more flexible "demand" feeding schedule, whereas a child who exhibits regularity is more suited to feeding at scheduled intervals.

In a classic longitudinal study of 136 children from infancy to adolescence (Chess & Thomas, 1987; Thomas, Chess, & Birch, 1970), nine temperamental characteristics were isolated. This model is still used by researchers today:

1. *Activity level*—the proportion of inactive periods to active ones
2. *Rhythmicity*—regularity of hunger, excretion, sleep, and wakefulness
3. *Distractibility*—the degree to which extraneous stimuli alter behavior
4. *Approach/withdrawal*—the response to a new object or person
5. *Adaptability*—the ease with which children adapt to their environments
6. *Attention span and persistence*—the amount of time devoted to an activity and the effects of distraction on the activity
7. *Intensity of reaction*—the energy of response, regardless of its quality or direction
8. *Threshold of responsiveness*—the intensity of stimulation required to evoke a response
9. *Quality of mood*—the amount of friendly, pleasant, joyful behavior, as contrasted with unpleasant, unfriendly behavior

It was found (Chess & Thomas, 1987; Thomas & Chess, 1977) that the 136 behavioral profiles were clustered in three general types of temperament. "Easy" children displayed a positive mood and regularity in body function; they were adaptable and approachable, and their reactions were moderate or low in intensity. At the other extreme, "difficult" children were slow to adapt and tended to have intense reactions and negative moods; they withdrew in new situations and had irregular body functions. Those in the middle, the "slow-to-warm-up" children, initially withdrew but slowly adapted to new situations; they had low activity levels and tended to respond with low intensity. These temperamental types could be recognized by the second or third month of life.

Although individual temperament seems to be established at birth, environmental factors play an important role in whether a person's style of behavior can be modified. Regarding this interplay of heredity and environment, if the two influences blend together well, one can expect healthy development of the child; if they are incompatible, behavioral problems are almost certain to ensue (Thomas & Chess, 1977, 1980).

Thomas and Chess (1977) recommended that parents adjust parenting styles to their offspring's temperament, although they emphasize that "a constructive approach by the parents to the child's temperament does not mean an acceptance or encouragement of all this youngster's behavior in all situations" (p. 188). Difficult children need consistent, patient, and objective parents who can handle their instability. For example, instead of expecting very active, distractible children to concentrate for long periods of time on their homework, parents can reward them for shorter periods of work with pleasurable breaks in between, as long as the task is finished. Slow-to-warm-up children do best with a moderate amount of encouragement coupled with patience; parents and teachers should let these children adjust to change at their own pace. Easy children tend to adapt well to various styles of child rearing. Thomas and Chess refer to the accommodation of parenting styles to children's temperaments as **goodness-of-fit.**

Infant temperament determines what kinds of interactions parents and infants are most likely to find mutually rewarding. For example, difficult children are more likely to accept change and enjoy new experiences if their parents are accepting, encouraging, and patient rather than critical, demanding, and impatient. Just because infants are born with certain temperaments does not preclude them from adapting to certain behaviors demanded of them; the key is how the parents frame those demands.

Initially, temperament mediates environmental input and individual responsiveness by setting the tone for interaction. Children who are sociable will communicate a different mood when they encounter people than will children who are more reserved. Next, temperamental differences determine the kinds of behaviors children initiate. Active children will experience more things because they are constantly "on the go," and they will probably have more social interactions because of their activities. Their temperamental differences may either encourage or discourage the responses of others. For example, if a parent accepts a child's frequent emotional expressions of joy, sadness, or even anger as normal behavior, that parent is likely to reward those behaviors by being attentive. But if the parent disapproves of overt displays of emotion, that parent is likely to punish those expressions by disapproval (Buss & Plomin, 1984).

Not only are children's temperaments influential, but parents' temperament affects their parenting styles and the way they respond to their children's behavior as well (Lerner, 1993). For instance, an active parent may be impatient with an inactive infant, a sociable parent may feel rejected by a withdrawn child, and a reserved parent may feel intimidated by an aggressive child. Thus, parents, due to their own temperaments, may encourage, ignore, or discourage certain exhibitions of their children's temperament (Buss & Plomin, 1984).

Points to Ponder

Heredity is partially responsible for our abilities and interests. Some believe that we seek out certain environments due to our genes. For example, someone who has musical ability might be involved in playing an instrument, singing, and listening to music. When that person creates a home environment for his or her child, will music be part of the parenting scene?

Gender. Parents provide different socializing environments for boys and for girls (Ruble & Martin, 1998), most likely due to their own socialization. Parents give children different names, different clothing, and different toys. Fathers, in particular, are more likely to act differently toward sons and daughters than are mothers (Fagot, 1995; Huston, 1983). Also, fathers tend to be more demanding of their children than are mothers (Doherty, Kouneski, & Erikson, 1998; Lamb, 1981). In one study, parents of school-age children were interviewed regarding parenting techniques used with their sons and daughters. Parents reported being more punishing and less rewarding with same-gendered children. Parents of girls emphasized cooperation and politeness; parents of boys emphasized independent and self-reliant behaviors (Power, 1987).

The types of play activities that are encouraged differ for boys and for girls. There is also some evidence that parents encourage girls to be more dependent, affectionate, and emotional than boys. In addition, as boys get older, they are permitted more freedom than girls—for example, they are allowed to be away from home without supervision more than are girls (Huston, 1983). Gender-role socialization is discussed in more detail in Chapter 12.

Presence of a Special Need. The presence of a special need, such as a disability, in a child influences family dynamics and parenting styles. Parental reactions to the diagnosis of a disability vary enormously, but can include grief, depression, and/or guilt (Meadow-Orlans, 1995). The nature, onset, and severity of the disability, as well as the availability of support systems, are factors in how the parents cope.

Another common reaction when a child is identified as disabled, is anger—anger with God, fate, society, professionals, oneself, the other parent, or even the child. In addition, parents may experience frustration as they seek an accurate diagnosis of or referral for a child who has a problem that is not so readily identifiable.

Society expects parents to love their children. When a parent experiences negative feelings at the birth of a child, that parent commonly feels guilt. Unable to accept feelings of rejection or hostility, this parent may blame him- or herself for experiencing emotions unbefitting a good and loving parent, especially with a child so in need of love and special care. Guilt may also be related to the parent's feeling that something he or she did, or failed to do, caused the child's disability.

Parenting is a difficult and complicated task, and parenting children with disabilities is even more so. Although most people will tolerate a 2-year-old's temper

Parenting a child with disabilities is a challenge.

tantrum in a grocery store, they are apt to stare at, or even make remarks about, a 10-year-old behaving in the same manner. Many parents have difficulty from time to time finding responsible babysitters, but parents of children with disabilities have even more. It is a challenge to change the diapers on a preadolescent, or care for a blind preschooler, or calm down a hyperactive child.

Not only is parenting children with disabilities more complicated and difficult, it is also more likely to cause major psychological stress in parents, resulting in disturbed family interactions. According to Ann and H. Rutherford Turnbull (1997), the parents of a child born with disabilities may lose self-esteem. This can be transmitted to the child as overprotection, rejection, or abuse. The child may experience ambivalence, sometimes feeling love and sometimes anger. The expenses and frustrations of parenting a child with disabilities can overburden anyone, as can worries about the future of their child. Some parents dedicate themselves totally to their child with disabilities, which can lead to marital conflicts, neglect of other children, and family disruption.

Children with disabilities also have some psychological hurdles to overcome. They must adapt to being different: "Why do I have to use crutches?" "Why am I this way and my brother isn't?" "Will I still have to use crutches when I grow up?" These children may feel guilty about the inconveniences they perceive themselves to have caused—the financial burden (for example, the cost of special equipment), the extra work and care, and the inability to measure up to parental aspirations. And the attention given children with disabilities may be resented by siblings, who may make these children feel guilty.

Siblings may also experience emotions such as sorrow, anger, and guilt. In addition, they may feel embarrassment and resentment and, as a result, not want to be identified as a relative of the child with disabilities. According to one study on siblings of children with disabilities (Simeonsson & Bailey, 1986), the most central concern is avoiding identification with them. In addition to being ashamed, siblings fear others questioning their normality, and they may wonder about themselves (Bernstein, 1984).

Siblings may also resent the amount of time and/or money directed toward a brother or sister with disabilities. They may feel deprived of attention or resources they want and need. Although sibling responses to a brother or sister with disabilities may be negative in certain respects, positive reactions are common, too. These include increased maturity, compassion, tolerance for individual differences, patience, sense of responsibility, and appreciation for family and health (Heward, 1999).

Family Characteristics

Characteristics that influence family dynamics and consequent parenting style are size (number of siblings), configuration (birth order, spacing, and gender of siblings), and parents' stage of life, marital quality, and abilities to cope with stress (Cowan, Powell, & Cowan, 1998).

Size.   Both parents and children are affected by the number of children in the family. The more children there are, the more family members interact, but the less likely there is to be individual parent–child interaction. Children in large families may have many resources to draw on for company, playmates, and emotional security. They may also have increased responsibility in the form of doing chores or caring for younger siblings. Parents in larger families, especially those with limited living space and economic resources, tend to be more authoritarian, more likely to use physical punishment, and less likely to explain their rules than are the parents of smaller families. The emphasis is on the family as a whole rather than the individuals within it (Bossard & Boll, 1956; Elder & Bowerman, 1963; Furman, 1995). However, the effects of family size on parenting style are mediated by parental education, occupation, social class, intactness of the family, and ethnic orientation (Blake, 1989).

Configuration.   Not only does the number of children in a family affect child-rearing practices, but the spacing and gender of the siblings also influence parent–child interactions. With the birth of each sibling comes different temperaments, and new relationships for parents to handle.

A number of studies (Furman, 1995; Sutton-Smith, 1982) have shown the parenting practices of first-born and later-born siblings to be different even when each was the same age. Firstborns received more attention, affection, and verbal stimulation than their later-born siblings. They also were disciplined more restrictively and were coerced more by their parents. More mature behavior was expected of them than of their siblings.

Research has also shown that mothers helped their firstborns in solving problems more frequently than they did their later-borns. And mothers of firstborns applied more pressure for achievement than they did on their later-borns (Zajonc, 1976).

It is much more difficult to predict the sibling effects on later-borns than first-borns because, with later-borns, there are more variables to take into account, such as number of siblings, the space between them, and the gender distribution. For example, the interactions with parents of the youngest male born after two females differ from the interactions of the youngest male born after two males. The patterns change, too, if there are 6 years between siblings versus 2 years.

Dunn (1988, 1992, 1993) has examined the socialization effects siblings have on each other. Whereas most such studies investigate bidirectional influences of siblings on parenting behavior and differential parenting on siblings (McHale, Updegraff, Jackson-Newsom, Tucker, & Crouter, 2000), Dunn added the perspective on social understanding—children's recognition of the feelings of others, their ability to interpret and anticipate the behavior and relationships of others, and their comprehension of the prohibitions and accepted practices in their developmental contexts (such as the family)—to what goes on inside families. Siblings provide opportunities for cooperation, competition, empathy, aggression, leading, following, and so on. Older siblings function as tutors or supervisors of younger brothers or sisters (Parke & Buriel, 1998). Dunn has shown that from age 18 months on children understand how to hurt, comfort, and exacerbate a sibling's pain. They understand what is allowed or disapproved of in their families. They even can anticipate the responses of adults to their own and others' misbehavior, and can comment on and ask about the causes of others' actions and feelings. Dunn concludes that children's ability to understand other people and the social world is closely linked to their activities and relationships with siblings and parents. It is important that parents monitor sibling interactions and intervene in conflicts. By explaining the concepts of rights and fairness, and by interpreting differences in abilities according to age, parents can contribute to positive relationships between siblings. A longitudinal study of sibling influences on gender development in middle childhood and early adolescence confirms the modeling influence of older siblings on younger siblings' gender-related behavior (McHale, Updegraff, Helms-Erikson, & Crouter, 2001).

What about only-children? Are they more pressured to grow up or are they babied? Do they suffer socially and emotionally from not having sibling relationships, with their closeness, compromises, and conflicts?

Only-children experience more parent–child interaction, and their relationships with their parents are more positive and affectionate than those of children with siblings (Falbo & Polit, 1986). In a study of 2-year-olds interacting with an unfamiliar peer in a laboratory room, Snow, Jacklin, and Maccoby (1981) observed that only-children were more advanced socially than children with siblings in that they showed more positive behavior, as well as assertive-aggressive behavior; second-borns showed the least. Only-children have also been shown to perform better academically than children who have siblings (Falbo & Polit, 1986).

Thus, being an only-child does not seem to be harmful to development; rather, it may be beneficial. There are disadvantages, however, such as too much pressure from parents to succeed, feelings of loneliness, or a lack of help in caring for aging parents.

Parents' Life Stage, Marital Quality, and Ability to Cope with Stress. The need for parenting practices to change in response to children changing over time has already been discussed. According to Ellen Galinsky (1981), parents go through six stages of changes in their expectations of and practices with children from infancy to adolescence: (1) image making, (2) nurturing, (3) authority, (4) interpretation, (5) interdependence, and (6) departure. Parents, too, are in the process of developing over time (Cowan et al., 1998). As they get older, parents must cope with health concerns, career changes, responsibilities toward their parents, and so on.

A generational area of research is the impact of parents' childhood and adulthood relationships with their parents on their own parenting practices (Cowan et al., 1998). For example, mothers who reported having had an insecure childhood relationship with their parents have less effective parenting strategies with their preschool children than mothers who reported having had a secure relationship. Apparently, having a good "working" model to emulate influences parenting.

Marital quality contributes to children's development in that the parents form a coparenting alliance, cooperating with and supporting each other (Cowan et al., 1998). Parents who are united are less subject to "manipulation" by their children. What child hasn't tried to get one parent to "give in" when the other parent has refused a request?

Research shows that children whose fathers are involved in their care do better socially and academically than children whose fathers play a marginal parenting role (Coontz, 1997). McHale (1995) found that marital distress observed in a two-way problem-solving discussion was associated with hostile-competitive coparenting with sons and differing levels of involvement with daughters.

Marital conflict culminating in divorce disrupts relationships among all members of the family (Kelly, 2000). As was discussed in Chapter 3, divorce affects the parenting style of both the custodial and noncustodial parent, with the custodial parent (usually the mother) becoming more authoritarian and restrictive, and the noncustodial parent (usually the father) becoming more permissive and indulgent, at least initially. Divorce also affects children's behavior, with children becoming more aggressive, rebellious, and manipulative.

There is evidence that stressors outside the family—such as economics, work problems, illness, and peer relationships—disrupt the parent–child relationship, thereby interfering with children's optimal development (Patterson & Capaldi, 1991). Conversely, the availability of social support has a buffering effect and lessens the strain (Cowan et al., 1998).

Parents who are tired, worried, or ill, or who feel they have lost control of their lives, are likely to be impatient, lacking in understanding, and unwilling to reason with their children. To see whether and how stress affects child rearing, a stressful situation was created in which parents were observed interacting with their toddlers and preschool-age children. A laboratory playroom was equipped with play materials that were complex enough to require the children to request help. It was also equipped with such items as a breakable vase, a filled ashtray, and a stack of index cards. The parents were given mental tasks to perform while the children played in the room. It was found that when the parents were preoccupied with their task they became less responsive to their preschool children (less likely to play with them, talk to them, or help them) and more interfering, critical, and authoritarian with their toddlers (Zussman, 1980).

What are the effects of real-life stress on parental interaction with children—for example, divorce, illness, death, abuse, or financial problems? In one study (Patterson, 1982), the researcher obtained daily reports from a group of mothers concerning the occurrence of crises of varying magnitudes, including an unexpectedly large bill, a car breaking down, the illness of a family member, and a quarrel between spouses. The mothers were asked to note their moods at the time. Family interactions were also observed. The number of crises experienced was found to be a positive predictor of maternal irritability. It was hypothesized that the more often a mother became irritable, the less likely she was to deal with family problem solving. In addition, as unsolved problems accumulated, stress levels increased. Further, disrupted family interaction can lead to an intolerant discipline style, which, in turn, fosters antisocial behavior in children (Patterson & Dishion, 1988).

Unemployment and consequent economic deprivation also increases family tension. A considerable body of research shows an association between paternal job loss and intrafamily violence, such as partner abuse and child abuse (Luster & Okagaki, 1993; McLoyd, 1998). The possible explanations offered are the greater amount of time the father spends at home, which increases the possibility of conflict; a possible increase in the father's discipline role; a reaffirmation of the father's power in order to save face; and tension resulting from diminished economic resources.

However, crises or stress do not always disrupt family functioning. The type of stressor, the personalities and relationships within the family, and the presence of social support networks outside the nuclear family are influential factors (Cochran, 1993; Yogman & Brazelton, 1986).

Parenting Styles

Parenting style encompasses the emotional climate in which child-rearing behaviors are expressed (Cowan et al., 1998). Parenting styles are usually classified by the dimensions of acceptance/responsiveness (warmth/sensitivity) and demandingness/control (permissiveness/restrictiveness) (Maccoby & Martin, 1983). Parents who are accepting and responsive give affection, provide encouragement, and are sensitive to their children's needs. Parents who are unaccepting and unresponsive are rejecting, critical, and insensitive to their children's needs. Parents who are demanding and controlling set rules for children and monitor their compliance. Parents who are undemanding and uncontrolling make few demands on children and allow them much autonomy. See Figure 4.3 for variations on the major dimensions of parenting styles.

MICROSYSTEM INFLUENCES: BETWEEN PARENT AND CHILD

A microsystem effect on children is the bidirectional parent–child relationship within the family. Research has shown that parenting styles have an impact on children's behavior, and vice versa, in such areas as attachment, self-regulation, prosocial behavior, competence, and achievement motivation. **Attachment** is an affectional tie that one person forms to another, binding them together in space and enduring over time. **Self-regulation** is the process of bringing one's emotions, thoughts, and/or behavior under control. **Prosocial behavior** refers to actions that benefit another person. **Competence** involves behavior that is socially responsible, independent, friendly, cooperative, dominant, achievement oriented, and purposeful.

Figure 4.3

Dimensions of Parenting Styles

Source: Based on Maccoby and Martin, 1983.

| | | Acceptance/Responsiveness | |
		High	Low
Demandingness/Control	High	**Authoritative:** Reasonable demands, consistently enforced, with sensitivity and responsiveness to the child	**Authoritarian:** Many rules and demands; few explanations and little sensitivity to the child's needs
	Low	**Permissive:** Few rules and demands; the child is allowed freedom and indulgence	**Uninvolved:** Few rules and demands; parents are uninvolved and insensitive to the child's needs

Achievement motivation refers to the tendency to approach challenging tasks with confidence of mastery.

Parenting styles are usually described in terms of three dimensions or degrees: (1) **authoritative** (democratic), (2) **authoritarian** (parent-centered), and (3) **permissive** (child centered). (See Appendix B for more detailed definitions of the basic parenting styles.) Another parenting style dimension, **uninvolved** (disengaged), is discussed later in the context of inappropriate parenting practices. It must be realized that parents never simply fit into one category or go to one extreme, rather, they are a mixture. Parenting is so complex that often many factors—the particular situation (including stress); the child's age, gender, birth order and siblings; the child's temperament, including how the child responds to parental demands; the parent's previous experience (Dunn, Davies, O'Connor, & Sturgess, 2000), including how the parent was parented; and the parent's temperament—influence parenting. To better understand the effects of parenting styles on children's behavior, researchers base their findings on the parenting styles observed most frequently in various situations.

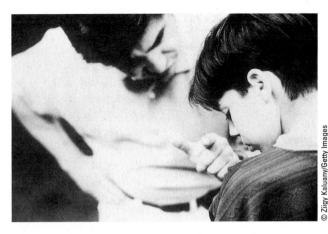

The scolding a child gets from a parent for wrongdoing exemplifies the authoritarian parenting style.

Attachment

As mentioned in Chapter 2, attachment is an outcome of sensitive, responsive caregiving. It is the basis for socialization in that infants who are securely attached are willing to comply with parental standards.

The verbal give-and-take between this mother and daughter exemplifies the authoritative parenting style.

Parenting behavior toward infants influences attachment. When a parent responds appropriately, being sensitive and responsive to the infant's signals, the infant forms a secure attachment; when a parent responds inappropriately, inconsistently, or not at all, the infant tends to form an insecure attachment. According to Ainsworth and colleagues (Ainsworth, Blehar, Waters, & Wall, 1978), appropriately responsive caregiving involves paying attention to the infant's signals, interpreting them accurately, giving appropriate feedback, and responding promptly (enabling the infant to learn that his or her stimuli cause a response).

Parents of securely attached infants also synchronize their interactions according to the infant's activity (DeWolff & van IJzendoorn, 1997). When the infant is alert and active, they stimulate. When the infant is fussy, they soothe. When the infant is tired, they put him or her to sleep.

Parents of an insecurely attached infant may ignore his or her signals or respond ineffectively or inappropriately. For example, a mother may give her infant a bottle or her breast when she or he is hungry, but be talking on the phone or reading rather than gazing at the infant to adjust to her or his needs.

To measure the quality of attachment in infants age 1–2, a classic experiment, "the Strange Situation" (Ainsworth et al., 1978), is commonly used. In the Strange Situation, the parent brings the child to a laboratory playroom equipped with toys: Does the infant explore the room using the parent as a secure base? The parent leaves the room briefly: Does the infant continue to explore, do nothing, or cry? A stranger enters the room: Does the infant ignore the stranger, seek comfort, or cry? The stranger leaves and the parent returns: How does the infant react?

The following are types of attachment that have been observed in the Strange Situation:

- *Secure attachment (secure).* The infant actively explores the environment in the mother's presence, is upset when she leaves, and seeks contact when she returns (the infant may accept the stranger's attention when the mother is present).
- *Resistant attachment (insecure).* The infant stays close to the mother, doesn't explore, becomes upset when the mother leaves, is wary of strangers, and resists physical contact with the mother when she returns.
- *Avoidant attachment (insecure).* The infant shows little distress when the mother leaves, may ignore or avoid the stranger, and ignores the mother when she returns.
- *Disorganized/disoriented attachment (insecure).* The infant is very upset by the strange situation and appears confused about whether to approach or avoid the stranger; when the mother returns, the infant may seek contact and then withdraw (Main & Solomon, 1990).

The significance of the quality of attachment is that it correlates with later intellectual and social development (Lamb, Hwang, Ketterlinus, & Fracasso, 1999). Securely attached infants tend to be more attentive, curious, and confident, exploring various physical environments, exhibiting more social competence with peers, and being more compliant with adults in the preschool years.

Self-Regulation and Prosocial Behavior

Baumrind (1966, 1967, 1971a, 1973) studied parenting practices by observing the behavior of preschool children, and rating their behavior according to degree of impetuosity, self-reliance, aggressiveness, withdrawal, and self-control.

The parents of groups of preschool children were observed and interviewed to determine how their parenting styles differed. Baumrind found that the parents of so-called competent, contented children were controlling and demanding, as well as being warm, rational, and receptive to the child's communication. She labeled this combination of high control and positive encouragement of the child's autonomous and independent strivings "authoritative." Parents of so-called withdrawn, discontented children were detached, controlling, and somewhat less warm than the other parents. Baumrind labeled this group "authoritarian." Parents of so-called immature, impulsive children were noncontrolling, nondemanding, and relatively warm. Baumrind labeled this group "permissive" (see Table 4.1).

Later studies (Brophy, 1989; Forman & Kochanska, 2001; Hart, DeWolf, & Burts, 1992) offer supported for Baumrind's findings that parenting style affects children's behavior. For example, children of authoritarian parents showed little independence and scored in the middle range on social responsibility. Children of permissive parents conspicuously lacked social responsibility and were not very independent. Children of authoritative parents were independent and socially responsible. In sum, children of affectionate, responsive parents want to please them and so are motivated to learn and behave according to parental expectations.

According to Baumrind, both the authoritarian and permissive parents in her studies had unrealistic beliefs about young children. Whereas the strict or authoritarian

Table 4.1

Relationship of Parenting Styles to Children's Behavior
Sources: Based on Baumrind, 1967, 1971a,b, 1991.

PARENTING STYLE	PARENTS' CHARACTERISTICS	CHILDREN'S BEHAVIOR
AUTHORITATIVE (DEMOCRATIC)	Acts controlling but flexible Is demanding but rational Is warm Is receptive to child's communication Values discipline, self-reliance, and uniqueness	Is self-reliant and self-controlled Is explorative Acts content Cooperates
AUTHORITARIAN (ADULT-CENTERED)	Exercises strict self-control (self-will curbed by punitive measures) Evaluates child's behavior and attitudes according to absolute standards Values obedience, respect for authority, and tradition	Acts discontented Seems aimless Is withdrawn, fearful, and distrustful
PERMISSIVE (CHILD-CENTERED)	Is noncontrolling and nondemanding Accepts the child's impulses Consults with child on policies	Lacks self-reliance Acts impulsive and aggressive Is hardly explorative Has poor self-control
UNINVOLVED (DETACHED AND WITHDRAWN)	Is noncontrolling and nondemanding Is indifferent to child's point of view and activities	Has deficits in attachment, cognition, emotional and social skills, and behavior Exercises poor self-control Has low self-esteem

parents viewed their children's behavior as constrained, the permissive parents tended to see their children's behavior as natural and refreshing. Neither group seemed to take into account the children's stages of development—for example, the desire in early childhood to model parental behavior or the inability in early childhood to reason when given a parental command. Thus, Baumrind and others (Steinberg, Mounts, Lamborn, & Dornbusch, 1994) endorsed the authoritative parenting style for adapting to the Euro-American values of independence, individualism, achievement, and self-regulation. Authoritative parents take into account both their children's needs and their own before deciding how to deal with a given situation. They exert control over their children's behavior when necessary, yet they respect their children's need to make their own decisions. Reasoning is used to explain parenting policies, and communication from the children is encouraged. Children experience democracy at home.

Most earlier parenting research took place with young children, but more recently, studies that include adolescents in order to reveal the long-term effects of parenting styles have been implemented (Baumrind, 1991; Holmbeck, Paikoff, & Brooks-Gunn, 1995). Dornbusch and colleagues (Dornbusch, Ritter, Herbert, Roberts, & Fraleigh, 1987) found that authoritative parenting is positively correlated with adolescent school performance, whereas authoritarian and permissive parenting are negatively correlated. Steinberg and colleagues (Steinberg, Elman, & Mounts, 1989; Steinberg et al., 1994) confirmed the relationship between authoritative parenting and academic performance. They explained it as being due to the effects of authoritativeness on the development of a healthy sense of autonomy and, more specifically, on the development of a healthy psychological orientation toward work. Thus, authoritative parenting influences not only how children behave in the early years but also how they deal with responsibility in adolescence.

Authoritative parenting is *not* the norm among various ethnic groups in the United States and other countries. More common is the authoritarian style utilized by Asian Americans, Hispanic Americans, and African Americans (Greenfield & Suzuki, 1998). Certain conditions, such as lacking social supports or living in dangerous neighborhoods, may make strict discipline necessary to protect children from becoming involved in antisocial activities (Brody & Flor, 1998; Ogbu, 1994).

Whereas authoritarian parenting is perceived by Americans and Europeans to be strict and regimented, stressing adult domination, it is perceived by Chinese people to be a means of training *(chaio shun)* and governing *(guan)* children in an involved and physically close way (Chao, 1994). The Chinese concept of authoritarianism has its roots in the Confucian emphasis on hierarchical relationships and social order. Standards exist, not to dominate children, but to preserve the integrity of the family unit and assure harmonious relations with others (Greenfield & Suzuki, 1998). Thus, Baumrind's definition of authoritarian parenting (see Appendix B) and child development outcomes (discontent, withdrawal, distrust, lack of instrumental competence) do *not* always apply cross-culturally.

Competence and Achievement Motivation

Burton White (1971) and his colleagues at Harvard (White & Watts, 1973) studied the relationship between parenting styles and the development of competence versus incompetence in preschoolers. First, they had preschool teachers rate their children, age 3–6, representing different socioeconomic statuses, as competent or incompetent (see Table 4.2). Then, to find out when the differences in competence

CHARACTERISTICS OF COMPETENT CHILDREN	CHARACTERISTICS OF INCOMPETENT CHILDREN
Get attention in socially acceptable ways	Remain unnoticed or are disruptive
Use adults as resources	Need a lot of direction to complete a task
Get along well with others	Have difficulty getting along with others
Plan and carry out complicated tasks	Lack the ability to anticipate consequences
Use and understand complex sentences	Have a simplistic vocabulary

Table 4.2

The Harvard Preschool Project: Differences in Learning

appeared, the researchers went into the homes of the competent and incompetent children who had younger infant siblings, in order to observe mother–child interactions from infancy to age 3.

No differences in competency were found among newborns who were siblings of the competent and incompetent children. Yet by 10 months of age, differences in competency began to show up; and by age 2, and often as early as 18 months, children could be classified as competent or incompetent. What is so significant about the period of development between 10 and 18 months? This is the time when children begin to talk, walk, explore, and assert themselves. It is during this time that the parenting style is revealed, a good example of the bidirectionality of the parent–child relationship.

How did the parenting styles differ? The mothers of the competent children designed a safe physical environment at home so their children could explore and discover things on their own. They also provided interesting things to manipulate—pots and spoons as well as toys. Surprisingly, these mothers spent no more than 10 percent of their time deliberately interacting with their children, yet they were always "on call" when needed. They made themselves available to share in their children's exciting discoveries, answer their questions, or help them in an activity for a few minutes while they went about their daily routines. They enjoyed their children and were patient, energetic, and tolerant of messes, accidents, and natural curiosity. They set limits on behavior and were firm and consistent in their discipline. The mothers of the competent children used distraction with infants under age 1, distraction and physical removal of either the child or the object from age 1 to 1½, and distraction, physical distance, and firm words after age 1½.

The mothers of the incompetent children were diverse. Some spent little time with their children; they were overwhelmed by their daily struggles, and their homes were disorganized. Others spent a great deal of time with their children, acting overprotective and pushing their children to learn. Still others provided for their children materially, such as giving them toys, but restricted their children's instinct to explore by ruling certain places and possessions out of bounds. The mothers of the incompetent children used playpens and gates extensively.

In sum, White's research shows that human competence develops between 10 and 18 months, and it is the parenting style that fosters competence. This parenting style includes arranging the environment, sharing enthusiasm with children, having a lot of energy, setting reasonable limits according to children's developmental level, and being available as a resource when needed. According to White (1995, p. 4), "The informal education that families provide for their children makes more of an impact on a child's total educational development than the formal educational system." Such an informal initial education essentially enables children to "learn how to learn," or be motivated to achieve (White, 1995). Research on school-age children confirms the connection between parenting style and competence/achievement in school (Grolnick & Ryan, 1989).

To assess the relationship of the environment provided by families to the achievement motivation and consequent intellectual development of children, Caldwell, Bradley, and colleagues (Bradley, Caldwell, & Rock, 1990; Caldwell & Bradley, 1984) developed an assessment scale called HOME (Home Observation for the Measurement of the Environment), which contained 45 items in six areas:

1. *Emotional and verbal responsiveness.* The parent responded to the child's vocalizations with verbal responses.
2. *Avoidance of restriction and punishment.* The parent did not interfere with the child's actions or prohibit him or her more than three times during the observation.
3. *Organization of the physical and temporal environment.* The child's play environment was accessible to her or him and was safe.
4. *Provision of appropriate play materials.* The child had toys that were safe, and age-appropriate, and that stimulated play.
5. *Parental interaction with the child.* The parent kept the child within visual range and looked at, touched, or talked to him or her frequently.
6. *Opportunities for variety in daily stimulation.* The parent read stories or plays games with the child.

Studies examining the relation between young preschoolers HOME scores and their IQ scores, as well as their later academic achievement, showed a strong positive correlation (Bradley & Caldwell, 1984; Bradley et al., 1990). Also, as White's group discovered, the most critical time for influencing a children's achievement motivation and intellectual development is the first 2 years of life.

Does the same relationship between home environment and children's achievement motivation and intellectual development apply in non-Western cultures? To find out, Sigman and colleagues (1988) observed the home interactions experienced by 110 Embu children age 15–30 months in a rural Kenyan community. The results were similar to those of White and Watts, and Bradley, Caldwell, and Rock. That is, children who were talked to frequently, whose vocalizations were responded to, and who engaged in sustained social interactions passed more items on the Bayley Scales of Infant Development (a common test of infant perceptual, motor, and memory abilities) at 24 and 30 months than did those who did not receive such attention. Performance on specific items (responding to a sound, building a tower of cubes, naming a picture) is compared to norms or averages for same-age children. Children who were carried a great deal between 15 and 30 months of age scored poorly. The researchers suggest that carrying a child after he or she can walk may restrict exploration of the environment.

MESOSYSTEM INFLUENCES: BETWEEN PARENT AND OTHERS

The impact of parental socialization techniques is enhanced by supportive links with other microsystems, such as the school and the community (Bronfenbrenner & Morris, 1998) (see Table 4.3). Collaborative values are more likely to lead to positive child outcomes than are conflicted values. When family and school or community values differ, the child is at risk for school failure, delinquency, and substance abuse (Wang, 2000). An example of where family and community values, especially those of the business community, are likely to differ is in the amount of consumerism thrust at children via advertising, promotional games and rewards, and displays of products.

CHILD CHARACTERISTICS Age Temperament (easy, slow-to-warm-up, difficult) Gender Presence of a special need	
FAMILY CHARACTERISTICS Size (number of siblings) Configuration (birth order, spacing, gender of siblings) Marital quality Abilities to cope with stress	

COMMUNITY CHARACTERISTICS
Supportive social environments
   Informal network—"gemeinschaft" relationships
   Formal network—"gesellschaft" relationships	

Table 4.3

Ecological Influences on Parenting Styles

School

Families' links to schools via parent education, parent–teacher conferences, and parental participation in school activities can have positive impacts on families (Epstein, 1995). Adolescents whose parents take time to talk to them about school, homework, and activities, and who show support for and confidence in their abilities, are achievement oriented (Wang & Wildman, 1995). Aspects of family involvement in schools are discussed in Chapters 6 and 7.

An example of how the school and families can work together is when parents and teachers plan a special graduation party or event that only those students not partaking of alcohol or drugs can attend. Similarly, parents and teachers might work together to devise a plan for consumer education for children so they learn how to spend money wisely and don't feel they have to compete with their peers for possessions. This plan might include giving lessons in comparative shopping, studying advertising techniques, and reaching consensus on the role of allowances as a reward for chores accomplished.

Community

The community is considered here to include social environments outside the family context of parenting. These environments can be supportive in that they help parents cope with stress (Crnic & Acevedo, 1995). Relatives and friends are examples of *informal* supports; psychologists and employers are examples of *formal* supports. Each of these types of social support system can provide instrumental physical and financial support, emotional support, and informational support (Bugental & Goodnow, 1998). Formal support systems are discussed in Chapter 10.

The neighborhood in which a family resides can influence parenting practices in terms of how the family responds to various neighborhood ecologies (Bugental & Goodnow, 1998), such as rural or urban, safe or unsafe, or stable or mobile. It has been found that, when parents perceive their neighborhoods to be dangerous and low in social control, they place more restrictions on their children's activities (O'Neil & Parke, 1997). To illustrate, residence in a neighborhood characterize by high levels of crime, low levels of economic opportunity, poor transportation, and weak marital support can impact a single mother's commitment to seek employment and find child care (Duncan & Raudenbush, 2001). In contrast, parents in lower-risk neighborhoods with neighbors who have similar norms, expectations, and values related to child rearing are less likely to need so many restrictions (Parke & Buriel, 1998), because they feel connected and are more likely to intervene for the common good (Small & Supple, 2001).

Appropriate Parenting Practices

Appropriate parenting practices involve knowledge of child development—what a child is capable of physically, emotionally, cognitively, and socially—as well as preventive and corrective methods for misbehavior. An objective and standardized risk assessment instrument, Child at Risk Field (CARF), is used by child protection agencies to define parenting practices on a continuum from appropriate at one end to inappropriate at the other. Appropriate parenting is that "which takes into account the child's age capacity; possesses reasonable expectations for the child; understands and acts on the child's strengths/limitations/needs; uses varied and acceptable disciplinary approaches; provides basic care, nurturing, and support; demonstrates self-control" (Depanfilis, Holder, Corey, & Olson, 1986, p. 273).

The National Institute of Child Health and Human Development (2002) has put the results of decades of parenting research into an easy-to-read booklet, "Adventures in Parenting," which enables parents to make informed decisions based on the applicability of child development principles to their children. The main principles for parents are to (1) respond to children in an appropriate manner, (2) prevent risky behavior or problems before they arise, (3) monitoring children's contact with the surrounding world, (4) mentor children to support and

Mother and son exhibit close physical contact and face-to-face interaction.

© Myrleen Ferguson Cate/Getty Images

encourage desired behaviors, and (5) model their own behavior to provide a consistent and positive example for children.

DEVELOPMENTAL APPROPRIATENESS

Developmental appropriateness involves knowledge of children's normal growth patterns and individual differences. Appropriate parenting practices are influenced by parents' understanding of what is developmentally appropriate behavior in their children. Appropriate parenting practices can also reflect a knowledge of socialization methods (described in Chapter 2). For example, when is it appropriate to use guidance, a preventative socialization method, as opposed to discipline, a corrective socialization method?

Understanding why children misbehave can help parents choose the appropriate method. Children sometimes misbehave because they are tired, hungry, uncomfortable, or sick. Sometimes children don't understand what is expected of them or why something they did was wrong. Children may react to parental demands with anger, such as when they are told they can't have the candy displayed at the supermarket. They may misbehave when they are fearful, such as when they are left in a new and strange place. They may be jealous when a new sibling arrives and misbehave to get attention. They may feel hurt or disappointed when adults let them down, such as by not fulfilling a promise or even divorcing, and seek revenge.

GUIDANCE AND DISCIPLINE

Guidance involves direction, demonstration, supervision, and influence; the person who guides "leads the way." **Discipline** involves punishment, correction, and training that develops self-control; the person who disciplines enforces obedience or order. Both guidance and discipline are necessary socialization methods in child rearing. Sensitivity to the situation, the child's temperament, and the desired outcome are some of the factors involved in which method is appropriate at a particular time (see Figure 4.4).

Inappropriate Parenting Practices

Inappropriate parenting practices include uninvolved parenting, and child maltreatment. Uninvolved parenting is characterized by aloofness and distancing. Usually, parents who display this style are so overwhelmed by their own stressors and problems that they have little energy left to devote to child rearing (Maccoby & Martin, 1983). With regard to children of uninvolved parents, preschoolers exhibit aggressive and externalizing behaviors, such as temper tantrums; school-agers perform poorly academically and display conduct disorders; and adolescents tend to be hostile, selfish, and rebellious, and to commit antisocial acts, such as delinquency and vandalism, and to abuse substances (Weiss & Schwarz, 1996).

Inappropriate parenting, as objectively defined by the CARF to determine potential risk, is that which "is based on the parent's needs; demonstrates expectations that are impossible for the child to meet; ignores the child's strengths/limitations/needs; shows an aversion to parenting; employs extreme/harsh disciplinary approaches, including violence, threats and verbal assaults; generally does not provide basic care and/or support; deliberately takes frustrations out on the child; is self-righteous" (Depanfilis et al., 1986, p. 273).

Figure 4.4

*Parental Practices:
Guidance and Discipline*

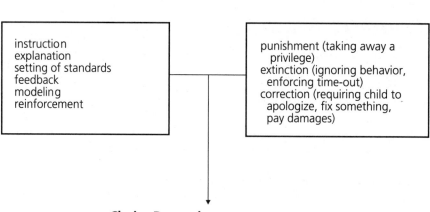

Guidance Methods
(Preventive Socialization)

instruction
explanation
setting of standards
feedback
modeling
reinforcement

Discipline Methods
(Corrective Socialization)

punishment (taking away a
    privilege)
extinction (ignoring behavior,
    enforcing time-out)
correction (requiring child to
    apologize, fix something,
    pay damages)

Choice Depends on:
age/gender of child
presence of a special need
temperament of child/parent
sociocultural/political context of
    society in which child is being raised
parents' socioeconomic status
parents' occupation
parents' ethnic orientation
family size/number of siblings
family configuration (birth order,
    spacing, gender of siblings)
family stress and coping abilities
parents' understanding of child
    developmental and behavioral norms

CHILD MALTREATMENT: ABUSE AND NEGLECT

Maltreatment is any intentional harm to or endangerment of a child, including unkindness, harshness, rejection, neglect, deprivation, abuse, and/or violence (Barnett, Manley, & Cicchetti, 1993). A broader concept than abuse and neglect, maltreatment can be viewed on a continuum with homicide at one extreme and parental force for disciplinary purposes at the other (Kalichman, 1999; Pagelow, 1982). Cultures may differ in what constitutes maltreatment (Goodman, Emery, & Haugaard, 1998). However, it is generally agreed that maltreating parents fail to meet the physical or emotional needs of the developing child and, in many cases, betray the trust the child places in them (Starr, 1990). Child maltreatment constitutes inappropriate parenting in that it may result in child maladaptation (Bolger & Patterson, 2001; Rogosch, Cicchetti, Shields, & Toth, 1995). Child maltreatment occurs in all economic, social, ethnic, and religious groups. Estimates of the number of children who are neglected, physically abused, sexually abused, or psychologically abused vary, but most observers agree that abuse and neglect are marks of significant risk for later development of aggressive behavior, emotional or psychological problems, and competency defects (Goodman et al., 1998; Shonk & Cicchetti, 2001).

Research suggests that maltreatment during childhood has far-reaching consequences in adulthood (Cicchetti & Lynch, 1993; Starr, 1990), such as inability to trust, low self-esteem, depression, relationship problems, sexual problems, learning difficulties, eating disorders, and alcohol or drug problems. The lack of normal nurturing during childhood may result in the adult need to replace the missing love and sense of security with externals, such as drugs, alcohol, food, material objects, sex, and gambling (Farmer, 1989).

EXAMPLE Ellen's addictions began when she was a teenager. "In high school, I used alcohol and drugs to numb myself just so I wouldn't have to feel anything," she states flatly. "I just couldn't deal with the pain, with the insanity of it all. I'd walk around all the time depressed" (Farmer, 1989, p. 7).

What can be done to help children who are maltreated? Although parents in our society have the fundamental right to raise their children as they see fit, the Fourteenth Amendment to the U.S. Constitution, which states that *everyone* has equal protection under the law, warrants legal intervention when the safety of children is in jeopardy. Intervention may involve the filing of criminal charges, referral to community agencies for counseling and treatment, and/or removal of the child from the care and custody of the parent, guardian, or caregiver. Every state has child protective laws with varying procedures.

To better understand the forms child maltreatment may take, each is examined separately even though they may occur simultaneously. **Abuse** is defined as maltreatment, involving physical, sexual, and psychological or emotional assaults. **Neglect** is defined as maltreatment involving abandonment, lack of supervision, improper feeding, lack of adequate medical or dental care, inappropriate dress, uncleanliness, and lack of safety.

Physical Abuse

Physical abuse is maltreatment involving deliberate harm to children's bodies—for example bruises, wounds, or burns. Some physical abuse takes place under the guise of discipline. The places on children's bodies where they are wounded and the shapes of the wounds can give clues that indicate abuse rather than accidents. Physical beating with a hand or an object such as a belt or hairbrush is the most common type of physical abuse; other forms include kicking, shaking, choking, burning with cigarettes or scalding in hot water, freezing, and throwing the child around.

Physical abuse of children is more likely to occur in families in which there is domestic violence—verbal conflicts or physical aggression between partners (Dodge, Bates, & Petit, 1990; Straus, 1992). Research shows a direct relation between physical abuse, aggressive behavior in children, and juvenile delinquency in adolescents (Rogosch et al., 1995). This may be due, in part, to modeling and, in part, to deficient abilities to process social information (Dodge et al., 1990). In other words, these adolescents attribute hostile intentions to others, and they lack strategies to solve interpersonal problems.

Sexual Abuse

Sexual abuse occurs whenever any person forces, tricks, or threatens a child in order to have sexual contact with him or her. This contact can include such "non-touching" behaviors as an adult exposing him- or herself or asking a child to look at pornographic material. It includes behaviors ranging from the sexual handling of a child (fondling), to actual genital contact, to intercourse, to violent rape. In all instances of child sexual abuse, the child is being used as an object to satisfy the adult's sexual needs or desires.

Children who are sexually abused often go through phases of (1) secrecy, (2) helplessness, (3) entrapment and accommodation, (4) delayed, conflicted, and unconvincing disclosure, and (5) retraction (Goodman et al., 1998). These phases reflect the victim's vulnerability to a more powerful and knowledgeable adult. The adult demands secrecy and threatens the child if he or she tells: "I'll take your cat away," or "Your mom will spank you." Thus, to enable child victims to share their experiences, caring adults must ensure a supportive and nonpunitive response.

The most common forms of sexual abuse of children are fondling and oral stimulation; physical injury is rare. The offender often uses bribery, manipulation, appeals to secrecy, threats, and psychological power over the child because most sexual abusers are adults whom the child knows and trusts (Finkelhor, 1984). Although some sexual abuse occurs between adult women and children, in a majority of cases, it is the adult male who is the perpetrator of child sexual abuse. Both girls and boys are victims.

Because children, by their very nature, are trusting and obedient, and because of their age and lack of experience, as well as their dependence upon adults, they are vulnerable to incest and molestation. Most sexual assaults follow a gradually escalating pattern whereby the perpetrator first attempts to gain the child's trust and affection before attempting sexual contact (Koblinsky & Behana, 1984).

Child victims may experience feelings of guilt, anxiety, confusion, shame, embarrassment, fear, and sadness, and a sense of being bad or dirty. Every child reacts differently. Some child victims do not understand that the abuse is "sexual" in nature; therefore, they may find some elements of the abuse pleasant if the abuse was not forceful or scary.

The way certain adults view children provides a clue as to why sexual abuse takes place. These adults feel children in their care are their property, to do with as they wish. A great myth of child abuse is that the child wants sex (O'Brien, 1984). Child sexual abusers also exhibit characteristics of low self-esteem, poor impulse control, and childish emotional needs (Koblinksy & Behana, 1984). They themselves likely were abused as children.

Incest deserves special attention. The closer the victim and offender are emotionally, the greater trauma the victim experiences. Ongoing incest, or sexual abuse by someone close to the family, can disrupt necessary psychological development in children. Victims may develop poor social skills with peers their own age, feel unable to trust people—yet desperately want to trust—and become depressed, suicidal, self-destructive, and confused about their sexuality. A high percentage of drug abusers, juvenile runaways, and prostitutes were sexually abused as children.

Psychological or Emotional Abuse

Psychological or **emotional abuse** is maltreatment involving a destructive pattern of ongoing nonphysical attack by an adult on a child, hindering the victim's development of a sense of self and social competence; forms of abuse include rejecting, isolating, terrorizing, ignoring, and corrupting (Garbarino, Guttman, & Seely, 1986). Psychological or emotional abuse can occur when parents are inconsistent in their talk, rules, or actions; when they have unrealistic expectations of their children; when they belittle and blame their children; when they do not take an interest in any of their children's activities; or when they do not ever praise their children. For example, a mother leaving a dance class with her sobbing 5-year-old daughter said, "Why can't you learn the positions like the others? You always embarrass me. Sometimes I can't believe you're really my daughter."

Parents who psychologically abuse their children are prompted not by the misbehavior, but by their own psychological problems. They are usually people who received inadequate love and nurturing from their own parents (Helfer & Kempe, 1989; Kempe & Kempe, 1978). Parents may provide a steady stream of verbal abuse that discounts the child's achievements and blows out of proportion every act of misbehavior. Words like *always, never,* and *should* imply that the child invariably fails to live up to parents' expectations. Psychologically abusive parents may display irrational expectations, so that normal behavior is seen as a deficiency on the part of the child and a failure on the part of the parent. For example, failing to give the parent change from lunch money may be viewed as stealing rather than merely forgetting.

Psychological abuse is also associated with physical and sexual abuse. Exposure to domestic violence, a form of psychological abuse, also results in emotional, social, behavioral, and learning problems (Margolin, 1998; Straus, 1992).

Neglect can be physical and/or emotional. Physical neglect encompasses poor hygiene, inappropriate dress for weather conditions, hunger or malnourishment, and lack of supervision in potentially dangerous situations or over time. Emotional neglect involves lack of sensitivity and responsiveness to children's needs.

Things Parents Should Never Do

1. Never call children derogatory names.
2. Never threaten to leave your child.
3. Never say, "I wish you were never born!"
4. Never sabotage the parenting efforts of your spouse.
5. Never punish when you've lost control of yourself.
6. Never expect a child to think, feel, or behave like an adult.

CORRELATES AND CONSEQUENCES OF CHILD MALTREATMENT

To understand the causes of child abuse and neglect, we need to examine not only the family interactions but also the cultural attitudes sanctioning violence and aggression, as well as the community support system (Rogosch et al., 1995). Figure 4.5 provides a model to illustrate the interaction between child, family, community, and cultural factors involved in maltreatment. For example, influences on child maltreatment include the temperament of the child, marital distress, unemployment, and lack of community support, as well as cultural values such as tolerance for violence and a view of the child as property (Belsky, 1993; Emery, 1989).

Before predicting maltreatment, risk and resilient factors must be weighed (Cicchetti & Lynch, 1993; Kalichman, 1999). *Risk* factors include those that are ongoing, such as parental history of being abused, as well as those that are transient, such as a parent's loss of a job. *Resilient* factors include both ongoing ones, such as the child's easy temperament, and transient ones, such as an improvement in the family's financial status.

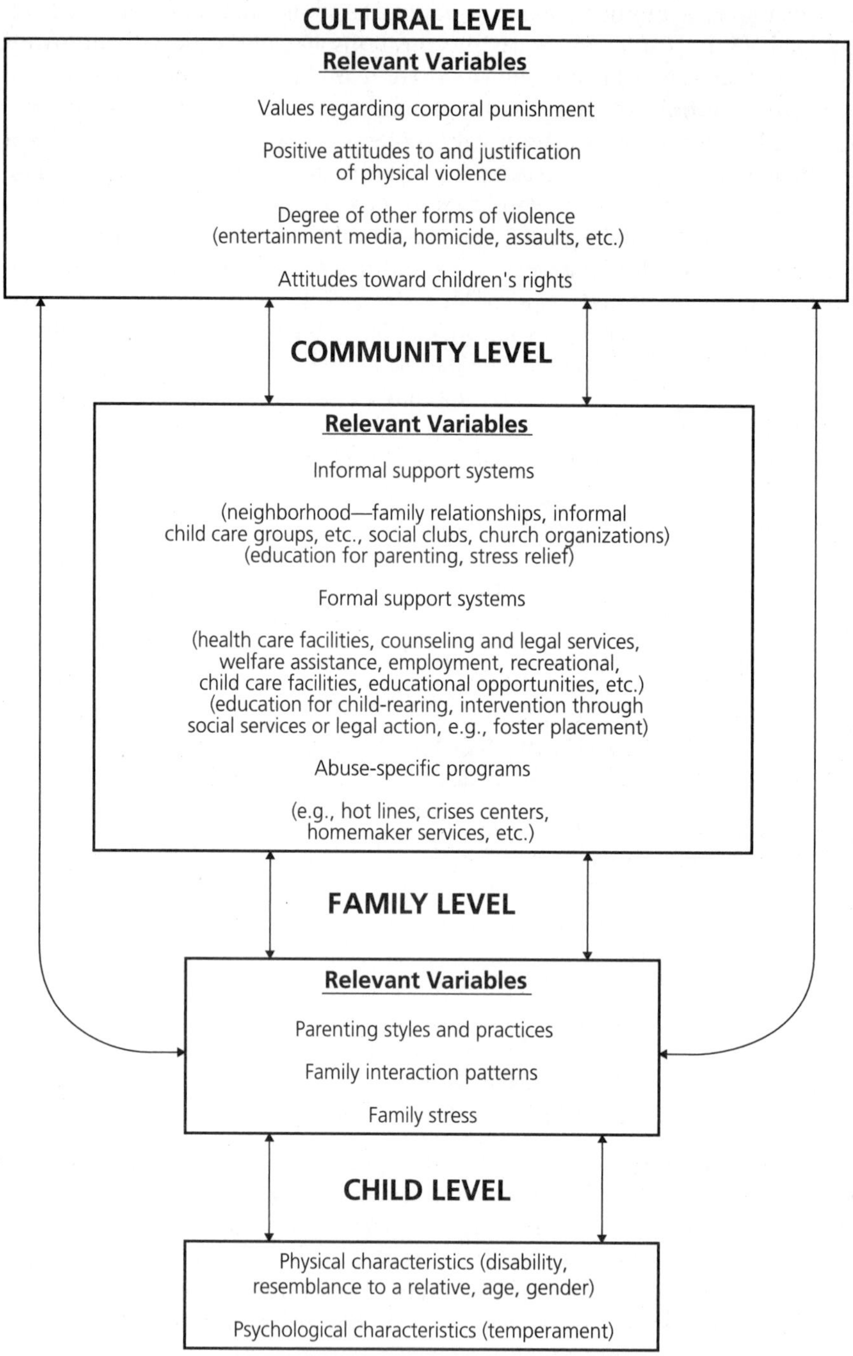

Figure 4.5

An Interaction Model of Risk and Resilient Factors in Child Maltreatment
Sources: Adapted from Parke and Lewis, 1981; and Cicchetti and Lynch, 1993.

CULTURAL LEVEL

Relevant Variables

Values regarding corporal punishment

Positive attitudes to and justification of physical violence

Degree of other forms of violence (entertainment media, homicide, assaults, etc.)

Attitudes toward children's rights

COMMUNITY LEVEL

Relevant Variables

Informal support systems

(neighborhood—family relationships, informal child care groups, etc., social clubs, church organizations) (education for parenting, stress relief)

Formal support systems

(health care facilities, counseling and legal services, welfare assistance, employment, recreational, child care facilities, educational opportunities, etc.) (education for child-rearing, intervention through social services or legal action, e.g., foster placement)

Abuse-specific programs

(e.g., hot lines, crises centers, homemaker services, etc.)

FAMILY LEVEL

Relevant Variables

Parenting styles and practices

Family interaction patterns

Family stress

CHILD LEVEL

Physical characteristics (disability, resemblance to a relative, age, gender)

Psychological characteristics (temperament)

The Family and Maltreatment

As has been discussed, the process of parenting is very complex—at once potentially stressful and frustrating as well as rewarding. Parenting involves the ability to continually give love, support, and guidance. Some individuals, because they themselves never received love, support, or guidance, do not know how to provide them to their own children.

Many abusers have a family history of being maltreated (Rogosch et al., 1995; Starr, 1990). When individuals are maltreated, they feel unworthy, inadequate, unacceptable, which results in low self-esteem. Members of the next generation tend to model the parenting and attitudes to which they were exposed. Therefore, unless it can be broken, maltreatment becomes a self-perpetuating cycle.

When children grow up under negative conditions and are constantly scapegoated, belittled, and criticized, they cannot develop their full potential or grow to be competent adults. They live out all the negative feelings they have developed as a result of the self-image they received from their parents or caregivers, and are thus prone to character and behavior disorders, self-doubt, and internal anger. They also have difficulty regulating their emotions and may avoid displaying their feelings; they have difficulty forming attachments and tend to avoid intimacy; they display more aggressive behaviors; and their cognitive development is often impaired (Lowenthal, 1999).

When life's stressors are added to adults' feelings of inadequacy and lack of parenting skills, child abuse and neglect may result. Parents who have emotional and financial problems, excessive stress, and lack of knowledge about child development, and who are immature, may neglect or abuse their children. Abusive parents lack understanding of child development and consequently often have unrealistic expectations. They expect their children to eat when they are fed, to be quiet and neat and obedient, and to give love. When children do not behave like adults, their parents lash out at them because their inability to conform to their parents' expectations serves as a reminder to parents of their own inferiority (Farmer, 1989). When parents were themselves abused as children, their ability to control their feelings, in addition to their perspective on parenting, is affected.

EXAMPLE Vicky was reported for child abuse. She had tied her 3-year-old son to the bed because, earlier that morning, he had gone to his friend's house and had not telephoned his mother to report his whereabouts. The little boy sobbed, "But Mommy, I forgot my number." Often, abusive parents believe that their child's behavior is deliberate and purposeful (Helfer & Kempe, 1989). "She spit up on my new blouse because she was mad at me," said a mother of her 1-month-old daughter. "He ran in the street just to frighten me," said a mother of her 2-year-old son.

Parents who abuse their children often have psychological problems. Depression and alcoholism have been linked to abuse (Farmer, 1989; Small, 1987). Abusive parents are emotionally immature and need nurturing themselves, and so they look to children to meet their needs (Farmer, 1989). This behavior, called "role reversal," is the most commonly observed psychological characteristic in abusive parents (Farmer, 1989). Parents who are abusive, instead of seeing themselves as nurturers of children, expect children to meet their needs for love. When children fail to meet this expectation, abuse results (Belsky, 1993). As one mother of a 3-week-old said, "When he cried all the time no matter what I did, that meant he didn't love me, so I hit him." These parents also lack appropriate knowledge of behavior management and developmental norms. Physical, or corporal, punishment is their only source of control.

Parents who are abusive often have a low threshold of stress and frustration (Farmer, 1989). There may be financial problems and marital discord; they may suffer from overload and lack support networks in the community (Belsky, 1993). Many of these parents are unprepared for possible financial indebtedness, the constant demands children make, and the responsibilities that keep them from other activities.

The Child and Maltreatment

Certain physical and psychological characteristics have been associated more often with children who are abused than with those who are not (Belsky, 1993)—for example, behaviors such as crying, hyperactivity, and inability to give an acceptable response to a parent. Disabilities such as mental retardations have also been found to be associated with abuse. Additionally, a child's appearance or behavior that reminds the parents of their own unhappy childhoods or of negative characteristics in themselves was found to contribute to negative parent–child relationships. Such children may become scapegoats for buried negative feelings.

In sum, children who are more difficult than average to care for seem to be the victims of more maltreatment (Rogosch et al., 1995). These children may be demanding, whiny, weepy, stubborn, resistive, sickly, or negative. High rates of mistreatment of premature babies, as well as those with developmental difficulties, have been reported (Fontana, 1992). Such children are commonly sensitive to all stimuli; they are restless, distractible, and colicky, and are disorganized sleepers (Maidman, 1984). Not only do these children require more care than average, their parents likely receive less support, encouragement, and advice in caring for them. Also, parents who don't have the opportunity to form an attachment with the child after birth (as in the case with premature babies or babies with medical problems who must remain in the hospital for a time) are at more risk for neglect or abuse (Kennell, Voos, & Klaus, 1976). The main reason is that children who require more than average nurturance, such as children who are premature, sickly, or colicky, tend to make their parents feel less successful.

When infants are irritable, difficult to soothe, and difficult to make eye contact with parents tend to blame themselves and may take it out on them or withdraw from relating to them. Depending on the parents' knowledge about child development and their emotional needs, such child behaviors may weaken the initial attachment process.

Older children's reactions to discipline may, in turn, evoke harsher discipline, possibly culminating in abuse. Studies have shown that of the various responses children make to being disciplined (ignoring, pleading for another chance, apologizing, expressing defiance), defiance is most likely to lead to harsher discipline (Patterson, DeBaryshe, & Ramsey, 1989).

The Community and Maltreatment

Researchers have reported that a significant characteristic of abusive families is their isolation from the community (Emery, 1989; Garbarino, 1977) and consequent lack of support. Frequently, there are no close relatives nearby, or the parents have few friends. Therefore, they have no one to turn to for guidance, comfort, or assistance when they need advice or have a problem. In addition, they have no one to relieve them of child care responsibilities when they need to get away from the house occasionally.

The line between physical abuse and acceptable discipline sometimes depends on the interpreter (Kalichman, 1999). Society expects parents to socialize their children to behave acceptably; therefore, to foster acceptable behavior, some parents use physical, or corporal, punishment. Although occasional spankings cannot legally be classified as child abuse, parental use of corporal punishment as a means of dealing with behavioral problems may have future undesirable consequences, such as teaching children to be aggressive to resolve conflicts. To help determine whether corporal punishment should be interpreted as abuse, Garbarino and Gilliam (1980) suggest that maltreatment be viewed as inappropriate and damaging "acts of omission or commission by a parent or guardian" judged as such by professionals in the community.

Poverty, unemployment, social isolation of families, transient lifestyles, lack of recognition of children's rights, cultural acceptance of corporal punishment, and limited help for families in crisis—are all environmental factors that correlate highly with abuse (Garbarino & Gilliam, 1980; Thompson, 1994). The most frequently reported environmental stressors for families that are abusive and/or neglectful is their lower socioeconomic status (McLoyd, 1998) and their exposure to community violence (Barry & Garbarino, 2000). Community support programs for child and family maltreatment are discussed in Chapter 10.

Epilogue

Parenting occurs in context. It is affected by cultural, family, and personal values. It is also affected by knowledge of child development and socialization methods as to what is appropriate for different ages and situations. Midas's and the Ramseys' parenting styles were both influenced by their materialistic values. Apparently, neither Midas nor the Ramseys had knowledge of child development or developmentally appropriate practices. However, Midas eventually learned appropriate parenting through his daughter, illustrating bidirectional socialization.

Summary

Parenting means implementing a series of decisions about the socialization of children. There is little consensus today in the United States about what children should be like when they grow up and what parents need to do to get them there.

Parenting is conducted within various macrosystems, such as political ideology, culture, and economics. Political ideology impacts parenting in that children have to be raised to function as citizens in society when they become adults. All cultures have parenting goals, but these vary in importance. Different economic systems have different family structures and different formulas for appropriate adult social behavior, which are transmitted to children.

The socioeconomic status of families influence parenting styles. Generally, parents of a lower socioeconomic status are more punitive, emphasizing obedience, whereas parents of a higher socioeconomic status use more reasoning, emphasizing independence and creativity.

Parental occupations (exosystems) influence parenting styles in that skills required at work tend to be emphasized at home—for example, bureacratic jobs tend to emphasize getting along, whereas entrepreneurial jobs tend to emphasize self-reliance.

Various ethnic and religious groups differ in parenting styles and practices. These can be classified as a cooperative/interdependent (collectivistic) orientation on one end of the spectrum and a competitive/independent (individualistic) on the other. These parenting styles differ in their socialization of children according to authority roles, communication, display of emotion, discipline/guidance, and emphasis on skills.

Parenting is affected by chronosystem influences such as historical trends and family dynamics. Historically, children were regarded as existing solely for their contribution to their family's welfare, and parenting styles were strict. Contemporary ideas of parenting regard children as individuals whose development must be nurtured and protected by the family. Parenting practices in the twentieth century were influenced by "experts," who ranged from strict to permissive to democratic.

Family dynamics involve the continuous bidirectional interactions affecting parents and children. Some variables involved are child characteristics (age, temperament, gender, and presence of a disability) and family characteristics (size, configuration, parents' stage of life, marital quality, and ability to cope with stress).

Parenting styles include microsystem influences (between parents and children) and mesosystem influences (between parents and others). There are four dimensions of parenting styles: authoritarian (adult-centered), permissive (child-centered), authoritative (democratic), and uninvolved. Parenting styles affect children's attachment, self-regulation, prosocial behavior, competence, and achievement motivation.

Mesosystem influences on parenting styles include links with the school and the community, which can be collaborative or conflicted.

Appropriate parenting practices are influenced by parental understanding of developmental appropriateness, as well as guidance/discipline socialization techniques. Parents respond to their children's development by changing their expectations and parenting tasks. Parents also need to know when it is appropriate to use guidance and discipline. Guidance techniques are preventative, whereas disciplinary techniques are corrective.

Inappropriate parenting is maltreatment, which involves intentional harm to or endangerment of children. It includes abuse and neglect. Parents who maltreat their children fail to meet their physical or emotional needs. Whether families resort to maltreatment depends on ongoing and transient risk and resilient factors.

Children who are neglected are those who are abandoned, lack supervision, do not receive proper nutrition, need medical or dental care, are frequently absent or late for school, do not have appropriate or sufficient clothing, are unclean, or live in unsafe or filthy homes.

Children who are physically abused are those who are intentionally bruised, wounded, or burned. Physical abuse is often related to domestic violence. Children who are sexually abused are those who are forced, tricked, or threatened into having sexual contact with an individual. Children who are psychologically or emotionally abused are those who are exposed to unreasonable demands that are beyond their capabilities. This abuse may include persistent teasing, belittling, or verbal attacks.

The parents in families that abuse tend to have been abused as children. These parents also tend to have unmet emotional needs. Generally, they have unrealistic expectations for children and often lack knowledge of child development processes. In many cases, they believe that their children's behavior is deliberate and meant to hurt them. These parents also often have very low self-esteem. Depression and alcoholism have been linked to abuse.

Parents who are abusive tend to be isolated from the community in that they lack a supportive network of relatives and/or friends upon whom to rely when in need of help or support. They also have a low tolerance for handling stress, in addition to financial, emotional, and health problems. Corporal punishment is often their only means of dealing with misbehavior. There is a documented relationship between poverty and neglect.

Activity

PURPOSE *To examine your values relating to parenting.*

1. Write the appropriate requirements for a parenting license. Include physical (health status, age, etc.), psychological (temperament, educational status, etc.), and social (marital status, finances, etc.) requirements, as well as experience with children.
2. As a parent, what would you do in the following situations?
   a. Three-year-old Charles spills his milk all over the table and begins to cry.
   b. Just as you walk out of the grocery store, you notice your 5-year-old daughter eating a candy bar that you did not purchase.
   c. Bill, age 10, has recently begun to ignore your requests to put his things away. He also has been "forgetting" to do his regular chores.
   d. Your 8- and 10-year-old children seem to be arguing about everything. When they have nothing specific to argue about, like a toy, a game, or a television show, they tease each other.
   e. Your 6-year-old daughter does not want to go to school. You talk to the teacher to find out what the problem is. The teacher says your daughter is shy and will not participate in class or interact with the other children.
   f. Your 9-year-old son is watching the news on television and asks, "What does 'rape' mean?"
   g. Your 2-year-old has been coming into your bedroom for the past three nights about 3:00 A.M.
   h. Your 11-year-old daughter asks to spend the night at a friend's house, but you have never met the friend's parents.

Research Terms

Authoritarian parenting
Authoritative parenting
Developmental appropriateness
Maltreatment
Permissive parenting
Resilient children
Uninvolved parenting

Related Readings

Brazelton, T. B. (1992). *Touchpoints*. Reading, MA: Addison-Wesley.
Brooks, R., & Goldstein, S. (2001). *Raising resilient children: Fostering strength, hope, and optimism in your child*. Lincoln, IL: Contemporary Books.

Christophersen, E. R., & Mortweet, S. L. (2003). *Parenting that works: Building skills that last a lifetime.* Washington, DC: American Psychological Association.

Cleverly, J., & Phillips, D. C. (1986). *Visions of childhood: Influential models from Locke to Spock* (rev. ed.). New York: Teachers College Press.

Dodson, F. (1974). *How to father.* New York: New American Library.

Dodson, F. (1987). *How to single parent.* New York: Harper & Row.

Dreikurs, R. (1964). *Children: The challenge.* New York: Hawthorn.

Faber, A., & Mazlish, E. (1982). *How to talk so kids will listen and listen so kids will talk.* New York: Avon Books.

Faber, A., & Mazlish, E. (1988). *Siblings without rivalry.* New York: Avon Books.

Garbarino, J., & Eckenrode, J. (1997). *Understanding abusive families.* San Francisco: Jossey-Bass.

Gordon, T. (1991). *Discipline that works: Promoting self-discipline in children at home and at school.* New York: Plume.

Hewlett, S. A., & West, C. (1998). *The war against parents: What we can do for America's beleaguered moms and dads.* Boston: Hougton Mifflin.

Ilg, F. L., Ames, L. B., & Baker, S. M. (1991). *Child behavior* (rev. ed.). New York: Harper & Row.

Satir, V. (1988). *The new peoplemaking.* Mountain View, CA: Science and Behavior Books.

Snow, R. L. (1997). *Family abuse.* Boulder, CO: Perseus.

Steinberg, L., & Levine, A. (1990). *You and your adolescent: A parent's guide for ages 10–20.* New York: Harper Perennial.

Turecki, S., & Wernick, S. (1994). *Normal children have problems, too.* New York: Bantam Books.

White, B. L. (1995). *The new first three years of life.* New York: Simon & Schuster.

Chapter 5

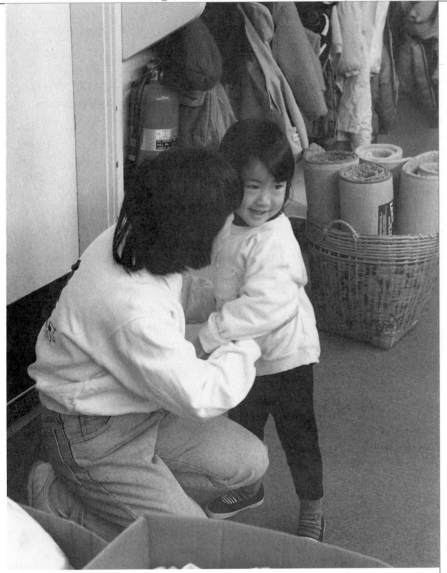

© Elizabeth Crews

Ecology of Child Care

Give a little love to a child, and you get a great deal back.

—JOHN RUSKIN

Prologue: Then and Now

Child Care
What Is Quality Care?
Macrosystem Influences
on Child Care
Chronosystem Influences
on Child Care

**Correlates and
Consequences of Child
Care**
Child Care
and Psychological
Development
Child Care and Social
Development
Child Care and Cognitive
Development

**Mesosystem Influences
on Child Care**
Child Care and the School
and Community
Child Care and the
Government and
Business

**Child Care and
Socialization**
Socialization Effects of
Different Preschool
Programs
Socialization Effects of Child
Care Ideologies

**Developmentally
Appropriate Caregiving**
Collaborative Caregiving
Caregivers and Child
Protection

Epilogue

Summary

Activity

Research Terms

Related Readings

COLLABORATIVE CAREGIVING

THEN A classic fictional caregiving story, *Mary Poppins*, by Mary Shepard and Pamela Travers, tells of the adventures that Mary, the magical nanny, shares with Jane and Michael Banks. Jane and Michael are the sullen, spoiled children of wealthy parents who have no clue as to how to raise them because they always have delegated the caregiving of their children to various nannies. Everything changes when Mary arrives: She is firm, strict, and demanding . . . but she is also loving and fun. After the children complete their schoolwork or chores, she takes them on fantastic adventures, such as stepping into the drawings made with chalk on the sidewalk. She also does silly things with them, like having tea upside down on a ceiling. When Mary feels confident that Mr. and Mrs. Banks have absorbed the caregiving skills they need, and that Jane and Michael have achieved some self-reliance, she leaves to become a nanny at another needy family's home.

NOW A true caregiving story is that of Helen Keller, who was born in Alabama in 1880. She was a normal, healthy baby during early infancy. However, at 18 months of age, she became ill. This resulted in the loss of her sight and hearing. Her parents hired a teacher, Anne Sullivan, who after many attempts finally reached Helen by having her put her hand under the water pump faucet and spelling "w-a-t-e-r" in her hand—the breakthrough of learning to sign in order to communicate. The under-standing that everything had a name awakened Helen's curiosity and desire to learn.

KEY QUESTIONS

- Should parents seek caregiving help (full- or part-time, babysitter, nanny, day care)?
- How can parents and caregivers collaborate for optimal socialization and developmental outcomes in children?

Child Care

Child care—or as it is sometimes called, **day care**—refers to the care given to children by persons other than parents during the parts of the day when parents are absent. Child care can begin as early as birth and extend into the school years (after school and on vacations) until children are old enough to care for themselves. Most states have laws regarding the age at which children can legally be left unsupervised by an adult. Child care for school-age children (school-age child care) is sometimes referred to as **extended day care.**

The care of children today, for a significant part of the day, is more likely to be provided by caregivers other than parents. Specifically, 13 million preschool children—including 6 million infants and toddlers—spend all or part of their day in a nonparental care setting. Millions of school-age children have no supervised care at all during times when school is closed (Children's Defense Fund, 2001). Because children are spending significant socialization time in nonparental care settings,

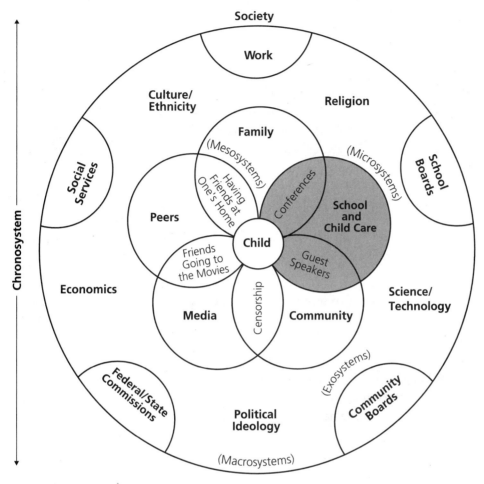

Figure 5.1

An Ecological Model of Human Development

Child care has a significant influence on children's development.

and at very young ages, this chapter examines the influence of child care settings on development. Figure 5.1 shows an ecological model of the systems involved in the process.

The availability, affordability, and adequacy of child care has become an increasingly serious concern over the past 25 years. In the mid-1970s, approximately 30 percent of mothers with children under age 6 were employed, as were more than 50 percent of mothers of school-age children. By the year 2000, these percentages had grown to about 65 percent and 77 percent, respectively (Children's Defense Fund, 2001). And in the twenty-first century, these numbers will climb even further due to the rising cost of living, which forces many parents to contribute to the family income jointly.

There are several different types of child care. A friend, relative, or sitter may come to the home and care for the child(ren). The family may hire a nanny (someone who has received child care training) to live in. Families may cooperate and provide care by taking turns. Independent caregivers may provide care for children in their homes (family day care). Parents may take children to a center for care during the day. According to data from the National Center for Education Statistics (2000), 38 percent of children age 5 or younger receive care on a regular basis from parents only. The remaining 62 percent of children are in one or more arrangements, including care by other relatives (24 percent), nonrelatives (17 percent), or center-based programs (34 percent). Children age 3–5 are more likely than children younger than 3 to be cared for in a center-based program; children under age 3 are more likely to be cared for by parents, relatives, or independent caregivers in the child's home or that of the caregiver's.

Regardless of the type, *quality* child care involves certain basics: (1) a caregiver who provides warm, loving care and guidance for children and works with the family to ensure that children develop in the best way possible; (2) a setting (home or center) that keeps children safe, secure, and healthy; and (3) developmentally appropriate activities that help children develop emotionally, socially, mentally, and physically (Clarke-Stewart, 1993). Many states require fingerprinting for caregivers so that background checks can be run through local law enforcement agencies.

The terms *nursery school, preschool, early childhood education,* and *child development program* are sometimes used to describe certain types of programs for young children. Because all care for children has an impact on their socialization or education, the terms *child care* or *day care* will be used to refer to nonparental caregiving.

WHAT IS QUALITY CARE?

Due to the patchwork of services that currently exists and the projected need for future child care, quality child care has become an issue of concern among working parents, professionals who deal with children, and policy makers (Ghazvini & Mullis, 2002; Lamb, 1998, 2000).

Because "quality" tends to reflect a subjective evaluation, research has approached the problem of an objective definition by closely examining the many aspects, both physical and social, of the child care settings. For example, the federal government initiated the National Day-Care Study (Ruopp, Travers, Glantz, & Coden, 1979) for the purpose of ultimately constructing national child care standards. The task was to identify key child care components that best predicted positive outcomes for children and to develop cost estimates for offering those components within programs.

According to the study, the components of child care that are the most significant predictors of positive classroom dynamics and child outcomes are (1) the size of the overall group, (2) the caregiver–child ratio, and (3) whether the caregiver has specialized training in child development or early childhood education. In classrooms that had smaller groups and those in which the teacher had specialized training, teachers could engage in more social interaction with children. Thus, the children were more cooperative, more involved in tasks, more talkative, and more creative. They also made greater gains on cognitive tasks.

Today, measures such as the Early Childhood Environment Rating Scale (Harms & Clifford, 1980) are available to assess quality. Later studies confirmed and expanded on the National Day-Care Study findings (Ghazvini & Mullis, 2002; Hofferth, 1992; National Institute of Child Health and Human Development [NICHD], 1996, 2000). Specifically, caregivers with specialized training in child development and developmentally appropriate practices have a more authoritative, rather than authoritarian, attitude toward child rearing, use more planned activities, are less stressed, and tend to communicate regularly with parents (Ghazvini & Mullis, 2002; NICHD, 2000).

In spite of such research on "quality" and positive child outcomes, recent studies of child care centers reveal that typical quality is still considerably below what is considered good practice (Fragin, 2000; Love, Schochet, & Meckstroth, 1996; NICHD, 2000). For example, the Cost, Quality, and Child Outcomes Study (1995) reported that in more than 400 centers studied in four states, only 8 percent of infant programs and 24 percent of preschool programs were of good or excellent quality. In 40 percent of infant programs and 10 percent of preschool programs, quality was rated as poor.

Factors that contribute to less-than-optimal quality include the following:

- The education credentials of caregivers who work in child care centers are often inadequate relative to the skills required. The NICHD Early Child Care Research (1996) found that only a third of infant care providers had any specialized training in child development, and only 18 percent had a bachelor's degree or higher. According to a survey by *Working Mother* magazine (Fragin, 2000), only 50 percent of all states require training in child development for caregivers.
- Staff turnover is high, ranging from 25 to 50 percent each year. This means that children are continually adapting to new caregivers, and administrators are constantly training new staff (Fragin, 2000; Whitebook, Howes, & Phillips, 1989).
- Staff compensation, including wages and benefits, is exceptionally low. Child care staff are among the lowest paid of all classes of workers in the United States. Worker compensation is significantly related to the quality of care provided (Whitebook, et al., 1989).

In recent years, a number of studies have examined the effects of varying levels of quality on children's behavior and development. A common conclusion is that a significant correlation exists between program quality (safe, stimulating environment) and socialization outcomes for children (Fragin, 2000; Frede, 1995; NICHD, 2000). Outcomes related to quality care include cooperative play, sociability, ability to resolve conflicts, self-control, as well as language and cognitive development.

Although most studies on quality care have focused on effects on children, a few have examined effects on the parental sense of well-being, because the emotional state of the parents influences the choice of child care, the level of satisfaction at work, and the quality of parenting (Phillips, 1992). For example, Mason and Duberstein (1992) found that the objective factors of availability and affordability of care overshadow the subjective factor of quality in parents' sense of well-being and, hence, their choice of child care. Also impacting the parental sense of well-being is ease of communication with caregivers. Informal, frequent communication, such as a daily face-to-face chat, was found to be favored over formal, infrequent communication, such as a written monthly report (Ghazvini & Mullis, 2002).

Advocacy for Quality Care

Because national standards for "quality" care do not exist, the National Association for the Education of Young Children (NAEYC), an organization of professionals involved in early childhood education, took on the task of setting its own criteria. A position statement on criteria for high-quality early childhood programs was published in 1984. Briefly, a high-quality program is

> one which meets the needs of and promotes the physical, social, emotional, and cognitive development of the children and adults—parents, staff, and administrators—who are involved in the program. Each day of a child's life is viewed as leading toward the growth and development of a healthy, intelligent, and contributing member of society. (NAEYC, 1984, p. 7)

Child care programs that meet the criteria can apply to the National Academy for Early Childhood Programs (a division of NAEYC) for accreditation, thereby receiving national recognition for high-quality standards and performance.

In 1986, the NAEYC expanded its position on quality. With the proliferation of programs for young children and the introduction of large numbers of infants and toddlers into group care, the NAEYC felt the need for a clear definition of *developmentally appropriate practice,* a term often used in the criteria for quality early childhood programs. In response to the trend (seen in many programs) toward increasing emphasis on formal instruction in academic skills, the NAEYC published specific guidelines for developmentally appropriate practices for programs serving children from birth through age 8 (Bredekamp, 1986, 1993; Bredekamp & Copple, 1997). **Developmental appropriateness** involves knowledge of children's normal growth patterns and individual differences. Research in human development indicates that there are universal, predictable sequences of growth and change in childhood, adolescence, and adulthood. These predictable changes take place in all domains of development—physical, emotional, social, and cognitive. Knowledge of typical development of children within the age span served by a given program provides a framework from which caregivers create the appropriate learning environment and plan appropriate experiences. Play is viewed as the primary indicator of children's development. Each child is viewed as a unique person with an individual pattern and timing of growth, as well as individual temperament, learning style, and family background. Both the program and interactions should be responsive to individual differences. Learning in a developmentally appropriate program emerges as a

These preschool children are engaged in a developmentally appropriate "hands-on" activity.

result of the interaction between the child's thoughts and experiences with materials and other people. The curriculum should match the child's developing abilities while also challenging the child's interests and understanding (Bredekamp, 1986, 1993).

After much hard work, debate, and compromise involving numerous child advocate organizations, a federal child care bill was eventually passed in 1990. The bill included a Child Care and Development Block Grant to state governments, requiring them to designate a lead agency to direct their child care programs, to set health and safety standards, and to allow eligible low-income families to choose any licensed child care provider. In addition, the bill granted tax credits for working families with children if they have child care expenses for one or more children under age 13 and pay for child care in order to work.

To address the concerns of parents about the ability to balance family and work responsibilities, the government passed the Family and Medical Leave Act (FMLA) in 1993. The FMLA requires all public employers and private employers with 50 or more workers to provide up to 12 weeks of unpaid leave per year to employees who need to care for a new child (own, adopted, or foster) or a seriously ill family member, or who themselves become seriously ill. Some states are considering legislation for paid leaves.

Accreditation of Child Care Programs

Voluntary systems exist nationally to establish higher-quality standards than are required by law for child care centers and in-home day care, as well as the nanny industry (Helburn & Howes, 1996). In 1984, the NAEYC developed an accreditation system for child care centers involving self-evaluations by staff and parents. Professional validators from the NAEYC conduct visits to determine whether standards have been met; if they have, the program is accredited for 3 years. Standards are designed for programs serving children from infancy through age 8 in centers caring for more than 10 children; school-age programs are eligible if a majority of children are age 8 or younger.

The standard criteria, based on research and professional consensus, address staff qualifications and training, administration and staffing patterns (group size and adult–child ratios), the physical environment, health and safety issues, and nutrition and food service. For example, for children age 12 months or less, the standard is 6–8 children per group with an adult–child ratio of 1:3 to 1:4; for children age 4–5 years, the standard is 16–20 children per group with an adult–child ratio of 1:8 to 1:10.

In 1988, the National Association for Family Day Care (now the National Association for Family Child Care, or NAFCC) began a program for voluntary accreditation for in-home child care services. The process includes both self-evaluation and external validation of aspects of program operation: health and safety, nutrition, indoor and outdoor play environments, interactions, and professional responsibility. Continuing education for caregivers, such as cardiopulmonary resuscitation (CPR), is also required.

The oldest professional nanny organization in the United States is the International Nanny Association (INA). It includes nannies, nanny employers, nanny placement agencies, and nanny educators. Since 1987, the INA has worked to professionalize the nanny industry by maintaining high standards of conduct, respecting and supporting families in their task of nurturing children, and promoting continuing professional growth. Background checks, referrals, conferences, and newsletters are among the services provided by the INA.

MACROSYSTEM INFLUENCES ON CHILD CARE

Generally, child care and educational practices have been affected by four distinct macrosystems: (1) political ideology, such as social responsibility (enable cultural assimilation by helping immigrants adapt), competition (provide learning opportunities to young children to prepare for the future), and equal opportunity, including the responsibility to aid poor families and include children with special needs; (2) culture/ethnicity, such as sensitivity to diversity; (3) economics, such as the need for both parents to work to keep up with the cost of living; and (4) science/technology, such as the pressure to impart academic skills to all children as early as possible. In terms of macrosystems, child care was used during the twentieth century to provide social services, for immigrants, enrichment and interventions for preschoolers, employability for parents, and school readiness for elementary-age students.

The first day nurseries were established to cope with the children of masses of immigrants to the United States during the mid-nineteenth century. Day nurseries were also established to care for the children of women who worked in factories and hospitals during World War I and II. The motivation to establish these day nurseries was to provide social services for neglected children; the care provided was custodial (Clarke-Stewart, 1993).

The first cooperative nursery school was inaugurated at the University of Chicago in 1915. The purpose was to give the children of faculty members opportunities to play in a supervised environment, where they could develop impulse control, verbal skills, and knowledge about the world. Parent participation was required. Such nursery schools were popular with middle-class families from the 1930s to the 1960s. In the late 1960s, due to child development research and political pressure for the United States to compete globally (specifically, to keep pace with Russian scientific advances), a new purpose was incorporated into nursery school programs—to stimulate intellectual growth (Clarke-Stewart, 1993).

Meanwhile, in the 1960s, civil rights groups demanded equal opportunities in education, jobs, and housing. Thus, in 1964, the Economic Opportunity Act was passed to provide educational and social opportunities for children from low-income families. Preschool programs were instituted to compensate for the perceived physical, social, and academic disadvantages of children who came from families of low socioeconomic status or ethnic minority status, or who were identified as having disabilities or having experienced abuse. The purpose of such intervention was to provide the children with skills they were unlikely to acquire at home to enable them to succeed in school and avoid poverty in adulthood. Such intervention programs are usually comprehensive in that they provide health and nutrition services, social services, and parental involvement. An example of a federally funded comprehensive preschool intervention program is Head Start. Its goal is to enable children from qualified families to enter school ready to learn. The rationale for such early intervention came from research concluding that early experiences stimulate intellectual development (Hunt, 1961). Public money spent to enhance the early childhood years, the argument goes, is more beneficial than public money spent to correct a deficiency in the later childhood years.

In addition to contributing to child development research, the political activism in the 1960s provided part of the rationale for early intervention. President Lyndon Johnson believed that the only way to break the cycle of poverty was through education. Intervention programs seemed to be the way to equalize opportunities, with education ultimately enabling people to get jobs to support themselves, rather than depend on welfare. Today, part of welfare reform is government funding of child care to enable mothers of young children to work.

Child care services allow women to seek job training and/or employment outside the home (Lamb, 1998). The increase in the cost of living and in single-parent families has resulted in a growing reliance on nonparental care by many families in the United States. Recent welfare reforms to increase employability have been implemented. For instance, the 1996 welfare law allows recipients of Temporary Assistance to Needy Families (TANF) to collect federal benefits for a maximum of 60 months. States can modify requirements for funds by extending the time if special hardship circumstances such as illness warrant it. Recipients of TANF must be engaged in work-related activities (training, job search, job) within their state's time limit. The immediate effect of the imposed time limit for welfare has been to increase the demand for available, accessible, affordable child care.

Some people who believe that child care is synonymous with early childhood education also believe that the period from birth to age 5 is a critical time for developing the physical, emotional, social, and cognitive skills children will need for the rest of their lives. In his State of the Union Address of 2002, President George Bush outlined his plan for educational reform—the "No Child Left Behind Act"—whereby the public schools will teach students what they need to know to be successful in life. Included is the need to prepare children before they start school. The Bush administration has also proposed a new early childhood initiative—"Good Start, Grow Smart"—to help states and local communities fund programs to teach young children the skills they will need to be ready to learn in school—for example, prereading and language skills.

In sum, due to macrosystem influences, child care has become a service to families to provide custodial care, to stimulate learning experiences, to provide socialization opportunities, to enable parents to work, and to implement early childhood education principles.

CHRONOSYSTEM INFLUENCES ON CHILD CARE

The various child care contexts in which children have been cared for and the early childhood educational practices employed throughout history are examined here to better understand the impact of changes in child care (chronosystem influences) on socialization.

Day care for children is neither new nor unique to the United States (Lamb, 1998). As touched on previously, in the mid-nineteenth century, industrialization was accompanied by the growth of factories and cities, and a flood of immigrants fleeing the famine in Ireland and the revolution in Germany. Many of these immigrants settled in the cities so they could work in the factories. At the same time, many women had to work to help their families survive. Thus, for example, the first day nursery in the United States was opened in 1838 by Mrs. Joseph Hale to provide care for the children of seamen's working wives and widows (Clarke-Stewart, 1993).

In the twentieth century, child care expanded, with day care usually set up in converted homes. Most child care could be classified as custodial; in other words, children's basic needs for food, shelter, sleep, and supervision were met. The caregivers cooked, cleaned, and washed clothes, and watched the children. Some programs taught children cleanliness and manners, trying to instill obedience and a belief in hard work and punctuality. Some even hired teachers to come in for a few hours each day to teach reading, spelling, sewing, and weaving. Others offered classes for the mothers in child rearing, English, cooking, and sewing, as well as providing assistance with family problems (Clarke-Stewart, 1993). Thus, the underlying philosophy of child care in the nineteenth and early twentieth centuries was to provide a support service for families in need.

In 1933, President Franklin Roosevelt initiated the Federal Economic Recovery Act and the Works Progress Administration (WPA) to alleviate the effects of the Depression. Public funds became available for the first time to expand day care programs, and jobs then became available for unemployed teachers, nurses, cooks, and janitors.

Beginning in 1938, when the WPA was disbanded, day nurseries declined until World War II. Then, with the massive mobilization of women into war-related industries, day care once again flourished to accommodate the children of women employed outside the home to assist in the war effort. Child care centers were established with federal funds by the Lantham Act of 1942.

Even though the Lantham funds were withdrawn in 1946, child care facilities continued to exist. Some were run by charitable organizations emphasizing social work and serving families with financial and other problems. Others were private, paid for by mothers who worked outside the home. Still others were set up for the purpose of enriching children's development (Clarke-Stewart, 1993).

As the twentieth century progressed, the underlying philosophy of child care evolved from a support service for families in need to a developmental service for all children. Child care programs began to flourish in the United States in the 1960s. There were several reasons for this, including a positive change in public attitude toward women who worked outside the home, the realization that provision of day care allowed more women to get off the welfare rolls, and research studies showing that children learned more rapidly during the early years of life. Thus, federal funding for preschool programs for children who were poor increased.

The 1971 White House Conference on Children pointed to the need for quality child care as the most serious problem confronting families and children. Unfortunately, as the twenty-first century begins, we still have no official national policy or federal standards aimed at establishing a high-quality system of child care. In addition, child care standards continue to vary widely from state to state and family to family. Why is this so?

One reason is that according to traditional views of parenting the primary responsibility for child care rests with the family. Some people in government and business promote the value of "individualism"—the idea that each family should be able to care for its own without outside assistance (Schorr, 1997).

Another reason is the fear of government involvement in what is considered a basic personal right: to bring up one's children according to one's values, religion, and culture. Federal involvement in private matters is viewed by some as teetering on socialism. Is the underlying fear that if the government foots the bill for child care then it will call the shots?

In general, the federal government has not yet committed itself to implementing universal child care standards (except for programs in which federal funds are involved). This means that the task is left to the states, local communities, private enterprise, professional organizations, and consumers (see Appendix C, "How to Choose a Good Early Childhood Program").

Since nonparental child care has become a fact of life, the question from the 1980s and 1990s, which was "Is day care helpful or harmful to children?" needs to be reframed to "What ecological model of child care is most supportive of children and families?" (Ghazvini & Mullis, 2002; NICHD, 2000).

There are a variety of opinions among professionals and laypeople as to whether children should be enrolled in day care. There are also opinions about the age at which children should be enrolled and whether such care should be full- or part-time. There are even opinions on the types of program that should be offered. For example, some believe the preschool experience should focus on children's learning how to get along with others, exploring the environment, and dealing with feelings; others believe the preschool experience should focus on academic skills such as reading and math. The debate goes on.

Correlates and Consequences of Child Care

Much of the early controversy regarding the effects of child care on children's development revolved around the fear that separation from the mother, especially in infancy, would disrupt the natural mother–child bond of attachment and result in psychological and social problems. Thus, most of the original research studies examined the effects of separation on children. It should be noted that the infant separation studies were done in residential institutions, rather than in child care centers as we know them today. More recent studies have examined the overall effects of different child care settings (home versus alternative) on children—for example, children's social relationships with other children, their relationships with their mothers, and changes in their intellectual development. The most recent studies have used an ecological approach combining family factors and child care factors (Clarke-Stewart, Allhusen, & Clements, 1995; NICHD, 2000), as well as cultural factors (Lamb, 1998), that work together to affect children's development. It is now accepted that "childrearing has become a collaborative endeavor with children moving back and forth . . . between their homes and child care" (Phillips & Howes, 1987, p. 9). The mesosystem links may be supportive, competitive, or neutral.

CHILD CARE AND PSYCHOLOGICAL DEVELOPMENT

What is the effect of separating infants from their mothers? One of the first studies to report the detrimental effects of separating infants from their mothers was conducted by physician Rene Spitz in 1946. He compared the development of infants raised by caregivers in a foundling home (a home for abandoned babies) to infants raised by their mothers in a prison. Each caregiver in the foundling home was responsible for at least eight infants. The prison mothers, who were all either mentally retarded or emotionally disturbed, were responsible for caring only for their own infants. The infants raised in the foundling home had poor appetites, lacked interest in their surroundings, and exhibited severe depression. As a result, their physical growth and mental development lagged behind norms. The infants raised by their mothers in prison, in contrast, developed normally. Even though the mothers in the prison were socially deviant, the one-on-one care and nurturance they gave their infants enabled the infants to exhibit normal development. For their part, even though the caregivers in the institution were professionally trained, they had eight babies to nurture and probably could not establish emotional attachments with each one. Not surprisingly, Spitz endorsed "nature" care provided by birth mothers over the "nurture" care in the foundling home.

In 1952, psychiatrist John Bowlby (1966, 1969, 1973) wrote that maternal love and care are the most important influences on infants' development. After reviewing studies on infants separated from their mothers, he concluded that any break in the early mother–child relationship could have severe emotional, social, and intellectual consequences. What Bowlby meant by "any break" was the loss of the mother in infancy due to death or the separation of the mother from the infant because of hospitalization, employment, or other circumstances such as neglect (being physically present but emotionally absent). He went on to say that deprivation of the early mother–child relationship would cause the infant to become depressed, physically and mentally retarded, and/or delinquent. Bowlby, too, supported "nature" care.

A 30-year longitudinal study completed in 1966 by psychologist Harold Skeels demonstrated that it is the quality of care (nurture) that affects children's development, not the relationship of the person (nature) who provides it. Thus, the care can come from someone other than the birth mother. Skeels studied 25 infants who were institutionalized because they were deemed mentally retarded. Of these, 13 were later transferred to the institution for retarded women, where the infants were "adopted" by small groups of residents, who lavished care and attention on them. The remaining 12 infants stayed where they were. After 2 years, the transfer group had gained an average of 28.5 points on an IQ test, whereas the control group had lost an average of 26.2 points.

Thirty years later, Skeels did a follow-up study on the original 25. He found that 11 out of the 13 transferees to the institution for retarded women had been adopted by families, and that 12 out of the 13 had achieved an education and become responsible, self-supporting adults. Their own children had average IQs. As for the control group, 11 out of the 12 children had survived. Four of these were in institutions, one was a vagrant, one was a gardener's assistant at an institution, three were dishwashers, one was a part-time worker in a cafeteria, and one was a domestic worker.

This study showed (1) that children need care and nurturance to develop normally (in this respect, Skeels agrees with Spitz and Bowlby), (2) that the care and nurturance can be provided by someone other than the mother (here Skeels disagrees with Spitz and Bowlby), and (3) that infants who are initially deprived can grow up normally if intervention by a caring, nurturing person is provided (Spitz and Bowlby did not even consider this possibility). Skeels supported "nurture" care.

Skeels's study has implications for society. If deprivational effects caused by neglect in infancy can be reversed by intervention, then we can enable many children to grow up to be independent, self-sufficient, responsible adults who are assets to society rather than liabilities. But there are still unresolved questions: Which children qualify for intervention? When does intervention take place? What type of intervention is best? What kind of programs are provided, and for how long? Is day care worth paying for? Does the government or some other agency have the right to intervene? Is society willing to pay for the intervention? These questions will be discussed in more detail later.

Selma Fraiberg (1977), a psychologist and author, defends mothering. The mother, she asserts, is the primary caregiver for the infant; good maternal care "is every child's birthright," so society's intervening role should be to help inadequate mothers improve their relationships with their infants, rather than subsidizing alternatives to mothering such as day care. But Sandra Scarr (1984), another psychologist and author of *Mother Care/Other Care*, provides evidence that babies and young children can be successfully reared by qualified others.

What exactly is so special about the early mother–child relationship? During the first year of life, children become attached to their primary caregivers—the persons who hold them, comfort them, feed them, and play with them. This caregiver is usually the mother, but it can be the father, a grandparent, an older sibling, or another person not related to the child. Feelings of attachment distinguish this caregiver from others. When children are in strange situations or not feeling well, they want to be near the person they are attached to; no one else will do.

As was discussed in Chapter 4, researchers access the level of attachment to mothers by putting their children in a strange or stressful situation—for instance, leaving the child alone in a room with a stranger and observing her or his reactions to the mother's presence, her departure, and her return. An *insecure* attachment is indicated when the child clings to the mother when she leaves or cries hysterically until the mother returns. An insecure attachment is also indicated when the child ignores the mother when she leaves and avoids her when she returns, or when the child clings to the mother one moment and rejects her the next. A *secure* attachment is indicated when the child is able to leave the mother's side to explore the toys in the

This child clings to his mother when left at child care because he is attached to her.

room—obviously, however, preferring the mother's company to the stranger's. When the mother leaves, the child shows concern or becomes mildly upset but gets over it quickly. When she returns, the child greets her happily (Ainsworth, 1973, 1979; Ainsworth & Bell, 1970).

Belsky (1988, 1992) has reported that babies less than 12 months old who receive nonmaternal care for more than 20 hours a week are at a greater risk of developing insecure relationships with their mothers; they are also at increased risk of emotional and behavioral problems in later childhood. Youngsters who have weak emotional ties to their mothers are more likely to be aggressive and disobedient as they grow older.

Others (Clarke-Stewart, 1988, 1992; Phillips & Howes, 1987) take issue with Belsky, saying that the evidence is insufficient to support the claim that infants in full-time day care are at risk for emotional insecurity. That day care infants exhibit different attachment behaviors than home care infants may simply mean that they have developed a coping style to adapt to the different people who care for them and to the daily separations and reunions. In addition, the assessment of attachment procedures commonly used may not be an accurate way of comparing differences in attachment between infants reared in such diverse environments. Thus, not all children who begin day care in infancy are insecurely attached, aggressive, or noncompliant; nor are they necessarily intellectually advanced. There are individual differences for day care children just as there are for children reared at home (Clarke-Stewart, 1989, 1992; Honig, 1993).

Finally, recent data on the psychological functioning of children who have attended day care in infancy frequently are confounded by the child's temperament and gender, family socioeconomic status, parental marital status, parent–child relationships, number of hours daily in care, and quality of care, including the sensitivity and responsiveness of caregivers (McCartney & Galanopoulos, 1988; NICHD, 1997, 2000; Phillips, 1992). According to Lamb (1998), who reviewed the research, day care in itself does not reliably affect mother–child attachment. Adverse effects occur only when poor-quality day care concurs with such risky conditions as insensitive and unresponsive maternal behavior (NICHD, 1997). In sum, children in a quality child care program and children cared for at home attach to their mothers similarly.

CHILD CARE AND SOCIAL DEVELOPMENT

Children in day care may be with peers from infancy. Infants stare at and touch each other. Toddlers may smile at each other, share toys, and fight over toys. Three-year-olds may play games, share, take turns, argue, and fight. Four-year-olds may role-play: "Let's play house—you be the mommy, and I'll be the baby."

A number of studies on the social development of preschool children have concluded that children attending some form of child care program interact more with peers—both positively and negatively—and that they are less cooperative and responsive with adults than are children in home care (Clarke-Stewart et al., 1995; Field, Masi, Goldstein, & Perry, 1988; NICHD, 1998).

Specifically, children who have had experience in child care programs seem to be more socially competent than those who have not had such an experience. They are more self-confident and outgoing and less fearful. They are also more assertive and self-sufficient. They know more about the social world—assuming gender roles, taking the perspective of others, solving problems regarding getting along with another child, and assigning emotional labels ("cheater," "crybaby," "bully"). They are not only more socially competent, but sometimes are less polite, less respectful of others' rights, and less compliant with adult demands, as well as more aggressive and hostile toward others (Clarke-Stewart, 1989; Clarke-Stewart et al., 1995; Lamb, 1998). Early individual differences in social competence have been found to remain stable through the school-age years and early adolescence (Campbell, Lamb, & Hwang, 2000).

CHILD CARE AND COGNITIVE DEVELOPMENT

Generally, the intellectual performance of children who attend a quality day care program is higher than that of children from similar family backgrounds who do not attend a day care program or who attend one of poor quality. For example, it has been shown that children, especially from low-income families, who attend a quality preschool program for children age 2½–5, even part-time, are more verbally expressive and interact more with adults than children who do not (Burchinal, Peisner-Feinberg, Bryant, & Clifford, 2000; Clarke-Stewart, 1993; Honig, 1993). It has also been demonstrated that children who attend quality child care programs are better able to meet the requirements in the primary grades of elementary school and function at an increased intellectual capacity during their initial years of schooling; their IQ scores increased up to 10 points by the end of program implementation. Academic achievement for these children continues to be better through high school than for those who did not attend a quality preschool (Cost, Quality, & Child Outcomes [CQO], 1999; Karoly, 1998; Schweinhart & Weikart, 1993). Although longitudinal studies have shown the increase in intelligence test scores of children from low-income families were not permanent, there was a significant reduction in

This father is influencing his daughters' competency and total educational development through his interest and involvement in their learning.

the number of children held back and in the need for placement in special education programs (CQO, 1999; Karoly, 1998; Schweinhart & Weikart, 1993).

Intervention Programs

Most research on the effects of day care on children's cognitive development focuses on intervention programs, which provide compensation for skills perceived to be lacking, rather than enrichment of abilities, as do traditional preschool programs. "Compensation" means making amends for what is lacking. Intervention programs attempt to make up for the perceived academic, physical, and social disadvantages of children who come from families of low socioeconomic-status or families of diverse ethnic backgrounds, or who have disabilities, or who have been abused. The purpose of intervention is to prevent, or compensate for, perceived disadvantages that impede achievement in public schools. Intervention preschool programs are usually comprehensive in that, in addition to education, they provide health and nutrition services and social services, and encourage parental involvement. An example of such a comprehensive program is Head Start, the federally funded preschool intervention program for qualified families intended to enable children to enter school ready to learn.

Many types of intervention programs were implemented in the 1960s and 1970s, using different curriculum models (discussed later). Although children enrolled in such programs fared better academically, socially, and emotionally than their nonparticipant counterparts (Karoly, 1998), the debate as to which type of intervention is best, for whom, for how long, and where (home or school) remains unresolved (NICHD, 2000).

Even though there are many variations of intervention programs, most investigators concur that, in order to enable children to become competent members of society, their families must be involved. Thus, the best type of intervention (among government-funded programs) is one that reinforces the strengths of the family as a child-rearing system. Specifically, it enables the family to be the primary educator of its children, links the family to the formal educational system through involvement, and steers the family to resources in the community so that the family can receive needed health and social services. These are known as family support programs. An example of such a program is the Child and Family Resource Program (CFRP), which began in 1973 as part of Head Start. CFRP enrolled qualified families of children from birth through age 8, rather than only the children. It provided diagnostic medical, dental, nutritional, and mental health services, as well as treatment. It also provided prenatal care and education for pregnant mothers, assisted parents in promoting the development of infants and toddlers, and offered comprehensive Head Start services for children age 3–5. It eased the transition from preschool to elementary school and offered special development programs for children with disabilities. Finally, it provided services such as counseling, referrals to community agencies, family planning assistance, and help in dealing with emergencies or crises.

Family support programs exist today under the Comprehensive Child Development Program (CCDP). These programs promote more developmentally appropriate behavioral expectations for children by the mothers and more prosocial behaviors by the children (Greenfield & Suzuki, 1998).

In sum, accurately predicting the socialization outcomes of intervention programs is difficult due to the many variables that must be taken into account. These include the quality of the mother–infant relationship, socioeconomic status of the family, educational level of the parents, stressors on the family and its coping skills, available family supports, temperament and gender of the children, spacing of the siblings, age at which children enter the program and the number of hours per day, quality of the caregiver–infant relationship, caregiver–parent communication, and quality of the program (see Table 5.1).

Mesosystem Influences on Child Care

The challenge of the future is for society to provide more choices in quality child care services, given the increased need. Availability, accessibility, and affordability remain a problem (Children's Defense Fund, 2001). The types of child care most often used for infants and toddlers (younger than age 3) have been relatives, family day care homes (care in the home of a nonrelative), and centers. Preschoolers (age 3–4) have been most frequently cared for in a child care center and by relatives, whereas the most common types of care (excluding self-care) for school-age children (age 6–12) have been family day care homes and relatives (see Figure 5.2). However, a more striking trend is the substantial growth in use of center-based care for all-age children, especially by full-time employed mothers (Hofferth, 1996; Willer, Hofferth, Kisker, Divine-Hawkins, Farquhar, & Glantz, 1991).

If center-based care is the trend, how can such child care options be increased? For families, the communities in which they live, the government to whom they pay taxes, and the businesses by which they are employed must make a commitment to provide quality day care.

Table 5.1
Variables Influencing Child Care Socialization Outcomes

CHILD CARE VARIABLES
Type of care (in-home, family day care, center care)
Type of program (compensatory, enrichment)
Compensation of caregivers
Caregiver stress levels
Stability of caregivers
Adult–child ratio
Quality of day care setting
Sensitivity and responsivity of caregivers to children
Caregiver education/training
Caregiver ideology and attitudes toward child rearing
Caregiver–parent communication
Part- or full-time day care

FAMILY VARIABLES
Socioeconomic status
Ethnicity
Family structure (single, step, extended)
Parental educational level
Mother employed part- or full-time
Mother's attitude toward work
Mother's attitude toward child care
Mother's sensitivity and responsiveness to child
Roles and relationships between parents
Father's involvement in child care
Parenting styles
Stress/coping strategies
Availability of social supports in community

CHILD VARIABLES
Age at entry into day care
Gender
Health
Temperament
Security of attachment to mother

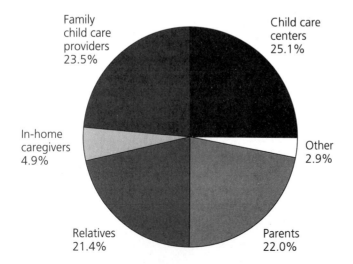

Figure 5.2
Who's Watching the Children?
Source: *The State of America's Children Yearbook 2001.* Reprinted with permission of the Children's Defense Fund.

CHILD CARE AND THE SCHOOL AND COMMUNITY

One way to increase child care options is for elementary schools to extend their services to include children younger than age 5 and to extend the hours they are normally in session. As mentioned previously, a majority of school-age children whose parents are employed care for themselves before and after school. Other children may be cared for by a neighbor, and still others may participate in a community program. Unsupervised children, contrary to popular belief, are not most likely to be found in impoverished, minority communities; rather, self-care is most common when mothers work full-time and parents are divorced or separated, regardless of family income (Lamb, 1998). Indeed, extended day care can be an effective link among children, family, and school as it complements and extends the school's educational mission and supports the family in its education and nurturance of children. To illustrate, according to Schorr (1997), Edward Zigler, one of the founders of Head Start, envisioned the schools of the twenty-first century as providing full day care, as well as being the hub of social services for families. Bowling Park Elementary School in Norfolk, Virginia, is such a school. It provides services for infants and preschoolers and their parents, responding to family needs. A breakfast club exists at which parents can discuss parenting issues, children's books, and so on, and adult education courses are offered, too. The goal is for children to feel connected to people who care.

Another extended day care program that is a cooperative community venture involves some urban public school district and the YMCA. The school district provides several schools as sites for the program, and the Y supplies trained recreational leaders and transportation (if an extended program is not available at their school, the children are bused to a nearby site after school). The male and female recreational leaders offer care that promotes the physical, social, emotional, and cognitive development of children. Games, crafts, and help with homework are some of the activities. An added bonus of this program for some children is the opportunity to develop a relationship with a male role model, which can be important for children living with single mothers.

Adult-supervised, extended day care is important in light of research reporting that both boys and girls in fifth through ninth grade are more susceptible to peer pressure when they are in an after-school situation in which there is no consistent adult control (Lamb, 1998; Steinberg, 1986).

Child care affects not only children and families but communities as well, exemplifying mesosystem linkages. A common misconception is that children in home settings must be experiencing caregiving from one or more adults who are committed to meeting the children's needs and capable of supervising safe, developmentally appropriate activities. This assumption is invalid in many homes, as is illustrated by data from the U.S. Census Bureau (2000) indicating that about 5 million children age 5–14 are left alone to care for themselves outside of school hours while their parents work. There are no exact data for children under age 5 who are left alone all day, but a significant number are cared for by a sibling under age 14. Children who are unsupervised by adults after school—sometimes referred to as **latchkey children** because they carry keys to let themselves into their homes—are more likely to become involved in antisocial acts in their neighborhoods than are children who attend an after-school program (Children's Defense Fund, 2001; Steinberg, 1986; Vandell & Su, 1999). Children involved in self-care are discussed in Chapter 10.

Thus, when examining the effects of child care on the community, we must ask: How does day care affect those children whose families' other alternatives are no care or inadequate care? Only then can we make a responsible decision regarding the economic costs of child care to the community versus the social (and economic) costs to the community resulting from inadequately socialized children who may need government social services, such as welfare, when they grow up.

The quality of family life in communities is often elevated by the provision of child care (Garbarino, 1992). For example, Barry and Garbarino (2001) found that support for child care in certain neighborhoods correlated significantly with a lower incidence of child abuse and neglect. Thus, the effect of child care on the community was that it helped prevent child maltreatment and, in so doing, resulted in a reduced need for more costly government social services to protect at-risk children, such as foster care.

Finally, child care affects the economics of communities in that it enables adults to work. In some societies, the government fully funds child care for such a purpose— for example, in China, France, and Belgium. Likewise, some U.S. businesses have become involved in supporting child care to attract and keep employees (Galinsky, 1992; Lamb, 1998).

The question of whether child care is a public, private, or individual concern remains unresolved in the United States. A key issue is, Who will pay? But if child care needs in the United States are so great, why is cost such a problem? Child care costs depend on the age of the child, whether the care is part- or full-time, and the type of care. Next to housing, food, and taxes, child care is parents' biggest expense.

CHILD CARE AND THE GOVERNMENT AND BUSINESS

The current official policy in the United States is that the government will pay for child care for disadvantaged families (defined by specific criteria) and will grant tax credits to other families up to a maximum set by Congress. It is less costly for the government to fund child care for certain children than it is to fund other services such as special education, welfare, or programs for juvenile delinquents. Government-subsidized child care enables parents to work. Also, research shows that certain types of child care have the potential to break the cycle of poverty in which families in need find themselves (Lamb, 1998).

For example, Karoly and colleagues (1998) examined nine early-intervention programs (including Ypsilanti, Michigan's, Perry Preschool Project [Schweinhart & Weikart, 1993], begun in 1962), following 123 African American children from poor families for 25 years from age 3 or 4 to age 27. Compared with nonparticipating peers (children were randomly assigned to groups), children who had attended a "quality preschool" significantly outperformed those who had not. Specifically, Karoly reported the following for participants in the programs:

- Gains in emotional or cognitive development for children, typically in the short run, or improved parent–child relationships
- Improvements in educational processes and outcomes for children
- Increased economic self-sufficiency, initially for parents and later for children, through greater labor force participation, higher income, and lower welfare usage
- Reduced levels of criminal activity
- Improvements in health-related indicators, such as child abuse, maternal reproductive health, and maternal substance abuse

Thus, preschool, or child care as it has been referred to, does have lasting effects. It is beneficial for children because it starts them off on a more positive track. From

Figure 5.3

High/Scope Perry Preschool Project: Major Findings at Age 27

Source: "Success by Empowerment: High/Scope Perry Preschool Project: Major Findings at Age 27," by J. L. Sweinhart and D. P. Weikert in *Young Children,* 49(1), p. 54. Copyright ©1993 by High/Scope Press. Reprinted by permission.

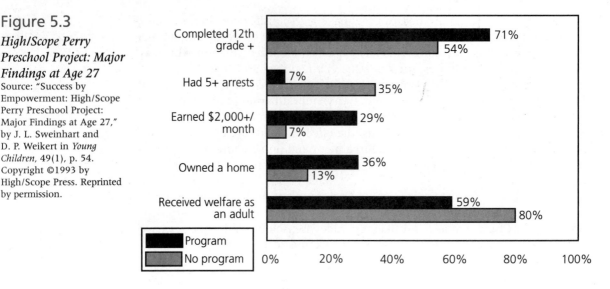

the beginning, they experience greater success in school, which leads them to have more pride in themselves. This reinforces them to become more committed to school, and in so doing, they are less disruptive. Preschool is beneficial for society because it is cost-efficient, according to Schweinhart and Weikart (1993) and Karoly (1998), due to the reduced need for special education and the lessened likelihood of dropping out of school and ending up on welfare or becoming delinquent (see Figure 5.3). In terms of tax dollars, child care appears to be worth the expense (Karoly, 1998; Schweinhart & Weikart, 1993)—and the government and businesses are beginning to concur.

The federal government has recently committed to expanding existing programs, such as Head Start, to include more children. It has given block grants to states to develop programs according to need. For example, in North Carolina, the Abcedarian Project offers individualized instruction for children, links with the public schools, and services for families; Georgia has initiated public preschool for all 4-year-olds.

Some businesses provide assistance in child care for employees, such as parental leaves, flexible scheduling, lists of community resources for parents to choose from (known as "resource and referral"), start-up costs for contributions to community child care centers in return for preferential admission for employees' children, financial assistance to pay for child care, and on-site child care. Employer-sponsored day care has several benefits: New employees are easier to recruit, employee absenteeism is lower, employees have a more positive attitude toward their work, and the job turnover rate of employees is lower (Galinsky, 1992). In addition, day care facilities located at parents' workplaces can provide a beneficial link between family and community for children. For example, parents can visit children during breaks, and children can learn about the work their parents do by touring the business and meeting employees. Some of the innovations businesses have implemented to support family life are outlined in Table 5.2.

- Child care, elder care, and ill-dependent assistance programs
- National resource and referral service networks
- Flextime programs to allow employees to adjust their workdays by as much as 2 hours in either direction
- Extended leave-of-absence policies permitting up to 3-year break from full-time employment with part-time work in second and third years
- Work-at-home programs
- Family-issues sensitivity training for managers and supervisors
- School partnerships, including donations of equipment, time for employees to volunteer, or time for parent–teacher conferences
- On-site employee-staffed child care centers
- Job-sharing programs
- Parent education seminars

Table 5.2

Exosystem Link: Business Support for Families

Child Care and Socialization

As has been discussed, there are different types of child care: (1) care provided by an individual in the child's own home (in-home care), (2) care provided in someone else's home (family day care), and (3) care provided in a center either part- or full-time (center-based care). See Table 5.3 for a summary of the socialization effects of types of child care. Children who care for themselves—self-care children—are discussed in Chapter 10.

There are also different educational practices, or curriculum models, that are implemented in center-based care. The **curriculum** includes the goals and objectives of the program, the teacher's role, the equipment and materials, the space arrangement, the kinds of activities, and the way activities are scheduled.

SOCIALIZATION EFFECTS OF DIFFERENT PRESCHOOL PROGRAMS

Many child care programs, especially center-based ones, follow a curriculum. Keep in mind, however, that some programs select only certain facets of the various curriculum models. A curriculum translates theories about learning into action; consequently, different curricula have different socialization effects. Curricula can be generally categorized as **teacher directed** (learning activities are planned by the teacher for all the children), or **learner directed** (learning activities emerge from individual interest and teacher guidance). The curriculum models used in child care programs that we will discuss are the cognitively oriented, direct instruction, Montessori, and developmental interaction.

The Cognitively Oriented Curriculum

The **cognitively oriented curriculum,** developed by David Weikart and associates at the High/Scope Educational Research Foundation in Ypsilanti, Michigan, represents an attempt to translate Jean Piaget's theory of cognitive development into an educational program. It blends the virtues of purposeful teaching with open-ended, child-initiated activities. It thus is classified as learner directed.

Table 5.3

Socialization and Types of Quality Child Care[a] for Young Children[b]

	IN-HOME CARE (PRIVATELY FUNDED OR VIA RELATIVE)	FAMILY DAY CARE (PRIVATELY FUNDED)	CENTER-BASED CARE (PRIVATELY AND PUBLICLY FUNDED)
PHYSICAL SETTING	Adult oriented (valuable and breakable items moved)	Adult oriented but some specific child materials and play areas	Child oriented (toys, educational materials, specific areas for play provided)
CAREGIVER SPECIAL TRAINING	Unlikely	Some	More likely to have college courses related to and experience with children (especially in public centers)
ADULT–CHILD INTERACTION	Frequent and personal	Close	Mostly adult directed and shared with other children
ACTIVITIES	Mostly unplanned (generally around housekeeping chores)	Some planned	Planned curricula (group and individual)
PEER INTERACTION	Little	Varied	Much
DEVELOPMENTAL DIFFERENCES[c]	Scored lowest on assessments of cognitive ability, social understanding (taking another's perspective and empathizing), cooperation, friendliness, and independence from mother	Scored highest on assessments of friendliness and lowest on assessments of independence from mother	Scored higher on assessments of cognitive ability, social understanding (taking another's perspective and empathizing), cooperation, friendliness, and independence from mother
SOCIALIZATION OUTCOMES	One-to-one interaction and training by adult	Experience in complex interactions with different age children	Increase in social competence, maturity, and intellectual development

[a]These are general differences *between* types of care; there are also differences *within* each type of care (Clarke-Stewart, 1987; Clarke-Stewart, Allhusen, & Clements, 1995).
[b]Age 2–4.
[c]Based on a series of tests done in a laboratory playroom and observations at home.

Piaget believed that humans adapt mentally to their environments through their interactions or experiences with people, objects, and events. He viewed the child as an active learner who explores, experiments, and plans, thereby constructing knowledge. Learning, or mental adaptation to one's environment, occurs through **assimilation** (incorporation) of experiences and **accommodation** (reconciliation of differences) of experiences. An example of assimilation is seeing a bluebird for the first time. The experience is incorporated into the viewer's mental concept of a bird. An example of accommodation is seeing a butterfly, calling it a bird, and being told that it is not a bird but a butterfly. Through experience, the person adjusts the original mental concept of butterfly to accommodate the concept that all things that fly are not always birds. When an individual can assimilate *and* accommodate new information, leading to **equilibrium** (or balance, according to Piaget), the information can then be incorporated.

We assimilate and accommodate throughout our lives, but we do not always reach equilibrium. When we cannot accommodate some new information at the time we encounter it, we reject it. To minimize rejection in children's learning experiences, Piaget recommended that all new experiences be planned in such a way that children can make connections to previous experiences. The implications of this recommendation for education are significant. For example, if teachers can assess the cognitive structures of all children through parent conferences, observation, interviews, and tests, they can select learning activities and tasks that will promote cognitive growth. Otherwise, if a child lacks the cognitive structure for a given task, the child will fail; the new information will be rejected because he or she cannot accommodate it at that particular time. For example, 4-year-olds generally have a poor understanding of equality. Thus, trying to convince a preschooler that the piece of cake on his plate is the same size as his sister's, even though her plate is smaller, thereby making the cake on her plate look larger, will be useless.

In addition to experiences or interactions with people, objects, and events, motivation is a factor in intellectual development. According to Piaget, all children mature in a certain order. At first, they understand their environment only through their senses and motor abilities, which enable them to explore. He called this stage the **sensorimotor** (thinking is action). It involves understanding only the here and now. As children develop language, they begin to understand what words symbolize, but they mistakenly think everyone understands things the same way they do. They can also consider only one characteristic of a thing at a time. Piaget called this stage the **preoperational** (thinking is based on appearances). Children in this stage make judgments based only on how things appear. By the time children reach school age, their understanding of the world expands to incorporate concepts related to time, equality, weight, distance, and so on, but their understanding is limited to concrete, or actual, things they can see or manipulate. Piaget called this stage **concrete operations** (thinking is based on reality). Although children in this stage can apply logical, systematic principles to specific experiences, they still cannot distinguish assumptions or hypotheses from facts. It is not until adolescence that children come to understand abstract concepts such as government and are able to employ logical thinking. Piaget called this stage **formal operations** (thinking is based on abstractions). In this stage, children can think logically about both hypotheses and concrete facts.

In the cognitively oriented curriculum, children are encouraged to become actively involved in constructing their own learning. The teacher observes children individually and questions and evaluates them in order to identify the developmental level. Knowing the developmental level enables the teacher to organize the environment so that children can choose from an array of developmentally appropriate materials and activities. The teacher encourages goal setting and problem solving by asking the children to plan what they are going to do and how they are going to do it. Meanwhile, the teacher is exposing the children to experiences that stimulate thinking processes, language development, and social development.

Thus, children learn to make decisions, set goals, and solve problems by finding alternatives to plans that did not work out as anticipated (Hohmann & Weikart, 1995). For instance, a preschooler's goal might be to build a road with blocks, and a third-grader's goal might be to make a book of the planets, with descriptions and drawings.

In a cognitively oriented program, the children's emerging abilities are broadened and strengthened rather than merely taught. In other words, once an ability is recognized by the teacher, it is nourished by the activities the teacher provides. Children are not pushed to achieve at another developmental level, nor are they taught facts per se; instead, they learn to think for themselves. The focus is on self-direction rather than external reinforcement from others (as is emphasized in behavioral programs). For example, a child may choose to make an airplane at the workbench. The teacher asks the child what materials are needed to carry out the project. When the airplane is complete, the teacher asks the child to describe how the airplane was made. A discussion about how airplanes fly might follow.

The Direct-Instruction Curriculum

The **direct-instruction curriculum** is based on behaviorist principles of dividing learning tasks into small, progressive segments and reinforcing mastery of them. The theories of behaviorist B. F. Skinner (1954) provide the foundation for the direct-instruction curriculum. **Behaviorism** is the doctrine that observed behavior, rather than what exists in the mind, provides the only valid data for psychology. The direct-instruction curriculum is classified as teacher directed. Also known as academic preschool, the curriculum was initially developed at the University of Illinois in the 1960s by Carl Bereiter and Siegfried Engelmann. It was later elaborated by Engelmann and Wesley Becker at the University of Oregon. The program was based on the idea that waiting for children to become academically ready is not a sound educational practice, especially for children from lower socioeconomic groups. Those who subscribe to behaviorism believe that it is possible to ensure learning and that schools can create readiness through behavioral principles of reinforcement and individualized instruction, whatever the IQ or background of the child. Therefore, in the behavioral approach to education, learning involves mastery of specific content. The content and sequence are determined by the teacher or the school—whoever is responsible for planning the curriculum. Learners receive immediate feedback for their responses. Incorrect responses require repetition of the task; correct responses are reinforced, and the learner progresses to the next task.

The Bereiter–Engelmann (1966) preschool program, which was specifically designed for children from low-income families, implements the behavioral approach to learning. According to Bereiter and Engelmann, children from low socioeconomic backgrounds are behind in language development. This lag causes them to have difficulty understanding what is required of them in school. To catch up with their age-mates, they need intense instruction in structured, detailed, sequential skill building. Concepts are organized explicitly and concisely in presentation books for teacher use, and the teacher presents the lessons exactly as shown in the book. The Bereiter–Engelmann program also prescribes classroom manage-

This activity exemplifies those typically found in a teacher-centered classroom, such as direct instruction.

ment techniques, such as rewards for correct responses, instructional pacing (how much time to spend on a topic or with a child), and group management—for example, using hand signals to cue students to respond. The program is designed to foster IQ gain and improve achievement test performance in the early school years (Horowitz & Paden, 1973).

A revised form of the Bereiter–Engelmann program for use in elementary schools is the Engelmann–Becker program, which stresses hard work, focused attention, and achievement in reading, language, and arithmetic. The direct-instruction curriculum uses few of the play materials normally found in many early childhood programs. The goal is to minimize environmental distractions that could tempt children to leave the task at hand and "go exploring." Children are expected to be quiet, respond to the teacher, and not interrupt or leave their seats without permission.

The Montessori Curriculum

Dr. Maria Montessori was a physician in Italy at the turn of the twentieth century. She developed methods of working with children who were mentally retarded and later adapted them for use with children of normal intelligence in her school *Casa del Bambini* (House of Babies). Her principles of education were described in a journal in the United States in 1909 and eventually became very popular in many parts of the world. Trainers were sent to her school to learn her methods and apply them in early childhood programs. However, philosophical differences in the United States prevented Montessori's curriculum from "taking off." In the 1960s, interest in the Montessori curriculum by parents and teachers was renewed.

Montessori (1967) believed that children should be respected and treated as individuals and that adults should not impose their ideas and wishes on them. Children must educate themselves. The Montessori curriculum thus is classified as learner directed.

Children naturally absorb knowledge simply by living. However, there are sensitive periods when children absorb knowledge most easily. Thus, the role of adults is to recognize these sensitive times and prepare the children's environment for the optimum use of these periods of learning (Montessori, 1967). In order, then, for teachers to take advantage of these sensitive periods, they must be keen observers of children's behavior. They also have to know when to encourage children, when to divert them, and when to leave them alone.

The **Montessori curriculum** involves children of different ages. The teacher, called a directress or director, prepares a classroom environment in which children can do things independently. Sometimes the younger children learn from the older ones. The teacher introduces materials to children by demonstrating the correct way to use them. The children are then free to choose any materials they wish to work with. Children work on the floor or on child-sized furniture. The Montessori program provides materials designed for exercises in daily living, sensory development, and academic development (Miller & Dyer, 1975). Exercises in daily living include gardening, setting the table, buttoning buttons, and folding clothes. Sensory development involves work with shapes, graduated cylinders, blocks, and puzzles. Academic materials include large letters, beads and rods for counting, and equipment for learning about size, weight, and volume. All the materials are designed in such a way that children can determine whether they have succeeded in using them properly. Rewards for success and reprimands for failure are nonexistent in Montessori schools (unlike behavioral programs). Rather, each child is encouraged to persist as long as possible on a chosen task because each child is respected as a competent learner.

The Montessori curriculum fosters reality training. For example, items stimulating pretend role-play, such as dress-up clothes, are not included. Children use real things, not "play" things, and perform real tasks, such as setting the table with real silverware and ironing with a real iron.

Only one of each type of equipment is provided in a Montessori classroom, which means other children must wait until the child using a particular piece of equipment is finished. The goal is to help children learn to respect the work of others and cope with the realities of life.

The Developmental-Interaction Curriculum

The Bank Street curriculum, developed by Elizabeth Gilkeson and associates at the Bank Street College of Education in New York City in 1919, focuses on the development of self-confidence, responsiveness, inventiveness, and productivity (Gilkeson & Bowman, 1976). It is classified as learner directed. This approach is also referred to as the **developmental-interaction curriculum** because it is individualized in relation to each child's stage of development while providing many opportunities for children to interact and become involved with peers and adults. The curriculum was influenced by the writings of educator John Dewey (1944), who believed that children are naturally curious and learn by exploring their environment, and Sigmund Freud (1938), who believed that the interactions in the first 5 years of each child's life are significant in forming the child's personality.

The curriculum is designed to help children understand more fully what they already know. Learning is organized around children's own experience bases. Gradually, children's orbit of knowledge and understanding is enlarged by enabling them to explore in greater depth things already familiar to them. Teachers must continually assess children's progress in order to challenge them to experience new levels of complexity (a feature similar to the Montessori curriculum).

The classroom is arranged to include a variety of interest centers where children can pursue special projects, ample and accessible storage space for children's materials, a quiet area for reading, and a library, musical instruments, and art materials. There are also places for the care of animals and plants.

All areas of the curriculum are integrated through the development of themes or units—for example, community helpers, animals, and seeds. Concepts are built around themes. For example, seeds grow into plants such as wheat; plants such as wheat are used to make ingredients for food such as flour; ingredients are combined and cooked to make food such as bread. Similarly, activities are built around concepts. For example, seeds might be planted, and bread might be baked. And activities lead to other learning engagements. For example, cooking leads to math—measuring, counting, adding, weighing, and so on. In addition, children might read books about seeds or take a trip to a bakery. Motivation to learn comes from the pleasure inherent in the activities themselves; extrinsic rewards, such as praise or tokens commonly used in behavioral programs, are generally not used in the Bank Street curriculum to influence children's learning, choice of activities, or behavior. The teacher gains the children's cooperation by showing care, concern, and support.

The results of various studies showed that children from the teacher-directed programs (in which there was more drill-and-practice, direct praise for good work, and time spent in reading and math activities) scored higher on reading and math achievement tests. They also showed more persistence in the ability to do this kind of work and took responsibility for their failures. Children from the learner-directed programs (in which there were more varied materials, more opportunities for choice and exploration, and more interpersonal contact) scored higher on nonverbal reasoning and problem-solving tasks. They also expressed responsibility for their successes. The children from these classrooms were involved in more cooperative work with other children and were more independent (Miller & Dyer, 1975; Schweinhart & Weikart, 1998; Schweinhart, Weikart, & Larner, 1986a; Stallings, 1974).

SOCIALIZATION EFFECTS OF CHILD CARE IDEOLOGIES

An **ideology** involves concepts about human life and behavior. It has been well documented, as discussed in past chapters, that cultural or ethnic ideology influences socialization practices. People from different cultural and economic backgrounds hold different views of what constitutes appropriate child care (Honig, 1995), yet much of the existing literature on child care practices has focused on a monocultural model of optimum care (Bromer, 1999; Greenfield & Suzuki, 1998; Miller, 1989).

Miller (1989) examined the nature of early socialization taking place in quality day care centers serving infants and toddlers from families of different social classes. She reported differences in language and social interaction according to the socioeconomic status of the center's clientele. She also discovered that parents tend to seek out and employ caregivers outside the family whose child care ideologies generally match theirs.

The centers in Miller's study included Center A (Alphabet Academy), which served a relatively low-income clientele, mostly working class; Center B (Balloons and Bunnies Learning Center), which served a clientele with modest incomes, mostly middle class; Center C (Color-Coordinated Country Day School), which served a highly educated professional clientele with affluent means; and Center E (Le Exclusive Enfants School), which served an elite, very wealthy clientele—mostly business executives. Miller focused on the verbal interactions and role expectations between adults and children because language, according to Bernstein (1961), mediates and is mediated by people's perceptions of reality and their social roles. Thus, the language of caregivers who spend much of the day talking and responding to children has an impact on the development of values, roles, and culture-specific behaviors.

Caregivers in the centers gave evidence of differing perceptions of the needs of babies (Miller, 1989). In Centers A and E, crying was not necessarily perceived to indicate a need, and so it wasn't responded to as such. For example, in Center A a baby who cried for days was said to have "just wanted her mama." A bottle or pacifier was not given to soothe the baby because doing so was not allowed. The attitude was that the children "holler for a few days and then they forget about them [their mothers]." In Center E, crying was perceived as a simple annoyance typical of babies and sometimes was indulged and sometimes ignored. In Centers B and C, crying was almost always perceived to indicate a need. In Center B, whenever several babies started to cry, they were said to be either hungry or tired, although not much was done except to tell the babies to stop. In Center C, when a baby cried, the adults were responsible for finding a solution, and if nothing they came up with worked, the parents were called.

According to Miller, the caregivers' response to babies' crying represents the world as they perceive it. If they see the world as a warm, gentle, and compliant place, that is the way they interact with the children—meeting their needs, comforting them, and giving verbal encouragement: "You'll be fine; I'm here now." But if caregivers perceive the world to be cold, hard, and unbending, they respond to children with epithets—"You scaredy-cat," or "You naughty boy"—pointing out their failures and denying indulgences as a way of habituating, and thereby protecting them from, future hurts and disappointments and avoiding false expectations.

Children socialized to exist in a setting of poverty and inequality may have low expectations and low self-esteem but highly effective coping skills. Children socialized to exist in a protected, middle-class environment might be confident, verbal, and creative but be unprepared for life's daily hazards, especially when the real world proves colder and harsher than expected.

That humans replicate for their children their own perceptions of social reality based on their experiences in the larger society was demonstrated by the different expectations communicated to children by caregivers in Miller's (1989) study. For example, although caregivers in both the low- and high-income centers reported that they would have toddlers "clean up" spilled milk, the one in the former said she would "make" them clean it up while the one in the latter said she would "invite" them to do it.

In Center C, the center serving affluent, highly educated professional/managerial parents (doctors, lawyers, professors)—there was a high level of give-and-take among caregivers and children. Children negotiated with caregivers for autonomy when caregivers made demands. Caregivers regarded children's resistance to obey as an indication that perhaps their expectations were unwarranted or the children's primary needs were not being met. Thus, the caregivers adjusted their expectations and demands to gain cooperation. In this sense, children were treated with respect. Because achievement of responsible independence was a goal for children in Center C, the rights and interests of individual children were the focal point of curriculum decisions. These children were being socialized to fit into the world of their privileged parents, who were primarily employed in self-directed, creative, and highly respected occupations.

In Center E—the center serving primarily very wealthy, elite, executive parents—the degree of measurable performance by children in academic tasks was the focal point of curriculum decisions. Children were positively reinforced for absorbing as much memorized information as they could reasonably handle via abstract symbols for quantities, letters, and geometric shapes. Adults controlled most of the use of time, space, and objects. Children who resisted authority demands were first ignored and then firmly redirected if they persisted. Compliance, receptivity, and attentiveness were valued by caregivers, but so was high-quality performance. These caregivers were socializing the children to fit into their parents' world, in which compliance, loyalty to the company, and ability to perform on cue help individuals rise through the hierarchy of power and money.

In Center B—the center serving middle-income families—children were expected to depend on caregivers, compete with peers for attention, and take events in stride. Children's resistance to caregivers' demands was tolerated. Promotion of safety, avoidance of conflict, adherence to set routines, and maintenance of the status quo seemed to be the criteria for curriculum decisions. The attitude was that development and learning would take their normal courses in a safe, nurturing environment. Thus, these caregivers were socializing the children to fit into their parents' world, where they were middle-level supervisors in factories, small-business owners, and participants in other occupations in which individuals may be less able to control the circumstances surrounding their work and more at the mercy of superiors or economic trends. People's occupational success in such circumstances may depend on avoidance of conflict and adherence to set procedures.

Finally, in Center A—the center serving mainly semiskilled and unskilled, working-class families—children were treated as underlings with few rights. Teachers were to be obeyed without question even though resistance was expected, and resistance was arbitrarily punished. Conformity and group cohesion, along with rote memorization, were the bases for curriculum decisions, and academic work was monotonous. The children were not overprotected or directly controlled during rowdy physical playtimes, and they were adept in dealing with the physical environment. These children learned to cope with environmental dangers, long periods of boredom, and lack of material resources. They learned to tolerate discomfort, care for the physical needs of one another, suppress impulses, and passively resist authority. They also became used to punishment while also becoming impervious to it. These children were being socialized to live in their parents' world, which generally consisted of doing menial and repetitive work while being at the mercy of forces beyond their control.

The significance of Miller's description of socialization in child care facilities for children under age 3 is its attempt to analyze different cultural ideologies that may be typical of various socioeconomic statuses and may unwittingly contribute to structures of social inequity in the larger society. Also, when nonparental child care complements family ideology and behavior, it is more likely to be beneficial for children; when it differs, it is more likely to be harmful (Lamb, 1998). This also applies to differences between caregiver and parental attitudes regarding child-rearing practices—for example, authoritative versus authoritarian (Ghazvini & Mullis, 2002).

Developmentally Appropriate Caregiving

Caregivers or teachers who implement developmentally appropriate practices

> must know about child development and the implications of this knowledge for how to teach, the content of the curriculum—what to teach and when—how to assess what children have learned, and how to adapt curriculum and instruction to children's individual strengths, needs, and interests. Further, they must know the particular children they teach and their families and be knowledgeable as well about the social and cultural context. (Bredekamp & Copple, 1997, p. 16)

Some aspects of developmentally appropriate caregiving involve observation, sensitivity to children's needs, and responsiveness. Teachers create a stimulating environment, plan engaging activities, enable children to initiate learning, and facilitate self-regulatory behavior in children. To enhance children's development, ongoing assessment of their learning must take place and be reflected in the planned activities. Collaboration with families is essential.

Points to Ponder

"Maturation" refers to developmental changes due to the process of aging. There are individual differences within the "average" ages when children reach certain developmental milestones, such as walking, talking, and controlling bladder and bowels. Sometimes a child might be labeled as too "immature" for child care or preschool. What does that mean?

COLLABORATIVE CAREGIVING

To provide a beneficial caregiving environment for children, it is critical for professionals who care for infants and children to collaborate with families regarding ideologies and socialization goals (Bromer, 1999; Greenfield & Suzuki, 1998). At different ends of the individualism–collectivism continuum are cultural frameworks (ideologies) for socialization (see Figure 5.4). The primary goal in an individualistic society is independence—children are encouraged to be autonomous and self-fulfilled, and social responsibilities are motivated by personal choice. The primary goal in a collective society is interdependence—children are encouraged to be subordinate and responsible in relating to others, and achievements are motivated in terms of service to the group, usually the family (Greenfield & Suzuki, 1998). In a diverse society, such as the United States, both parents and caregivers represent different degrees of individualism and collectivism. These can be observed in such attitudes as sleeping arrangements (Should the baby sleep alone or with its parents?), carrying (Should the baby be carried in a baby carrier close to his or her mother's body, or put in an infant seat to be physically separate but in view of his or her mother?), and feeding (Should the baby be fed whenever he or she cries, or should a certain schedule be adhered to?) (Bhavnagri, 1997).

	Independence Oriented ← → Interdependence Oriented	
Values	Individual achievement is valued. • Competition is encouraged. • Toys promoting individual enjoyment or mastery are provided. • Self-help skills are reinforced.	Group cohesiveness is valued. • Mutual help is encouraged. • Toys promoting turn taking or collaboration are provided. • Helping others is reinforced.
Activities	Object-focused activities are emphasized. • Children are stimulated and learn from playing with toys and things. • Babies are put on mats or in playpens to play with things.	People-focused activities are emphasized. • Children are stimulated and learn from observing and interacting with people. • Babies are held by adults most of the time.
Communication	Communication of feelings is openly expressive. • Children are encouraged to talk about feelings of happiness, sadness, fear, or anger. • Children are permitted to question rules and authority figures.	Communication of feelings is restricted. • Children are expected to subordinate their feelings to promote the harmony of the group. • Children are not permitted to question rules or authority figures.

Figure 5.4

Some Cultural Frameworks for Socialization in Caregiving Settings
Source: Adapted from Bromer, 1999.

© Wadsworth/Thomson Learning

These parents and teacher are collaborating on an activity with their children.

Diversity in socialization goals can also be observed in communication styles with infants. An American mother is likely to label objects verbally so her child learns the names of things in the environment: That's a car. It's red. Look! It has four wheels." A Japanese mother is likely to focus more on the sharing of an object than on labeling it: "Here's the car. I give it to you; you give it to me. Thank you!" (Greenfield & Suzuki, 1998).

Some experts suggest that parents and nonparental caregivers set aside "transition time" when children enter a child care setting. During this time, parents and caregivers can observe each other interact with the children and discuss socialization goals, methods, and outcomes. Observation and discussion should take place at regular intervals. Support for this practice comes from a study of child care facilities in three Canadian cities with substantial immigrant populations (Bernhard, Lefebvre, Kilbride, Chud, & Lange, 1998). The investigators found that parents and teachers were unaware of their basic differences in socialization goals, particularly respect for authority, social skills, and learning. Also, there were substantial disagreements over what constitutes appropriate parenting at home. Thus, there needs to be more linkages between home and child care in order to provide developmentally appropriate practices for diverse groups of children (Bredekamp & Copple, 1997).

Collaborative caregiving also refers to the support child caregivers can provide to parents based on their knowledge of child development and developmentally appropriate practices. Support includes the following:

- Listening to parents
- Empathizing
- Translating emotional responses into concrete ones that can be acted upon
- Modeling methods of guidance and discipline
- Providing opportunities for support groups and parent education
- Enabling the family to link with services in the community

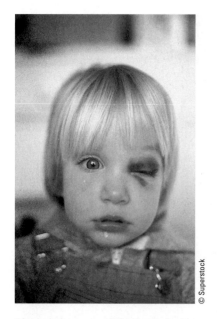

Physical abuse, exemplified by the bruise on this child's eye, must be reported to child protective services.

CAREGIVERS AND CHILD PROTECTION

According to the current political ideology in the United States (a macrosystem), children should be protected from harm and maltreatment. If the family doesn't do this, then the government must. Child protective laws, such as the Child Abuse Prevention and Treatment Act (CAPTA) of 1974, have been passed. CAPTA defines maltreatment and identifies professionals who must report suspected cases to their local child protective agency. Child caregivers and educators are among the mandated reporters. Sometimes caregivers notice that a child's appearance, behavior, or way of interacting differs from that of the other children. Caregivers with child development training and experience are able to recognize deviations from what is considered normal development. Although states vary in their specific definitions of maltreatment and their procedures as to when and how to report it, the box "Indications of Possible Maltreatment" provides useful general information. Intervention programs are discussed in detail in Chapter 10.

Indications of Possible Maltreatment

Physical Abuse
Physical Indicators

Bruises

- Unexplained bruises and welts on the face, lips, mouth, torso, back, buttocks, or thighs, which often reflect the shape of the object used to inflict the injury—for example, electric cords, belts, buckles, and sticks. ("Normal" bruises or welts do not usually cause lacerations, deep discoloration, or other trauma to the extent injuries from abuse do.)
- Bruises that regularly appear after absences, weekends, or vacations.

Burns

- Burns in unusual places, especially on the soles of the feet, palms of the hands, back, or buttocks. (These are often caused by cigars or cigarettes.)
- Burns resembling socklike or glovelike markings on the hands or feet or "doughnut" burns on the buttocks or genital area. (These burns are caused by forced immersion in scalding liquids.)
- Appliance or tool burns that leave a pattern mark of the object (iron, electric burner, fireplace tool, etc.)
- Rope burns on the arms, legs, neck, or torso. (These appear when children are tied to beds or other structures.)

Fractures and Other Injuries

- Unexplained fractures (particularly to the nose or facial structure) in various stages of healing. Fractures that are a result of child abuse frequently cannot be explained by one episode of trauma. They often have not healed properly and have some additional patterns of stress in terms of growth that are evident upon examination.
- Multiple fractures appearing in different parts of the body (ribs, vertebral compression or spinal fractures).
- Injuries that are in various stages of healing, are clustered, or form regular patterns over the same injured area.
- Unexplained swelling of the abdomen, localized tenderness, and constant vomiting.
- Human bite marks, especially when they are recurrent and/or appear to be adult size.

Behavioral Indicators

- Unexplained behavior patterns, such as fear of adult contact, apprehension when other children cry, fear of parents, or fear of going home.
- Chronic tardiness, poor attendance, increased withdrawal, preoccupation, or simply the need to talk to someone.
- Inability to establish good peer relations and, often, aggressive acting-out behavior.
- Restlessness or inability to sit down.

Physical Neglect

Physical Indicators

- Constant hunger.
- Poor hygiene.
- Inappropriate dress for weather conditions.
- Unattended physical or medical needs.
- Lack of supervision in especially dangerous situations or activities over long periods of time.

Behavioral Indicators

- Alcohol or drug abuse.
- Begging for or stealing food; making statements that indicate there is no guardian or parent at home.
- Extended stays at school (early arrival or late departure).
- Constant fatigue, listlessness, or falling asleep in class.

Sexual Abuse and Exploitation

Even though sexual abuse is often deceptively nonviolent, it is disabling and emotionally harmful. It involves the employment, use, or coercion of any child to engage in sexually explicit conduct. It includes indecent exposure, obscene phone calls, pornographic pictures (viewing or taking), fondling, oral or genital stimulation, and sexual intercourse. It may occur over a long period of time, beginning gradually, or it may occur as rape.

Physical Indicators

- Difficulty in walking or sitting.
- Torn, stained, or bloody underclothing.
- Complaints of pain or itching in the genital area.
- Bruises or bleeding in external genital, vaginal, or anal area.
- Venereal disease in the genital area, mouth, or eyes.

Behavioral Indicators

- Unwillingness to change clothes for gym class or to participate in physical education class.
- Bizarre, sophisticated, or unusual sexual behavior or knowledge in younger children, including withdrawal, fantasy, or infantile behavior.
- Verbal reports by the child of sexual relations with a caregiver or parent.
- Fear of certain people or places.
- Withdrawal.
- Clinging to parent more than usual.
- Behaving as a younger child.
- Acting out the abuse with dolls or peers.
- Excessive masturbation.

Emotional Abuse

Just as physical injuries can scar and incapacitate a child, emotional cruelty can similarly cripple and disable a child emotionally, behaviorally, and intellectually. Obviously, individual incidents of emotional abuse are difficult to identify and/or recognize and are, therefore, not mandated reporting situations. However, the interests of the child should be primary, and if it is suspected that the child is suffering from emotional abuse, it should be reported. Furthermore, if there is an indication that emotional abuse is being inflicted willfully and causing unjustifiable mental suffering, reporting is required. Regardless of whether the situation is one requiring mandatory reporting, cases should be diverted to some sort of treatment as soon as possible.

Behavioral Indicators

- Withdrawn, depressed, apathetic behavior.
- Antisocial or 'acting-out' behavior.
- Other signs of emotional turmoil (repetitive, rhythmic movements; inordinate attention to details; no verbal or physical communication with others).
- Unwitting comments about own behavior: "Daddy always tells me I'm bad."

Emotional Deprivation

Like emotional abuse, emotional deprivation can leave serious scars on a child. It, too, is difficult to recognize or identify, and is only a mandated reporting situation if willfully intended and if serious mental suffering results. However, the same precautions apply: In the best interests of the child, suspected emotional deprivation should be reported and/or referred for some type of intervention treatment.

Physical Indicators

- Speech disorders.
- Lag in physical development, frailty, and/or refusal to eat.
- Failure to thrive.

Behavioral Indicators

- Thumb or lip sucking (habit disorders).
- Constantly "seeking out" or "pestering" other adults for attention and affection.
- Attempted suicide.
- Antisocial or destructive behavior.
- Sleep disorders, inhibition of play, or neurotic traits.
- Behavior extremes (such as compliant/demanding, passive/aggressive).
- Hysteria, phobias, or compulsive traits.

Parental Attitudes

Some noticeable indicators in parental behavior that may indicate abuse are as follows:

- Blaming or belittling the child.
- Overly defensive or abusive reaction when approached about problems concerning the child.
- Apathetic or unresponsive attitude.
- Showing little concern for the child—as evidenced by lack of interest in what the child is doing in school and lack of participation on parent's or child's part in school activities.
- Finding nothing good or attractive in the child.

Sources: Crime Prevention Center, 1988, National Clearinghouse on Child Abuse and Neglect, 2002.

Children who are maltreated do not usually "tell." They may be distrustful of all adults. They may even be unlikely to express hatred toward abusing parents. In any case, there is little understanding of the parents' behavior. Often children believe the abuse occurred because they did something wrong. Thus, they may be confused and even frightened by another adult's concern. They may also worry about their parents' reaction if they tell (O'Brien, 1984). With this understanding, child caregivers and educators can be involved in identifying victims, offering support, providing a stable environment, and modeling ways to express feelings appropriately and resolve conflicts.

Epilogue

Child care is a significant socialization setting. Family involvement is essential to caregivers in socializing children; it is thus a collaborative effort. Mary Poppins modeled appropriate practices with the Banks children, as did Anne Sullivan with Helen Keller. Both Mary and Anne were available to the parents as consultants. Both were sensitive, responsive, and stimulating to the children in their care, enabling psychological, social, and cognitive development.

Summary

Child, or day, care refers to care given to children by persons other than parents during the day or part of the day. It can be at the child's home, at another home, or in a center.

Quality care involves (1) a caregiver who provides warm, loving care and guidance for the child and works with the family to ensure that the child develops in the best way possible; (2) a setting that keeps the child safe, secure, and healthy; and (3) activities that help the child develop emotionally, socially, mentally, and physically. Quality care is also judged by whether the program is developmentally appropriate. Objective measures of quality include size of the overall group, caregiver–child ratios, and caregiver training in child development. Voluntary accreditation systems exist nationally to establish higher-quality standards than are required by law for both child care centers and family day care homes.

Child care and early childhood educational practices have been affected by macrosystems—political ideology, culture/ethnicity, economics, and science/technology.

Chronosystem influences in child care are evidenced by historical changes in the United States. Child care began in this country at the beginning of the nineteenth century as a social service for immigrants who were poor and for mothers employed outside the home. It was mainly custodial. Some middle-class families viewed child care as potentially enriching. By the 1960s, child care programs were flourishing because of the increase in the number of mothers of young children entering the labor force and the recognition of the importance of the early childhood years for subsequent development. Giving children from low-income families an opportunity to develop learning skills before entering public school also became a priority. Along with the increase in child care programs came a concern with their quality.

The correlates and consequences of child care on children include emotional, social, and intellectual ones. Basically, children who attend quality day care programs do not differ from children cared for at home in their attachments to their mothers. Children in day care programs differ somewhat from other children in their relationships with peers. Children in day care programs are more self-sufficient, outgoing, and aggressive with others than children who are not. Generally, the intellectual performance of children who attended day care is higher than that of children from similar family backgrounds who did not attend a quality child care program. This is especially true of children from lower socioeconomic statuses.

A federally funded program for children who are disadvantaged, Head Start, provides intervention to enable such children to enter school ready to learn. The rationale for government intervention comes from research on the importance of early experience on intellectual development, as well as political attitudes regarding the prevention of poverty. Even though there are many kinds of intervention programs, most investigators seem to agree that, for the child to become a competent member of society, the child's family must be involved. Also, the earlier and longer the intervention, the better the results. The problem, however, with assessing the socialization outcomes of intervention programs is that so many variables pertaining to the child, the family, and the day care program must be taken into account.

A mesosystem influence on child care includes links with the school and community. Schools can extend hours to care for children and include those under the age of 5. Child care impacts the community as well as families. Child care fosters future contributors to society. Economically, it is less costly to fund child care programs with tax dollars than it is to fund other services such as special education, welfare, and programs for juvenile delinquents. Child care also provides work for adults in the community, thereby contributing economically.

Another mesosystem influence on child care is links with the government and businesses. The government funds child care and offers tax credits to families using child care. Business can provide services for their employees, such as leaves, flextime, financial assistance for child care, resources and referrals, in-kind contributions to child care facilities in the community, and/or on-site care.

Different types of child care (in-home care, family day care, center-based care) have different effects on socialization due to the varying opportunities for interacting with adults, other children, and materials. Having several adults with whom to interact, in addition to other children, in a safe, orderly, stimulating environment is related to subsequent intellectual and social competence.

Curriculum models found in preschool programs include cognitively oriented, Montessori, direct instruction, and developmental interaction. Curriculum influences socialization in that the specific skills a program emphasizes are likely to be the ones exhibited by children. Teacher-directed curricula such as direct instruction generally produce children who score higher on achievement tests. Learner-directed curricula, such as Montessori and developmental interaction (as well as the cognitively oriented curriculum) generally tend to foster autonomy, problem-solving skills, and cooperation.

Caregivers influence socialization by their cultural ideologies. These ideologies affect caregivers' language and social interaction with children. Thus, caregivers in child care centers serving clienteles of varying socioeconomic statuses may have different expectations of children, which, in turn, can affect the socialization practices and outcomes in the centers.

Caregivers or teachers who implement developmentally appropriate practices must know about child development and how to teach curriculum accordingly. To provide a beneficial caregiving environment for children, it is critical for professionals who care for infants and children to collaborate with families regarding socialization goals, ranging from individualism to collectivism. Collaborative caregiving refers to the support provided to parents based on knowledge and experience.

According to the political ideology in the United States, children should be protected. By law, caregivers and educators must report child maltreatment, which includes physical abuse, neglect, sexual abuse and exploitation, and emotional abuse and deprivation.

Activity

PURPOSE *To assess the socialization that occurs in the child care facilities in your community.*

1. Look in the phone book and choose two child care facilities in your community to visit. Note whether they are half- or full-day facilities and whether they serve infants/toddlers, preschoolers, and/or school-agers.
2. Describe each facility—physical setting, teacher–child ratio, ages of children, hours, fees, equipment (outdoor and indoor), toys, and creative materials.
3. Observe the interaction between the adults and the children. Describe.
4. Observe the interaction between the children. Describe.
5. What kind of curriculum is implemented? Describe.
6. Is there parent involvement and/or education in the program? Describe.
7. Are there support services (health, nutrition, counseling, referrals) for families of the enrolled children? Describe.

Research Terms

Quality child care
Early childhood education
Developmental appropriateness
Cognitively oriented curriculum
Direct-instruction curriculum
Montessori curriculum
Developmental-interaction curriculum
Head Start
NAEYC

Related Readings

Baker, A. C., & Manfred-Petitt, L. A. (1998). *Circle of love: Relationships between parents, providers, and children in family child care.* St. Paul, MN: Redleaf Press.

Bender, J., Flatter, C. H., & Sorrentino, J. (1998). *Half a childhood: Quality programs for out-of-school hours.* Nashville, TN: School Age Notes.

Besharov, D. J. (1990). *Recognizing child abuse.* New York: Free Press.

Clarke-Stewart, K. A. (1993). *Daycare* (rev. ed.). Cambridge, MA: Harvard University Press.

Cochran, M., & Larner, M. (1990). *Extending families.* Cambridge, MA: Cambridge University Press.

Elkind, D. (1987). *Miseducation: Preschoolers at risk.* New York: Knopf.

Forward, S., & Buck, C. (1988). *Betrayal of innocence* (rev. ed.). New York: Penguin Books.

Garbarino, J., Guttman, E., & Seely, J. W. (1986). *The psychologically battered child: Strategies for identification, assessment and intervention.* San Francisco: Jossey-Bass.

Helfer, R., & Kempe, C. H. (1987). *The battered child* (4th ed.). Chicago: University of Chicago Press.

Hohmann, M., & Weikart, D. P. (1995). *Educating young children: Active learning practices for preschool educators and child care programs.* Ypsilanti, MI: High/Scope Press.

Kontos, S. (1992). *Family day care: Out of the shadows and into the limelight.* Washington, DC: National Association for the Education of Young Children.

U.S. Department of Education and U.S. Department of Health and Human Services. (2002). *Teaching our youngest: A guide for preschool teachers & child care & family providers.* Washington, DC: U.S. Government Printing Office.

Chapter 6

Prologue: Then and Now

The School's Function as a Socializing Agent

Macrosystem Influences on Schools
  Factors in Educational Decisions
  School Choice
  Diversity and Equity: Gender, Ethnicity, Religion, and Special Needs

Chronosystem Influences on Schools
  Adaptations to Social Change
  Technology
  Violence
  Substance Use/Abuse

Mesosystem Influences
  School–Child Linkages
  School–Family Linkages
  School–Peer Group Linkages
  School–Media Linkages
  School–Community Linkages

Epilogue

Summary

Activity

Research Terms

Related Readings

© Bob Daemmrich/Stock, Boston Inc./PictureQuest

Ecology of the School

The direction in which education starts a man will determine his future life.

—PLATO

LEARNING: INSTINCT OR INSTRUCTION? PROCESS OR PRODUCT?

THEN *Emile*, a classic novel by Jean-Jacques Rousseau (1762), tells of a plan for a child's education from infancy to adulthood. Emile's education was to take place on a country estate under the guidance of a tutor who would nurture his natural abilities. Emile was not to be exposed to societal influences that might corrupt him, such as books and other people's words.

The plan was for Emile to first learn about the world through his senses. According to Rousseau, the senses are the first teachers and, therefore, are more efficient and desirable than formal learning in a schoolroom with a teacher and a curriculum. By observing his environment, Emile would acquire knowledge of nature, geography, and science.

Emile was indeed a child of nature in that he was to be allowed to follow his instinctive curiosity, express himself as he desired, and deviate from society's morals or the usual ways of teaching subjects. Rousseau believed that formal education was based on symbols—for example, words, numbers, and maps. Thus, a child could learn the names of countries and cities but not know how to navigate his way to town without getting lost. Emile would learn by doing—his eyes would be his compass, adding information to his repertoire as he became capable of understanding and as the information became necessary. By the time Emile was 13 years old, he would have enough practical experience to be ready for formal schooling. He would also be able to deal with the "corrupt" influences of government, economics, business, and the arts because, at this age, he would be capable of evaluating information based on real experiences.

NOW The "deschooling" philosophy described in *Emile* is ongoing today. Many children like Emile are being educated at home, as it is legal for parents to take charge of their children's education from kindergarten through high school. A primary reason for home schooling is to protect children from the "corrupt" influences of school—drugs, alcohol, sex, violence. A second reason is to teach values and morals, especially religious ones, that are synonymous with those of the family. Public schools must offer a nonsectarian education. A third reason is to maintain children's natural curiosity. Home schooling enables children's learning to be more individualistic and spontaneous, according to their interests. For example, if a child is fascinated with dinosaurs, a trip to the museum is easier to arrange than it would be in a school setting, in which approval and planning for a class field trip must take place.

KEY QUESTIONS

- What and how should children learn?
- Is learning a process or a product?
- Should content or curiosity drive the curriculum?
- Should schools teach society's accumulated knowledge (a "core" curriculum)

or stress skills related to learning how to learn (a focus on individualism and creativity)?

- How should children's learning be motivated?

The School's Function as a Socializing Agent

The school is society's formal institution where learning takes place. This chapter examines the school as a microsystem in which children develop. To better understand the socialization functions of the school, macrosystem influences (political ideology, economics, culture/ethnicity, religion, and science/technology), and their changes over time (chronosystem influences) are discussed. Also relevant to understanding the school's function as a socialization agent are the linkages, or mesosystems, between school and family, school and peer groups, school and media, and school and community. (Figure 6.1 shows an ecological model of the systems) involved in the process.

The school functions as a socializing agent by providing the intellectual and social experiences from which children develop the skills, knowledge, interest, and atti-

Figure 6.1

An Ecological Model of Human Development
The school is a significant influence on children's development.

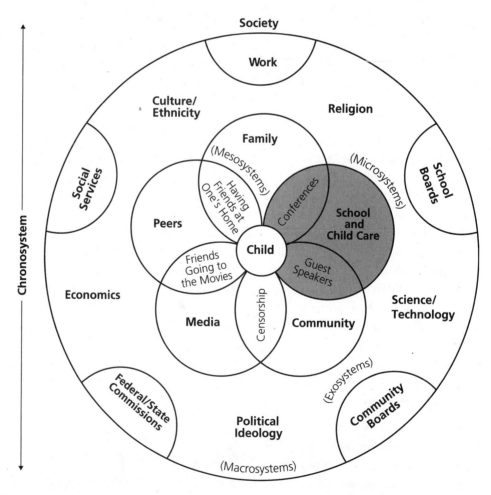

ACADEMIC GOALS
- Mastery of basic skills (learn reading, writing, arithmetic) and fundamental processes (communicate ideas, use information resources)
- Intellectual development (accumulate general knowledge; think rationally, independently, and critically; solve problems; be curious)

VOCATIONAL GOALS
- Career/vocational education (select a suitable occupation based on interests and abilities, develop appropriate work attitudes and habits, become economically independent and productive)

SOCIAL, CIVIC, AND CULTURAL GOALS
- Interpersonal understandings (acquire values, develop relationships, appreciate culture)
- Citizenship participation (understand history and representational government, make informed choices, contribute to the welfare of others and the environment)
- Enculturation (become aware of values, behavioral norms, traditions, achievements of one's culture and other cultures)
- Moral and ethical character (evaluate choices and conduct, develop integrity)

PERSONAL GOALS
- Emotional and physical well-being (develop self-awareness, coping skills, time management skills, healthy habits, physical fitness)
- Creativity and aesthetic expression (develop originality in problem solving, be tolerant of new ideas, appreciate various forms of creativity)
- Self-realization (evaluate abilities and limitations, set goals, accept responsibility for decisions)

Table 6.1

Goals for Schooling in the United States
Sources: Goodlad, 1984; Johnson, Dupuis, Musial, and Hall, 2003.

tudes that characterize them as individuals and that shape their abilities to perform adult roles. Schools exert influence on children (1) by their educational policies leading to achievement, (2) by their formal organization of the introduction of students to authority, and (3) by the social relationships that evolve in the classroom. Some of these influences are intentional, such as instruction in a specific subject; others are unintentional, such as competitive grading, possibly leading to low motivation.

The primary purpose of education, from *society's* perspective, is the transmission of the cultural heritage: the accumulated knowledge, values, beliefs, and customs of society. To transmit the culture and maintain it, society must be provided with trained people who can assume specialized roles, as well as develop new knowledge and technology. The purpose of education from the *individual's* perspective is to acquire the necessary skills and knowledge to become self-sufficient as well as able to participate effectively in society.

The school's function in the United States can be described as universal (it is open to all), formal (it follows convention), and prescriptive (it provides directions based on custom). Society's expectations are expressed in goals: academic, vocational, social, civic, cultural, and personal (see Table 6.1). These goals emerged from a detailed study of schooling, led by John Goodlad (1984), in a sample of communities across the United States representing urban, suburban, and rural areas, as well as different socioeconomic statuses. Elementary, junior high, and high schools were included in the study. Questionnaires were given to teachers, parents, students, and administrators regarding their goals for education.

Points to Ponder

Habituation/dishabituation is considered an innate form of learning due to the brain's response to stimuli. Habituation means an infant has become accustomed to a particular stimulus (the noise of the vacuum cleaner or TV) and no longer responds as he or she originally did (crying). Dishabituation means the infant's response (crying) can be elicited by a new, similar stimulus (the noise of the dog barking). Habituation usually occurs with repetition or sameness, and dishabituation usually occurs with novelty. From your experience, what did school do to foster habituation/dishabituation?

Macrosystem Influences on Schools

The school reflects macrosystem influences of society—specifically, its traditional values and future goals. The citizens of the society implement these values and goals. In a democratic society, the role of the school is continually debated by its citizens until a consensus is reached regarding funding, curricula, teacher education, class size, attendance requirements, and so on. Influential factors in educational decisions are political ideology, economics, culture/ethnicity, religion, and science/technology.

FACTORS IN EDUCATIONAL DECISIONS

The basic political ideology for which the United States of America stands is democracy—as Abraham Lincoln stated, "government of the people, by the people, and for the people." A democratic society presumes freedom from government oppression. Citizens in a democratic society, although diverse, are presumed to have equal rights and equal opportunities. As Thomas Jefferson wrote in the Declaration of Independence, "We hold these truths to be self-evident, that all men are created equal, that they are endowed by their Creator with certain unalienable Rights, that among these are Life, Liberty, and the Pursuit of Happiness."

For a democracy to function, its citizens must be educated to discuss and compromise on issues pertaining to them as individuals and as a group. They must be able to select competent leaders to rule by the will of the majority. And they must be able to evaluate the equity of the rules and the leaders' implementation of them. Citizens' exercising their right to vote, thereby participating in decision making, is how this occurs. It wasn't until after the Civil War, however, that schooling became public, thereby availing all children, regardless of socioeconomic status, an equal opportunity to be educated and to exercise their voice in government. The concept of equality has been expanded since the days of the writing of the Constitution to include race, creed, color, gender, age, national origin, and disability—as has been implemented in various laws, discussed in following pertinent sections.

How much society is willing to pay for the education of its citizens is influenced by values of equality of opportunity, concepts of knowledge and skills required for the future, and opinions about the affordability of programs and curricula. Educational policies are under the jurisdiction of the states, rather than the federal government, so there is a wide range of expenditures spent per pupil throughout the country, among and even within the states. For example, New Jersey, ranked first among the states for public education, spends about $9700, and Utah, ranked

Scientific knowledge is one of the national education goals recently formulated by government, business, and educational leaders.

last, spends about $4000 per pupil (Children's Defense Fund, 2001). A major cause of school funding inequalities is that most states rely heavily on local property taxes to finance education. Thus, property taxes in wealthier districts usually generate adequate monies, but property taxes in poorer districts do not. Another cause of funding inequalities is states' policies on school accountability for student learning. Some states, such as California, give "bonus" financial rewards to schools that have boosted students' scores on state achievement tests.

The school imparts traditional cultural values through the curricula and through classroom management. A challenge facing educators is how to balance equity (assimilation into a common culture) with diversity (maintenance of a distinctive heritage or identity). This challenge is exemplified by what information is included in textbooks, such as what is the Native American Indian perspective on Thanksgiving versus that of the descendants of the colonists who came to America from Europe?

The first amendment to the Constitution guarantees freedom of religion and requires separation of church and state. This means that public schools cannot promote a particular religion, nor can they inhibit religious beliefs. This line between church and state has been debated throughout history, as exemplified by controversies over educational policies regarding school prayer, appropriate science curriculum, extracurricular activities on public school facilities, and school vouchers (tax rebates to families who choose a private education instead of a public one).

Finally, advancements in science and technology have impacted not only school curricula but the methods of teaching. Technological aids for teaching include television, videodisc recorders, CD-ROMS, computers, and modems. Children learn how to use such equipment to enhance learning and to develop skills. Scientific research on how children process information has broadened teaching methods to include active participation and discovery in addition to passive recitation and rote learning.

SCHOOL CHOICE

Macrosystem influences are evidenced by society's policies regarding school choice. Generally, students are assigned to a public school in their local district. Educational decisions—teachers and staff, curricula, attendance time required, textbooks, assessment procedures, class size and composition, extracurricular activities, school expenditures, rules and regulations—are made bureaucratically by the school district in compliance with state requirements.

Many people believe that private schools have more successful educational outcomes than do public schools, due to less bureaucracy, more family involvement, smaller classes, and students' backgrounds (Levine & Levine, 1996). Families who send their children to private school must pay both tuition and school taxes for public schools. There was much political pressure, beginning in the 1970s in various states, to give public financial support to private schools. One mechanism is the voucher—a coupon in the amount the school district normally spends on an individual child's education—to be "spent" at whatever school the family chooses, public or private. The argument is that in a free-market system private schools should have as much right as public schools to be supported by the government and that the best schools will attract the most students, thereby thriving, while the worst schools will improve to attract "customers" (Tozer, Violas, & Senese, 2002).

The voucher system came under legal scrutiny in a court case in Cleveland, Ohio, in 1997, when the system was declared unconstitutional because of inappropriate church–state separation; most of the vouchers (public money) were being used for religious schools. However, the concept of vouchers as a school choice option is still viable, as evidenced by the No Child Left Behind Act of 2001, which tries to balance flexibility with accountability in schools receiving federal funds under Title I of the Elementary and Secondary Education Act (ESEA). The act grants parents certain rights, such as to inspect instructional material and assessments; it provides guidelines for school choice and vouchers, and for school prayer; and it stipulates requirements for funding school improvements, teacher qualifications, and testing.

In response to the controversy surrounding vouchers, many states have recently passed legislation to enable families to choose schools for their children—hence, the creation of charter schools. A **charter school** is established when a school district grants a group of people, which could include parents, community members, and teachers, a charter, or authorization, to open a school that reflects their shared educational philosophy. The district then funds that school like any other public school. Charter schools provide entrepreneurial opportunities for those who design the curricula. There is explicit responsibility for improved achievement, as measured by standardized tests.

Some families believe that any mechanisms involving public schools will not benefit their child and so choose to provide home-based education. States do require home schools to have credentialed teachers and to follow a prescribed curricula; however, specific requirements vary from state to state. Some home-based education is combined with that provided by charter schools. Many families who choose home schooling do so because they believe it's the parents' right to control their children's education and to teach morals and values (usually religious) as they see fit (Kantrowitz & Wingert, 1998).

DIVERSITY AND EQUITY: GENDER, ETHNICITY, RELIGION, AND SPECIAL NEEDS

All the macrosystem influences discussed previously relate to how diverse groups in society, such as those characterized by gender, ethnicity, religion, and special needs, have equitable opportunities to achieve. We examine the effects of those macrosystem influences here; in the next chapter, we focus on how such diverse groups are treated as part of the general student population in the classroom.

Gender

Until 1972, when Title IX of the Education Amendments Act was passed, there were inequities in schools based on gender. These inequities included different curriculum opportunities for males and females (boys took "shop" and girls took "home economics"), different academic and career advisement, different amounts of money allocated to athletic and extracurricular activities, and different portrayals in textbooks. The opening section of Title IX states:

> No person in the United States shall, on the basis of sex, be excluded from participation in, be denied the benefits of, or be subjected to discrimination under any education program or activity receiving federal financial assistance.

Every public school and most colleges and universities in the United States are covered by Title IX, which prohibits discrimination in school admissions, in counseling and guidance, in competitive athletics, in student rules and regulations, and in access to programs and courses, including vocational and physical education. Title IX also applies to sex discrimination in employment practices, including interviewing and recruitment, hiring and promotion, compensation, job assignments, and fringe benefits.

Ethnicity

The macrosystem ideology that the school is responsible for socializing ethnically diverse groups is wedded to American immigration policy. That is, those who live and work here must learn good citizenship, accept democratic values, and adhere to the laws and principles of the Constitution.

Macrosystem philosophies influencing how diverse ethnic groups should be socialized, especially by the school, are assimilation (microcultures assume attributes of the macroculture), melting pot (all cultures blend into one), and cultural pluralism (micro- and macrocultures coexist).

Assimilation involves the process whereby one group gives up its characteristics and takes on those of another group. The school has traditionally served the socialization needs of the majority culture. For a long time, it was felt that, for diverse ethnic groups to be assimilated into society, they had to adapt to the majority culture's ways. Examples of assimilation are English as the official language on public documents, English-immersion programs in schools, and celebration of American holidays. An important influence in this attitude was Elwood P. Cubberley (1919), a historian of U.S. education and an educational leader. Cubberley advocated an intensive effort to Americanize the children of immigrants. He felt that it was the obligation of the public schools in areas of immigrant concentrations to assimilate the children of the newcomers into the superior "American race." His view was generally accepted by school administrators and teachers.

Later, the idea of America as a melting pot became a popular approach to socializing immigrants and ethnic minorities. The melting-pot concept was first expressed by Hector Saint-John de Crevecoeur, who wrote in 1756, "Here in America individuals of all nations are melted into a new race of men" (quoted in Krug, 1976). Advocates of the melting-pot theory deplored the hatreds and feuds that the immigrants brought with them from Europe and perpetuated in the United States, but they acknowledged that there was much good in their respective ethnic groups. They believed that the emerging U.S. culture must be built not on the destruction of the ethnic values and mores of the various immigrant groups, but on their fusion with existing U.S. civilization—which, itself, was never purely Anglo-Saxon but was a product of the interaction of Anglo-Saxon elements with the French, Spanish, Dutch, Native American, and African American ones.

The melting-pot concept presupposes respect for the ethnic heritage of immigrants because it accepts their intrinsic values and their potential contributions to the cultural mingling process that was—and is—taking place in the United States. This process points to the emergence of a new American people. Melting-pot theorists reject the idea of Anglo-Saxon superiority expressed by Cubberley and others. In the melting pot, all ethnic groups are equal, and all are to be reshaped into a new entity.

An example of the melting-pot philosophy is Esperanto, a language invented in 1887 for international use. It is based on word roots common to the main European languages. Currently, there is an Esperanto League of Cyberspace. Another example is intermarriage between people of different races or religions.

Today, the approach to the socialization of ethnically diverse groups has become associated with **cultural pluralism,** which accepts the existence of a mainstream "American" culture, or macroculture. Kallen (1956) maintained that the dominant culture benefits from coexistence and constant interaction with the cultures of other ethnic groups—in other words, "unity in diversity." Thus, the various ethnic groups, or microcultures, should accept and cherish the common elements of U.S. cultural, political, and social mores as represented by the public schools, but they should also support supplemental education for their young to preserve their ethnic awareness and values.

> [This philosophy] embraces the ideals of mutual appreciation and understanding of various cultures in society; cooperation of diverse groups; coexistence of different languages, religious beliefs and life styles; and autonomy for each group to work out its own social purposes and future without interfering with the rights of other groups. (Ornstein & Levine, 1982, p. 245)

An example of the socialization philosophy of cultural pluralism is the concept of bilingual/multicultural education, which will be discussed later.

Ideological Backgrounds for Socialization. In general, children from ethnically diverse or minority families are much more likely to be poor and, therefore, at greater risk for negative developmental outcomes than are other children (Reed & Sautter, 1990). "Minority" refers to an ascribed (given) social status, and not necessarily a statistical (actual) one. Sometimes the label "minority" can be a self-fulfilling prophecy (Garcia, 1998). For example, workers from some ethnic minority families find it hard to get work when the economy slows down, and they are usually paid less for the work they do than are Euro-Americans (Levine & Levine, 1996). In addition, the educational level of certain ethnic groups, in general, is lower than that of Euro-Americans (Cohen, Pettigrew, & Riley, 1972; Coleman, 1966; Levine & Levine, 1996).

Because education is an increasingly important requisite for employment success, children from some ethnic minority families are generally disadvantaged in their quest for the so-called American dream—equal opportunity to achieve one's inborn potential. In other words, their capacity for achievement is handicapped because of their ascribed social status as minorities in U.S. society. A long history of prejudicial attitudes has been difficult to change. These attitudes are discussed in Chapter 11.

Until recently, the general philosophy in the United States of socializing ethnic minorities was assimilation. Those who did not learn the language or "American" ways failed to become effective members of the larger society because they could not achieve in school—which meant that their knowledge of the world about them remained limited, as did the opportunities available to them as adults. Thus, their statuses remained low.

Various societal measures have attempted to address the unique socialization needs of ethnically diverse groups to enable resiliency and success. Laws have been passed, such as the Civil Rights Act of 1964, which prohibits discrimination on the basis of race, gender, or national origin in public accommodations, federally assisted programs, and employment. Funding has been allocated to schools and to community agencies to provide services to ethnic minorities, such as bilingual educational programs. And parents have been required to become involved with schools in the socialization of their children.

Historically, it has been very difficult to break the cycle of inequality of opportunity. Because ethnic minority parents were denied equal political rights, they were not involved in community affairs. They were not elected to school boards or city councils, nor were they appointed to committees or commissions, which were usually dominated by Euro-Americans. Further, ethnic minority representation on higher-education faculties was rare. Thus, until recently, ethnically diverse groups had no place in decision-making bodies, such as government or education, or in advisory capacities. Not only could they not be advocates for themselves, they could not provide leadership role models for their children.

To try to break the cycle of inequality, and as part of President Lyndon Johnson's War on Poverty, the U.S. Office of Education commissioned a study on the equality of educational opportunity. This concern with educational opportunities illustrated society's view in the 1960s regarding its obligation to meet the special socialization needs of ethnic minorities—the idea that diverse groups should have educational opportunities in accordance with their talents and abilities.

James Coleman (1966), a sociologist at Johns Hopkins University, was given prime responsibility for surveying nearly a million pupils in 6000 schools across the nation to determine whether students were succeeding in accordance with their ability and, if not, why not. It was the first study to examine what attributes children bring to school that influence learning, rather than what educational methods schools employ that affect learning (Tozer et al., 2002). This famous survey, known as the Coleman Report, found that nonwhite and white students usually attended different schools. Nonwhites did less well than whites in verbal and nonverbal skills, reading comprehension, arithmetic skills, and general information acquisition. And the difference became greater as they progressed through school. Coleman found that the school's social composition had the most influence on individual achievement. In other words, children were influenced by their classmates' social class backgrounds and aspirations. For instance, African Americans from low socioeconomic statuses attending school with Euro-Americans from low socioeconomic statuses did not achieve as well as African Americans from low socioeconomic statuses attending school with Euro-Americans from middle socioeconomic statuses.

Some interpreted the report as concluding that the integration of schools and communities would eventually resolve the problem of unequal achievement. They reasoned that if African American children from poor families interacted with Euro-American children from middle-income families their achievement would improve. Others, who felt that integration either was unattainable or would take too long, advocated compensatory education. They reasoned that the achievement of African American children from poor families would improve if they were given more educational and related services, such as tutoring, reading programs, preschools, and parental participation. As discussed in Chapter 5, various types of compensatory educational programs appeared in the 1960s, with varying results.

Given the Coleman Report's strong association between children's achievement levels and their attitudes, which were rooted in their family backgrounds, it was felt that parental participation in school and parental control over educational decision making might make a difference in children's achievement. In fact, research (Lazar, 1977; Schorr, 1997; Schorr & Schorr, 1988) has shown that early intervention programs that include parents (participation and education) result in improved test scores of participants. However, it has also been shown that these improvements peter out in elementary school unless intervention is continued (Bronfenbrenner, 1977; Levine & Levine, 1996).

Students from ethnically diverse backgrounds who perform poorly in school do so for a number of reasons, some linked to ethnicity and others to social class (Bennett, 2003; Ornstein & Levine, 1989; Sadker & Sadker, 2003). Potential reasons include the following:

- *Inappropriate curricula and instruction.* The lessons teachers plan and the kinds of materials they have been trained to use are often inappropriate for some children from ethnically diverse groups. Often the children are unfamiliar with the terminology and concepts, and many are unfamiliar with the language.
- *Differences between parental and school norms.* Because the parents of children from ethnically diverse groups are likely to be unfamiliar with school norms and learning experiences, they are unlikely to reinforce such behaviors as creative thinking, reasoning, and self-direction.
- *Lack of previous success in school.* Failure to achieve in the early grades leads to low self-esteem and a lack of feeling of control over what happens in school. Consequently, the motivation to try harder and to achieve is diminished, and learned helplessness (giving up effort) results. Such motives and attributes are discussed in detail in Chapter 11.
- *Teaching difficulties.* Teachers of children from ethnically diverse groups often become frustrated because of the lack of success in the classroom. The students who do not succeed in school can exhibit behavioral problems. This provides an additional burden for the teacher, especially given that most teachers are not adequately trained in dealing with behavioral problems.
- *Teacher perceptions and standards.* Because of published data and their own experiences, teachers of children from ethnically diverse groups are likely to have low expectations. These perceptions often result in a self-fulfilling

prophecy, in that standards are lowered and students' low performance levels are reinforced. In other words, teachers who believe that their students cannot learn are less likely to motivate them beyond their current performance level; therefore, the students do not succeed. Teachers who believe that their students can learn are more likely to design appropriate learning experiences that stimulate them to succeed.

- *Segregation.* Children from ethnically diverse groups are more likely to attend school with their ethnic minority peers; or, if they attend an integrated school, they are more likely to be placed in special classes than are Euro-American children. Consequently, they are reinforced by peers from similar backgrounds, with similar educational needs, and with similar school performance levels. Thus, there is no motivation to succeed within the peer group because high performance by an individual makes that individual different from his or her friends. And the price to pay for nonconformity—ostracism—is too great for many children to handle.

- *Differences in teacher/student backgrounds.* Teachers from middle-class backgrounds may experience particular difficulties in understanding and motivating their students from lower-class backgrounds. Problems may also occur when teachers are from one ethnic group and students are from another. Schools reflect the communities from which they draw their students and their teachers (Garcia, 1998). Sometimes a wide range of socioeconomic statuses are represented in classrooms. Although ethnic minority groups are represented in greater numbers than are Euro-Americans in the lower socioeconomic classes, the disparity between oppression and privilege affects all.

The differential treatment of groups of people because of their class background, and the reinforcement of those differences through values and practices of societal institutions such as schools, is known as **classism.** Socioeconomic class, as discussed in Chapter 3, is based on income, educational attainment, occupation, and power. Where a family falls on the continuum from poor to rich affects how its members live, how they think and act, and how others react to them (Gollnick & Chinn, 2002).

Our society socializes children in "a world of contradictions." On the one hand, children learn that everyone is "created equal," that each individual has the right to "pursue happiness" (the Declaration of Independence), and that we as a nation are united to provide for the "common good" (the Constitution). On the other hand, in the community, children observe that certain groups of people are exploited while others compete for resources and power. "Despite its egalitarian principles, the United States has been moving away from, not toward, more equitable distribution of wealth, especially during the last two decades" (Ramsey, 1998, p. 45).

Dealing with life's inevitable inconveniences is dependent on class. For example, if your car breaks down, do you bring it to a service station for repairs, rent a car, and go about your business? Or do you ask a relative or friend to help you fix it while you depend on others and public transportation to take you where you need to go? For another example, when you get sick, do you go to a doctor knowing that, whatever the treatment, it will be covered by your insurance? Or do you go to bed and try to heal yourself? Likewise, in the classroom, children who have access to books and computers can navigate more successfully through school projects than can those who have few resources at home.

The consequences of classism in school are subtle but significant. One consequence is that a large number of students from lower socioeconomic statuses are more likely to be assigned to low-ability groups in their early years, setting them on a track that is difficult to alter (Gollnick & Chinn, 2002; Levine & Levine, 1996). Another consequence is segregation of peer groups along socioeconomic lines, especially in middle or junior high school (Davidson & Schniederwind, 1992). The possessions students have, the neighborhoods they live in, the clothing they wear, the language and vocabulary they use—all can interfere with positive social interaction, thereby reinforcing inequality in society.

Bilingual/Multicultural Education. An increasing number of children from ethnically diverse groups with limited English proficiency (LEP) are attending U.S. schools and are at risk for failure. Research shows that disproportionately high numbers of ethnic minority students do not finish school, and disproportionately high numbers of those who do remain in school are achieving far below their potential (Bennett, 2003). Through legislation, the federal government has tried to equalize opportunities for diverse groups. The basis for a variety of legislative acts and court decisions is Title VI of the Civil Rights Act of 1964, which states, "No person in the United States shall, on the grounds of race, color, or national origin, be excluded from participation in, be denied the benefits of, or be subjected to discrimination under any program or activity receiving federal financial assistance."

In 1974, Congress passed the Equal Educational Opportunity Act requiring schools to take "appropriate action" to overcome the language barriers of students who could not communicate in English. Also in 1974, the Supreme Court in *Lau v. Nichols* held that schools receiving federal funds could not discriminate against children with limited or no English-speaking ability by denying them language training. The Court ruled that the civil rights of the students involved in the suit had been violated because the school had not provided an equal educational opportunity for them. The Court gave school districts a choice of providing instruction in the child's native tongue while learning English (bilingual education), training in English as a second language (ESL), or other specialized services. The purpose of **bilingual education** is to help students achieve both communicative and academic competence (Garcia, 1998).

Many schools have added a multicultural component to bilingual education. A major goal of **multicultural education** is to prepare culturally literate citizens who can function effectively in their own microculture, other microcultures, and the macroculture (Banks, 2002). We live in a world that is becoming increasingly interdependent on other cultures about which most of us are culturally illiterate. Thus, it is both desirable and necessary that we understand diversity and impart this understanding to our children. Multicultural education should meet the needs of all children so that they can progress to their fullest potential in this ever-changing world.

Do bilingual/multicultural programs meet the unique socialization needs of children from ethnically diverse groups? There are still some issues that need to be resolved before this question can be answered (Levine & Levine, 1996). At one end of the continuum are those who believe that the language and culture of diverse ethnic groups must be preserved to develop and maintain positive individual and group identities in an equitable society. At the other end are those who believe that ethnic minority children will be better prepared to compete in society if they are immersed as soon as possible in English-language instruction. In between are a variety of approaches to enable LEP students to make the transition from their native language to English.

The research on the effects of bilingual/multicultural education is inconclusive. Some research shows that learning in individuals' native language facilitates achievement in English; other research shows that the earlier students learn English, the more likely achievement is to occur in that language (Sadker & Sadker, 2003). Many factors in addition to language proficiency contribute to children's success in school, including individual learning ability, socioeconomic status, family involvement, and effective teaching. A response to the lack of clear results from bilingual/multicultural education is the emergence of "English only" movements across the United States, which involve state or local laws stating that English is the official language and must be used in public institutions and on public documents.

Students from different ethnic groups have notably different experiences in school. For example, Chinese, Japanese, and some Southeast Asian children have succeeded in American schools, whereas some other Asian, Pacific Rim, and Native American children are less successful (Tharp, 1989). Because teachers are generally from the majority culture and invoke the ways of the majority culture, educational underachievement by minority groups is usually blamed on incompatibilities between a child's culture and that of the school (Levine & Levine, 1996).

Research indicates that children's learning styles may be related to their ethnic socialization, and teachers should respond accordingly (Banks, 2002). However, teachers often communicate in the style of their own culture. For example, researchers compared the time a teacher waited for a child to respond to a question and the time the teacher waited before talking again for a Euro-American and a Navajo teacher of the same group of third-grade Navajo students (White & Tharp, 1988). The Navajo teacher waited considerably longer than the Euro-American teacher after the child responded before talking again. What was perceived by the Euro-American teacher as a completed response was often intended by the child as a pause, which the Euro-American teacher had interrupted. For their part, native Hawaiian students preferred "negative" wait times, with the listener speaking without waiting for the speaker to finish (White & Tharp, 1988). This is often interpreted by teachers from other ethnic groups as rude interruption, but in Hawaiian society, it demonstrates involvement (Tharp, 1989).

Another variation related to ethnic socialization is behavior. For example, Euro-American children are usually taught to look directly at an adult when being spoken to, whereas many African American, Mexican American, and Asian American children are taught to lower their eyes—behavior that may be interpreted as disrespect. Teachers must develop an awareness of how ethnic background affects actions. Chapter 7 explores the ecology of teaching a diverse student population.

Religion

As discussed in Chapter 3, religion is a significant socializing mechanism in the transmission of values and behavior. Traditions, rituals, and religious institutions reinforce those values taught in families.

Religious pluralism flourishes in the United States. There are about 2000 different religious groups, and with the influx of immigrants from Asia, Africa, and the Middle East, non-Western religions such as Islam, Hinduism, and Buddhism are joining the ranks of Protestanism, Catholicism, and Judaism (Gollnick & Chinn, 2002).

Although the political ideology in the United States advocates separation of church and state (including public school), the two often intersect. For example, the words "One nation, under God" are in the Pledge of Allegiance, and the statement "In God we trust" appears on U.S. currency. The degree to which religious ideologies intersect with public school curricula and policies is significant in the socialization of all children who attend public school. Controversial issues include school prayer, the curriculum (teaching evolution and sex education), censorship of certain books, and the celebration of certain holidays. Teachers need to be sensitive to the values of the families in the community in the context of a diverse society while at the same time implementing the educational goals of the school district.

Sometimes the line between secular and nonsecular education is a fine one and must be adjudicated in the courts. Legally, schools may teach the Bible as part of the history of literature, but they may not teach it as religion. Reading scripture and reciting prayers are also violations of the law. Public schools may teach the scientific theory of evolution, but not creationism. Dismissing children an hour early from public school for religious instruction is permitted.

How are secular and nonsecular divided? Perhaps a quote from the late author Chaim Potok aptly explains how the Bible may be viewed as nonsecular literature:

> Literature presents you with alternative mappings of the human experience. You see that the experiences of other people and other cultures are as rich, coherent and troubled as your own experiences. They are beset with suffering as yours. Literature is a kind of legitimate voyeurism through the keyhole of language, where you really come to know other people's lives—their anguish, their loves, their passions. (quoted in Johnson, 2002, p. B13)

The Bible assumes secular or religious characteristics when it is taught as dogma.

Special Needs

Due to changes in the law that reflect the prevailing public attitude—that education is a *right*, not a *privilege*—the school has become a designated agent for identifying children with special needs, such as disabilities, and including them in educational activities that are available to all children (mainstreaming). Therefore, the attitudes, history, and laws regarding individuals with disabilities are discussed here.

Disability refers to the reduction of function or the absence of a particular body part or organ. **Impairment** refers to diseased or defective tissue. **Handicap** is defined as something that hampers a person—a disadvantage or a hindrance.

Children with disabilities are those who have been evaluated as being mentally retarded, hard of hearing, deaf, speech impaired, visually impaired, seriously emotionally disturbed, autistic, orthopedically impaired, other health impaired, deaf-blind, multidisabled, or traumatically brain injured, or as having specific learning disabilities, and who, because of those impairments, need special education and related services.

The terms *disability* and/or *impairment* are used today instead of *handicap* in order to dispel negative stereotypes. For instance, people in wheelchairs are disabled; they are handicapped only when they try to enter a building with steps. A person may be handicapped in one situation but not in another. For example, Ray Charles is handicapped in *reading* music because he is blind, but he certainly is not handicapped in *playing* music. Thus, for children with disabilities, the main aim of socialization should be to minimize the effects of their disabilities and to maximize the effects of their abilities.

There are some common views about individuals with disabilities that affect interaction with them. For example, assuming that individuals with disabilities are helpless can lead to solicitude or overprotectiveness, and assuming that individuals with disabilities are incapable can lead to ostracism or neglect.

Assumptions and practices that promote the deferential and unequal treatment of people because they are different physically, mentally, or behaviorally is called

handicapism. The word *handicap* is thought to be derived from the practice of beggars who held "cap in hand" to solicit charity, thereby reflecting a dependent position (Biklen & Bogdan, 1977). The media have contributed to certain attitudes associated with disabilities. For example, children's stories tell of evil trolls, hunchbacks, old, deformed witches, thus promoting an attitude of fear. Although handicapism has a long history, the current trend is to include people with disabilities in TV shows and advertisements. Teachers need to be sensitive to handicapism and to view children as individuals with abilities and with disabilities, if applicable.

Ideological Background for Socialization. Historically, we can delineate four stages of attitudes toward people with disabilities that have affected their socialization (Hallahan & Kauffman, 2002; Kirk, Gallagher, & Anastasiow, 1997):

1. During the pre-Christian era, people with disabilities tended to be banished, neglected, and/or mistreated.
2. As Christianity spread, they were protected and pitied.
3. In the eighteenth and nineteenth centuries, institutions were established to provide separate education.
4. In the latter part of the twentieth century, there was a movement to accepting people with disabilities and integrating them into the mainstream of society to the fullest extent possible (full inclusion). Currently, laws enable individuals with disabilities to receive a free and equal education and to compete for jobs without discrimination.

In colonial time, there was no concept of classification according to type of disability. The concept of individual differences, as we know it today, was not understood or appreciated. In those years, there were no public provisions for people with disabilities. Such individuals were "stashed away" in charitable houses or remained at home without educational opportunities.

In the early 1800s, residential schools were established in some states for people with disabilities. These institutions offered training in a protective environment, often spanning the life of the individual. As the population of the United States increased and large numbers of people congregated in the growing cities, the population of children with disabilities in any one place also increased. Parents and educators sought ways of keeping the children with disabilities in their home communities because residential schools tended to be remote, making it difficult for parents to visit their children. Therefore, in the latter part of the nineteenth century, special classes were introduced in the public schools.

The most significant force in special education has been the advocacy of the parents of children with disabilities. They have raised money for treatment and research centers, and lobbied government for new legislation providing funding for research, professional training, treatment, transportation, financial assistance, community health, and many other related needs.

As the special-class movement grew, so did the body of research on the effectiveness of special-class placement. Some research indicated that such placement provided a more supportive and sheltered social environment for exceptional children, but other researchers reported that it did little to increase the learning and achievement of children (Dunlop, 1977).

In 1968, Lloyd Dunn wrote a classic article in the field of special education that drew serious widespread attention to the issue of special-class placement. The article questioned the appropriateness of special classes for many children labeled "educable mentally retarded." Dunn estimated that 60 to 80 percent of the pupils enrolled in classes for the mildly retarded were from low-socioeconomic-status backgrounds, "including Afro-Americans, American Indians, Mexicans, and Puerto Rican Americans, those from nonstandard English-speaking, broken, disorganized and inadequate homes, and children from other non middle-class environments" (p. 5). In 1973, Jane Mercer reported that, among children labeled "retarded" by the public schools, there were twice as many African Americans and more than four times as many Mexican Americans as might be expected from their proportion in the general population. Conversely, only half as many Euro-American children were labeled "retarded." Were the public schools using the special classes as a dumping ground for children who were not successful in the regular classroom, regardless of the reason?

Studies done during the late 1960s and early 1970s (Avery, 1971; Beez, 1968) indicated that teacher expectations were lower for labeled children than for others. Lowered expectations tend to reduce the chances of reaching optimal developmental capacity. A strong impetus for inclusion of students with disabilities into regular classes came from parents who claimed that their children were not developing to their full potential in special classes because not much was expected of them—they were receiving a "watered-down" curriculum.

The prevailing attitude into the mid-1970s was that the school's role was to educate the majority. Thus, any students who might interfere with that role were isolated if possible, or else not accommodated. Those accommodated students were put in special classes taught by experts. Those students whose needs could not be met by the public schools generally received no education at all, unless their families could afford a private tutor.

In 1975, Congress passed the Education for All Handicapped Children Act, which required that children age 3–21 with disabilities be educated in a regular public classroom wherever possible. In 1986, an amendment was passed to serve children from birth to age 3 in order to minimize the risks of developmental delays due to lack of appropriate services early on. In 1990, the name of the Education for All Handicapped Children Act was changed to the Individuals with Disabilities Education Act. In 1991, the Americans with Disabilities Act was passed to ensure nondiscriminatory treatment of people with disabilities in areas such as employment, public facilities, transportation, and telecommunications.

The Individuals with Disabilities Education Act (IDEA). In 1990, the Individuals with Disabilities Education Act (IDEA) was passed. It provides federal money to states and local agencies to educate children with disabilities age 3–21. Because of the possible effects of early categorization, the IDEA allows states to use the category "developmental delay" for preschool children with special needs. Each state has specific criteria and evaluation procedures for determining children's eligibility for early intervention and special services, including what constitutes developmental delay (Wolery & Wilbers, 1994).

Many children are diagnosed early by physicians as having specific conditions such as cerebral palsy or spina bifida. However, many other children, due to environ-

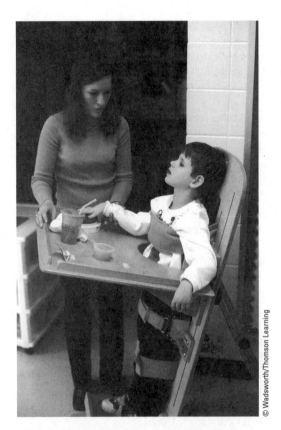

© Wadsworth/Thomson Learning

Children with disabilities can be integrated into the classroom with the support of special equipment and assistance from the teacher.

mental variables such as abuse, exposure to toxins or disease, or poverty, are at risk for developmental delays or disabilities not only because of their environments but also because they are often not identified as such prior to their contact with social workers or teachers (Wolery & Wilbers, 1994). Thus, early childhood professionals are significant identifiers of children with special needs. This identification can occur through informal observations of children, screening with developmental scales, and vision and hearing screening (Meisels & Wasik, 1990).

The IDEA requires nondiscriminatory evaluations, appropriate to a child's cultural and linguistic background, of whether the child has a disability and, if so, the nature of the disability. A reevaluation must occur every 3 years. Parental approval is required.

The main purpose of the act is to guarantee that all children with disabilities have access to a free and appropriate public education. The principal method of guaranteeing the fulfillment of that purpose is via the **Individualized Education Program (IEP).** Any child receiving special education services must have an IEP written at the beginning of each year and reviewed at least once a year. The IEP is basically a form of communication between the school and the family. It is developed by the group of people responsible for the child's education—parents, teachers, and other involved school personnel. The exact format varies, depending on the particular school district; however, all IEPs must include the following:

- A statement of the child's present levels of educational performance
- A statement of annual goals, including short-term objectives
- A statement of the specific special education and related services to be provided to the child, and of the extent of the child's participation in regular education environments, including initiation dates and anticipated duration of services
- Required transition services from school to work or continued education (usually by age 14–16)
- Objective criteria, evaluation procedures, and schedules for determining whether instructional objectives are being met

Inclusion. The IDEA also requires that students with disabilities be placed in the least restrictive environment (LRE). This means that such students should be included in school programs with students who are not disabled to the maximum extent appropriate. Supplementary help in the form of attendants, tutors, interpreters, transportation, speech pathology and audiology, psychological services, physical and occupational therapy, recreation, and medical and counseling services enable inclusion. Supplementary aids such as wheelchairs, crutches, standing tables, hearing aids, embossed globes, braille dictionaries, and books with enlarged print also enable inclusion. Inclusion can be for the entire day or certain portions of the day.

Inclusion is the educational philosophy of being part of the whole—that children are entitled to fully participate in their school and community. But is such a concept appropriate for *all* children with disabilities? Some believe in full inclusion (Stainback, Stainback, East, & Sapon-Shevin, 1994), advocating appropriate support services as needed by all children. Others believe in partial inclusion, providing a continuum of services and integration in regular classrooms and regular activities whenever possible. They acknowledge the need for special, supplementary services or even separate schooling if necessary (Smith & Bassett, 1991). The rationale for the availability of comprehensive special services is that students with disabilities may need

Figure 6.2

*Meeting the Special
Socialization Needs
of Children
with Disabilities*

Source: Adapted from
"Special Education as
Developmental Capital" by
E. Deno, 1979. *Exceptional
Children, 37*, pp. 229–237.
Copyright 1970 by the
Council for Exceptional
Children. Reprinted with
permission.

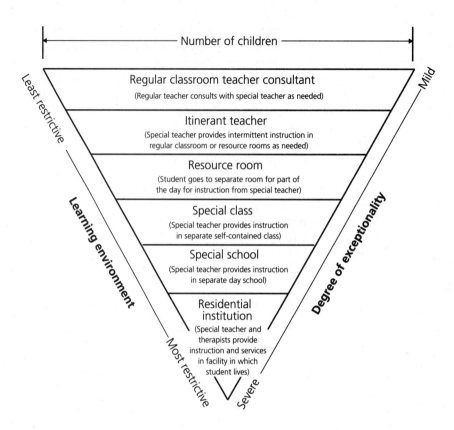

more intensive, individualized instruction, and it helps ensure that students without
disabilities in the regular classroom get an appropriate education (Kaufman,
1989). Figure 6.2 shows how varying degrees of inclusion and separation might
be implemented.

The debate regarding optimal socialization environments for those with disabilities goes on. Many schools nationwide serving children age 3–21 are experimenting with various educational reforms, especially using peers as socialization agents
in an integrated or mainstreamed classroom (Fulton, 1994).

Chronosystem Influences on Schools

Chronosystem influences on the school include its adaptation to societal change in
general and its adaptation to specific developments, such as technology, violence,
and substance use/abuse. In a changing society, the challenge continually facing
educators, in addition to preparing individuals for the future, is how to transmit the
society's diverse cultural heritage. What aspects of past knowledge must be taught
for survival in the present, and what coping skills must be taught for survival in the
future? With new knowledge emerging every day, choices have to be made. For
example, most jobs being created today require workers who can (1) read, write,
and compute at high levels, (2) analyze and interpret data, draw conclusions, and
make decisions, and (3) function as part of a team.

From its inception, the public school system was intended to be a vehicle for
social change. Schools, however, do not execute their functions in a vacuum. As

discussed previously, they are affected by macrosystems such as political ideology, economics, culture/ethnicity, religion, and science/technology, and are linked to other microsystems such as the family and community. They must teach children from diverse backgrounds with diverse skills. Therefore, to equalize opportunities, schools must implement a variety of programs in addition to basic reading, writing, and arithmetic (Levine & Levine, 1996).

> Policy mandates like desegregation and mainstreaming dramatically changed the social environment of the school. These forces have expanded and complicated the mandate of the public school well beyond the traditional academic "three Rs," identifying multiple and sometimes conflicting goals. The school has become a potential intervention site for almost every social problem affecting children. (Linney & Seidman, 1989, p. 336)

Schools are supposed to offer preventative programs such as sex education to help students avoid unplanned pregnancies, as well as AIDS and other sexually transmitted diseases; health classes that discuss the dangers of substance abuse; and conflict resolution to reduce violence. Schools are also supposed to keep up with technology by teaching computer literacy.

ADAPTATIONS TO SOCIAL CHANGE

Elementary schools traditionally taught academic skills and good citizenship. Gradually, concepts related to critical thinking, individuality and the self, and interpersonal relationships crept into the curricula. The reasons for the gradual changes were many. The classic writings of John Dewey (*Democracy and Education*), Jean Piaget (*To Understand Is to Invent*), B. F. Skinner (*The Technology of Teaching*), and Carl Rogers (*Freedom to Learn*), to name a few, influenced educational practices. More recently, the work of Lev Vygotsky (*Mind in Society*) has been adapted for the classroom.

The political climate from the late 1950s to early 1970s, as evidenced by the passage of legislation providing federal funds for new programs, was also supportive of change. For example, the Economic Opportunity Act of 1964 provided federal aid for preschool programs for disadvantaged children, the Elementary and Secondary Education Acts of 1965 (Title I) provided federal aid to education, and the Education for All Handicapped Children Act of 1975 (revised in 1990 to become the Individuals with Disabilities Education Act) mandated a free and appropriate education for all children with disabilities. Thus, government support allowed schools to serve more children by individualizing programs to meet individual needs. It also enabled schools to experiment with new programs to meet those needs. For instance, bilingual education was mandated in school districts with high rates of children whose native language was not English. Children in such programs were taught the specified curriculum in their native languages while they learned English as a second language. The philosophy behind bilingual education is that it prevents non- or limited-English-speaking children from being academically disadvantaged due to not understanding the language of the teacher. During the 1980s, however, federal aid to education was reduced as responsibility for public education shifted to the states. This appeared to some to reflect a lack of "national purpose" in education.

A 1993 report titled *A Nation at Risk: The Imperative for Educational Reform,* by the National Commission on Excellence in Education (NCEE), helped create a public demand for change in the public schools. The report charged that U.S. citizens "have lost sight of the basics of schooling" and that "the educational foundations of our society are presently being eroded by a rising tide of mediocrity that threatens our very future as a nation and a people" (NCEE, 1983). The report advocated a number of directions for reform, including the following (Chafel, 1997):

- There must be a greater consensus by Americans on the goals of schooling.
- There must be renewed emphasis on "the basics" (reading, communicating, and computing) in learning.
- Standards of excellence must be established.
- More capable people must be motivated to enter and stay in the teaching profession.
- The U.S. economic position in the world community necessitates higher levels of education for *all* students.

As the twenty-first century approached, the debate regarding the functions of school continued. To address the charges in the NCEE report, government, business, and educational leaders developed six national education goals, announced in 1990 and reconfirmed in 1999 via the Educational Excellence for All Children Act (National Educational Goals Panel, 1999):

1. All children in America will start school ready to learn.
2. The high school graduation rate will increase to at least 90 percent.
3. American students will leave grades 4, 8, and 12 having demonstrated competency in challenging subject matter including English, mathematics, science, history, and geography; and every school in America will ensure that all students learn to use their minds well, so they are prepared for responsible citizenship, further learning, and productive employment in our modern economy.
4. American students will be first in the world in science and mathematics achievement.
5. Every adult American will be literate and will possess the knowledge and skills necessary to compete in a global economy and exercise the rights and responsibilities of citizenship.
6. Every school in America will be free of drugs and violence and will offer a disciplined environment conducive to learning.

Although all of these goals have not yet been reached, they remain targets worth striving for. The hope is that schools and students will rise to the expectations and standards set for them.

For any education strategy to be implemented and for school socialization to be effective, children must come to school ready to learn. To assess what exactly was involved in "school readiness," the Carnegie Foundation for Advancement in Teaching examined the influences of a healthy birth on family, involvement in children's learning, child care arrangements, the workplace, and community supports (Boyer, 1991). Children's readiness to learn is discussed later in the chapter.

Reaching the goals will require significant improvements in a wide range of services for children, including health care, child care, parent education, and family support. It will also require many changes in schools, teacher education, and testing. Finally, it will require the involvement of businesses, communities, government, colleges, and universities. For example, to address the transition from school to work, especially for high school graduates who don't go on to college or for drop-outs, some states have established funding for apprenticeship programs in areas such as health care, machine tooling, and entrepreneurship.

TECHNOLOGY

Schooling for the future includes being prepared for the world of work and technological change. Learning to use computers is essential to successful functioning in any society. This is a good example of the impact of a macrosystem (technology) and a chronosystem (change) on a microsystem. For instance, both mechanics and doctors now use computers to assist with diagnoses. Along with television and telephones, computers have revolutionized communication. Computers enable users who have access to the Internet to get information from anywhere in the world. In response to technological change, most schools (high, middle, elementary, and even pre-) have purchased computers to serve as educational tools.

The computer is an interactive tool that enhances learning in a variety of subjects. It can present and store information, motivate and reward learners, diagnose problems and prescribe solutions, provide drill and practice, and individualize instruction (Levine & Levine, 1996; Oppenheimer, 1997). It can support a wide range of learning styles because it enables children to construct their own knowledge (Haugland & Wright, 1997; Papert, 1993). The effectiveness of computers as a tool for learning depends on how they are used by teachers and students, as well as the software selected.

Computers are not really new to education. In the past, computers were used mainly for programmed instruction, which involved reading information and answering questions. Depending on their responses, students branched into different program areas or went back for more information and practice. The learning that occurred was determined by reacting to the program rather than exploring by learners, although sometimes they discovered different ways to obtain the same result by experimenting with different commands. Today, software, interactive games, Web sites, and e-mail discussion groups all enhance education.

How does computer education affect children? Do computers foster independence at the expense of developing social skills? Do computers enhance certain skills at the expense of creativity? Computers deal with facts; they do not convey or receive emotions. If computers become a primary medium of communication, especially in school, what happens to the socializing impact of the teacher through attachment and modeling? What happens to other mechanisms of socialization such as reasoning and group pressure?

According to Healy (1991, 1998), the computer provides visual and sometimes auditory stimulation. However, optimal learning occurs, especially for preschoolers, when several senses are involved. Young children need to manipulate things, as well as see them, to construct an understanding of the world.

Computers can be used as an adjunct to regular classroom activities, rather than a replacement. For example, computers can facilitate children's creative writing by using word processing to help simplify physical aspects of writing, and to correct errors (Daiute, 1983). When students don't get stuck on handwriting, spelling, and grammar, they are freer to express thoughts. However, some children exhibit *parallel* thinking (like hypertext) rather than *sequential* thinking (Oppenheimer, 1997). That is, they don't connect their thoughts in a logical way; they merely list things without understanding the relationships (Healy, 1991, 1998).

Creating software programs can encourage problem-solving skills and logical thinking. For example, Papert (1999) developed a system using a computer language called LOGO, in which children learn mathematics by *being* mathematicians. LOGO is programmable, unlike direct-manipulation software. By controlling the movements of the "Turtle," children as young as age 3 learn about numbers, shapes, velocities, and rates of change, as well as problem solving. Various LOGO applications are

Technological advances affect what and how children learn.

used today in school for biology, physics, and driver's education, to name a few (Papert, 1993). Designing computer programs requires users to think hypothetically: "If I choose this command, then this will happen." Programmable software, such as LOGO, thus enables users to construct knowledge.

Computers can also be used for collaboration and research. Students can network with each other in the classroom on projects. With a telephone hookup, they can access information from libraries, universities, government databases, and any online services subscribed to by their school. With computer-interactive multimedia capabilities, such as graphics, sound, and compact discs, students can "visit" museums, planetariums, and other countries, or go back in history. New software is being developed for learning via computer simulation. For example, the standard biology laboratory experiment of dissecting a frog can now be simulated, and some driver education programs start students on computer simulations.

In sum, computers contribute to schooling for the future in several ways: (1) They can individualize instruction to accommodate different learning styles; (2) they can be used for routine tasks, thereby freeing teachers to provide more creative ones; (3) they can help develop self-directed learners, logical or hypothetical thinkers, and problem solvers; and (4) they can provide access to vast stores of information. Parents and teachers must enable children to develop critical thinking skills to evaluate various software, as well as the plethora of information on the Internet. In doing research on the Internet, students must learn to distinguish facts from opinions and reliable resources from unreliable ones.

Finally, computer technology has been utilized to link home or hospital to school for ill children, school to school for specialized instruction, and business to school for "virtual field trips." Such utilization is known as "distance education."

VIOLENCE

The National Academy of Sciences defines **violence** as "behaviors by individuals that intentionally threaten, attempt, or inflict harm on others" (Elders, 1994). Parents, teachers, students, and communities are very concerned about the rise in school violence in recent years. The shootings of 12 students and a teacher in 1999 at Columbine High School in Colorado alerted society to the negative outcomes of being rejected by peers, of being victims of bullying, and, most importantly, of being disengaged from family, school, and community.

To have an optimal environment for learning, schools must be safe. Violence transcends all socioeconomic statuses, and its roots are as much a part of families' dysfunctional problem solving as communities' racism, sexism, classism, and high unemployment. If children grow up in families that characterized by spousal or child abuse or neglect, they are more likely to exhibit aggressive behavior in school. They may also model the violent behavior they see in their neighborhoods (Verdugo, Kuther, Seidel, Wallace, Sosa, & Faber, 1990). Many people believe that the pervasiveness of violence in society and in the media, and its portrayal as the normal means of conflict resolution, sends children the message that violence is an acceptable and effective way to solve problems (Elders, 1994).

There is a rising incidence of hate-motivated violence (National Education Association [NEA], 2001). The NEA defines hate crimes as "offenses motivated by hatred against a victim based on his or her beliefs or mental or physical characteristics, including race, ethnicity, and sexual orientation." Not only has there been an increase in the incidence of hate-fueled violence in schools, but Web sites promoting intolerance have proliferated. The NEA believes that preventing hate-motivated violence requires a comprehensive, coordinated educational effort in schools and communities in conjunction with federal legislation.

The availability of guns and knives enables individuals to vent anger physically. Children have turned to gangs and weapons for the protection they believe they have not received from parents, teachers, and/or community members (Children's Defense Fund, 2001).

Children who grow up in violent communities are at risk for emotional and psychological problems because living in a constant state of fear makes it difficult for them to establish trust, autonomy, and social competence (Wallach, 1993). Likewise, growing up in impoverished neighborhoods that lack recreational and employment opportunities, and successful adult role models leads to alienation of children. Children do not develop feelings of safety and nurturance; instead, they often develop feelings of hopelessness (National Research Council, 1993), leading to 'learned helplessness.' In addition, poverty appears to inhibit the capacity of families to parent and hence to achieve social control over adolescents (Sampson & Laub, 1994). Although violence does occur in suburban and rural communities, it is more prevalent in urban communities (Verdugo et al., 1990).

What is being done? Some schools have hired security guards, installed metal detectors and cameras, required students to carry photo identification, and/or given teachers cellular phones, but these are reactive measures to a problem whose roots lie in a "socially toxic environment." To be proactive and eradicate those roots, all of children's ecological systems must participate.

How can micro-, meso-, exo-, and macrosystems work to combat violence?

The macrosystem, or government, can implement laws, such as stricter policies on gun control and the portrayal of violence in the media (both of which are objectionable to a significant number of people). It can also increase law enforcement in communities and provide funding for preventative programs in schools and families. Violence prevention in schools might involve having more counselors available to students and training teachers to intervene with children who are social isolates, bullies, or victims. Violence prevention in families might involve parent education and/or counseling.

The exosystem, such as businesses, can provide jobs, financial assistance to rebuild impoverished communities, and role models for youths. Businesses can support schools by donating time, providing opportunities for field trips, supplying guest speakers, and funding after-school activities.

School violence has become a national concern: These students must be searched.

© Michael Newman/PhotoEdit

The mesosystem, exemplified by the link between schools and families, can empower families to share the responsibility for creating a safe school environment (Stomfay-Stitz, 1994). This means accompanying children to and from school and being involved in school activities. The mesosystem, exemplified by the link between communities and families, can provide services to support families (examples are given in Chapter 10), thereby proactively contributing to the prevention of violence.

The microsystem, referring here to the school itself, can implement, as a curricular priority at all grade levels, instruction and guidance in anger management (learning when angry feelings threaten to get out of control and how to deal with them appropriately) and conflict resolution (learning positive strategies to resolve differences). Consistent behavior standards and consequences, as well as academic expectations, must be established. Classes for parents in parenting methods and violence prevention should be available. Teacher in-service training should include methods for dealing with disruptive or uncooperative behavior before it escalates. Teachers need to be more responsive to bullies, victims, and social outcasts at all school levels. Teacher training should also include working with diverse groups and learning how to connect with appropriate community resources (medical, psychological, and economic). Children should learn to respect differences and be empathetic to others (Verdugo et al., 1990).

Preventing Violence in Young Children

Strategies to help children resolve conflicts before they escalate into violent behavior include the following:

1. *Emotional regulation:* Enable children to verbalize angry feelings and presumed causes (young children may need some suggested words). Also, redirect anger to appropriate physical activity (pounding play-doh, running)
2. *Empathy:* Role-play to get the other person's perspective.
3. *Problem solving:* Discuss various solutions to conflict that are agreeable to all involved parties.
4. *Mediation:* Involve adults or trained peers, listen to all perspectives, and give assistance in working out a compromise.

SUBSTANCE USE/ABUSE

Substance use and abuse remains a major problem among high schoolers and an increasing one among middle schoolers (American Academy of Pediatrics [AAP], 1995). Substances include tobacco, alcohol, and various drugs, as well as performance-enhancing supplements. The use of mind- and body-altering chemicals has dangerous effects on development and deleterious effects on school performance. Students under the influence of such substances are not in a state of readiness to learn, and they may suffer long-term impairment of cognitive abilities and memory. Substance abuse is frequently associated with lack of motivation and self-discipline and with reduced school attendance (National Commission on Drug-Free Schools, 1990). Substance abuse is also correlated with antisocial and violent behavior. Furthermore, studies indicate that users are more likely to engage in risk-taking behavior and sexual experimentation when under the influence of various substances (AAP, 1995).

The use of substances in school by some students impairs the educational environment for others. Along with families and communities, schools must be involved in dealing with the substance use/abuse problem. The U.S. Department of Health and Human Services (1991) and the U.S. Department of Education (1989) have identified ways for schools to participate in promoting the health of children and preventing substance abuse:

- Schools must provide factual information about the harmful effects of drugs.
- Schools must collaborate with parents and community members to support and strengthen students' resistance to substances.
- Schools must provide such services as confidential identification, assessment, and referral to appropriate treatment programs for users and abusers.
- Schools must monitor substance use and establish clear guidelines and penalties for usage.

Can schools require students to submit to random drug tests in order to participate in extracurricular activities (sports, drama, band, decathelon, and so on)? Random drug testing typically involves selecting students at random, calling them out of class, and directing them to a bathroom where they must provide a urine sample in a container. Teachers usually wait outside the bathroom stall and seal the container for transport to the testing lab. In 2002, the Supreme Court (in *Earl vs. Board of Education of Tecumseh, Oklahoma Public School District*), ruled that drug testing did not violate students' rights under the Fourth Amendment to be free from warrantless searches. The rationale in the decision was that students in public schools are under the temporary custody of the state and, therefore, have limited privacy rights, especially when a search is deemed necessary for their protection.

Macrosystem/Chronosystem Influences on the School

In a changing society, the challenge continually facing educators is how to transmit the society's diverse cultural heritage, as well as prepare individuals for the future.

Political Ideology

Laws mandating equitable funding and programs for diverse groups

Value of equal opportunity leading to intervention programs for social problems, compensation, financial aid, and scholarships

Achievement and competitiveness issues resulting in more early academics, an increase in advanced classes in high school, and more work/study programs

Economics

Cost-effectiveness impacting programs, curricula, class size, and school improvements

Accountability (testing) enhancing preparation of students for future employability

Gender, Ethnicity, Religion, and Special Needs

Diverse student population resulting in more individualized approaches to learning
Inclusion leading to adaptation

Science/Technology

Scientific advancement leading to increased knowledge and approaches to learning
Computers resulting in increased access to information and more opportunities for
   skill development

Violence and Substance Use/Abuse

Safety/security issues vying with privacy rights

Mesosystem Influences

Mesosystem influences on the school include its linkages with other ecosystems. Children in the United States spend approximately 180 days per year, for approximately 12 years, in school (and more if they attend preschool), so the schools they attend and the teachers they encounter play significant roles in their socialization. The school, in designating programs and curricula, selects which experiences children will have. In other words, the school determines which aspects of culture are transmitted.

By exposing children to different experiences, both directly and vicariously, the school opens new avenues to them. A direct experience might be playing a part in a play; a vicarious experience might be seeing a documentary about another country. The effect of these experiences on children's development often is influenced by the children themselves, their families, peer groups, media experiences, and the community. Whereas the school is the *formal* system in which children learn, children learn *informally* in these other contexts. To optimize the socializing influence of the school, supportive linkages, or mesosystems, must be developed with these other ecosystems.

In theory, public education in the United States enables any child, according to his or her abilities, to acquire the skills necessary to fulfill virtually any role in society. In reality, however, today's students are so diverse that educational opportunities are not equal. For example, factors such as family income, family structure, and parents' education have been correlated with children's repeating grades, requiring special services, and dropping out of school (Young & Smith, 1997). Also, because schools have different resources, different philosophies of education, and different teachers, children's learning abilities are affected accordingly.

SCHOOL–CHILD LINKAGES

Certain psychological characteristics of children, such as learning style, may determine which type of learning environment is optimal for each child's development (Bennett, 2003; Levine & Levine, 1996). **Learning style** is defined as

> that consistent pattern of behavior and performance by which an individual
> approaches educational experiences. It is the composite of characteristic cognitive,

affective, and physiological behaviors that serve as relatively stable indicators of how a learner perceives, interacts with, and responds to the learning environment. It is formed in the deep structure of neural organization and personality that molds and is molded by human development and the cultural experiences of home, school, and society. (Bennett, 2003, p. 186)

Learning style, then, is an aspect of socialization. How schools and teachers respond to children's learning styles affect their educational experiences. Learning styles can be observed in children by various criteria. For example, does the child learn best by watching? By listening? By moving his or her body? Does the child achieve more alone or in a group? Is the child better at breaking down a whole task into components (analysis) or relating the components to each other to form a new whole (synthesis)? Is the child motivated by a desire to please the teacher? By concrete rewards? By internalized interest? Does the child need much or little structure to carry out a task?

Psychologist Howard Gardner's theory of multiple intelligences has attracted attention in recent years. Gardner (1999) delineates a variety of intelligences: linguistic, logical-mathematical, spatial, musical, bodily-kinesthetic, interpersonal, intrapersonal, existential, and naturalist. Historically, schools have primarily focused on the linguistic and logical-mathematical. Gardner's theory has significant implications for meeting the individualized needs of various children. For example, different ethnic groups tend to value and develop different areas of intelligence related to problem solving. Thus, by assessing children's learning styles, in addition to developing learning profiles describing their strengths and weaknesses according to Gardner's categories of intelligences, teachers can empower all children to succeed.

SCHOOL–FAMILY LINKAGES

Whereas socialization of children begins in the family, the school extends the process by formal education. The outcome of this joint effort depends considerably on the relationship between family and school. Many research studies, from preschool to elementary school to high school (Cochran & Henderson, 1986; Epstein & Dauber, 1991; Henderson & Berla, 1994; Lazar & Darlington, 1982; Nettles, 1990), have provided evidence showing that, when schools work together with families to support learning, children tend to succeed in school and afterward. These studies point to family involvement in learning as a more accurate predictor of school achievement than is socioeconomic status. Specifically, when families (1) create a home environment that encourages learning, (2) express high (but not unrealistic) expectations for their children's current achievement and future careers, and (3) become involved in their children's lives, at school and in the community, children from low-socioeconomic-status and ethnically diverse families fare comparably to middle-class children.

The effectiveness of the school as a socializing agency depends to a large degree on the kinds of families its children come from (Coleman, 1966; Levine & Levine, 1996; Sadker & Sadker, 2003). As discussed previously, the school has been less effective in educating children from low-socioeconomic-status families. Such children, in addition to being poor, are often from minority groups. The reasons generally attributed for the school's lessened effectiveness are the fewer resources available for education in poorer communities, the expectations of the teachers (most teachers are from the middle class), and the lack of certain preschool experiences expected of children their age by public schools. For example, sitting still at the table when working or eating is generally expected of school-age children, but some children do not have a table at home large enough to accommodate all family members at one time, so there are no formal sit-down meals; instead, family members eat "on the run." Consequently, these children have trouble in school until they learn to sit still and conform to other school-expected behaviors.

It has been demonstrated that the effectiveness of the school as a socializing agent depends on the degree of consistency, or supportive linkages, between children's home environments and their educational environment (Levine & Levine, 1996; Minuchin & Shapiro, 1983). This may help explain why schools generally are less effective in educating children from lower socioeconomic levels. Beginning in the 1960s, the federal government attempted to remedy some of the inequities in educational opportunities by providing intervention programs for children from lower classes. The rationale behind such programs was to provide learning experiences and skills disadvantaged children lacked due to their environments. Most federally funded programs require that schools and families work together.

The school's influence in the socialization process differs according to the value placed on school by the family (Gordon, 1971; Schaefer, 1991). In other words, if a family believes that the school is important in imparting the cultural heritage (accumulated knowledge, values, and so forth) to their children, the family will support the school. The family will tell children that school is important, that school will help them achieve in life, and that the teacher knows best. Parents will see that children do their homework and will respond to teachers' requests for behavioral change. Studies have shown that parental involvement is related to children's school performance, and the degree of involvement is related to the level of education attained by the parents (Levine & Levine, 1996).

If, however, the family does *not* believe that the school is a significant socializing agent, parents will not take much interest in the work children bring home; they may ignore the teacher's requests for help to change children's behavior; and they may even relate negative experiences they had at school to children.

Family Involvement

How can families become involved in school? There are three major ways: (1) decision making—determining school programs and policies; (2) participation—working in the classroom as paid and volunteer instructional assistants; and (3) partnership—providing home guidance to their children to support learning and extend school goals. For example, Yale University psychiatrist Dr. James Comer (1988) found that, by involving parents of children from minority groups in these three ways, parental distrust of the school was overcome. Students were viewed as having unmet needs rather than as having behavioral problems. The children in Comer's program were served by a mental health team and by resource teachers. There was a Crisis Room, where counselors provided positive alternatives to antisocial behavior. There was a Discovery Room, where teachers motivated learning based on children's interests and curiosity. Comer's program thus joined social and intellectual skills. Parents' help was enlisted, and the school became a source of self-esteem and community pride.

Families also become involved in the school and education when they vote. They elect people to serve on the local school board to make decisions about educational goals, school facilities, budget allocations, personnel, student standards of achievement and conduct, and evaluation methods. Obviously, this interaction is indirect, but it is nonetheless influential (see Figure 6.3). Direct interaction occurs when families go to the school their children attend and talk to administrators and teachers.

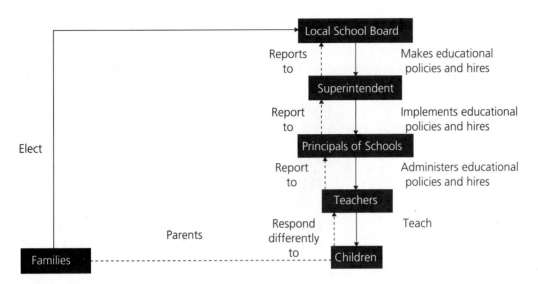

Figure 6.3
Child–Family–School Linkages

For example, schools that have turned around truancy rates dramatically let the students know they care about them. In some cases, schools use a system in which each student is assigned a teacher who makes sure the student gets to school. The teacher makes wake-up calls and occasionally even drops by the child's home on Saturdays to express the school's ongoing interest. If there is any sign of reluctance about going to school, the teacher explores why and, if necessary, refers the student to appropriate social services. Successful schools, then, really work on human connectedness (Henderson, 1990; Steinberg, 1996).

However, the effectiveness of the school or family can be eroded by conflict, confusion, lack of consensus in goals, or mismatch in motivation or cognitive skills (Hess & Holloway, 1984; Levine & Levine, 1996). For example, a mismatch in the way language is used in a community and in school can result in learning problems (Banks, 2002; Heath, 1983). Thus, a child who communicates in Black English dialect will have difficulty in a classroom in which standard English is the norm.

Why is family involvement in schools so important to the school's ability to socialize? When families are involved, children benefit by having a more positive attitude toward learning, better attendance, fewer placements in special education, better grades, and increased likelihood of graduating from high school and going to work or continuing their education. When families are involved, they gain confidence in the school, the teacher, and themselves. Often they are motivated to continue their own education. For its part, the school benefits by having community support, higher teacher morale, and better student achievement.

Thus, the school needs to interact with the family so that socialization goals for children are complementary rather than contradictory. For example, in several studies of students in early grades (Kelly-Vaace & Schreck, 2002; Tizard, Schofield, & Hewison, 1982), those children (of all reading levels) who were asked to read to their parents gained in reading skills (a school goal), whereas the control group of children did not.

This parent supervises the child's homework, emphasizing the importance of effort and hard work.

The key to forming complementary goals for children is communication. The school and the family need to talk to each other about their attitudes regarding education and parenting. What are the parents' expectations for children's achievement and behavior at school? What are the school's expectations for children's activities at home?

Studies report that parents of young children with some college education and in the middle to upper socioeconomic statuses have the most involvement in school (Berger, 1995; Epstein, 1995). As children progress from elementary school to upper grades, parental contact with school diminishes. Inner-city parents, single parents, dual-earner parents, and parents of secondary schoolchildren express both a desire to be more involved and frustration that the school and teachers are not more accessible.

To collaborate with and empower parents, Indianapolis schools implemented weekly tutoring sessions, assignment monitoring, and workshops that enable parents to learn how to help their underachieving children. The program demonstrated that the school cared about the parents and the success of their children (Hyde, 1992).

However, not all parents are interested in becoming involved with their children's school. Why? Perhaps some disliked school as children, and their attitude prevents them from wanting to communicate with their children's teachers. Some may feel that parents are called to the school only when there is a problem. Perhaps some are so involved with work and careers that they are too tired to make the effort. Or perhaps some do not speak English fluently enough to feel comfortable talking to the teacher.

What can teachers do to break through these barriers to communication? Probably the most effective course of action is to allay the fears underlying that barrier. For instance, if parents will not come to school because they are afraid to hear bad things about their child, the teacher can make it a habit to send positive notes home and to call parents to let them know their child is doing well. If parents are very involved in their work, they might share their work with the class—visit the class, arrange a trip for the children to visit their workplace, or share information with their child so he or she can share it with the class. If the parents' English is limited, the teacher can invite them to visit the class to see their child's work. Their language facility is unimportant; what's important is that the teacher let them know that she cares about their child.

Basically, parents need confidence, support, and praise. Parenting is hard work. In the business world, hard work is recognized by praise from supervisors, salary raises, and/or commissions, but in the home, the hard work of child rearing often goes unrecognized. A teacher who is able to communicate to parents the positive outcomes of their jobs as parents is, in effect, building their self-esteem and breaking down their doubts about their competence as parents. A teacher who can communicate respect for parents has taken the first step in motivating them to become involved. The sustenance of that involvement then depends on the teacher's genuine and constant interest. Workshops for teachers to enhance school–family partnerships are often provided by school districts as in-service training.

Family–School Linkages and Children's Readiness to Learn

Illustrating the significance of child, family, and school linkages, the nation's primary educational goal is that all children will come to school "ready to learn." The challenge of reaching this goal for macro-, micro-, and mesosystems is to employ the following strategies (Boyer, 1991, pp. 136–143):

1. *A healthy start.* Good health and good schooling are inextricably interlocked, and every child, to be ready to learn, must have a healthy birth, be well nourished, and be well protected in the early years of life.
2. *Empowered parents.* The home is the first classroom. Parents are the first and most essential teachers; all children, as a readiness requirement, should live in a secure environment in which empowered parents encourage language development. Specifically, parents must do the following:
   a. Speak frequently to children and listen.
   b. Read to children.
   c. Build a bridge between home and school.
3. *Quality preschool.* Because many young children are cared for outside the home, high-quality programs are required that not only provide good care but also address all dimensions of school readiness.
4. *A responsible workplace.* If each child in America is to come to school ready to learn, we must have workplace policies that are family friendly, ones that offer child care services and give parents time to be with their young children. Here employers can:
   a. Provide available leave time.
   b. Have flexible scheduling.
   c. Enable job sharing.
   d. Link with community child care services.

5. *Television as a teacher.* Next to parents, television is probably the child's most influential teacher. School readiness requires television programming that is both educational and enriching. Thus, it's important to:
   a. Require commercial companies selling children's products to help underwrite quality programming.
   b. Establish a ready-to-learn cable channel.
6. *Neighborhoods for learning.* Because all children need spaces and places for growth and exploration, safe and friendly neighborhoods are needed, ones that contribute richly to the child's readiness to learn. Thus, neighborhoods can:
   a. Have well-designed indoor and outdoor parks.
   b. Provide readiness programs in libraries, museums, and zoos.
   c. Establish ready-to-learn centers in malls where college students can volunteer their services.
7. *Connections across the generations.* Connections across the generations will give the child a sense of security and continuity, contributing to school readiness in the fullest sense. The task here is twofold:
   a. Build bridges between child care and senior citizen centers.
   b. Build bridges between child care and community teacher programs.

In sum, children who are ready to succeed in school are healthy, immunized against disease, well nourished, and well rested. Their early experiences have given them a head start in learning to cooperate, exercise self-control, articulate their thoughts and feelings, and follow rules. They are trusting and have a feeling of self-worth. They explore their environment actively and approach tasks with enthusiasm (U.S. Department of Education, 1991b).

SCHOOL–PEER GROUP LINKAGES

Children's attitudes about learning can be influenced by the peer group to which they belong. The peer group can thus help or hinder the school's role in socialization.

Brian was not too sure of his status with his peers in class. The high school he attended had a strong tradition of academic excellence and many intramural scholastic competitions. Brian's peers expected best efforts, which were rewarded by social recognition. Those who lagged were put down. Brian worked very hard academically to meet the standards of his peer group.

Todd, in contrast, had a group of friends who believed it was not "cool" to carry books, give evidence of having done homework, or work hard academically. Todd, in choosing a group of friends whose value it was to "keep cool," probably was not working up to his full potential academically.

That peers influence the educational process was demonstrated by Coleman (1961) in his classic study on adolescents in schools. He found that in most high schools boys value athletic ability and girls value popularity. This is still true today as evidenced by the labeling of peer groups in junior high school and high school (Kinney, 1993)—"brains" or "nerds," "jocks," "populars" or "normals" or "unpopulars." Thus, students who are dependent on their peers for approval are less likely to endorse school and family values of academic success.

Research has established that under certain circumstances, such as attaining a superordinate goal (a group grade), the use of peers in a cooperative learning setting (in which students share responsibility for solving academic tasks and preparing reports) increases student achievement more than does a teacher-directed set-

Businesses and the media link with schools by advertising products and sponsoring activities, such as a "read-a-thon."

ting. In addition, working together in a cooperative learning setting improves student self-esteem, social relations (particularly in the area of ethnic relations), and acceptance of students with disabilities who have been mainstreamed (Johnson & Johnson, 1999; Slavin, 1991).

SCHOOL–MEDIA LINKAGES

Schools are linked to media via use in the classroom and by media-related experiences students have outside the classroom that may influence their learning.

Many schools and teachers use the Public Broadcasting Service (PBS) to complement their lessons. PBS offers a service called "Teacher Source," which provides educational support for prekindergarten through twelfth-grade classes. Schedules of local broadcasting of PBS shows are available online, as are related lesson plans and activities. PBS videos on arts and literature, health and fitness, math, science and technology, social studies, history, and early childhood can be purchased.

An example of media materials that can be used with preschoolers is *Barney & Friends,* which was developed to address the interests and needs of children age 2–5. The show is designed to enhance the cognitive, emotional, social, and physical development of young children. Music, stories, examples, repetition, and positive reinforcement are some of the techniques used to teach social interaction, cooperation, sharing, language development, and ways to cope with new experiences, such as going to the dentist, moving, or going to school.

An example of media materials that can be used with high schoolers is the opera adaptation of *Romeo and Juliet.* Related activity ideas include having students research the Shakespearean era, write an opera that addresses a problem, and compare the original version with modern adaptations for films.

Many schools and teachers subscribe to *Channel One,* a for-profit TV news program, including commercials, beamed directly into America's secondary schools. Participating schools receive satellite dishes, wiring, VCRs, and television monitors for each classroom. The programs, which must be shown in class, consist of news sprinkled with ads aimed at teens—for example, Gatorade, Phisoderm, and bubblegum.

SCHOOL–COMMUNITY LINKAGES

Communities allocate resources for schools. They may use tax money to fund school construction or services. They may pass laws requiring builders to include a school in a new housing development. They set school boundaries (districts), thereby influencing the economic and/or ethnic composition of schools.

Generally, large schools are found in large communities, and small schools in small communities. Communities with ample budgets can afford to have more schools per student capita, and hence smaller schools and classes. Studies have been done relating the size of a school to socialization. Specifically, researchers (Barker & Gump, 1964; Linney & Seidman, 1989) have found that students in small schools engage in a greater variety of activities than students in large schools. Students in small schools also hold more leadership positions than those in large schools. Although there may be more choices of activities in large schools, students have to compete to make teams and participate in extracurricular activities like the school paper. Consequently, many students don't "try out." Thus, the size of the school influences the kind of socializing experiences students have in that participation in extracurricular activities contributes to leadership skills, a sense of responsibility, cognitive and social competence, and personality development.

The size of the classes within a school also influences socialization. Classes are considered "large" if they have over 25 students, "small" if they have less than 20 students, and "regular" if they are in between. In large classes, as the size of the group increases, participation in discussion by each child decreases, as does interaction with the teacher (Barker & Gump, 1964; Linney & Seidman, 1989). In small

Communities provide many learning experiences for children and their families, as exemplified by this museum.

© Davis Barber/PhotoEdit

classes, more learning activities take place, and the increased interaction among students enables them to understand one another, which results in an increase in cooperative behavior. Teachers have more time to monitor students' on-task behavior and can provide quicker and more thorough feedback. Also, potential disciplinary problems can be identified and resolved more quickly (Pate-Bain, Achilles, Boyd-Zaharias, & McKenna, 1992).

That the size of the learning environment affects socialization was demonstrated in a large-scale experiment (Finn & Achilles, 1990) in which kindergarten students and teachers were assigned randomly to small and large classes within each participating school. Students remained in these classes for 2 years. At the end of each school year, they were given standardized tests in reading and mathematics. The students in reduced-size classes in both subject areas outperformed students in the regular-size classes. Minority students in particular benefited from the smaller class environment. As a result of the studies on class size, the federal government has mandated a maximum number of students per teacher depending on the grade.

Local businesses can support schools by donating resources and time ("Adopt-a-School"). For instance, a business can donate equipment, provide expert guest speakers, host field trips, and/or offer apprenticeship training to students. Such supportive linkages enable children to understand the connection between school learning and the world of work, and to discover new role models to emulate (Swick, 1997).

Communities may also have certain traditions that are reflected in the schools. For example, San Juan Capistrano, California, celebrates the return of the swallows every spring. There is a parade in which the local schools participate—students decorate floats, bands play, and drill teams perform.

Characteristics of Effective Schools and Schooling

- *Schooling goals.* The school provides clear standards of achievement and excellence.
- *School–child linkages.* Psychological characteristics of child temperament, motivation, and learning style influence the ability to learn.
- *School–family linkages.* The family provides resources according to its socioeconomic status and attitudes to schools to become involved and ensure that children come to school ready to learn.
- *School–peer group linkages.* Cooperative activities increase learning.
- *School–media linkages.* Schools use TV, videos, and computers appropriately, teaching critical thinking skills.
- *School–community linkages.* The community provides resources to support schools; the size of schools and classes influences adult–child interactions.
- *Safety.* The school provides protection for children and is proactive in violence prevention.
- *School programming.* Traditional (teacher-directed) and modern (learner-directed) programs have different socialization effects (see Chapter 7).
- *Teacher characteristics.* Successful teachers are democratic leaders and good classroom managers; are warm, enthusiastic, and generous with praise; have high status and positive expectations; and respond sensitively to gender, ethnicity, religion, and special needs (see Chapter 7).

Epilogue

The school's basic function in society is to develop future contributing citizens. What is important to impart to children varies as societies change. Philosophies on teaching and learning also vary as to the best way to accomplish this. Rousseau's philosophy was learner directed (let the child's natural curiosity determine what is learned); formal traditional schooling is teacher directed (the teacher determines what is learned by the child); home schooling can be either or both.

For the school to be an effective socializer, the family and community must be involved in the child's education.

Summary

The school is an agent of socialization in that it is a setting for intellectual and social experiences from which children develop the skills, knowledge, interests, and attitudes that characterize them as individuals and that shape their abilities to perform adult roles.

Schools exert influence on children by their educational policies, by their formal introduction of students to authority, and by the social relationships that evolve in the classroom.

The primary purpose of education from society's perspective is the transmission of its cultural heritage—the accumulated knowledge, values, beliefs, and customs of the society. To transmit culture and maintain it, society must be provided with trained people who can assume specialized roles, as well as develop new knowledge and technology. The function of education from the individual's perspective is to acquire the necessary skills and knowledge to become self-sufficient and able to participate effectively in society.

The school's function in the United States is universal, formal, and prescriptive. Society's expectations of schools are expressed in academic, vocational, social, civic, cultural, and personal goals. The school's function as a socialization agent is affected by the larger macrosystem context—political ideology, economics, culture/ethnicity, religion, and science/technology. Macrosystem influences are evidenced by society's policies regarding school choice (public or private schools, vouchers, charter schools, home schooling). Macrosystem influences also are demonstrated by society's policies regarding diversity and equity as they relate to gender, ethnicity, religion, and disability.

The school's response to gender equity involves implementation of Title IX of the Education Amendments Act, which prohibits sex discrimination. The school traditionally has served the needs of the majority culture. For a long time, the attitude toward the socialization of ethnic minorities was assimilation—teaching them to adapt to the ways of the majority culture. Later, the idea of a cultural blending (the melting pot) became popular. Today, the socialization approach has become associated with the theory of cultural pluralism—that the mainstream of the majority culture should coexist and interact with the various cultural minorities for the benefit of all. Bilingual/multicultural education is an example. However, "English-only" programs are gaining popularity. The school must be sensitive regarding which religious values intersect with educational goals. Controversial issues involve school prayer, curriculum, required books, and holiday celebrations.

The school's response to children with disabilities is to provide special education and related services as required. The history of socialization of individuals with disabilities ranges from banishment and neglect, to pity and protection, to segregation and education. Currently, the trend is toward integration or inclusion into the mainstream of society. Thus, the Individuals with Disabilities Education Act guarantees that all children with disabilities will have available to them a free and appropriate education. The act requires nondiscriminatory evaluations to determine whether a child is disabled. The act also requires that an individualized education program (IEP) be written for each child, which is developed by school personnel in conjunction with parents. Students with disabilities must be placed in the least restrictive environment (LRE), and supplementary aids and services must be provided as necessary.

Chronosystem influences on the school involve its adaptation to societal change in general and its adaptation to specific developments, such as technology, violence, and substance use/abuse.

In a changing society, the challenge continually facing educators is how to transmit the cultural heritage, as well as prepare individuals for the future. Educators have approached this dilemma differently. Some believe that only academic skills, cultural heritage, and good citizenship should be taught; others believe that critical thinking skills, development of self-concept, and interpersonal relationship skills should be part of the mix.

Schooling for the future involves being prepared for the world of work and for technological change; knowing how to use computers and software is essential to successful functioning in our society. The effectiveness of the computer as a learning tool depends on how it is used by teachers and students, as well as on the software selected.

To have an effective environment for learning, schools must be safe. Violence is rooted in families and communities. Children model parents' behavior and view the violence they see in the media and in the community as a way to solve conflicts. They also have access to guns and knives, and turn to gangs for protection. Children who are rejected by their peers are at risk for violent behavior, as are children who are disengaged from caring adults.

Substance use/abuse remains a problem in schools. Issues of health and safety, the learning environment, and privacy are involved.

Mesosystem influences on the school include its links with other ecosystems: school–child, school–family, school–peer group, school–media, and school–community. Linkages supportive of education have beneficial socialization outcomes for children.

Family involvement in the school is the most important influence on children's educational success, because the family is the primary socializer of children. Some of the benefits of family involvement in the school for children are positive attitudes toward learning, higher academic achievement, and higher aspirations. Some of the benefits for the family members who are involved are higher self-esteem and more interaction with their children.

Family involvement can occur through decision making, participation, and/or partnership. Families need encouragement and support from teachers. Teachers need good communication skills to work collaboratively.

Activity

PURPOSE *To understand the school's role in influencing the socialization of children.*

1. Attend a school board meeting at which a controversial issue (school rules, dress code, curriculum, extracurricular activities, use of federal funds) is discussed. Agendas can be obtained in advance by contacting the school district office.
2. Describe the issue in at least a paragraph, giving background information if possible.
3. Explain the views of (a) the board, (b) the school administration, (c) the teachers, and (d) the parents and/or students.
4. What was the outcome of the discussion?
5. What was your opinion of the experience?

 Research Terms

Bilingual/multicultural education
Charter schools
Home schooling
Inclusion
Learning style
Literacy
Multiple intelligences

Related Readings

Berger, E. H. (1999). *Parents as partners in education: Families and schools working together* (5th ed.). Englewood Cliffs, NJ: Prentice-Hall.

Caroll, M. K. (1998). *What did you do at school today? A guide to schooling and school success.* Springfield, IL: Charles Thomas.

Darling-Hammond, L. (2001). *The right to learn: A blueprint for creating schools that work.* San Francisco: Jossey-Bass.

Dewey, J. (1944). *Democracy and education.* New York: Free Press.

Epstein, J. L. (1996). *School and family partnerships.* New York: Basic Books (Westview Press).

Farnham-Diggory, S. (1990). *Schooling.* Cambridge, MA: Harvard University Press.

Gardner, H. (1999). *Intelligence reframed: Multiple intelligences for the 21st century.* New York: Basic Books.

Goodlad, J. I. (1984). *A place called school: Prospects for the future.* New York: McGraw-Hill.

Gollnick, D. M., and Chinn, P. C. (2002). *Multicultural education in a pluralistic society* (6th ed.). Upper Saddle River, NJ: Prentice-Hall.

Hallahan, D., & Kauffman, J. (2002). *Exceptional learners: Introduction to special education* (8th ed.). Boston: Allyn & Bacon.

Healy, J. (1991). *Endangered minds: Why children don't think and what we can do about it.* New York: Touchstone.

Holt, J. (1970). *How children learn.* New York: Dell.

Kozol, J. (1991). *Savage inequalities: Children in America's schools.* New York: Crown.

Lareau, A. (2000). *Home advantage.* Lanham, MD: Rowman & Littlefield.

Papert, S. (1999). *The children's machine: Rethinking school in the age of the computer* (2nd ed.). New York: Basic Books.

Rothenberg, P. S. (1998). *Race, class, and gender in the United States: An integrated study* (4th ed.). New York: St. Martin's Press.

Stewart, E. C., & Bennet, M. J. (1991). *American cultural patterns: A cross-cultural perspective* (rev. ed.). Yarmouth, ME: Intercultural Press.

Chapter 7

© Will Hart/PhotoEdit/PictureQuest

Ecology of Teaching

The ideal condition would be, I admit, that men should be right by instinct; but since we are all likely to go astray, the reasonable thing is to learn from those who can teach.

—SOPHOCLES

Prologue: Then and Now

The Teacher's Role as a Socializing Agent

Teacher Characteristics and Student Learning
Teachers as Leaders
Teachers as Managers
Teacher Expectations

Student Characteristics and Teacher Interaction
Gender
Ethnicity
Learning Styles
Disability
Children at Risk: Poverty, Substance Abuse, and Violence

Macrosystem and Chronosystem Influences on Teaching
Philosophies of Teaching and Learning
Socialization Outcomes of Different Classroom Contexts

Accountability and Standardization

Mesosystem Influences on Teaching

Families Empowering Student Success: Involvement in Learning

Schools Empowering Student Success: Developmentally Appropriate Learning and Assessment

Epilogue

Summary

Activity

Research Terms

Related Readings

| *Then and Now*

EXECUTING AN EFFECTIVE EDUCATION

THEN The Greek philosopher Socrates *(469–399 B.C.)*, is known for stimulating other's thoughts by questioning their statements in order to elicit more information and to lead them to a certain conclusion. This technique, known as the "Socratic method," was employed by Socrates as he traveled around Athens teaching students. Dedicated to the search for truth, Socrates questioned government policies. Eventually, he was brought to trial for inciting the people against the government. His sentence was a choice: End his teaching or be put to death. Socrates chose death, poisoning himself, and thereby becoming a martyr for the cause of education. Socrates' fundamental principle, "Knowledge is virtue," has been adopted by teachers throughout history.

NOW The psychologist Burrhus Frederic (B. F.) Skinner (1904–1990) believed that observable behavior, rather than thoughts, indicate learning. He formulated "behavior learning theory," proposing that students can be conditioned to learn any subject a teacher desires to teach, provided that the tasks involved are divided into small, sequenced steps and that the learner is appropriately reinforced for desired behavior (for example, the correct answer). Skinner used principles from his theory to design teaching machines, the forerunner of computer-assisted instruction. The subject software is divided into bits of sequenced information, with relevant questions, so that mastery increases as learners proceed through the program. Skinner's teaching technology is used in many classrooms today.

KEY QUESTIONS

- Does effective teaching involve eliciting what students already know and enabling them to apply that knowledge to form new concepts?
- Does effective teaching involve choosing from all available information and shaping that knowledge so that it can be assimilated by students?
- Does effective teaching involve knowing one's students individually, so that one can combine various methods?

The Teacher's Role as a Socializing Agent

For the past 20 years or so, I have been asking my students to think back over their education in elementary, middle, and high school, and to remember the characteristics of their best teachers and their worst ones. Although the exact wording differs, without fail, the "best" teachers are interesting, competent, caring, encouraging, and flexible, yet have demanding standards; the "worst" teachers, in contrast, are boring, incompetent, distant, demeaning, and rigid, with inflexible standards, or inconsistent, with lax standards. After exploring the reasons for students' choices, the message becomes quite clear: The "best" teachers

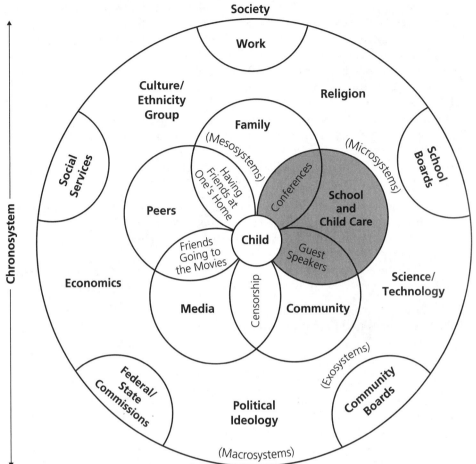

Figure 7.1

An Ecological Model of Human Development
All children are affected by how exosystems and macrosystems provide support for their diverse socialization needs.

make students want to learn and reinforce their efforts, whereas the "worst" teachers turn students off.

Interestingly, the results of my informal surveys correspond to the formal research on effective role models. According to Albert Bandura (1986, 1989), models whom children imitate are perceived as being warm, having prestige, wielding control over resources, and having the potential to reinforce or punish behavior. And according to other research, primary grade students characterized good teachers as caring, responsive, and stimulating (Daniels, Kalkman, & McCombs, 2001).

This chapter examines the teacher's role as a socializing agent and the impact on learning of the teacher-student bidirectional relationship. Figure 7.1 shows an ecological model of the systems involved in the process. Students come to school with a unique family background, learning style, abilities, motives, and interests. Teachers come to school with certain abilities and characteristics, such as teaching style, management techniques, and expectations. Student–teacher interactions take place in a classroom environment that may enhance or detract from learning. Additional factors in learning the prescribed curriculum include other students, personal problems, and difficulty with standardized tests.

The most powerful socializing influence of the school lies in those who translate program goals into action—the teachers (Brophy, 1992). Teachers provide the environment for children's learning. They understand children's needs, interests, and abilities, and they can empathize with children's fears of failure. Teachers have the ability to encourage children to explore, to satisfy their natural curiosity, and to value learning—so much so that it becomes part of their lives forever. Teachers also play a major role in helping children learn to deal with individuals in positions of authority, to cooperate with others, to cope with problems, and to achieve competence.

Teachers are responsible for selecting materials relevant to learners, for managing the group dynamics in the classroom, and for interacting individually with each child. When teachers interact with their students, they communicate attitudes about learning and behavior, as well as feelings about individuals. Specifically, effective teachers do the following (Levine & Levine, 1996):

1. Provide time and opportunity to learn, and pace instruction accordingly.
2. Communicate high expectations for student success.
3. Involve all students in learning activities by engaging them in discussion and providing motivating work.
4. Adapt levels of instruction to the learning needs and abilities of students.
5. Ensure success for students as they progress through the curriculum.

The teacher–student relationship represents a different social experience for each child and so leads to different developmental outcomes.

Points to Ponder

Perception is a biological construct that involves interpretation of stimuli by the brain. Factors such as maturation, attentiveness, past experiences, and emotions influence people's perception of things, events, and interactions. How did a teacher influence your perception of an event such as a Shakespeare play or the attack on the World Trade Center?

Teacher Characteristics and Student Learning

What characteristics of teachers foster student learning? Teachers who work closely with each child and who understand group dynamics are more likely to provide a successful and rewarding learning environment. For example, studies (Agne, 1992; Brophy & Good, 1986; Daniels, Kalkman, & McCombs, 2001) have found that successful, or effective, teachers are warm, enthusiastic, and generous with praise, and have high status. Also, successful teachers communicate well with and are responsive to students. Teachers who are warm and friendly in their relationships with children are likely to encourage favorable rather than aggressive behavior and constructive, conscientious attitudes toward schoolwork. Conversely, unsuccessful, or ineffective, teachers are aloof, critical, and negative. They tend to communicate in ways that are difficult for students to understand and are unresponsive to students' needs.

When teachers communicate with children, learning is influenced; when teachers ask questions, verbalization from children is elicited. For example, teachers'

This teacher has a powerful influence on learning through the ability to stimulate the children's interest and engage their involvement.

verbal styles have been found to have an impact on the development of language skills in preschool children (Schickedanz, 1990). Teachers who use expansive verbal descriptions and who encourage children to converse with each other effect an increase in their students' verbal skills. In addition, teachers who use reinforcement (verbal praise, smiles, touch) foster the learning of certain tasks. And preschool children who were observed in the presence of a friendly, approving adult behaved in a more exploratory, inquisitive manner than they did when a critical, aloof adult was present (Moore & Bulbulian, 1976).

The relationship of teachers' characteristics to their degree of success and their impact on socialization can be explained by the classic research of Bandura and Walters (1963) on modeling, as discussed in the introduction to the chapter. They point out that "models who are rewarding, prestigeful or competent, who possess high status, and who have control over rewarding resources are more readily imitated than are models who lack these qualities" (p. 107).

Students who model their teachers pick up subtle behaviors and attitudes related to learning. It would follow, then, that the most important influence on students' achievement is the competent teacher. More specifically, the competent teacher is committed to work, manages the classroom well, provides a positive role model with whom students can identify, is enthusiastic and warm, works toward self-improvement in teaching, possesses skill in human relationships, and can adapt his or her skills to specific contexts (Good & Brophy, 2003; Linney & Seidman, 1989).

TEACHERS AS LEADERS

The teacher is a leader in that he or she directs, guides, and sets an example. However, teachers have different styles of leadership to accomplish their goals. To illustrate, a classic study done by Lewin, Lippitt, and White (1939) compared the effects of three leadership styles—authoritarian, democratic (or authoritative), and laissez-faire (or permissive)—on three groups of 10-year-old boys. The boys were assigned randomly to one of three after-school recreational groups engaged in craft activities. The groups were led by three adults who behaved in different ways. In the **authoritarian** situation, the leader determined the group's policy, gave step-by-step directions, dictated each boy's particular task, assigned children to work with one another, was subjective in praising the children's work, and stayed aloof from group participation. In the **democratic** situation, the leader allowed the boys to participate in setting group policy, gave the boys a general idea of the steps involved in the project, suggested alternative procedures, allowed the boys to work with whomever they wished, evaluated them in a fair and objective manner, and tried to be a member of the group. In the **laissez-faire** situation, the leader gave the group complete freedom to do as they wished, supplied materials or information only when asked, and refrained almost completely from commenting on the boys' work.

The style of leadership was shown to have a definite effect on the interactions within each group. The boys in the authoritarian situation showed significantly more aggression toward one another and were far more discontented than were the boys in the democratic condition. They also produced more work than the other two groups. The boys in the democratic group acted less hostile, showed more enjoyment, and continued to work even when the leader left the room, which was not true of the other two groups. Finally, the laissez-faire group accomplished relatively little; the boys were frequently bored and spent much time "fooling around."

Do teachers' leadership styles influence the learning environment in the classroom? In several studies, Good and Brophy (1986) reported that teachers who are clearly the leader and authority figure and who direct the class toward specific goals (direct instruction) promote achievement. In this learning environment, little emphasis is placed on discussion, student ideas, discovery learning, or other types of indirect instruction. However, Jonathon Kozol, in *Savage Inequalities* (1991), disagreed. He describes the plight of inner-city children trying to learn from teachers who used direct instruction that was correlated to their students' experiences. Contributing to the teachers' effect on learning was overcrowded schools with dilapidated equipment. Herbert Kohl, in his classic book *36 Children* (1967), describes the remarkable progress in language and thinking abilities made by the inner-city children in his class when he brought books, art supplies, and play materials to class and allowed the children to explore them freely and make discoveries. Kohl acted as a facilitator, a helper in the acquisition of knowledge, and in so doing enabled the children to participate in their own learning. Kohl (1984) concluded that children, regardless of economic background, learn best from teachers who act as role models and who love learning.

Still another way of viewing the teacher's leadership role is as a mentor who guides participation (Rogoff, 1990). For example, when a teacher shows a child how to be more successful at doing arithmetic problems by putting the numbers in the boxes on graph paper, the teacher is not only guiding the child's participation but also providing support for success from one level to the next. In this way, teachers facilitate children's capacities to reach their full potential. Vygotsky (1978) called the space between what a learner can do independently and what he or she can do while participating with more capable others the **zone of proximal development (ZPD).** The effective teacher is sensitive to students' zone of development and provides appropriate independent, as well as collaborative, activities to enhance learning.

> **EXAMPLE** My mother wanted to learn how to use the word processing program on my computer. I demonstrated a few commands and let her practice, telling her to call me if she got stuck. When she felt she had mastered the basics, I showed her how to do more complicated things. With my assistance, my mother was able to learn more quickly than she would have on her own.

TEACHERS AS MANAGERS

Teachers' ability to manage a classroom affects their effectiveness as socializing agents. For example, Kounin's (1970) classic research on classroom management showed that the key to successful management lay in *preventive* rather than *consequential* measures. That is, successful classroom managers plan and prepare instruction, thereby reducing inattention and boredom.

Kounin found that student inattentiveness and misbehavior were often linked to problems of discontinuity in lessons, which, in turn, were linked to inadequate preparation by teachers. For example, a teacher who is giving instructions on how to do a book report but stops to find the appropriate books is likely to have lost the students' attention by the time the books are located. In contrast, if the teacher has the relevant books displayed on a table while delivering the book report instructions, inattentiveness is likely to be prevented.

Did you ever have teachers who had "eyes in the back of their heads"? Such teachers seem to know what their students are doing without having to look and therefore are quick to react to potential problems. Kounin (1970) refers to this type of teacher behavior as "with-itness." Teachers who are "with it" respond immediately to incidents rather than waiting, quash minor problems before they turn into major ones, do not overreact to incidents, and focus on the individuals involved in the incident rather than blaming someone wrongly. When students realize that the teacher knows what is going on, they are less likely to become involved in unproductive behavior.

Another characteristic of successful classroom managers is the ability to "overlap"— that is, to deal with more than one activity at the same time (Good & Brophy, 2003). For example, while working with a group of students in one corner of the room, a teacher may provide an appropriate motivating statement to a child who is wandering about, not involved in an activity. Also, transitions from one activity to the next are smooth, not disruptive: "When you complete the chapter, you may work on the computer" rather than "All books away; it is time for your test now."

In sum, then, effective classroom managers prevent most potential problems from occurring and move activities along or give presentations without confusion or loss of focus. They also provide activities that are at the appropriate developmental level for students and are interesting enough to hold their attention. And they monitor the entire class continuously, doing two or more things simultaneously without disrupting the flow of learning (Brophy & Good, 1986; Good & Brophy, 2003).

TEACHER EXPECTATIONS

Do teachers' expectations affect the achievement and behavior of students? Rosenthal and Jacobson (1968), in their book *Pygmalion in the Classroom*, describe a classic experiment in which they had all the teachers in an elementary school give a test to their students that was designed to identify intellectual "bloomers" (those who would show an academic spurt during the year). Actually, the test was a nonverbal IQ test that, unknown to the teachers, did not predict future intellectual growth. After the test, the researchers provided the teachers with a list of supposed bloomers. However, the list was not based on the test results; instead, it was a random list of names from the teachers' rolls. Eight months later, all the children were retested with the same IQ test. The designated bloomers did, in fact, demonstrate significant intellectual growth, with children in the first and second grades showing the most growth. This study raised an important question: Are teachers trapped by their own self-fulfilling prophecies?

Rosenthal and Jacobson's study generated much controversy because of methodological weaknesses and the inability of others to replicate the original results. Brophy and Good (1986) suggested that attempting to influence teacher expectations by providing phony information generally has not yielded results. However, studies of actual teacher behavior in the classroom have shown the effects of teacher expectations (Sadker & Sadker, 2003). For example, in a longitudinal study of more than 1500 middle school students, teacher predictions of students' performance in math had a greater impact on future math achievement for low achievers than for high achievers. Teachers' overestimation of performance had a greater—and more positive—influence on achievement than did underestimation (Madon, Jussim, & Eccles, 1997). In sum, the study demonstrated the power of "living up to expectations."

Brophy and Good explain the reality of teacher expectations as follows: Teachers usually receive data about students at the beginning of the school year (test scores, past grades, family and health information, comments by previous teachers), which influence their expectations of students for achievement and behavior. Based on these expectations, teachers tend to treat students differently. Students then react to the teacher differently, with the students' behavior and achievement reinforcing the teacher's expectations. Gradually, the students' self-concepts, motivation, levels of aspiration, and performance come to reflect these expectations. In addition to students' past records of achievement and behavior, teachers' expectations can be influenced by certain student characteristics, such as socioeconomic class, ethnicity, gender, personality, physical attractiveness, speech characteristics, and handwriting (Brophy & Good, 1986; Good & Brophy, 2003; Proctor, 1984).

EXAMPLE Mrs. Levins had a student named Roy in her third-grade class who had moved several times and had below-normal achievement scores for his age recorded in his cumulative folder. As Mrs. Levins reviewed the folders of other children in her class, she found that there were three—Sarah, Andrew, and Cary—who consistently scored well above normal on achievement tests and whose folders also contained notes from previous teachers about what a joy each one was to teach. By midyear, Mrs. Levins was giving Roy less time to answer her questions than she did Sarah, Andrew, or Cary. She was also more critical of Roy than she was of the others and demanded less of him in terms of work.

Of course, not all teachers translate their expectations into the type of behavior described in the example. Some teachers do not form expectations that continue throughout the year; rather, they alter their expectations on the basis of students' performances. Teacher expectations about students do not, by themselves, have a direct impact on student behavior. It is only when the expectations are communicated to the students and when selective reinforcement results in shaping their behavior that they have an impact. Therefore, only when teachers become aware of possible biases in their behavior, caused by their expectations, can they interact objectively with each child.

Student Characteristics and Teacher Interaction

Teacher–student interaction is bidirectional, with teachers eliciting responses in students, and students, according to their behavioral, cognitive, and affective qualities, eliciting responses in teachers (Bloom, 1982). According to Katz (1984), teacher–student interaction is specific and limited in that it relates to school matters. The intensity of affect between teacher and student is supposed to be low and somewhat detached, because teachers cannot get too emotionally involved with their students; otherwise, they lose objectivity (in their ability to evaluate, for example). Teachers must maintain rationality and intentionality in their curriculum goals. They must also exhibit impartiality toward individual students, as their scope of responsibility is toward the group. Teaching a group of students from diverse backgrounds is a big challenge, especially when the group is large. The bidirectional relationship of teacher and student, which, in turn, affects socialization, is a complex issue reflecting factors such as gender, ethnicity, learning styles, and disability.

GENDER

Research has shown that teacher–student interaction differs according to the gender of the student (the gender of the teacher does not seem to matter), although most teachers are unaware of any inequities (Sadker & Sadker, 2003). Studies consistently show that boys have more interventions with teachers than do girls (Streitmatter, 1994). For example, it has been found (Serbin, O'Leary, Kent, & Tonick, 1973) that teachers are more responsive to the disruptive behavior of boys than girls and more likely to reprimand boys. When children request attention, teachers generally respond to boys with instructions and to girls with nurturance. In addition, girls receive more attention when they are physically close to the teacher, whereas boys are given attention from a distance.

It has also been found that the feedback received by boys and by girls on the intellectual quality of their work differs. For example, boys receive considerable criticism for failing to obey the rules, whereas girls receive criticism related to their performance. Boys attribute their failure to do well to lack of effort, whereas girls attribute it to a lack of ability (Dweck, Davidson, Nelson, & Enna, 1978). Do some girls, then, give up trying to succeed when they reach high school due to the responses their elementary teachers have given them?

It is well established that girls generally perform better academically than boys in elementary school but falter in high school. For example, girls do not do as well as boys in science and math by the time they reach adolescence (American Association of University Women [AAUW], 1991; Maccoby & Jacklin, 1974). In addition, girls typically take fewer advanced math classes than do boys in high school and college (AAUW, 1991; Sadker & Sadker, 1994, 2003). Even though Title IX of the Educational Amendment Act of 1972 obliged schools to provide equal treatment for males and females, schools are still shortchanging girls according to a report by the

AAUW (1991). Although more girls are now involved in athletics (Eisenberg, Martin, & Fabes, 1996), the contributions and experiences of females are not as visible as are those of males in textbooks. Furthermore, the pace of change is slow in gender-segregated enrollment patterns in vocational education, with girls primarily enrolled in office and business-training programs, and boys in programs leading to higher-paying trade jobs. Sexuality and the realities of sexual activity (pregnancy, disease, rape) are rarely discussed in schools, although, by law, sexual harassment is defined and consequences delineated (Chmielewski, 1997).

Teachers must be trained to foster assertive and affiliative skills in both girls and boys. School curricula and textbooks should be monitored for gender stereotypes and provide positive role models for both girls and boys. Gender-role socialization is discussed in more detail in Chapter 12.

ETHNICITY

Ethnicity is a factor in teacher–student interaction in that both teachers and students bring to the relationship certain socialization experiences reflecting their values, morals, attitudes, motives, behaviors, roles, and so on. Also, the role of teacher and school is to implement the values and traditions of society, such as the belief that national strength and unity come from the diversity of individuals. Symbolizing this value is the Great Seal of the United States, used on many official documents and coins, containing the motto "E pluribus unum" (one out of many). Thus, to help maintain a strong society, the school takes on the responsibility of acculturation.

The United States is composed of many ethnic groups. According to the U.S. Bureau of the Census (2000), although the majority of individuals in the United States classify themselves as non-Hispanic White, many citizens are of Hispanic, Asian–Pacific Island, African American, Native American, other origins. Americans speak many languages. More than 32 million speak a language other than English at home, including Spanish, French, German, Chinese, and Italian (U.S. Bureau of the Census, 2000). And, according to projections, based on life expectancies, fertility rates, and immigration patterns, by the year 2050, the gap between majority and minority ethnic groups may be closed. This fact, plus the movement toward a global economy (discussed in Chapter 1), points to the importance of understanding ethnic diversity.

> **EXAMPLE** As the preschool teacher was helping the children settle down on their mats for naptime, she noticed red marks on Jenny Truong's neck and forehead. When she asked Jenny how she got them, Jenny replied that her father had put them there. The teacher, suspecting child abuse, reported it to the authorities. Unknown to the teacher, people from various Asian cultures believe that internal "winds" cause illness. However, by bringing the winds to the surface, the illness can be banished and the person healed. This is done by "scratching the wind away," or "coining." That is, a coin dipped in oil or menthol is vigorously rubbed against the head, neck, chest, or back—wherever the symptoms are exhibited—until the skin turns red (Dresser, 1996).
>
> One day the fifth-grade teacher noticed that Juanita, normally a tidy youngster, had a brown smear of dirt on one arm. That day and the next, the teacher said nothing. However, when Juanita came to class with the mark on her arm for a third day, the teacher told her to go wash it off. When Juanita replied that her arm was not dirty, the teacher told her not to argue and to do as she was told. Juanita complied. Several

days later, Juanita was taken out of school by her parents to attend the funeral of her sister. When two weeks had passed and Juanita still had not returned to school, the principal went to her home to find out why. Juanita's mother explained to the principal that when someone was ill each family member placed a spot of oil and soil somewhere on the body: "We are one with nature. When someone is ill, that person is out of balance with nature. We use the oil and soil of our Mother, the earth, to show her we wish our sick one to be back in balance with nature. When Juanita's teacher made her wash her arm, our oneness with nature was broken. That is why her sister died. The teacher caused her death; Juanita can never return to her class" (Garcia, 1998).

Respect for cultural and ethnic differences requires teachers to be sensitive to a variety of customs. Asking appropriate questions and listening carefully to the answers can help avoid misunderstandings. The National Association for the Education of Young Children (NAEYC) (1996a) has taken the following position:

> For optimal developmental and learning of all children, educators must *accept* the legitimacy of children's home language, *respect* (hold in high regard) and *value* (esteem, appreciate) the home culture and promote and encourage the active involvement and support of all families, including extended and nontraditional family units. (p. 5)

Teacher sensitivity can help children learn to be tolerant and respectful of differences. For example, when a kindergarten boy from India was called "garbage head" by his classmates because his hair smelled of coconut oil, the teacher planned a series of activities in which she and the children compared coconut oil to a variety of shampoos, conditioners, mousses, and gels. After much discussion about all the different things people put on their hair, the children came to realize that everyone's hair has a particular smell and that coconut was simply one of a vast array (Ramsey, 1998).

Understanding diversity in microcultures, or minorities, involves examining the macroculture, or majority. Historically, political and social institutions in the United States developed from a western European tradition. For instance, the English language and American legal system were derived from English common law. The American political system of democratic elections likewise has primarily English roots (Gollnick & Chinn, 2002). Thus, American formal institutions (representing the macroculture), such as government, schools, business, and health and welfare agencies, reflect White, Anglo-Saxon, Protestant (WASP) influences, often referred to as the **Protestant ethic.**

Despite the fact that the macroculture includes many people who are not White, Anglo Saxon, or Protestant, certain basic values are shared to some degree by all members of the macroculture. Generally, the American macroculture is characterized by the following (Arensberg & Niehoff, 1975; Stewart & Bennett, 1991; Williams, 1960b):

- Emphasis on active mastery rather than passive acceptance—individuals are responsible for what happens to them.
- Valuation of the work ethic—industriousness, ambition, competitiveness, individualism, and independence are desired traits, and status is based on occupation, education, and financial worth.
- Stress on assertiveness and achievement—achievement is valued above inheritance.
- Valuation of fairness—equal opportunities are provided in social, political, and economic institutions.

- Interest in the external world of things and events rather than the internal world of meaning and feeling—achievement and success are measured by the quality of material goods purchased.
- Emphasis on change, flow, and movement—new and modern are better than old and traditional, and emphasis is on the future rather than the past or present.
- Belief in rationalism rather than traditionalism—things are accepted not because they have been before, but because there is a logical reason for doing so.
- Emphasis on peer relationships rather than superordinate-subordinate ones—the ideal is equality, or horizontal relationships, rather than hierarchy, or vertical relationships.
- Focus on individual personality (individualism, independence) rather than group identity and responsibility (collectivism, interdependence)—an adaptive and outgoing personality, rather than a conventional, introverted one, is the model.
- Emphasis on open relationships with others (impersonal or objective)—communication is direct or confrontational.
- Valuation of clearcut moral values—personal life and community affairs are based on principles of right and wrong rather than shame, dishonor, or ridicule.

How are these values exemplified in young children's behavior? "Most children in the United States learn that nature is something you conquer and exploit. In the sandbox they often 'build roads' or 'dig to the other side of the world'" (Ramsey, 1998, p. 61). Children are also encouraged to be actively engaged in activity rather than be "bored," as verified by the quantity of toys parents bring on long car rides.

© SW Productions/Index Stock Imagery/PictureQuest

This child is learning by observing and modeling her mother and by working cooperatively on a task.

The degree to which individual U.S. citizens subscribe to the general values of the macroculture depends, in part, on the values of the microculture, or ethnic group, to which they belong. It may also depend on the extent to which they must interact with formal societal institutions for support (Gollnick & Chinn, 2002). For example, if a person receives a government loan to further his or her education, she or he has to comply with regulations by proving attendance at a college or university and following the prescribed schedule for repayment. To better understand possible areas of differences between macroculture (individualistic) and microculture (collectivistic) values in school, consider these generalities about microcultures:

- The orientation is toward the extended family. Children are considered important members of the family group; the family provides a psychological support system throughout individuals' lives. Also, cousins are considered as close as brothers. Emphasis is placed on cooperating with others, helping those in need, and respecting elders. Family matters may take precedence over school attendance.
- Sharing and group ownership are valued. This means that, to children who have not been socialized to understand individual ownership ("These are *your* crayons"), *your* may mean belonging to the group. For example, if Juan cannot find his pencil, he may borrow Lee's without asking because whatever belongs to the group the child regards as his or hers, too.
- Children are taught not to "show up" their peers. Thus, they may not exhibit competitive behaviors in classroom settings ("Who has the best work?"). However, when performance is socially defined as benefiting the peer society, these compete well ("Which group has read the most books?").
- Children learn by observing and being patient. At home, they may not be rewarded for curiosity and for asking questions; parents may even use legends and fables to discourage curiosity.
- Children are taught to drop their heads as a sign of respect and compliance rather than look directly at the adult.
- Status is based more on who one is (family name) than what one has.
- Time orientation is generally more present-oriented than future-oriented. Time is viewed as a continuum, with no beginning and no end. Ceremonies, for example, begin when the participants are ready, rather than punctually, at the scheduled time.

Until recently, most of the research on child development was carried out in the context of the dominant macroculture, which has an individualistic orientation. Consequently, the development of children from Euro-American, middle-class families has come to be considered the norm for all children regardless of the ethnic, cultural, or economic context they inhabit (Bennett, 2003). However, to promote understanding of diverse ethnic children, it's important to be aware of the socialization backgrounds of collectivistic versus individualistic cultures. According to Turnbull and colleagues (2001),

> The continuum of individualism/collectivism represents the degree to which a culture emphasizes individual fulfillment and choice versus interdependent relations, social responsibility, and the well-being of the group. Individualism makes the former a priority, collectivism, the latter. (p. 4)

Generally, the schools are oriented toward the Euro-American values and traditions of individualism, while most other ethnic groups are oriented toward those of collectivism. Trumbull and colleagues (2001) give an example of how the values of different cultures might be applied in the classroom:

> At the end of the school day, when it is time to clean up, Salvador isn't feeling well. He asks his friend, Emanuel, to help him do his assigned job for the day, cleaning the blackboard. Emanuel isn't sure he'll have time to do his job and help Salvador.
>
> *Individualistic response:* The teacher gets a third person to do Salvador's job, as Emanuel has his own responsibility.
>
> *Collectivistic response:* The teacher tells Emanuel to help Salvador with his job. (p. 6)

Some Contrasts Between Individualism and Collectivism Impacting Teaching

Objects/people. Children socialized in individualistic cultures generally learn about physical objects as a means toward independence. Parents give children toys and teach them how to use various materials so they can amuse and help themselves. Parents use direct language to communicate instructions. Children socialized in collectivistic cultures generally are amused and helped by other people. Holding, touching, and modeling tend to be the dominant forms of communication. In school, where verbal instructions are often given, children who are not accustomed to that manner of learning may have difficulty. Demonstrating processes and working alongside such students may be more helpful.

Possessions. In collectivistic cultures, the emphasis is on social relationships, and communal possessions. Personal items, such as clothing, books, and toys, are often considered family property and are readily shared. In individualistic cultures, the emphasis is on having and taking care of one's own things: "That's mine!" In school, where students are expected to produce their own work and keep their things tidy in their desks, children who are use to shared tasks and property may have difficulty adjusting. Teachers might incorporate cooperative activities in the classroom to allow such children an opportunity to contribute.

Achievement. Individualistic cultures tend to stress individual achievement and competition: "Who read the most books?" Related is the sense of self-expression and personal choice: "Who knows the answer?" or "Which club do you want to join?" Collectivistic cultures tend to stress group affiliation and cooperation: "How is your friend feeling today?" or "Let's let him hold your teddy bear." Related is the belief in the need for group harmony and "saving face": "We need to help Maria with her math so she won't be embarrassed in class." Teachers thus should be cognizant of their use of praise for children in front of the group. Although this is thought to reinforce desired achievement and competition, as well as to foster self-esteem, it may have the opposite effect in children who interpret it as a threat to group harmony and a source of embarrassment.

Social roles. Children socialized in collectivistic cultures are generally taught to respect a hierarchy of authority, with grandparents, parents, teachers, and other adults possessing knowledge and worthy of respect. Thus, they may not be very responsive if a teacher asks their opinion (their low status in the age hierarchy implies that they do not know enough to have one) or inquires whether they have questions (any indication that the material the teacher taught might not have been understood is considered disrespectful). Children socialized in individualistic cultures are generally taught egalitarian principles in social roles; everyone has certain rights that must be respected, such as the right to voice an opinion. Collectivistic cultures, in addition to relatively rigid hierarchical roles, also usually have more rigid gender roles than do individualistic cultures. For instance, when I taught preschool, some little girls would always arrive clothed in pretty dresses, in spite of the suggestion to all the parents that their children wear clothes suitable for outdoor activities and easily washable. Teachers might accommodate for socialization in collective culture by using cooperative group structures and group leaders in various learning activities. Children in the group help each other and ask pertinent questions via the group leader, who serves as mediator between the group and the teacher. As the children become more competent with various school subjects, they can experience being a group leader.

LEARNING STYLES

Children have preferred ways of learning, and teachers have preferred ways of teaching. For example, when I was in school, I liked listening to interesting lectures, and liked organization and analysis. When I had difficulty, I appreciated help from a neighboring student. I disliked being put into groups and given a task, and I hated laboratory assignments. My daughter, in contrast, loved working in groups and hated analytical tasks. She also liked writing creative stories but was not too fond of lab work. I liked teachers who were structured and followed a plan; my daughter liked teachers who were innovative in their approaches to the curriculum. Student learning styles and teacher teaching styles can be viewed as bidirectional, with one influencing the other. Learning styles have been studied along cultural lines, and teachers are encouraged to accommodate their style to match the students'

This child is learning how to play a game of strategy coached by a more expert peer.

to facilitate academic success (Marshall, 2002). However, given the broad spectrum of human characteristics, in reality, this is difficult.

Some children learn more effectively by observing, modeling, and apprenticing than through receiving verbal instruction, the teaching method most commonly used in American schools.

EXAMPLE Growing up in the Northwest, Joan learned how to prepare salmon as a child. After watching her mother, she was allowed to gradually take on portions of the task and to ask questions only if they were important. Once she told her mother that she didn't understand how to do "the backbone part." So her mother took an entire fish and repeated the deboning because, according to her, it is not possible to understand "the backbone part" except in the context of the whole fish.

Researchers (Hilliard, 1992; Ramirez & Castaneda, 1974; Tharp, 1989) suggest that children develop learning or cognitive styles based on the socialization they receive in their families and peer groups—although there are still many unanswered questions about cognitive styles. Children from families structured so that members have defined roles, have specific times set aside for activities such as eating and sleeping, and have experiences with formal styles of group organization (relating to a leader, following rules, receiving feedback) have been observed to have an *analytical* cognitive style. In contrast, children from families that are less structured, in that the roles are shared, and members eat when hungry and sleep when tired, are more likely to exhibit a *relational* cognitive style.

According to several studies (Bennett, 2003; Hale-Benson, 1986), some children are more oriented toward feelings and personal interaction and are more proficient at nonverbal communication than other children. For example, some African American children, as well as children from other ethnic groups, get a lot of experience interacting with people (Hale-Benson, 1986). Communication in these interactions may differ from that of Euro-American children, with conversation jumping from topic to topic rather than following a linear sequence from the beginning of the story to the end (Ramsey, 1998). Euro-American children tend to be more oriented toward objects and usually have frequent opportunities to manipulate objects and discover properties and relationships. These experiences help prepare them for school, which is also object-oriented (books, computers, learning centers, and so on).

Some children exhibit a holistic, concrete, social approach to learning (Bennett, 2003; Ramirez & Castaneda, 1974). This style of learning, often referred to as field-dependent, usually implies that the person works well in groups and perceives things in terms of the larger context. A field-independent learning style, in contrast, refers to an analytic and logical approach to tasks and usually implies that the person relates well to impersonal, abstract information, independent of the context. For example, Hispanic American and Native American children tend to be more field-dependent than Euro-American children because they are socialized to be open, warm, mutually dependent, cooperative, sensitive to the feelings of others, and respectful of adults and social conventions (Escobedo & Huggans, 1983; Greenfield & Suzuki, 1998; Ramirez & Castaneda, 1974; Soldier, 1985). In general, Native American children also prefer holistic to analytic learning. In community storytelling, for example, Navajo children are not asked to recite details of a story or to dissect it; instead, they are expected to listen quietly to the long telling of stories (Tharp, 1989).

Another illustration of learning styles comes from studies of Native American children that demonstrate the importance of visualization in learning (Bennett,

2003). These children generally learn through careful observation—for example, noticing the behavior and expressions of adults, the changing weather conditions, or the terrain. After observing an adult perform a task, the child takes over small portions of the task under the guidance of the adult; the child becomes an apprentice. When the child feels ready to do the whole task, he or she practices it in private. Thus, failures are not seen and don't cause embarrassment, but success is demonstrated for the adult with pride (Vasquez, 1990).

Compared with the research on learning styles of other ethnic groups, there is a scarcity of information on Asian American learners. Children who come from a country in which many do not get a formal education (for example, the Hmong) have different ways of approaching cognitive tasks required in school than those children from countries in which formal education is necessary for success (Bennett, 2003; Thuy, 1983). Japanese Americans, for example, have the highest literacy rate of any ethnic group in the United States, tend to do well professionally and financially, and have been assimilated into the macroculture (Bennett, 2003). Similarities between the Buddhist-Confucian ethic of hard work and that of the Protestant ethic may be part of the explanation.

According to studies (Stevenson & Lee, 1990; Stevenson, Siglor, Lee, Kitamura, & Kato, 1986), Japanese students consistently are top performers on achievement tests in both math and science. One possible factor is the time spent on homework: Japanese children are expected to practice all their lessons at home, and the mother is present to supervise and help. Another possible factor is the emphasis Japanese parents place on the value of effort and hard work.

Japanese and American families tend to provide different socialization experiences to prepare children for the classroom (Hess, 1986). For example, Japanese mothers are likely to interact with their children in a way that promotes internalization of adult norms and standards, whereas American mothers are likely to rely more on external authority and direction. Similarly, Japanese mothers tend to demonstrate how to perform a task correctly, providing gentle and supportive guidance, whereas American mothers tend to rely more on verbal instructions, external rewards, and punishment.

Although Asian children may do very well on tests and homework assignments, they may not participate in class discussions, and be reluctant to work with other students on group projects. This is because, generally, such children have been socialized to view the teacher as the complete source of knowledge. Their job is to listen, take notes, memorize, follow directions, and recite. Students' ideas are not solicited, nor are they valued. Such students are taught not to ask questions, argue, or challenge the teacher (Dresser, 1996).

Because all children learn differently, Howard Gardner (1999) recommends that teachers adapt the curriculum to the various multiple intelligences he believes encompass human capability:

- *Logical-mathematical*—skills related to solving logical problems and performing mathematical calculations (generally qualities of scientists and mathematicians)
- *Linguistic*—skills related to the meanings, sounds, and rhythms of words, as well as the use of language (generally qualities of authors, journalists, and poets)
- *Bodily-kinesthetic*—the ability to coordinate parts of the body and manipulate objects skillfully (generally qualities of athletes, dancers, and surgeons)
- *Musical*—the ability to produce pitch and rhythm and to appreciate musical expression (generally qualities of musicians, composers, and singers)

- *Spatial*—the ability to form a mental model of concrete objects and manipulate parts in relation to each other (generally qualities of architects, engineers, and artists)
- *Interpersonal*—the ability to analyze and respond to behavior, feelings, and motives of other peoples (generally qualities of psychologists, teachers, and salespeople)
- *Intrapersonal*—the ability to understand people's feelings and motives, using such knowledge to adapt one's own behavior accordingly (generally qualities of actors and lawyers)
- *Naturalist*—the ability to discriminate among living things and be sensitive to the natural environment (generally qualities of botanists, zoologists, and ecologists)

DISABILITY

Teacher–student interaction regarding disability is another dimension of the bidirectional relationship. As discussed in Chapter 6, recent legislation has enabled individuals with disabilities to be included in the mainstream of society. Equal access to educational opportunities has become highly significant in the socialization of children with disabilities, enabling them to become optimally functioning adults and resilient to the risk of negative developmental outcomes.

Not only have laws been passed to give individuals with disabilities certain equal-access rights, but educators have modified the teaching environment to include the following (Hallahan & Kauffman, 2002):

- *Individualized instruction,* whereby children's abilities, rather than prescribed academic content, provide the basis for teaching techniques
- *Adaptation of the curriculum to various learning styles,* whereby visual, auditory, and tactile learners are motivated to succeed
- *Collaboration with various professionals,* whereby services such as medical, physical, and speech therapy, and counseling are provided
- *Peer tutoring,* whereby children with greater abilities help those who are in need

Some examples of how the educational environment and teaching strategies can be modified to include children with disabilities are given in Appendix D.

The Individuals with Disabilities Education Act (IDEA), discussed in Chapter 6, requires that children with disabilities be placed in the "least restrictive environment." This means inclusion in the classroom with nondisabled peers wherever possible. In order to determine and maintain optimal placement, the IDEA requires that an **Individualized Education Program (IEP)** be written annually and reviewed by (1) the child, (2) his or her parents, (3) his or her teacher, (4) the professional who has most recently evaluated the child, and (5) the principal or school district special resource person. The IEP must specify educational goals, methods for achieving those goals, and the special educational/resource services to be provided to meet the child's needs.

Because the IEP enables children with disabilities to interact with peers who do not have disabilities, teachers must provide appropriate interactive activities. An example of an appropriate interactive activity is cooperative learning, discussed in Chapter 6. It involves organizing students into small groups of five or six and giving them a task to perform or a problem to solve together. This encourages students to learn problem-solving techniques and to constructively work with others. The child with disabilities can be part of the group, making contributions according to ability (Kirk, Gallagher, & Anastasiow, 2000). Cooperative learning structures also provide opportunities for reinforcement and tutoring.

Reinforcement increases the chance of a behavior being repeated. Thus, children without disabilities can reinforce certain behaviors in children with disabilities (for example, sharing tends to be repeated when it is appreciated), and children with disabilities can do likewise (for example, helping tends to be repeated when it results in a positive outcome).

While helping children to learn, peer tutoring or direct instruction also provides an opportunity for close social interaction. The learner receives instruction, and the tutor gains sensitivity to others, develops communication skills, and has an opportunity to nurture. The learner also benefits from individual attention and an opportunity for cognitive growth, while the tutor gains self-confidence and self-esteem.

Identification and Assessment of Children with Disabilities

In 1986, Congress passed PL 99-457, which addressed the needs of infants, toddlers, and preschoolers with disabilities. It also recognized that families play a large role in the socialization of children with disabilities. Consequently, PL 99-457 provides that, whenever appropriate, the preschooler's IEP will include instruction for parents; it then becomes an Individualized Family Service Plan (IFSP). A variety of programs are available to meet the needs of preschool children with disabilities—both home- or center-based, and full- or part-time.

An early-intervention program was authorized by PL 99-457 to establish state grants for infants and toddlers from birth to age 2 who are at risk for special needs. In this context, "at risk" refers to children who are not currently identified as impaired or disabled but who are considered to have a higher-than-normal chance of developing a disability due to conditions surrounding their birth or home environment (Heward & Orlansky, 1994). Examples of at-risk conditions are discussed in the next section.

PL 99-457 is supported by evidence showing that providing early educational and therapeutic programs for children with disabilities and their families reduces the number of children requiring intensive or long-term help (Lerner, Mardell-Czudnowski, & Goldberg, 1987). Therefore, it is crucial to diagnose and assess children who have special socialization needs as soon as possible.

For children with certain kinds of disabling conditions, identification can occur at birth—for example, Down syndrome and various physical abnormalities. Behaviors not usually exhibited by normal infants can be identified shortly after birth—for example, extreme lethargy, continual crying, convulsions, and paralysis. There are, however, many disabling conditions that are not readily apparent and may not be suspected until later—for example, learning disabilities.

Because more and more children are attending various types of preschool programs, teachers and other workers in such programs are in a unique position to assess young children. By observing and recording specific behaviors that occur excessively or in lieu of appropriate behavior, preschool personnel can identify children who may have potential disabilities.

Teachers and parents can observe behavior through a variety of techniques:

- *Anecdotal records* report a child's adaptive behavior in various situations.
- *Checklists and rating scales* are used to compare a child's development against the norms or averages.

- *Time samples* record everything a child does for a certain period of time each day (for example, from 9 to 10 o'clock for five consecutive days).
- *Measurements of behavior* record the frequency, duration, antecedents, and consequences of the behavior.

The teacher observation form (an assessment of general development for pre-school children—see Appendix E) provides a model that can be used to indicate the necessity for referral to other professionals. These might include a pediatrician for health problems; an otologist for auditory problems; an ophthalmologist for visual problems; a neurologist for neurological problems; an orthopedist for bone, joint, or muscle problems; and a psychologist or psychiatrist for emotional problems.

There are many other assessment devices available, in addition to the teacher observation form provided in Appendix E. Some are designed for a particular population, and others assess specific areas of development. For example, a medical assessment consists of a medical history and a physical examination. The medical history includes specific information about the prenatal and postnatal development of the child, as well as unusual aspects of the family's health history. Complications during pregnancy and birth, illnesses in the early years, and developmental milestones (such as the age the child walked or talked) are also included in the assessment. The physical examination focuses on developmental normalities and abnormalities.

A psychological assessment includes a psychological evaluation and a measurement of intelligence. The evaluation assesses perceptual, motor, language, social, and emotional development. The intelligence test used depends on the child's age. For an infant, the tests usually measure sensorimotor development; however, the accuracy of predicted intelligence from such tests is debatable. After age 2, intellectual development can be assessed more accurately.

Assessment, of course, is meaningless unless adequate follow-up and services are provided for children who need them. Services include corrective or supportive medical treatments and/or special educational programs. Corrective or supportive medical services may involve prosthetic devices and/or medication, and physical and/or psychological therapy. Special educational programs may involve services at home (a professional works with the parent and child, and the parent carries on the program between visits by the professional), services in a center (the child attends a center for several hours a day for education and therapy), or supportive services enabling the child to be mainstreamed (transportation, tutoring, interpreting).

Services may also involve training, social work, or counseling. For example, certain prescribed medical treatment that is to be carried out at home may necessitate training the parents—for example, in dialysis, diet therapy, physical therapy. Social or counseling services may include **advocacy** for the child—informing the family of the services to which the child is legally entitled. Thus, the professional serves as an educator, a supporter, and a resource.

Assessment is an ongoing process, necessitating the use of IEPs and IFSPs. When children are continually assessed, their performance can then indicate the need to modify special programs.

Any program designed to meet the special needs of children with disabilities must involve the family, for several reasons (Gargiulo & Graves, 1991; Hauser-Cram, Warfield, Shorkoff, & Krauss, 2001; Heward, 1999):

- Because parents of a child with disabilities will often be responsible for implementing the educational program at home, they may need additional training.

© Wadsworth/Thomson Learning

A child with disabilities can attend school using special transportation services.

- Parents can contribute much valuable information to program staff regarding the behavior and performance of their child.
- In order for professionals to work with parents for the optimal development of the child, the particular dynamics of the family must be understood—the emotions (hopes, disappointments, frustrations, joys) and the interactions.

The recognition that parents are family members with myriad responsibilities and individual needs and preferences has a profound influence on parent–professional relationships in special education settings. The same concept of individuation embraced by the field of special education as pertinent to children and youths also applies to parents and other family members.

Inclusion

The community, via legislation, has facilitated integration of individuals with disabilities into society. Not only do those with disabilities have the right to an appropriate education, they also have the right to equal employment opportunities and the full range of services provided by the community. The macrosystem behind such legislation is rooted in the principles of equal opportunity, independence, and economic self-sufficiency (Hardman, Drew, & Egan, 1999). Thus, schools and teachers must help prepare all students for inclusion in the community.

The Vocational Rehabilitation Act of 1973 (PL 93-112), amended in 1992, serves as a "bill of rights" for individuals with disabilities in order to guarantee equal opportunity. It requires that federal agencies and all organizations holding contracts with or receiving funds from the U.S. government have affirmative action programs to hire and promote qualified persons with disabilities. It enforces an earlier law requiring that all buildings constructed with federal funds or owned or leased by federal agencies provide ramps, elevators, handrails, wide aisles, or other barrier-free access for persons with disabilities. It also prohibits discrimination against qualified persons with disabilities—students, employees, and recipients of health and other services—in all public and private institutions receiving federal assistance. For example, employers can ask about a person's ability to perform a job but cannot inquire if she or he has a disability. In 1990, the Americans with Disabilities Act (ADA) was passed. This law bars discrimination in employment, transportation, public accommodations, and telecommunications, and guarantees access to all aspects of life—not merely those that are federally funded—for people with disabilities. The law specifies that "reasonable accommodations" must be made according to the disability a person has. For example, telephone companies must provide services so that individuals with hearing or voice impairments can use ordinary telephones; all new buildings or renovated facilities must be accessible to those with disabilities; and employers must restructure jobs and modify equipment as reasonably required to accommodate all potential employees.

Because opportunities have opened up for individuals with disabilities, schools and support services must be involved in enabling those persons to make the transition from home to community. This means inclusion in leisure and social functions as well. The community not only has to make physical accommodations, such as designated parking spaces and ramps, but also has to open up leadership and/or advisory positions on boards, provide sensitivity training to businesses, and be more welcoming to individuals with disabilities in the neighborhood. For example, in one community, the Performing Arts Center installed special headphones in every seat for anyone who might be (or might become) hearing impaired.

CHILDREN AT RISK: POVERTY, SUBSTANCE ABUSE, AND VIOLENCE

A growing number of children, with and without disabilities, are at risk for psychological, social, or academic problems (Children's Defense Fund [COF], 2001; Hardman, Drew, & Egan, 1999). They come from families that may lack social support networks, experience unemployment, exhibit depression, engage in substance abuse, have poor marital relations, and/or practice domestic abuse (Rogosch, Cicchetti, Shields, & Toth, 1995).

Children at risk are vulnerable to negative developmental outcomes, such as dropping out of school, substance abuse, violence, teenage pregnancy, unemployment, and suicide. Risk factors affecting infants and children can be classified as *genetic* (such as mental retardation), *prenatal* (such as drug exposure), *perinatal* (such as health care), and *environmental* (such as poverty) (Rickel & Becker, 1997).

Resilience refers to the ability to recover from or adjust easily to misfortune or change. Studies of psychological resiliency have identified factors that enable children to thrive despite difficult or traumatic environments (Garbarino, 1995b; Rickel & Becker, 1997). For example, psychologist Emmy Werner began studying infants at risk in Hawaii over 40 years ago (Werner, 1993). The children came from families that were chronically poor, alcoholic, and/or abusive. Expecting negative developmental outcomes for the children, she was surprised to find that approximately one-third of them grew into emotionally healthy, competent adults. They had close friends and supportive spouses, attained a high level of education, and mastered vocational skills.

What enabled these children to become resilient to a traumatic childhood? They had a sense of autonomy and personal responsibility; they related to others positively; and perhaps most significantly, they had established a bond with an adult caregiver or mentor. Apparently, the "substitute" parent and positive relationships and experiences act as buffers against negative developmental outcomes:

> These buffers make a more profound impact on the life course of children who grow up under adverse conditions than do specific risk factors or stressful life events. They appear to transcend ethnic, social class, geographical, and historical boundaries. Most of all, they offer us a more optimistic outlook than the perspective that can be gleaned from the literature on the negative consequences of perinatal trauma, caregiving deficits, and chronic poverty. They provide us with a corrective lens—an awareness of self-righting tendencies that move children toward normal adult development under all but the most persistent adverse circumstances. (Werner & Smith, 1992, p. 202)

The implications of such research are profound. The findings mean that parents, schools, community services, and others can help children develop into emotionally healthy, contributing adults by working together to build a socially nourishing environment (CDF, 2001; Garbarino, 1995b).

Certain groups have traditionally been oppressed: children of diverse ethnicity, children with disabilities, and children from families with identified risk factors—for example, poverty, substance abuse, domestic abuse, and maltreatment. Schools can provide optimal socialization experiences and foster resiliency for these children. Most importantly, schools must work with families as well as children (Connors & Epstein, 1995; Funkhouser & Gonzales, 1997). Specifically, when families get involved in school, their children (1) get better grades and higher test scores, (2) graduate from high school at higher rates, (3) are more likely to pursue higher education, (4) behave more positively, and (5) are more achievement-oriented.

Developing Parent–Teacher Partnerships

A collaborative relationship between parents and teachers depends on a number of factors:

- Trust: "I know you will inform me if John is having problems with his homework."
- Mutual respect: "I admire your patience."
- Open communication: "I don't understand the requirements."
- Honesty: "I had hoped for more challenging work for Suki."
- Active listening: "I understand you to mean . . ."
- Openness: "Conferences make me nervous, too."
- Flexibility: "If you can't come tomorrow, the next day will be fine."
- Caring: "I hope you are feeling better."
- Understanding: "I'm sure you must be disappointed with Shawon's grade."
- Shared responsibility: "Let's work together drilling Matt on his multiplication tables."
- Full disclosure of information: "Here are all of Marie's standardized test scores since first grade."

Source: Martin and Waltman-Greenwood, 1995.

Poverty

According to the CDF (2001), one out of six children are classified as "poor." Poor families face many challenges in addition to their standard of living. These include a lack of parental supervision and a reliance on outside child care, inadequate health care, malnutrition, a lack of affordable and adequate housing, and unsafe communities. In his book *Savage Inequalities*, Jonathan Kozol (1991) describes many poor neighborhoods and schools as being near chemical plants and sewage dumps, in ill repair, and plagued by crime and drugs.

One potential impact on the teacher–student relationship for these children is their lack of preparedness for school. Poor families tend not to have physical or emotional resources for educational support. Many resources and experiences taken for granted in middle-class families, such as books, computers, and trips, are unavailable to poor families. Because poverty can be a self-perpetuating cycle, poor parents may not have received an adequate education themselves growing up, and, so lack knowledge of school readiness and supportive educational activities to provide for their children, such as language stimulation, reading, and games. A study comparing the home language environments of 3-year-olds from professional and poor families revealed that more than three times as many words were used in interactions between parents and children in professional families as in poor families (Hart & Risley, 1995).

Another potential impact on the teacher–student relationship is the inadequacy of support for teachers from the community due to economics and values. As discussed in Chapter 6, schools in poor communities often lack money to improve schools, purchase supplies, access resources, and so on. Teachers also have to encourage students who have **learned helplessness**—the perception that effort has no effect on outcomes (to be discussed in more detail in Chapter 11)—to be motivated to achieve. The difficulty rests in the belief, common in poor families, that there is little connection between educational achievement and employment opportunities (Levine & Levine, 1996). Thus, delinquency and dropping out present additional challenges to teachers.

Poverty is a societal problem that must be addressed by macrosystems (political ideology, economics), exosystems (business, communities), and mesosystems (linkages), as well as the microsystems of school and family. As discussed in Chapter 6, the "No Child Left Behind Act" of 2001 is an example of a macrosystem response—governmental support of education. Included in the act are provisions for mental health counseling, gifted and talented education, safe and drug-free schools, community learning centers, reading and literacy programs, math and science education, testing and accountability, discipline, hate crimes, and parental rights. An example of various mesosystems supporting education comes from a study on what makes adolescents feel connected to schools (McNeely, Nonnemaker, & Blum, 2002). The researchers found students' connections with their schools to be associated with several factors:

- *School size*. The smaller the school (down to 600 pupils), the more connected students felt.
- *Discipline policies*. The harsher the discipline, such as zero tolerance, the less connected (if safer) students felt.
- *Student friendships*. The more friends they had, the more connected to school students felt, because they were less socially isolated.

Substance Abuse

The teacher–student relationship is also influenced by children's exposure to the use/abuse of substances by family members. Substance abuse has been consistently linked with poor parenting and poor family functioning; addicted parents' primary relationship is with drugs, and not their children (Thompson, 1998).

Prenatal Substance Exposure. One group of children at-risk are those who were prenatally exposed to their mother's abuse of drugs or alcohol. Commonly abused drugs include crack cocaine, heroin, marijuana, tranquilizers, and stimulants. Substance-exposed infants exhibit low birth weights, sleeping and eating disorders, and increased irritability (Hardman, Drew, & Egan, 1999), as well as psychological and behavioral problems.

> **EXAMPLE** Five-year-old Jeffrey's foster parents were at their wits' end. Jeffrey had hit the neighbor's cat with a golf club. Fortunately, the cat was quick to move, so its tail got the brunt of the blow. Jeffrey was in perpetual motion most of his waking hours. He even had a hard time sitting still while eating or watching TV. He was also prone to bursting into tears or laughter, or entering trancelike states that could last an hour or more (Green, 1990).

Jeffrey is a victim of his mother's addiction to crack cocaine, which she smoked during her pregnancy. And Jeffrey's situation is hardly unique. About 15 percent of women of child-bearing age are substance abusers, and the incidence of prenatal exposure to illicit drugs is at least 11 percent of live births (Hardman, Drew, & Egan, 1999).

Implementing interventions for mothers and their babies who have been exposed to drugs is challenging and expensive. Many drug-exposed babies are placed in foster care, which is costly, too. There is also the cost of special education and services, which can be two or three times the amount spent on children in regular public school programs (about $5000 per year).

Due to his mother's addiction to drugs, Jeffrey was removed from her care shortly after birth and placed in foster care. Jeffrey's antisocial behavior is likely related to the effects the drugs had on his developing brain in utero; cocaine causes blood vessels to constrict, thereby reducing the vital flow of oxygen and other nutrients to the brain and other organs. Because fetal cells multiply rapidly in the first few months of development, the fetus is thus deprived of an optimal blood supply for normal growth.

Prenatal cocaine exposure affects brain chemistry as well. The drug alters the action of neurotransmitters, the substances that travel between nerve cells and help control people's moods and emotional responses. Such changes may explain the unusual behavior, including impulsiveness and moodiness, seen in some prenatally cocaine-exposed children as they mature (Toufexis, 1991).

Caring for prenatally cocaine-exposed babies is frustrating because they respond differently to natural adult overtures such as cooing, tickling, and bouncing. Whereas normal babies gurgle and laugh in response to such stimuli, babies prenatally exposed to drugs stiffen or scream. The mother feels rejected and ends up avoiding further contact unless she is taught how not to overstimulate the infant (Toufexis, 1991; Tyler, 1992).

When these children reach preschool and school age, they often don't relate to other children or adults appropriately. They tend to ignore rules, have temper outbursts, act aggressively, and are unable to concentrate (Green, 1990; Hardman, Drew, & Egan, 1999). Thus, they have special socialization needs, and their caregivers need to learn techniques to optimize their development.

Alcohol. Another group of children at risk for negative developmental outcomes are those whose parents abuse alcohol. According to the American Academy of Child and Adolescent Psychiatry (AACAP) (1999), one in five adult Americans lived with an alcoholic parent while growing up. **Alcoholism** is a chronic, progressive, and potentially fatal disease. It is characterized by excessive tolerance for and physical dependency on alcohol or by pathologic organ changes, or both—all the direct or indirect consequences of the alcohol ingested.

Alcohol is so prevalent in our society that we seldom think of it as a drug, yet beer, wine, and liquor are all central nervous system depressants. They are similar to barbiturates and other sedative drugs in that they slow down metabolic functions such as heart rate and respiration.

Alcohol consumption during pregnancy can produce abnormalities in the developing fetus. Specifically, alcohol interferes with the delivery of nutrients to the fetus, impairs the supply of fetal oxygen, and interferes with protein synthesis.

A cluster of abnormalities appearing in babies exposed prenatally to alcohol abuse (heavy drinking) was described and named "fetal alcohol syndrome" (FAS) by Jones and his colleagues (1973). Among the distinguishing features of this syndrome are prenatal and postnatal growth retardation; facial abnormalities, including small head circumference; widely spaced eyes; short eyelid openings; a small, upturned nose; and a thin upper lip. Most FAS children are mentally retarded. FAS is the leading known preventable cause of mental retardation.

Behavior problems associated with maternal alcohol consumption appear in infancy and persist into childhood; the most common are irritability, hyperactivity, poor concentration, and poor social skills. Affected children can display physical problems as well, such as defects of the eyes, ears, heart, urinary tract, or immune system (Aaronson & MacNee, 1989).

Children whose parents abuse alcohol are frequently victims of incest, child neglect, and other forms of violence and exploitation (Leershen & Namuth, 1988). These children are also prone to a range of psychological difficulties, including learning disabilities, anxiety, suicidal behavior, eating disorders, and compulsive achieving. However, the problems of most such children remain invisible because their coping behavior tends to be approval seeking and socially acceptable. They do their work, do not rock the boat, and do not reveal their family secret. Many are high achievers and eager to please. Yet their adaptation to the chaos and inconsistency of an alcohol-abusing family often involves development of an inability to trust, an extreme need to control, an excessive sense of responsibility, and denial of feelings—all of which results in low self-esteem, depression and guilt, a sense of isolation, and difficulty maintaining satisfying relationships. And these and other problems often persist throughout adulthood (Leershen & Namuth, 1988; Tubman, 1993).

Janet Geringer Woititz (1990), in her classic book *Adult Children of Alcoholics*, and Claudia Black (1991), in her classic book *It Will Never Happen to Me*, discuss some common traits exhibited by adult children of alcoholics. These include attempting to guess what is "normal" behavior, having difficulty following a project from beginning to end, lying instead of telling the truth, having difficulty enjoying themselves, constantly seeking approval, feeling they are different from others, and tending to lock themselves into a course of action without considering the consequences. As adults, the wounded child within impairs emotional expressions, because feelings are repressed, and development of relationships, because trust is difficult.

These children often are embarrassed by and ashamed of their parents. They do not invite friends home and are afraid to ask anyone for help. They also feel anger toward the alcoholic parent for drinking and may be angry with the nonalcoholic parent for lack of support and protection. They may even experience feelings of guilt, viewing themselves as the cause of the parent's drinking (AACAP, 1999).

Although these children try to keep the alcoholism a secret, teachers, friends, relatives, and other caring adults may sense that something is wrong. The following behaviors may signal a problem (AACAP, 1999):

- Truancy
- Failure in school
- Lack of friends or withdrawal from classmates
- Delinquent behavior, such as stealing or violence
- Frequent physical complaints, such as headaches or stomachaches
- Abuse of drugs or alcohol
- Aggression toward other children
- Risk-taking behaviors
- Depression or suicidal thoughts or behavior

Whether or not their parents are receiving treatment for alcoholism, these children can benefit from programs such as Al-Anon and Alateen. Therapists can help them understand that they are not responsible for the drinking problems of their parents. Therapists can also help the family develop healthier ways of relating to one another, particularly when the alcoholic has stopped drinking. For example, a common problem during recovery stems from the familial responsibilities undertaken by children during active parental alcoholism. When parents are drinking, children may run the household and care for younger siblings. But when the recovering alcoholic tries to reassume these responsibilities, children are expected to become children again instead of "little adults" or "parents." Because they are unaccustomed to behaving like children, the transition back to more traditional familial roles may cause conflict (AACAP, 1999).

The consequences of living in an alcoholic family are particularly problematic for young children and adolescents because alcoholism affects the process of socialization of values, morals, attitudes, behavior, gender roles, self-control, and self-concept. The effects of alcoholism depend on the child's age, gender, and relationship to the drinking and nondrinking parents, other family members, and other social networks.

Violence

Violence in families includes child maltreatment and domestic abuse. Various types and observable signs of maltreatment were explained in Chapter 4; here, the focus is on the masked effects that interfere with children's development. Less obvious developmental consequences include difficulty in regulating emotions, insecure attachments, problems in achieving autonomy, aggressiveness with peers, noncompliance with adults, and lack of readiness to learn (Rogosch, Cicchetti, Shields, & Toth, 1995).

Children exposed to domestic violence are at risk for negative developmental outcomes. "Domestic violence" can be defined as "the systematic abuse by one person in an intimate relationship in order to control and dominate the partner" (Kearny, 1999, p. 290). Abusive behavior can be physical, emotional, mental, and/or sexual. Domestic violence occurs in all socioeconomic classes and cultures (Greenfield, 1998). Most is directed at women although some men experience it, too (Kearny, 1999). The government plays a significant role in preventing negative outcomes from domestic violence. It has passed laws making violence against women a crime and provided funding for shelters, counseling, and hot lines (National Coalition Against Domestic Violence, 1999).

Children who are exposed to domestic violence often experience the following feelings (Kearny, 1999, p. 291):

- *Anger.* They are angry at the abuser for the violence, at the victim for tolerating it, or at themselves for not being able to stop the violence.
- *Fear/terror.* They are afraid that the mother or father will be seriously injured or killed, that they or their siblings will be hurt, that others will find out and then the parents will be "in trouble," or that they will be removed from the family.
- *Powerlessness.* They experience a sense of loss of control because they are unable to prevent the violence from happening or to stop it when it occurs.
- *Loneliness.* They are unable or afraid to reach out to others, feeling "different" or isolated.
- *Confusion.* They are confused about why it happens, what they should do, and who is "right" and "wrong." They are also confused about how the abuser can sometimes be caring and other times violent.
- *Shame.* They are ashamed about what is happening.
- *Guilt.* They feel guilty because they think they may have caused the violence or should have been able to stop it.
- *Distrust.* They don't trust adults because experience tells them that adults are unpredictable, that they break promises, and/or that they don't mean well.

Strategies for Teachers of Children Exposed to Domestic Violence

Breaking the silence surrounding domestic violence and providing appropriate intervention can help. Specific preventative strategies include the following:

- *Identification.* Be alert to changes in emotional, social, and/or learning behaviors. Ask the child, "What is wrong?" (Does the child not want to go home? Is the child unusually attached to his or her teacher? Is the child withdrawn? Is the child aggressive or a bully?)
- *Support.* Be available to listen to the child and acknowledge his or her feelings without being judgmental. Help the child to develop ways to release her or his feelings appropriately.
- *Modeling.* Exhibit nonviolent, cooperative ways of solving problems.

Children living in a violent environment often exhibit similar behavior with their peers. Chapter 6 listed some strategies to resolve conflicts before they escalate into violent behavior; these include emotional regulation, empathy, problem solving, and mediation.

Macrosystem and Chronosystem Influences on Teaching

Macrosystem and chronosystem influences on teaching include philosophical and theoretical foundations of teaching and learning, classroom and curriculum contexts affected by school administration, and policies and procedures regarding accountability for achievement (standardization and individuation).

PHILOSOPHIES OF TEACHING AND LEARNING

There are many types of educational programs, based on various philosophies of teaching and learning. For the sake of simplicity, the programs discussed here are categorized according to their emphasis on who takes responsibility for the learning that takes place—the teacher or the learner (see Table 7.1). In reality, however, most programs emphasize both teacher and student responsibility for learning, but to varying degrees. Because different programs provide different learning environments, experiences, and interactions, each school's program influences children's development and socialization in a particular way.

Proponents of *teacher-directed* educational environments (sometimes referred to as "traditional") subscribe to the philosophy that the functions of the school are to impart basic factual knowledge (reading, writing, arithmetic) and to preserve the American cultural heritage (Sadker & Sadker, 2003; Toch, 1996). Those who support this philosophy believe that education should include homework, tests, memorization, and strict discipline, and that the school is a place for hard work and obedience. Furthermore, the curriculum should be structured and subjects chosen based on the teacher's, school's, or community's goals.

The roots of teacher-directed learning can be traced back to Plato's *Republic* (fourth century B.C.), in which he stated that the mind is what it learns. In this sense, the content of curricula is vital for an educated society.

Proponents of *learner-directed* educational environments (sometimes referred to as "progressive" or "modern") subscribe to the philosophy that the function of the school is to develop the whole child. The curriculum emerges from children's interests and abilities, and knowledge is constructed as they are capable of processing it

© Spencer Grant/PhotoEdit

This classroom is organized to provide for various learner-centered activities.

Table 7.1

Teacher- Versus Learner-Directed Classroom Contexts
Source: Adapted from George H. Morrison (1980). *Early childhood education today* (2nd ed.). (Columbus, OH: Merrill), pp. 146–149, 152–153.

TEACHER-DIRECTED (TRADITIONAL)	LEARNER-DIRECTED (MODERN)
STRUCTURE The day is organized by the teacher and divided into time segments according to subject.	The program is prepared by the teacher based on student abilities and interest; time spent on activities depends on interest; activities are not divided into specific subjects.
MANAGEMENT There are many rules for appropriate behavior (being moral, having manners, following directions, paying attention, being quiet, sitting still, being neat).	The teacher encourages children to discuss standards of conduct and take responsibility for their behavior.
CURRICULA Subject matter is predetermined by the teacher and/or textbook. The emphasis is on reading, writing, arithmetic, science, and social science. Knowledge is considered an end in itself; what is studied is preparation for life.	Subjects are determined by student ability and interest. Activities and problem-solving experiences are based on student interest. Knowledge is considered a means to an end, the process of living; subject matter grows out of experience.
MOTIVATION Extrinsic (grades)—success is mainly a function of how well required tasks are mastered according to the teacher's standards. Advancement is determined by subjects and tests passed or time spent in the system. The environment is competitive.	Intrinsic (child's interests)—success is mainly a function of self-evaluation (based on accomplishment of a self-chosen goal). Advancement is according to activities chosen and skills developed. The environment is cooperative.
METHOD The teacher teaches generally the same thing at the same time to all students or to a group of students. Teaching style is dominative. Content is taught. Children's participation is directly encouraged.	Learning is individualized, and students are responsible for their own learning. Teaching style is integrative. Process is taught. Children's participation is indirectly encouraged.

(Toch, 1996). This process is called "constructivism." Teachers support child-initiated learning via appropriate curriculum.

The roots of learner-directed learning can be traced back to Jean-Jacques Rousseau's *Emile* (1762). Rousseau emphasized the development of children, rather than the subjects to be taught, arguing that *how* learning occurs is more important than *what* is taught.

John Dewey (1859–1952), influenced by Rousseau, was the first progressive educator. He believed that education should place emphasis on children and their interests, rather than on the subject matter. Dewey also argued that education was a *process* of living, not a *preparation* for living. Those who subscribe to this philosophy believe that learning occurs spontaneously and takes place optimally when children interact with materials and people in their environment. Learning materials may be grouped in various centers, which children explore in a process of inquiry and discovery. They become involved in their own learning by making choices about what they will learn. Subject matter is thus integrated into student activities.

To determine the extent to which a given philosophy shapes teaching practices, Putnam (1983) observed classroom interactions in six inner-city kindergartens—three of which followed a traditional or teacher-directed approach to reading readiness and three of which favored an interactive or learner-directed view of reading. Teachers in the traditional kindergartens assumed that, prior to trying to read, children should develop a set of foundational skills—visual and auditory discrimination, letter naming, beginning word sounds, and so on—that would allow them to be successful when they actually learned to read in first grade.

EXAMPLE Mrs. Hall's kindergartners had just listened to a song about Mr. D., who loves *doughnuts, dogs, deer,* and other things that begin with *d.* Mrs. Hall then asked the children to name other things that began with the *d* sound. "Raise your hand; don't call out, speak in a sentence," she said. One child said, "I sit at a *desk.*" "Very good, '*desk*' begins with *d,*" replied Mrs. Hall. After several responses the children were given worksheets on which they were to circle pictures of items beginning with a *d.*

Thus, in this teacher-directed environment, the children were supposed to sit quietly, follow directions, listen attentively, and talk only when called on to answer a question. Discussion with classmates was frowned upon (Putnam, 1986).

In contrast, teachers in the interactive or learner-directed kindergartens created a reading environment in these ways:

- Giving children plentiful opportunities to listen to literature and nonfiction being read aloud
- Providing opportunities for children to act out and discuss the readings
- Allowing children to express their understanding of the readings through art
- Enabling the children to experiment with writing and reading their own "books"

There was some instruction in letter sounds, but most of the focus was on interpreting whole messages. The children were encouraged to collaborate with one another in talking, asking questions, and comprehending material. They spent time each day "reading" a book (looking at pictures, reciting the story, and trying to decode the words) or "writing" a story (drawing, inventing spelling, and talking about ideas). The teachers moved around listening to pretend readings, asking the writers to "read" their stories, helping with invented spelling, answering questions, and praising efforts. Thus, in this learner-directed environment, the children had a greater degree of control, choice, and responsibility (Putnam, 1986).

SOCIALIZATION OUTCOMES OF DIFFERENT CLASSROOM CONTEXTS

What does research say about the effects of teacher- and learner-directed programs on socialization? In a review of approximately 200 research studies on elementary school programs, Horowitz (1979) noted the different socializing effects of modern and traditional settings. In general, he found that children in modern settings tended to have a more positive attitude toward school and their teachers than did children in traditional settings. They were also more likely to have friends of both genders, to be involved in cooperative work, and to show autonomy, or self-reliant behavior. Horowitz did not find any significant differences in the academic achievement of children in modern and traditional settings. However, later studies (Good & Brophy, 1986; Chall, 2000) indicated that students in traditional, teacher-directed classrooms tended to perform better academically than students in modern learner-directed programs. It is difficult, however, to compare these results because standardized tests are based more on teacher-directed goals than on learner-directed ones.

Modern and traditional environments provide different opportunities for cooperative work. In traditional environments, teachers generally teach to the whole class and children work individually; sharing information is equated with cheating. In modern classrooms, in contrast, there is considerable small-group effort and emphasis on developing a cooperative work ethic (Atkinson & Green, 1990; Minuchin & Shapiro, 1983).

We can conclude, then, that different patterns of competence emerge as a result of the experiences children have in various programs (Daniels, Kalkman, & McCombs, 2001; Toch, 1996). More specifically, how students relate to each other and to teachers to accomplish educational goals also affect socialization outcomes.

Instructional settings can be organized into "goal structures" (Johnson & Johnson, 1999). There are three types of goal structures: (1) **cooperative,** in which students work together to accomplish shared goals; (2) **competitive,** in which students work against each other to achieve goals that only a few can attain; and (3) **individualized,** in which one student's achievement of a goal is unrelated to other students' achievement of the goal (see Table 7.2).

Each type of goal structure, according to Johnson and Johnson, leads to a different pattern of interaction among students. A cooperative goal structure promotes

These children are enjoying learning by working cooperatively on an activity that permits collaboration.

GOAL STRUCTURES	TYPE OF INSTRUCTIONAL ACTIVITY	IMPORTANCE OF GOAL FOR SOCIALIZATION	STUDENT EXPECTATIONS	EXPECTED SOURCE OF SUPPORT
Cooperative	Problem-solving; divergent thinking on creative tasks; assignments can be more ambiguous with students doing the clarifying, decision making, and inquiring	Goal is perceived as important for each student, and students expect group to achieve the goal	Each student expects to interact positively with other students; to share ideas and materials; to be supported for risk-taking; to make contributions to the group effort; to divide the task among group members; to capitalize on diversity among group members	Other students
Individualized	Specific skill or knowledge acquisition; assignment is clear and behavior specified to avoid confusion and need for extra help	Goal is perceived as important for each student, and each student expects eventually to achieve this goal	Each student expects to be left alone by other students; to take a major part of the responsibility for completing the task; to take a major part in evaluating his/her progress toward task completion and the quality of his/her effort	Teacher
Competitive	Skill practice; knowledge recall and review; assignment is clear with rules for competing specified	Goal is *not* perceived to be of large importance to the students, and they can accept either winning or losing	Each student expects to have an equal chance of winning; to enjoy the activity (win or lose); to monitor the progress of his/her competitor to compare ability, skills, or knowledge with peers	Teacher

Table 7.2

Classroom Management: Goal Structures and Socialization
Source: Adapted from David W. Johnson and Roger T. Johnson (1999). *Learning together and alone: Cooperative, competitive, and individualized learning* (5th ed.), pp. 6–8. Published by Allyn and Bacon, Boston, MA. Copyright © 1999 by Pearson Education. Adapted by permission of the publisher.

positive interpersonal relationships such as sharing, helping, trust, and acceptance; a competitive goal structure promotes comparisons and mistrust; an individualized goal structure promotes student–teacher interaction and responsibility for oneself.

An interesting application of the cooperative goal structure was described by Aronson and Patenoe (1996). The goal of the activity was to get students in a newly integrated classroom to interact positively with one another. The students were divided into small groups and given tasks in which they had to cooperate with group members to succeed. Each student was given a piece of information that the rest of the group needed in order to finish the task. All the members had to share their pieces of information with the others. Aronson called this the "jigsaw-puzzle method." The results were higher achievement, a decrease in insults, higher self-esteem, and improved attitudes toward school. Cooperative goal structures have been developed to include children with disabilities and ethnically diverse children and to prepare students for an increasingly collaborative workforce (Slavin, 1991).

Thus, the way teachers manage the classroom environment, including arranging the room, planning the activities, observing behavior, and organizing groups, affects the socialization taking place in that classroom.

ACCOUNTABILITY AND STANDARDIZATION

Accountability in education refers to the idea of making schools responsible for student learning, or achievement outcomes. It means that educational expenditures must be justified. Educational accountability is a result of rising costs, poor student performance in the business world, and the desire to compete in global markets and maintain leadership in science and technology.

The first formal mandate from the federal government for educational accountability was the passage of the Elementary and Secondary Education Act of 1965. This law required schools to produce documented results of educational attainment to receive public funding. Since then, state and local school districts have tied funding to performance. To measure performance, schools must set goals or standards, such as that all students completing first grade will be able to read and comprehend simple stories. The federal policy initiative Goals 2000, discussed in Chapter 6, provides a model for states to implement. Assessment instruments must then be devised to measure achievement of the goals. Another federal policy initiative that serves as a model involves standards-based education, with student achievement in reading, writing, math, and science tested every few years throughout elementary and middle school, and upon graduation from high school, although states and local school districts vary in specifics. The "No Child Left Behind Act" of 2001 requires annual testing in all states.

Although standardization is usually applauded by bureaucrats and taxpayers, teachers and advocacy groups for diverse interests call for more flexibility in assessments due to individual teaching and learning styles. A practice used in some schools is "authentic assessments," those based on *real* performance (building a model of a house) rather than *test* performance (figuring out the square footage of a house in a math problem).

Mesosystem Influences on Teaching

Mesosystem influences on teaching include community support and family involvement. Community support can be financial, as in donations and grants; it can be service-oriented, as in mental health counseling; and/or it can be learning based, as in field trips and guest speakers. Family involvement and collaboration with teachers is important throughout school, but especially before children begin formal schooling, so that appropriate attitudes toward future learning can be developed.

FAMILIES EMPOWERING STUDENT SUCCESS: INVOLVEMENT IN LEARNING

As noted previously, families and schools share a collaborative role in successful student learning. Families help ready children for school and support school goals.

Strategies for Teachers to Involve Families in Learning

1. Recognize and show that parents are significant contributors to their child's development. Call on parents for advice, help, support, and critical evaluations.
2. Present a realistic picture of what the child's program is designed to accomplish.
3. Maintain ongoing communication with parents. Provide written information regarding due process procedures and parent or parent–teacher organizations, as well as oral and written information about the child's progress.
4. Show parents you care about their child. Call, write notes, and spend time listening to parents' concerns.
5. Keep parents informed as to how they can help their child at home. Enable parents to enjoy their children.
6. Use parents' ideas, materials, and activities to work with their child.
7. Be familiar with community services and resources so you can refer parents when necessary.
8. Be yourself. Don't pretend to know all the answers when you don't; don't be afraid to ask for advice or refer parents to other professionals and resources.
9. Recognize that diverse family structures and parenting styles influence parental participation.
10. Help parents grow in confidence and in self-esteem (Gargiulo & Graves, 1991; Heward, 1999).

Strategies for Families to Prepare Children to Learn

1. Express love:
   a. Spend time with children.
   b. Talk and listen.
   c. Help children to be independent by letting them do things they are capable of.
2. Use everyday opportunities to teach about the world:
   a. Talk about scenery, weather, and news.
   b. Figure things out together—how much time has passed, how to divide the pie, or how to repair the toilet.
   c. Enable children to follow directions.
   d. Plan together (activities, goals).

3. Encourage questions: "How does this work?" and "Why did this happen?"
4. Give approval for trying new things:
   a. Reward accomplishments.
   b. Explain that mistakes happen and can be learned from.
   c. Stimulate creativity.
5. Instill a love of books:
   a. Model reading.
   b. Read to children.
   c. Answer questions.
   d. Visit the library.
   e. Tell stories, and have children tell them, too.
6. Get involved in school:
   a. Talk about school positively.
   b. Visit the school.
   c. Encourage attendance.
   d. Support homework.
7. Limit TV viewing:
   a. Select appropriate programs.
   b. Encourage reading and imaginary and physical activities.
   c. Discuss programs with children.
8. Encourage writing:
   a. Have children write and/or draw thank-you notes, messages, and stories.
9. Develop math concepts:
   a. Cook together.
   b. Play games.
   c. Give allowance money to save and spend.
10. Develop science concepts:
    a. Encourage collections.
    b. Observe plants and animals.
    c. Visit museums.
11. Develop social studies concepts:
    a. Discuss current events.
    b. Observe national holidays.
    c. Demonstrate good citizenship by being well informed, discussing political decision making, and voting.
12. Get involved in the community (Hatcher & Beck, 1997):
    a. Visit workplaces (post office, fire department, factory, office).
    b. Visit historical sites.
    c. Participate in community service.
13. Be a model of lifelong learning (Rich, 1992):
    a. Have confidence: "I can do it."
    b. Show motivation: "I want to do it."
    c. Give effort: "I'm willing to try hard."
    d. Model responsibility: "I follow through on commitments."
    e. Demonstrate initiative: "I am a self-starter."
    f. Show perseverance: "I finish what I start."
    g. Express caring: "I show concern for others."
    h. Show teamwork: "I work cooperatively with others."
    i. Use common sense: "I use good judgment."
    j. Practice problem solving: "I use my knowledge and experience effectively."

SCHOOLS EMPOWERING STUDENT SUCCESS: DEVELOPMENTALLY APPROPRIATE LEARNING AND ASSESSMENT

Many schools have interpreted the concept of "readiness to learn" to mean children's ability to succeed at school-related tasks and have used entrance testing to make this evaluation (Lewit & Baker, 1995). For example, **standardized tests,** those in which an individual is compared to a norm on specific items, have been developed to assess kindergarten readiness. However, the National Association for the Education of Young Children (1988) asserts that such tests are inappropriate for young children because each child comes from a unique set of family experiences, and what one family makes available for its children, another does not. For example, some children travel extensively, whereas others seldom go outside their immediate community. Some children speak a language other than English. Some have had preschool experiences, whereas others remained at home. Also, maturational differences influence children's ability to perform well on standardized tests—for example, the ability to listen and follow instructions, control a pencil, or sit still for a certain period of time.

Schools that embrace the concept of readiness can do more to individualize the curriculum and group children by developmental readiness instead of by age only (Lewit & Baker, 1995). Thus, children who are of the legal age to attend school but are not as "ready" as their peers to learn due to diverse family backgrounds can be provided with developmentally appropriate activities. In addition, **authentic assessments,** those which evaluate performance on actual tasks (for example, a portfolio of a child's writing or art), can be used, rather than solely relying on standardized paper-and-pencil tests.

In sum, the school should be ready for children to learn when they come to school, just as children should be ready to learn when they come to school.

Epilogue

The teacher–student relationship is a complex one. Both teacher and learner bring individual characteristics into a bidirectional relationship that is affected by the broader context of society, as well as the linkages within subcontexts. Teaching methods may have specific socialization outcomes, but the real influence comes from whether the teacher is a model for the student to emulate, thereby stimulating learning.

Summary

The most powerful socializing influence of the school rests in those who translate program goals into action—the teachers. Effective teachers are warm, enthusiastic, and generous with praise, and have high status. These characteristics lead to their becoming role models for children. Other characteristics of successful teachers include the ability to communicate well with and respond positively to students.

Teachers play a major leadership role in helping children learn to deal with positions of authority, to cooperate with others, to cope with problems, and to achieve competence. Leaders can be classified as authoritarian, democratic (authoritative), or laissez-faire (permissive).

Teachers are responsible for selecting materials relevant to learners, for managing the group dynamics in the classroom, and for interacting individually with each child. Goal structures—cooperative, individualized, or competitive—have different socialization effects.

Teachers' expectations of children often influence their interactions with them and, consequently, the children's performance. Teachers need to be aware of the effects of the self-fulfilling prophecy. Teachers also need to be aware of their responses to gender—teachers typically give more attention to boys for their work and to girls for appropriate behavior—as well as to children from diverse ethnic groups, social classes, and religions; to children with disabilities; and/or to those at risk for negative developmental outcomes due to poverty, substance abuse, or violence in the family. Children's backgrounds may impact the teacher–student relationship, which is bidirectional.

Gender equity remains an issue in schools. Teachers must be aware of differential treatment of males and females in terms of attention, curricular issues, role models in books, career counseling, and extracurricular activities.

Ethnic diversity needs to be understood because the United States is composed of many diverse ethnic groups, many languages are spoken in the United States, and the world is moving toward a global economy. The U.S. macroculture—usually defined as White, Anglo-Saxon, Protestant—generally shares certain values. The degree to which individual citizens subscribe to the general values depends, in part, on the microculture or ethnic group to which the individual belongs. It may also depend on how much individuals must interact with formal institutions (schools, government, health and welfare agencies) for support. Diverse ethnic groups can be classified according to where they best fit along a continuum of individualistic versus collectivistic orientations.

Learning, or cognitive, styles are aspects of socialization that have implications for education. Analysis, deductive reasoning, accuracy, individual and competitive work, and verbal communication are characteristics of an analytical, field-independent cognitive style. Viewing things in their entirety, approximations, a focus on people, simultaneous involvement in activities, and proficiency in nonverbal communication are characteristics of a relational, field-dependent cognitive style.

To enable children with disabilities to have positive developmental outcomes, society, schools, and teachers must provide support. Laws requiring individuals with disabilities to be included in the mainstream of society have been passed. Educational methods have been modified to include children with specific disabilities to optimize their socialization.

The Individuals with Disabilities Act (IDEA) requires that an Individualized Education Program (IEP) be written annually specifying educational goals, methods, and resources/services required to meet the child's needs. Also, PL 99-457 provides for a variety of programs for infants, toddlers, and preschoolers with disabilities and includes instruction for parents in the socialization of their child via an individualized family service plan (IFSP).

The community, via legislation, has aided integration of individuals with disabilities. The Vocational Rehabilitation Act of 1973 and, more recently, the Americans with Disabilities Act of 1990 guarantee certain rights to individuals with disabilities, such as affirmative action and access. Thus, schools and support professionals must be involved in the transition from home to community.

Children at risk for negative developmental outcomes, such as children from families experiencing poverty, substance abuse, and/or violence need special support from teachers and other adults to promote resiliency and motivate achievement.

Macrosystem and chronosystem influences on teaching include curriculum philosophies and policies on accountability and standardization. Philosophies of teaching and learning range from teacher directed to learner directed. Proponents of teacher-directed (traditional) educational environments usually subscribe to the philosophy that the functions of the school are to impart basic factual knowledge and preserve the cultural heritage. Traditional education features homework, tests, memorization, and strict discipline. Proponents of learner-directed (modern) educational environments subscribe to the philosophy that the function of the school is to develop the whole child—physically, socially, and emotionally, as well as cognitively. The curriculum emerges from children's interests and abilities and is constructed accordingly.

Socialization outcomes differ according to the setting. Children in traditional settings perform better on academic tasks and are "on task" more often than children in modern settings. Children in modern settings tend to have a more positive attitude toward school, are involved in more cooperative work, and show more autonomy than children in traditional settings.

Instructional settings can be organized into cooperative, competitive, and individualized goal structures, each leading to different student interaction patterns.

Schools and teachers are accountable for student learning and so must administer standardized achievement tests to receive public funding.

Linkages between the child, family, school, and community are necessary to optimize socialization and empower success. The significance of these mesosystems is reflected in the nation's top education goal: that all children will come to school "ready to learn." Families can enable children to be ready by nurturing, communicating, encouraging learning, and getting involved in school. Schools can enable readiness by individualizing the curriculum, providing activities that are developmentally appropriate, and using authentic assessments rather than relying on standardized tests.

Activity

PURPOSE *To understand the teacher's influence on socialization.*

1. Choose two elementary school classrooms (same grade) to observe. One should be primarily teacher directed, or traditional; the other should be primarily learner directed, or modern. (You may have to go to two different schools.)
2. Describe the physical arrangement of each classroom environment.
3. Describe the activity going on during the time of your observation in each classroom. How are simultaneous activities (computer work and reading groups, for example) handled? What about transitions from one activity to another?
4. Describe the social interaction (for example, warm/hostile, flexible/inflexible, caring/uncaring) between the teacher and children in each classroom. Note teachers' responses to gender and ethnic diversity (and disability, if included).
5. Can you draw any conclusions regarding the socialization of the children in each classroom?

ℱ Research Terms

Accountability
Cooperative learning
Disability
Family–school partnerships
Learner-directed (modern) curriculum
Standardization
Teacher-directed (traditional) curriculum

Related Readings

Bennett, C. E. (2003). *Comprehensive multicultural education: Theory and practice* (5th ed.). Boston: Allyn & Bacon.

Black, C. (1991). *It will never happen to me* (rev. ed.). New York: Ballantine Books.

Byrnes, D. A., & Kigler, G. (Eds.). (1996). *Common bonds: Anti-bias teaching in a diverse society.* Wheaton, MD: Association for Childhood Education International.

Chall, J. (2000). *The academic achievement challenge: What really works in the classroom?* New York: Guilford Press.

Farnham-Diggory, S. (1992). *The learning-disabled child.* Cambridge, MA: Harvard University Press.

Garbarino, J., Eckenrode, J., & Barry, F. D. (1997). *Understanding abusive families: An ecological approach to theory and practice.* San Francisco: Jossey-Bass.

Geffner, R. A., & Jouriles, E. N. (1998). *Children exposed to marital violence: Theory, research, and applied issues.* Washington, DC: American Psychological Association.

Ginott, H. (1972). *Teacher and child.* New York: Avon Books.

Gordon, T. (1974). *T.E.T.: Teacher effectiveness training.* New York: Wyden.

Heck, S. F., & Williams, C. R. (1984). *The complex roles of the teacher: An ecological perspective.* New York: Teachers College Press.

Ramsey, P. G. (1998). *Teaching and learning in a diverse world: Multicultural education for young children* (2nd ed.). New York: Teachers College Press.

Marshall, P. L. (2002). *Cultural diversity in our schools.* Belmont, CA: Wadsworth.

Wolery, M., & Wilbers, J. S. (Eds.). (1994). *Including children with special needs in early childhood programs.* Washington, DC: National Association for the Education of Young Children.

York, S. (1991). *Roots and wings: Affirming culture in early childhood programs.* St. Paul, MN: Toys 'n' Things Press.

Chapter 8

© David Young-Wolff/PhotoEdit

Ecology of the Peer Group

Without friends no one would choose to live, though he had all other goods.

—ARISTOTLE

Prologue: Then and Now

The Peer Group as a Socializing Agent
The Significance of Peers to Development
Psychological Development: Emotions
Social Development: Social Competence
Cognitive Development: Social Cognition
Peer Group Socializing Mechanisms

Macrosystem Influences on the Peer Group: Developmental Tasks
Getting Along with Others
Developing Morals and Values
Learning Appropriate Sociocultural Roles
Achieving Personal Independence and Identity

Chronosystem Influences on the Peer Group: Play/Activities
The Significance and Development of Play
Infant/Toddler Peer Activities (Birth–2 Years)
Early Childhood Peer Activities (2–5 Years)
Middle Childhood/Preadolescent Peer Activities (6–12 Years)
Adolescent Peer Activities

Peer Group Interaction
Development of Friendship
Acceptance/Neglect/Rejection by Peers
Peer Sociotherapy

Peer Group Dynamics and Social Hierarchies
Inclusion and Exclusion
Bullies/Victims
Gangs
Peer Collaboration, Tutoring, and Counseling

Mesosystem Influences on the Peer Group
Adult-Mediated Group Interaction
Adult Leadership Styles
Team Sports

Epilogue

Summary

Activity

Research Terms

Related Readings

| *Then and Now*

PEERS, PRESTIGE, POWER, AND PERSUASION

THEN William Golding's classic novel *Lord of the Flies* (1954) tells of a group of English schoolboys, ranging in age from 6 to 12, who are marooned on a desert island when their plane crashes. The adults are all killed, and the youngsters, despairing of rescue, set out to build their own society. At first, the older boys try to draw on their memories of English society, but they do not remember enough, and there are no elders they can turn to for guidance. Therefore, they establish their own system of socialization, first by investing authority in a leader chosen on the basis of appearance and perceived power (he possesses a conch shell), and then by developing rituals to provide order amid the chaos. In the beginning, the boys try to cooperate, making shelters, gathering food, and keeping signal fires going. Ralph takes on the leadership role, trying to impose order by delegating responsibility for survival chores. Piggy, Ralph's chubby, bespectacled friend, contributes logic and rationale to help Jack make necessary decisions, and his thick spectacles come in handy for lighting fires. However, disagreements and conflict soon give way to savagery. The other boys would rather play, swim, or hunt the island's wild pig population than plan for survival. Soon, they begin to ignore Ralph's rules, and Jack, the leader of a subgroup of savages, challenges them outright. Ralph and Piggy now become the hunted, instead of the hunters, as emotion replaces reason. Piggy, the continual reminder of adult standards of behavior, is brutally killed before the rescuers arrive. The children, *unintentionally* not remembering how they were socialized to appropriately resolve differences, resort to competition for status and power, using aggression as a means to obtain them.

NOW The "reality" TV series *Survivor* shows a group of adult castaways (chosen as contestants) marooned in a remote locale. Each week, the survivors compete in grueling physical competitions, as well as for resources to survive. The prize for which they are competing is to be the last one left on the island and, hence, the winner of a million dollars. What begins as fun, however, turns into manipulation and maliciousness. Every week, the group meets with its leaders in a tribal council to vote one contestant off the island. Everyone must explain the rationale behind his or her vote, and the ejected member must give a farewell speech describing his or her experiences and feelings. Here, the adults, *intentionally* not remembering how they were socialized to appropriately resolve differences, resort to competition for status and power, using manipulation as a means to get them.

KEY QUESTIONS

- What is the appeal of the peer group, making insiders want to remain members and outsiders wanting to become members?
- What makes one a leader, able to manipulate peers?

- How does social pressure influence people to conform to others?
- What influences cooperative versus competitive goals for the peer group?

The Peer Group as a Socializing Agent

The peer group is a microsystem in that it comprises relationships, roles, and activities. **Peers** are equals; they are usually of the same gender and age and have similar social statuses and interests. Although *outwardly* the peer group appears to be made up of equals, *inwardly* the dynamics of the peer group are such that some members are more equal than others (Adler & Adler, 1998; Steinberg, 1996).

Experiences with peers enable children to acquire a range of skills, attitudes, and roles that influence their adaptation throughout life (Rubin, Bukowski, & Parker, 1998). Peer groups are significant socializers, contributing beyond the influence of family and school, because (1) they satisfy certain belonging needs (Adler & Adler, 1998), (2) they often are preferred to other socializing agents (Harris, 1998), and (3) they influence not only social development but cognitive and psychological development as well (Ladd, 1999).

As more mothers are being employed outside the home, more and more children are being cared for in group settings. Today, children are experiencing social interaction with peers earlier and for longer periods of time than they were a generation ago. Also, school-age children and adolescents who are not supervised by adults after school are more likely to turn to their peers for support. In this chapter, we examine various peer group influences; Figure 8.1 shows an ecological model of the systems involved in the process.

THE SIGNIFICANCE OF PEERS TO DEVELOPMENT

Peer groups are significant because they satisfy certain basic human needs to develop optimally. These include the need to belong to a group and interact socially and the need to develop a sense of self (a personal identity). Belonging to a peer group enables children to interact socially with others and to have experiences independent of parents or other adults. By interacting socially with others, children derive an opinion of themselves. We referred to this concept of self in Chapter 2 as the "looking-glass self" (Cooley, 1964) and the "generalized other" (Mead, 1934). For example, we think of ourselves as having pretty hair, cute freckles, or a large nose because others tell us so; we think of ourselves as clever, as fast runners, or as good at drawing by comparing our skills to those of others.

Belonging Needs and Social Interaction

Although the need to belong to groups and interact with others is characteristic of humans, individual differences in intensity and amount exist. Some differences are due to nature, or temperament, and some are due to nurture, or socialization experiences. For example, child–peer bidirectional relationships are influenced by individual temperamental characteristics, such as shyness or sociability. These traits may also influence various parent–child interactions and social behaviors (Rubin, Bukowski, & Parker, 1998). Parents of shy children may have to provide them with more encouragement to have peer experiences than do parents of sociable children.

Figure 8.1

An Ecological Model of Human Development
Peers are a significant influence on children's development.

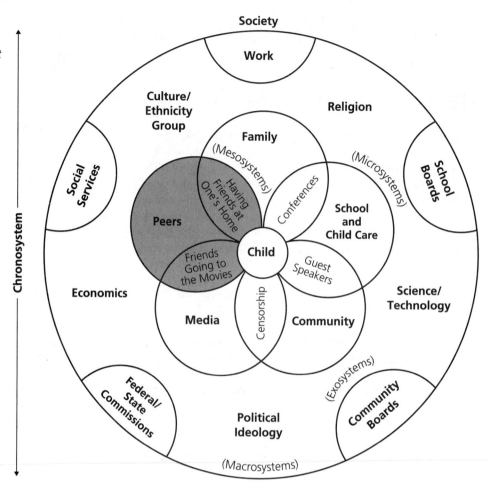

Also, parents who provide opportunities for their children to have contact with peers may also coach their children to interact positively and may intervene when negative behavior occurs (Pettit & Mize, 1993). Parent–child relationships from infancy to middle childhood, in particular, influence peer relationships.

Infancy/Toddlerhood (Birth to Age 1½ or 2). The sense of belonging develops first within the family. Babies get the feeling that they "belong" to the mother when she holds and soothes them and meets their needs. Babies whose mothers or caregivers are sensitive and responsive to their needs—for example, feeding them when they are hungry and comforting them when they are frightened—are securely attached (Ainsworth, 1979; Rubin, Bukowski, & Parker, 1998). The importance of attachment in socialization was discussed in Chapter 2. Attachment theory suggests that children who enjoy secure attachment relationships with caregivers are likely to possess a model to imitate for responsiveness to others (Schneider, Atkinson, & Tardif, 2001; Rubin, Bukowski, & Parker, 1998). In addition, a secure attachment may provide a secure base for exploratory behavior (Ainsworth, Blehar, Waters, & Wall, 1978). In other words, infants and toddlers who are secure in their relationship with their caregivers feel confident in leaving them to explore their environment (including objects and people) because they know their caregivers will be

These babies are already interested in each other as distinct human beings.

available to touch base with should the need arise. In contrast, babies who are insecurely attached, those who have experienced parental rejection or inconsistent care, tend to avoid peer relationships (Troy & Sroufe, 1987).

Babies who form secure attachments during their first year tend at age 3½ to 5 be socially involved with their peers. They approach others with positive expectations more readily than do children who are insecurely attached (Ainsworth, 1979; Jacobson & Wille, 1986; Rubin, Bukowski, & Parker, 1998), and they are often leaders proactively engaged in activities (Park & Waters, 1989). In contrast, children who have experienced insecure attachments in which their needs were met insensitively or inconsistently may have negative expectations toward peers, acting as if peers will be rejecting (Howes, Matheson, & Hamilton, 1994). Such children may exhibit withdrawal or aggressive behavior (Rubin, Bukowski, & Parker, 1998).

After toddlerhood, a gradual shift occurs in the relative importance of adults and peers in children's lives. Children who attend preschool increasingly look to their peers for attention and decreasingly seek proximity to caregivers (Hartup, 1983). This was demonstrated by Corsaro (1981) in a field study done in a preschool with children ranging in age from approximately 3–5. As field notes and videotapes indicated, the children rarely engaged in solitary play and that, when they found themselves alone, they consistently tried to join ongoing peer activities: "Can I play? I'll be your friend." Also, children who were involved in peer activities often protected the interaction by resisting those who attempted to gain access: "You can't play; you're not our friend." Thus, the more important peers become to children, the more expansive are their social experiences.

Early Childhood (Age 2 to 5 or 6). Preschool children's social interactions are affected not only by how secure they feel in their attachment to the mother but also by how willing adults are to provide opportunities for social interaction (Ladd &

LeSieur, 1995). For instance, where the family resides determines the number of same-aged children living nearby. Likewise, how willing parents are to invite other children to their home or to take their child to another's home, and whether the child attends a preschool program, affects the amount of social interaction that can take place.

Parenting style has been found to influence children's competence in interacting with peers. **Authoritative** (democratic) parenting has been associated with children's social and behavioral competence and confidence (Baumrind, 1973). **Authoritarian** (adult-directed), **permissive** (child-directed), and **uninvolved** (indifferent) parenting styles, in contrast, have been linked to low competence in social interaction (Ladd & LeSieur, 1995; Ladd & Pettit, 2002). It is likely that children model parental interactions with their friends.

Middle Childhood (Age 6 to 12 or 13). By school age, children's opportunities for social interaction increase. Children spend most of the day with other children—in class, on the school bus, and in the neighborhood—and they no longer need adults to structure their social interactions. In the middle years, children become more and more dependent on the recognition and approval of their peers, rather than that of adults. Their sense of belonging extends and expands. Interestingly, however, children whose parents took an active role in arranging and organizing their peer relations (inviting specific children to the home, encouraging their children to participate in a school or community group, discussing the children's friends and interactions) tend to develop closer, more harmonious ties with peers (Ladd & LeSieur, 1995).

Adolescence (Age 12 or 13 to 18 or so). Adolescents generally delineate their belonging needs and consequent social interactions according to the closeness of the relationship. The closest relationships and most intimate social interactions, such as sharing feelings, occur with one or two "best" friends; next are relationships with perhaps 6–10 peers who do things together (the "clique"); finally, there are relationships with the larger, more loosely organized peer group (or the "crowd") with which adolescents identify (Steinberg, 1996).

Sense of Self and Personal Identity

Peer relationships also contribute to the self-concept at various stages of development.

Infancy/Toddlerhood. Infants as young as 6 months look at, vocalize to, smile at, and touch other infants, thereby distinguishing themselves from others (Hay, 1985). As babies develop, relations with peers change, becoming more reciprocal. For example, at about age 1, their smiles, vocalizations, and playful activities are often imitated or reacted to (Howes & Matheson, 1992). During the second year, toddlers use words to communicate and can coordinate their behavior with that of playmates (Rubin, Bukowski, & Parker, 1998).

Early Childhood. When children begin to play in groups, generally after age 2 or 3, they have a chance to assume a variety of roles that were not available to them in the family context. Now they have to grapple with and work through issues of power, compliance, cooperation, and conflict (Kemple, 1991). Such issues contribute to the development of a sense of self and personal identity in that they give young children the opportunity to be assertive regarding ownership and to negotiate regarding desires: "That's my puzzle; you can't play with it," or "If you let me ride the bike, I'll let you hold my doll."

Middle Childhood. For middle-years children (age 6 to 12 or 13), the peer group is attractive because it provides opportunities for greater independence than does the family, thereby enhancing the sense of self. Did you ever build a fort or a tree house when you were a child? The underlying idea, of course, was for the group to have a place of its own, where it could be independent of adult supervision and where unwanted peers could be excluded.

In the peer group, children can say what they feel without being told, "You should not say things like that." Or they can make suggestions without being told, "You're too young to do that." Or they can do things without being told, "It will never work" (as an adult might say).

Middle-years children, especially as they approach preadolescence (age 11–13), long to find others like themselves—to know that others share their doubts, fears, wishes, and perceptions. The peer group is an important source of self-confirmation in that children learn, by comparing their thoughts and feelings with those of others, that they are not really different or "weird." Thus, belonging to a group clarifies their personal identity and enhances their self-esteem. The concern with acceptance in the peer group is often reflected in gossip. Teasley and Parker (1995) found that much gossip among middle-years children is negative, involving defamation of third parties. Children like to discuss who their friends and who their enemies are.

Peers also provide empathy and support for one another when their desires for independent actions are in conflict with adults' demands: "My father won't let me touch his CD player! He's so mean!" or "Can you believe Mrs. Millard made me clean the whole floor after school just because I shot one spit-wad? It's not fair!"

The peer group, in addition to clarifying and supporting children's identities, also provides models for what they can become. Peers show what is worth doing and how to do it. Think about it: It was probably your friends who taught you how to dance and what music to listen to, and influenced what style of clothes you wore.

Achieving a personal identity is a slow and difficult process during which children turn to their peers instead of their parents for certain kinds of support. However, entrance into the peer group creates some difficulties of its own (Grusec & Lytton, 1988). First, there is the change from protected to unprotected competition. At home, squabbles between children can be settled by adults; in the peer group, children must learn to protect themselves, whether it be getting to the video game first or not letting someone tease them. Second, the responses expected and rewarded at home and at school are different from those in the peer group. At home and at school, children are encouraged to be obedient and submissive. In the peer group, self-assertion and domination are the virtues that are rewarded.

Adolescence. Adolescence (about age 13–18) is a time in our society when peer group activities escalate, one reason being that adolescents are not yet fully included in the adult world of responsibility and recognition for contributions. Therefore, they turn to peers. Adolescents often face differences in the values of the family and those of the peer group. For example, academic achievement is an important value in some families, whereas among some groups of adolescents, athletic performance is far more important (Steinberg, 1996). Which values are adolescents more likely to adopt: their family's or their friends'? According to Sebald (1989, 1992), adolescents turn to their parents in regard to scholastic or occupational goals—in general, future-oriented decisions. They turn to their friends in regard to clothing, social activities, dating, or recreation—in general, present-oriented decisions. On moral issues, parental values dominate; on appearance, such as grooming, peer values dominate (Niles, 1981).

Parenting styles (discussed in Chapter 4) have been found to be associated with adult versus peer influences. Parents do influence with whom their children interact. The following findings link child–parent relationships to child–peer relationships:

- Authoritative parents, who are warm, accepting, neither too controlling nor too lax, and consistent in their child rearing, generally have children who are attached and who internalize their values. These children have little need to rebel or to desperately seek acceptance from peers (Fuligni & Eccles, 1993). They usually associate with friends who share their values, so they are not faced with negative peer influences (Fletcher, Darling, Steinberg, & Dornbusch, 1995).

- Authoritarian parents, who are strict and cold and who do not adjust to adolescents' needs for greater autonomy, typically have children who alienate themselves from parental values and are attracted to the peer group to gain understanding and acceptance (Fuligni & Eccles, 1993). These adolescents are at risk for negative peer influences.

- Permissive parents, who indulge their children by not providing standards, rules, or behavioral consequences and/or who ignore their children's activities, typically risk having adolescents who are attracted to antisocial peer groups (Dishion, Patterson, Stoolmiller, & Skinner, 1991).

- Uninvolved parents, who are emotionally detached and indifferent to their children's needs and activities, generally have children with poor emotional self-regulation, low academic achievement, and frequent anti-social behavior with peers in adolescence (Baumrind, 1991; Lamborn, Mounts, Steinberg, & Dornbusch, 1991).

Do these generalizations relating parenting styles to peer group attraction apply to diverse ethnic groups? This is a question still being researched. It is known that some ethnic groups place more emphasis on interdependence and social support networks than do Euro-Americans, who tend to emphasize independence and individuality (Greenfield & Suzuki, 1998). Social support networks include extended family members and friends. This was documented in a field observation study by Hutchison (1987) that took place in public parks in Chicago and involved 18,000 groups engaged in various leisure activities. In general, Whites engaged in more individualized activities, Hispanics engaged in the most combined family–peer activities, and Blacks engaged in the most peer-oriented activities.

Thus, the significance of peer group attraction may differ according to ethnic origin. Peer groups may provide connection to the community and positive social support regardless of parenting style; or, because of its attractiveness, the peer group may become a negative influence on values and behavior.

In sum, in achieving a personal identity, a major task for children is balancing group identification with personal autonomy while forging an individual role within the group. Participating in the activities of the group requires developing the skills for its games, as well as mastering the rules and agreements that govern its activities. In reaching a balance between group identification and personal autonomy, children must weigh loyalty to group norms against individual and parental norms.

They must also develop their roles in the group structure (leading or following, for example) and cope with feelings of being accepted and popular or unpopular and rejected (Grusec & Lytton, 1988; Minuchin, 1977; Rubin, Bukowski, & Parker, 1998). Thus, the peer group contributes to a sense of self.

PSYCHOLOGICAL DEVELOPMENT: EMOTIONS

Individuals who do not have normal peer relations are affected in their later psychological development. Studies have linked poor peer relations in childhood to the later development of neurotic and psychotic behavior and to a greater tendency to drop out of school (Asher & Coie, 1990; Hartup, 1983; Ladd, 1999, Rubin, Bukowski, & Parker, 1998). Psychologists actually find that sociometric measures (measures of patterns of attraction and rejection among members of a group, discussed later in the chapter) taken in the elementary grades predict adjustment in later life better than other educational or personality tests. The child's peer group seems to be a "sensitive barometer" of present and future adjustment problems (Asher, 1982; Hymel, Bowker, & Woody, 1993; Parker & Asher, 1987). Why is this so? Dealing with the social world requires communicative skills and the ability to coordinate actions with those of others, as well as reciprocity, cooperation, and competition. These competencies develop via interactions and experiences in the peer group. In addition, peer groups have certain norms for behavior—sometimes positive (cooperation, for example) and sometimes negative (exclusion of some children or rebelliousness, for example). Children learn to compete for status in the peer group by compliance with group norms ("followership") and creation of group norms (leadership) at appropriate times. Statuses, or social hierarchies, generally remain fairly stable in the group, with those who don't fit in being cast out or leaving on their own (American Academy of Pediatrics [AAP], 2002).

SOCIAL DEVELOPMENT: SOCIAL COMPETENCE

Social competence involves behavior influenced by the understanding of others' feelings and intentions, the ability to respond appropriately, and the knowledge of consequences of one's actions. Belonging to a social group involves conforming to group norms. The degree of social conformity that individuals exhibit depends on their age, situation, and stage of cognitive development, and on psychological factors, such as temperament, values and morals, motives, and self-esteem.

Studies (Berndt, 1979; Brown, Clasen, & Eicher, 1986; Foster-Clark & Blyth, 1991) have shown that children become most susceptible to the influence of peers in middle childhood and become less conforming in adolescence (see Figure 8.2). Even when they know it is wrong, middle-years children still go along with the majority opinion of the group (Berenda, 1950). In a classic study, 90 children age 7–13 were asked to compare the lengths of lines on 12 pairs of cards. They had already taken this same test in school. This time, however, the children participating in the experiment were tested in a room with the eight brightest children in their class, with answers given aloud. These eight children had been instructed beforehand to give 7 wrong answers out of 12. The results pointed to the power of group influence. Whereas almost all the subjects had given correct answers to the seven critical questions in the original test taken in school, only 43 percent of the 7- to 10-year-olds, and only 54 percent of the 10- to 13-year-olds gave correct

Figure 8.2

Conformity Peaks

Prosocial conformity peaks in the sixth grade; antisocial conformity peaks in the ninth grade.
Source: T. J. Berndt (1979). Developmental changes in conformity to peers and parents. *Developmental Psychology, 15,* 608–616. Copyright © 1979 by the American Psychological Association. Reprinted with permission.

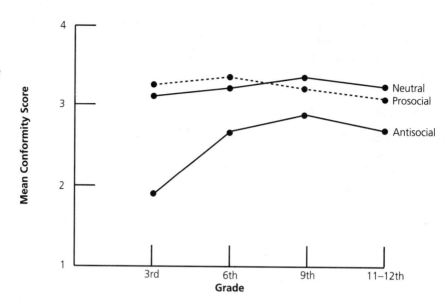

answers on the test in the group setting. The rest changed their former answers to match the group's, which were intentionally incorrect.

Such conformity is even more apparent in ambiguous situations where children are unsure about what they should do or are supposed to do (Cohen, Bornstein, & Sherman, 1973; Hartup, 1983; Steinberg, 1996). For example, Berndt (1979; Berndt & Ladd, 1989) gave a questionnaire to students ranging from the third to the twelfth grade, asking how they would respond to various hypothetical situations (prosocial, neutral, antisocial). A question exemplifying a prosocial situation asked the students whether they would help a classmate with a report if asked by their peers, instead of doing what they wanted to do, which was helping another classmate operate the film projector. A question exemplifying a neutral situation asked the students whether they would go to a movie if asked by their peers, even if they were not particularly interested in that movie. A question exemplifying an antisocial situation asked the students whether they would steal some candy if a peer wanted help in doing it.

One of Berndt's (1979) findings was that conformity to antisocial behavior and in neutral situations peaked in the ninth grade and then dropped off to previous levels. Another finding was that conformity to prosocial behavior peaked in the sixth grade and then dropped. In general, the sixth- to ninth-graders exhibited the most conforming behavior (see Figure 8.2). Berndt also found that whether students conformed to the group depended on the particular situation—how "good" or "bad" they felt about it. Students were more likely to conform to situations they did not feel very "bad" about. Thus, personal values do affect children's likelihood of conforming to the peer group.

According to Harris (1998), children learn not only the importance of conforming to be accepted by the peer group but also the dynamics of power, manipulation, and popularity (aspects of social competence). They learn how to compete for status within the group by combining "leadership" and "followership" skills (Adler & Adler, 1998). Thus, conformity exhibited at a given time may depend on whether the child is leading or following.

COGNITIVE DEVELOPMENT: SOCIAL COGNITION

As the various studies suggest, the peer group becomes an increasingly powerful socializing agent during the period of development between early childhood (age 2–5) and preadolescence (age 11–13). Why are children age 11–13 more susceptible to peer group influences than children of other ages?

Just as children interact with one another increasingly from infancy on, so the ability to cope with complex social messages increases with age. For example, children under age 7 do not have the cognitive ability even to be aware of peer pressure to conform or of the consequences for deviance. They have difficulty taking another's point of view and so cannot project what the peer group thinks of them. Research findings have been accumulating regarding the connection between social and cognitive development (Ladd, 1999). This connection is referred to as **social cognition:** the conceptions and reasoning about people, the self, relations between people, social groups' roles, and rules, and the relation of such conceptions to social behavior (Shantz, 1983). Collaboration with peers through language and play enables children to construct thoughts (Berk & Winsler, 1995). Social interactions with peers also contribute to children's cognitive understanding of their culture.

Young children age 7–11 are in the stage of cognitive development that the Swiss psychologist Jean Piaget (1952) termed the **concrete operations.** This stage is characterized by the ability to apply logical, systematic principles to help interpret specific or tangible experiences, but also by the inability to distinguish between intangible assumptions (hypotheses) and facts (reality).

According to Elkind (1981a), concrete-operational children make assumptions about situations and people that they are convinced are real and true—**"assumptive realities"**—no matter how illogical they are. For example, U.S. children of this age who have seen a globe at school might try to dig a hole in the ground to get to China, because China is on the other side of the globe (I used to do this at the beach), and no amount of adult logic can dissuade them. Concrete-operational children also assume that they are clever. Elkind called this **"cognitive conceit"**—the exhibition of too much faith in one's reasoning ability. The concept of cognitive conceit is illustrated in some favorite stories of children of this age—for example, *Peter Pan* (in which a child outwits Captain Hook, an adult) or *Alice's Adventures in Wonderland* (in which a young girl makes the queen look like a fool).

Because children under age 11 often think that they know it all, they sometimes feel that they do not have to pay attention to the opinions of others, be they adults or other children. In this context, "I don't have to" (a common remark at this age), then, represents not so much defiance as a statement of belief in their own abilities (Piaget, 1952).

About age 11, children become capable of logical thought. Piaget called this the stage of **formal operations** because individuals now understand the *form* behind a concept and can add ideas to or subtract them from it. This stage is characterized by the ability to think logically about abstract ideas and hypotheses, as well as concrete facts. Children can now construct all the possibilities of a proposition—the ones related to fact and the ones contrary to fact—and so can conceptualize their own thoughts and discover the arbitrariness of their assumptions. They also discover rules for **reality testing,** or testing assumptions against facts. This leads to diminished confidence in their own abilities, especially their cleverness. Preadolescent children are aware of the reactions of others and the need to conform to their expectations. This new awareness is reflected in the projection of an **imaginary audience**—the belief that others are as concerned with their behavior and appearance as they are themselves. Thus, preadolescent children believe they are the focus of attention. Because of this, they strive especially hard to be like their peers, so that they will not stand out.

As children approach adolescence (age 13–15), the imaginary audience comes to be regarded as an assumption to be tested against reality. As a consequence of this testing, adolescents gradually come to recognize the difference between their own preoccupations and the interests and concerns of others. Conformity decreases because adolescents realize that, although they are expected to conform to some situations, they can be independent in others. Adolescents have also developed improved social skills and a greater reliance on their own judgment.

One reason preadolescent children are more conforming than those in other age groups is that, even though they are capable of logical thought (that is, they can project how others will react to and evaluate their assumptions), they have not yet had the experience of testing their assumptions on reality.

EXAMPLE When my daughter began junior high school, she refused to take the backpack I had bought her for her books. She said, "All the kids will laugh at me; only kids in elementary school use backpacks." I asked her what the junior high kids used to carry their books. Exhibiting preadolescent assumptions, she did not know exactly (she had not been there yet), but she thought they used satchels. For the first week of school, she carried her books loosely in her arms. When the second week of school came, she grudgingly put her books in the backpack, saying she was tired of dropping books and that her arms ached. One day after school had been in session for about a month, I picked up my daughter at school. I noticed that a lot of kids had backpacks. I said nothing, but I thought to myself, "She assumed all the other kids would have satchels and she didn't want to be different. She had to make sure that enough other kids had backpacks before she would take hers to school." Can you remember being reluctant to do something before you saw others do it? What were your concerns?

Another reason preadolescent children are more conforming than other age groups is that they are entering Erikson's (1963) fifth psychosocial stage of development—identity versus identity (role) confusion ("Who am I, and what is my role in life?"). Erikson's stages were discussed in Chapter 2. In the process of finding an identity, preadolescent children repeat the crises of the earlier stages—trust versus mistrust ("Do I generally trust people, or distrust them?"), autonomy versus shame and doubt ("Am I confident I can be independent, or am I doubtful about my ability to be independent?"), initiative versus guilt ("Do I feel good about starting new things or meeting new people, or do I feel guilty?"), and industry versus inferiority ("Do I feel competent about my abilities, or inferior?").

> The growing and developing youths, faced with this psychological revolution within them, and with tangible adult tasks ahead of them, are now primarily concerned with what they appear to be in the eyes of others as compared with what they feel they are. (Erikson, 1963, p. 261)

They are trying out roles and using the reactions of others to judge how well the roles fit their self-concept. Thus, in the process of asking "Who am I?" children in this psychosocial stage of development tend to "temporarily overidentify to the point of apparent complete loss of identity, with heroes of cliques and crowds" (Erikson, 1963, p. 262).

Erikson explained the clannishness and cruelty of excluding those who are different from the group as a defense against a sense of identity confusion. Preadolescent children who are on the brink of entering the identity-versus-role-confusion stage look to the peer group for their identity. The group's symbols and rituals (ways of dressing, ways of behaving, attitudes, opinions), as well as its approval and support, help define what is good and what is bad, thereby contributing to the development of ego identity. Identifying with a group and excluding those who differ from its members help children identify *who they are* by affirming *who they are not.* As preadolescence gives way to adolescence, young people begin to derive an identity from the accumulation of their experiences, abilities, and goals. They begin to look within themselves rather than to others for their identity. The peer group, then, serves to mediate between individuals and society, playing a powerful role in shaping each individual's identity (Adler & Adler, 1998).

PEER GROUP SOCIALIZING MECHANISMS

What socializing mechanisms does the peer group employ to influence behavior? Typical methods include reinforcement (or approval and acceptance), modeling (or imitation), punishment (or rejection and exclusion), and apprenticeship (novice learns from expert).

Reinforcement

One important way in which children influence one another is through **reinforcement,** or giving attention. Approving another's behavior (smiling, laughing, patting, hugging, praising) increases the likelihood of that behavior recurring (Kindermann, 1998). The behavior could be sharing, or it could be acting aggressive (Martin & Pear, 1996). Reinforcement also involves acceptance into the group; criteria for acceptance will be discussed later.

That reinforcement increases behavior, and not the degree of friendship, was demonstrated in a study in which young children age 4 and 5 performed better at simple tasks when a child they disliked praised their performance than when a child they liked did so (Hartup, 1964, 1983).

Reinforcement can be unintentional but still effective. In one study (Patterson, Littman, & Bricker, 1976), some preschool children reacted to physical aggression (bullying) by becoming passive, assuming a defensive posture, bursting into tears, telling the teacher, retrieving their property, or retaliating with aggression. When the victim responded to the aggression with reinforcers such as passiveness, defensiveness, or tears, the aggression tended to be repeated. But when the victim responded with proactive behavior such as telling the teacher, retrieving property, or acting aggressive, the aggressor or bully tended to behave differently toward the former victim. Unintentional passivity in response to aggression, then, generally reinforces it toward the victim; action serves to redirect the aggression away from the victim.

To determine whether certain social stimuli function as reinforcers, Furman and Masters (1980) observed and recorded incidence of laughter and praise (positive reinforcers); tears, physical attacks, and disapproval (negative reinforcers); and other expressions (neutral reinforcers) in preschool children. They found that behaviors classified as positive reinforcers were twice as likely to be followed by similar affective behaviors; in contrast, punitive acts were more than five times as likely to be followed by negative behaviors. Parents and teachers need to be alert to patterns of peer reinforcement so that peers can be used to help change negative or disruptive behavior.

Modeling

Children also influence each other through **modeling,** or imitation (Kindermann, 1998). Modeling is related to conformity in that observing a child behave in a certain manner can affect another's consequent behavior in several distinct ways (Bandura, 1977, 1989):

- The observing child may learn how to do something new that she or he previously could not do (such as drawing a picture of a dog) or that she or he would probably not have thought of doing (such as riding a bike with "no hands").
- The child may learn the consequences of behavior by observing someone else. For example, pinching a classmate results in being punished by the teacher, or getting to the swings first results in getting the longest turn.
- A model may suggest how the child should behave in a new situation. For example, when the children lined up at the edge of the pool for their first dive, one girl was first. She said, "I can do it. I've watched my brother

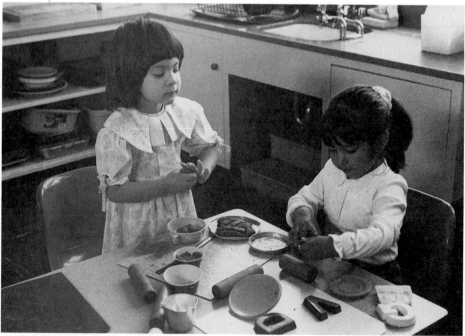

This child is intent on modeling her friend.

© Elizabeth Crews

hundreds of times." As the instructor was showing her how to hold her arms and keep her head down, the other children watched nervously. In a second, she hit the water, and in another few seconds, she popped up smiling. The others relaxed.

In a classic study by Bandura, Ross, and Ross (1965), children who were shown a film in which a model struck a doll, sat on it, and screamed at it later copied the model's aggressive behavior when given a similar doll to play with. Other researchers (Hartup, 1983; Hartup & Coates, 1967) studied a group of 4- and 5-year-old children who were asked to watch one of their classmates work out problems. The classmate (the model) received some trinkets for performing the task, some of which the model put aside for an imaginary child. The children who observed were then asked to do the problems. They were also given trinkets and offered an opportunity to save some for the "other child." Another group of 4- and 5-year-olds, who did not watch a model do the problems and exhibit altruistic behavior, were asked to do the same problems, were given trinkets, and were offered the opportunity to save some for the "other child." The children who observed altruistic behavior set aside more trinkets than those who did not.

Modeling does influence behavior, but the extent can depend on the situation. *Active* behavior is more likely to be imitated than *passive* behavior. The extent of the influence also depends on the observer's perception of the model. A model who is similar to the observer and has desirable or admirable traits is more likely to be imitated than one who is not very similar to the observer or who has traits not particularly desirable to the observer. In addition, the observer's ability to produce the observed behavior influences modeling (Bandura, 1977, 1989).

In one study, preschool children exhibited a great deal of imitation, some positive and some negative, of both verbal and motor acts in day-by-day interactions (Abramovitch & Grusec, 1978). Imitation seems to decrease from preschool age to age 10, perhaps because deferred, rather than immediate, imitation and other subtle forms of observational learning become more favored as children get older. Dominant children in a group are imitated more often by other members, but they imitate the others as well (Grusec & Lytton, 1988).

Compared with reinforcement, modeling as a socializing method has broader effects. A large number of children can be influenced by one carefully selected model, whereas direct reinforcement requires one-to-one interaction between teacher and learner. Modeling can provide a means of inducing behavior that otherwise might not occur. It may give children an idea for doing something never done before, or it may remind children of something done before and induce them to repeat it (Bandura, 1989). Using reinforcement as a behavior modification technique requires waiting for the behavior to appear and then reinforcing it (Martin & Pear, 1996).

Punishment

Still another way in which children influence one another is through **punishment**—teasing, physical aggression, or rejection by the group. An extreme of such punishment is being a victim of bullying. *Victims* are usually withdrawn, passive, shy, and insecure, and have difficulty asserting themselves in a group. *Bullies* are usually dominant, aggressive, impulsive, and angry, and have a low frustration tolerance. Bullying and victimization require adult intervention strategies, which will be discussed later (Crick, Casas, & Ku, 1999; Olweus, 1993).

Sometimes children are rejected or punished by peers because of physical characteristics (being overweight, for example) or behavioral characteristics (bragging, dominating, or criticizing, for example) (Adler & Adler, 1998; Coie, Dodge, & Kupersmidt, 1990; Parkhurst & Asher, 1992). The consequence of being punished by exclusion and teasing by the peer group are described in the box "Peers, Power, Pecking Order, and Punishment." The social dynamics of inclusion, exclusion, and social hierarchies are discussed later.

Peers, Power, Pecking Order, and Punishment

Peer groups in schools are manifested in the form of **cliques**—friends who view themselves as mutually connected and who do things together—and **crowds**—loosely organized reference groups of cliques. Cliques and crowds are significant contributors in children's and adolescents' quests for identity.

In elementary school, cliques are hierarchical friendship groups based on popularity and prestige. By the time children reach high school, the clique social hierarchy is stratified. Typically, one finds "jocks," "preppies" or "populars," "brains" or "nerds," and "unpopulars" (Eder, 1995). High school social life was popularized in the media by the TV show *Beverly Hills, 90210*. By interacting within and among friendship groups, children learn what kind of social competence they possess. The high-status clique is the "populars"; below them are the "wannabes" (the groups whose members hang around hoping for inclusion); next are smaller, independent groups; and at the bottom of the social hierarchy are the "social isolates" (those who only occasionally find playmates) (Adler & Adler, 1998).

Cliques are dominated by leaders. Cliques also are exclusive in nature, so that not all individuals who desire membership are accepted. Cliques maintain exclusivity through careful membership screening, with acceptance or rejection of potential new members linked to the power of the leaders. Leaders derive their power through popularity and use it to make decisions and influence social stratification (the pecking order) within the group (Adler & Adler, 1998).

In their observations of preadolescents in school, Adler and Adler (1998, p. 76) found that the popular clique "set the tone for, and in many ways influenced, the behavior of the entire grade." Maintaining membership required a concerted effort to conform to desires of the leaders. The exclusivity of membership was a reward for those who were "in" and a punishment for those who were "out." The "wannabes" tried to be "cool" by imitating the "populars"—wearing the same clothing and hairstyles, buying the same music, and using the same vocabulary (Eder, 1995). Their conforming behavior was reinforced because, occasionally, they were invited to participate in clique activities even though they were not fully accepted into the group.

Those who were "out," the "social isolates" ("loners," "drifters," "dweebs," "nerds"), were excluded because they were different in some way—appearance, behavior, and/or language. Those who were "in" or the "wannabes" teased and laughed at them. It is as though everyone in the pecking order offset his or her own insecurities by humiliating the individuals who were lower in status (Thorne, 1993). The exclusion of the "social isolates" from nearly all cliques' social activities, coupled with the extreme degradation they suffer, took a heavy toll on their feelings of self-worth.

The significance of these findings from peer group studies was manifested in 1999 at Columbine High School in Littleton, Colorado, where two social isolates, Eric Harris and Dylan Klebold, shot and killed 12 students and a teacher, as well as themselves. Interviews with students and community members pointed to harassment of Harris and Klebold by the "jocks," combined with their disengagement from caring adults (Wilson & Mishra, 1999). That such rage was acted out when cliques and cruelty have been around for years in children's groups raises a disturbing question. In 1961, sociologist James Coleman studied 11 high schools of varied socioeconomic statuses and found similar peer group stratification, similar values (with "jocks" having the highest prestige, and "brains" and "unpopulars" the lowest), and similar behavior. The adolescents in his study seemed to accept things as "normal" for high school life; so why did the Columbine tragedy occur?

According to Greenfield and Juvonen (1999), Harris and Klebold acquired knowledge from the broader society (macrosystem) beyond home and school: (1) They had role models (media showing heroes engaged in violence to accomplish goals); (2) they had tools (guns and assault weapons available for purchase along with internet instuctions on how to construct a bomb); (3) they had social validation from internet groups; and (4) they had opportunities to practice their objectives (via violent video games). Thus, peers are influenced by other ecosystems.

Apprenticeship

Throughout this chapter, references have been made to the influences of peers, such as in having introduced you to popular music, taught you to dance, or "educated" you about sex. The underlying idea is someone with more expertise (the expert) helping someone with less (the novice), as in an apprenticeship. The concept of **apprenticeship** as a method of socialization was discussed in Chapter 2. Traditionally, the word *apprenticeship* has been used in the world of work—a beginner becomes an apprentice under a master until he or she learns a trade well enough to succeed alone. .

Vygotsky (1978) postulated that a more knowledgeable person, such as a teacher or an expert peer, initially guides the learner's, or novice's, activity. Gradually, the two begin to share the problem-solving functions, with the novice taking the initiative and the expert correcting and guiding when the novice falters. Finally, the expert cedes control and becomes a supportive audience.

An illustration of Vygotsky's hypothesis might be your learning how to ride a bike from a friend who had mastered the skill. Your friend shows you how to get on the bike, how to keep your balance, how to pedal, and how to stop. You get on the bike while your friend supports it. Your friend holds on while you pedal. After several tumbles, you learn to balance and pedal at the same time, so your friend lets go (but runs alongside yelling instructions on how to stop).

Vygotsky believed that engaging in such apprenticeship activities advances novices' level of development. Vygotsky suggested that novices' boundaries lie between (1) their actual development, or what they can do independently, and (2) their potential development, or what they can do while participating with more capable others.

> **EXAMPLE** My husband has a talent for drawing. I persuaded him to take an art class to develop his ability further. The students in the class submitted their drawings every week for peer review and heard suggestions for improvement while the instructor served as a moderator. At the end of the course, my husband's drawings were significantly more elaborate and sophisticated than when he began the class. Peer review is a technique also used in other classes, such as writing or speech.

Vygotsky called the space between the learner's two boundaries the zone of proximal development (ZPD), as discussed in Chapter 2. Schools are implementing the concept of ZPD in cooperative goal structures (discussed in Chapter 6), peer collaboration, peer tutoring, peer counseling, and conflict resolution. Peer groups provide apprenticeships for learning many things; these, as noted previously, can be positive, neutral, or negative.

Points to Ponder

"Arousal" refers to heightened alertness, emotionality, or responsiveness to a stimulus. Although partially influenced by temperament, arousal levels can be heightened (anxiety) or lowered (depression) due to contextual factors, such as how your peers treat you. Growing up, what effects did your friends have on your state of arousal, and what was the outcome?

Macrosystem Influences on the Peer Group: Developmental Tasks

Developmental tasks, discussed in Chapter 2, are midway between an individual need and a societal demand. The macrosystem influences the peer group to reinforce the values and traditions of society. The peer group, in turn, provides the setting and the means for children to achieve some of the developmental tasks of early and middle childhood (Duvall & Miller, 1985; Havighurst, 1972; Zarbatany, Hartmann, & Rankin, 1990), especially social competence: getting along with others, developing morals and values, learning appropriate social and cultural roles, and achieving personal independence (Rubin, Bukowski, & Parker, 1998).

GETTING ALONG WITH OTHERS

Playing with children of the same age is a vehicle for socializing the capacity to "get along" by learning to give and take. Getting along involves recognition of the rights of others. The peer group provides children with opportunities for understanding the limitations that group life places upon the individual: "At my house I can play with my Legos all I want, but at preschool I have to share," or "When I'm with my friends, I can't always have my way. We talk about what we're going to do on Sunday, trying to please everyone. If Barbara, Joleen, and Cara want to go shopping and I don't, the group tells me if I come with them, they'll stop by my favorite ice-cream place on the way home. Even though I don't get my way, I get the feeling I'm wanted and that the group is trying to please me. I agree to go shopping."

The ability to get along is developmentally progressive in that it involves both seeing things from another's perspective and communicating verbally (Grusec & Lytton, 1988). It depends, then, on increasing cognitive abilities and social experiences. Some studies (Clarke-Stewart, 1992; Lamb, 1998) have shown that young children who are in child care centers are more socially competent than those who are cared for at home but are also more aggressive. It is likely that these children learn early how to "stick up" for themselves and compete for toys and other valued resources.

DEVELOPING MORALS AND VALUES

The development of **morals** (distinguishing right from wrong) and **values** (determining what is worthwhile) occurs in a social setting. By interacting with others, children come to know what is and what is not acceptable behavior. Children usually learn morals and values from parents and other adults via instruction, reasoning, modeling, reinforcement, and punishment. They usually learn morals and values from peers through actual experiences (learning by doing).

Most studies of the development of morals and values involve school-age children and adolescents, who are capable of articulating judgments about hypothetical dilemmas, as is discussed in Chapter 11. However, research by Dunn (1988) on the origins of social understanding, which is the cornerstone of moral development, has shown that, from 18 months on, children understand how to hurt, or comfort others. They also understand the consequences of their hurtful actions toward others in their own environment, and can anticipate the response of adults to their own and to others' misdeeds. Preschoolers enter the peer group setting with a rudimentary understanding of social rules influenced by their family context. As children develop, peer group experiences expand this understanding (Rubin, Bukowski, & Parker, 1998).

Understanding rules is part of moral development in that both involve rule formulation, rule following, cooperation, limit setting, division of roles, and territoriality: "Consciousness of rules cannot be isolated from the moral life of the child as a whole" (Piaget, 1965, p. 50). Rules are related to morals in that both have to do with established guides for conduct. In the peer group, common rules based on common experiences begin to emerge. These rules may be devised to meet a specific situation or copied from adults' rules or those of older children. Between age 3 and 7, children sometimes observe the rules of the group and other times do not. Even when playing together, children of this age play "each one on his own" (Piaget, 1965, p. 27)—everyone has his or her own views of the way the game is played—without any real regard for the codification of the rules.

Between age 7 and 8, children "begin to concern themselves with the question of mutual control and of unification of the rules" (Piaget, 1965, p. 27), even though their understanding of the rules may be rather vague. Between age 11 and 12, children establish the rules in their groups; everyone in the group understands and observes them. For example, in the game of four square, whoever misses the ball is out, as everyone knows. However, some groups will make rules regarding how the ball is returned, like "no babies." A "baby" is a ball bounced so lightly that it barely comes off the ground and so is almost impossible to get. Thus, children who want to belong to the group must respect and obey the rules. If "babies" are not allowed, players cannot use them if they wish to continue playing with the group. Learning

In game playing, children's moral development is influenced through such activities as following rules, cooperating, and setting limits.

the conditions attached to belonging to the group, then, is the way children are socialized to the requirements for participation. It is also a way in which children develop morality.

Piaget (1965) contrasted two types of morality. One type, **morality of constraint** (or heteronomous morality), consists of behavior based on respect for persons in authority. It is imposed by a prestigious and powerful source, usually a parent or other adult. This type of morality fosters the ideal that to obey the will of the authority is good and to obey one's own will is bad. Such morality is fostered in the family and in school. The other type, **morality of cooperation** (or autonomous morality), consists of behavior based on mutual understanding between equals. It involves the acceptance of rules because they are necessary for the continuance of group life. If one wants to participate in the group, one freely accepts the rules, and so these rules are imposed upon oneself by oneself. This type of morality emerges from the mutual respect of group members. Thus, peer group participation—participation among equals—helps foster morality of cooperation, whereas morality of constraint is more likely to be fostered in authoritarian, adult-dominated situations, such as in the family or school.

In our society, we must obey certain rules because they were imposed by an authority, whether or not we agree (registering with the Selective Service, for example). We also impose certain rules upon ourselves for the benefit of group life (compromising with a neighbor regarding the property line, for example). To participate effectively in society, then, children need both types of morality training. Studies (Devereaux, 1970; Ladd & LeSieur, 1995) have shown that children who came from homes with moderate to high levels of discipline and control and who had a great deal of peer group experience are autonomous and have strong moral character. In contrast, children who came from homes characterized by high permissiveness or high punitiveness and who had a great deal of peer group experience tend to be "peer conformists" or "chameleons." Studies on parenting styles, discussed in Chapter 4, have also shown that authoritative parents are more likely to have children who exhibit independence and social competence (Baumrind, 1973; Ladd & LeSieur, 1995; Ladd & Pettit, 2002).

It would seem, then, that the peer group helps children in the *process* of developing morals, whereas the *level* of moral development is greatly influenced by parenting styles. Recent research (Bogenschneider, Wu, Raffaeli, & Tsay, 1998) documents the importance of contingent linkages between parents and peers in moral behavior.

LEARNING APPROPRIATE SOCIOCULTURAL ROLES

Although the family imparts sociocultural roles, such as independence and interdependence, the peer group gives children opportunities to try out roles learned at home (Greenfield & Suzuki, 1998). Children thereby gain an understanding of individuals' responsibilities in a group situation. For example, do they exercise autonomy and respect peers' right to free choice ("I want to play Scrabble; what game do you want to play?"), or do they exercise empathy, anticipating the desires of peers ("I know you like to play Chess, so let's play")? Do they communicate in a direct, assertive manner ("I want to try your new bike") or in an indirect, passive manner ("That's a nice new bike you got")? Do they compete with peers for individual recognition or cooperate with peers for group recognition? Do they confront conflict or avoid it?

An example of how appropriate sociocultural roles are learned can be seen when children who have never had to share things at home or who have never had to take turns must learn to do so in the peer group or else be excluded. From the peer group, children receive feedback about their behavior and skills; their peers will not hesitate to tell them when they are acting dumb. Children not only learn the sociocultural roles of cooperation and appropriate behavior from each other, they also learn how to compete. They evaluate their skills in terms of whether they can do better than, as well as, or worse than others in the group. They also learn methods of conflict resolution. An example of cultural conflicts involves children who have been socialized by their families to value cooperation in the group or on a team trying to function with children who have been socialized to value competition. "Two immigrant Latina players talk about wanting the team to work as a unit. They complain that the Euro American girls just want themselves to look good sometimes even at the expense of the team's performance" (Greenfield & Sukuki, 1998, p. 1091).

The box "Development of Sociocultural Roles Through the Peer Group" illustrates how societal values influence what are considered appropriate sociocultural roles for young children.

Development of Sociocultural Roles Through the Peer Group

The peer group can provide a mechanism whereby the socialization goals of the macrosystem are implemented. Researchers investigating how preschools in China, Japan, and the United States shape their children found that each country viewed preschools as agents that preserve certain traditional cultural values even in times of social change (Tobin, Wu, & Davidson, 1989).

In China, a collective society that values interdependence, concerns about overpopulation caused the government to mandate that only one child be born to each family. Therefore, Chinese preschools are expected to provide experiences with peers that will counter the undivided attention that the only child gets from parents and grandparents.

In Japan, a society that values conformity and cooperation, preschools enable children to learn these traditional values by functioning in a large group. Social change in Japan has resulted in shrinking birthrates and movement of young people away from their extended families. When families were large and many relatives lived close by, Japanese children could learn social skills in their families and identify with members of a group; now preschools have become the vehicle.

In America, a society that values independence and individuality, social change has evidenced itself in heightened family mobility, increased employment of mothers, and the growth of single-parent families. Parents have turned to preschools to provide stability, enrichment, and guidance for children.

Preschools in all three cultures stressed the importance of learning to cooperate and being a member of a group. In addition, Chinese preschools especially value learning citizenship, self-discipline, and perseverance. Japanese preschools especially value learning sympathy, empathy, and concern for others. American preschools especially value learning self-reliance and self-confidence.

The Chinese children were taught citizenship via regimentation and orderly conduct. Children performed the same activities at the same time under the direction of the teacher, whether it was doing calisthenics, singing, or building with blocks. The children copied what the teacher does, and no talking was permitted. The children even lined up to go to the bathroom at a specified time. They were taught to regulate their bodily functions to synchronize with the group. Sociocultural roles of interdependence, order, and conformity were thereby reinforced.

Whereas Chinese preschools maintain order by direct adult control, Japanese preschools do so by relying on the peer group to deal with disputes and misbehavior. The children arrived at school and played with their friends until the "clean-up" song. They were led by the teacher in group exercises. Once seated at their tables, they began a workbook project. The teacher made no attempt to stop the talking, laughing, or even playful fighting that occurs. After their work, there was free play and then lunch. In one case, a little girl told the teacher about a particularly raucous boy, but the teacher merely encouraged her to deal with the problem herself. Eventually, the fighting ceased, and the children listened to a song before settling down to rest. Thus, the Japanese preschool experience involves children's learning to enjoy ties to peers, to transfer the warmth of the parent–child relations to other relationships, and to balance informality with formality, emotion with control, and family with society. Sociocultural roles of interdependence and harmony are thereby reinforced.

American preschoolers generally experience much freedom of choice and expression. The function of the preschool is to make young children more independent and self-reliant by promoting individuality, autonomy, problem solving, cognitive development, and friendship ties. Whereas Chinese preschools instill discipline primarily by providing regimentation, modeling appropriate behavior, and offering criticism and praise, and Japanese preschools do so by fostering a sense of concern for the group, American preschools instill discipline by fostering a sense of individual rights.

The American children began their day with free play until all the children arrived. The teacher then gathered everyone together for "show and tell," thereby encouraging individual expression. After a flannel board story and a song, the children could choose to go to any of the several learning centers set up for that day.

The children moved about freely, and the teachers assisted them in the learning activities. In one instance, a disruptive child was told by the teacher that his actions may have caused another child to get hurt and was told to sit in the "time-out" chair to think about what he had done. Sociocultural roles of independence and individual rights were thereby reinforced.

Thus, the peer group in preschool settings serves as a vehicle by which children learn certain cultural values. In China, children learn to conform to the group by the teacher's structuring the activities accordingly, criticizing those who don't conform, and praising those who do. In Japan, children learn to get along in the peer group by the teacher's encouragement and noninterference. In America, children learn to respect other children's rights by the teacher's interceding in conflicts, explaining why they are hurtful or unsafe, and providing a consequence (Tobin, Wu, & Davidson, 1989).

Gender Roles, Sex Education, and Sexual Activity

Gender role is another sociocultural role that the peer group helps teach children. Both boys and girls learn from their peers what is culturally acceptable and admirable (Best, 1983; Pitcher & Schultz, 1983; Thorne, 1993). For example, Jerry, age 4, wanted to join a group of girls who were playing with their dolls. Jerry had a doll at home that he bathed and dressed while his mother or father bathed his baby sister. When Jerry approached the girls, they said, "Boys don't play with dolls!" Peer pressure for appropriate gender-type play has been observed to begin as early as age 2 (Fagot, 1985; Maccoby, 1990, 2000; Serbin, Powlishta, & Gulko, 1993).

Peer groups generally segregate boys and girls beginning in preschool (Maccoby, 1990, 2000; Ruble & Martin, 1998). In the preschool years, girls become interested in small-group games in confined spaces, games that allow them to practice and refine certain social rules and roles (for example, playing "house" or "school"). Boys engage in larger-group games that are more physically active and wide ranging. These games tend to have more extensive sets of explicit rules and to involve striving to reach a defined goal. The games tend to be competitive (for example, the "good guys against the bad guys," in the form of Batman or Darth Vader, with the goal being "to save the world"). Thus, segregated peer group play leads to different outcomes for boys and girls in achievement motivations, personal relationships, and self-concepts (Dweck, 1981). Gender roles are discussed in more detail in Chapter 12.

The peer group is often the imparter of sex education. Children and adolescents share their knowledge with each other—knowledge they may have gained from their families, from the media, from school, or from friends. With their limited cognitive ability, however, they often have an incomplete understanding of sexual behavior, which, combined with their friends' incomplete understanding, distorts the picture of sexuality.

Observations of elementary school children in the United States reveal that girls and boys are very aware of the opposite gender (Best, 1983; Thorne, 1993). Children continually talk about who "loves" whom and who is "cute." As preparation for later heterosexual relations, children play chase-and-kiss games. Usually, the girls try to catch the boys and kiss them, announcing that they have "cooties."

In the United States, the onset of sexual activity is influenced by peers, gender, and ethnic orientation (Brooks-Gunn & Furstenberg, 1989). Children's peers establish the norms for initiating sex. Assumptions (rather than actual knowledge) about what their peers are doing has been found to be associated with sexual behavior (actual behavior is difficult to research due to disclosure reluctance). In teens age 15–19, early dating has been associated with early intercourse (Brooks-Gunn & Furstenberg, 1989). Historically, boys have been much more likely to engage in sexual intercourse earlier than girls. This may have been due to peer pressure to "become a man," as well as not having to bear the consequences of becoming pregnant. However, the gap between the onset of sexual activity by gender has narrowed (Miller, Christopherson, & King, 1993). This may be a consequence of media portrayals of females as sexual seductresses and to easier access to contraception. Parental influences on sexual behavior are believed to outweigh those of peers and the media if there is a feeling of connectedness and support and open communication (Brooks-Gunn & Furstenberg, 1989; Small & Luster, 1994).

Onset of sexual activity in teens differs according to ethnic orientation, especially as indicated by out-of-wedlock births. For example, according to the National Center for Health Statistics (2001), Hispanic American, African American, and Native American teenagers age 15–19 have higher birthrates than do Euro-Americans or Asian Americans (though overall births to teens have declined in the past several years). However, ethnicity may not be the sole factor (Adams, Gullotta, & Markstrom-Adams, 1994). As socioeconomic status decreases, sexual activity has been found to increase. Teens from single-parent families report a higher incidence of sexual activity; those who attend church, do well in school, and are on academic rather than vocational tracks report lower activity. Thus, other factors usually linked with ethnic orientation, in addition to possibly greater peer affiliation, could explain the ethnic differences found in the onset of sexual activity.

In the United States, adolescents receive information on sex and sexuality from parents, school, the media, and peers (Katchadourian, 1990; Thornburg, 1981). Topics such as love, contraception, ejaculation, homosexuality, intercourse, masturbation, petting, and prostitution are discussed with peers. Schools provide information on topics such as abstinence, sexually transmitted diseases, menstruation, semen production, and pregnancy. Parents transmit their attitudes about sex, love, and marriage. The media present the excitement of sex without the consequences. Thus, knowledge about sexual behavior apparently comes from peers and the media, whereas knowledge about the mechanics of reproduction apparently comes from parents and schools.

Regarding the danger of sexually transmitted diseases and the consequences of teen pregnancy, adults need to be "tuned in" to the role that peers and other socializing agents play in sex education. They need to talk to their children before they reach puberty about love, marriage, sex, and reproduction, and they need to communicate throughout adolescence, being "askable," available, and willing to answer questions.

ACHIEVING PERSONAL INDEPENDENCE AND IDENTITY

As discussed previously, peer groups enable children to become increasingly independent of adults. "Individuals juggle different and often conflicting images of self between the childish self shown to their families and the maturing self shown to their peers" (Adler & Adler, 1998, p. 198). In addition, as children grow older, peers become an increasingly important source of social support (Belle, 1989). **Social support** refers to the resources (tangible, intellectual, social, emotional) provided by others in times of need. Tangible support includes sharing toys, clothes, and

A place secluded from adults allows children to experiment with different roles, behaviors, and interactions.

money; intellectual support includes giving information or advice; social support involves companionship; emotional support involves listening and empathy.

Children develop their identities through meaningful interactions and accomplishments in the peer group. Children begin to view the peer group as a reference group beginning at about age 7 or 8 and increasing through adolescence (Levine & Levine, 1996). Specifically:

- Peers provide validation for the self: "Do you like my hair?" or "C'mon, let's play ball," or "I have a secret to tell you."
- Peers provide encouragement to try out new things: "I'll join Girl Scouts if you will too," or "Do you want to go camping with me and my dad?"
- Peers provide opportunities for comparison: "I beat Sam in the race," or "Sally made the team, but I didn't."
- Peers enable self-disclosure. Children are more likely to disclose their innermost feelings to trusted friends than to adults (Parker & Gottman, 1989): "I'm in love with Brad; I let him French kiss me."
- Peers provide identity: "I want to be a 'popular' when I go to high school next year."

In a study of high-risk adolescents (Ungar, 2000), the participating youths indicated that the adoption of the behavior and appearance of peers was a consciously employed strategy to enhance personal and social power. Identification with the peer group enabled them to avoid feelings of alienation, especially if there were family problems, in that peers served as a source of support. Peer groups were described by the participants as a means to assert both individual and collective identities. In other words, peer influence was bidirectional in that the members shaped the group and the group, in turn, shaped the members.

Chronosystem Influences on the Peer Group: Play/Activities

Chronosystem influences on the peer group involve changes in structure, activities, and relationships as peers grow and develop psychologically, socially, and cognitively. Because child-initiated play is the main activity that occurs in peer groups, it is discussed first; adult-initiated play is examined later.

THE SIGNIFICANCE AND DEVELOPMENT OF PLAY

"**Play** is behavior that is enjoyed for its own sake" (Evans & McCandless, 1978, p. 110). Play is significant to development for many reasons. Play, according to Piaget (1962), is the way children learn about their environment because its interactive nature promotes the construction of knowledge. Vygotsky (1978) and Berk and Winsler (1995) saw play as an imaginary situation governed by social rules. Play contributes to development in that it enables children to separate thought from actions and objects, and also enables them to move from impulsive activity to planned goals and self-regulation (instead of taking a desired toy, the child asks permission to play with it). Anna Freud (1968) viewed play as an acceptable way to express emotions and impulses. Groos (1901) described play as a way for children to practice skills necessary for adult life. These various functions of play enable therapists and educators to learn what children feel and understand by observing their play activities.

Years ago, in a classic study, Parten (1932) examined the developmental changes in children's social play according to types of social interactions. On the basis of observations of nursery school children at "free play," she described the following stages, or forms, of play, which are still applicable today:

- *Stage 1: Solitary.* Children play alone and independently, concentrating on the activity rather than on other children who may be nearby. Solitary play is typical of infants and toddlers.
- *Stage 2: Onlooker.* Children watch other children playing and perhaps initiate conversations. Though there is no actual engagement in the play being observed, children are definitely involved as a spectator. Two-year-olds engage in a considerable amount of onlooker play.
- *Stage 3: Parallel.* Children play alone, but with toys like those that other children are using or in a manner that mimics the behavior of others. Parallel play is common among 2- and 3-year-olds but diminishes as they get older.
- *Stage 4: Associative.* Children interact socially and communicate, but with little or no organization. They engage in play activities similar to those of other children; however, the children appear to be more interested in being associated with each other than in the tasks at hand. Associative play is common among 3- and, especially, 4-year-olds.
- *Stage 5: Cooperative.* Children interact in groups. The activity is organized, and the group has a purpose—for example, building a fort, playing "store," or playing baseball. Cooperative play is the prototype for the games of middle childhood. Cooperative play begins to be exhibited by 4- and 5-year-olds.

Contemporary research shows that these play forms emerge in the order suggested by Parten, but earlier forms may coexist with later forms, rather than being

These children are engaged in parallel play; they enjoy playing next to each other while engaged in a similar activity, but true interaction doesn't take place.

replaced by them (Howes & Matheson, 1992). However, the complexity of the form does change with age (Rubin & Coplan, 1992). Children will combine *type* of play with what Parten classified as *stage* of play. For example, when children pretend, they may do it solitarily or cooperatively (Hughes, 1998).

Sutton-Smith (1971) categorized play by type of activity:

- *Imitative.* During the first year of life, babies imitate the parents. In the second year, they put together parts of acts already imitated or observed in new combinations. In the third year, children imitate whole roles, such as mother or father. Between age 4 and 6, imitative social play tends to be characterized by one child acting as a central person and the others filling satellite roles, with children taking turns and alternating the roles, with all the children doing much the same thing at the same time.

- *Exploratory.* In the first year, babies explore—touching, tasting, and manipulating. In the second year, children also empty, fill, insert, put in and out, pull, stack, and roll. In the third year, they arrange, heap, combine, transfer, sort, and spread. Novel manipulations—of objects or of words—are a source of delight.

- *Testing.* In many types of play, children are actually testing themselves. During the second year, children test their motor skills—pulling wagons, lifting objects, climbing, running, and jumping. As children get older, they test themselves in games, competing with others to measure their skills, both physical and intellectual. They also test their emotions, such as fear and anger.

- *Model-building.* About age 4, model-building play becomes explicit, with blocks organized into buildings, trucks into highway traffic, and dishes into tea parties. Children begin to put elements of their experiences together in unique ways.

As can be seen, children's play becomes more complex and interactive with age. The increasingly social nature of their play requires a combination of physical/motor, interpersonal, and cognitive skills. Through play, children discover their capacities, exploring and testing their physical and mental abilities against their own standards and in comparison to others. Children often issue a challenge merely to see if they can make their bodies and minds do what they want them to: "I bet I can climb to the top of that tree"; or "I can figure out that puzzle in five minutes!"

Young children often engage in rough-and-tumble play—fighting, wrestling, and/or chasing. It is viewed more as "mock" aggression than "real" aggression (Hughes, 1998). Children in many cultures exhibit such behavior, as do young animals, which suggests that it may have evolutionary survival roots.

A common type of pretend play among young children is "superhero/heroine play" (Kostelnik, Whiren, & Stein, 1986). Superheroes and superheroines emerged in radio, comics, movies, and television. Examples include Buck Rogers (1920s), Superman and Batman (1930s), Wonder Woman (1940s), Captain Video (1950s), Captain Kirk (1960s), Luke Skywalker and Princess Leia (1970s), He-Man (1980s), Ninja Turtles and Power Rangers (1990s), and Spiderman and Catwoman (2000s). What supercharacters have in common is that they possess powers children wish they themselves had: They can fly, swim under water, change the shape of their bodies, and overcome all obstacles they may encounter. In other words, they are in control—no one tells them what to do, they know what is right, and they have respect from and approval of others. Unfortunately, in this kind of play, some children exert too much control, intimidating others and causing hurt feelings.

Superhero/heroine play allows children to experience power and prestige unavailable to them in their daily lives. It also provides them with concrete models whose behavior is easy to emulate, unlike real-life models, whose behavior is often too ambiguous or complex for children to figure out. Finally, it gives children a chance to experience concretely abstract values such as honor, justice, courage, honesty, and mercy. Although some preschools ban superhero/heroine play because it usually involves aggression, others use it to encourage children to be creative rather than imitative—for example, "How would Darth Vader fix that broken chair?" (Levin, 1998).

INFANT/TODDLER PEER ACTIVITIES (BIRTH TO AGE 2)

Peer groups emerge early in children's lives, although the timing varies according to the family situation, the availability of age mates, and their own temperament and social competence (Ladd, 1999; Parke, 1990). Research suggests that peer sociability is influenced by relationships with caregivers. When caregiving is sensitive and responsive, babies learn how to send and interpret emotional cues, which carries over to peer relationships (Mize & Pettit, 1997; Vandell & Mueller, 1995).

Observations of babies in institutions have shown that even at 2 months babies are oriented toward the movements of babies in adjoining cribs (Bridges, 1933). Between 6 and 8 months, babies look at and sometimes touch each other; between 9 and 13 months, they may fight, mainly over toys (Hay, 1985; Vincze, 1971). It has also been found that during the second year toddlers interact positively with peers, once conflicts over toys have been resolved (Hughes, 1998; Rubenstein & Howes, 1976). They imitate each other (Asendorpf & Baudoniere, 1993) and show responsiveness (Howes, 1988).

Children become increasingly able to empathize with others—first on an emotional level and then on a behavioral one. For example, it has been found that, by the end of the first year, babies often cry when they observe another baby crying; by the middle of the second year, they pat or hug the crying baby; and by the end of the second year, they offer specific kinds of help, like a toy or a Band-Aid (Saarni, Mumme, & Campos, 1998). At this time, they also begin to empathize cognitively. For example, Zahn-Waxler and Radke-Yarrow (1990) and Zahn-Waxler, Radke-Yarrow, Wagner, and Chapman (1992) showed that during the second year children's responses to distress of others become increasingly differentiated and their ability to comfort increasingly effective. They are more likely to empathize with family and friends than with strangers and to verbalize their empathy and respond sensitively: "Please don't cry; I'll let you play with my doll."

EARLY CHILDHOOD PEER ACTIVITIES (AGE 2–5)

From age 2 to age 5, peer interactions increase and become more complex (Rubin, Bukowski, & Parker, 1998). Sometime about age 3 or 4, children begin to enjoy playing in groups—at first, usually on an informal and transitory basis (Howes, 1988). Young children, however, are limited in their friends. Playmates come from the immediate neighborhood or from school if parents are willing to chauffeur or have friends over.

Successful social relationships depend on the ability of one person to take the point of view of another, the ability to empathize, and the ability to communicate. Generally, children under age 3 not only cannot take another's point of view or empathize but also lack the skills for effective two-way communication. Even though some children under age 3 do exhibit prosocial behaviors, such as empathy, they also exhibit antisocial behaviors, such as selfishness and aggressiveness. According to Dunn (1988), children begin to exhibit social understanding by about 18 months, in the family setting. They must then have experiences with peers to implement their understanding of social situations effectively.

Developmental advances in cognition and language enable preschoolers to engage in increasingly complex social interactions. They participate in more cooperative ventures, but they also exhibit more aggression. They direct more speech toward their peers as well (Rubin, Bukowski, & Parker, 1998).

MIDDLE CHILDHOOD/PREADOLESCENT PEER ACTIVITIES (AGE 6–12)

In the middle years, social interactions involving peers increase from approximately 10 percent for 2-year-olds to more than 30 percent for 6- to 12-year-olds. The remainder is spent with siblings, parents, and other adults (Rubin, Bukowski, & Parker, 1998). The settings of peer interaction also change during the middle years from supervised (home and preschool) to more unsupervised (neighborhood).

As children reach school age, they spend more time hanging out informally—talking, teasing, roughhousing, and bike riding. But they also often move spontaneously into group games, which involve the development of skill, understanding, and acceptance of rules, and the ability to cooperate as well as compete.

As children's physical and mental capacities mature and their interests, develop, the quality of their games changes. The games tend to reflect the culture and are apt to be more gender specific (Best, 1983; Hughes, 1998; Sutton-Smith, 1972). For example, girls traditionally played jump rope, hopscotch, dolls, and house or school; boys played baseball or football, cars and airplanes, chase, and action heroes. According to Sutton-Smith (1972), games involving verbal and rhythmic

In this soccer game, some girls seem to be enjoying themselves more than others.

content, such as guessing games, were played predominantly by girls, whereas physical games and organized sports were played mostly by boys. Chasing and teasing games are popular with both genders.

Game patterns change with cognitive development (Hughes, 1998), as children become more capable of handling complex rules and strategies. According to Sutton-Smith (1972), children age 6–9 enjoy simple games with dramatic content, while older children like games requiring strategy, such as checkers or chess, as well as organized team sports.

Games also change with children's psychological development. Sutton-Smith (1972) pointed out that in younger children's games, such as Simon says or giant steps, the person who is "it," operating from a home base, is safe and has power to control the moves of the others. The structure of these games provides a nonthreatening opportunity for children to venture into a leadership role. From about age 10 on, the games enjoyed involve a central figure who is vulnerable to attack by others who seek the leadership role (king of the castle). Older children also enjoy competitive games, in which one person wins and the others are defeated, because these types of games offer the experience of competence.

Children's games reflect the culture in which they live. For example, according to Parker (1984), competitive games, such as soccer, basketball, and football, offer practice in territorial invasion, and card games offer practice in bluffing and calculating odds. All games involve memory, manipulation, and strategizing. Games thus offer opportunities for children to practice skills they will need in adult life (Hughes, 1998).

Today, children generally spend less time in spontaneously organized play (stickball, hide-and-seek, marbles, jacks) than they did a generation or two ago, and more time on computer and video games. Likewise, the sandlot versions of baseball and football have given way, for many children, to organized sports supervised by adults, such as Little League or soccer. One reason is safety; parents fear letting their children play unsupervised because of traffic, crime, and kidnapping issues. Another reason is to provide structured time after school, especially when both parents are employed. Although children gain many physical, cognitive, and social skills from adult-organized play, they are getting fewer opportunities to experience developing their own rules and enforcing them with their peers.

ADOLESCENT PEER ACTIVITIES (AGE 13 AND UP)

Adolescents like to "hang-out"—talk, watch TV, listen to music, play video games, be seen, see who else is "hanging" with whom, wait for something to happen (Jaffe, 1998). When not engaged in school, athletic, or community activities, adolescents spend a lot of time working on their appearance—clothing, make-up, jewelry, body art—and connecting with friends via pagers, cell phones, and the Internet. In early adolescence, most activities occur with same-sex peers, whereas in later adolescence, activities that attract and include members of the opposite sex are favored, such as parties, sporting events, and concerts.

Peer Group Interaction

The relationships children form when interacting with peers, as well as the reasons some children are successful in making friends, vary based on a variety of factors.

DEVELOPMENT OF FRIENDSHIP

Like the activities children engage in as they develop, their social relationships and friendships become more complex and interactive with age.

Toddlerhood to Early Childhood

Howes (1988) studied the social interactions and friendship formations of young children in a child care setting. Although young children's social competence is limited by their cognitive development, early experience with peers seems to enhance interaction skills. She found that toddlers age 1–2 differentiated friends among available playmates. These friendships were marked by emotional responsiveness (happiness in seeing each other or comforting in times of stress). Children age 2–3 were able to distinguish between the emotional and play components of friendship by approaching different peers when in need of comfort and when wanting to run or wrestle.

Selman and Selman (1979) interviewed more than 250 individuals between the ages of 3 and 45 to get a developmental perspective on friendship patterns. They delineated the following five stages:

1. Momentary playmateship—early childhood (4 years)
2. One-way assistance—early to middle childhood (4–9 years)
3. Two-way, fair-weather cooperation—middle childhood (6–12 years)
4. Intimate, mutually shared relationships—middle childhood to adolescence (9–15 years)
5. Autonomous interdependent friendships—adolescence to adulthood (12 years and up)

Early Childhood

Most children under age 4 and some older ones are in the first stage—momentary playmateship. They are unable to consider the viewpoint of another person and can think only about what they want from the friendship. Friends are defined by how close they live: "He's my friend; he lives next door." Or they are defined by their material possessions: "She's my friend; she has a doll house and a swing set."

Early to Middle Childhood

The second stage is one-way assistance. Children age 4–9 are more capable of telling the difference between their own perspectives and those of others. However, friendship is based on whether someone does what the child wants that person to do: "He's not my friend anymore; he didn't want to play cars." Youniss and Volpe (1978), in a study of the friendships of children age 6–14, found that the 6- and 7-year-olds thought of friendship in terms of playing together and sharing material goods: "She plays dress-up with me," or "She always shares her candy with me."

Middle Childhood

In the third stage—two-way, fair-weather cooperation—children age 6–12 acknowledge that friendship involves give-and-take. However, they see friendship as serving individual interests rather than promoting a common interest: "We are friends. We do things for each other." Youniss and Volpe (1978) found that 9- and 10-year-olds regard friends as those who share with one another: "A friend is someone who plays with you when you don't have anyone else to play with." At this age, children emphasize similarities between friends, as well as equalities and reciprocities: "We all like to collect baseball cards. We trade them and give doubles to our friends who are missing those. No one brags." These children are beginning to recognize that friendship is based on getting along—sharing interests, ideas, and feelings.

Middle Childhood to Adolescence

The fourth stage is one of intimate, mutually shared relationships. Children age 9–15 are able to view friendship as an entity in itself. An ongoing, committed relationship that incorporates more than merely doing things for each other; friendship now tends to be treasured for its own sake and may involve possessiveness and jealousy: "She is my best friend. How can she go to the movies with Susan?" Youniss and Volpe (1978) reported that the 12- and 13-year-olds in their study carried the earlier principles of equality and reciprocity further: "If someone picks on me, my friend helps me," or "My friend does not leave me to go off with some other kids."

Adolescence to Adulthood

Finally, there is the stage of autonomous interdependent friendships. About age 12, children are capable of respecting their friends' needs for both dependency and autonomy: "We like to do most things together, and we talk about our problems, but sometimes Jason just likes to be by himself. I don't mind."

Are there gender differences in friendships? Generally, girls refer to best friends as someone they can have an intimate conversation with and who is "faithful" more than do boys; boys refer more to the companionship nature of best friends and the sharing of activities (Lever, 1976; Maccoby, 1990, 2000).

Is there a link between the ability to make friends in childhood and emotional adjustment in adulthood? A review of the literature on peer relationships verifies a link between problematic childhood peer interactions and adjustment difficulties in adolescence and adulthood (Bagwell, Newcomb, & Bukowski, 2000; Kupersmidt, Coie, & Dodge, 1990). In the next section, we look at some reasons for peer acceptance and rejection, as well as ways to help children be more successful in making friends. Generally, having friends and being accepted by the peer group are related in that children who are well liked by peers have many opportunities to make friends. However, not all children who are rejected by the peer group lack friends. Children who are rejected by the group but who have at least one friend have fewer problems later in life than do those who are rejected and also have no friends (Howes, 1988; Rubin, Bukowski, & Parker, 1998).

ACCEPTANCE/NEGLECT/REJECTION BY PEERS

The significance of being accepted, neglected, or rejected by peers came to the attention of the public in 1999 when two rejected adolescents shot 12 students and a teacher at Columbine High School in Colorado. Apparently, the athletes who repeatedly teased them were the targets for retaliation. Which children are readily accepted by the group? According to several studies (Asher, Gottman, & Oden, 1977; Dodge, 1983; Hartup, 1983; Rubin, Bukowski, & Parker, 1998), children's acceptance by peers and successful interactions with them depend on their willingness and ability to cooperate and interact positively with others. Children who are popular with their peers tend to be healthy and vigorous, capable of initiative, and well poised. They are also adaptable and conforming, as well as dependable, affectionate, and considerate.

Acting naturally, being happy, showing enthusiasm and concern for others, and demonstrating self-confidence but not conceit are other characteristics that lead to popularity (Hartup, 1983; Rubin, Bukowski, & Parker, 1998). Certain physical and intellectual factors can also affect children's popularity. Studies have shown that, on average, children who are physically attractive are more popular than those who are not (Adams & Crane, 1980; Adler & Adler, 1998; Ritts, Patterson, & Tubbs, 1992). In a study of 6- to 10-year-old boys (Hartup, 1983), the boys with muscular physiques were more popular than boys who were skinny or plump; perhaps this correlates with consistent findings that athletic ability is related to popularity (Adler & Alder, 1998; Coleman, 1961). Children who are more intelligent have been found to be more popular than those who are less intelligent (Berndt, 1983; Rubin, Bukowski, & Parker, 1998). Other studies have shown that the ability to use language and communicate ideas effectively promotes peer acceptance (Gottman, Gonso, & Rasmussen, 1975; Kemple, 1991). In general, popular children approach others in a friendly manner, respond appropriately to communications interpreting emotional states correctly, and are generous with praise and expressions of approval.

Prosocial behavior (being empathetic, cooperative, helpful) has been shown to be the most consistent correlate of peer group acceptance (Wentzel & Erdley, 1993). Socialization of pro- and antisocial behavior is discussed more thoroughly in Chapter 12.

Family interaction patterns play a role in children's successful integration into the group (Hartup, 1989, 1996). In the family, children learn to express and interpret various emotions, such as pleasure, displeasure, attachment, and distancing. Children also learn to respond to such emotional expressions to regulate their behavior according to family requirements. Thus, social competence, which leads to peer acceptance, begins in the family.

Table 8.1

Characteristics of Children Accepted or Neglected/Rejected by Peers

ACCEPTED	NEGLECTED/REJECTED
Cooperative	Uncooperative
Positive in interactions	Negative interactions
Capable of initiating interaction	Incapable of initiating interaction
Adaptable and conforming	Socially unskilled
Capable of understanding emotional expressions	Incapable of understanding emotional expressions
Concerned with others	Unconcerned with others
Ability to communicate effectively	Inability to communicate effectively
Happy	Whiny
Dependable	Undependable
Affectionate	Withdrawn
Considerate	Inconsiderate
Poised	Disruptive
Generous with praise	Miserly with praise
Intelligent	"Different" academically
Friendly	Unfriendly
Self-confident (not conceited)	Bossy
Physically attractive	"Different" physically, behaviorally
Athletic	Poor sport
Prosocial	Antisocial
Positive social reputation	Negative social reputation

Which children are neglected or rejected by the group? The shifts in children's likes and dislikes causes almost every school-age child to feel neglected or rejected at some point by other children. The child not asked to play, not chosen for the team, not invited to the party, or excluded from the club feels that his or her world has been shattered. Children may be neglected or rejected due to their shyness or lack of social skills. Children who do not know how to initiate a friendship, who are withdrawn, who misinterpret others' emotional states, who have difficulty communicating, who are bossy, who are disruptive in class, and/or who rarely praise their peers are not readily accepted by the group. Also, children who are poor losers, who cheat or whine, and/or who are aggressive are not welcome in most children's groups. Antisocial behavior is the most consistent correlate of peer rejection (Coie & Cillessen, 1993; Coie, Dodge, & Kupersmidt, 1990). Table 8.1 summarizes the characteristics of children accepted, neglected, and rejected by peers.

Sometimes children are rejected for reasons they cannot change or even understand. For example, *Blubber,* by best-selling author Judy Blume (1974), is about an overweight girl who is the brunt of her fifth-grade classmates' teasing and scapegoating: "She won't need a coat this winter; she's got her blubber to keep her warm." Sometimes children are teased and ostracized because they are different physically (weight, height, skin color), behaviorally (accent, speech impediment, style of dress, religious preference), or academically (learning disabled, gifted); they may even be shunned because of their names (Hartup, 1983; Langlois, 1986; Sandstrom & Coie, 1999).

EXAMPLE A 9-year-old boy named Alfonse wrote a letter to Senator Alfonse D'Amato (R-N.Y.), asking him how he got his name. The boy couldn't ask his father why he was named Alfonse, because his father had died. He wrote that he hated his name because the kids at school joked about it. D'Amato wrote back that the name

Alfonse means "prepared for battle," and when you're young, "you'd better be." D'Amato also wrote that when he asked his father why he was named Alfonse, his father replied, "Son, your Uncle Alfonse was a very wealthy man, and that's how we got the down payment on the house." The senator recommended that young Alfonse tell his friends to call him Al (*Los Angeles Times,* 1982).

Family problems can have damaging effects on children's peer relations (Baker, Barthelemy, & Kurdek, 1993; Burton, 1985; Ladd, 1999). For example, children whose parents are separated or divorced may act out feelings of anger and fear at school, eliciting rejection from peers in the process. Children who have a parent who is an alcoholic may avoid making close friends and be reluctant to bring friends home. Likewise, children who are abused or whose parents are homosexual, or whose parents have a disability or health impairment, may isolate themselves from others to avoid being judged by others.

Although many studies suggest that children's behavior and characteristics contribute to how well liked they are by peers, according to Kemple (1991), it is important to consider the role that peers play in maintaining children's level of social acceptance. Once a child establishes a reputation as someone who is fun to play with, acceptance is easy; in contrast, for a child who has a reputation for being unpleasant, acceptance is difficult.

In sum, factors linked to acceptance (initiating and maintaining a relationship) enable group belonging; factors linked to neglect and rejection (being unsociable, disruptive, or aggressive) make it difficult to belong to a group. Dodge and others (Coie & Dodge, 1998; Dodge, 1986) propose that these factors are influenced by how children cognitively process social information, including their ability to interpret stimuli, remember, and respond.

PEER SOCIOTHERAPY

Techniques known collectively as **sociometry** have been developed to measure patterns of acceptance, neglect, and rejection among members of a group. Sociometry originally was used in the classroom but is now widely applied in other settings, such as recreational facilities, the workplace, and prison. Contemporary researchers typically use sociometry to identify the extent to which children prefer to be with certain peers (Cillesen & Bukowski, 2000; Parkhurst & Asher, 1992).

A sociometric rating is easy to determine; it involves asking children questions anonymously about each other and tabulating the results. Examples include "Who is your best friend?" "With whom would you prefer and not prefer to work on a project?" and "With whom would you share a secret?" For preschoolers, it can be implemented by showing each child photographs of classmates and asking which ones he or she likes and dislikes playing with. Children with the most "liked" votes are popular; the ones with the most "disliked" votes are neglected or rejected.

Sociometric results can help adults facilitate the inclusion of neglected or rejected children into the group. By careful observations, adults can assess in which area the neglected or rejected child needs intervention (Kemple, 1991)—(1) social (Does the child cooperate? share? boast?), (2) emotional (Does the child interpret other's emotions correctly? empathize?), (3) lingual (Does the child make relevant responses to peers' communications? communicate desires clearly?), or (4) physical (Does the child resort to aggression to resolve conflicts?). Adults can choose appropriate intervention strategies.

Improving Children's Social Skills

By monitoring children's interactions, adults will enable them to do the following:

1. *Model:*
   a. Observe how others interact positively.
   b. Imitate behaviors and communications that were successful in promoting friendship.
2. *Participate:*
   a. Get involved with others.
   b. Get started on an activity, project, or game.
   c. Pay attention to the activity.
   d. Try to do your best.
   e. Help someone who is younger.
3. *Cooperate:*
   a. Take turns.
   b. Share the game, materials, or props.
   c. Make suggestions if there's a problem.
   d. Work out a mutually agreeable alternative if there is disagreement about the rules.
4. *Communicate:*
   a. Talk with others.
   b. Say things about the activity or about yourself.
   c. Ask a question about the activity.
   d. Ask a question about the other person.
   e. Listen when the other person talks.
   f. Look at the other person to see how he or she is doing.
5. *Validate and support:*
   a. Give some attention to the other person.
   b. Say something nice when the other person does well.
   c. Smile.
   d. Have fun.
   e. Offer help or suggestions when needed.

Selman and Selman's (1979) developmental stages of friendship have been used in **sociotherapy,** an intervention to enable children who have trouble making and keeping friends learn to relate to others. By assessing their levels of social relationships with others, therapists or teachers can sometimes help children to move on to the next developmental level.

Children who have difficulty making friends can be helped by giving them a chance to play with younger children. Some researchers (Bullock, 1992; Howes, 1988) have found that socially withdrawn preschoolers become more sociable after they have had a chance to play, one on one, with children a year or two younger than them during play sessions. The researchers conclude that being with younger children gives socially withdrawn children a chance to be assertive in initiating and directing activity. Once they experience success with younger children, they are better able to interact with children their own age.

Children who have difficulty reading other children's social cues may benefit from observing others who interact successfully. This can be done in real situations with an adult coach, or by watching a videotape, or by viewing a puppet show (Bullock, 1992).

Also, having a friend in a new situation, such as school, or in a stressful situation, such as a divorce, helps children cope with and better adjust to what is going on (Ladd, 1990, 1999). This is another reason it is important to help children to make friends.

In order to help children who are not readily accepted by their peers get along better, Oden and Asher (1977) identified four categories of social skills, based on the research on popularity: (1) participation (playing with others, paying attention), (2) communication (talking and listening), (3) cooperation (taking turns, sharing), and (4) validation support (offering encouragement or help). A group of unpopular school-age children were coached on these specific skills. The coaching sessions involved demonstration (instruction and role modeling), discussion (explanation and feedback), and reinforcement of desired behavior (behavior modification). A year later, the group of unpopular children who were coached showed more sociability toward and acceptance by peers than the control group of unpopular children who were not coached. Coaching strategies have been employed successfully with preschool and school-age children (Mize & Ladd, 1990).

According to another study (Sandstrom & Coie, 1999), elementary school children who were initially rejected could improve their statuses with peers by participating in extracurricular activities and by having their parents monitor their social interactions (arranging for play with cooperative peers, intervening in conflicts).

How Teachers Can Help Rejected Children Gain Acceptance

1. *Enable compromise.* For children to effectively implement newly learned social skills in the classroom, teachers must be able to offer on-the-spot guidance in various situations (Kemple, 1991). For example, in conflict situations, the teacher serves as a mediator, encouraging each child to voice his or her perspective and generate potential solutions leading to compromise (Bullock, 1992; Stein & Kostelnick, 1984).

2. *Enable communication.* Teachers can also provide on-the-spot guidance to help with communication patterns: "Joey, I don't think Jackson understands why you don't want to play fire engines; can you tell him why? Maybe you can say what you can both do together."

3. *Enable interpretation.* Teachers can guide children who have difficulty interpreting others' emotional states; "Look at Sarah's face; do you think she likes it when you push her?" Sometimes teachers might have to explain children's behavior to the group in order to facilitate acceptance. For example, a child who makes fun of a group playing a game may be doing so in order to be included: "I think Trey is trying to figure out how he can be an ambulance driver; if you don't need another one, maybe he can be the emergency room doctor."

4. *Enable family involvement.* Teachers' attempts to help disliked children find a niche in the peer group may sometimes be more successful if the children's families are involved (Sandstrom & Coie, 1999). Teachers can discuss skills being taught and request parents' support, as well as that of siblings and neighborhood peers (Kemple, 1991).

Peer Group Dynamics and Social Hierarchies

The peer group is a microsystem with dynamic roles and relationships impacting its participants. Unlike the microsystems of family, school, and community, the peer group generally is unencumbered by adult guidance. The peer group implements informal social mechanisms through which children create norms, statuses, and alliances; establish consequences; and develop feelings about themselves (Thompson, Cohen, & Grace 2002). These social mechanisms were illustrated in the discussion of *Lord of the Flies* and *Survivor* in the prologue.

INCLUSION AND EXCLUSION

According to Adler and Adler (1998), who studied groups of children age 8–12 in a predominantly White, middle-class community for 8 years, dynamics in peer cliques included techniques of inclusion (recruitment of new members, treatment of "wannabes," friendship realignment, ingratiation) and of exclusion (out-group and in-group subjugation, compliance, stigmatization, expulsion).

Recruitment of new members into a clique was usually by invitation—if a member met and liked someone, that individual was afforded "probationary" status until the other members agreed to include him or her. "Wannabes" sometimes gained entry by doing nice things for members of the clique or by doing something to gain their respect, such as helping the school team win. However, shifts in status and power in the hierarchical structure of the clique caused friendship loyalties to be compromised. Higher-status members often co-opted lower-status members to maintain their popularity. Lower-status members frequently abandoned their lower-status friends in order to gain favor with a higher-status member, thereby moving up in the social hierarchy. Ingratiation, or currying favors with clique members, was directed both upward, toward higher-status peers (for example, adulation), and downward, toward lower-status peers (for example, domination).

Out-group subjugation, such as teasing, picking on, and being mean to those outside the clique, served to solidify the cohesiveness of the group and assure the strength of the group's position relative to other groups. In-group subjugation occurred via high-level insiders harassing or ridiculing low-level insiders to maintain dominance. Compliance with leaders' or high-status members' wishes was manifested by lower-status members to gain favor. Stigmatization, or "branding" a member as a tattletale, cheat, crybaby, or whatever, was served as a means of disempowerment. Expulsion, or being cast out of the group permanently, occurred when a member engaged in a serious infraction of the group's rules or stood up for his or her rights against dominant members.

EXAMPLE Lloyd and Stuart were friends. They lived around the corner from each other and attended the same school. In first and second grade, they played GI Joe at recess and Nintendo games after school, sometimes spending the night at each other's houses. In third grade, a new boy, Brad, moved into the neighborhood. Brad invited Lloyd to go fishing with him and his dad, but Stuart was not invited. Lloyd went and, excited by the experience, began to collect "flies," the colorful lures placed on the end of a hook to catch fish. Brad liked to challenge the other kids to play games, offering his duplicate flies as prizes. The other kids were attracted to the decorative feathers, threads, and beads of the lures. Soon, Brad had co-opted several peers into following his lead in other activities.

Meanwhile, Stuart joined a Little League team and badgered Lloyd to try out. Lloyd did so after being pressured by his parents. He tried to be as coordinated as his team-mates, but they were obviously more physically advanced. Stuart kept encouraging him to practice.

Brad did not like Stuart, and he especially did not like sharing his friend, Lloyd. Brad began to tell his new cohorts at school negative things about Stuart: "Stuart won't go fishing because he's afraid of the water," and "He's afraid a shark will come and get him," and "Stuart is a fag; he has to play baseball to cover it up."

As Brad gave away more of his flies to select friends, they began to band together to tease Stuart and solidify their standing with Brad. Lloyd was faced with a dilemma: Abandon his long-time friend and retain high status with his new friend, or stick by his old friend and be ostracized by the other kids.

BULLIES/VICTIMS

An extreme example of the dynamics and social hierarchies occurring in peer groups involves bullies and victims. Olweus (1993) has extensively studied bullies and their victims at school. He defines victimization by bullies as being "exposed, repeatedly and over time, to negative actions on the part of one or more other students." Negative actions, or harassment, include threatening, taunting, teasing, name calling, and making faces or dirty gestures, as well as hitting, kicking, pinching, and physically restraining others.

Bullies tend to share certain characteristics. For example, they have domination needs—that is, the need to feel powerful and superior. Usually physically stronger than their peers, they also are impulsive and easily angered and frustrated. Furthermore, they generally are oppositional, defiant, and aggressive; not surprisingly, then, they have difficulty adhering to rules. Finally, they usually show little empathy toward others and engage in antisocial behavior. However, they tend to have a relatively high self-concept.

Victims tend to share certain characteristics as well. For example, they usually are physically weaker than their peers and are in poor physical condition. As a consequence, they tend to exhibit fear of being hurt or of hurting themselves. In addition, they generally are cautious, shy, sensitive, quiet, and passive, as well as anxious, insecure, and unhappy. Not surprisingly, then, they tend to have a relatively negative self-concept and have difficulty asserting themselves.

What can be done about bullies and their victims? First, teachers and parents must be aware of the problem and become involved in its solution. This means intervening directly with bullies to end the harassment. It also means establishing clear rules and consequences regarding appropriate behavior, offering training in alternative behavior (such as through role-playing and modeling), and providing cooperative learning experiences. For their part, victims must be the target of interventions as well—learning how

This child is being teased by the group leader.

to alter their negative self-concept, be more assertive, and respond in nonreinforcing ways to threats (for example, through humor or nonattention).

GANGS

Sometimes peer group dynamics can result in negative or antisocial behaviors. Why do peer groups sometimes engage in negative behavior? Peers (or, more specifically, the "wrong crowd") are often blamed for delinquency and substance abuse, but in reality, the single most consistent characteristic of delinquents is lack of support in and socialization by their families (Jackson & McBride, 1985; Rutter, Giller, & Hagell, 1998). Antagonistic relationships between parents are often found in families with antisocial children (Patterson, Reid, & Dishion, 1992; Rutter, 1971). When children's needs are not met in their families, they often turn to their peers. There is also a relationship between peer rejection and delinquency (Bagwell, Coie, Terry, & Lochman, 2000). And delinquent behavior is often socialized by peers (Dishion, McCord, & Poulin, 1999; Goldstein, 1991).

Poor neighborhoods with low-quality schools, limited recreational and employment opportunities, and adult criminal subcultures tend to be predictive of juvenile gang activity (Farrington & Loeber, 2000).

Social change, microsystems (family, school, community) under stress, and consequent lack of support for children tend to be associated with an increase in delinquency rates (National Research Council, 1993). Many young people lack positive adult role models. The gap between the consumerism promoted by the media and the reality of their circumstances may entice young people to turn to delinquency. Personality factors may also contribute to adolescents' delinquency. It is known that those who become delinquent are more likely to be defiant, ambivalent to authority, resentful, hostile, impulsive, and lacking in self-control (Goldstein, 1991; Thompson & Dodder, 1986). Those who get poor grades in school, have been reported for classroom misconduct, and have trouble getting along with other children and with teachers have been shown to possess a greater tendency to delinquency (Ladd & LeSieur, 1995; Landre, Miller, & Porter, 1997). Therefore, the peer group may be the setting in which preexisting antisocial behavior due to family factors, social change, personality characteristics, or noninterest in school is reinforced (Goldstein, 1991; Rubin, Bukowski, & Parker, 1998).

"A **gang** is a group of people who form an allegiance for a common purpose and engage in unlawful or criminal activity" (Jackson & McBride, 1985, p. 20). Gangs are of concern not only because of their antisocial activities but also because of their increasing membership (Goldstein, 1991). Gangs usually consist of males, although there are female gangs. Gang members identify themselves via names, clothes, tattoos, slang, sign language, and graffiti. The problem of gangs is spreading through our society like a plague, with gangs present in neighborhoods and schools, impacting businesses, recreation, and education (Landre, Miller, & Porter, 1997). Gang violence has tragic consequences; gangs deal drugs, steal, maim, and kill, and innocent bystanders are often victims (U.S. Department of Justice, 2000).

What is the appeal of gangs? Gangs offer members companionship, guidance, excitement, and identity (Goldstein, 1991). When a member needs something, the others come to the rescue and provide it (Landre, Miller, & Porter, 1997). Gang members have experienced failure and alienation in their lives. They tend to live in depressed or deprived environments, which their families may be helpless to change. Because they feel they can't accomplish anything individually, gang members band together in order to exercise influence over their lives (Jackson & McBride, 1985).

The homes of gang-oriented children are characterized by either high permissiveness or high punitiveness (Devereaux, 1970). The parents of such peer-oriented children also show less concern and affection, and through such passive neglect, rather than active maltreatment, push their children to look to their peers for support (Condry & Simon, 1974; Ladd & LeSieur, 1995). Youngsters living with both biological parents have been found to be less susceptible to pressure from peers to engage in deviant behavior than youngsters living in single-parent homes or in stepfamilies. Thus, the stability of the home is an important protector against pressure toward deviant behavior (Steinberg, 1987).

Gang members have significantly lower levels of self-esteem than their nongang peers. They also have fewer adult role models in their families and communities than their nongang peers (Wang, 1994).

In sum, sociological forces in the formation of gangs include the following (Jackson & McBride, 1985):

- *Racism.* Gangs are usually made up of members of one race, thereby being a source of identity and support.
- *Socioeconomics.* Gang members usually come from poor families in densely populated areas where there is fierce competition for resources, although there are increasing numbers of gangs from middle-class neighborhoods.
- *Family structure.* Gang members usually come from a family with minimal adult supervision; a mother-headed family; a two-adult family in which the father, stepfather, or boyfriend is a negative role model; or a family that has a gang lineage.
- *Belief system.* Gang members see themselves as victims and blame society for their problems. They also believe that because society hasn't helped them they are justified in "helping" themselves outside of society's rules.

PEER COLLABORATION, TUTORING, AND COUNSELING

Peer group dynamics, often with the help of adults, can result in positive outcomes for participants. Collaboration, tutoring, and counseling all enable peers to be supportive of one another. Peers who collaborate learn to solve problems through consensus. Peers who tutor learn how to analyze and synthesize information for others. Peers who counsel learn how to care for, help, and support others.

According to Piaget (1965), when children interact, they discover that others have opinions and perspectives different from theirs. As a result, they reorganize their cognitive structures to accommodate discrepant information. Thus, Piaget suggested, cognitive development is more likely to result from *conflict* with same-age peers than from interaction with older children and adults (Berk & Winsler, 1995). Vygotsky (1978), in contrast, argued that cognitive development results from *collaboration* with peers. Peer conflict contributes to heightened understanding only if the disagreement is resolved. Vygotsky emphasized the importance of mixed-age groups that provide children with opportunities to interact with more knowledgeable companions and give them a chance to serve as a resource for others. More expert peers can serve as mentors, models, or tutors; novice peers can be apprentices. Adults must guide collaborative activities, teaching social and problem-solving skills and intervening when necessary (Berk & Winsler, 1995).

Peer tutoring is exemplified by inclusion programs in which children with disabilities are assisted by classmates academically and/or socially (Vaughn, Bos, & Schumm, 1997). Peer tutoring provides a zone of proximal development (ZPD), as discussed earlier, in which what children are capable of learning independently is potentially increased by participating with more capable others.

An example of peer counseling is "positive peer culture" or PPC (Vorrath & Brendtro, 1985). PPC involves a group of peers with an adult leader. It is designed to "turn around" negative youth subcultures and mobilize the power of the peer group to foster positive behavior. Individuals are not asked whether they want to *receive* help, but whether they are willing to *give* help. As these persons become of value to others, they experience increased feelings of self-worth (Vorrath & Brendtro, 1985). The underlying belief is that delinquent youths, who are often rebellious and strong-willed, have much to contribute when redirected. Those who have encountered many difficulties in their lives may be in the best position to help others. PPC provides students with what they did not receive from other socializing agents: care and a sense of responsibility—for themselves and others.

EXAMPLE A group home for troubled girls had severe drug-abuse problems. The result of the many attempts to suppress this activity was a cold war between staff and youths. Searches were commonplace, and the atmosphere was restrictive. That was a year ago. Now staff members no longer police the girls for drugs, and the climate of suspicion and intrigue is gone. When a new girl enters the home, her peers confiscate any drugs she may have and tell her, "We don't have to use dope around here." Drug problems are dealt with openly in a helpful, matter-of-fact way. Group members state with strong conviction that when a person has good feelings about herself she no longer needs to get high on drugs.

Mesosystem Influences on the Peer Group

Adults play a significant role in "setting the stage" for peer group experiences. Earlier, the adult role was discussed in terms of providing secure attachments and arranging for friends to get together in the home. According to Steinberg (1996), the neighborhoods in which children live influence whether the peer group has positive or negative effects. Neighborhoods that include parents who are involved in schools, who participate in organized activities for children (sports, arts, scouts), and who monitor their children tend to have children who provide positive peer influences for one another. In contrast, neighborhoods that include parents who are disengaged from school and community activities tend to have children who provide negative peer influences for one another. Thus, parents can influence whether children's peer group experiences are positive or negative by knowing who their children's friends are and by being involved in their activities.

Peer groups linked to and structured by adults include team sports, clubs, Scouts, and church groups. Due to their organization, these groups differ from the informal peer groups (neighborhood or school groups of friends) discussed previously, which are formed and maintained by the children themselves. Whereas child-structured groups are casual and informal, adult-structured groups are purposeful and formal.

Adult-structured and child-structured groups also differ in their socializing influences on children. When adults organize groups, they provide rules, guidelines, or suggestions about appropriate or expected behavior. Adults supply the structure by offering verbal instructions, praise, criticism, and feedback about the activity or the child's performance, or by modeling ways to perform the activity. The structuring of the setting influences the behavior that goes on within it. For example, formal groups organized by adults encourage children to play according to established rules, to be compliant, and to seek guidance and recognition from adults; however, groups organized by children themselves encourage the children to be active and assertive with peers, to take the initiative, and to behave independently (Huston, Carpenter, Atwater, & Johnson, 1986). Studies of preschool children have found that girls prefer more adult-structured groups (Carpenter, Huston, & Holt, 1986; Powlishta, Serbin, & Moller, 1993). A similar pattern of gender differences has been shown to exist for school-age children (Carpenter, 1983; Huston, 1983; Maccoby, 1990, 2000).

Groups structured by adults are also characterized by the different values that are imparted to children. Clubs may be formed at church, at school, or in the community. The church club may serve the purpose of fellowship—getting to know children from similar religious backgrounds. School clubs may provide extracurricular activities for interested children—for example, computer club, chorus, or drama club. Community clubs may be for recreation (the Y) or for character building (Scouts). For instance, the ideology of the Boy and Girl Scouts of America is to foster patriotism, reverence, leadership, and emotional development. Children are encouraged to develop self-reliance by accomplishing certain tasks to earn badges—such as in water safety or cooking.

ADULT-MEDIATED GROUP INTERACTION

How adults mediate, or structure, the social interaction within a peer group—specifically, whether it is competitive or cooperative—influences children's behavior. To illustrate, psychologist Mustaf Sherif (1956) and his colleagues (Sherif, Harvey, White, Hood, & Sherif, 1961) conducted a series of naturalistic classic experiments in which middle-class, White, Protestant boys, age 11, were recruited and sent to a summer camp. He demonstrated that, within a few weeks, two sharply contrasting patterns of behavior in this sample of normal boys could be brought about by adult mediation. The camp was divided into two separate groups of boys (the Rattlers and the Eagles) who did not know each other. The counselors/observers were able to transform each group into a hostile, destructive, antisocial gang by various strategies, such as playing competitive sports, in which winning was all-important, and informing each group that the other group was "the enemy." Then the counselors/observers were able, within a few days, to change each group into cooperative, constructive workers and friends who were concerned about the other members of the community. Various problems at the camp were set up to foster a cooperative spirit. For example, a water line was deliberately broken so that both groups of boys would have to work together to fix it. Another time, the camp truck "broke down" on the way to town for food, and the boys had to help get the engine started.

Several findings emerged from Sherif's (1956) and his colleagues' (Sherif et al., 1961) naturalistic experiments regarding peer group behavior:

- Groups tend to stratify, with some individuals assuming more dominant roles and others more submissive ones.
- Groups develop **norms**—standards that serve to guide and regulate individuals' actions as group members.

- Frustration and competition contribute to hostility between groups.
- Competition between groups fosters cohesiveness within groups.
- Intergroup hostility can often be reduced by setting up a superordinate, or common, goal that requires the mutual efforts of both groups. When overriding goals that are real and important for all concerned need to be achieved, then hostility between groups diminishes.

The significance of these studies of peer group dynamics is that it suggests strategies for enabling children to work together. The findings on cooperation and competition were implemented by a team of researchers at Johns Hopkins University (Johnson & Johnson, 1999; Slavin, Devries, & Hutten, 1975). A team games tournament (TGT) was developed to see if cooperation in a competitive setting would increase academic achievement. In the TGT, four or five children of varying academic ability, gender, and race are put on a team. Individuals compete with individuals who are members of other teams, and each person's game score is added to those of the others on the team to form a team score. Team members cooperate by studying as a group and helping each other prepare for the tournament. The TGT has had positive effects on mathematics achievement in the junior high school, on language arts achievement in elementary school, and, in general, on attitudes toward subject matter and classroom procedures. The TGT has also promoted increases in class solidarity and in helping friendships among girls and boys and among children of differing ethnic backgrounds. In addition, children who succeeded as team members were liked more than when they succeeded as individuals.

ADULT LEADERSHIP STYLES

Groups led by adults can differ markedly in the kind of leadership provided. Leadership style influences socialization, as illustrated by a classic series of studies (Lewin, Lippitt, & White, 1939; Lippitt & White, 1943) that distinguished three kinds of adult leadership and measured their effects on groups of 10-year-old boys. The boys were organized into clubs and worked on such activities as soap carving, mask making, and mural painting. Several kinds of adult leadership were identified:

- *Authoritarian.* Policies, activities, techniques, and delegation of tasks were dictated by the leader. Praise and criticism of the group members' work was subjective: "You are good at that." The leader did not actively participate in the group's activities.
- *Democratic (authoritative).* Policies and activities were determined by group discussion. Techniques and delegation of tasks were presented by the leader in terms of alternatives from which the group members could choose. Praise and criticism were objective: "Your soap carving has a lot of detailed work; it must have taken you a lot of time to do that." The leader participated in the activities.
- *Laissez-faire (permissive).* Policies, activities, techniques, and delegation of tasks were left up to the group members. The leader supplied materials for the projects and was available for help, if requested. Comments about the group members' work were very infrequent. The leader did not participate in the group's activities.

Because each adult in the studies rotated the three leadership styles, differences in the group's behavior were determined to be a function of the style of leadership, rather than the leader's personality. The boys in the groups with authoritarian lead-

ADULT LEADERSHIP STYLE	CHILDREN'S CHARACTERISTICS
Authoritarian	Aggressive or submissive Discontented Competitive
Democratic (authoritative)	High morale Cooperative Self-supporting, cohesive
Laissez-faire (permissive)	Disorganized Frustrated Nonsupporting, fragmented

Table 8.2

Socialization Effects of Leadership Styles
Source: Lewin, Lippott, and White, 1939.

ers became either submissive or aggressive, and they tended to be competitive with one another. They were discontented with the activities and worked less constructively when the leader left the room. The boys in the groups with democratic leaders had high morale. They were involved in their group goals and were cooperative, and they sustained their level of activity even when the leader left the room. The boys in the groups with laissez-faire leaders were disorganized and frustrated. They made efforts to mobilize themselves as a group but were unable to sustain their efforts.

In all three situations, the behavior of the adult set the tone for group effort (see Table 8.2). Within each situation, children received different messages about how to make decisions and work with others toward a goal.

TEAM SPORTS

Sports are "organized interactions of children in competitive and/or cooperative team or individual enjoyable physical activities" (Humphrey, 1993, p. 3). In the United States, sports are not only a major form of recreation but also a means of achieving physical health. Sports are regarded as a way for children to learn leadership skills, loyalty, and other desirable traits, and as valuable training in competitiveness and give-and-take relationships. In addition, organized sports are a vehicle for promoting the development of talent.

Sports are a pervasive part of American culture. Sports lingo—"competition, teamwork, winning the game"—is widely used in the corporate world (Murphy, 1999).

The American attitude toward sports is revealed by the statistics: Over 20 million U.S. children, age 6 and older, play on organized sports teams—over 2.5 million in Little League, more than 1 million in organized football, and the other 17 million in such sports as hockey, soccer, swimming, track, and gymnastics (Poinsett, 1997).

Do all children benefit from the experience? According to Murphy (1999), many do not. Some children do learn a lot about themselves and their capabilities, about their potential for improvement (however modest), about the value of teamwork, about the fun of sports, and about the lifelong importance of physical fitness (Poinsett, 1997). Other children, unfortunately, are humiliated by their experiences in organized sports. Perhaps they are being pushed to succeed by their parents; unable to live up to their parent's expectations, they become discouraged and end up hating the sport or themselves. I remember watching many Little League games while my son was involved. It was not uncommon to hear a father yell to his son from the stands, "You dummy, how could you miss that ball? Wake up!"

> **EXAMPLE** When I was 11 years old, I was on a softball team. I desperately wanted to be the pitcher, but I wasn't chosen. My throwing was accurate, but it wasn't fast enough. The coach put me in centerfield because I was also a good fielder. I was so crushed that I almost quit. What I didn't understand then was that the team already had a good pitcher, but the shortstop made a lot of errors and the right- and leftfielders were daydreamers. The coach's logic was to put me in centerfield because I could catch and throw, and because I could also run fast, I could get to the balls missed by the others. It took me quite a few games to understand that teamwork makes everyone play better because teamwork coordinates all the individual abilities. No matter how good one person on the team is, if the others are not playing well, the team can't win. I wanted to be the pitcher because I wanted to be the star. I learned that stars don't succeed without the support of the cast.

In some cases, coaches place more emphasis on winning than on playing. Winning can mean several things. It can mean self-improvement and a sense of accomplishment when players' performances improve, or it can mean beating the other team. When winning is narrowed down simply to beating the other team, undue pressures are put on children (Galton, 1980; Humphrey, 1993). If children are ridiculed, belittled, or threatened when they make a mistake, or if the coach pays attention only to the better players, then some children are not benefiting from participating on that team. In contrast, if the coach gives extra support to those lacking in confidence, they benefit in more ways than merely improving their athletic skills. Thus, sports can help children develop an attitude of positive thinking and strive to attain goals beyond what they think they can presently do. Coaches need to consider the developmental needs of children and foster an environment based on respect for effort, rather than focusing solely on winning (Murphy, 1999).

> **EXAMPLE** At a gymnastics competition I saw a girl fall off the bar. She was not hurt, but her confidence was shaken. Her coach explained her mistake to her and made her do the routine again correctly even though it would not count for points. The girl took a deep breath, focused, and completed her flip on the bar. Everyone applauded. The girl learned not to give up if perfection was not achieved on the first attempt, and also that effort can be as appreciated by the audience just as much as performance.

Epilogue

Peers are significant socializers. Acceptance by the group influences self-concept, behavior, and values. Rejection by the group can have damaging developmental and real consequences, as exemplified by the killing of Piggy. A desire to be part of the group and have status within helps explain why children conform. Children compete within the group for power and leadership roles; leaders make the rules and manipulate the others, as exemplified by Ralph and the last survivor. Peer group dynamics are powerful influencers on later relationships.

Summary

The peer group is a microsystem in that it comprises relationships, roles, and activities. Peers are a group of equals, usually of the same age, gender, and socioeconomic status, who share the same interests. Experiences with peers enable children to acquire a wide range of skills, attitudes, and behaviors that influence their social adaptation throughout life.

Peer groups are significant because they fill children's needs for belonging and social interaction, as well as promoting a sense of self and personal identity.

The need to belong is first established in the family via attachment. Infants and toddlers who are securely attached are more likely to interact socially with others. Opportunities for social interaction are influenced by parents.

The peer group influences the sense of self in that it provides opportunities for comparisons with others. It also influences personal identity in that it provides opportunities to gain independence from adults and allows children to "learn by doing." Children in peer groups work through issues of power, compliance, cooperation, and conflict.

As children enter the middle years of childhood (age 6–12 or 13), the peer group becomes increasingly important. Children become more susceptible to the influence of peers in middle childhood (especially around preadolescence, age 11–13) and become less conforming in adolescence. The reasons for this have to do with children's cognitive level (the transition from Piaget's stage of concrete operations to formal operations) and stage of personality development (the entrance into Erikson's psychosocial stage of identity versus identity confusion). Also, children's social cognitive abilities are becoming more complex.

The relative importance of adult and peer influences depends on parenting style, particular values, and ethnicity. Children of authoritative parents are less likely to be influenced by peers than are children of authoritarian or permissive parents. Parents, in general, are more likely to influence future decisions and values; peers are more likely to influence present ones. Ethnic groups valuing interdependence are more group-oriented than ethnic groups valuing independence.

In achieving a personal identity, a major task for children is to balance group identification with personal autonomy while forging an individual role within the group. The socializing influences of peer groups relate to psychological (emotions), social (social competence), and cognitive (social cognition) development.

The socializing mechanisms that peers employ to influence one another's behavior are reinforcement (approval and acceptance), modeling, punishment (rejection and exclusion), and apprenticeship.

Macrosystem influences on the peer group enable children to accomplish certain developmental tasks: getting along with others, developing morals and values, learning appropriate sociocultural roles (including gender roles, sex education, and sexual activity), and achieving personal independence and identity.

Chronosystem influences on the peer group involve changes in structure, activities, and relationships as children develop and have new experiences. When children get together in informal groups, they play. Play has cognitive, social, psychological, and adaptive functions for adult life.

Categories of play based on social interactions include solitary, onlooker, parallel, associative, and cooperative. Types of play based on activities are imitative, exploratory, testing, and model building. As children develop, their play, as well as their social relationships, becomes more complicated. Stages of friendship include momentary playmateship; one-way assistance; two-way, fair-weather cooperation; intimate, mutually shared relationships; and autonomous, interdependent friendships.

Children who are readily accepted by the peer group tend to be healthy, vigorous, initiating, poised, adaptable, conforming, dependable, affectionate, considerate, happy, enthusiastic, concerned for others, and self-confident. Family interaction patterns play a role in children's successful integration into the group.

Children who are neglected or rejected by the peer group tend to have difficulty initiating a friendship, to have problems communicating, to rarely praise their peers, to be shy, and to be poor losers, cheaters, whiners, or aggressors. Sometimes children are rejected because they are different physically, behaviorally, or academically. Family problems can have damaging effects on children's peer relations. Rejected children tend to be attracted to deviant peer groups.

Sociometry is a set of techniques to measure acceptance, neglect, and rejection among members of a group. Children who have trouble making and keeping friends can sometimes be helped to move on to the next developmental level. Ways to help children improve their social skills and be more acceptable to their peers include modeling, participation, communication, cooperation, and validation/support. Children coached in these categories are more sociable and acceptable to their peers than those who are not coached.

Peer group dynamics and social hierarchies involve norms, statuses, alliances, consequences, and outcomes that are related to self-esteem.

Peer groups can have negative effects on children. Bullies who victimize children can cause psychological and physical harm. Delinquency usually occurs in the peer groups whose members lack family support and live in poor, unsupportive neighborhoods. Gangs are allegiances whose members engage in unlawful activities.

The influence of peers can be positive, too. Peer groups can be used to solve problems, educate members, and help others with appropriate adult guidance. Examples are peer collaboration, tutoring, and counseling.

Mesosystem influences on peer groups emerge from links with adults. Groups structured by adults differ from those structured by children in that adults provide values, rules, and suggestions. Examples of adult-structured peer groups are Scouts, church groups, and team sports. Team sports can be influential for children in teaching competitiveness and cooperation and promoting self-esteem.

Groups led by adults can differ markedly according to the kind of leadership provided by the adult. Children in groups with authoritarian leaders tend to become either submissive or aggressive. Children in groups with democratic (authoritative) leaders tend to cooperate and have high morale. Children in groups with laissez-faire (permissive) leaders tend to be disorganized and frustrated.

How adults mediate, or structure, social interaction within a peer group (competitive or cooperative) influences children's behavior. For example, frustration and competition contribute to hostility between groups, competition between groups fosters cohesiveness within each group, and intergroup hostility can often be reduced by setting a superordinate, or common goal that requires the mutual efforts of both groups.

Activity

PURPOSE *To understand peer influences at different ages on attitudes, values, and behavior.*

1. Choose at least six children (two preschoolers age 4–5, two elementary school children age 7–9, and two middle-school children age 11–13). Separately ask each one the following questions, marking parents (P) or peers (pr) in the appropriate column in the accompanying chart.
2. Write a one-page summary on which choices were most influenced by parents and which were most influenced by peers. Explain. Did you notice an age difference regarding peer influence? Explain. Did you notice a personality difference, such as being shy or outgoing, in those children who chose peers over parents—or vice versa? Explain.

	PRESCHOOL	ELEMENTARY SCHOOL	MIDDLE SCHOOL
1. Whom do you tell about what happened at school—your mom or dad, or your friends?			
2. Whom do you ask about which TV show you should watch?			
3. Who has helped you decide what you want to be when you grow up?			
4. Who most often helps you decide who your friends should be?			
5. Whom do you talk to most about games or sports you would like to play?			
6. If someone hurts your feelings, whom do you talk to about it?			
7. Who suggests books to you to read (or toys to play with)?			
8. Whom do you ask about what you should wear?			
9. If something exciting happens to you, whom do you tell first?			
10. Who tells you about snack foods to try?			

☝ Research Terms

Bullies
Conformity
Friendship
Gangs
Leadership
Peer pressure
Play
Team sports
Victims

Related Readings

Adler, P. A., & Adler, P. (1998). *Peer power: Preadolescent culture and identity.* New Brunswick, NJ: Rutgers University Press.

Asher, S. R., & Gottman, J. M. (Eds.). (1981). *The development of children's friendships.* Cambridge: Cambridge University Press.

Bukowski, M. W., Newcomb, A. F., & Hartup, W. W. (Eds.). (1996). *The company they keep: Friendship during childhood and adolescence.* New York: Cambridge University Press.

Dunn, J. (1988). *The beginnings of social understanding.* Cambridge, MA: Harvard University Press.

Garvey, C. (1990). *Play.* Cambridge, MA: Harvard University Press.

Goldstein, A. P. (1991). *Delinquent gangs: A psychological perspective.* Champaign, IL: Research Press.

Harris, J. R. (1998). *The nurture assumption.* New York: Free Press.

Herron, R. E., & Sutton-Smith, B. (1971). *Child's play.* New York: Wiley.

Kerns, K. A., Contreras, J. M., & Neal-Barnett, A. M. (2000). *Family and peers: Linking two social worlds.* Westport, CT: Praeger.

Landre, R., Miller, M., & Porter, D. (1997). *Gangs: A handbook for community awareness.* New York: Facts on File Inc.

Olweus, D. (1993). *Bullying at school: What we know and what we can do about it.* Cambridge, MA: Blackwell.

Thompson, M., Cohen, L., & Grace, C. O. (2002). *Best friends, worst enemies: Understanding the social lives of children.* New York: Ballantine Books.

Chapter 9

©Michael Newman/PhotoEdit

Ecology of the Mass Media

The medium is the message.

—MARSHALL McLUHAN

Prologue: Then and Now

Understanding Mass Media

Chronosystem Influences on Mass Media

Macrosystem Influences on Mass Media

Pictorial Media: Television and Movies
Concerns About Television and Movies
Mediating Influences on Socialization Outcomes
Mesosystem Influences

Print Media: Books and Magazines
The Power of Print Media: Literacy
How Books and Magazines Socialize Children
Concerns About Books and Magazines
Books, Socialization, and Developmental Levels of Children

Sound Media: Popular Music

Interactive Media and Multimedia

Computers and the Internet

Computerized Video/CD Games

Epilogue

Summary

Activity

Research Terms

Related Readings

| *Then and Now*

MESSAGES, METAPHORS, AND MIMES

THEN Long before people recorded events as history, the medium used to share group traditions and values was oral stories, which were passed from one generation to the next. People expanded this media form to include folktales and myths in an attempt to explain natural phenomena and to make sense out of human nature. If a lesson or useful message was added to the story, it was called a fable.

A famous storyteller in ancient Asia Minor was Aesop, who served King Croesus as an entertainer, mime, and diplomat. Aesop's fables featured animal characters with human qualities to deliver his messages; that way the tales would not offend those for whom the lesson was intended. His fables traveled by word of mouth from one country to another and from old people to young.

A very popular tale was *"The Boy Who Cried Wolf."* It tells of a boy who is employed to tend sheep but who is often bored with the task. One day he decides to create a little excitement by running into the village crying, "Wolf! Wolf!" When the villagers come to the rescue with clubs and pitchforks, they see nothing but grazing sheep. This is such fun for the boy that a few days later he cries, "Wolf!" again; once more the villagers came to help him and leave empty-handed.

Several days later, a wolf actually wanders out of the forest, and the boy cries, "Wolf! Wolf!" This time, however, the villagers ignore him, believing it to be just another one of his tricks. Meanwhile, the wolf has a hearty meal of sheep.

The moral of the story is, one who habitually lies will not be believed even when one speaks the truth.

NOW Today's messages are not only spread orally but also via print, pictures, and the Internet. A modern fable is Roald Dahl's (1964) tale, *Charlie and the Chocolate Factory*. The moral message in this elaborate story of five children, similar to that of *"The Boy Who Cried Wolf,"* is that it pays to be honest and good.

Willy Wonka offers a tour of his chocolate factory and a lifetime supply of Wonka Bars to the lucky five children who find a golden ticket in their chocolate bars. The winners are Augustus Gloop, a greedy boy; Veruca Salt, a spoiled girl; Violet Beauregarde, a girl who constantly chews gum; Mike Teavee, a boy who does nothing but watch television; and Charlie Bucket (the hero), a kind and caring boy (he tends for his ailing relatives).

On the appointed day, the children, accompanied by their parents, show up at the chocolate factory for a tour. As they visit each room, one by one all the children, except Charlie, get into trouble because of their bad habits. For every mischievous deed, the factory workers—the Oompa Loompas—sing and mime the appropriate lesson to be learned.

For example, Mike Teavee, the TV buff, is fascinated by Willy Wonka's television chocolate room. Willy invented a machine to send chocolate to people's homes much the same way TV sends images. The children are told not to disturb anything in the room, but while Willy is demonstrating the machine, Mike disobeys and steps in front of the camera. He is instantly zapped and reduced to tiny particles that disappear into the air, later to reappear on the TV screen as a miniature Mike Teavee.

The Oompa Loompas then sing the following message (Dahl, 1964, pp. 145–147):

> The most important thing we've learned,
> So far as children are concerned,
> Is never, Never, NEVER let
> Them near your television set—
> Or better still, just don't install
> The idiot thing at all.
> In almost every house we've been,
> We've watched them gaping at the screen.
> They loll and slop and lounge about,
> And stare until their eyes pop out. . . .
> But did you ever stop to think,
> To wonder just exactly what
> This does to your beloved tot?
>
> IT ROTS THE SENSES IN THE HEAD!
> IT KILLS IMAGINATION DEAD!
> IT CLOGS AND CLUTTERS UP THE MIND!
> IT MAKES A CHILD SO DULL AND BLIND
> HE CAN NO LONGER UNDERSTAND
> A FANTASY, A FAIRYLAND!
> HIS BRAIN BECOMES AS SOFT AS CHEESE!
> HIS POWERS OF THINKING RUST AND FREEZE!
> HE CANNOT THINK—HE ONLY SEES! . . .
>
> What used the darling ones to do?
> How did they keep themselves contented
> Before this monster was invented?
> Have you forgotten? Don't you know?
> We'll say it loud and slow:
> THEY . . . USED . . . TO . . . READ! They'd READ, READ, AND READ.

At the end of the factory tour, the only child left who has not gotten into trouble is Charlie. Willy Wonka bequeaths the factory to Charlie because he has proved himself to be trustworthy. The other children go home with their lifetime supplies of chocolate bars, the promised reward for having found the lucky tickets in their candy.

Although the two stories are similar in that they are fables intended to teach moral behavior to those who hear or read them, they differ in the socialization methods employed to enable children to learn not to misbehave. The boy who misbehaves by crying "Wolf" for fun is ignored by the villagers when his cry is for real and ends up losing his sheep to the wolf (learning by doing). In contrast, even though all the children who misbehave in Willy Wonka's factory do get their supply of chocolate as promised, they do not get the actual chocolate factory (learning via punishment).

KEY QUESTIONS

- Does the form of the medium (oral fable, printed story, television show) make a difference in the message's impact on the audience?
- Do media shape culture, reflect it, or transform it?
- Do media stimulate critical thinking or inhibit it?
- Is media access to information a cultural equalizer or cultural divider of the information-rich and the information-poor?

Understanding Mass Media

"Media," the plural of *medium,* refers to a type of communication. A "medium" is an intervening means through which a force acts or an effect is produced. This chapter focuses on socialization and **mass media,** forms of communication whereby large audiences quickly receive messages via an impersonal medium between sender and receiver—for example, radio, television, movies, videos, DVDs, books, newspapers, magazines, popular music, computers, and various multimedia. Figure 9.1 shows an ecological model of the systems involved in the process.

What are the shared effects of various media on children in general? What are the diverse effects on children as individuals who experience media at different ages, with varying backgrounds and perceptions? What are immediate and long-term effects of so much media exposure? How many children fantasize or build their dreams around what they have seen on television or read in books? How many young people have unrealistic expectations about the world of work, family life, and relationships? For example, many books, TV programs, and movies that appeal to teenagers portray teenagers as wise and adults as dumb. Such a portrayal gives adolescents the unrealistic expectation that they can assume an adult identity without much effort (Elkind, 1984). Some classic media examples are Peter Pan and Pippi Longstocking; some contemporary ones are Harry Potter and Madeline.

The outcomes for children of mass media experiences are sometimes difficult to sort out because of the many variables involved, change over time and may be bidirectional (Anderson, Huston, Schmitt, Linebarger, & Wright, 2001). Child variables include age, cognitive ability, gender, social experience, and psychological needs. Family variables include economics, such as what media are purchased (videotapes, books, CDs, computers); time, such as what alternative leisure activities are pursued (games, sports, museums, trips); and/or mediation, such as how much adult supervision accompanies media exposure (Dorr & Rabin, 1995). Bidirectional variables include what children bring to the media experience to change it (for example, computer knowledge can enable them to program software such as Photo Shop) and how the media experience changes children (for example, surfing the Internet can provide them with vicarious experiences such as travel). "It is not what the media does to people but what people do with the media" (Lull, 1980, p. 198).

Communications theorist Marshall McLuhan's (1964) famous aphorism "The medium is the message" means that media are extensions of humans and "the 'message' of any medium is the change of scale or pace or pattern that it introduces into human affairs" (p. 8). New media create new environments, as well as new ways of looking at that which exists. Thus, the mass media are both shapers and

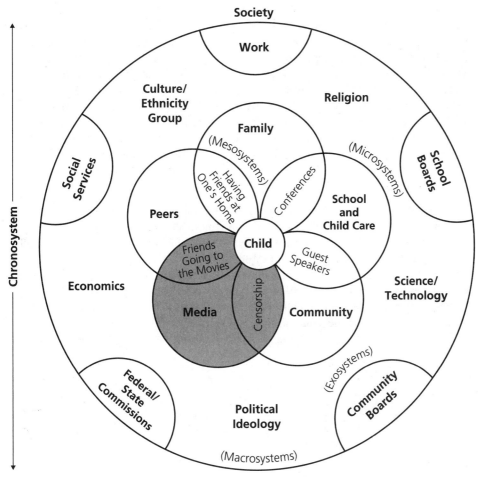

Figure 9.1

*The Media Contribute
to the Socialization
of Children*

spreaders of **culture,** which includes the knowledge, beliefs, customs, skills, and patterns of behavior of a group of humans. The mass media are shapers of culture in that their form and content affect us in some way (the products we buy, for example). The mass media are spreaders of culture in that they extend our capacity to process information and, in so doing, transform us in some way (our ability to multitask, for example).

Media and their messages can change experience, enhance experience, or interfere with experience. Books or television, for example, can change the neutral experience of going to sleep into a frightening one for children, by showing monsters coming out from under a bed. Movies can employ computer graphics and simulations to alter reality. Television can enhance the experience of a parade by providing close-up shots, supplying comments, and increasing the pace of the action. Computers equipped with the multimedia of graphics and sound can enable users to make infinite combinations and projections with the available information, thereby enhancing the experience. Television and movies can also interfere with the experience of imagining what a storybook character looks like by choosing an actor with certain characteristics to play the role.

Extending our human capacity to process information changes the way we perceive reality. We can, via television, "see and hear things happening at the other end of the world" (Esslin, 1982). Satellite communications have transformed the world into a "global village" by compressing time and distance. According to McLuhan (1989), our global village has become a global theater. Because of the electronic media revolution, we perceive ourselves differently than people did 50 years ago. Whereas learning about the world through reading is solitary, single-sensory, and gradual, learning about the world through television, videos, and computers is massive, multisensory, and immediate. For example, how many of you were "at" the World Trade Center in New York September 11, 2001?

What television does for us was accurately described almost 40 years ago in *TV Guide* and is still applicable today:

> What I think must be said is that television is not just a great force in modern life, but that it virtually is modern life. What, one might ask, doesn't it do? It gives us—be we rich, poor, snowbound, bedridden, or slow-witted—the time, the weather, the small news, sports news, now in spoken headlines, now in pictured narrative, now at the very scene of the crime or the coronation itself. It plays, sings, whistles, and dances for us, takes us to movies and theaters, concerts and operas, prize fights and ball games, ski jumps and tennis tournaments. . . . It teaches you French, rope dancing, bird calls, and first aid; provides debates and seminars and symposiums, quizzes and contests, and it tells you jokes, gags, wheezes, wisecracks, jokes and jokes. (Krononberger, 1966, p. 15)

Not much has changed about what TV does except for its availability, choices, and pervasiveness (Andreasen, 2001). Most children growing up today have access to multiple channels, videotapes, and computer discs. This technology enables viewers to choose what they will watch and when they will watch it. It also allows for use in many settings—home, school, business, transportation, and so on.

Most research on the role of mass media in socialization has been concerned with pictorial media, especially television, but print and sound media also have an impact. Television and movies have been criticized for violent and/or sexual content, but as we will see later in this chapter, some books and music offer the same. Although books enhance language and cognitive development, many of them stereotype gender and ethnic groups. The medium of music also can influence children. We all know from personal experience that setting words to music makes them easier to remember, and many commercials take advantage of this concept (Rosenfeld, 1985). We also know that music can alter our mood—make us relaxed or get us excited. Music has been used as therapy—for example, in breaking through the psychological isolation of autistic children (Rosenfeld, 1985). Popular music has been a staple in the media diets of children and adolescents, with many using it to identify with peer groups (Roberts & Christenson, 2001). That computers can connect to the Internet, are interactive, and have multimedia capabilities makes them a potentially influential socializing agent (Wartella & Jennings, 2000). Other new technology, such as cell phones, enables instant communication and easier links with family and friends. Even though the availability of multimedia clearly has boosted our abilities to multitask, it's less clear what it has done to our ability to process information analytically and critically.

Chronosystem Influences on Mass Media

McLuhan (1974) viewed media as extensions of humans in that "any technology gradually creates a totally new environment" (p. vi). Media technology has been undergoing change over the past 100 years—from books to radio to movies to television to computers to multimedia. The widespread use of communications satellites has enabled almost instantaneous delivery of media content and has changed mass communication from a national to a global enterprise (Perse, 2001). Cable and satellite dishes have increased the available programming, and the VCR and World Wide Web have added to the choices. And the decreasing costs of such technologies have afforded families the opportunity to own multiple sets.

Even though media technology has changed, concerns regarding its influence on children remain the same: "In general proponents of media innovation argue that the new technology benefits children by opening up new worlds to them, while opponents argue that new media might be used to substitute for real life in learning ethical principles undermining children's morality" (Wartella & Jennings, 2000, p. 32).

Research on children and media has focused on which demographic groups of children were gaining access to new technologies, what their preferences were for different genres, and how much time was being spent and what other activities were being displaced, and how the content of various media exposure might be affecting them (Anderson et al., 2001).

The introduction of broadcast radio in the 1920s, while touted as a source of educational and entertainment benefits, provoked parental concerns about the decrease in family communication and the effect of violence in programming (Wartella & Jennings, 2000). When television emerged as a mass medium in 1948, critics said:

> It brought the world to everyone's living room, but most particularly it gave children an earlier look at far places and adult behavior. It became the greatest and loudest salesman of goods, and sent children clamoring to their parents for boxtops. It created heroes and villians, fads fashions, and stereotypes, and nowhere so successfully, apparently, as with the pliable minds of children. (Schramm, Lyle, & Parker, 1961, pp. 11–12)

Dominating the media scene today are interactive media, such as computers, video games, and cell phones. Although these technologies offer the potential for expanded learning and socialization of children, they also increase the risk of exposure to content and experiences that may be inappropriate for children (Wartella & Jennings, 2000). The influence on children's development of active participation in such media, compared to passive participation in radio and television, is a concern. Research on interactive media is discussed later.

Of special interest in the evolution of media technology is the effects of multimedia usage—for example, television and computers. Computer scanning recorders can be attached to TV sets. These personal video recorders (PVRs) scan all television programs available to households for specific shows, content, topics, or personalities.

The computerized recorder finds and records user-selected items for playback at the convenience of the consumer making the selection. Thus, broadcast and cable channels provide the programs, but viewers control programming choices and times (Andreasen, 2001). Will parents, then, take more control over what their children view? Will there be too much information to critically evaluate options before making a choice? How will commercials, which depend on large audiences to generate sales, adapt?

Chronosystem influences on media involve not only technological changes but content changes as well. As we will discuss, there have been increases in portrayals of violence and sex and in advertising over time. Media appeals to different age groups and diverse populations have also changed. For example, there are television shows and movies geared toward children and adolescents. There are shows available in different languages and shows with closed captions for people with hearing impairments. Nontraditional relationships are more visible. Scripted and nonscripted dialogues compete for audiences. Reality-based entertainment is becoming more popular, especially when viewers can participate by calling or e-mailing their opinions to the broadcaster.

Macrosystem Influences on Mass Media

The impact of the media on children depends in part on macrosystem influences (politics, economics, technology)—in other words the broadcast systems under which radio and television operate (Leibert & Sprafkin, 1988; Levin, 1998). Politics involves the laws under which the media operate. Economics relates to the corporate sponsors for shows. Technology includes the type of medium and its message, or content.

The mass communication system in the United States is characterized by private ownership and the drive for corporate profits (this does not, of course, apply to public TV). The broadcast media are subject to regulation by the Federal Communications Commission (FCC), which controls the frequencies, transmitting power, and transmitting times of radio and TV. During the 1930s, Congress established the principle that the airwaves belong to the people. Therefore, the government, through the FCC, can issue licenses and control transmitters in the interest of the people. In addition to federal regulations, there are also state and local laws pertaining to broadcasting. Cable television, which does not use the public airwaves, is not under the same obligation to serve the public interest as broadcast television.

The FCC can award a license to broadcast when such an action is "in the public interest, convenience, or necessity." However, there are no clear standards for what constitutes serving the public interest. When frequencies are available, they are auctioned to the highest bidder. The FCC is thus supposed to encourage competition, and it is also prohibited from censoring program content. However, broadcasters must refrain from airing obscene material and, until recently, had to regulate the amount of time allocated to commercials. There are no comparable FCC rules for cable (pay) television or videocassettes. In 1984, the FCC lifted some of its restrictions under the general movement of the Reagan administration to deregulate various industries and to reduce government intervention.

The FCC held that marketplace competition could best serve children's interests. Two trends resulted from this shift in policy: (1) Educational content declined, and

(2) advertising increased. These developments led Congress to enact legislation known as the Children's Television Act of 1990. This law imposed a limit of 10 1/2 minutes of TV commercials per hour for children's programming on weekdays and 12 minutes per hour on weekends. In 1996, the FCC expanded this act by ruling that all commercial stations must broadcast at least 3 hours of children's educational or informational programs per week.

In 1997, most of the television industry implemented a rating system intended to give parents advance information (see the box entitled "Parental Guidelines") about the content of programs. Specifically, the guidelines address the amount of violence, foul language, and sexually suggestive content. Television manufacturers are now installing V-chips—computer chips that can be programmed to block undesirable programs—in all new sets. They are also available as add-ons for existing TVs. These V-chips will enable families to set their own viewing standards.

Radio and TV make their profits from advertising. Broadcasters sell time to advertisers, which choose the vehicles—the programs—that will appeal to the demographic audience best suited for their commercials. In this system, control over content really rests with the audience. If the audience is not interested in the content of a program, the program is dropped. Thus, the tastes and interests of viewers and listeners serve as indirect but powerful controls.

The main emphasis of mass communication in the United States is on entertainment (Huston, Zillman, & Bryant, 1994; Perse, 2001). Generally, the major media aim their content at the broadest spectrum of viewers in order to win the attention of the largest number of consumers to the products advertised on their programs. This means that the broadcast media must continually produce a "mass culture" geared to popular or majority tastes. However, with new technologies, such as cable, satellite, video, and computers, audiences have become more fragmented, so advertisers have to target their products to special interests. Audience fragmentation increases as family income increases (Dorr & Rabin, 1995). This is because there are more TV sets and more choices of available technologies in families with higher socioeconomic status.

Yet, as long as the broadcast media in the United States are designed to attract audiences to whom to sell products, they will convey messages that are likely to influence attitudes and behavior (Huston, Zillman, & Bryant, 1994; Perse, 2001). Parents, then, must be cognizant of what is and is not appropriate for their children to watch.

Parental Guidelines: TV and Movies

Television

There are two categories of ratings, one for children's programs and one for programs not specifically designed for children. The following categories apply to programs designed solely for children:

 All Children. This program is designed to be appropriate for all children. Whether animated or live action, the themes and elements in this program are specifically designed for a very young audience, including children age 2–6. This program is not expected to frighten young children.

Directed to Older Children. This program is designed for children age 7 and above. It may be more appropriate for children who have acquired the developmental skills needed to distinguish between make-believe and reality. Themes and elements in this program may include mild fantasy or comedic violence, or may frighten children under the age of 7. Therefore, parents may wish to consider the suitability of this program for their very young children. Programs containing fantasy violence that may be more intense or more combative than other programs in this category are designed as TV-Y7-FV.

The following categories apply to programs designed for the entire audience:

General Audience. Most parents would find this program suitable for all ages. Although this rating does not signify a program designed specifically for children, most parents may let younger children watch this program unattended. It contains little or no violence, no strong language, and little or no sexual dialogue or situations.

Parental Guidance Suggested. This program contains material that parents may find unsuitable for younger children. Many parents may want to watch it with their younger children. The theme itself may call for parental guidance and/or the program contains one or more of the following: moderate violence (V), some sexual situations (S), infrequent coarse language (L), or some suggestive dialogue (D).

Parents Strongly Cautioned. This program contains some material that many parents would find unsuitable for children under age 14 years of age. Parents are strongly urged to exercise greater care in monitoring this program and are cautioned against letting children under the age of 14 watch unattended. This program contains one or more of the following: intense violence (V), intense sexual situations (S), strong coarse language (L), or intensely suggestive dialogue (D).

Mature Audience Only. This program is specifically designed to be viewed by adults and therefore may be unsuitable for children under 17. This program contains one or more of the following: graphic violence (V), explicit sexual activity (S), or crude, indecent language (L).

When a program is broadcast, the appropriate icon should appear in the upper left corner of the picture frame for the first 15 seconds. If the program is longer than one hour, the icon should be repeated at the beginning of the second hour. Guidelines are also displayed in TV listings in a number of newspapers and magazines.

Movies

G	**General Audiences**	All ages admitted.
PG	**Parental Guidance Suggested**	Some material may not be suitable for children.

PG-13	**Parents Strongly Cautioned**	Some material may be inappropriate for children under 13.
R	**Restricted**	Anyone under 17 requires an accompanying parent or adult guardian.
NC-17	**No One 17 and Under Admitted**	

Pictorial Media: Television and Movies

Television includes network and cable shows broadcast on the TV set. Movies include productions made for the theater and available for home viewing on the TV set in video or DVD format. According to a report titled *Kids and Media and the New Millennium* (Kaiser Family Foundation, 1999), the American family remains strongly connected to television even though other media are available. Families use TV for entertainment, education, news, and consumer information.

TV Viewing Patterns

- Preschoolers (age 2–5) view about 15 hours of TV per week. Most of their viewing time is on weekdays from 10 A.M. to 4:30 P.M. and in the evening from 8 P.M. to 11 P.M.
- School-age children (age 6–11) watch about 23 hours of TV per week. Most of their viewing time is in the evening.
- Saturday morning "kid vid" viewing accounts for only about 14 percent of the total time children spend watching TV.
- Two-thirds of children age 8 and older have a TV set in their bedrooms, as do one-third of children age 2–7.

Sources: Comstock and Sharrer, 2001; Kaiser Family Foundation, 1999; Nielson, 2000.

Television and movies have evoked many concerns, especially about their content, their socializing effects on children, and potential public responses. Television has certain properties that distinguish it from other media, including its attention demands, the brevity of its sequences, the rapid succession of presented material, and its visual orientation (Singer, Singer, & Zuckerman, 1990).

Children are a special audience in regard to the medium of television (Dorr, 1986; Levin, 1998). Because of their cognitive immaturity, they are generally assumed to be more likely than adults to believe that the images they see are real; that violence is the way to solve problems; that viewers should buy what is advertised; and that the values, stereotypes, and behavior portrayed on TV constitute the way people should be. "Television is a particularly appealing medium to young children in part because many of its images and modes of representation are readily understood; it does not require the child to learn a complicated system of decoding as does reading, for example" (Huston, Zillman, & Bryant, 1994, p. 5). As a result, television has important socializing potential.

CONCERNS ABOUT TELEVISION AND MOVIES

Advances in television broadcasting have created changes in the sleep habits, meal arrangements, leisure time pursuits, and conversation patterns of millions of U.S. families (Andreasen, 2000; Huston, Zillman, & Bryant, 1994; Leibert & Sprafkin, 1988). Mass communications have also created changes in our culture. New products advertised via television, magazines, newspapers, and the Internet can proliferate in a very short time. The rapid spread of other cultural forms, such as fashions, hairstyles, and types of music or sports, can be stimulated by the media. All of these changes have understandably given rise to concerns:

> It has never been much of a secret . . . that movies influence manners, attitudes, and behavior. In the fifties, they told us how to dress for a rumble or a board meeting, how far to go on the first date, what to think about Martians or, closer to home, Jews, blacks, and homosexuals. They taught girls whether they should have husbands or careers, boys whether to pursue work or pleasure. They told us what was right and what was wrong, what was good and what was bad; they defined our problems and suggested solutions. (Biskind, 1983, p. 2)

Effects on Other Activities and Relationships

The statistics on TV viewing habits indicate that, on average, children spend 3–5 hours a day in front of the television set, often with little parental monitoring (Comstock & Sharrer, 2001; Kaiser Family Foundation, 1999; Nielson, 2000). Young children from economically and educationally disadvantaged backgrounds spend even more time watching TV than do children from more affluent, better-educated families (Dorr, 1982; Huston & Wright, 1998).

If children are spending that much time in front of the television set, VCR, or DVD player, activities that they might otherwise be engaged in, such as reading, pursuing hobbies, or playing games or sports, and family or peer interactions likely are being neglected. As Urie Bronfenbrenner (1970c) said in an address to the National Association for the Education of Young Children:

> Like the sorcerer of old, the television set casts its magic spell, freezing speech and action, turning the living into silent statues so long as the enchantment lasts. The primary danger of the television screen lies not so much in the behavior it produces— although there is danger there—as in the behavior it prevents: the talks, the games, the family festivities and arguments through which much of the child's learning takes place and through which his character is formed. Turning on the television set can turn off the process that transforms children into people.

Family Rituals and Interactions. Rituals are shared customs or ceremonies that give life meaning (Bria, 1998). Author Marie Winn (1977), in *The Plug in Drug*, discussed what has happened to family life and rituals with the advent of television. She defined family rituals as "those regular, dependable recurrent happenings that gave members of a family a feeling of belonging to a home . . . those experiences that act as the adhesive of family unity" (p. 124).

EXAMPLE When I was a small child, my grandmother had weekly family dinners, at which we children got to tell all the adults about our achievements and then gloried in their praise. We also got to listen to adult gossip. When we got bored by the conversation, we'd explore my grandmother's house. She had drawers full of old clothes, pictures, and letters—she never threw away anything. Or we'd play cards, and if we lost, we could always hustle a game with one of the adults, who would see to it that we'd win. That was before my grandmother bought a TV.

Although television may have replaced extended family conversations around the dinner table, card games, and the like, it has become an integral part of family life in that viewing often occurs with other family members, especially for young children. Parents and siblings provide a model of how to use television, and children are exposed to what their parents and siblings view simply because they are in the same household (Huston & Wright, 1998). A generation ago, when only about 50 percent of homes had more than one TV set, families assembled to watch shows together. Now, with the majority of households having multiple sets, opportunities for shared experiences have decreased (Nielson, 2000).

Time spent watching TV affects family interactions—the development of relationships, the process of communication, and the resolution of problems. Interpersonal relationships take work. To get along with others, individuals must be able to communicate their own feelings and wishes, as well as acknowledge other persons' feelings and wishes. When these feelings and wishes are compatible, the two individuals are said to "get along"; when they are incompatible, the two must compromise in order to get along. The compromise may involve taking turns or modifying individual desires. Although parents and children are often in close proximity when watching TV, sometimes touching and hugging, they tend to talk less to one another when viewing TV than when performing other activities (Wright, St. Peters, & Huston, 1990).

The values of working at interpersonal relationships as part of children's development are numerous. The children receive language training, in that they must use words to express feelings and wishes. They must also receive messages, process them, and respond to them. By having to listen to others' messages, they also move away from egocentrism (such as the inability to see things from another's point of view). Finally, they are involved in problem solving if compromises have to be reached.

Physical Activity. Time spent watching TV is time that potentially can be used for physical activity. According to one study, children who watched 4 or more hours of TV per day were significantly more obese than children who watched an hour or less (Crespo et al., 2001). In another study of preschoolers (age 1–4), their risk of being overweight increased by 6 percent for every hour of television watched per day. And if the children had a TV in their bedrooms, the odds of being overweight jumped an additional 31 percent for every hour watched. Preschool children who had TVs in their bedrooms watched an additional 4.8 hours more of TV or videos per week than those who did not (Dennison, Erb, & Jenkins, 2002).

Effects on the Liability to Distinguish Between Reality and Fantasy

According to Piaget (1962), young children think very differently from adults. They believe that everything that moves is alive, that the sun follows them when they go for a walk, and that dreams come in through the window at night when they sleep. Preschool children believe that the cartoon characters and the actual people they see on television are equally "real" and live inside the television set. This is because they have difficulty conceptualizing the distinction between a pictorial representation and an actual one. They also have difficulty understanding pretense or false claims (as in some advertisements) (Flavell, Miller, & Miller, 2001). Preschool children believe that they can turn off a program and that the same show will be on when they turn on the set again (as if one were putting a marker inside a book). For preschoolers, reality (*actual* objects) and fantasy (*images* of objects) tend to be interchangeable. Flavell (1986) demonstrated the difficulty that preschoolers have in distinguishing appearance from reality. For example, 3-year-olds assert that a rock-shaped sponge really is a rock, whereas children over age 5 can make the distinction.

In addition, preschool children usually cannot distinguish the commercial from the program. This may be because they can only deal with one "script" at a time (Flavell, Miller, & Miller, 2001). They also accept the message literally and uncritically. At this stage of cognitive development, preschoolers are unable to understand that advertisements are intended to sell products rather than entertain them. This gullibility can lead to dangerous consequences. A number of children each month are brought to hospital emergency rooms with broken bones from leaping from the tops of buildings or smashing objects with bare hands—a sad way to find out one is not Superman. One 4-year-old spent several days in intensive hospital care after swallowing 40 children's vitamins—the TV commercial said vitamins would make him "big and strong real fast" (Leibert, Neil, & Davidson, 1973). It is not until about age 7 that children realize ads are intended to be persuasive messages. And although ability to evaluate advertising claims increases with age, even adolescents exhibit gullibility (Dorr & Rabin, 1995).

Because young children confuse reality and fantasy, many of their ideas about the world beyond their home and neighborhood come from television programs and movies (Cantor, 1998; Greenfield, 1984; Perse, 2001). The more limited their life experiences or economic circumstances, the more likely they are to believe what they see on television. Although some people believe that fantasy on television can lead to imaginative and creative expression, it also permits children (especially troubled ones) to retreat from real-life situations and can encourage them to seek immediate gratification of their impulses or instant solutions to problems (Comstock & Paik, 1991).

"Television substitutes its own image of reality (usually made to the specifications of adult media executives) for the image of reality the child is beginning to form as he develops his capacity for symbolic activity" (Gatz, 1975, pp. 415–418). In effect, TV is saying, "This is the world the way it is." Because children have not experienced much of the real world, they accept what TV portrays as the truth and neglect to test it against reality.

As children get older (age 5–7) and have more experience with different types of TV programming, as well as reality, they learn to recognize form and content cues denoting fact and fiction on TV (Wright, Huston, Reitz, & Piemymat, 1994). By about age 7 or 8, children can distinguish between things that are real and those that are make-believe on television. At first, they judge according to format (cartoons are make-believe, and live-action shows are real). Then they come to realize that certain things portrayed on TV—whether animated or live—are physically impossible (people can't fly like Superman). They come to evaluate reality on TV based on whether things in the story match what exists in the real world (a police story is real because police are present in the community). By about age 10, chil-

These children are engaged in imaginative play.

dren begin to understand that some programs are script-acted for the purpose of telling a story and that others show real events that actually happened, such as news and documentaries (Cantor, 1998).

Effects on Imagination

Piaget (1962) believed that the thinking process involves a balance between the demands the outside world makes on us (objectivity) and the demands we make on the outside world (subjectivity). When this balance is shifted in the direction of the data presented by the world, we *imitate*. When it is shifted in the direction of our interpretation, we *imagine*. "Imaginative play," wrote Piaget (1962), "is a symbolic transposition which subjects things to the child's activity without rules or limitations" (p. 87). When a child plays, the world bends itself to the child's wishes.

> **EXAMPLE** Five-year-old Tammy went to her room after lunch, having come home from kindergarten. She didn't nap anymore, but her mother felt she needed some quiet time alone before going outside to play with her friends. Tammy got out her model horses and "galloped" them around her bed on the floor. The horses spoke to each other—they were arguing over where to graze. Tammy then got out her blocks and attempted to build a barn for one of the horses. She succeeded in building the sides but could not get the roof to stay on without collapsing on the horse. The play then abruptly changed to a rodeo, and the blocks used to build the barn became an obstacle course. The horses, no longer arguing, took turns jumping and turning corners, complete with sound effects. Forty-five minutes had passed, and Tammy emerged from her room cheerful and ready to play with her friends.

Television makes imagination subservient to imitation. Furthermore, TV's images become reality for children, who are then unable to later break through that mindset when they experience the real world. For example, studies by Singer and Singer (1990) found that children age 3–8 whose play themes reflected specific references to TV cartoons, superheroes, and action/detective shows were more likely to be aggressive. The researchers found that the children with the least imagination watched television with large amounts of violence and were most likely to imitate the aggression in school. They also found that the imaginative children were less likely to engage in impulsive acts or gross aggression.

Although television does not ordinarily stimulate imaginative play and creativity, children do find ideas for make-believe play in everything around them, including television. In a review of the research, Van der Voort and Valkenburg (1994) found that television's influence on imaginative play depended on the type of program. Benign, nonviolent programs did not directly affect imaginative play, whereas programs with high levels of violence reduced imaginative play. However, certain educational programs were exceptions in that they did enhance imaginative activities.

Children's imaginative play and creativity may be reduced by heavy viewing. But if adults watch TV with children, they can stimulate children's imagination by asking questions about the show, interpreting words and actions on the screen, and suggesting various alternative solutions to what is happening.

Effects of the Prevalence of Violence

"Television and movies, by their very nature, have the ability to introduce children to frightening images, events, and ideas, many of which they would not encounter in their entire lives without the mass media" (Cantor, 1998, p. 3). An example is **violence,** defined as the "overt expression of physical force against others or self, or compelling action against one's will and pain of being hurt or killed or actually hurting or killing (Gerbner, Gloss, Jackson-Beck, Jeffries-Fox, & Signorielli, 1978). Violence on TV is measured in terms of prevalence (the extent to which violence occurs in the program), rate (the frequency of violent episodes), and role (the number of characterizations of violence or victimization). Violence is a concern because, over the years, there has been an increase in violence on children's Saturday morning programs, as well as on prime-time television (8–11 P.M.) (Center for Communication and Social Policy, 1998; Mediascope, 1996). The National Television Violence Study (NTVS) (Mediascope, 1996) has demonstrated that not all violence portrayed on TV has similar effects on children. Characterizations in which the perpetrators are attractive are more likely to influence viewers' identification and modeling. When violence is justified, goes unpunished, or causes no harm or pain to victims, it is also more likely to influence viewer behavior.

According to the Center for Media and Public Affairs (CMPA) (1999), TV viewers and moviegoers see scenes of serious violence (physical force) every 4 minutes (CMPA, 1999). In 1998–1999, a majority of the 10 most violent television movies carried a PG-13 rating, and a majority of the 10 most violent television shows were rated TV-PG. The concern is not only the prevalence of violence but also its depiction as necessary and relatively harmless (Comstock & Sharrer, 1999).

Although it may be difficult to prove that excessive viewing of televised violence can or does provoke violent crime in any *one* individual, if children who watch a great deal of televised violence clearly are more prone to behaving aggressively than children who do not watch TV violence (Geen, 1994; Perse, 2001). The NTVS (Mediascope, 1996) demonstrated that the context in which most violence is presented on TV poses certain risks for viewers: (1) learning to behave violently, (2) becoming more desensitized to violence, and (3) becoming more fearful of being attacked. Characteristics of children such as age, real-life experiences, temperament, and cognitive developmental level influence the impact of viewing violence.

Observational Learning. Observational learning is based on Bandura's (1974, 1989) social cognitive theory: People learn by observing and imitating behavior. According to this theory, role models, especially attractive ones, act as stimuli to produce similar behavior in observers of the role model. The behavior is learned by being imitated, rewarded, or reinforced in a variety of ways. Responses produced often enough and over long enough periods maintain the behavior. Bandura outlined four steps necessary for this process: (1) attention to the stimulus, (2) retention of the observed behavior and consequences, (3) ability to reproduce the behavior, and (4) motivation to perform the observationally learned behavior.

Are children likely to learn and remember new forms of aggressive behavior by watching them on TV? And if they learn and remember, will they practice the behavior? Research has shown that children do learn and remember novel forms of aggression seen on TV or in films. They are more likely to remember the behavior learned by observation if they have tried it at least once. Whether children actually practice the behavior depends on the similarity of the observed setting and their real setting. That is, if they imitate an observed aggressive act and it "works" (is reinforced) in solving a problem or attaining a goal, it is likely to be repeated. For example, a young child who sees Superman punching a criminal to retrieve a bag of money and prevent innocent bystanders from getting shot, might try the observed aggressive behavior to take a toy away from another child, not having comprehended the concept of the Superman scene—that aggression is justifiable for protection. If the child's aggressive behavior results in getting the toy, she or he is likely to repeat the behavior. Thus, children may learn aggressive behavior from TV, but whether they actually perform it depends on personality factors and on the situation (Huston & Wright, 1998; Leibert & Sprafkin, 1988; Perse, 2001).

Attitude Change. Television viewing influences people's attitudes. The more television children watch, the more accepting they are of aggressive behavior. It has been shown that persons who watch a lot of television tend to be more suspicious and distrustful of others; they also believe there is more violence in the world than do those who do not watch much television (Comstock & Paik, 1991; Pearl, 1982; Perse, 2001).

In psychological theory, attitudes are attributions, rules, and explanations that people gradually learn from observations of behavior. Therefore, for individuals who watch a great deal of television, attitudes will be built upon the basis of what they see, and these attitudes will, in turn, have an effect on their behavior.

Apparently, young children are more willing to accept the aggressive behavior of other children after viewing violent scenes (Paik & Comstock, 1994). However, studies have shown that children's attitudes can be changed if adults discuss the programs with them (Huston & Wright, 1998). In an experimental study (Huesmann, Eron, Klein, Brice, & Fisher, 1983), one group of children who regularly watched violent programs were shown excerpts from violent shows. They then took part in discussions about the unreality of television violence and alternative methods to solve conflicts. Another group, which also had watched many violent programs, was shown nonviolent excerpts followed by a neutral discussion of content. The group that took part in the sessions on unreality and alternative strategies was significantly less aggressive than the control group.

Arousal. Arousal theories examine the physiological changes and subsequent emotions that result from viewing violent episodes. One response might be desensitization.

Does viewing violence on TV decrease sensitivity to it in real life? Research has shown that, as a result of the repetition of violence in the media, classical desensitization takes place. **Desensitization**—the gradual reduction in response to a stimulus due to repeated exposure—is practiced in behavior therapy to overcome fears. There was a story in the news several years ago characterized by this very kind of desensitization. A masked burglar gagged a woman and tied her to a chair while he robbed her home of valuables. He had told her 5-year-old son to watch television and not to call the police until the show was over. Four hours later, the boy phoned. Apparently, his emotional sensitivity to the real event was so reduced that he did not react immediately. Also, the boy may have been so accustomed to seeing similar events on TV that he was not cognizant of the seriousness of the real event.

In yet another study, school-age boys who regularly viewed violent programs showed less of a physiological response when they looked at new violent programs (Pearl, 1982), compared with boys who were not used to viewing much violence (Condry, 1989). If viewing violence desensitizes individuals to aggression, then the content will have to be more and more graphic in order to keep the audience attentive. Some TV critics believe this is exactly what has occurred.

Another response might be increased aggression due to the increase in general arousal, which occurs because viewing televised violence releases socialized constraints on individuals' behavior. Thus, televised aggression can have a disinhibiting effect, making subsequent aggression, after viewing violence, more likely, especially in certain situations (Condry, 1989; Perse, 2001).

Effects of Advertising

Every hour of television programming is carefully planned to contain enough minutes for commercial messages. By selling commercial time to advertisers, TV stations are able to defray the costs of their programs. Commercials are cost-effective. Even though seconds of broadcast advertising cost thousands of dollars, mailings to individuals would cost much more. The federal agency responsible for regulating TV commercials is the Federal Trade Commission (FTC). The Better Business Bureau, to which most advertisers belong, has a self-regulatory Children's Advertising Review Unit.

Annually, on average, children age 2–11 are exposed to between 20,000 and 40,000 television commercials. And the number of product commercials has increased steadily (Center for Media Education [CME], 1997; Condry, Bence, & Scheibe, 1988; Kerkman, Kunkel, Huston, Wright, & Pinon, 1990). On a typical Saturday morning, the average young viewer may see over 100 child-directed commercials, including ads for toys, cereal, snacks, and beverages.

Why advertise to children? Children have decades of buying power ahead of them, and unlike adults, they have no preconceived product preferences. They are open to suggestion and are impulsive (Stabiner, 1993). Advertisers report that children start asking for brand names as early as age 2. One successful way to gain a child consumer is to give him or her a sense of empowerment or importance. For example, Kool-Aid was marketed as a product "just for kids"; also, it contained coupons that children could save and trade in for toys (Stabiner, 1993).

Gorn and Goldberg (1982) directly tested the effects of exposure to commercials for sugared snacks on children's actual food selections. The study was conducted in a summer camp setting with children age 4–8. During each of 14 consecutive days, the children viewed a different half-hour, Saturday morning cartoon. Four experimental groups were devised according to the nature of the commercials: (1) sweetened snack foods, such as candy, Cracker Jacks, and Kool-Aid; (2) fruit and fruit products, such as orange juice or grapes; (3) public service announcements that emphasized the value of eating a balanced, nutritional diet; and (4) no commercials. The commercials took up 4 1/2 minutes of each half-hour show. Snack choices were made available each day immediately after the television viewing. The snack choices consisted of orange juice, Kool-Aid, two fruits, and two candy bars. The children exposed to the sweetened snack food commercials selected Kool-Aid and candy more often than did members of the other groups. The children exposed to the fruit commercials selected the most orange juice and more fruit than sweetened snack foods.

Marketing products to children has become common.

According to several studies, "Television is remiss in helping its audience to attain better health or better understanding of health practices." These studies cited evidence showing a disproportionate number of commercials for sweet and snack foods, compared with nutritious foods (Fox, 2000; Hill-Radimer 1997; Pearl, 1982). Subsequent research has documented that children who watch a lot of TV are fatter than children who watch less (Dorr & Rabin, 1995; Huston & Wright, 1998). This is partially due to lack of physical activity and partially due to the tendency to snack when watching TV.

Young children take things literally, rather than figuratively, which makes them more vulnerable to advertising messages (Stabiner, 1993). Although most children by age 3 can distinguish program content from commercials, children below age 8 seldom understand that the purpose of the ad is to sell something. Research suggests that repeated exposure to ads turns children into minisalespersons who make demands on their parents for what they see advertised on TV (Kunkel & Roberts, 1991). Their parents, in turn, complain that advertising causes conflict in the parent–child relationship ("I want" versus "You can't have").

Children below age 8 do not understand the persuasive intent of advertising and so are particularly vulnerable to its appeals. Children over age 8, who are more aware of the purposes of advertising, are still apt to be persuaded by appeals that are subtly deceptive or misleading (Huston, Watkins, & Kunkel, 1989). For example, they don't understand product disclosures or disclaimers, comparative claims, the real meaning of endorsements by famous characters, or the use of premiums, promotions, and sweepstakes (Council of Better Business Bureaus, 2000).

To illustrate the fact that young children do not critically evaluate the commercials they see, researchers (Atkin & Gibson, 1978) showed children an advertisement in which two cartoon characters, Fred Flintstone and Barney Rubble, said the cereal was "chocolatey enough to make you smile." When asked why they wanted the cereal, two-thirds of the children mentioned its chocolate taste, three-fifths said it would make them smile, and over half said it was because Fred and Barney liked it. Another study (Atkin & Gibson, 1978) reported that children who saw a cereal advertisement with a circus strongman lifting a heavy weight believed that eating the cereal would make them strong, too.

Despite increased awareness of the purpose of advertising, even older children find commercials convincing. In a sample of 8- to 14-year-old boys, celebrity endorsement of a racing toy made the product more attractive; including live racetrack footage led to exaggerated estimates of the toy's features and to decreased awareness that the race was staged (Ross et al., 1984).

A recent development in children's programming is the production of programs that feature characters corresponding to toys (Levin, 1998)—"toy tie-in" marketing. In essence, these program-length commercials constitute unfair soliciting of children, according to Action for Children's Television (Condry, 1989; Huston & Wright, 1998; Leibert & Sprafkin, 1988). Product-related programming is of concern for reasons other than its commercial intent. Its content is "formulaic" and stereotyped (Huston & Wright, 1998). Children's play with program-featured toys tends to be more imitative and less imaginative than play with other toys (Greenfield, Yut, Chung, & Land, 1990). Another development causing concern is interactive TV programming. Children buy the required toy, such as a gun, aim it at the screen, and exchange fire with on-screen enemies (Tuchscherer, 1988). Recently, interactive toys ("Teletubbies") have been developed for children as young as 1 year.

Adolescents are affected by TV commercials, too. According to the Centers for Disease Control and Prevention (1994), by glamorizing smoking, cigarette smoking by movie stars increases the likelihood that teenagers will experiment with cigarettes. The same holds true for alcohol (Perse, 2001; U.S. Department of Health and Human Services, 1992).

If children are influenced by TV ads for toys and foods, what about all the medication commercials? Although ads for medicine are not intentionally directed at children, they are nevertheless exposed to them. Do the ads give children the perception that drugs give quick relief for all pain, stress, or discomfort? Does exposure to such advertising increase the likelihood that children will turn to drugs when they have problems? These questions are being researched. What is known so far is that children in stressful families (characterized by divorce, alcoholism, abuse, and/or economic problems) watch more television, reportedly to escape their problems (Dorr & Rabin, 1995). According to Neil Postman (1994), New York University professor of communication arts and sciences,

> a commercial teaches a child three interesting things. The first is that all problems are resolvable. The second is that all problems are resolvable fast. And the third is that all problems are resolvable fast through the agency of some technology. It may be a drug. It may be a detergent. It may be an airplane or some piece of machinery, like an automobile or computer. (pp. 43–45)

The essential message of commercials, then, is that people have problems—lack of confidence, lack of friends, lack of money, lack of health, and so on—and these are solvable through the products advertised.

According to James McNeal (1987), author of *Children as Consumers*, advertisers are attuned to children's developmental stages and their need for peer approval, status, and independence. The basic advertising message being communicated, then, is "Things make the person."

Commercialism not only invades the home but is present in the school as well. Chapter 6 discussed some advertising strategies implemented in school (Channel One, fundraisers, sponsorships of clubs and sports). Are the promotional messages and commercial influences undermining the integrity of children's education? Studies have shown that students in schools with Channel One show a greater consumer orientation and intent to purchase products than students not exposed to Channel One (Huston & Wright, 1998).

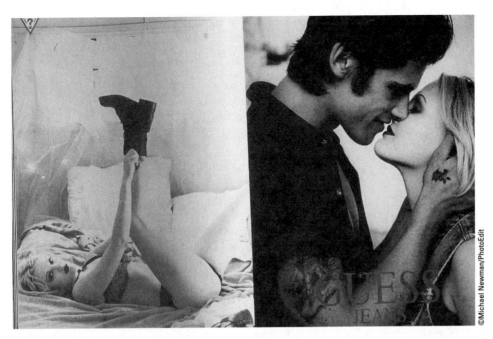

Advertising sells more than products; it sells a message. These ads exemplify equating sexual desirability with purchasing the product.

Perpetuation of Values

Values refer to qualities or beliefs that are viewed as desirable or important and that influence attitudes, motives, and behavior. Of concern here is how behavioral, sexual, and stereotypical values portrayed on TV are interpreted by children.

As has been discussed, children watch not only "kid vid" but "adult" programs (action shows, dramas, situation comedies, news). The problem with this is that adults know about certain aspects of life—its tragedies, contradictions, inequities, mysteries, and joys—whereas children do not have the intellectual capabilities or the life experiences to comprehend these aspects. What television does, then, is communicate the same information to everyone simultaneously, regardless of age, education, or experience. And, in the quest for new material to hold audiences, television has been increasingly exposing its audiences to life experiences previously considered forbidden: sexuality, adultery, domestic abuse, incest, corruption, extreme violence, pornography, and horror. Consequently, with TV's relentless revelation of all adult secrets, it is not inconceivable that in the near future we shall return to the thirteenth- and "fourteenth-century situation in which no words were unfit for a youthful ear" (Postman, 1994, p. 89). If so, what values are being perpetuated?

Behavior. According to Dr. Isidore Ziferstein, a fellow of the American Psychiatric Association, television has presented to children a set of "antivalues" regarding behavior (Larrick, 1975). Examples include the following:

- *Anti-interpersonal relations values:* A woman kills her husband in order to get his insurance.
- *Anticooperation values:* Life is presented on television as consisting of conflicts, strife, and war.
- *Antidemocratic values:* Heroes succeed by operating outside the law.

But viewers get much less information on cooperation, peace, and lawfulness. A television show often contains more excitement, adventure, power, and violence than the average person experiences in a lifetime. By comparison, everyday life seems boring (Huston & Wright, 1998).

Not all shows present negative values; some exhibit socially desirable behaviors that benefit others. Studies have shown that children who watch altruistic behavior (generosity, selflessness, cooperation) on television become more altruistic themselves (Comstock & Paik, 1991; Perse, 2001). For example, children who watched a prosocial episode of *Lassie,* in which Lassie's master risked his life by hanging over the edge of a mineshaft to rescue Lassie's puppy, exhibited more prosocial behavior than did children who watched a neutral episode of *Lassie* (Sprafkin, Leibert, & Poulos, 1975). Although many children's TV shows today feature prosocial behavior, there are few *lasting* effects unless adults watch the shows with them, discuss the positive behavior, and encourage the children to model it. Unfortunately, not many adults do so (Dorr & Rabin, 1995).

According to the late Fred Rogers, long-time host and producer of *Mister Rogers' Neighborhood:*

> So much of what we see on television is so terrifically limited. Just think of the problem solving on television that people are exposed to and how in so many instances, it is so uncreative. If somebody gets angry with somebody else, he just annihilates that other person. Children look to adults to discover how they solve problems. . . . It would be helpful for kids to see that there is a wide variety of ways to deal in a constructive fashion with what the world hands out. (quoted in Boyer, 1983, p. 1)

Sexuality. Presentation of behaviors, lifestyles, and attitudes believed to be harmful to children has led some parents to organize into groups to protest what they consider to be assaults on family and religious values. For example, TV is bolder in depicting sexual activity than it was several decades ago (Perse, 2001). The shows of the 1970s that caused a furor only talked about sex, whereas shows in the late 1980s began to present actual sex acts. Men and women are now routinely shown in bed together. Moreover, these presumably copulating couples are typically not married to each other. Finally, sex acts previously considered taboo, such as sexual abuse, incest, rape, and prostitution, are now openly discussed and depicted on TV (Greenberg, 1994; Leibert & Sprafkin, 1988).

A significant portion of adolescents' sex education comes from prime-time programming. Watching shows depicting premarital, extramarital, or nonmarital sex affects the moral values of young teens, who report that they find such sexual behavior to be acceptable. However, family discussions of values can help promote alternative view points (Bryant & Rockwell, 1994).

Young people today are exposed to an incessant flow of sexual images. Television and movies have increasingly included nudity, profanity, and sexually explicit activities, and glamorized sex appeal and sexual activity. Unfortunately, much less attention is paid by the media to the potential consequences of casual sexual behavior. For example, if wasn't until 1995 that TV and radio carried ads for condoms (Jaffee, 1998).

Stereotypes. Stereotypes are oversimplified representations of members of a group; they generally conform to a pattern of dress or behavior that is easily recognized and understood. Generally, stereotypes are less real, more perfect or imperfect, and/or more predictable than their real-life counterparts. Some stereotyping on television may be unavoidable, due to the format; 30- or 60-minute programs do not allow for full character development. Many minority groups—women, older people, African Americans, Italians, Hispanic Americans, Asian Americans, Native Americans, and Middle Eastern Americans—claim that television and movies either ignore them or distort them. In a study (Scheibe, 1989) of 2135 commercials containing more than 6000 characters, it was shown that men outnumbered women. However, females represented the majority of characters in commercials for cleaning and hygiene/beauty products, apparel, and toys; males dominated in ads for alcohol, cars, leisure/travel, and financial services. TV commercials also overrepresented young adults by three to one. The large majority of characters on TV commercials were white, and nearly all the rest were African American. Other ethnic groups were underrepresented relative to their true demographic distribution in the population. Finally, TV commercials overrepresented white-collar, managerial, and professional occupations while underrepresenting blue-collar occupations.

In situation comedies or action dramas, ethnic minorities are most often associated with violence, servile occupations, or comic roles. Studies have shown that both African American and Euro-American children accept television's stereotypes of ethnic minorities and their lifestyles as realistic. In contrast, the portrayal of ethnic minorities on children's programs has become more and more favorable. Prosocial programs reflecting ethnic variety tend to have a beneficial effect on children's perception of and interactions with minority groups (Comstock & Paik, 1991).

Gender stereotypes have decreased on TV but are still common in depictions of behavior, relationships, and occupational roles (Comstock & Paik, 1991; Huston & Wright, 1998; Perse, 2001). Males outnumber females on children's TV, and they dominate in action roles, wielding authority, displaying bravado, or demonstrating competence or expertise. Females dominate in nurturing roles and dependent behavior. A metanalysis shows correlations between television viewing and gender-role stereotyping (Signorella, Bigler, & Liben, 1993). Children who have stereotyped beliefs are likely to be attracted to stereotyped shows. However, in a classic study, the television show *Freestyle*, with boys in nurturing roles and girls as mechanics, changed the perceptions of its middle-school viewers (Johnston & Ettema, 1982). When classroom viewing was accompanied by class discussions, changes in attitudes about stereotypes endured 9 months later (Huston & Wright, 1998).

Both the young and the old are represented differently from reality on TV (Condry, 1989). The typical female on television is young (under age 35), whereas males are generally older. Elderly women are portrayed on TV as victims of crime 30 times more often than is the case in real life, whereas older men tend to be portrayed as successful and powerful. These stereotypes lead children to assume that the real world mirrors that of TV unless they have actual experiences to alter this perception (Dorr & Rabin, 1995).

How do children perceive ethnicity and class as represented by the media? According to a study of 1200 children representing African American, Asian American, Hispanic American, and Euro-American ethnic groups (Children Now, 1998), the children believed it is very important to see their own ethnic group on television. Euro-American children reported seeing members of their group most frequently, followed by African American children; Asian American and Hispanic American children reported doing so much less frequently. All groups recognized the media's use of stereotypes, frequently attributing positive traits and roles to Euro-American characters and negative traits and roles to minority group members.

Effects on Children's Reading and Communication Skills

In addition to watching TV, children learn about the world through reading and communicating. There is concern that time spent in front of the TV has been responsible for the general decline in reading levels and test scores on standardized tests, such as the Scholastic Aptitude Test (Healy, 1998; National Commission on Excellence in Education [NCEE], 1983). Certainly, TV viewing takes time away from other activities, such as reading, pursuing hobbies, attending concerts, and visiting museums—all of which enhance intellectual development.

According to reviews of the research (Neuman, 1991; Winn, 1977), children read fewer books when television is available to them. This is probably because it is human nature to opt for the activity requiring less effort (passively viewing) rather than the one requiring more effort (actively perusing). However, family values regarding what constitutes "useful" leisure activities can influence what children choose to do (Neuman, 1991).

Television actually has the potential to motivate reading. For example, an award-winning show, *Reading Rainbow,* broadcast on public television, encourages reading: Once a book is spotlighted on the show, libraries and bookstores report an increase in demand (Trelease, 2001).

Many educators report that children who watch a lot of television have a low tolerance for the frustration involved in learning. Watching television accustoms children to being entertained. Programs such as *Sesame Street* and cartoons designed for children "tend to give students unrealistic expectations of teachers. Kids are so used to being entertained by personalities on TV that they expect teachers to do the same" (Fiske, 1980, p. 55). Furthermore, students accustomed to being entertained by "show biz" techniques become bored with schoolwork that requires complex thought or sustained concentration, and they may have attention and listening problems (Healy, 1998). Again, adult involvement in viewing shows and discussing them can stimulate children to think about what they have seen (Dorr & Rabin, 1995).

Reading is an active process in that it involves the creation of images in readers' minds through symbols—the printed words. Television viewing, in contrast, does not involve the decoding and transformation of symbols; the entire sensory message and experience are there all at once. **Information processing** involves selecting content to attend to based on interest, past experiences, and level of cognitive development (Huston & Wright, 1998).

Until recently, there was little research on how the brain absorbs information from TV. TV primarily stimulates the right half of the brain, the part that specializes in emotional responses, rather than the left half, which specializes in analytical thinking. After connecting viewers to instruments that measure brain waves, one researcher found twice as much right-brain activity as left-brain activity (Mann, 1982). Because reading demands complex mental manipulations, readers must concentrate far more than television viewers. Readers also control the pace; if they do not understand the material, they can reread it, slow down, or go to other sources for elucidation before continuing. Similarly, if the material is familiar or easily understood, readers can skip over it, speed up, or skim it. And, if the material evokes an emotional reaction, they can stop and experience their feelings, and then return to it without having lost anything.

Television's pace cannot be controlled by viewers—another reason it impacts their ability to concentrate (Healy, 1998). TV programs continually move forward; what is misunderstood by viewers remains so, and what evokes delight cannot be slowed down or reviewed. The increased use of VCRs and DVD players may counter this limitation in that viewers can slow down, stop, and repeat videos and DVDs. Television is essentially a visual medium; although words are spoken, it is the images that contain the most important meaning. Because the rapid succession of images doesn't allow time for viewers' own reflections, some researchers have speculated that television viewing leads to an impulsive rather than reflective style of thought and to a lack of persistence in intellectual tasks (Greenfield, 1984; Healy, 1998).

Effects on Academic Achievement

A longitudinal study (Anderson et al., 2001) following over 500 children from preschool to adolescence found that the content of television shows has a significant impact on academic achievement. Specifically, viewing educational programs as preschoolers was correlated with higher grades in school, an increase in reading, a higher value on achievement, greater creativity, and less aggression. These associations were more consistent for boys than for girls, with the exception of girls who watched violent programs as preschoolers. These findings held true even after taking into account family background. These findings underscore the potential positive influence of television.

Children and adolescents actively choose media and assimilate their messages into their own systems of meaning (Brown & Cantor, 2000). Television has made significant contributions to children's realms of experience, their vocabulary, and their ability to communicate. The challenge for educators and parents, then, in regard to improving academic skills, is to capitalize on the useful aspects of children's viewing experiences.

MEDIATING INFLUENCES ON SOCIALIZATION OUTCOMES

In a comprehensive review of research on the effects of television on children, Comstock and colleagues concluded that television is indeed a major socializer of children (Comstock & Paik, 1991; Comstock & Scharrer, 1999). However, it is difficult to pinpoint the exact effects of television on behavior because of other mediating or intervening influences, such as viewers' cognitive developmental levels, psychological needs, attitudes, motives, habits, interests, values, morals, beliefs, and experiences (Huston & Wright, 1998; Perse, 2001) (see Figure 9.2). For example, teens who need to feel part of the group are more influenced by ads touting "in" clothes, perfume, or CDs than are adults whose needs for belonging have been met. For another example, some of my students who watch certain talk shows said they could not relate to some of the topics because what was being discussed was against their moral beliefs. These mediating influences determine what viewers will selectively attend to in their environments.

Thus, media effects are bidirectional:

> Children are not just recipients of media messages; they choose the content to which they are exposed, and they interpret the content within their own frames of reference. They receive media messages in contexts of family, peers, and social institutions, all of which may modify or determine how children integrate messages into their existing store of information and beliefs (Huston & Wright, 1998, p. 1027)

Selective Attention

Our senses (sight, hearing, touch, taste, smell) enable us to respond to stimuli in the environment. However, it is impossible to pay attention to everything going on

Figure 9.2

*Mediating Influences
Affecting the Outcomes
of Media Messages*

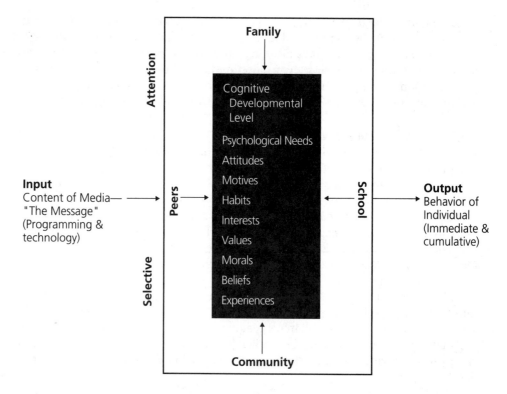

about us; thus, we select, or consciously attend to only some of the available stimuli. Research has been done on infants and children in order to identify what parts of their environment they attend to. **Selective attention** is crucial to learning because children's perceptions and concepts of the world depend on which aspects of it get their attention. The following are examples of classic research findings that illustrate the role of selective attention in learning.

Babies respond to movement. For example, a 5-day-old who is sucking on a pacifier will stop sucking if a light moves across her or his visual field (Haith, 1966). Babies also respond to novelty. For instance, 1-day-old babies will look longer at a patterned surface than at a plain one (Fantz, 1965). Children between age 2 and 3 years tend to pay more attention to the color of the object than to the form, whereas children age 4–6 tend to prefer form to color (Stevenson, 1972). As children grow, their attention tends to focus on what they judge to be the important aspects of a situation. Eight-year-olds are more capable than 4- to 6-year-olds of deliberately ignoring irrelevant information when confronted with a problem (Bjorklund, 1994; Osler & Kofsky, 1965).

Although children become increasingly better at selective attention as they get older due to attentional strategies they have developed, it is not until about age 7 that they can purposely ignore "attention grabbers" (Bjorklund, 1994), such as images or songs in advertisements.

As children approach adulthood, they selectively attend to those messages that are related to their individual interests, are consistent with their attitudes, are congruent with their beliefs, and are supportive of their values. For example, children will spend more time watching families on television that are similar to theirs in regard to ethnicity or single- or step-parenthood (Dorr & Rabin, 1995; Huston & Wright, 1998).

Condry (1989) summarized what specific aspects of television children attend to in his book *The Psychology of Television*. Starting in infancy, the amount of time children spend looking at a TV set while it is on increases steadily with age. The largest increase comes between age 2 and 3. Preschool children show elevated attention to women, puppets, animation, strange voices, lively music, auditory changes, and rhyming, repetition, and alliteration, and they pay less attention to men, animals, inactivity, and still pictures. Commercials capitalize on these findings.

Older children pay attention to more complexities as they gain in cognitive development. They are now able to understand story plots and characters, and they are attracted to action adventure shows and situation comedies. School-agers need to attend to visual techniques more so than do adolescents to understand the story line (Comstock & Paik, 1991). In general, media cues that attract attention are "outstandingness," novelty, contrast, and the relationship of cues to viewers' frames of reference.

Points to Ponder

Selective attention involves the ability to focus on relevant aspects of a task while ignoring irrelevant or distracting stimuli. As choices increase in every area of life (new products, technologies, services, and opportunities), how do you make decisions regarding relevancy? Similarly, every time I want to go on the Internet, I am swamped with advertisements, trivia information, and opinions. The movies have also become a forum for the information glut, and this has been occurring for years on television. How do you choose what to selectively attend to out of all the stimuli bombarding you?

Adult Involvement

Just as we selectively attend to our environment from infancy onward, so we selectively attend to the messages communicated by television. Television programmers may be able to manipulate the level of "outstandingness," novelty, or contrast, or to attract the audience's attention by controlling the input. However, it is up to viewers to decide whether those messages belong in their frames of reference by being aware of the mediating influences (cognitive developmental levels, needs, attitudes, motives, habits, interests, values, morals, beliefs, and experiences).

Parents, especially, can mediate the amount of attention given to TV by their children by being the primary socializers in their children's frames of reference. Children are more likely to attend to messages on TV that conform to their family's interests, attitudes, beliefs, and values. Parents, teachers, and older siblings are probably most important in determining television programming effects on children (Comstock & Paik, 1991; Pearl, 1982). Early evidence of this importance was found in a first-year evaluation of *Sesame Street*. The researchers showed that those children who watched the show with their mothers and talked to them about it learned more than did other children (Ball & Bogatz, 1970). This finding was supported by later research on the vocabulary development of preschoolers (Rice, Huston, Truglio, & Wright, 1990).

Parents can mediate television viewing by (1) controlling the number of hours of television exposure, (2) checking ratings and evaluating what kinds of programs may be viewed, (3) viewing television with their children and discussing the

By viewing TV with their children, these parents can mediate the messages being broadcasted.

programs, and (4) arranging family activities other than television viewing. Several studies (Dorr & Rabin, 1995; Huston & Wright, 1998; Perse, 2001) support the value of significant others' involvement in children's television viewing. For example, one study (Wilson & Weiss, 1993) showed that co-viewing a show with older siblings increased preschoolers' enjoyment of and decreased their level of arousal in response to a scary program. Another study (Haefner & Wartella, 1987) showed that coviewing changed 6- and 7-year-olds' evaluations of certain characters in two programs.

Why is mediation by significant others or adults important? For one thing, children do not "see" television in the same way adults do; according to Marieli Rowe, executive director of the American Council for Better Broadcasts, "The impact television has on a viewer depends to a great extent on what the viewer brings to TV" (Condry, 1989; Perse, 2001; Skalka, 1983). Adult viewers can analyze and evaluate content, tune out irrelevancies, absorb complicated plots, and understand underlying messages. For the most part, children cannot.

For another thing, as mentioned previously, young children cannot distinguish fantasy from reality; their understanding is based on appearances. They do not know what is fact and what is opinion. They have not had the experiences, nor do they possess the knowledge, to enable them to comprehend the basis of many events that occur in the world. Yet they are exposed to the whole world through the television screen before they have even developed an understanding of their own immediate world. We do not expect children to read a book before they can recognize letters. Adults, then, must develop strategies to mediate children's television viewing according to their own values and their children's cognitive developmental level.

MESOSYSTEM INFLUENCES

Mesosystem influences on television and movies consist of linkages with the community, the school, and the family. These linkages affect the pervasiveness of media exposure, the type of media and content, adult mediation, and the impact of socialization outcomes.

Community–Media Linkages

It is generally agreed that TV is here to stay. Even though some alternatives to broadcast (free) TV are available, it is the programs transmitted over the airwaves "in the public interest" that have stimulated community concern:

> Children and families live in a media environment that is not of their own making. They can select from what is available, but they do not have many opportunities to change the menu. Decisions about production and distribution of most mass media are made by private corporations. In this country, because of the First Amendment to the Constitution, those decisions are protected from government interference except in unusual circumstances. (Huston, Zillman, & Bryant, 1994, p. 9)

The community's response, therefore, has been to develop alternatives to commercial television, such as the Public Broadcasting Service and cable and satellite

TV, to use new technologies to record particular shows and to view selected movies, and to form public interest groups.

The Public Broadcasting Service (PBS). One response to the perceived deficiencies of commercial television was the establishment of the Public Broadcasting Service (PBS), through the Public Broadcasting Act of 1967. PBS is an alliance of local community and educational stations financially supported by the Corporation for Public Broadcasting and by annual membership fees of licensees, as well as by advertisers. Supplemental funds come from grants from the National Endowment for the Humanities, from universities, and from corporations, with the aim of providing more specialized, diversified, and high-quality programs to reach specific age, social, and cultural groups.

Some examples of children's programs broadcast on PBS are *Sesame Street*, designed for preschoolers (programs are creative and educational); *Wishbone*, designed for school-agers (adaptations of excellent children's literature promote reading), and *Scientific American Frontiers*, designed for young adolescents (programs stimulate scientific discoveries).

The main problem that public television faces is financial; specialization is costly. If the public wants the quality PBS provides, it has to financially support its local community PBS station.

Cable and Satellite Television. Families that pay for cable television or have purchased satellite dishes can view certain channels that show movies, sports, and educational programs. One such channel, available only through cable TV, is Nickelodeon—a television channel for children. Every day there are shows for children age 2–15. For example, there are songs for young children, adventures for middle-years children, and talk shows for teenagers.

Cable TV also provides music television on channels like MTV, CMT, and VH1. For example, MTV shows videos in which rock groups and rappers "act out" their songs. Occasionally, the portrayals are surrealistic, have sexual imagery, and/or violence (Greenberg, 1994). Many religious and parental groups have sought to ban such videos and recordings because the lyrics were said to have a bad influence on children (Cocks, 1985; Strasburger & Hendren, 1995). Particularly active has been the Parents Music Resource Center (PMRC), which charged in a congressional hearing that rock music promotes sexual activity, violence, drug use, and Satanism (Gore, 1987). Recently, however, MTV and the American Psychological Association (APA) joined forces to enlighten viewers to the dangers of violence on TV. The research on popular music is discussed later in this chapter.

Videocassette Recorders and DVD Players. The business community has provided expanded uses of television. In many homes, television sets are used as display terminals for videotapes or discs and video games. Over three-quarters of the TV households in the United States own videocassette recorders or DVD players. Families that have home videocassette recorders can play a more active role in selecting and managing their leisure time. A home video recorder enables individuals to rent selected movies or instructional tapes and to record shows they don't want to miss.

Schools use videocassette recorders, too. Teachers can record television shows and play them back in their classrooms. The advantage of such a medium is that the video can be stopped at any point for discussion. Sometimes videos are used to illustrate literature. For example, viewing Zeffirelli's *Romeo and Juliet* aided my son's understanding of Shakespeare's play.

The proliferation of videos makes movies produced for the big screen accessible and affordable. Unless adults mediate, however, young people can be exposed to the same violence, sexuality, and "antivalues" as on TV.

Public Interest Groups. Another response to what were felt to be the deficiencies of commercial television was the formation of public interest groups. These groups pressure broadcasters for change, lobby the government for regulations, and/or educate the public to monitor its own viewing habits and those of its children. They have been influential in developing the rating system for television and movies.

One such group is Action for Children's Television (ACT), which was founded in 1968 by a concerned parent, Peggy Charren, who mobilized 30 friends for the purposes of reducing violence on children's TV, limiting the number of commercials on children's shows, and preventing program hosts or celebrities from advertising on their shows. ACT is now a national organization that encourages networks to provide more and better-quality programming for children by giving annual awards to broadcasters that have made significant contributions to children's television and by providing parents, teachers, and others with educational materials. Other advocacy groups, such as the Center for Media Education, have followed suit. These organizations were influential in pressuring the FCC in 1996 to strengthen the Children's Television Act of 1990 by mandating that commercial television stations broadcast at least 3 hours of educational/informational (E/I) programming per week for children. These programs must be labeled and advertised in a TV schedule. There are also mechanisms for public accountability whereby parents can rate the shows.

Another example of a public interest group is the National Citizens' Committee for Broadcasting (NCCB), which distributes information outlining public TV rights and methods for legislation. The NCCB's annual "violence index" was instituted to increase public awareness of advertisers that sponsor shows with a high incidence of violence.

Finally, the national Parents and Teachers Association (PTA) has become involved in educating parents and teachers on how they can help children develop critical viewing skills (see the box "Strategies for Television Viewing").

School–Media Linkages

Public broadcasting airs a variety of programs specifically developed for the classroom, referred to as educational television (ETV). Teachers nationwide use ETV as part of their curriculum, and millions of school-age children receive a portion of their regular instruction through television. Supporters of television in the classroom suggest that ETV provides memorability, concreteness, and emotional involvement, and also stimulates reading, encourages class discussion, and promotes student interactions (Greenfield, 1984). However, ETV has also been criticized because many programs are financed by corporations that advertise their products on the show; the argument is that the classroom should not be a marketplace.

Schools have tried various tactics to control children's viewing habits. Some schools ask parents to keep children away from TV entirely; others recommend setting limits on the number of viewing hours per day or allowing only certain shows to be watched. Some schools have taken steps to educate parents on the effects of TV on academic performance, rather than making across-the-board rules. Parents are encouraged, then, to develop their own family policies. Still other schools give suggestions to alternative activities to TV viewing.

Some schools work with parents to develop critical viewing skills in children. The television networks have cooperated with the schools in this regard by producing detailed study guides for teachers to use as learning aids. The scripts of some shows are available to schools to stimulate interest in reading. An example of such a show broadcast by CBS was *Skeezer*, based on the book by Elizabeth Yates. ETV provides related curriculum aids to teachers. PBS also has literature, history, and science programs and videos available to schools; teachers and parents can obtain a schedule of local programming.

Obviously, the success of the school efforts to ban, limit, provide alternatives to, or develop critical viewing skills for television depends on the cooperation of the family.

Family–Media Linkages

There can be no doubt that television as a medium of communication and information is of extreme potential value. Shows such as *The American Experience, Nova,* and *National Geographic* enrich viewers by exposing them to history, culture, geography, science, and travel—providing perspectives of life that they may never have experienced. Shows such as *Barney, Sesame Street,* and *Mister Rogers' Neighborhood* provide children with models of cooperation, altruism, self-control, and empathy. Research has shown that exposure to television programs that provide models of prosocial behavior enhances children's prosocial tendencies (Friedrich & Stein, 1973; Leibert & Sprafkin, 1988). Parental coviewing of prosocial programs and subsequent discussions of them are even more enhancing (Dorr & Rabin, 1995; Huston & Wright, 1998; Perse, 2001).

Parents must exercise primary responsibility in regulating and monitoring their children's viewing habits. In a democratic society, it is ultimately the viewers who bear responsibility for the effects of television; families must accept that responsibility by not viewing what is offensive and/or by supporting public interest groups.

Unfortunately, several studies (Dorr & Rabin, 1995; Huston & Wright, 1998; Perse, 2001) have indicated that parental involvement in children's viewing is infrequent. Many children are allowed to watch what and when they want. Some children are restricted as to how early and how late they may watch, and others have restrictions on their total viewing time per day. And some children are restricted to viewing certain approved shows. Although many shows are viewed with other family members, especially siblings, two intensive, longitudinal studies of young children and their families concluded that parents did not use the time to mediate the shows (Desmond, Singer, & Singer, 1990; St. Peters, Marguerite, Huston, Wright, & Eakins, 1991.

Parental involvement is difficult for many families because both parents work. In some families, children come home after school to an empty house and turn on the television for companionship. In other families, the television unintentionally becomes an "electronic babysitter" while parents are busy doing chores, caring for other children, or engaging in some other activity. In these families, then, the messages children get from television are not mediated by significant adults in their lives. Thus, television becomes a powerful socializing agent for these children. Parents who rely on television to occupy children while they are busy might consider using selected videotapes and/or purchasing a channel blocker (V-chip). However, all parents should teach their children how to watch TV selectively and critically.

Strategies for Developing Critical Viewing Skills in Children

1. *Know what your children watch and when.* A log of how much time they spend in front of the tube often speaks for itself about whether TV is playing too large a role in their lives. Also be alert to the content of the programs, as well as the commercials. Notice ways in which viewing affects your children's behavior:
   a. Do they become transfixed after watching for a while?
   b. Does viewing make them tense and lead to fighting?
   c. What effects does it have on family communication when you all watch together?
   d. How are ethnic groups, gender roles, and age groups presented?
   e. How are conflicts resolved?
2. *Know the ratings and choose what to watch.* Don't leave watching to chance—you wouldn't put a refrigerator in your children's room and allow them to eat what they wanted on the chance they would eventually meet their nutritional requirements. Learn to turn off the set when your selected show is over.
3. *Set limits.* Talking over a set of guidelines with family members, agreeing upon them, and sticking to them is effective in establishing a new routine for viewing TV. For example, your family may choose to ban TV during dinner, to allow viewing only after other responsibilities (homework, chores) have been met, or to allow each family member to select one program each week. Also, help children choose activities to do when the TV is off (read a book, draw a picture, play a game).
4. *Whenever possible, view with children.* When watching with young children, point out what is real and what is fantasy. When values presented on TV conflict with your family values, say so! When values agree, say so, too!
   a. Discuss the differences between fantasy and reality.
   b. Discuss conflict situations and ways problems could be solved without violence.
   c. Discuss situations involving cooperation, and note behaviors your children might imitate.
   d. Point out characters who represent a variety of ethnic groups.
   e. Point out men and women who represent a variety of occupations.
   f. Discuss food advertisements in terms of what is healthy and nutritious.
   g. Discuss toy advertisements in terms of play potential, safety, and age appropriateness.
5. *Use the time in front of the TV to benefit children:*
   a. Television can be a rich source of vocabulary development—explain new words to children.
   b. Television can expand children's horizons—talk about other places in the world, other cultures, and new experiences.
   c. Television programs can stimulate reading of related material—encourage children to do so.
   d. Television can stimulate discussion on sensitive topics with older children, such as drugs, rape, and teenage pregnancy—take advantage of this opportunity to discuss such topics.

Source: Action for Children's Television, n/d.

Print Media: Books and Magazines

Compared with pictorial media, such as television, print media are more difficult to investigate experimentally because they are often long, have complex structures, and provoke more individual imagery than does television. Thus, it is difficult to separate the socializing effects of the *content* of the book or magazine from the socializing effects of the *interpretation* of the reader.

Unlike the pictorial media, in which the visual image is provided, the print media describe in words the images of the writer. These words must then be translated into visual images by readers. Obviously, reading is much more personal than is television viewing because the visual images readers conjure up from printed words depend on their vocabulary, reading ability, and real-life experiences.

Also, it is difficult to compare the effects of books and TV on socialization because, until children gain a fair amount of reading skill, adults usually read books to them. This means that the adults are present to explain material, answer questions, and adjust the tempo to children's level of understanding and interest. In addition, adults choose most of the books young children read. Parents and relatives buy books, teachers assign certain books, and librarians choose which books will fill the library shelves. Thus, adults play a large role in determining the influence books will have on children; this has not been the case with television viewing.

The print media play an important role in socialization in passing on culture to the next generation. The print media teach history, values, morals, ideals, and attitudes. Former Secretary of Education William Bennett felt so strongly that American children should be exposed to the basic human values of self-discipline, compassion, responsibility, friendship, work, courage, perseverance, honesty, loyalty, and faith that he edited *The Book of Virtues: A Treasury of Great Moral Stories* (Bennett, 1993). He believed that stories are the way children learn what virtues look like, what they are in practice, how to recognize them, and how they work.

THE POWER OF PRINT MEDIA: LITERACY

Literacy—the ability to communicate via reading and writing—is at the core of the educated person. According to Postman (1986, p. 2), "The written word endures, the spoken word disappears." Print media make a powerful contribution to literacy because cognition and socialization are involved in interpreting printed words, stories, and information.

Different media elicit different thinking skills (Healy, 1991). Meringoff (1980) and colleagues (Char & Meringoff, 1981) compared the abilities of young children to comprehend and reproduce narratives presented in different media (stories in print versus those on television and radio). They found that, even when the same soundtracks were used, television focused children's attention on actions of characters whereas radio and books directed attention to the quality of the language. Children were more likely to consider television as an experience apart from themselves when answering questions about the program, and they were more likely to include their own personal experiences when answering questions about stories in books. Thus, print and pictorial media require different ways of processing information.

The print media have more potential to socialize because of the greater involvement of adults. Adults motivate children to notice print by pointing out signs and

By reading aloud to children, adults can enhance children's language development and their desire to read on their own.

PhotoDisc Collection/Getty Images

labels. They also read books to children and encourage them to recognize letters and to write:

> The development of literacy is a social process, embedded in social relationships, particularly in children's relationships with parents, siblings, grandparents, friends, caretakers, and teachers. These people serve as models, provide materials, establish expectations, and offer help, instruction, and encouragement. (McLane & McNamee, 1990, p. 7)

When adults become involved in children's experiences with print, children are exposed to certain values, attitudes, behaviors, and skills; they learn how to derive meaning from print (McLane & McNamee, 1990). The ability to glean meaning, then, opens up the world of history, culture, science, and so on to children. As Vygotsky (1978) observed, children's learning is increased with the help of an expert, a phenomenon referred to earlier in the book as the "zone of proximal development."

HOW BOOKS AND MAGAZINES SOCIALIZE CHILDREN

History and culture have been passed on first orally, then via writing (hieroglyphics, letters, diaries), then via print, and now also via computers. We can, therefore, conclude that the print media is a significant socializer.

Books are written language. Language, as was discussed in Chapter 2, enables socialization to take place. Language makes ideas and communication of these ideas possible; language also makes it possible to replace action with thoughts. Language is a vehicle by which individuals can express emotions (Rovenger, 2000). Language enables humans to internalize attitudes of others. Language is the means of passing on the cultural heritage from one generation to the next.

Magazines are written language, too, but they are infused with pictures and advertisements; this means that one socializing effect is consumerism. Magazines usually cater to special interests, such as fashion, sports, computers, science, and pets, and so contribute to the knowledge base of their readers.

Jim Trelease (2001), in *The Read-Aloud Handbook*, cites evidence stressing the importance of reading for building knowledge. Reading aloud improves children's listening comprehension, a skill that must be developed before reading comprehension can take place. It is the activity of reading aloud to children that, in turn, enables them to become successful readers. Reading aloud is so important because it enhances attachment, and socialization begins with personal attachment. Reading aloud provides a model for children to imitate:

> Children who are not spoken to by live and responsive adults will not learn to speak properly. Children who are not answered will stop asking questions. They will become incurious. And children who are not told stories and who are not read to will have few reasons for wanting to learn to read. (Haley, 1989, p. 19)

Ellen Spitz (1999), in *Inside Picture Books*, analyzes books that adults have read to children for generations, such as *Goodnight Moon* (Brown, 1947) and *Where the Wild*

Things Are (Sendak, 1963). She discusses how well-known picture books transmit psychological wisdom, convey moral lessons, and shape tastes. Hidden in these familiar stories are the anxieties of childhood, such as fear of separation and loss, or threat of aggression. Reading to children builds a special bond between reader and listener.

Influences on Development

The way children use their brains causes physical changes in their neural wiring. Children who are stimulated and are actively engaged in experiences have more neural connections than children who have fewer experiences (Begley, 1997). These neural connections allow for different functions, so children with more connections not only can master more skills but also are more adaptable in learning them. Analogously, one can get to a destination more successfully if one knows alternative routes to use in case of road work or traffic.

Language and Reading Development. Books enhance language development. Studies have shown that children who are read to often and who read a lot on their own are more advanced in their language development than children who are rarely read to and who do not read much on their own (Chomsky, 1972; McLane & McNamee, 1990).

Part of the explanation for the effect of reading on language development, compared with talking and/or other media, is that written language is more structured and more complex. The language in children's books, then, is more complex and richer in syntactic patterns than the language used in children's television programs (Healy, 1991; Postman, 1992). Television engages children in a passive way with language, whereas books and stories engage children in an active way. Active use of language has a greater impact on language development than passive listening (Barclay, Benelli, & Curtis, 1995).

Not surprisingly, books also enhance reading development. Research indicates that children who are read to and who have someone to answer their questions learn to read earlier and more easily than children who are not read to (Barclay, Benelli, & Curtis, 1995; Schickedanz, 1986; Teale, 1984). Although most children learn to read at school, preschoolers who are read to learn about reading by developing emergent literary skills—for example, that words tell stories and words are made up of different letters (Whitehurst & Lonigan, 1998). Letter recognition has been found to correlate with future reading achievement scores (Lonigan, Burgess, & Anthony, 2000).

Cognitive Development. Books nourish cognitive development. Not only do they provide information and concepts, they also provide vicarious experiences and stimulate children's imagination. For example, *The Very Hungry Caterpillar* (for preschoolers) by Eric Carle (1986) helps teach children what the days of the week are, how to count to five, and how a caterpillar becomes a butterfly, all in bright pictures.

Books can be used to help children gain an understanding of themselves and others across time and space (Norton & Norton, 2002). For example, *The Three Pigs* (for preschoolers) by David Weisner (2001) was a 2002 **Caldecott Medal** winner, an award given annually for the most distinguished American picture book for children. The book is an adaptation of the classic folktale, in which the pigs are huffed and puffed off the page into a new world. Transformations occur as the pigs boldly enter new stories, make new friends, and ultimately control their own fate.

Psychosocial Development. Books provide models for children—models of behavior, gender roles, and occupational roles (Rovenger, 2000). For example, *Mothers Can Do Anything* (for preschoolers) by Joe Lasker (1972) demonstrates the variety of jobs mothers can hold, including scientist, engineer, artist, and lion tamer.

Books can also be used to impart a desired value system (Bennett, 1993). For example, Linda Sue Park's (2001) *A Single Shard* (for school-agers) was the 2002 **Newbery Medal** winner, an award presented annually for the most distinguished contribution to American literature for children. The book is about dedication to one's dreams. The story takes place in twelfth-century Korea where Tree-ear, an orphan, becomes fascinated by the artistry and craft of some potters who live nearby. Despite great odds, Tree-ear's courage, honor, and perseverance enable him to become an apprentice to the master potter, Min. He achieves great happiness by fulfilling his dream of becoming an artist.

Literature can be of value in helping children cope with and overcome problems in their lives (Bettelheim, 1976; Cashdan, 1999; Rovenger, 2000). For example, some fairy tales and folktales deal with aggressive and negative traits of human beings and indicate ways of coping with them. Folktales and fairy tales lie at the roots of every culture and, despite geographical differences, have many similarities in theme (Norton & Norton, 2002): tribal history, local history, myth, legend, and trickster. Folktales and fairy tales are appealing to children because they explain things in terms to which children can relate.

Books offer children the opportunity to explore and understand their own feelings and the feelings of others (Rovenger, 2000). For example, in *The Hundred Dresses* (for school-agers), a classic by Eleanor Estes (1944), a group of schoolchildren realize too late that their cruelty has destroyed the happiness of a poor girl, Wanda Petronski, and her family, who immigrated to the United States from Poland. Wanda attempts to win a place in the group by telling of the hundred dresses she owns. However, she wears the same faded dress to school every day and is teased by the other girls because of it and because she has a funny name. The ostracism that the Petronski family experiences compels them to move away. Soon afterward, Wanda's hundred dresses—that is, her drawings of 100 dresses—are presented in an art contest. The girls finally understand Wanda's feelings, but it is too late to undo that cruelty. This book helps children understand what values are truly important and also that mistakes cannot always be rectified.

Literature, then, can help children understand the realities of life. It can provide them with models of behavior that are useful in dealing with problems and help them understand the consequences of certain behaviors.

CONCERNS ABOUT BOOKS AND MAGAZINES

Books can elicit some of the concerns described earlier in this chapter regarding television, such as the confusion of fantasy with reality, violence, the perpetuation of certain values and stereotypes, and even commercialism (toy tie-ins, clothing, or movies). The degree to which children's books should reflect reality is a source of controversy regarding how the characters solve problems and how they are portrayed (Norton & Norton, 2002).

Fantasy and Reality
Some books feature young characters who overcome obstacles, apparently caused by adults, through real problem solving or through fantasy (Norton & Norton,

2002). For example, Maurice Sendak's *Where the Wild Things Are* (1963) illustrates Max's imagination when, because of his misbehavior, his mother sends him to his room without supper. This book was banned in some schools because its illustrations were regarded as "frightening" to young children and because of its message. Others highly recommend the book because readers can identify with Max and his strong feelings, expressed through fantasy.

The Goosebumps books, a series of monster mysteries for the under-12 set, by R. L. Stine, were introduced to school-agers through school book clubs. There are five basic plotlines, written in a clipped style, replete with thumps and gasps. The books are advertised on TV, and the publisher also offers games and toys for children to act out the plots, thereby blurring the boundaries of fantasy and reality (Gellene, 1996). Critics say the books don't promote literacy but do promote commercialism.

A popular series for the over-12 set is the Harry Potter books (and movies), by J. K. Rowlings. These best-sellers stimulate children's imaginations through their blend of fantasy, magic, mystery, and reality. The attendance at the movies and the number of video purchases attests to the series' popularity.

Some classic juvenile series books have been criticized for being formulaic, such as the Nancy Drew and Hardy Boys books, by Edward Stratemeyer. The dominant themes are danger, mystery, and excitement. Stratemeyer's formula consisted of capturing the readers' interest on the first page, providing a dramatic highpoint in the middle of each chapter, and ending each chapter with a cliff-hanger. Romances, westerns, and mysteries usually contain a great deal of action; the characters are ideal types, and the endings are happy. However, such books purvey an unrealistic view of life, based on the following questionable assumptions (Carlsen, 1980, pp. 52–53):

- Children and adolescents are more perceptive than adults; if they could switch places with adults, they could do a better job at everything adults generally do.
- Dramatic changes, such as in personality or personal appearance, can occur in a short period of time.
- Premonitions turn out to be accurate.
- There is a solution for every problem, and it is usually a simple one.
- One's physical appearance indicates one's character.
- People are either good or bad. Good always wins over bad, and bad people are punished.
- It is OK for the good people to use deceptive or illegal techniques because they have the right goals—"The end justifies the means."
- Heroes and heroines are the culture's male and female stereotypes (handsome, brave males and pretty, dainty females). They also tend to have anglicized names (Nancy Drew).
- Villains are different from the cultural ideal stereotypes. They may be fat, hairy, or dark. They also tend to have foreign-sounding names (Fu Manchu).
- The wealthy tend to be corrupt, whereas the lower and middle classes tend to be good.

Books, as has been noted, are agents of socialization. As psychologist Bruno Bettelheim (1976) wrote, "The acquisition of skills . . . becomes devalued when what one has learned to read adds nothing of importance to one's life." Books should help children examine values, sort them out, and make decisions. Reading stereotyped and formulatic fiction is unlikely to achieve such ends. Research has shown that children's attitudes and achievements are affected by certain biases in books (Norton & Norton, 2002). As a response, Bennett (1993) compiled his book of moral stories and poems to influence children's values.

Violence

Children were exposed to violence in stories and fairy tales long before there was television, and it has been shown that children imitate aggression from storybooks, just as they do from television (Neuman, 1991). Bettelheim (1976) and Cashdan (1999) have suggested that fairy tales help children cope with their strong emotions on an unconscious level:

> It seems particularly appropriate to a child that exactly what the evildoer wishes to inflict on the hero should be the bad person's fate—as the witch in "Hansel and Gretel" who wants to cook children in the oven is pushed into it and burned to death . . . . (Bettelheim, 1976, p. 144)

In *The Witch Must Die,* Sheldan Cashdan (1999) explores how fairy tales help children project their own inner struggles with good and evil onto battles enacted by characters in the stories. Thus, the violence we, as adults, see in literature for young children, especially in fairy tales, is a **catharsis,** a mechanism for the release of strong feelings. According to Charlotte Huck (Huck & Helper, 1996), however, a well-written book enables readers to empathize with the human suffering caused by people's inhumane acts, whereas television or films are more apt to concentrate on the act itself.

A well-written book can provide a perspective on people's pain and suffering because the author has time to develop the characters, which is not true of television. Thus, readers get to know the motives and pressures of each individual and can understand and empathize with the characters (Norton & Norton, 2002).

Stereotyping

Stereotypes continue to appear in children's books, textbooks, and magazines, just as they do on TV. Males, Euro-Americans, and middle-class families tend to be overrepresented. Men and boys are more likely to be active and presented in adventuresome or exciting roles; females are more likely to be passive or dependent and presented in inconspicuous or immobile roles. Fairy tales, especially those made into Disney movies, are good examples (*Cinderella, Snow White and the Seven Dwarfs,* and *Beauty and the Beast*). Minority groups are underrepresented, and when they are shown, members are usually portrayed as conventional and middle class (Dougherty & Engle, 1987; Gollnick & Chinn, 2002).

Recently, however, children's literature has made progress. Specifically, award-winning books have begun to present more equitable portrayals of gender and cultural diversity (Dellman-Jenkins, Florjancic, & Swadener, 1993; MacLeod, 1994). A study by Dougherty and Engle (1987) assessed the gender-role distribution of characters in a sample of Caldecott Medal books from 1981 to 1985. They compared their findings to those from a similar study done 14 years earlier by Weitzman (1972) of Caldecott Medal books from 1967 to 1971. The early study found that males in the titles of picture books outnumbered females 8 to 1; the later study found males still outnumbering females, but in a ratio of 12 to 1. And whereas the early study found males to be portrayed as active and females as passive, the later study found instances of females being portrayed as active and independent; in these instances, the females occupied central roles in the story. Comparable findings were reported in an analysis of sexism in Newbery Medal award books from 1977 to 1984 (Kinman & Henderson, 1985).

Similar changes have occurred in elementary school textbook gender-role stereotyping. Since 1972, when Scott, Foresman became the first publisher to issue guidelines for improving the image of women in textbooks, all major publishers have made recommendations for reducing inequities in instructional materials (Levine & Levine, 1996). However, Myra and David Sadker (1994), in their research on sexism in schools, found twice as many boys and men as girls and women pictured in language arts textbooks; and in a 631-page history text, only 7 pages were related to women.

Reality is still misrepresented in children's books as well (Britton & Limpkin, 1983; Gollnick & Chinn, 2002). For example, in an attempt to correct an imbalance of ethnic minority males, who in reality make up about 6 percent of the labor force, these figures are overrepresented in basal readers in that they are depicted in 17 percent of the working roles. Individuals with disabilities, in contrast, are underrepresented: Whereas about 10 percent of the population are disabled, only 2 percent are shown in basal reader series. People over age 55, who make up over 20 percent of the population, are not only underrepresented but often are shown walking in parks, rocking in chairs, and being cranky. Finally, less than 1 percent of the families portrayed in basal readers have single parents even though about half of the children reading these books are likely to spend at least part of their childhood with only one parent.

A problem in solely depending on textbooks for classroom instruction is that sometimes the validity of their content is not questioned. Gollnick and Chinn (2002) recommend critically examining the following in textbooks:

- *Invisibility*—the underrepresentation of certain groups
- *Stereotyping*—the attribution of rigid roles to certain groups
- *Selectivity and imbalance*—the interpretation of issues and situations from only one perspective
- *Unreality*—the exclusion of sensitive and controversial topics
- *Fragmentation and isolation*—the separation from rather than the integration into main instructional materials issues, information, and contributions of certain groups
- *Linguistic bias*—the omission of feminine and ethnic group references, pronouns, and names

Concern about the effects of school textbooks on gender-role stereotyping, attitudes toward ethnic minorities and people with disabilities, and acquisition of values has caused some state boards of education to adopt guidelines for purchase.

Ten Quick Ways to Analyze Children's Books for Ethnic and Gender Stereotypes

1. Check the illustrations. Look for stereotypes and tokenism (presentation as a symbol with no real significance), and note who is doing what.
2. Check the story line. What is the standard for success? How are problems presented, conceived, and resolved in the story? What is the role of women?
3. Look at the lifestyles.

4. Weigh the relationships between people.
5. Note the heroes.
6. Consider the effects on children's self-image.
7. Consider the author's or illustrator's background.
8. Check out the author's perspective. Is the perspective patriarchal or feminist? Is it Euro-centric, or do minority ethnic perspectives also receive attention?
9. Watch for loaded words (those that ridicule or have insulting overtones).
10. Look at the copyright date. Books with minority themes began appearing in the mid-1960s, but they were usually written by white authors. Not until the 1970s did children's books begin to reflect the realities of a multiethnic society and exhibit more gender equity.

Source: Council on Interracial Books for Children, n/d.

Magazines for teenagers have been around for decades. For example, *Seventeen,* a magazine for teenage girls, was first published in 1944 and still dominates sales (Palladino, 1996); it has articles on fashion, cosmetics, celebrities, and relationships. Teenage boys prefer to read magazines about sports, cars, or computers (Jaffe, 1998).

In one study (Evans, Rutberg, Sather, & Turner, 1991), researchers sampled 10 issues each of three widely circulated female-oriented magazines (*Seventeen, Sassy,* and *YM*) to identify messages directed at teenage girls and the ways in which they related to female identity. The underlying message was that the road to happiness for girls is to attract males by physical beautification (presumably by purchasing the products advertised in the magazine). Many articles implied that female self-esteem should be related to body image, physical attractiveness, and satisfaction with one's weight. Relatively few articles discussed personal enhancement through professional development or leadership, and few promoted intellectual or athletic pursuits or discussed the social issues most women face.

BOOKS, SOCIALIZATION, AND DEVELOPMENTAL LEVELS OF CHILDREN

The developmental level, or cognitive stage, of a child influences the socializing effect of books on that child. How children selectively attend to their environment, perceive information, process it in their brains, remember it, and apply it are influential factors. Several authors (Huck, 1996; Norton & Norton, 2002) believe that children's favorite stories (usually the ones that endure from one generation to the next) correspond to their stages of cognitive development.

Preoperational Stage (About Age 2–7)

Children in the preoperational stage (about age 2–7) are unable to deal with more than one aspect at a time or with complex relationships or abstractions. Thus, folktales, for example, which repeat each event from the beginning—such as "The Gingerbread Boy"—are very appealing to preoperational children, especially 2- to 4-year-olds. Such folktales are cumulative; that is, they bring all previous events into the present to establish visible scenes for readers. Examples of classic books that appeal to older preoperational children are *Blueberries for Sal* by Robert McCloskey (1948) and *Harry the Dirty Dog* by Gene Zion (1956).

As preoperational children begin to understand seriation (arranging things in a sequence), they become interested in stories that have characters of increasing size, such as "The Three Bears," or stories that denote growth, such as the classic *Peter's*

Chair by Ezra Jack Keats (1967). Books can extend and reinforce children's developing concepts—the sequence of time, for example.

Concrete Operational Stage (About Age 7–13 or 15)

As children move from the preoperational to the concrete operational level of thought (about age 7–13 or 15), their ability to understand literature expands. At this level, thought is more flexible and reversible, so they can understand stories within stories, as in Leo Lionni's (1968) classic *The Biggest House in the World.* They can also understand flashbacks and shifts in time periods, and so project themselves into the past and future. Finally, they can more easily identify with other points of view and understand a wide variety of books. Informational books can expand their interests and experiences, and biographies can provide them with models with whom to identify.

Formal Operational Stage (About Age 13)

The intellectual developmental stage of formal operations (about age 13) is characterized by abstract, logical thought. Children in this stage can reason from hypotheses to conclusions. They can hold several plots or subplots in their minds simultaneously and see interrelations among them. They can also interpret abstract symbols and different meanings in literature. They can analyze and evaluate what they read, understand the values presented in books, and examine various issues presented from different viewpoints. For example, in Marjorie Rawlings' (1938) classic *The Yearling,* Jody's parents reluctantly consent to his adopting an orphan fawn because he is so lonely. The two become great friends, but when the fawn destroys the family's meager crops, Jody realizes he must sacrifice the fawn. In giving up what he loves, he leaves behind his own yearling days. Books can provide role models, morals, and attitudes for these children to explore. Books play an important role in socialization at this time because formal operational children are beginning to develop a sense of self, including a gender-role identity, a moral code, and a set of values.

Sound Media: Popular Music

Music expresses aspects of the culture as it changes through history—for example, from "Yankee Doodle," to jazz, to rock (Sklaroff, 2002). What sets today's popular music apart from television and books is that it is an expression of the subculture of youths and that it effectively alienates many adults (Elkind, 1994; Jaffe, 1998). "Popular" music usually refers to rock even though other types of music may go in and out of vogue.

According to a review of the research on popular music (Christenson & Roberts, 1998), children's interest in rock music accelerates in about the third and fourth grades, and by the time of early adolescence, teens listen to music (radio, CDs, tapes, music videos) from 2 to 5 hours each day. Girls listen more than boys, and African Americans and Hispanics watch more music videos than Euro-Americans.

Music taste preferences become more specific as children get older. Boys generally prefer the louder forms of rock, whereas girls generally prefer softer, more romantic forms. Ethnicity and socioeconomic status also play a role in music choice. Young African Americans report a preference for rap and hip-hop; Hispanics lean toward salsa; Euro-Americans say they like all types of rock, as well as rap and hip-hop. The lyrics are a socializing influence in that they espouse certain values while

Teens at this rock concert are enjoying each other's company as well as the music.

engaging attention and emotions with the sound (American Academy of Child & Adolescent Psychiatry [AACAP], 1997; Jaffe, 1998). However, motivation, experience, knowledge, and self-concept are factors in the interpretation of the lyrics. For example, some researchers (Prinsky & Rosenbaum, 1987; Thompson, 1993) have discovered that preadolescents and adolescents often don't understand or attend to the underlying themes in the lyrics. Other studies (Larson, 1995) frame music listening as a fantasy experience to explore possible selves (images of power and conquest, rescue by an idealized lover). This effect is magnified by music videos with their visual as well as audio components (Strouse, Buerkel-Rothfuss, & Long, 1995) and reduced by the presence of family members who disapprove (Thompson & Larson, 1995).

Throughout time and across cultures, people have always created and listened to music. It was a form of communication and emotional expression, an art and celebration, a tradition and source of enjoyment. The media of records, radio, television, and videos provided the ways and means for popular music.

Teenagers in the 1950s were attracted to a form of popular music known as "rock 'n' roll." The term was coined by the late Alan Freed (1922–1956) on his radio show in 1951. Teens liked the dance beats and rhythms, the wailing guitars, and the emotional vocal tones of the singers (Gay, 1998). The music and dance often celebrated sexuality and other freedoms beyond what most adults considered to be acceptable boundaries (Gay, 1998). The general themes of the lyrics were alienation, romantic longing for an ideal partner, and frustrated sexuality (Jaffe, 1998). As teenagers demanded more rock music be played on the radio and purchased more records, the genre spread to other media (TV, movies, audiotapes, videotapes, and compact discs). By the 1960s, rock music was featured in movies about gangs and juvenile delinquents, reinforcing an association between teenage music and alienation (Jaffe, 1998):

> With its origins in the music of slaves and other downtrodden groups, rock music has always spoken to values and points of view outside the mainstream, values frequently divergent from or in opposition to adult culture. . . . Rock music offers an antidote to and an escape from the unrelenting socialization pressures that emanate daily from family and school. Popular music does not tell its listeners to delay gratification and prepare for adulthood. Rather, it tells young people that the concerns they have today are of importance, that they merit expression in music, and that one ought to value one's youth and not worry so much about the future. (Larson, Kubey, & Colletti, 1989, pp. 584, 596–597)

Does listening to music about sensual gratification or reckless behavior influence teenagers' behavior, or are troubled teens attracted to such music because it reflects their state of confusion? Consistent with the hypothesis that solitary music listening allows adolescents to explore their possible selves, one study (Took & Weiss, 1994) concluded that heavy metal and rap music empower male teenagers and provide them with an identity "complete with clothes and hairstyle." Such music also offers a peer group with only similar music taste as a requirement for entry.

Some authors (Arnett, 1991; Roberts & Christenson, 2001) suggest that adolescents' fascination with the despairing lyrics of heavy metal music is a *symptom* of alienation, not its *cause*. For some teens, drug use and careless behavior provide an escape from a chaotic family environment. Acting on the lyric suggestions reflects an absence of parental supervision. For most fans, heavy metal music serves not as a source of anger and frustration, but as a release.

Popular music provides many adolescents with a means of identifying with a particular group or performer (AACAP, 1997; Larson, 1995), especially when positive role models are lacking in their lives. Going to concerts, collecting the stars' music, wearing certain clothing, adopting certain hairstyles, getting tattooed or body pierced can all be part of adolescents' search for identity—it's a style to "try on," a group of which to be a part. Performers are powerful image makers; their effect on children depends on the role of other significant socializing agents, such as family and friends.

The question that remains is whether the songs *reflect* the values of a particular generation or whether they *influence* that generation's values. Concern centers on the issue of **contagion,** the phenomenon whereby individuals exposed to a suggestion will act on it. For example, there is a real concern about the subgenre of hard rock focused on sex and violence (AACAP, 1997). Groups of adults have formed in opposition to this "rockporn"; a number of wives of government officials have formed the Parents' Music Resource Center (PMRC). Along with some PTAs and others, they have pressured the recording industry and the National Association of Broadcasters not to record or air controversial songs or videos and to establish a rating system similar to the ones used for TV and movies. Some recording companies now identify recordings that possess certain explicit lyrics, and some radio stations do not air controversial music (Rice, 2001).

Such a rating system, however, may attract young people to the very material they are being warned against. Keep in mind, though, that a medium's influence as a socializing agent, whether it be television, books, or music, depends on its ability to capture the attention, emotions, and motivations of its audience.

A highly controversial media because of their ability to captivate young audiences are music videos. The issue has its origins in MTV, or Music Television, which was first introduced in 1981 as a 24-hour rock music, cable television channel that promoted new songs by accompanying them with visual dramatization. Music videos now can be found all over the cable dial—from MTV and VH1 to CMT and BET, and beyond. Music videos have been criticized for their violence, sexism, substance abuse, and sexual content (American Academy of Pediatrics, 1996), as well as for stereotyping ethnic groups (Rich, Woods, Goodman, Emans, & DuRant, 1998). "Shake Your Bon Bon," by Ricky Martin (1999), exemplifies sexism and sexual content in that it shows a group of guys on the street looking up at a girl dancing in front of a window in her underwear.

Mental images once fueled by rhythm, beat, and perceived lyrics are now created by special effects on video. That these images are often sexual and/or violent leaves us with this question: Do they influence teen behavior, or are they an outlet for fantasy and aggressive feelings? Another concern is commercialism. Music videos show images that sell the product (Gay, 1998); therefore, what messages are really being promoted must be questioned. For example, many preadolescents and adolescents are influenced by the clothing, hairstyles, and body art of rock and rap stars.

According to the AACAP (1997), the following are troublesome themes found in songs and videos:

- Advocacy and promotion of drugs and alcohol abuse
- Images and lyrics presenting suicide as an "alternative" or solution
- Graphic violence
- Sexual imagery focusing on control, sadism, masochism, incest, devaluation of women, and violence

Interactive Media and Multimedia

Interactive media and multimedia are those which enable the users to participate and/or change, such as computers, video games, and cell phones.

COMPUTERS AND THE INTERNET

The Internet, formerly known as the Arapnet and created by the U.S. Department of Defense, was first established to provide a communications network that would always be operable under any form of attack because there was no central distribution point. This network soon was being used by universities to share information with each other and then by the private sector. The Internet created public space and removed barriers to communication, such as time and space. This public site is neither owned nor controlled by any individual or institution; free speech prevails. The Internet is an international network and so represents many different cultures. Web sites, shopping and trading, e-mail, instant messaging, chat rooms, and newsgroups make for what McLuhan called the "global village."

The Internet is a pool of information. What may be of interest to any individual potentially is there, no matter how major or minor. Information is typically stored on Web pages posted by individuals and content producers. Because Web sites are not categorized, search engines emerged as a means to locate, sort through, and index the sites. Web sites sometimes provide means for feedback from visitors, and forums can be created wherein collaboration can take place. It can be a challenge, however, to distinguish objectivity from subjectivity (Alexander & Tate, 1999).

Information on the Internet is multidimensional rather than linear in that topics can expand in different directions due to hyperlinks among Web sites. Users thus have to be careful not to get distracted.

Some of the problems with Internet technology are (1) piracy issues related to the illegal transfer of copyrighted material, (2) privacy issues regarding the ability to track online usage patterns and gain access to personal data, (3) access issues related to the capacity to hack into unauthorized information, (4) viruses and worms, which can destroy data on computers, and (5) unsolicited "junk mail."

Over two-thirds of U.S. children have access to computers at home, and virtually all have access at school. There is concern, however, regarding the disparity in opportunities for children of different socioeconomic statuses to learn to use computers and to experience enriched learning in the classroom (Shields & Behrman, 2000). Some children may lag behind in the very skills needed to succeed in our increasingly computer-dependent society. Are we creating a gap between the information-rich and information-poor?

As noted previously, computers enhance instruction by presenting information, enabling students to practice skills, promoting creativity by reducing time spent on mechanics, and allowing for assessment. The interactive capabilities of computers with CD-ROMS and modems allow for practically unlimited access to information.

Computers are also an excellent medium for learning by doing (Papert, 1993). For example, some programs enable children to create figures, plan strategies, and solve problems. However, parents and educators must be selective in choosing educational software that will enhance, not detract, from cognitive development. As Healy (1998) points out, because many programs allow users to select tasks and set the level of difficulty, adults need to mediate such selections. Also, "hands-on" learning should precede computer use, and virtual reality should not replace genuine experience.

What about the socializing effects of computers outside the educational domain? What are the influences on children's development of playing computer games? How do children cope with access to all kinds of information on the Internet without having developed critical thinking skills? What about access to material contrary to family values, such as pornography? How can children discern commercial interests from educational ones?

One concern is that children who have home computers will become social isolates and choose solitary activities over interactive ones. One study (Sleek, 1998) of people who regularly logged onto the Internet found that, as use of the Internet increased, the number of social activities engaged in and overall social support experiences decreased. At the same time, children often use computers to attract playmates, and they also use them in the classroom to do collaborative activities (Crook, 1992; Haugland & Wright, 1997; Weinstein, 1991).

Another concern is that children will access information that negates their family's values. Individuals can easily connect to banks, businesses, government agencies, stores, libraries, universities, people with certain interests, and so on. How does such access affect children? Most likely, it depends, as with all media, on the involvement of parents. Parents have to enable children to develop critical thinking skills to evaluate the information and services accessible on the Internet. Using certain software, parents can block out parts of the Internet (pornography, for example) to which they don't want their children exposed. The problem with such "filter" software is that it blocks access to Web sites via certain banned words, which means, for example, that it may block "breasts" links to cancer as well as to pornography. Recently, the Federal Trade Commission (FTC) set privacy rules to protect children from data-gathering online marketers, requiring them to obtain parental permission prior to soliciting information.

As Postman (1992) eloquently elaborates in his book *Technopoly: The Surrender of Culture to Technology,* we must take charge of the technology that is running our lives and place it within the larger context of desirable goals and values. The American Academy of Child and Adolescent Psychiatry (1997) and the Center for Media Education (1997) suggest the following Internet safety rules for children:

1. Never give a name, address, phone number, or school name to anyone met online.
2. Never go into a new online area that will cost extra without parental permission.
3. Never give out a credit card number online.
4. Always tell parents or a trusted adult if something online is scary or confusing.
5. Never arrange to meet anyone in person met online.

Video games actively engage children in media technology.

Computerized Video/CD Games

Video games are a popular alternative to television. Some games can be educational in that they reinforce certain skills, such as math, spelling, and reading, or require players to use certain strategies: "Video games are the first medium to combine visual dynamism with an active participatory role for the child" (Greenfield, 1984, p. 101). It is estimated that 67 percent of households with children own a video game system (Subrahmanyam, Kraut, Greenfield, & Gross, 2001).

Video games represent the fusion of the media technologies of television and computer. The major forces in the current entertainment video game market are Nintendo and Pokémon, although many other interactive systems are available, some in videotape format and others in disc format. Pokémon is an example of a multimedia phenomenon (Solomon, 1999)—a popular TV show and also a video game, a card game, and a toy. The most popular categories of video games are fantasy violence, sports, general entertainment, human violence, and educational (Cesarone, 1994).

The main concern with these interactive games is the prevalence of aggression and gender-role stereotyping, as well as their rule-bound logic designed by the programmers (Dietz, 1998; National Institute on Media and the Family, 2001; Provenzo, 1991).

Males play video games more than females (Cesarone, 1994), and TV producers and video game manufacturers may produce violent games for this audience. The demand for such games may arise from a need to have strong role models, rather than from male hormones.

Studies have shown an increase in the aggressive feelings of children after having played certain games. Whether these games help children let off steam or encourage hostile behavior remains uncertain (Cooper & Mackie, 1986; Griffiths, 1991), but they do contribute to children's acceptance of violence as a way to solve problems (Levin, 1998).

Another concern regarding electronic games, computers, and the Internet is the increasing opportunity to substitute virtual experiences for real ones. Multimedia enable children to interact with simulated characters, assume multiple identities, and chat with strangers who also may have simulated identities (Subrahmanyam et al., 2001). How do children shift from reality to simulation and back to reality, and what is the outcome?

In a review of the research on video game playing, National Institute on Media and the Family (2001) summarized the positive and negative influences on children. On the positive side, games provide an introduction to information technology and give practice in following directions, solving problems and applying logic, and using fine motor and spatial skills. Games also provide an opportunity for adults and children to play together. On the negative side, violent games may contribute to aggressive behavior and to stereotyping, and restrict opportunities for independent thought or creativity. In addition, academic achievement may be negatively related to overall time spent playing video or computer games.

In sum, adults need to be cognizant of available technology, software, and games. They can use video game ratings to select developmentally appropriate games for their children. They should also limit the time spent playing games, with homework and chores done first. And they should discuss the game content with children, explaining discrepancies between reality and fantasy.

Epilogue

Media transmit cultural values via oral tradition, pictures, print, sound, and computer. For example, both the boy who cried "wolf" and Charlie Bucket learned the value of being truthful, albeit in different ways. Media users must cultivate critical thinking skills to evaluate how media messages relate to personal and family values. Adults must be involved in children's media use, just as adults were involved in socializing the boy who cried "wolf" and Charlie Bucket. The villagers taught the boy a lesson by ignoring his third wolf cry, and Willy Wonka taught Charlie a lesson by bequeathing him the chocolate factory for being kind and caring.

Summary

Mass media—including broadcast television, books, movies, magazines, popular music, computers, video games, and multimedia—are shapers, spreaders, and transformers of culture.

Chronosystem influences on media are primarily related to new technology. Children's changing interests and abilities as they develop contribute to the media they select and to the media's outcomes (bidirectional effects).

Macrosystem influences on mass media include politics (laws), economics (corporate sponsors), and technology (medium and message). Whatever is broadcast on the airwaves in the United States must be in the public interest. The responsibility of determining what constitutes public interest rests with broadcasters, which must find sponsors to make their programming cost effective. Some government regulations exist regarding children's television, which are monitored by the Federal Communication Commission, the agency that grants licenses to broadcasters. Recently, a rating system has been developed for TV viewers.

Television in the United States is mostly perceived as a form of entertainment. Television's multisensory nature forces its audience to employ selective attention. Selective attention depends on viewers' frame of reference—their psychological needs, attitudes, motives, habits, interests, values, morals, beliefs, and experiences. These mediating or intervening effects of selective attention make research on television's direct effects on children confusing. It is difficult to separate the content of a show from the viewing experience. Parental or older sibling involvement has also been shown to have a mediating effect.

Concerns regarding pictorial media include time spent watching TV and movies, changes in family rituals, the blurring of reality with fantasy, the effects on imagination, the prevalence of violence, the effects of advertising, the perpetuation of certain values (sexuality, stereotyping), the effects on reading and communication skills, and the effects on academic achievement.

Mesosystem influences on media include linkages to the community, school, and family.

The community's linkage to media is to develop alternatives to broadcast television, such as the public broadcasting system, cable and satellite TV, video recorders, and computerized video games. Another response is the formation of public interest groups to pressure broadcasters to change programming, lobby the government for regulations, and educate the public regarding the importance of monitoring its television-viewing habits, especially those of children.

The school's linkage to media is to teach critical viewing skills and to provide educational programs in the classroom, such as educational television.

The family's linkage to the media is to mediate children's television viewing and help them develop critical viewing skills by knowing the ratings, knowing what children watch and when, choosing what to watch, setting limits, viewing shows with them whenever possible, and using the time in front of the TV to benefit them.

Print media (books and magazines) are more difficult to investigate experimentally than are pictorial media (television and movies). Unlike the pictorial media, in which the visual images are provided, the print media describe in words the images of the writer. These words must then be translated into visual images by the reader. The visual images readers conjure up depend on their vocabulary, reading ability, and real-life experiences. The print and pictorial media require different ways to process information.

It is difficult to compare the socializing effects of print and pictorial media because adults are more likely to mediate books than television. Until children gain a fair amount of reading skill, adults usually choose their books and read to them.

Reading is important for building knowledge. Reading aloud to children enables them to become successful readers. Reading aloud enhances personal attachment, which is a basic ingredient of socialization. It also improves listening skills, which are necessary for reading comprehension. And it provides a model for children to imitate.

Print plays a role in socialization in that it passes on culture to the next generation. It teaches history, values, morals, ideals, and attitudes. Books also socialize children by influencing language development, cognitive development, and psychosocial development. One of the criteria influencing the effect of books on children's socialization is their developmental level, or cognitive stage.

Some concerns regarding the influence of print media on children revolve around certain themes and values perpetuated in comic books, juvenile series books, romances, westerns, mysteries, and magazines. Other concerns involve unrealistic life views, violence, consumerism, and stereotyping.

Sound media (popular music) are a socializing influence in that they engage listeners' attention and emotions with the sound while espousing certain values with the lyrics. Whether children's values and behavior are influenced by the lyrics is uncertain, because other mediating factors, such as relationships and self-concept, are involved. Popular music provides many adolescents with a means of identifying with a particular group or performer. Such identification may affect dress, behavior, friends, and self-concept.

Interactive media—computers, video games, and multimedia—have provoked many questions regarding their socializing effects. Although their use in the classroom to assist instruction generally enhances learning, the effects of their use at home is under debate. Current concerns focus on diminished social interaction, reduced time spent on other activities, aggressive and stereotypical games, the prevalence of rule-bound logic at the expense of creative thought, the confusion of reality with fantasy, and access to information negating family values.

Activity

PURPOSE *To increase your awareness of television's impact.*

1. Monitor a child's (or your own) television viewing behavior for a week, using the accompanying as a model.
2. Note the total viewing hours for the week.
3. Keep track of the time spent on other leisure activities for a week.
4. Analyze your findings to determine what types of shows are viewed and what the impact of their content and commercial messages on viewers might be.

DAY AND TIME	NAME AND TYPE* OF SHOW	DESCRIPTION OF ACTION (CONFLICTS COOPERATION)	DESCRIPTION OF ROLE PORTRAYAL (ETHNIC, GENDER, OR OCCUPATIONAL)	NUMBER AND KIND† OF ADVERTISEMENTS

*Type—comedy, sports, news, drama, cartoon, musical, mystery, and so on.
†Kind—food, toy, beverage, medicine, public service, and so on.

Research Terms

Educational Television (ETV)
Fairy tales
Folk literature
Internet
Literacy
Mass media
Music Television (MTV)
Public Broadcasting Service (PBS)

Related Readings

Bryant, J., & Bryant, A. J. (Eds.) (2001). *Television and the American family* (2nd ed.). Mahwah, NJ: Lawrence Erlbaum.

Cantor, J. (1998). *"Mommy, I'm scared": How TV and movies frighten children and what we can do to protect them.* San Diego: Harcourt Brace.

Carlsen, G. R. (1980). *Books and the teenage reader.* New York: Harper & Row.

Cashdan, S. (1999). *The witch must die: How fairy tales shape our lives.* New York: Basic Books.

Cassell, J., & Jenkins, H. (Eds.). (1999). *From Barbie to Mortal Kombat: Gender and computer games.* Cambridge, MA: MIT Press.

Comstock, G., & Scharrer, E. (1999). *Television: What's on, who's watching, and what it means.* San Diego: Academic Press.

Haugland, S. W., & Wright, J. L. (1997). *Young children and technology: A world of discovery.* Needham Heights, MA: Allyn & Bacon.

Healy, J. (1998). *Failure to connect: How computers affect our children's minds—for better and worse.* New York: Touchstone Books.

Levin, D. E. (1998). *Remote control childhood? Combating the hazards of media culture.* Washington, DC: National Association for the Education of Young Children.

Levine, M. (1996). *Viewing violence: How media violence affects your child's and adolescent's development.* New York: Doubleday.

Lull, J. (Ed.). (1987). *Popular music and communication.* Newbury Park, CA: Sage.

Norton, D. E., & Norton, S. E. (2002). *Through the eyes of a child: An introduction to children's literature* (6th ed.). Upper Saddle River, NJ: Prentice-Hall.

Perse, E. M. (2001). *Media effects and society.* Mahwah, NJ: Lawrence Erlbaum.

Postman, N. (1992). *Technopoly: The surrender of culture to technology.* New York: Vintage Books.

Provenzo, E. F., Jr. (1991). *Video kids: Making sense of Nintendo.* Cambridge, MA: Harvard University Press.

Spitz, E. H. (1999). *Inside picture books.* New Haven, CT: Yale University Press.

Trelease, J. (2001). *The read-aloud handbook* (5th ed.). New York: Viking Press.

Chapter 10

©Michael Newman/PhotoEdit

Ecology of the Community

No man is wise enough by himself.

—Titus Maccius Plautus

Prologue: Then and Now

Community: Structure and Functions

The Community's Influence on Socialization
Physical Factors
Economic Factors
Social and Personal Factors

The Community as a Learning Environment

The Community as a Support System
Chronosystem and Macrosystem Influences on Community Services
Preventive, Supportive, and Rehabilitative Services

Creating Caring Communities
Economic Assistance
Health Care
Support for Families
Special Child Care Services

Mesosystem Influences: Linking Community Services to Families and Schools

Involvement and Advocacy
Types of Advocacy Groups
Child Protection and Maltreatment

Epilogue

Summary

Activity

Research Terms

Related Readings

Prologue | *Then and Now*

THE CONCEPT OF COMMUNITY—UTOPIAN OR UTILITARIAN?

THEN *Plato (427–347 B.C.:)* described the ideal community, a utopia, in *The Republic*. In such a utopia, everyone fulfills his or her function and works for the good of all. Socialization and education prepare individuals for their particular functions in the community and for citizenship in the republic.

In Plato's ideal republic, rational, ethical leaders rule because they understand what is good in human life; they "know" that what is beneficial for the community is likewise beneficial for the individual. Specifically, the community agrees on common social rules concerning such things as safety, theft, truth telling, and promise keeping because these protect individuals. However, Plato's vision was criticized in his day, as it is today. Can such a utopia exist in reality, in that its leaders are truly rational and ethical? Can it be utilitarian, or practical, in that there is agreement among citizens on what is beneficial for all?

NOW George Orwell expressed his anti-utopian views in his satirical 1946 novel *Animal Farm*. In his story, it is the very nature of leadership that fosters disagreement. Having been treated poorly, the animals on Manor Farm oust their drunken human master and take over the management of the farm. At first, the animals share a collective spirit. Everyone willingly works overtime, productivity soars, and there is plenty to eat. The rules for the new community are painted on the barn:

The Seven Commandments

1. Whatever goes upon two legs is an enemy.
2. Whatever goes upon four legs, or has wings, is a friend.
3. No animal shall wear clothes.
4. No animal shall sleep in a bed.
5. No animal shall drink alcohol.
6. No animal shall kill any other animal.
7. All animals are equal. (p. 33)

Within the first season, the pigs appoint themselves to be the leaders because of their assumed intelligence (or could it be they were "pig-headed"?): "We pigs are brain workers. The whole management and organization of the farm depend on us. Day and night, we are watching over your welfare. It is for your sake that we drink that milk and eat those apples" (p. 42). Having succumbed to the temptations of privileges and power, the pigs begin to edit the rules to benefit themselves while rationalizing their violence and greed: "Some animals are more equal than others." They sell the old dog, Boxer, to the glue factory for money to buy liquor. Once again, the rest of the animals are left hungry and exhausted, no better off than they were when humans ran the farm.

Whereas Plato envisioned benevolent, idealistic leaders (a utopian community), Orwell envisioned manipulative, practical leaders (a utilitarian community). Plato focused on the benevolent, empathetic side of human nature: Orwell was more concerned with the malevolent, selfish side.

Since the establishment of the United States as a republic, the government, via legislative policies, has helped shape communities and the services they provide. Throughout history, some leaders have been motivated by altruistic concerns, and others by selfish ones. Political ideologies, pressures from special interest groups, and fluctuations in funding have all played a role in the number and types of programs government leaders have made available to support families and children. A key question has been, Should leaders do what is best for certain persons, or should they do what is best for all? How should the motto of the United States (printed on all its currency)—*"E. pluribus unum"* (one out of many)—be interpreted?

KEY QUESTIONS

- How can we approach the concept of an ideal community while oscillating between values of individualism and collectivism, independence and interdependence, and equality and competition?
- Does the individual shape the community, or does the community shape the individual?
- How can we know what is best for all, who is qualified to decide, and what policies will best help those in need?

Community: Structure and Functions

John Donne (1572–1631) wrote, "No man is an island entire of itself; every man is a piece of the continent; a part of the main. . . ." A community is a group of people having something in common. A community is created because no individual is self-sufficient; we all have many needs, so we turn to others to help satisfy those requirements to survive. Indeed, the word *community* derives from the Latin *communis*, which means "shared." The concept of sharing can refer to space, norms, values, customs, beliefs, rules, and obligations. The spatial aspect of community can be small and limited, as when one refers to one's neighborhood; or it can be large and far-reaching, as when one refers to one's country or to society in general. Thus, a **community** is a group of people living in the same geographic area (neighborhood, town, city) under common laws; it is also a group of people having fellowship, a friendly association, a mutual sharing, and common interests. **Community ecology** comprises the psychological and practical relationships between those people, and their social and physical environments. Therefore, the crucial components of a community are the relationship of people to one another and the sense of belongingness and of obligation to the group.

The community is a microsystem in which much socialization and development take place. It also represents an expansion of family and friendship ties, commonly described as a "sense of community." The sense of community was graphically exhibited in New York City when the twin towers of the World Trade Center and several thousand people within and around them were horrifically destroyed. My cousin was one of those who perished. Although shocked, people did not hesitate to help one another. Strangers risked their lives to try to save individuals buried in the rubble. Doctors, nurses, firefighters, police officers, and many others donated their time. People from all over the country came to dig for bodies so that families could identify their loved ones. Others came to help clean up the debris. And even after the last embers had died out and the last of the foul air had dissipated, people stayed connected. This terrible tragedy was felt all around the globe. It made people realize the importance of community—the idea that people need people to survive. Will this profound sense of community stay with us, or will it erode over time, perhaps due to feelings of helplessness? According to prior reviews of the research (Schorr, 1997), community ties had eroded almost everywhere, for several reasons:

- Fear of violence deters people from gathering informally in public spaces.
- Advances in transportation and communication enable people to move far from family and friends in order to work.
- Technological advances make it less necessary to leave home for entertainment.
- The larger scale of most institutions and businesses makes it harder for individuals to connect with others.

Perhaps research on the aftermath of September 11, 2001, will show that we will have learned some lessons.

The need for community is both psychological and practical. Psychologically, humans need companionship—the emotional security that comes from belonging to a social group whose members share the same ideas and patterns of behavior. Practically, humans need to cooperate with others in order to attain the necessities of life—food, shelter, and security. Therefore, communities are structured to serve five functions (Warren, 1983):

1. *Production, distribution, consumption.* The community provides its members with the means to make a living—for example, in agriculture, industry, or services.
2. *Socialization.* The community has the means by which it instills its norms and values in its members, (through tradition, modeling, and/or formal education).
3. *Social control.* The community has the means to enforce adherence to community values, such as through group pressure to conform and/or formal laws.
4. *Social participation.* The community fulfills the need for companionship, in neighborhoods, churches, businesses, and so on.
5. *Mutual support.* The community enables its members to cooperate to perform tasks too large or too urgent to be handled by a single person. Supporting a community hospital with tax dollars and donations is an example of people cooperating to accomplish the function of health care.

Communities, small or large, perform these functions in many different ways. The ways in which a particular community does so influence the socialization of children growing up there. In this chapter, we examine how different factors—physical, economic, social, and personal—characterizing a community might influence socialization. Figure 10.1 provides an ecological model of the systems involved in the process.

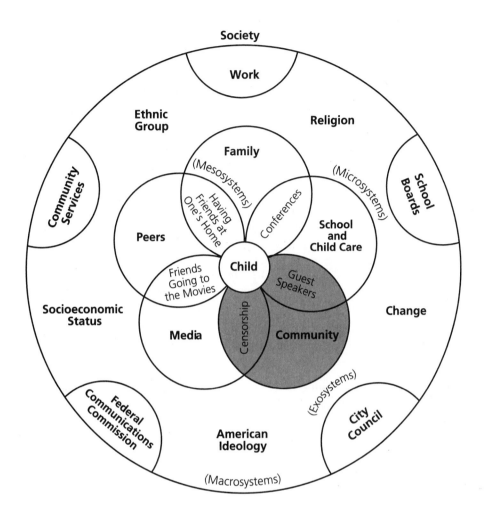

Figure 10.1

An Ecological Model of Human Development
The community in which the child grows up is a significant influence on his or her development.

The Community's Influence on Socialization

The neighborhood or neighborhoods (nearby geographic areas) in which we grew up conjure up vivid images of what constitutes a sense of community. We may picture a small town with several stores, a gas station, a diner, a movie theater, a school, and a church or two, with homes widely spaced. We may recall apartment houses grouped closely together, with the bus stop on the corner and the park and school several blocks away. We may envision acres of farmland, with the town miles away, and perhaps a mall that we visited only once a week. Or we may picture a large housing tract with lawns, cars, bicycles, and no sidewalks.

Points to Ponder

Survival is probably the most basic of all human instincts. People develop survival, or coping, skills through both experiences and biological instincts. Over the millennium, people have survived by living in groups, helping one another, and repelling intruders. How do your experiences in a community exemplify aspects of the survival instinct?

How did the people in the neighborhood in which we grew up earn a living? We may envision farmers harvesting crops, shopkeepers tending stores, laborers working in factories or mines, or people rushing to and from work dressed in business suits.

How did the people in our neighborhood instill in us their norms and values? We may visualize the schools we attended or the clubs we belonged to. We may remember community traditions like the Fourth of July picnic, when everyone brought food to share, or the annual school music festival, when every class had certain songs to sing.

How did our community enforce its rules? We may picture everyone watching over everyone else and knowing that if we did something wrong someone would surely tell our parents. We may recall the police officer on the corner or the sheriff's car patrolling the streets. We may remember the neighborhood bully beating up someone for being a "rat fink."

How did the people in our neighborhood socialize with one another? We may visualize our mothers gathered in someone's kitchen or on the sidewalk in front of someone's house. We may envision a group of men entering the corner bar after work or a group of adults dancing at the church social. Or we may remember our homes filled with company on various occasions.

How did the people in our neighborhood help one another? We may recall the flurry of activity after one family's house burned down, when everyone contributed clothing, food, and household items. We may think of another family after their 2-year-old was run over by a car, with people crowded in the house, talking quietly and offering condolences. We may picture the hospital room where a parent spent several weeks—filled with plants, flowers, and cards. We may remember the people waiting in line to fill out forms at a government office.

The community is a socializing agent because it is where children learn role expectations—for adults and for themselves. It is in the community that children get to observe, model, and become apprentices to adults; it is in the community that children get to "try themselves out." Socialization requires active involvement:

> For the things we have to learn before we can do them, we learn by doing them. We become just by doing just acts, temperate by doing temperate acts, brave by doing brave acts . . . states of character are formed by doing the corresponding acts. (Aristotle, *Methaphysics* [Book 1, Ch. 1])

According to a survey of leaders from 90 cities and towns across the United States by the National League of Cities (Meyers & Kyle, 1998), five main characteristics make a community "family friendly": (1) education (quality academic pro-

The community in which a child grows up is a significant influence on his or her development.

grams and safe schools), (2) recreation (facilities and opportunities), (3) community safety, (4) citizen involvement, and (5) physical environment (clean, safe, and attractive). Other important factors are employment opportunities (good jobs and economic growth) and neighborhood quality (affordable housing, good government, cultural opportunities, supports for children and families).

PHYSICAL FACTORS

Research has shown that certain characteristics of the physical environment of the community influence behavior (Bell, Greene, Fisher, & Baum, 2000). These include population density and characteristics, noise, arrangement and types of housing and play settings.

Population Density and Characteristics

"Population density" refers to the number of people occupying a certain area of space. High population density can have positive effects on social relationships in that people have many opportunities to mingle, provided there are spaces (places to sit or play) to do so (Etzioni, 1993). But high population density can also have negative effects, such as excessive social contact, reduced behavioral freedom, scarcity of resources, personal space violations, and inability to maintain desired privacy (Bell et al., 2000).

People who have excessive or unwanted social interactions and insufficient privacy have been observed to socially withdraw. The consequence of social withdrawal is a breakdown in socially supportive relationships (Evans, Palsane, Lepore, & Martin, 1989).

Rodin (1976) demonstrated the relationship between residential density and susceptibility to **learned helplessness**—the condition of people who have developed a sense of apathy due to their perception that they have no control over events. This occurs when they feel that their actions no longer influence outcomes. (Did you ever get low grades no matter how hard you studied in a class and so didn't put forth your best effort on the final because you figured, "What's the point"?)

Rodin (1976) found that children who lived in high-density areas were less likely than those in low-density areas to try to control the amount of rewards they received for performing certain tasks. She also found that, when initially given a frustrating task that was not related to getting rewards, these children did worse on a subsequent task that was related to getting rewards than did those who lived in low-density areas.

Density thus influences learned helplessness. The density of the environment tends to affect people's perception of their control over that environment: the higher the density, the less control they believe they have. For example, fires, floods, earthquakes, hurricanes, and tornadoes are much more damaging in high-density environments. In addition, they serve as reminders of how vulnerable people are to natural forces they cannot control, no matter how technologically advanced society becomes. When people continually experience loss of control, which apparently occurs more often in high-density areas, they are likely to lose the motivation to act; they become helpless.

Additionally, high-density communities have been associated with higher rates of violence and crime than low-density communities (Limber & Nation, 1998). For example, Sampson (1983) found that the rates of victimization were three times greater in high-density than low-density neighborhoods, even after holding other demographic variables constant. Sampson also identified a relationship between multifamily housing units and crime rates. Thus, continual exposure to violence and crime most likely contributes to feelings of helplessness.

The rate of population turnover in a neighborhood influences the interactions with newcomers, as well as the level of community involvement (Bell et al., 2000; Garbarino, 1992). The degree of transience in a neighborhood affects both those who remain and those who move. When people do not plan to remain in a neighborhood more than a few months or years, they tend not to get involved in community activities. And those who do remain in the neighborhood make fewer efforts to establish close personal ties with newcomers whom they expect to depart.

Neighborhoods differ in the extent to which they include people of differing ages, income levels, and religious, ethnic, or educational backgrounds (Garbarino, 1992). *Homogeneous* neighborhoods include people of similar backgrounds; *heterogeneous* neighborhoods include people of differing backgrounds.

Children who grow up in homogeneous neighborhoods—like many suburban neighborhoods—have few opportunities to interact with children or adults who differ in backgrounds and values. Children whose neighborhoods are accessible to a larger town only by car have little opportunity to even observe the work world of adults. Children who grow up in heterogeneous neighborhoods—like many urban neighborhoods—are more likely to have opportunities to interact with children of differing backgrounds at school or on the playground. Because stores and businesses are more accessible, children have more opportunities to interact with adults in their work roles.

Noise

Noise is simply "unwanted sound" (Bell et al., 2000). High levels of noise can lead to hearing loss, cause increases in arousal levels and stress, and interfere with attention.

Cohen, Glass, and Singer (1973) studied children living in a high-rise apartment complex situated adjacent to a noisy highway in New York City. Controlling for other factors such as social class and air pollution, the researchers found that the children on the noisier lower floors had poorer hearing discrimination than the children on the upper floors. Moreover, the hearing problems of the children on the lower floors may have been related to their poorer reading performance in school.

Similarly, a study conducted by the California Department of Health Services linked freeway noise to poorer school test scores (Savage, 1983). The study compared third- and sixth-graders in nine sets of pairs of comparable schools, one set located near a freeway and one farther away. The children in the noisy schools generally did less well academically in reading and mathematics than their counterparts in quieter schools. One sixth-grader commented, "We can't hear the teacher, and she gets mad because we don't hear what she says." Another child said, "You can't concentrate when the trucks are passing." Noise interferes with verbal communication and may affect productivity (Bell et al., 2000).

In another study (Evans, Hygge, & Bullinger, 1993), third- and fourth-graders children who lived near the Munich (Germany) International Airport, and thus were chronically exposed to airport noise, had higher stress levels (measured by blood pressure, heart rate, and hormones) when performing cognitive tasks than children who lived in quieter neighborhoods.

In sum, whether noise hurts or helps performance depends on the type of noise, the complexity of the task, and individual factors such as personality and adaptation level (Bell et al., 2000).

Arrangement and Types of Housing

The way housing and streets are arranged affects the interactions between people in a neighborhood (Bell et al., 2000; Garbarino, 1992). When housing faces the street or shares a courtyard, people have a common place of contact. Children living in such a setting usually play on the courtyard or sidewalk or in the street, provided there is not much traffic. This direct access to the outside world maximizes the potential for parental supervision (Taishido Study Group, 1984/1985). In other words, people can monitor children from indoors simply by looking out. In contrast, housing that lacks a common area, such as an apartment building minimizes the potential for parental supervision. When children leave such dwellings to play, they cannot be supervised unless they are accompanied by a parent, other adult, or older sibling or neighbor.

Play Settings

Play settings influence socialization in terms of the types of activities that occur in them and the presence or absence of adults to supervise. Some neighborhoods provide playgrounds for children, and the type of equipment available appears to affect their use (Rivkin, 1995). A study (Hayward, Rothenberg, & Beasley, 1974) comparing different playground settings (traditional, modern, adventure) reported a relation between the availability of the play materials and the type of play activity. The *traditional* playground setting had swings, a slide, a teeter-totter, and a sandbox; the *modern* playground had various sculptures upon which children could climb, crawl, and slide; the *adventure* playground had old lumber, tires, crates, bricks, and rocks.

Children were interviewed and observed in each of the settings. Preschool children, often accompanied by adults, used the traditional and modern playground more often; school-age children and teenagers used the adventure playground more often. The children in the traditional and modern playgrounds were involved with using the equipment, whereas the children in the adventure playground were involved in expressing ideas and fantasies.

ECONOMIC FACTORS

Economic factors in a community play a central role in shaping the daily lives of families who live and work there. Local economic systems vary depending on the jobs, goods, and services provided by the business sector of the community. When a local plant closes, the employees are forced to find work elsewhere, often at lower wages, which means they have to bridge the income gap by working more hours. Thus, wage earners have fewer hours to spend with their families.

Community economics affect the costs of housing, transportation, education, and health care, all of which have risen steadily since the 1970s and today consume substantially more of a typical family's income than they did then. In recent decades, the average working family's tax burden has also risen.

Partly in response to economic changes in the community, more than two-thirds of mothers with young children are now in the labor force (U.S. Bureau of the Census, 2000). When mothers work, adjustments have to be made in the workplace and in communities. The main adjustments involve businesses becoming more responsive to families and, as discussed in Chapter 5, communities providing quality child care.

Obviously, children's economic well-being is directly related to that of their families. When families have an adequate income, they are better able to meet their children's material, intellectual, and emotional needs and help them become healthy, productive adults. Yet today, children, especially those in single-parent families, are at the highest risk for poverty (Children's Defense Fund [CDF], 2001; McLoyd, 1998). Failure to address the economic needs of families, especially the threat of poverty, leads to social consequences affecting individuals, families, and communities. Consequences include more crime and delinquency, more substance abuse, more school failure, more child abuse and neglect, more teenage childbearing, more unhealthy children, and lower productivity by tomorrow's labor force. These problems impose enormous costs on the community, including expenditures for treatment of illnesses and chronic health conditions, special education, foster care, prisons, and welfare (CDF, 2001; National Commission on Children [NCC], 1991). Social problems and their costs are discussed in more detail later.

Community economics (specifically, unemployment) is related to how children in families are socialized. Evidence suggests that economic hardship threatens the psychological well-being of parents and undermines their capacity for supportive child rearing. When parents who are having difficulty coping financially share their problems with their children, children experience increased psychological distress (McLoyd, 1998; McLoyd & Wilson, 1990).

Many inner-city neighborhoods are plagued by the highest levels of joblessness since the Great Depression of the 1930s (Wilson, 1995). Unemployment, as experienced in different neighborhood settings, has different connotations for, and hence effects on, children. A jobless family that lives in an area of relatively low employment and poverty differs from a jobless family that lives in a predominantly poor neighborhood. Neighborhoods plagued with high levels of joblessness tend to have high levels of crime, gang violence, and drug trafficking. The decline of legitimate employment opportunities tends to provide added incentives to sell drugs (Fagan, 1993). For example, children see the drug dealers driving expensive cars, wearing fancy clothes, and flashing wads of money, things they don't see at home. They also have trouble connecting the role of education to postschool employment because most of the adults in their community don't work in spite of having gone to school (Wilson, 1995).

Surprisingly, the effect of unemployment on children has not always been found to be negative. A classic longitudinal study by sociologist Glen Elder (1974), discussed in Chapter 1, demonstrated that adolescents whose fathers lost their jobs had to assume certain responsibilities to keep the families functioning. This contribution to family welfare helped the adolescents to adjust successfully to adult life. They did well in school, were satisfied with their marriages, and had successful careers. However, such positive outcomes did not occur for children under age 14 whose fathers lost their jobs. Instead, they were resentful, lost respect for their fathers, and generally adjusted poorly to adult life. They were vulnerable to impaired development because, at the time when the economic crisis hit their families, they were most dependent and in need of a role model.

Interaction with a variety of people is possible in this highly populated neighborhood; however, some people may experience a feeling of being crowded.

The different findings regarding economic conditions and children's development may be due to the types of supportive relationships children or adolescents had with relatives and nonrelatives during the time of economic hardship (Coleman, 1990). These social supports include common values of neighborhood residents to maintain effective social control, supervising children's activities, monitoring their behavior, and motivating them to be productive.

SOCIAL AND PERSONAL FACTORS

In addition to physical and economic factors, certain other characteristics of the community, less tangible and more individualistic, influence socialization. These are the neighborhood setting and the patterns of community interaction.

The Neighborhood Setting

The neighborhood is the geographic setting in which children generally spend their unstructured time (Garbarino, 1992). It is where children explore, interact with other children, observe adults engaged in work or other activities, and have various experiences themselves.

Neighborhood settings differ not only in the physical environments (streets, parks, facilities) available for children but also in the social environments (other children with whom to interact). Because children are minimally mobile, they play close to home and interact with those who live close by. Medrich and colleagues (Medrich, Roizen, Rubin, & Buckley, 1981) studied how children in different neighborhoods spent their time after school. Five neighborhoods (their names were changed for publication) exemplify how different settings affect children's daily experiences and hence their socialization. Were any of these similar to neighborhoods you grew up in?

EXAMPLE **Mountainside.** Mountainside has no sidewalks, and its streets are hilly. The houses are set back from the road, which contributes to a feeling of isolation. The shops, library, school, park, and recreation center are clustered in "the village" at the base of the hill, several miles from most of the houses. Children spend most of their free time close to home because it's not easy to get around in this neighborhood—the hills are too steep for bicycles. They play baseball and soccer in diamonds painted on the streets. They build tree houses and hang rope swings and share them with other neighborhood children. The children interact with few adults other than their parents, which doesn't seem to bother them. They have to rely on their parents to drive them to lessons or recreational facilities.

Rosewood. Rosewood is a neighborhood with sidewalks and connecting streets on which the children ride their bicycles and play ball. There are few boundaries between the houses. The neighborhood is centered on the school. Anyone can get there within a 7-minute walk, and many children use the playground as a meeting place. Rosewood is heterogeneous in character and dense with children. The majority of children are Euro-American, but a large proportion are African American. Friends are chosen on the basis of similarities in age and race.

Bancroft. Bancroft is a neighborhood with no sidewalks or street lamps. The roads are narrow and patched with asphalt. Most houses cannot be seen from the street, and, yards are separated by fences. Both parents are apt to work, and children frequently are left on their own when not at school; they are expected to stay close to home after school so their parents know where they are. Children's time is often spent in the company of brothers and sisters. They rarely leave their block except to go to school, run an errand, or keep an appointment. This may be because the school and park both front on streets heavy with traffic.

Glenn. Glenn begins where the trucking companies and warehouses along a freeway exit end. The houses look like fortresses, and there are lots of apartments. Neighbors lounge on front steps, and children hang around in the streets. Although buses and trucks pass through town continually, there are no stop signs. Shops and churches are located mostly in one area; all have gated locks because vandalism rates are high. There is a park with a recreation center that many people frequent. The neighborhood has strong ethnic ties—most families are African American or Hispanic, and few are Euro-American. Friendships seem to be formed along ethnic lines, and tightly knit adolescent gangs are common.

Eastside. Eastside is a neighborhood with stark streets and debris collecting at the curbs. Yards are fenced, and most lack trees. Despite its physical appearance, the neighborhood is vibrant with street life. Many Eastside families migrated from the South and talk with one another about relatives back there or recent visits. The children congregate on the street. Many go to the community center, where they are eligible for free lunches. Friendships are formed easily according to whoever is nearby. Not only are peers considered to be friends to children, but so are neighbors and shopkeepers. Children thus have comfortable relations with various adults. The schoolyard can be reached in 5 minutes, and children often gather there to play. Age doesn't seem to matter regarding playmates, but skills count. It is not uncommon to find a broad age range of children getting together to play ball.

Patterns of Community Interaction

Community interaction is an important factor in development because, according to Bronfenbrenner (1979, 1989), the developmental potential of a setting—in this case, the community—is enhanced as a function of the number of its supportive links with other settings children might be in, such as the family or school. Patterns of interaction vary considerably according to the size of a community. In a small town, one person may interact directly with almost every other person in a given week or month. In contrast, a resident of a large city might conceivably roam the streets without ever seeing a familiar face.

The social density, or degree to which an environment contains diverse roles and experiences for children to learn from and for parents to draw upon, affects families and children. A dense setting typically contains a variety of businesspeople, as well as people of various ages and ethnic groups. Such a setting provides many opportunities for children to learn what community relations are all about. It also affords families a choice of social networks upon which they can rely for support (Garbarino, 1992; Hareven, 1989).

Interaction in a small town involves close contact with relatives, friends, and acquaintances. Because of this, people in such communities tend to be involved in each other's lives—their marriages, children, illnesses, employment, and so on are subjects of discussion, concern, and gossip. Interaction in a large city, in contrast, involves less personal contact and more impersonal interactions. For example, interactions with co-workers, bank tellers, clerks, bus drivers, and the like may occur daily, but only in the context of the specific roles they perform. For personal interactions, city dwellers usually rely on immediate family members and voluntary associations (church, PTA, lodge, club).

Some neighborhood designs foster interpersonal interaction.

The norms of a small town are more homogeneous than those of a large city and are also more widely understood and accepted (Garbarino, 1992). Because of this consensus, socialization of children tends to proceed more smoothly in a small town than a large city. In a small town, shared convictions about what is right or wrong, and proper or improper, tend to be passed on from generation to generation and become institutionalized. In other words, the unwritten local customs become the common law. The community, then, is the medium through which the basic values, norms, and customs of society are interpreted and reinforced through repeated interaction of community members.

An example of an institutionalized *value* mediated by the community might be the maxim "Honor thy father and mother," meaning that community members ask children if their parents know where they are before inviting them into their homes. An example of a *norm* mediated by the community might involve certain ways of dressing—it may not be appropriate to wear shorts certain places in town. An example of a *custom* mediated by the community might be how people greet one another: "Hello, how are you?" or "Hi, y'all," or "What's happening?"

Unlike a small town, a large city brings together people from a variety of ethnic, religious, regional, educational, and occupational backgrounds, and they are all products of their own socialization. The majority of residents may have similar values, but their norms and ways may have not been institutionalized. Therefore, large cities must rely more on formal rules and regulations than on informal methods to influence behavior. For example, in a small town, it is highly unlikely that someone would play a stereo loudly at 11 P.M., simply as a courtesy to the neighbors. In a large city, however, where neighbors often do not know each other, behavior might have to be regulated by rules restricting loud noise to certain hours.

Mechanisms of social control differ in small towns and large cities. In a small town, residents know they are under constant surveillance and that any misconduct will become a matter of community concern. Social control is rooted in fear of rejection and gossip. In large cities, the police and courts are more often relied on to provide social control, through formal sanctions.

Industrialization and urbanization were accompanied by increasingly impersonal forms of interaction, according to German sociologist Ferdinand Tonnies (1957). His book *Gemeinschaft und Gesellschaft*, considered to be a classic, defines two basic types of social relationships. ***Gemeinschaft*** relationships are mutually dependent and caring: People relate to each other because they are kin, because they live in a particular locality, or because they are like-minded and share common goals. *Gemeinschaft* relationships thus are close, informal, interpersonal, and intimate, characterized by trust, concern, and cooperation. ***Gesellschaft*** relationships, in contrast, are independent and contractual: People relate to each other because it is a practical way of achieving specific objectives, like paying for services rendered. *Gesellschaft* relationships thus are associative and formal, characterized by individualism and mutual distrust. Children who primarily experience *gemeinschaft* relationships have socialization experiences very different from those of children who primarily experience *gesellschaft* relationships (see Table 10.1).

The decline of contemporary morality has been blamed on too much *gesellschaft* or "individualism" in communities and not enough *gemeinschaft* or "communalism" (Etzioni, 1993; Hayes & Lipset, 1993/1994). Those who favor communalism do so because they believe that the norms of responsibility common to *gemeinschaft* communities should be emphasized to "counterbalance" the selfishness of individualism. Those who favor individualism do so because it is embedded in the American culture and because they believe that Americans should use the tools with which their individualistic culture provides them (efficiency, specificity, or practicality, for example) to fix the social problems (such as crime, substance abuse, or homelessness) common to *gesellschaft* communities. What kind of social relationships did you primarily have in the community or culture in which you grew up, and how did they influence you?

Table 10.1

Two Types of Social Relationships

GEMEINSCHAFT	GESELLSCHAFT
Mutually dependent	Independent
Caring	Contractual
Informal	Formal
Intimate	Associative
Trusting	Mistrusting
Focus on kin, friends, neighbors	Focus on employers/managers, employees, business associates
Collectively oriented	Individually oriented

The Community as a Learning Environment

The community is a potential source of much learning (Decker & Decker, 2001). Libraries, museums, zoos, farms, businesses, and collectibles (family heirlooms, antiques, photographs, and so on) are all rich sources of intellectual stimulation, as are people's experiences (Hatcher & Beck, 1997).

To illustrate the community's potential for learning, the city of Philadelphia experimented with a "school without walls" (Brenner & Von Moschzisker, 1971). Students in grades 9–12 were chosen by lottery from eight school districts; neither economic nor academic background was a factor. Instead of school buildings, each of the eight areas had a headquarters with office space for staff and lockers for students. All teaching took place within the community. Thus, art was studied at the art museum, biology was studied at the zoo, vocational education took place at various business locations, and so on. A higher-than-average percentage of students who took part in the program went on to college.

Many school districts have so-called alternative schools that follow this model. The philosophy of **alternative education** is that "the child, like the adult, learns the art and technique of citizenship, not through admonitions or through lectures on civics, but from involvement in real issues" (Ward, 1978, p. 184; see also Hatcher & Beck, 1997). Some high schools and colleges have combined work–study programs, in which students can apply theoretical knowledge acquired in school to real-life work settings. Existing schools can find many ways of using the community as an educational resource—for example, inviting guest speakers to class, sponsoring field trips, and working on community projects (planting trees, participating in parades, raising money for the needy, and so on).

Today, many high schools around the country require students to perform community service in order to graduate. This was a result of the passage of the National and Community Service Act of 1990, which gave grants to schools to develop and implement student involvement projects (Levine & Levine, 1996). For instance, students can become involved in conservation, work in hospitals or child care facilities, law enforcement or volunteer in social service agencies, to name but a few opportunities.

Part of the National School Goals 2000 reform strategies, discussed in Chapter 6, is the commitment of communities to learning. The business community can facilitate child socialization by fostering educational and recreational projects in several ways. Members of the business community can provide schools with materials, financial aid, human resources, and professional support. (Some communities refer to such programs as "adopt-a-school.") They can serve on school advisory councils or on school boards. They can provide schools with business settings for job placement or offer field sites for work experience programs. A specific example of a cooperative business–school venture to facilitate child socialization is operated by the Boston Private Industry Council Partnerships. John Hancock, an insurance company, collaborates with various schools in the Boston area to motivate disadvantaged minority children toward academic and career achievement. Classes of eleventh- and twelfth-graders are transported twice a week to the company, where they learn business skills to give them a head start for permanent positions at John Hancock or another firm. In addition, Hancock employees volunteer at the schools, and the company sponsors workshops to work with parents on "partnering" and to help students to find summer jobs.

In sum, the community becomes a resource for learning when citizens (parents, educators, businesspeople, religious leaders, service providers, legislators) are committed to mutually beneficial goals that focus on the growth and development of children (Decker & Decker, 2001; Pagano, 1997).

The Community as a Support System

The community can provide informal support to families, as when neighbors watch each other's children or share things (*gemeinschaft*), or it can provide formal support via publicly or privately funded community services (*gesellschaft*). Why are community services necessary? The following are some reasons:

- *The increasing population.* More people are competing for available resources to survive—job assistance, housing assistance, financial support, food subsidies, and medical care. As people live longer, the number of years that they are likely to depend on Social Security payments for support in their retirement years, and on Medicare and Medicaid for their health insurance increases. People also may have diseases or disabilities that prevent them from working, which means that they need financial assistance and other services to survive.
- *The changing nature of the family.* More births to teenagers, more divorces, more single-parent families, and more employed mothers translate into a heightened need for financial assistance, social services, and child care. The mobility of families has caused separations from relatives, so families turn to the community for support.
- *The increasing urbanization of communities.* The centralization of industries in certain areas and the consequent migration—from rural to urban areas—of people seeking employment has increased the number of people living in smaller geographic areas. Therefore, city dwellers must turn to the community for various kinds of services. When employment decreases, people must rely on social services provided by the community to survive.

CHRONOSYSTEM AND MACROSYSTEM INFLUENCES ON COMMUNITY SERVICES

Chronosystem influences on community services involve changes in the macrosystem due to political ideology and economics. Political ideology might relate to what services government leaders believe to be worthy of support—for example, the Head Start preschool program launched under President Lyndon Johnson in the 1960s. Political ideology also refers to legislation. For example, in 1975, the Education for All Handicapped Children Act was passed, ensuring that all children, regardless of disability, had a right to a free and appropriate education. Economics relates to funding sources for a community service. Agencies providing services can be public, private, or a combination.

Public agencies are financed by tax revenues and administered within the legal framework of the local, state, or federal government. For example, an outcome of the 1910 White House Conference on the Care of Dependent Children was the establishment of the U.S. Children's Bureau, the oldest federal agency for children, for the purpose of protecting children from harm. Since then, the role of government in the protection of children has expanded. The Children's Bureau is now administered by the U.S. Administration for Children and Families in the

Department of Health and Human Services. The bureau works with state and local agencies to develop programs that focus on preventing the maltreatment of children, protecting them from abuse, and providing permanent placement if their home environments are not safe.

Private agencies are financed by donations, membership dues, corporate contributions, consultation fees, investment income, foundation grants, publication sales, and conference fees. They are established by individuals or philanthropic, religious, fraternal, or humanitarian groups and managed by boards of directors. One of the nation's oldest and largest membership-based child welfare organizations is the Child Welfare League of America ([CWLA] 2002), founded in 1920. The CWLA's member agencies provide at-risk children and families with services in the areas of child abuse prevention and treatment, kinship care, juvenile justice, family foster care, adoption, youth development, residential group care, child day care, and adolescent parenting and pregnancy prevention. The CWLA's trained staff address such issues as behavioral health care, substance abuse, housing and homelessness, and HIV/AIDS.

Combination agencies have public and private sources of funding. They may obtain government grants to conduct research or implement programs and private donations to provide services beyond what are covered by the grant. For example, the Office of Community Services, run by the Administration for Youth and Families, was set up by the federal government to work in partnership with state, community, and other agencies to provide a wide range of human and community development services and activities. Various agencies, public or private, can submit applications for funding.

PREVENTIVE, SUPPORTIVE, AND REHABILITATIVE SERVICES

Community services, whether publicly or privately funded, can be categorized according to their primary function as preventive, supportive, or rehabilitative:

- *Preventive services* lessen the stresses and strains of life resulting from social and technological changes and to avert problems.
- *Supportive services* maintain the health, education, and welfare of the community.
- *Rehabilitative services* enable or restore people's ability to participate in the community effectively.

Preventive Services: Parks, Recreation, and Education

The purpose of preventive services is to provide for people's needs for space, companionship, physical activity, and mental stimulation. Children need room to play and explore; family members need places to relax and enjoy each other's company; everyone needs space to exercise. And many community residents take classes to learn new skills or to broaden their perspectives on life (culturally, historically, technologically, linguistically, and so on).

Open spaces have been set aside for people's use and enjoyment as far back in history as ancient Greece and Rome. Later, as European cities grew, parks and plazas were established. The first land in America to be designated for public use was established in 1660, and as the colonies grew, so did the number of parks. One of the best-known parks, which was established in the 1850s, is Central Park in New York City; its 843 acres of land were reserved for the purpose of recreation and relief from urban conditions. Other cities followed New York's example (Rivkin, 1995).

This city park is available for all to enjoy.

In the 1890s and early 1900s, the public began to pressure the government to assume greater responsibility for community recreation. This pressure was probably due to the growth of the cities and the lack of play space for children. Thus, by 1900, some 14 cities had made provisions for supervised play, and in 1906, the Playground and Recreation Association of America (now called the National Recreation Association) was established to promote community recreational facilities and programs.

Community recreational programs provide and maintain natural or designed environments, promote physical fitness, and offer classes to enable people to pursue interests, develop skills, and to enhance their employability. The environments provided and maintained by parks and recreation departments include playgrounds, nature trails, museums, zoos, botanical gardens, planetariums, and aquariums. Programs promoting physical fitness and skills development include organized sports and classes in tennis, fishing, sailing, photography, and arts and crafts. Opportunities for camping and other trips may be provided. Special events, such as hobby shows and pet shows, may be sponsored by parks and recreational programs. And many communities offer classes in computers, languages, parenting, art, and astronomy, to name but a few.

In addition to state and local agencies, many federal agencies for administering recreational programs—for example, the National Park Service and the Cooperative Extension Service. The National Park Service, created in 1916 under the auspices of the U.S. Department of the Interior, is the federal agency responsible for managing the nation's 29 national parks. In addition to working to keep parklands as natural as possible, the service sometimes reconstructs historical sites to provide visitors with a feeling of "what it was like then."

The Cooperative Extension Service, a branch of the Department of Agriculture, was originally designed to benefit the rural economy by providing educational services and information to farmers. The service works through state agricultural schools and county agricultural agents to provide community services. For example, one popular service involves 4-H clubs, in which many children participate. They learn farm, home, and camping skills, and participate in various recreational activities. The mission of 4-H (head, heart, hands, and health) is to enable young people to become self-directing, productive, and contributing members of society through hands-on experiences.

Many state agencies responsible for park and recreational services have functions similar to their federal counterparts. However, certain functions can vary from state to state, such as the actual services provided to local communities, the laws regarding protection and conservation of wildlife and natural resources, and the maintenance of lands and waters for public use.

Private and voluntary groups providing recreational services to children in the community include the Boy and Girl Scouts of America, the Boys' and Girls' Clubs of America, the American Red Cross, and the Young Men's Christian Association (YMCA). These agencies foster certain values, emphasize learning by doing, and promote personal development; their leaders come from the community and serve as role models. For example, the Boy Scouts of America encourages young people to do things for themselves and for others, training the boys in self-reliance, courage, and citizenship. For another example, the Boys' and Girls' Clubs of America serve boys and girls age 6–18 who are at risk for behavioral, social, or academic problems, providing programs and services to enhance their lives and enable them to develop skills to become employable. The clubs also teach youths how to engage in positive behaviors and safe health practices, and to become responsible citizens.

Supportive Services: Family and Child

The purpose of **supportive services** is to preserve healthy family life by promoting harmonious family relationships. In helping families, supportive services must be aware of the influences that ethnicity, religion, and patterns of organization have on families (Feldman & Scherz, 1987; Schorr, Both, & Copple, 1991).

Referrals. Problems that threaten the stability of family life include domestic discord (between husband and wife, or between parent and child), illness, accidents, economic hardship, desertion, delinquency, teen pregnancy, and alcohol or drug abuse. Family services provide referrals to specific agencies dealing with these specific problems. They also offer counseling on such issues as budgeting, home management, vocational opportunities, and family relationships.

Economic Assistance. Both public and private social agencies provide family services. Generally, public agencies offer services based on economic need; that is, families must meet eligibility requirements to qualify for assistance—for example, in receiving financial assistance, getting a job, locating affordable and suitable housing, obtaining food and medicine, and finding child care. Private family service agencies are concerned primarily with the personal problems and emotional maladjustment of family members, and not economic problems. Private agencies do, however, provide financial help in emergencies—especially when a family is waiting to see if it qualifies for public assistance or when it has recently immigrated to the United States and does not qualify for public assistance. Family agencies may deal with personal problems involving an economic commitment, such as the placement of children in special schools or camps or the placement of adults in mental institutions or homes for the aged.

Counseling. Family services include marriage counseling, prenatal and family planning, family life education, homemaker services, and senior citizen services. Counseling services help spouses meet their marital responsibilities and resolve

Table 10.2

*Two Approaches
to Family Services*
Source: *The State of
America's Children
Yearbook 1994.* Reprinted
with permission of the
Children's Defense Fund.

CHARACTERISTICS OF FAMILY SUPPORT AND PRESERVATION SERVICES	CHARACTERISTICS OF TRADITIONAL SERVICES
Build on family strengths	Emphasize family deficits
Focus on families	Focus on individuals
Respond flexibly to family needs	Allow program and funding sources to dictate services
Reach out to families	Have strict eligibility requirements
Treat families as partners in goal setting	Let workers set goals and solutions
Offer services in home or homelike setting	Offer office-based services
Respond quickly to needs	Have waiting lists

conflicts. They may also help individuals with emotional maladjustment problems, such as lack of communication between parents and teenagers, or with problems adjusting to divorce. Prenatal care and family planning services promote the mental and physical health of children (and mothers), and provide birth control education. Child guidance services include family therapy and parent training.

Family Preservation. The Family Preservation and Support Services Program, enacted by the federal government in 1993, provides states with funding to develop family preservation and support services. Thus, the government has changed the way services are delivered to families (see Table 10.2).

The purposes of family preservation services are (1) to keep families safe, (2) to avoid unnecessary placement of children in substitute care and the consequent high human and financial cost, and (3) to improve family functioning so that the behavior that led to the crisis will be less likely to reoccur (CDF, 2001; Cole & Duva, 1990). Family preservation services offer a mix of counseling, education, referrals, concrete assistance, and advocacy. For example, family life education includes training in home economics and management, parenting skills, and family relationships. Homemaker services send trained personnel to the home when the mothers is temporarily unable to care for her family. These services enable families to stay together and carry on in crises such as a family members' hospitalization, chronic illness, or impairment due to a disabling condition.

Keeping families together means promoting children's safety in the home and strengthening families' abilities to deal with their problems. Family preservation programs may include intensive family-based crisis intervention services. For example, when a child is at risk for abuse, rather than remove the child from the family, a trained professional goes to the home to give practical assistance on immediate problems, provide parenting training, and link the family with other support services in the community.

A fatherhood training curriculum has recently been implemented by the government to teach support personnel in local communities how to engage and involve fathers in their children's lives.

Senior Citizens. Senior citizen services may include economic assistance, in-home care, day care, institutionalization, recreation, Meals on Wheels (a program that delivers meals to the housebound), "friendly" visits, and "adopt a grandparent"— (for example, a child care center might welcome the experience and extra help senior citizens could provide for the children).

Child Health and Welfare. The term *child welfare* encompasses care for youngsters who may be indigent, neglected, abused, deserted, sick, disabled, maladjusted, or delinquent. The purpose of child welfare agencies is to protect the physical, intellectual, and emotional well-being of children (Zaslow, Tout, Smith, & Moore, 1998). Specifically, child welfare services entail providing (1) economic and personal aid to children living in their own homes, (2) foster care for children who have no home or cannot remain with their own families, and (3) institutional care when children cannot be placed in a foster home or cannot remain with their own families (CWLA, 2002).

Traditionally, children whose families could not care for them, due to death, illness, poverty, or incarceration, were placed in institutions. Private agencies and charitable organizations assumed responsibility for child welfare. Today, however, children are removed from their homes only as an emergency measure—for example, in cases of abuse or the absence of suitable relatives for care.

The need to provide financial aid to mothers in order to preserve the family was initially emphasized at the White House Conference on the Care of Dependent Children in 1910. The first national child welfare legislation was passed as part of the Social Security Act of 1935 (Zaslow et al., 1998). Public funds are available through the Temporary Aid to Needy Families (TANF) program to help families provide shelter, food, clothing, and medical care for their children. And in 1998, as part of the Family Support Act, the Job Opportunities and Basic Skills Training (JOBS) program was implemented to provide education and job training, as well as child care, for mothers with young children. The Personal Responsibility and Work Opportunity Reconciliation Act of 1996 sets time limits for the transition from government assistance to independence.

The states enact maternal and child health programs with the financial support of the federal government. These programs include family planning services, prenatal clinics, well-baby clinics for regular medical examinations of young children, hearing and vision screening, and, nursing, dental, and mental health services.

The states also administer programs for children with disabilities, partially financed by matching funds from the federal government. Specific services include identifying children with disabilities (physicians, nurses, and teachers do the referrals); performing medical, surgical, and corrective procedures; providing facilities for diagnosis, hospitalization, and rehabilitative care; and supplying aids and prosthetic appliances, physiotherapy, and medical social services.

Protective Care. There is a need for services that protect children from abuse and neglect. Protective services are usually invoked upon a report of potential maltreatment from a teacher, doctor, or neighbor. An investigation of the family takes place, and depending on the findings, the child may be removed from the home and temporarily placed in foster or institutional care until the parents demonstrate that they can care for the child appropriately. Often, the parents must obtain counseling and take classes in child development and parenting.

These services also entail the care and protection of children born to unmarried mothers. Typical services for unmarried mothers include financial assistance, prenatal care, hospitalization, and counseling. Educational programs (child development, parenting, health and nutrition, vocational, and academic education) are often provided as well.

Child Care. Child care centers serve preschool children whose parents are employed. Most care is for children age 2–5, but more and more centers are serving infants and toddlers as well. Some centers offer health and educational services as part of their programs. Extended day care programs serve school-age children whose parents are employed. Children come to the center before and after school, as necessitated by their parents' work schedules. Extended day care programs may be located in elementary schools or in community centers. When necessary, the extended day care program provides transportation between school and center. Child care costs, minus a tax credit, generally are borne by parents; however, if the family meets government financial criteria, all or part of the cost is publically funded.

Foster Care. Foster care services are provided for children who are neglected or abused and, therefore, need protection, as well as for children whose parents are temporarily unable to care for them. Foster homes are carefully selected by the community social service agency. Children placed in these homes are closely supervised by the agency, which provides money for room and board, clothing, and medical and dental care, and often grants an allowance for the children. Counseling services are for the foster parents.

Adoption. In contrast to foster care, **adoption** is a social and legal process by which a child becomes a permanent member of the adopting family, with legal rights, including that of inheritance. The social process of adoption seeks to provide children of incapacitated or deceased natural parents with a healthy home environment. Separation from natural parents is resorted to only when absolutely necessary and only on the basis of consent, if the parents are alive. Social agencies arranging for adoption conduct investigations to match child and adoptive family. Character, motivation, age, finances, and sometimes ethnic and religious background of the family are important considerations.

Rehabilitative Services: Corrections, Mental Health, and Special Needs

The purpose of **rehabilitative services** is to enable or restore individuals' capacities to effectively participate in the community by correcting behavior, addressing mental health issues, and/or providing needed services to those who have a disability or who have recently immigrated to this country.

Corrections. Correctional services are provided for children, youths, and adults who have difficulties abiding by the legal rules of the community. What constitutes deviant behavior varies among different social groups. Some children may be encouraged by their friends and neighbors to behave delinquently—for example, stealing may be a prerequisite to being accepted by the neighborhood gang. Children in another neighborhood who behave similarly may be referred to a social agency, such as a child guidance clinic, and others may be arrested and brought before the juvenile court.

Because human behavior is influenced in part by the customs of the society in which people live, some deviant behavior may stem from conflicting values within and between ethnic groups (Garbarino, 1992). For example, different ethnic groups may have different attitudes toward fighting. Societal mores, as expressed by the U.S. legal system, punish aggressive acts, especially if the aggression harms someone or someone's property. However, some ethnic groups may believe that aggression is the only acceptable way to respond to an insult or a slight. One explanation for "machismo" behavior, or male physical dominance, in Hispanic culture is that it represented a survival response, evolved during the time of the Spanish invasion of Mexico, to defend the honor of victimized females (Vigil, 1980). Or aggression may be a reactive strategy to neighborhood dangers, disrespect, an awareness of stereotypes, a lack of social supports, and/or a distorted personal orientation (feeling of "superiority") (Spencer, 2001).

Children under age 18 who are deemed neglected or delinquent are under the jurisdiction of the juvenile justice system. The juvenile court is not a criminal court per se; it does not file charges against the child, and so there usually is no jury to determine guilt or innocence. Rather, the court investigates the causes for the particular maladjustment or deviant behavior and determines which steps must be taken for rehabilitation (for example, probation, diversion or detention). Thus, the court looks at the child and his or her family background, as well as the physical, socioeconomic, and cultural conditions under which he or she is living. Statutes vary by state regarding sentencing, rehabilitation, and parental liability, as well as the age at which a juvenilve may be tried in adult court.

EXAMPLE Sometimes, to join a gang, adolescents will get tattoos even though technically it is illegal for anyone under age 18 to get one. When these kids want to leave the gang, they have to either move out of town or get the tattoo removed, so they won't be identified and harmed by rival gang members.

A juvenile officer in Monrovia, California, has established a corrective program, funded by private donations, in which he helps remorseful gang members get tattoos removed in a medical facility with a laser. The youths must write an essay on the reasons they got the tattoo, problems regarding it, and the reasons they want it removed. The officer then interviews the youths and tells them the requirements of the program: parental involvement, periodic contact for 3 years, and acceptable grades.

Juvenile court judges may place children under the supervision of their parents in their homes, with the stipulation that the family receive counseling. Or children may be removed from their homes and placed in foster care or institutions. Judges may even require children (or their parents) to pay for damages caused by the delinquent behavior.

Mental Health. Children are usually referred to local mental health and child guidance clinics by teachers, medical personnel, or the courts. Behavioral problems indicating the need for referral include truancy, running away, lying, stealing, vandalism, arson, and extreme aggressiveness. Other behaviors may include shyness, apathy, daydreaming, withdrawal, fearfulness, bed-wetting, eating disorders, and nightmares. In coordination with the schools, these clinics provide medical and psychological examinations for the child; parents and siblings may come in for treatment as well.

Special Needs. Services for recent immigrants to the United States encompass education (English, American history, government, and culture), financial assistance, housing assistance, and vocational counseling, as well as referrals to other agencies providing specific services.

Services for people with disabilities emphasize inclusion. Self-help and productive work are the goals of **rehabilitation.** These services encompass evaluation, special education, financial assistance, counseling, vocational training, recreation, and referrals for treatment (Epps & Jackson, 2000). (Table 10.3 lists the main types of community services.)

Table 10.3

Types of Community Services

PREVENTIVE	SUPPORTIVE	REHABILITATIVE
Parks	Family and child services	Corrections
Recreation	Referrals	Mental health
Education	Economic assistance	Special needs
	Counseling	
	Family preservation	
	Senior citizens	
	Child health and welfare	
	Protective care	
	Child care	
	Foster care	
	Adoption	

Creating Caring Communities

Even though communities may offer a variety of services, many do not provide enough to adequately meet the needs of all children and families. Sensitizing individuals, especially those on decision-making bodies, to the unmet needs of children and to society's obligation to respond to those needs is known as "child advocacy." In general, **advocacy** refers to the process of supporting a person, group, or cause. "Society" can mean public agencies, such as the government or the school; private agencies, such as religious groups or businesses; or concerned members of the community.

To publicize the need for advocacy for children, in 1977 the Carnegie Council on Children, under the leadership of Kenneth Keniston, published *All Our Children: The American Family Under Pressure*. This report described how the effects of U.S. social policy (or the lack thereof) had been detrimental to family life. The Children's Defense Fund (CDF) publishes reports on *The State of America's Children* annually. The purpose of such reports is to educate the nation by drawing attention to the need for better public policies regarding children and families—for example, by citing the high infant mortality rate in the United States compared with many other nations. The CDF (2001) points to the lack in our country of a social policy that guarantees adequate health care to mothers and children.

The CDF (2001) also emphasizes that the United States is the only modern democracy that lacks a system of income supports for families with children. It calls attention to the high number of children living below the official poverty line—the bare-bones income level that the federal government estimates is necessary to meet a family's minimal subsistence needs.

The National Commission on Children ([NCC] 1991) points to the school system in the United States, which is supposed to equalize opportunities for all children, as manifesting a tremendous gap by the time children reach the twelfth grade. This gap is evident between those who are rich and those who are poor, and between individuals with ethnic minority backgrounds and those with Euro-American backgrounds.

If the life chances for children are to be improved, then parents and other community members must become involved in public policy; they must become advocates for children. According to many concerned with the welfare of children and youths, the United States has made a minimal investment in caring for its future citizens (CDF, 2001; NCC, 1991).

The NCC was created by Congress and the president "to serve as a forum on behalf of children of the Nation." The commission, comprised of parents, grandparents, teachers, health care and child development experts, business leaders, professionals, and elected officials, became official in 1989. Their mandate was to assess the status of children and families in the United States and to propose new directions for policy and program development in order to improve the opportunities for every young person, regardless of circumstances, to become a healthy, secure, educated, economically self-sufficient, and productive adult. The commission's final report, *Beyond Rhetoric: A New American Agenda for Children and Families* (NCC, 1991), made recommendations in nine general areas:

1. Ensuring income security
2. Improving health
3. Increasing educational achievement
4. Preparing adolescents for adulthood
5. Strengthening and supporting families
6. Protecting vulnerable children and their families
7. Making policies and programs work
8. Creating a moral climate for children
9. Providing financing for programs

Specific recommendations included a refundable tax credit for children; a government-guaranteed minimum child support payment, as well as tough enforcement; procedures; continuation of the job training program, as well as child care and health insurance to help low-income families make the transition from welfare to employment; and community responsibility for health care and education programs. Other recommendations included development of a universal system of health insurance, expansion of Head Start to all income-eligible children, and higher-quality education and increased accountability. The commission also suggested that public support for family services be continued; that businesses develop family-oriented policies; that the quality, availability, and affordability of child care services be improved; that community-based family support programs be developed and expanded; and that salaries and training opportunities in early childhood and welfare fields increase. Finally, the commission asserted that there needs to be more diligence in the public and private sectors in terms of giving children and adolescents clear, consistent messages about personal conduct and responsibility to others, and that the allocation of financial resources be shared by the private and public sectors.

ECONOMIC ASSISTANCE

Poverty

One in six children in the United States are living in poverty—that is, in families with incomes below the federally designated poverty line ($17,000 for a family of four in 1999). The poverty rate for African Americans is about 37 percent, for Hispanic Americans about 34 percent, for Asian Americans and Pacific Islanders about 18 percent, and for Euro-Americans about 15 percent (CDF, 2001; U.S. Bureau of the Census, 2000). Many families are poor even though one or both parents are employed. And many families that are poor are large and represent various ethnic minority groups, although the largest recent increase in poor families has been among Euro-Americans under age 30 (U.S. Bureau of the Census, 2000). Both family structures and the labor market affect the duration of childhood poverty

(Corcoran & Chaudry, 1998). A common feature of families that are poor is that the head of household is less educated than are heads of households that are not poor. A large proportion of poor families are headed by single women; these families are more likely to be poor due to the cost of child care and the lower average wage paid to women than men (CDF, 2001).

EXAMPLE Rafael Gomez works as a gardener for a landscape company. He earns $350 per week. He and his wife have five children, ranging in age from 6 months to 12 years. Mrs. Gomez stays home to care for the family. Their rent for a three-bedroom apartment in a dilapidated building is $425 per month. The Gomez children wear hand-me-down clothes from each other and from relatives. The family does not own a car or have medical insurance.

Joan Thomas, age 20, has three young children. She gets government assistance for welfare, food, and medical services. Her husband recently deserted her. She first became pregnant while in high school and never completed her education. Because her education is lacking, so are her job opportunities. She would like to work but knows that the job would be low-paying because of her lack of skills, and she worries about the cost of child care and her ability to juggle all the responsibilities.

Federal programs that attempt to alleviate some of the conditions of poverty include the following:

- *Temporary Assistance for Needy Families (TANF)*—provides temporary financial support for families with children through a federal and state matching program. Eligibility and work requirements, and time limits for benefits are established by individual states. (This welfare reform program replaced Aid to Families with Dependent Children [AFDC].)
- *Unemployment compensation*—covers all workers in the labor force. Financed by employers' contributions, it is intended to maintain about 50 percent of a worker's income for a temporary period of involuntary unemployment. The program is administered by federal and state governments.
- *Social Security survivor or disability benefits*—is administered by the federal government. Payments come from the Social Security Trust Fund, through taxes on employer and employee. The benefits of individuals covered by Social Security, but who die or become disabled are paid to their survivors or dependents.
- *Supplemental Security Income (SSI)*—provides a guaranteed minimum income for the aged and disabled.
- *Veterans' benefits*—is paid by the federal government to survivors or dependents of veterans who die or are disabled in the service.
- *Child Nutrition Services*—consists of federally funded programs administered by the states. These are intended to improve the nutritional standards of low-income families. Included are the Food Stamp Program, in which participants buy food stamps, according to a formula based on income and family size, for a cost less than the value of the food to be bought, and then use the stamps to purchase food; the National School Lunch Program; the Special Supplemental Food Program for Women, Infants, and Children (WIC); and the National School Breakfast Program.
- *Other services*—represents a variety of social services funded through state grants, according to Title IV and Title XX of the Social Security Act.

Large proportions of these funds provide day care for children of employed mothers and other child welfare services. Title I of the Elementary and Secondary Education Act and the Head Start program provide educational and related services to low-income children. Child health programs and Medicaid also provide services to poor families.

Why have the federal programs not succeeded in alleviating poverty? According to the CDF (2001), five main factors have been pushing more and more children and families into poverty: (1) the persistently high rate of unemployment among parents, (2) the inability of parents to earn enough to escape poverty, (3) the growing number of female-headed households due to divorce and out-of-wedlock births, (4) inadequate education and job training, and (5) the reduction in funding for government programs. Each of the factors exemplifies how exosystems and macrosystems affect children.

Unemployment and low-wage employment have outcomes other than poverty: loss of a sense of self-worth, increased family tensions, alcoholism, domestic violence, drug abuse, and lower academic achievement of children. When the economic support system of a family breaks down, often so does its ability to provide emotional support (Behrman, 2002; Huston, McLoyd, & Coll, 1994).

Ross and Sawhill (1975), as well as others (Huston, McLoyd, & Coll, 1994; Wilson, 1995), reported that family disintegration increased in families whose head was unemployed for a long period, compared with similar families not experiencing long-term unemployment. For example, at a congressional hearing, the former president of the United Automobile Workers testified that as unemployment increased so did the number of people seeking assistance because of alcoholism and child abuse (Marcossen & Fleming, 1978).

Which public policies are designed to overcome the effects of economic problems, especially unemployment? In addition to unemployment compensation, the federal government creates jobs and provides tax exemptions. To create jobs, local governments (cities, towns, counties) can apply for federal funds to pay for local public construction—for example, road improvements or building additions. The local community thus both reduces unemployment and improves the infrastructure. The federal government also creates jobs by allocating funds to local governments to hire unemployed individuals. Thus, public services are provided (clerks, park attendants), and jobs are created for those in need.

Tax exemptions are provided for those receiving unemployment compensation. They are also granted to businesses hiring certain individuals, such as those with disabilities or those in government work-training programs, and for child care as required by the mother's employment.

Even though welfare reform has contributed to declining poverty rates, problems regarding government support for poor families with children remain. These include the income level at which the government considers a family poor enough to receive assistance and funding for welfare-to-work programs, job training, child care, housing, and health care (Behrman, 1997a, b, 2002).

Homelessness

Related to poverty is the inability of many families to obtain shelter. Families with children are the fastest-growing segment of Americans who are homeless, now accounting for more than one-third of the nation's homeless population (CDF, 2001).

The incidence of families that are homeless has increased greatly.

The threat of homelessness is even graver than the statistics suggest because millions of families are just one crisis—an unexpected expense, illness, disability, or job loss—away from losing their homes. Other families are at risk for homelessness because they spend most of their income on housing and have no financial cushion if their rent goes up or their income falls even slightly (CDF, 2001).

Homelessness is the result of many simultaneous trends: shrinking incomes for many young families, rising housing costs, a decreasing supply of low-cost housing, a decline in government housing assistance, and deinstitutionalization of those with mental disorders (CDF, 2001). A significant number of homeless youths have run away from or been kicked out of their homes (Levine & Levine, 1996). An alarming trend is the number of homeless youths who were formerly in foster care (Balk, 1995). Nearly all state child protective services stop foster care payments when children reach age 18; few young people have the skills at this age to be self-supporting.

Other problems associated with homelessness are poverty, poor health, inadequate education, poor employment prospects, and social isolation (CDF, 2001). Children who are homeless suffer psychological, behavioral, and educational, consequences (McCormick & Holden, 1992).

EXAMPLE Thomas Green, age 6, took his stuffed dog and lay down on the mattress with his sister, Eva, age 3, who was already asleep. The mattress was a piece of foam rubber donated to the church that was to be Thomas's home for the next few months (his town had no public shelter for the homeless). Thomas's mother, Vicki, had been living in motel rooms with the children and whomever was her current boyfriend until he left or was arrested. Vicki took odd jobs in between boyfriends to support herself and the children, but being a high school dropout, her skills were limited, as were her work opportunities.

In the morning, Vicki took Thomas to the nearby school to enroll him in kindergarten. He had to repeat it because he moved so many times in the previous year and missed so much school that he wasn't ready for first grade. Eva was invited to go to the church preschool while Vicki spent the day looking for work.

Local governments frequently have been unable or unwilling to deal effectively with the problems of familes and children who are homeless, and the federal government also has provided only limited assistance (CDF, 2001). The federal government does allocate funds to states for temporary shelters and to schools to assure that children who are homeless have access to free public education.

Teachers need to be sensitive to potential characteristics of homeless children, such as depression, anxiety, severe separation problems, poor-quality relationships, shyness, aggressiveness, sleep disorders, temper tantrums, and short attention spans (McCormick & Holden, 1992). Many homeless parents have substance abuse problems, are victims of domestic violence, and have fragmented social support networks (McCormick & Holden, 1992).

HEALTH CARE

As a nation, we spend enormous amounts of money on health care. For insured persons, we have an excellent health care system that focuses on crises and serious illnesses, but we have inadequate preventative and public health care (CDF, 2001). There are also serious inequities in health standards for low-income families and those from ethnic minorities, as well as too few medical resources in rural and inner-city communities, too little prenatal care for many women, and not enough regular immunizations against disease (CDF, 2001; NCC, 1991). To address these inadequacies, the Children's Health Insurance Program (CHIP) was enacted in 1997. Federal funds are granted to states to develop and implement programs.

EXAMPLE Thu Truong, age 7, developed a high fever and a cough one Saturday night. His mother gave him aspirin and some cough syrup, but on Sunday morning, the fever was still high and the cough was worse. Mrs. Truong decided to take Thu to the emergency room; she has no regular doctor and relies on health clinics for medical care. It took her an hour and a half by bus to reach the hospital. Because Thu was not "critical" (bleeding profusely, or unable to breathe, for instance), he had to wait an hour before a doctor was available to examine him.

Lara Michaels had her third baby several weeks prematurely, and the baby remained in intensive care for 2 months. Al Michaels' insurance policy did not cover newborn health care, so the Michaels face an enormous hospital bill that will keep them in debt for years.

The most important factors influencing child health occur before birth. A baby is likely to grow into a healthy child when the mother had good nutrition during her own childhood and during pregnancy, received prenatal care early in pregnancy, is age 20–35, is in good health, has not been pregnant recently, and does not abuse drugs or alcohol. A baby is more likely to have a low birthweight (under $5\frac{1}{2}$ pounds) and/or to suffer from birth defects or to die when its mother was poorly nourished, had no prenatal care, is under age 18, is in poor health (has a sexually transmitted disease, for example), has recently been pregnant, smokes, and abuses drugs or alcohol. The infant mortality rate in the United States remains high compared with other industrialized nations (CDF, 2001). Thus, females need to be educated *before* they get pregnant about their future child's health.

Early and continuous health care for young children saves lives and helps minimize long-term health problems. High-quality preventive, primary, and remedial pediatric health care can ensure that problems that might develop during infancy, such as respiratory, neurological, or orthopedic impairments, are detected and treated. Health professionals working with schoolchildren from low-income families have found that they are twice as likely as children from middle- and upper-income families to suffer from one or more untreated medical conditions. Untreated vision, hearing, and dental problems, as well as anemia and mental health and developmental conditions, can impair children's school performance, thereby affecting their later life (CDF, 2001; NCC, 1991).

In addition, children exposed to drugs or alcohol while in utero are especially vulnerable to serious physical and mental disabilities and to behavior problems and learning impairments. Acquired immune deficiency syndrome (AIDS) threatens a growing number of children each year, primarily through transmission from their mothers before or at birth. The risk of human immunodeficiency virus (HIV), which can develop into AIDS, is also growing among adolescents who are intravenous drug users or sexually active (NCC, 1991).

Human-made environmental hazards increasingly threaten the health of all children. For example, absorption or inhalation of lead causes damage to the central nervous system, mental retardation, and blood and urinary tract infection. Thus, technological advances must continually be monitored regarding their impact on health and safety.

Government programs promoting children's health include the following:

- *Medicaid*—provides matching funds to the states to pay for medical services for the indigent and medically needy. Children who are eligible for Medicaid receive early and periodic screening, which involves diagnoses and treatment.
- *Maternal and Child Health Services*—provides federal funds to states for programs to reduce infant mortality, improve the health of low-income mothers and children, and provide comprehensive health care to low-income children up to age 21, dental care for low-income children, and outreach, diagnosis, and medical and related services for low-income and medically indigent children who are physically disabled. There are also neighborhood health centers, migrant health centers, and Native American health services.
- *Centers for Disease Control*—provides federal funds to the states for the purchase of vaccines.
- *Child Nutrition Services*—includes school lunch and breakfast programs and special food programs for low-income children and children with disabilities in day care or other nonresidential settings. Also included is the Women, Infants, and Children Program (WIC), which provides nutritious food to low-income pregnant and lactating women and to children under age 4 who are at nutritional risk.

SUPPORT FOR FAMILIES

Traditionally, many U.S. family services have been aided by private charitable organizations. In recent years, more and more public agencies have begun to play a role in providing services to families. Unfortunately, the combination of public and private social services is often fragmented and uncoordinated, though there are successful collaborative examples across the country (Schorr, 1997).

Government programs providing support for families include the following:

- *Child Welfare Services*—fund state efforts to preserve families by strengthening members' abilities to address their problems, and avoid unnecessary foster care, and to reunite with their parents children who have been placed in foster care.
- *Social Services Block Grant (Title XX)*—provides various preventive, counseling, and other support services for low-income, and vulnerable, abused, and neglected children and their families.
- *Child and Adolescent Service System Program*—helps ensure that youths with serious emotional problems receive needed mental health services by improving coordination among the many agencies responsible for them.

EXAMPLE Jill Sanger, age 15, lives in a suburban town. Her father is an engineer for an aerospace company and often works late. Her mother is not employed but is involved in school and community activities, as well as in caring for Jill's 10-year-old twin brothers and 6-year-old sister. Jill has been reported truant from school on several occasions. She refuses to communicate with her parents and has become involved with drugs. Her parents want to get help.

Helen Black, recently divorced, has two young children. Her ex-husband is lax in sending child support payments. Helen wants to become a computer programmer and feels confident she can get a job. Someday, she would like to buy a computer and work at home. Meanwhile, however, she must go to school, and so needs child care.

Jack Baker, (age 13), and his sister Sally, (age 12), have been cared for and supported by their mother since their father deserted them when Sally was a year old. When Jack was 6 and Sally was 5, however, their mother became very ill. She had to be hospitalized for 3 months and then recuperated for 6 months. Having no relatives, the children were placed in foster care. When their mother could again care for them, they were returned to her. A year later, however, their mother suffered a relapse, and the children were placed in another foster home. This time, they were separated because a home was not available that would take both of them.

Two changes in family structure have accelerated tremendously in recent years—the increase in the number of women employed, especially mothers of young children under age 6, and the growth in the number of children living in families headed by one parent, primarily the mother. Among the family supports that can respond to the needs of mothers who are poor, employed, and/or single, and to the needs of the children, is a system of quality child care services, in home or center settings.

As discussed in Chapter 5, families seeking child care for their children can choose (where available) child care centers, family day care homes, or home care by a relative, neighbor, or paid person. Even though some centers and some day care homes are licensed, this is no guarantee of quality, because enforcement of licensing standards may be minimal.

Self-Care by Children

Mothers who are employed outside the home and have school-age children often do not or cannot make provisions for after-school care. These children sometimes are referred to as **latchkey children**—children who have to let themselves into their homes with a key. Unsupervised by adults, children who care for themselves tend to be vulnerable to delinquency, vandalism, injury, rape, and drug use (Collins, Harris, & Susman, 1995).

There are other problems, as well, for children in self-care. In studies comparing self-care children age 5–12 with their supervised counterparts, researchers have found that children who are left alone to care for themselves and/or siblings often feel apprehensive regardless of their age, capabilities, or parents' assurances (Behrman, 1999; Belle, 1999; Long & Long, 1982). Perhaps their fearfulness stems from warnings and cautions about strangers coming to the door or about various household problems that might occur.

Self-care children usually are restricted to their homes until their parents return and are prohibited from having friends over. Sometimes, older children are given the responsibility of caring for younger siblings.

It took a tragedy to bring national attention to the problems surrounding self-care children. A 5-year-old boy, left alone in his home while his mother worked, was accidentally shot and killed by a police officer who mistook the background noise of the television and the shadow on the wall of the toy gun as threats to his life. He didn't see the little boy until it was too late.

Government programs assisting families experiencing such changes include the following:

- *Income tax breaks*—allow deduction of child care expenses by employed mothers.
- *Subsidized day care (such as Head Start and Title XX)*—provides federal and state matching funds for a wide variety of social services, including day care.

Although some children flounder when forced to be responsible for themselves, many others (especially children over age 10) flourish. They enjoy the independence and the experience of having to deal with various situations, such as a stranger coming to the door, the electricity going out, and so on (Belle, 1999). Apparently, developmental outcomes from self-care depend on children's characteristics (Are they mature? self-confident?) family circumstances (Is someone available by phone?), and neighborhood features (Is it safe?) (Vandell & Su, 1999).

Is This Child Ready for Self-Care?

- Is the child mature enough to care for him- or herself?
- Has the child indicated that he or she is willing to try self-care?
- Is the child able to solve problems?
- Is the child able to communicate with adults?
- Is the child able to complete daily tasks?
- Is the child generally unafraid to be alone or to enter the house alone?
- Can the child unlock and lock the doors to the home unassisted?
- Is there an adult living or working nearby whom the child knows and can rely on in case of an emergency?
- Is there adequate household security?
- Is the neighborhood safe?

If the answer to any of these questions is "no," then plans to leave the child in self-care should be delayed or abandoned (Long & Long, 1983).

SPECIAL CHILD CARE SERVICES

Some children have special needs—for example, they have disabilities, are maltreated or abandoned by their families, are orphans, or have run away from desperate situations.

Julie was born prematurely and required special care when her mother brought her home from the hospital a month after she was born. After a week at home, Julie had lost a significant amount of weight and was listless. She was diagnosed as suffering from "failure to thrive" due to neglect and was placed in foster care. Her mother, just 18 years old, had a history of drug abuse. She also had trouble keeping track of medical appointments, filling prescriptions, and meeting Julie's needs. In a single year, Julie was shifted three times from her mother's care to foster care. Julie's current foster mother wants to adopt her, but the biological mother will not sign the papers.

Kenny, age 13, is the oldest of four children. Both his parents are alcoholics. Kenny has been involved in some stealing incidents in the neighborhood, but he was never reported to the police because the shopkeepers felt sorry for him. Kenny stole when his father spent his paycheck on booze and there was no food in the house. Recently, however, Kenny has been hanging around with some older kids who deal drugs. Kenny sees this as an easy way to make money and get out of the house. The first time he tries to make a sale, though, he gets caught.

Mike was born without hip sockets. In order for him to walk normally and use his legs, he needs several surgeries. In addition to the surgeries, he will need special equipment such as a walker until he heals. He will also need daily physical therapy to strengthen his muscles. Unfortunately, Mike's father deserted the family after Mike's birth; he couldn't deal with having a disabled son. Mike's mother has to work to support Mike and his two older sisters. She has no medical insurance, nor does she have the time or energy to give Mike the special care he needs.

Children who are abused and neglected have recently received more national attention, due in part to the establishment in 1974 of a National Center on Child Abuse and Neglect. Children who are abused, neglected, or abandoned, as well as those who are orphaned and sometimes those who run away, may be placed in foster homes. Foster care is funded by federal, state, and local sources. Foster arrangements provide temporary care when children cannot be cared for in their own homes due to the death or illness of a parent, divorce or desertion, inadequate financial support, abuse or neglect, and/or behavioral problems with which the parent(s) cannot cope. The problems with foster care placement are several. Relatively few foster parents have training in dealing with maltreated children; some children placed in foster care drift from one home to another, never returning to their own homes; and some children are abused by their foster parents.

In spite of the fact that many children placed in foster care are eligible for adoption, it seldom happens. Present legislation mandates the loss of federal support for foster children if they are adopted by the family with which they reside. Support is not only financial; it includes medical, dental, and clothing allowances. Many private insurance companies will not cover preexisting medical conditions that some of these children have. However, the government Adoption Assistance Program provides financial grants to families adopting "hard-to-place" children, such as those with health problems (physical or emotional) or disabling conditions and those with an ethnic minority background.

Table 10.4

*Key Federal
Assistance Programs
and Services
for Children
and Families*

POVERTY	CHILD HEALTH	SUPPORT FOR FAMILIES	CHILD CARE NEEDS
Temporary Assistance for Needy Families (TANF)	Medicaid	Child Welfare Services	Foster care
Unemployment compensation	Maternal and Child Health Services	Social Services Block Grant (Title XX)	Adoption Assistance Program
Social Security survivor or disability benefits	Children's Health Insurance Program	Child and Adolescent Service System Program	Child Abuse Prevention and Treatment Act
Supplemental Security Income (SSI)	Centers for Disease Control (CDC)	Income tax deduction for child care expenses	Family Violence Prevention and Services Program
Veterans' benefits			
Child Nutrition Services	Child Nutrition Services		
Various child-care educational, and health services	Head Start	Subsidized child care	Head Start
Homeless assistance			

In many states, terminating parental custody is very difficult; therefore, children cannot be legally adopted. Often, this is damaging to children's emotional health because they do not know to whom they really belong (Nazario, 1988).

In addition to foster care funding and adoption assistance, governmental programs for children with special needs include the following:

- *The Child Abuse Prevention and Treatment Act*—authorizes grants to states to assist them in developing and strengthening programs to prevent child abuse and neglect while providing treatment for its victims.
- *The Family Violence Prevention and Services Program*—supports local programs that provide immediate shelter and related services to family violence victims and their children.

(Table 10.4 summarizes key federal assistance programs and services for children and families.)

Mesosystem Influences: Linking Community Services to Families and Schools

To be effective in supporting children's development, community child care services need to link with health care, nutrition, social, and education services for children and their parents (CDF, 2001; Decker & Decker, 2001). Such collaboration strengthens the immediate environment of vulnerable children, making them more resilient to stress (Hurd, Lerner, & Barton, 1999).

Characteristics of Effective Community Services

- The earlier intervention is undertaken in children's lives, the better the outcome.
- Comprehensive approaches are more effective than limited interventions.
- Services must be easily accessible to individuals, and aggressive outreach may, in some cases, be required.
- Staff involvement in and knowledge of the situation are critical.
- Stable, caring adults, including mentors, are important role models.
- Parental involvement is crucial to success with children.
- Involvement in the school system is a key element of successful intervention.
- Highly structured programs are the most successful.

Source: Rickel and Becker, 1997, pp. 7–8.

Examples of comprehensive service linkages between children, families, and schools are the Head Start Preschool Program (discussed in Chapter 5) and the Brookline (Massachusetts) Early Education Program (BEEP) for prekindergarten children in the public schools. Head Start addresses children's physical, emotional, cognitive, and family support needs; BEEP focuses on family involvement and empowerment in children's education.

Examples of service linkages between children, families, and communities are child care resource and referral agencies (providing information to parents regarding child care arrangements, health and social services, parent education, and family friendly businesses) and university programs (providing model schools, teacher training, and collaboration with schools in the community) (Decker & Decker, 2001; Hurd, Lerner, & Barton, 1999).

How Communities Can Help to Optimize Children's Development

1. *Establish a local commission for children and families.* This commission should find out what is being done in the community and what needs to be done for children and families. More specifically, it should examine the adequacy of existing programs, such as maternal and child health services, social services, day care facilities, and recreational opportunities. The commission should include representatives of the key institutions dealing with children and families, as well as business, industry, and labor representatives. Older children, who can speak from their own experience, should also be included.
2. *Establish a neighborhood family center.* A place that provides a focal point for leisure, learning, sharing, and problem solving should be established in a school, church, or other community building. To eliminate the fragmentation of services, the center should be the place where community members receive

A neighborhood family center provides social and recreational services.

information on family health, social services, child care, legal aid, and welfare. The center should emphasize cross-age rather than age-segregated activities.

3. *Foster community projects.* Projects involving cleaning up the environment; caring for the aged, sick, or lonely; and organizing parades, fairs, and picnics are excellent ways for community members of all ages to learn to work together and appreciate each other's talents and skills. Such projects give young people an opportunity to act as collaborators rather than subordinates.

4. *Combat alcohol and drug use and violence.* Children need positive community role models. Thus, it's important to work with families and schools to give children skills to solve problems without having to resort to substance abuse or violence, and to provide strong sanctions for substance abuse and violence.

5. *Foster youth participation in local policy bodies.* Every community organization affecting children and youths should include teenagers and older children as voting members. These include such organizations as school boards, recreation commissions, health boards, and welfare commissions.

6. *Plan communities with the children who will be growing up in them in mind.* When planning and designing new communities, factors to consider include shops and businesses located so that children can have contact with adults at work, recreational and day care facilities readily accessible to parents as well as children, provision for a family neighborhood center and family-oriented facilities and services, and availability of public transportation, and "places to walk, sit, and talk in common company."

Sources: Bronfenbrenner, 1980; Garbarino, 1995b; U.S. Department of Education, 1994.

Involvement and Advocacy

Lisbeth Schorr (1997), in her book *Common Purpose,* quotes anthropologist Margaret Mead: "Never doubt that a small group of thoughtful, committed citizens can change the world; indeed, it is the only thing that ever has." Schorr gives examples of community services (family, educational, and welfare) throughout the country that have succeeded by injecting flexibility and creativity into bureaucratic policies that govern their existence.

TYPES OF ADVOCACY GROUPS

Advocacy groups can form to solve and monitor specific problems, or they can be a source of ongoing support for children's problems in general. An example of an ongoing children's advocacy group, mentioned earlier, is the Children's Defense Fund (CDF), developed in 1973 to provide a strong and effective voice for all the children in America who cannot vote, lobby, or speak for themselves. Particular attention is paid to the needs of poor and minority children and those with disabilities (CDF, 2001).

The CDF's goal is to educate the nation about the needs of children and to encourage preventive investment in children before they become ill, drop out of school, experience family breakdowns, or get into trouble. The CDF monitors the development and implementation of federal and state policies (CDF, 2001).

Being an effective advocate requires knowledge of both the facts and the law. Advocacy involves not only research and pressure for legislative reform but also follow-up on implementation of the reform. CDF staff includes specialists in health care, education, child welfare, mental health, child development, adolescent pregnancy prevention, family income, and youth employment.

The work of another ongoing children's advocacy group, the Child Welfare League of America (CWLA), also discussed earlier, is grounded in the knowledge and understanding of the needs of children and their families. The CWLA takes the position that advocacy is an important responsibility of child welfare agencies. According to the league's philosophy, social agencies today cannot merely be providers of services. They must also be concerned with the general welfare policies of the community and take into account the external forces and conditions that affect people's ability to function. Child welfare agencies are expected to help change community conditions that affect children and their families adversely (Goffin & Lombardi, 1988). In this respect, the CWLA employs an ecological approach to human development.

Agencies that belong to the CWLA must be committed to securing the fullest measure of services and rights to which children are entitled. This means halting processes and procedures that are adverse to children's interests, promoting humane and rational response by government and others to the needs of children and families, discovering gaps in services and proposing ways to fill them, and focusing public attention on the nature and extent of problems and on possible solutions (Whittaker, 1983).

Many children's advocacy groups exist on the local level as well. In some cases, local groups join together to form a national coalition in order to influence national public policy. A familiar example of this is the National Congress of Parents and Teachers, comprising local PTAs, which is devoted to improving relations between home and school on behalf of children.

In addition to the unmet needs of children examined previously, there are many others, such as child maltreatment, a less-than-humane system of juvenile justice, and a lack of transition programs for young people leaving protective community services to become independent, functioning adults. If these things bother you and you want to do something about them, you need to know how to become an advocate (NAEYC, 1996b; Phillips, 1981):

1. *Make a personal commitment.* Speak out, write, and be heard regarding a certain problem or need.
2. *Keep informed.* Do research and get facts. For example, if the problem in your neighborhood is lack of after-school care for children, find out how many families could benefit from such a service, what facilities would be available, what licensing requirements exist, what the cost would be, and so on. Find out what is currently being done to alleviate the problems or meet the need (publicly and privately). For instance, do any public schools in your areas remain open after regular hours?
3. *Know the process.* Determine what must be done, set priorities, and have a plan of action for how to use the information most effectively.
4. *Express your views.* Write letters, send e-mail, make telephone calls, and talk in person to those in decision-making roles.
5. *Get support.* Seek allies both outside and within the system—people or organizations that have the power to make changes.
6. *Be visible.* Be physically present at community hearings and meetings in legislators' offices.
7. *Show appreciation.* When those in power respond positively to your requests by taking action or speaking publicly, send a "thank you" message immediately.
8. *Monitor implementation.* Continue to watch the specifics in order to correct misinterpretations or problems; legislation often outlines intent and directions, and is a result of compromise. Also, analyze budgets.
9. *Build rapport and trust.* Be a reliable source of information to those in power so you will be trusted, volunteer to help your elected officials, and influence legislation.
10. *Educate your legislators.* Meet new decision makers, keep them informed by sending them articles, and invite them to speak at meetings and visit targeted programs, and influence appointments to advisory boards.

CHILD PROTECTION AND MALTREATMENT

Inappropriate parenting practices resulting in child abuse or neglect were discussed in Chapter 4, and the role of caregivers in protecting children who might be maltreated was discussed in Chapter 5. In this context, advocacy for children is exemplified in the law (macrosystem influence) and in the community services provided to help families in need of emotional support and parenting skills, as well as the children who have been maltreated (mesosystem influence of linkages between the community and families). The National Clearinghouse on Child Abuse and Neglect (2002) recommends the following:

1. *Know your state's child abuse/neglect laws.* All states require that suspected child abuse be reported, but each state defines abuse differently and has dif-

ferent reporting procedures. You can get a copy of your state's laws from a department of social services; a law enforcement agency; a state, district, city, or county attorney's office; or a regional office of child development.

2. *Know who must report abuse and neglect.* Injury, sexual molestation, death, abuse, or physical neglect that is suspected of having been inflicted upon any child under age 18 by other than accidental means *must* be reported by each of the following:

- physician
- surgeon
- teacher
- child caregiver
- dental hygienist
- ophthalmologist
- pharmacist
- commercial film and photographic print processor
- dentist
- chiropractor
- osteopath
- podiatrist
- nurse
- hospital intern or resident
- foster parent
- group home worker
- marriage, family, or child counselor
- school personnel
- social worker
- county medical examiner
- psychologist
- law enforcement officer
- audiologist
- clinical laboratory technician
- speech pathologist
- others having responsibility for child care

3. *Know how to report abuse and neglect according to the law.* The box in Chapter 5 titled "Indications of Possible Maltreatment" describes physical and behavioral indicators of potential abuse. If you notice several of the indicators over time, you have valid reason to report your observations.

Treatment or Intervention Programs for Child Maltreatment

Every state requires that a report of suspected child abuse be made "immediately" or "promptly." This means that as soon as an individual suspects abuse, she or he must inform the appropriate agency. The person taking the call is trained to determine whether it is an emergency situation and an immediate response is required or whether it can wait a few days. The response depends on how old the child is, how severe the abuse is, and how accessible the child is to the perpetrator. In a typical protective services investigation of alleged maltreatment, the professional must decide not "Has this child been maltreated?" but rather "Is this maltreatment extreme enough to justify community intervention?"

Once a social worker and a police officer investigate, they determine whether to place the child in protective custody. If the child is removed, he or she is placed in an institution until the court decides on final placement. The court hearing must take place within a specified time (usually 72 hours) after the child has been taken into protective custody. The child and the accused abuser(s) are assigned different lawyers. The court can require participation in a family preservation program, such as counseling or parent education, along with supervision by a social worker. The court also can order that the child be placed in an institution or in foster care for a specified time while the accused undergo rehabilitation. Then another hearing is held to determine whether the family is ready for reunification.

Individuals who report abuse or neglect do have legal protection. That is, those who report in good faith are granted immunity from civil and criminal court action, such as lawsuits, even if the report, when investigated, turns out to be erroneous. There are cases in which persons have been wrongly accused of child abuse or neglect. Family members who are wrongly accused can suffer emotional tur-moil, so it's important to observe and take notes to document observations before reporting the suspected abuse. A national organization for victims of child abuse laws, called VOCAL, exists to address their concerns.

Beyond identifying and assessing maltreatment, agencies and practitioners con-front the challenge of providing effective treatment programs. In order to protect children, *legal* intervention is the first requirement (Goodman, Emery, & Haugaard, 1998). The following are types of therapeutic intervention or treatment used with families that are abusive, depending on the particular case (Goodman, Emery, & Haugaard, 1998; Wolfe, 1994). The individual child, the family, and the community context (what is available and/or ethnically amenable) must be considered in decid-ing on the most effective treatment (Garbarino, Guttman, & Seely, 1986).

- *Family preservation.* The child remains at home under the supervision of the protective agency, with the child protective worker visiting the home on a scheduled basis. The worker may also teach child development and child management to the parents.
- *Homemaker services.* A person employed by the appropriate community agency helps the family with home management and child care.
- *Parent education.* The parents take a formal parenting course.
- *Child care.* The child is cared for during the day at a center or in a family day care home.
- *Family therapy.* A therapist addresses the family's interaction patterns.
- *Kinship care.* The child is temporarily (or permanently) placed in the care of grandparents or other close relatives.
- *Foster care.* The child is temporarily placed in another home until his or her family can provide adequate care.
- *Parent groups.* The parents are required to join a support group, such as Parents Anonymous (a voluntary organization of child abusers), and/or become involved in their child's school.
- *Institutionalization.* The child is temporarily placed in an institution for abused/neglected children until his or her family can provide adequate care.
- *Residential family care.* The whole family moves into a supervised environment.
- *Adoption.* When returning the child to his or her home is unwise or impos-sible, the child is put up for adoption. This avoids interminable foster care.

Support. The goals of treating an abusive family are to help both parents and chil-dren with their problems and to improve the relationship between parents and chil-dren in order to prevent further abuse (Cole & Duva, 1990).

Before any changes can be made in the abusive adults' behavior, they must rec-ognize that they may have unmet needs and need to be "parented" themselves before they can become adequate parents to their children. This support can come from therapy, a parent aide, or a group such as Parents Anonymous. Also, the par-ents have to *want* to make changes in their behavior; they have to understand their own self-destructive patterns and the consequences of them.

Parents Anonymous, founded in 1970, now has chapters all over the country. Parents can join on their own or can be ordered to do so by the courts. When parents join Parents Anonymous, they are given instruction in how to handle anger or frus-tration—for example by going into a room alone and then screaming, kicking, or pounding, thereby venting their aggression on objects so that no one gets hurt. Members share their difficulties and try to develop solutions to their problems and learn to feel better about themselves. They also maintain a network of telephone con-tacts so that they can call one another for support when they feel a crisis coming on.

Parents are children's primary role models, the most important people in their lives. Much of what children learn about dealing with stress and conflict is pat-terned on their parents' behavior (Iverson & Segal, 1990). Thus, Children's Village, a treatment facility in Dobbs Ferry, New York, for children who have been abused and their families, and other programs like it reflect the current attitude among social service professionals that treatment for abuse should include reeducating the parents and strengthening the family wherever possible while making sure that the child who is victimized is protected.

Parents who are abusive need to alter their behavior in these ways:

- *They have to learn to deal appropriately with emotions and stress.* They need to increase their repertoire of coping mechanisms in dealing with frustra-tion—to become less isolated and to turn to others when in need of help or support. This should result in improved self-esteem and increasing abil-ity to enjoy life.
- *They need to develop more realistic expectations of themselves and of others.* They also must work on breaking potentially self-destructive patterns of inter-personal relationships. For example, a mother must learn not to continu-ally become involved with passive-aggressive men, who tend to resist the demands of others in an indirect way—for example, procrastination, inef-ficiency, forgetfulness, or complaints.
- *They must learn what is age- and developmentally appropriate behavior for chil-dren.* They must also learn to tolerate and understand children's negative behavior. They need to view children as an individual, and not as objects of personal-needs-satisfaction. To do this, they have to learn to empathize with and respect children's individuality. Finally, parents must learn to express affection toward children, both verbally and physically.

Prevention. Social agencies have developed various programs to help families with problems. Since the passage of the Child Abuse Prevention Act in 1974, gov-ernment funds have been available for research on preventive programs. Some programs are based on parent effectiveness training, which concentrates on devel-oping good communication between parents and their children. Proponents of these programs theorize that abuse often occurs because parents do not understand or know how to react to their children's expressions of need and affection. Other programs teach behavior modification techniques. The aim of these programs is to teach alternatives to physical punishment when disciplining children. Parents are trained to notice when their children behave appropriately and to reward them accordingly. In some communities, hot lines provide counseling advice, available any time of the day or night.

Still other programs concentrate on preventing abuse, even before birth. For example, Johns Hopkins University has such a preventive program for high-risk mothers. These women are sought out while pregnant, counseled, and given the option of abortion. Those who choose to have their children are enrolled in classes in parenting, health, and nutrition. They are also counseled in planning their future education and career and in learning how to use the community services available to them.

Epilogue

A community can be both utopian (idealistic) and utilitarian (practical)—utopian in the sense that it values families and children, and utilitarian in the sense that it requires widespread citizen involvement to support families and children, balancing individualism and collectivism *(E. pluribus unum).* If children are to grow up to be contributing members of society, they need positive role models, mentors, and leaders. They need support from caring adults. And they need to experience democracy in action—involvement, discussion, collaboration, and compromise.

Summary

The community comprises a group of people living in the same geographic area under common laws who have a sense of fellowship among themselves. Community ecology refers to the relationship between those people and their environment. The need for community is both psychological and practical.

The community is structured to serve five functions: production/distribution/consumption, socialization, social control, social participation, and mutual support. These functions are performed in different ways by different communities, and the ways these functions are performed affect the socialization of the children involved.

The community influences socialization through the role models it provides for adults, such as ways of earning a living, socializing with one another, and helping one another. The community also influences socialization through members' ways of instilling norms and values in children and ways of enforcing its rules. Finally, the community is where children can "try themselves out" and, by so doing, learn the consequences of their behavior.

Physical factors in the community that have an impact on socialization include population density and characteristics, noise, arrangement and types of houses, and play settings.

Economic factors in a community play a central role in shaping the daily lives of families who live and work there. Economics affects unemployment rates, mothers' employment, the ability of young adults to afford homes of their own, and the cost of living.

Certain social and personal factors, such as the neighborhood setting and patterns of community interaction, influence socialization. The neighborhood setting affects children's mobility, exposure to adults, friendship patterns, and types of play. Community interaction is important to the development of children because of its supportive links to the family or school. Community relationships can be classified as informal, mutually dependent and caring (*gemeinschaft*), or formal, independent, and contractual (*gesellschaft*).

Children can be involved in the community in order to learn. Libraries, museums, zoos, farms, and businesses, as well as people's experiences, are all rich sources for involvement and education. The community is a more valuable resource for children if the schools view it as an educational resource and if the community itself (the business community, for example) opens itself to children.

The community represents a formal support system through its community services. Community services are necessary because of the increasingly diverse population, the changing nature of the family, and increasing urbanization.

Chronosystem influences on community services involve changes in the macrosystem, such as political ideology and economics. Community agencies can be public, private, or a combination. Some community services are preventive, such as parks, recreation, and education agencies; some are supportive, such as family and child services; and some are rehabilitative, such as corrections, mental health, and special needs agencies.

Mesosystem influences link community services to families and schools. These links can be fostered by establishing a local commission for children and families, creating a neighborhood family center, fostering community projects, encouraging youth participation in local policy bodies, and planning communities with the children who will be growing up in them in mind.

Community services have attempted to meet the needs of children and families, but many needs are still unmet, such as economic, health care, support, and special child care needs.

Child advocacy is the process of sensitizing individuals and groups to the unmet needs of children and to society's obligation to provide a positive response to those needs. To be an advocate, one must make a personal commitment, keep informed, know the process, express one's views, obtain support, be visible, show appreciation, build rapport and trust, and educate one's legislators.

Child maltreatment must be reported to police or social agencies. Professionals and persons responsible for child care are required by law to report suspected cases of child abuse or neglect immediately. In turn, they are granted immunity from legal action if the investigation turns up no evidence.

Treatments for abusive parents include therapy, training in child development and child management, parent education, support groups, and supervision by a child protective agency. Treatments for abused children include hospitalization, residential care, child care, foster care, adoption, and therapy. The choice, as well as the effectiveness, of an intervention program depends on the individual child, the family, and the community context. The main goal in treating the abusive families is to improve the relationship between parents and children in order to prevent further maltreatment.

Activity

PURPOSE *To learn about the services in your community.*

1. The following 10 hypothetical case studies involve families and children in a community. Read each of these case studies, and then select one family. (Or make up your own hypothetical one that you would like to help. Possibilities include-at-risk infants [premature or drug- or alcohol-exposed], a relative with a terminal disease, 18-year-olds no longer eligible for special or protective services, and disaster victims [tornado, fire, hurricane, earthquake].

2. Provide the family with a list of three agencies that may be helpful in their particular situation. Your list should include the following information about each agency:
   a. Name
   b. Address

      c. Telephone number

      d. Hours

      e. Services provided

      f. Eligibility requirements

      g. Fees

      h. Area served

3. Choose one of the three agencies on the list, call to make an appointment to visit the agency, and interview one person employed there (for example, director, counselor, teacher, therapist, or caseworker). In this section of your report, be sure to include the following information:

    a. The services provided by the agency and the steps the agency would take to help this hypothetical family (person)

    b. For the person interviewed, the requirements for the job, educational background, previous experience, job satisfactions/ dissatisfactions, and so on

    c. For the agency itself, the number of employees, physical layout, number of people served, and so forth

---

CASE STUDY 1: THE WILSON FAMILY. Matt Wilson is 67 years old, and his wife has recently died. His daughter and her family live in another state, and they have persuaded Matt to sell his home and move to their town. Matt has found an apartment and gotten somewhat settled, he seems to be having a difficult time adjusting. He is generally depressed and sometimes confused. He does not leave his apartment often (although he has a car and drives), he spends his days watching television, and he doesn't seek out other people. He is also not eating properly, and his family is afraid that his physical, as well as mental, health will begin to decline rapidly. Is there help available for Matt in your community? What would you recommend to Matt's family in order to help him?

CASE STUDY 2: THE JOHNSON FAMILY. You are a first-grade teacher at an elementary school. You are especially worried about one of the students in your class, Michael Johnson. He always arrives at school early (usually about 30 minutes). He is never dressed appropriately for the weather, and his general appearance is sloppy. His schoolwork is on grade level, but his behavior often is aggressive and hostile (especially toward classmates). On several occasions, you have noticed bruises on Michael, and when you've asked him about these, he was evasive. During your first parent–teacher conference, you share your concerns with his mother, Yolanda. She breaks down and tells you that her husband, Michael's stepfather, is very hard on him. He is sarcastic, always belittling Michael, and at times gets physically violent with him. Yolanda asks you for help. What is your role as a teacher? What assistance is available to Michael and to his family in your community?

CASE STUDY 3: THE PETERSON FAMILY. Mary Peterson is a single parent living in your community. She has three teenage children, Pam, Brian, and Lynn. Mary works full time, and the three children all attend school. Mary's oldest daughter, Pam, age 16, has always been a good student, has had a nice group of friends, has rarely had any problems that could not be worked out easily. Recently, however, she has been withdrawn and moody. She spends a lot of time in her room, and Mary suspects that she is crying a lot. When confronted, Pam gets emotional and shouts at Mary, "Mind your own business and leave me alone!" Mary questions her other children about Pam's behavior. Finally, Lynn informs her that Pam thinks she is pregnant. Where would you suggest that Pam and Mary go for help in this situation? What kind of assistance is available to them in your community? Who can help Pam explore her options and make a decision about this pregnancy?

CASE STUDY 4: THE MEYERS FAMILY. Paula and Larry Meyers live in your community with their two children, Kelly, age 4, and Lisa, age 18 months. Lisa is not showing the normal development Kelly did at this age, and Paula is concerned. Lisa is not yet standing or walking. She does not respond to the family with love and affection and often seems to be in her own little world. Their pediatrician has suggested that the Meyers take Lisa to a neurologist for testing. After extensive tests, it is determined that Lisa has cerebral palsy. Paula and Larry want to provide Lisa with every possible opportunity for a normal life. What services are available to Lisa and her family in your community? Where would you recommend that the Meyers go for assistance?

CASE STUDY 5: THE SIMMONS FAMILY. Martin Simmons lives in your community with his wife, Sue, and their 14-year-old son, Steve. Martin has worked for a large engineering firm in the area for the past 12 years. Recently, due to cutbacks, Martin lost his job. He has been unemployed for the past 8 months, and his family is feeling the pressure of his job loss. Martin had been actively looking for a job for the first few months of his unemployment. Lately, however, he has begun drinking more and more and looking for work less and less. Since he began drinking, his relationships with Sue and, especially, with Steve, have suffered. Sue is convinced that Martin is becoming an alcoholic and is settling deeper and deeper into a depressed state. Steve is angry with his father, and they are continually fighting with each other. Sue has asked you to help her find assistance for herself and for her family. What agencies would you suggest the Simmons family contact for assistance?

CASE STUDY 6: THE HERNANDEZ FAMILY. During lunch break on the junior high school playground, you notice a group of boys in a small circle intently examining something. As you approach the group, Roberto hastily shoves something in his pocket. In the panic, a joint drops on the ground. You pick it up and escort the group to the principal's office. You learn that Roberto had gotten the marijuana from his older brother, who is in a gang, and brought it to school to show his friends. Roberto's parents are called, and a conference is scheduled. After explaining the situation to the parents, where do you refer this family for help?

CASE STUDY 7: THE LAMBERT FAMILY. Mrs. Lambert waits to speak to you after picking up her daughter at the day care center. She tells you her husband has been laid off and that his unemployment checks will stop next week. She can't pay the tuition at the center, and she has no other place to leave her daughter while she works. She must work to pay the rent and buy food. She hopes her husband will find work soon (he spends all day looking), because there are unpaid bills piling up. The family no longer has medical insurance since Mr. Lambert lost his job. They have several doctor bills to pay for a severe ear infection their daughter had last month. The family car's tire treads are so worn that driving is unsafe, yet the car is the family's only means of transportation to work, the day care center, and the store. Mrs. Lambert is terrified of having her family become homeless. Where would you refer her for help?

CASE STUDY 8: THE SULLIVAN FAMILY. You are a prekindergarten teacher at a local preschool. Five-year-old Brian's behavior in class is causing problems for you and the other students. He has difficulty sitting still, attending to stories, completing activities, and keeping his hands to himself. Brian is easily frustrated and is prone to temper tantrums and outbursts of aggression. His mother, a single parent, has experienced the same problems with Brian at home. What could be the cause of Brian's behavior, and where would you refer this family for help?

CASE STUDY 9: THE NGUYEN FAMILY. A child enters your public school preschool class the first day and speaks no English. You wait for his mother to pick him up so you can get some information about the child. The mother's English is very limited. You resort to communicating in simple words combined with gestures. You even draw pictures in order to communicate. You learn that the family has recently emigrated from Vietnam and is staying with relatives who were sponsored to come to the United States the previous year. The father works in a local electronics factory, and the mother is expecting another child in 3 months. The mother is most anxious that her son, as well as she and her husband, learn English and the "American way" as quickly as possible. Where do you refer this family for help with American culture?

CASE STUDY 10: THE HORVATH FAMILY. For the past 2 years, Mr. Horvath has dropped off and picked up his two children, age 4 and 5, at the children's center. You have never met the mother. One day a woman comes to the center claiming that she is the children's mother and demanding that they be released to her. You refuse because her name is not on their information form. She produces a court document stating that she has legal custody of the children. You assign someone to watch the children while you call the police and the father (immediate attention is required by the legal authorities). The father admits that the mother was granted legal custody but claims that she was continually drunk, so he took them. He has had them for 2 years, and she has never even visited them once. What do you advise him to do?

ℱ Research Terms

Advocacy
Adoption
Child maltreatment
Child welfare
Family preservation
Foster care
Juvenile justice
Medicaid
Temporary Assistance to Needy Families (TANF)

Related Readings

Belle, D. (1999). *The after-school lives of children: Alone and with others while parents work.* Mahwah, NJ: Lawrence Erlbaum.

Decker, L. E., & Decker, V. A. (2001). *Engaging families and communities: Pathways to educational success* (2nd ed.). Fairfax, VA: National Community Education Association.

Etzioni, A. (1993). *The spirit of the community: The reinvention of American society.* New York: Touchstone.

Garbarino, J. (1995). *Building a socially nourishing environment with children.* San Francisco: Jossey-Bass.

Goffin, S. G., & Lombardi, J. (1988). *Speaking out: Early childhood advocacy.* Washington, DC: National Association for the Education of Young Children.

Nazario, T. A. (1988). *In defense of children: Understanding the rights, needs, and interests of the child.* New York: Scribner.

Rickel, A. U., & Becker, E. (1997). *Keeping children from harm's way: How national policy affects psychological development.* Washington, DC: American Psychological Association.

Rivkin, M. S. (1995). *The great outdoors: Restoring children's rights to play outside.* Washington, DC: National Association for Education of Young Children.

Schorr, L. B., & Schorr, D. (1997). *Common purpose: Strengthening families and neighborhoods to rebuild America.* New York: Anchor Books.

Warren, R. L., & Lyon, L. (1983). *New perspectives on the American community.* Homewood, IL: Dorsey Press.

Whittaker, J. K., & Garbarino, J. (1983). *Social support networks: Informal helping in the human services.* New York: Aldine.

Chapter 11

Prologue: Then and Now

Values
    Values, Decisions,
        and Consequences

Attitudes
    Development of Attitudes
    Influence of Significant
        Socializing Agents on
        Attitude Development
    Changing Attitudes
        About Diversity

Motives and Attributes
    Achievement Motivation
    Locus of Control
    Learned Helplessness
    Self-Efficacy

Self-Esteem
    Development of Self-
        Esteem
    Influences on the Develop-
        ment of Self-Esteem

Epilogue

Summary

Activity

Research Terms

Related Readings

© Billy E. Barnes/PhotoEdit

Affective/Cognitive Socialization Outcomes

What gives life its value you can find—and lose. But never possess. This holds good above all for "The Truth about Life."

—DAG HAMMARSKJOLD

POTENTIAL AND PERSONAL AGENCY

THEN In *Anne Frank: The Diary of a Young Girl* (1993 [1947]) the title character demonstrates the attribute of **personal agency**—the realization that one's actions lead to certain outcomes. The sense of personal agency has the positive potential for developing into achievement motivation, self-efficacy, and high self-esteem or negative potential for developing into learned helplessness, low self-esteem, and depression. Anne Frank exemplifies personal agency, self-efficacy, and high self-esteem in the most dire environmental conditions. Hers is the story of a Jewish teenager who died during World War II in Bergen-Belsen, Germany, in 1945.

Born in 1929, Anne received a blank diary for her thirteenth birthday. Soon afterward, when the Nazis occupied Amsterdam and began rounding up Jews to put in concentration camps, Anne, her family, and another family went into hiding in the "secret annex" of an old office building. Cut off from the outside world, Anne documented her impressions for two years, vividly recounting the claustrophobic, sometimes quarrelsome intimacy with her parents and sister and the other family.

The diary is unique in that it describes the details of confinement during the war (constant fear of discovery and death, hunger, and boredom), yet it is universal in its discussion of typical adolescent emotions (everyone criticizes me, no one knows "the real me," and so on).

Anne exhibits personal agency, self-efficacy, and high self-esteem in her interpersonal relations even though, because of the circumstances of war, she was "at risk" for many of the psychological disorders plaguing today's teens (depression, anxiety, substance abuse, self-mutilation, eating disorders, and/or suicide). What enabled her to be resistant to such negative developmental outcomes? Anne Frank's short life was experienced in a very close family and community; she lived and breathed their values. To survive, hope was the only elixir.

NOW Exemplifying learned helplessness, low self-esteem, and depression are the adolescent girls struggling with identity development examined in Mary Pipher's book *Reviving Ophelia: Saving the Selves of Adolescent Girls* (1994). The title was inspired by the character of Ophelia in Shakespeare's *Hamlet.* Ophelia loses her sense of self-efficacy when she falls in love with Hamlet. Rather than have direction in her own life, she does everything for the approval of her father and Hamlet. Ultimately, torn by her efforts to please both, she commits suicide.

In *Reviving Ophelia,* Pipher describes the adolescent girls whom she sees in therapy because they have become inefficacious and exhibit learned helplessness, as well as depression:

> Girls become fragmented, their selves split into mysterious contradictions. They are sensitive and tenderhearted, mean and competitive, superficial and idealistic. They are confident in the morning and overwhelmed with anxiety by nightfall. . . . They try on new roles every week—this week the good student, next week the delinquent, and the next, the artist. (1994, p. 20)

Pipher believes that these girls are experiencing a conflict between their autonomous selves (their sense of personal agency and self-efficacy) and their need to be feminine (their perception of a stereotypic cultural attitude of helplessness).

According to William Pollack (1999), author of *Real Boys: Rescuing Our Sons from the Myths of Boyhood,* not only is Ophelia at risk for negative developmental problems, but so is Hamlet. Hamlet, too, becomes inefficacious, vacillating between acting on his feelings toward Ophelia and wreaking vengeance on his uncle, who has seized the throne after killing Hamlet's father. Hamlet cannot bring himself to act on his anger; he pretends to be insane to cover his real motives.

Meanwhile, Ophelia's brother, spurred by the king (Hamlet's uncle), challenges Hamlet to a duel. After both he and Hamlet are stabbed during the duel, Hamlet finally owns up to his feelings and actions—"This above all: To thine ownself be true"—killing the king before dying himself.

Hamlet's pretenses and vacillations resemble the conflicted values and attitudes facing today's adolescent boys. According to Pollack, boys are at risk for violence, substance abuse, depression, and suicide. Pollack attributes this to the stereotypic value associated with following "the Boy Code"—the pretense that everything is fine. The Boy Code dictates conformity to the cultural stereotype of the "real" male as silent, unemotional, tough, and independent. Indeed, many social agents teach that it is unacceptable for males to be fearful, uncertain, lonely, or desirous of comfort or help.

KEY QUESTIONS

- How can the microsystems in society provide children with humanitarian values and attitudes, rather than stereotypic ones?
- How can the microsystems in society cooperate to foster achievement motives and attributes?
- How can young people's self-esteem be supported?

Values

The outcomes of socialization that are examined in this chapter and the next can be categorized as primarily affective/cognitive (such as values, attitudes, motives, attributes, and self-esteem) or primarily social/behavioral (such as self-regulation/behavior, morals, and gender roles). These outcomes are the result of child, family, school, peer, and community interactions (mesosystems). Also influencing the development of these outcomes are exosystems (such as parents' work or school board policies), factors in individuals' macrosystem (such as religion, ethnicity, or economics), and changes in society or in individuals (the chronosystem, such as today's sexual norms compared with those of one's grandparents). Figure 11.1 provides an ecological model of the systems involved in the process.

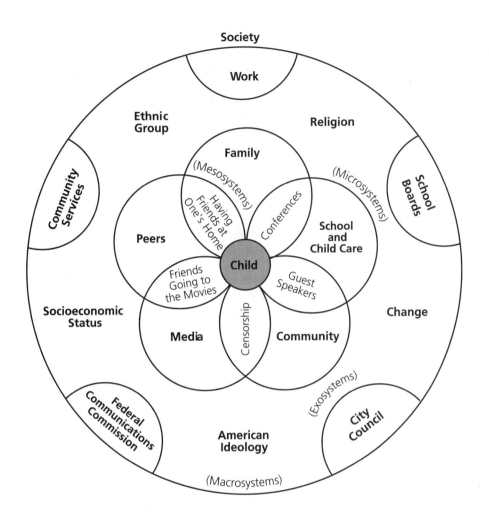

Figure 11.1
*An Ecological Model
of Human Development*
The child's values, attitudes,
motives, attributes, and self-
esteem are outcomes of his or
her socialization.

Recall that **values** are qualities or beliefs that are viewed as desirable or important. They can include such related characteristics as attitudes and morals, which
affect behavior. Values are outcomes of socialization. Some values reflect the values
of people's parents, teachers, religion, culture, profession, or friends; others reflect
what people have read, or seen on TV or film, as well as what they have directly
experienced.

Values, whether societal or personal, change over time. According to professor of
social work Sophie Freud (1999), the concept of "normality" is socially constructed
based on what norms society expects at a given time and on who is perceived as
deviating from those norms. What society does about deviations is also influenced
by values. In the United States, individuals who deviate from "normal" may be
counseled by psychologists or social workers who believe that their professional support can alleviate the "problem," or they may be referred to psychiatrists who believe
medication is what is needed. However, in other times and in other cultures, individuals rarely divulge confidences and personal feelings to strangers. The persons

experiencing problems might keep the problems to themselves, as divulging deviance would be shameful; or they might rely on family and/or religion for help. In order to provide formal and appropriate help (diagnosis and treatment), it is common in the United States to label deviations. These labels are value judgments regarding what is "normal," which change in response to chronosystem factors such as politics, economics, and technology. For example, the American Psychiatric Association's *Diagnostic and Statistical Manual* no longer lists "homosexuality" as a mental disorder; added to the list of pathologies are attention deficit hyperactivity disorder (ADHD) and post traumatic stress disorder (PTSD).

EXAMPLE Tammy wants to have a party for her graduation from high school. The neighborhood where she lives with her family has a recreation center, which is rented out for a nominal fee to various groups for meetings, club functions, and parties. Tammy's parents, Tom and Cheryl, agree to let Tammy have the party provided the rules for rental are followed. For instance, parties for minors must be chaperoned, no more than 50 people can attend, the room must be cleaned after the party, and no alcohol can be served to minors. Tammy agrees to all but the last: "How can you have a graduation party without beer? C'mon, get real . . . no one will come!" "Sorry," says Tom, "you want a party, you have to abide by the rules." "OK, OK, but we better have great food," Tammy grumbles.

One week before the party, Cheryl gets a phone call from a parent of a girl she does not know. The parent wants to confirm that there is, in fact, a party; that beer will be served; and that the cost of a formal invitation to enter is $10. Cheryl can hardly contain her shock and anger. Apparently, a flier was distributed at school "advertising" the party. Cheryl thanks the parent and says there will be no such party.

Cheryl tells Tom what happened, and together they confront Tammy. Tammy says it was one of her friends who distributed the flier (she won't tell who). Tom says he is extremely disappointed that she didn't stop her friend, as they had agreed to the rules for the party—especially no alcohol—in advance. As a result, there will be no party. Tom explains that advertising the party, especially one in which beer will be served, is setting up her parents for trouble—uninvited kids, angry neighbors, the police, and alcohol-related accidents. Tammy understands her father's position but says that he and Cheryl are out of touch with reality (all graduation parties have booze) and that they don't understand her position (she can't have a party and not do what is expected). "Well, then, I guess the party is off," says Tom, "because we have expectations, too."

The next evening several of Tammy's friends come over to beg Tom and Cheryl to reconsider. They claim that drinking is going to occur on graduation night whether or not Tammy has the party. Tammy's having the party will at least keep the kids from driving around drunk, and the best way to prevent alcohol-related accidents is to let Tammy have the party, take everyone's car keys, and have all the kids spend the night.

Cheryl replies, "That's an interesting argument but, first, I feel morally wrong serving kids alcohol; second, the recreation room belongs to the community, and the rules cannot be broken; and third, it is illegal for kids under twenty-one to drink in this state."

Tom shakes his head and says to Cheryl, "The values of this generation are so different from those of ours. Why does booze have to be the essential ingredient for having a good time?"

As this example demonstrates, Tammy places more value on what her friends think than what her parents think. Her parents, in contrast, place more value on obeying the law and following community policy in regard to minors drinking alcohol than on Tammy's saving face with her friends.

In the pop culture, as portrayed by the media, there is much value placed on drinking alcohol as a means of having fun, whereas in certain religious and ethnic groups, drinking alcohol is considered sinful. Thus, some people might experience conflict in social situations.

As soon as children can understand language, they have access to their parents' and their culture's values (Damon, 1988). As children develop cognitively and can interpret the meaning of their social interactions and experiences, they begin to construct their own values, which will change and be redefined as they get older.

Points to Ponder

Language is a unique biological capacity of humans. The ability to communicate thoughts and ideas verbally to others enables adults to teach values to children. "Other," or social, speech becomes internalized and "self," or inner, speech drives children's behavior. Can you remember some messages you heard over and over again while growing up that still influence you: "Money doesn't grow on trees!" or "Work before play," or "Don't get into trouble!"?

VALUES, DECISIONS, AND CONSEQUENCES

How do individuals come to know what is personally important? One technique is known as **values clarification**—the process of coming to know what is personally worthwhile or desirable in life at any particular time. This can help individuals understand their own personal moral codes, their attitudes and motives, their prosocial or antisocial behavior, and their gender roles. For example, in a class about the founding of America, a factual discussion might explore dates and events; a conceptual discussion might focus on emigration and freedom of religion; a values discussion might address questions like these: What is so important to you that if it were taken away you would leave your country? And if you left, what would you take with you?

Values clarification involves making decisions—choosing among alternatives. Sometimes the process is difficult because values may conflict. For example, Tom and Cheryl must choose between their values of respect for the law and family harmony; Tammy must weigh her value of preserving friendship against that of respecting the law. Other

Many adolescents in this culture equate alcohol with having a good time.

© Bill Aron/PhotoEdit

times, the process of values clarification is easy because certain basic human values are enshrined in the laws of most civilized societies. The Ten Commandments are an example of basic human values, some of which ("Thou shalt not kill") are also found in laws. In addition, certain values are basic to a particular society. An example of a basic societal value is the Bill of Rights, which lists the rights and freedoms (freedom of speech, for instance) assumed to be essential in our society.

Human values and societal values are part of people's cultural heritage, with many of their decisions based on such learned values. Still other values are personal in that they develop through experiences and relationships. Differences in social and personal interactions make for a wide divergence in human values. For example, some people value money over leisure time. They would rather spend most of their time working in order to earn money to afford a large house or an expensive car. Other people prefer to schedule their work so that they have some time for leisure—time to enjoy their families, their homes, or their environments—even if, in so doing, they earn less money.

Divergence in values is manifested in parenting styles, as discussed in Chapter 4. Some parents believe that the most effective way to raise children is to be authoritarian; others believe an authoritative style is best; still others favor a permissive style. Values in adolescents, exemplifying socialization outcomes, have been found to be related to delinquency, substance abuse, and sexual activity (Goff & Goddard, 1999). Teens valuing fun/enjoyment and security were strongly identified with delinquency and substance abuse, whereas those valuing self-respect, a sense of accomplishment, and warm relationships with others exhibited a low incidence of delinquent behavior and substance abuse. At the same time, sexual activity was found to be related to a desire for warm relationships with others.

Divergence in values is also manifested in governmental policies. For example, during the 1960s, many social programs emerged as part of the War on Poverty; in the 1980s, many social programs were scaled back or eliminated as a way to achieve the goal of a balanced budget. In the 1990s, a goal was to build a "nation of learners," a process that continues in the 2000s as the "Leave No Child Behind" act is implemented.

Values of specific groups have an impact on governmental decisions and consequent policies, as mentioned in the discussion on advocacy in Chapter 10. A pertinent example of how group values influence public policy is the Human Capital Initiative, launched by professional associations in the behavioral sciences (National Science Foundation, 1994). This initiative calls for government funding to support research on the processes that shape individuals' intellectual, physical, and psychological capacities for productive citizenship. The National Science Foundation supports research in six priority areas, as recommended by the representatives of the behavioral sciences:

1. Building strong neighborhoods
2. Educating for the future
3. Employing a productive workforce
4. Fostering successful families
5. Overcoming poverty and deprivation
6. Reducing disadvantages in a diverse society

Since the 1970s, many people have questioned the role of the federal government in providing services to children and families (Children's Defense Fund, 2001; Schorr, 1997). Some believe that many of the nation's more expensive public health and public welfare programs (child abuse and neglect programs, residential and outpatient psychotherapy, rehabilitation following avoidable accidents) might be greatly reduced if parents were more effective in nurturing and socializing their children. Whereas most people value the importance of the family to children, few supported the 1980 White House Conference on Families' proposal to implement universal parent education in the schools (Caldwell, 1986). Thus, although people share a value, they might not agree as to how to implement it.

Attitudes

Socialization outcomes related to values (include attitudes, motives, attributes, self-esteem, self-regulation/behavior, morals, and gender roles).

> **EXAMPLE** Bill Pratt loves football. He's anxious about Saturday's game because it is for the league championship. Since Bill made the team last year as a high school sophomore, he has been more conscious about his diet and sleep habits. He has also neglected his schoolwork a bit. Bill's younger sister, Julie, hates football; she thinks it's a stupid game in which everybody simply piles up on everybody else. Bill's dad was the star quarterback for his high school team, and he is still devoted to the game. It was he who encouraged Bill to try out for the team, and it was he who used to toss a football to little 3-year-old Bill. Bill's mother's attitude toward football is one of fear. She is proud of her son's accomplishments but would rather he participated in a different sport. She worries about the possibilities of injury, and she is also concerned about Bill's falling grades.

An **attitude** is a tendency to respond positively (favorably) or negatively (unfavorably) to certain persons, objects, or situations. Bill's dad has a positive attitude toward football, whereas Bill's sister has a negative one.

Prejudice, which means "prejudgment," is an attitude. It generally refers to the application of a previously formed judgment to some person, object, or situation; it can be favorable or unfavorable. Usually, prejudice comes from categorizing or stereotyping. Bill accuses his mother of being prejudiced against football when she objects to his joining the team.

A **stereotype** is an oversimplified, fixed attitude or set of beliefs about members of a group. Stereotypic attitudes usually do not allow for individual exceptions. Bill's sister stereotypes football players as "dumb jocks." And when she hears her mother prodding Bill about his grades, she teases him: "See? You're turning dumb just like the other goons."

Attitudes are composed of beliefs, feelings, and behavioral tendencies. Most psychologists agree that attitudes determine what individuals attend to in the environment, how they perceive the information about the object of their attention, and how they respond to that object. Thus, attitudes guide behavior. For example, if someone has the attitude that intelligence is genetic, then she or he will not support educational programs for children with learning problems.

DEVELOPMENT OF ATTITUDES

The development of attitudes is influenced by age, level of cognitive development, and social experiences (Van Ausdale & Feagin, 2001). For example, according to researchers (Derman-Sparks, 1989; Goodman, 1964; Van Ausdale & Feagin, 2001), ethnic attitudes develop in the following sequence:

- Phase 1—awareness of ethnic differences, beginning about age 2–3
- Phase 2—orientation toward specific ethnic-related words and concepts, beginning about age 4
- Phase 3—true attitudes toward various ethnic groups, beginning about age 7

This sequence is probably due to the reaction of others to children's appearance, in that remarks about skin color, hair, and facial features alert them to the fact that people look different. Cognitive development and social experience also enter into the equation.

As children develop cognitively, they are better able to categorize (assimilate and accommodate) similarities and differences. In reviewing studies of Euro-American children's attitudes toward other groups, Aboud (1988) found that 4- to 7-year-old Euro-American children were already aware that "white" is the ethnic identity favored by the society. They referred to other groups as "bad" or as having negative characteristics: "He's lazy because he's colored." Many African American children felt ambivalent about being African American and were envious of Euro-American children; Hispanic children followed a similar pattern. After age 7, however, children of all ethnic groups were found to be less prejudiced toward other groups and to have more positive attitudes toward their own group. Aboud explained young children's prejudicial attitudes as due to cognitive immaturity rather than malice.

Social experiences, including observation and interaction, provide children with a perspective on the macrosystem in which they live (Hirschfeld, 1997). Children become familiar with attitudes about ethnicity, religion, socioeconomic status, gender, disability, and age by watching TV, by listening to significant adults talk and seeing how they behave, and by noticing differences in neighborhood facilities (schools, theaters, sidewalks) and practices (employment, discrimination, violence). Exemplifying how color attitudes can be transmitted subtly, a 1993 Caldecott Honor Book (recognition given for pictures), *Seven Blind Mice*, by Ed Young (1992), is about seven blind mice, each a different and brilliant color, whose task is to identify an object. The white mouse solves the riddle, correctly identifying the object as an elephant. Many have criticized the book, complaining that the white mouse is portrayed as the "savior," thereby perpetuating prejudicial attitudes of "white supremacy" (Jacobs & Tunnell, 1996). Furthermore, children abstract attitudinal concepts from their social experiences and try them out. For example, in wanting to control the space in the sandbox, one youngster might assert that only people who speak Spanish are allowed; experimenting with a racial epitaph, another might discover that he can be dominant by hurting other's feelings (Van Ausdale & Feagin, 2001).

Whether children act on messages from the media depends on their real-life experiences and interactions, especially with parents. Studies of young children have shown that those with the most prejudicial attitudes have parents who are authoritarian, who use strict disciplinary techniques, and who are inflexible in their attitudes toward right and wrong (Aboud, 1988; Boswell & Williams, 1975; Katz, 1975). Thus, rigid parental attitudes influence similar ones in their children.

Prejudicial attitudes are found with regard to disabilities as well. In a longitudinal study of children's attitudes toward those with mental *illness*, Weiss (1994) found that, by the time children entered kindergarten, they already had stigmatized attitudes, which remained stable 8 years later. However, perception of those with mental *disabilities* had changed, from stigmatization to greater acceptance. Perhaps the inclusion of children with mental disabilities in schools and communities, and in the media, has influenced the attitude change.

Stages in the Development of Prejudice

- *Awareness*—being alert to, seeing, noticing, and understanding differences among people even though they may never have been described or talked about.
- *Identification*—naming, labeling, and classifying people based on physical characteristics that children notice. Verbal identification relieves the stress that comes from being aware of or confused by something that you can't describe or no one else is talking about. Identification represents children's attempt to break the adult silence and make sense of the world.
- *Attitude*—thoughts and feelings that become an inclination or opinion toward other people and their ways of living.
- *Preference*—valuing, favoring, and giving priority to a physical attribute, a person, or lifestyle over another, usually based on similarities and differences.
- *Prejudice*—preconceived hostile attitude, opinion, feeling, or action against a person, race, or their way of being in the world without knowing them.

Adapted with permission from *Roots & Wings: Affirming Culture in Early Childhood Programs* by Stacey York. Copyright © 2003 Stacey York. Redleaf Press, St. Paul, Minnesota. www.redleafpress.org.

INFLUENCES OF SIGNIFICANT SOCIALIZING AGENTS ON ATTITUDE DEVELOPMENT

Family, peers, media, community, and school all influence children's attitudes toward those who are similar and those who are different.

Family

Parents have a large impact on children's attitudes and values. Studies have shown that the attitudes of children tend to resemble those of their parents; for example, 76 percent of a national sample of high school seniors favored the political party favored by both of their parents (McGuire, 1985). Ethnic prejudice also follows this general pattern. The ethnic prejudices of Euro-American elementary school children tend to resemble those of their parents, as do the ethnic prejudices of African American elementary school children (Aboud, 1988).

Modeling. One explanation for the similarity of children's and parents' ethnic attitudes is that children develop attitudes through role modeling, identifying with models they view as powerful and admirable. Thus, through the process of identification, they begin to assume attitudes of the people they would like to emulate—parents, relatives, friends, fictional heroes or heroines, television and movie characters, rock stars, and so on.

Instruction. We often think of the ethnic majority as being prejudiced against ethnic minorities. However, prejudice is present in ethnic minorities, too. The following description illustrates how a Jewish boy's parents tried to socialize him to be prejudiced against Christians because they had been persecuted by prejudiced Christians:

> My first impressions of Christianity came in the home, of course. My parents brought with them the burden of the Middle Ages from the blood-soaked continent of Europe. They had come from the villages of Eastern Europe where Christians were feared with legitimate reason.
>
> When occasionally a Jewish drunk was seen in our neighborhood, our parents would say, "He's behaving like a Gentile."
>
> For in truth, our parents had often witnessed the Polish, Romanian, Hungarian, and Russian peasants gather around a barrel of whiskey on Saturday night, drink themselves into oblivion, "and beat their wives." Once in a while the rumor would spread through the tenements that a fellow had struck his wife, and on all sides we heard the inevitable, "Just like a Gentile."
>
> Oddly enough, too, our parents had us convinced that the Gentiles were noisy, boisterous, and loud—unlike the Jews. It is indeed strange how often stereotypes are exactly reversed.
>
> If we raised our voices, we were told, "Jewish boys don't shout." And this admonition covered every activity in and out of the home: "Jewish boys don't fight." "Jewish boys don't get dirty." "Jewish boys study hard."
>
> It wasn't until I was in school and was subjected to the influence of Gentile teachers and met Gentile social workers and classmates that I began to question these generalizations. Then I began to read and I found myself finally dismissing all prejudice from my mind. (Golden, 1962, p. 210)

The example illustrates one way children learn attitudes—by instruction. Young children accept as true the statements of their parents and others they admire because, with their limited experience, they are not apt to have heard anything different.

According to Ramsey (1998), children assimilate ethnically related attitudes, preferences, and social expectations at an early age. They see the world in terms of absolutes and overgeneralizations. Therefore, because of their cognitive level of development, they are receptive to the stereotypic and prejudicial comments of adults. For example, in one experiment (Bigler, Brown, & Markell, 2001), 7- to 12-year-olds attending a summer school program were randomly assigned to groups denoted by yellow or blue T-shirts. The status of each group was artificially manipulated by the teachers, who created posters showing the yellow-group members as having won more spelling and athletic competitions, and thereby achieving higher status than the blue group. Teachers called attention to the different statuses, using them as a basis for seating arrangements, task assignments, and class privileges. When the children were asked to evaluate each other, those in the yellow group rated each other higher, and those in the blue group rated each other lower. Children in the control group, who were not exposed to the artificial evaluative judgment of adults, did not express prejudice toward each other.

Reinforcement and Punishment. The socializing techniques of reinforcement and punishment are also involved in the way children learn attitudes. For example, it has been demonstrated that attitudes toward ethnic groups can be influenced simply by associating them with positive words (reinforcement), like *happy* or *suc-*

cessful, or negative words (punishment), like *ugly* or *failure* (Aboud, 1988; Lohr & Staats, 1973). For another example, negative attitudes about individuals with disabilities, such as that they are vocationally limited or socially inept, are reinforced when such individuals are excluded from the mainstream of society (Gollnick & Chinn, 2002).

Peers

Peers are influential regarding attitudes and behavior in that children compare the acceptability of their own beliefs with those of their friends. Thus, for example, children and adolescents whose peers are academically motivated are more likely to do well in school (Eccles, Wigfield, & Schiefele, 1998).

Coleman's (1966) classic study showed how attitudes were molded among high school students. He surveyed students in 11 high schools representing a wide range of social class backgrounds and found popularity with peers to be more important than academic achievement. Subsequent studies (Goodlad, 1984; Kinney, 1993) confirmed Coleman's findings. Margolis (1971) found that the main factor affecting African Americans' association with Euro-Americans was how they thought their African American friends would react.

Peers are also very influential in the development of gender-role attitudes, as discussed in Chapter 8, as well as influencing who is accepted into or rejected by the group based on similarities and/or differences. Because preadolescent children have a strong need to identify with the peer group, those who are ethnically different or who have a disability often are excluded (Gollnick & Chinn, 2002). Other attitudes influenced by peers involve dress, dating, personal problems, and sex (Sebald, 1986, 1989).

Because peer opinion is important to children, peers can be used to influence attitudes regarding achievement. Cooperative learning settings enable peers to help each other learn by sharing resources and modeling academic skills. Also, inclusion of diverse children in cooperative learning groups reduces stereotypic and prejudicial attitudes (Eccles, Wigfield, & Schiefele, 1998).

Mass Media

Television and Movies. Children and adolescents frequently cite television as a source of information that influences their attitudes about people and things (Comstock & Paik, 1991; Perse, 2001). "You see so much violence that it's meaningless. If I saw someone really get killed, it wouldn't be a big deal. I guess I'm turning into a hard rock," said an 11-year-old. "When I see a beautiful girl using shampoo or a cosmetic on TV, I buy them because I'll look like her. I have a ton of cosmetics," said a 13-year-old. Several studies have reported that middle and high school students rate the mass media as their most important source of information and opinions, even more so than their parents, teachers, and friends (Perse, 2001). Television, as discussed in Chapter 9, is a source of social stereotypes. Although the occupational roles of African Americans have become more varied than the subservient roles of the past, other minority groups are often typecast as villains or victims (Leibert & Sprafkin, 1988). For instance, Arab Americans have experienced negative stereotyping in movies, frequently portrayed as villains, criminals, or terrorists, and violating taboos of American society (Bennett, 2003).

Although television and movies have a reputation for perpetuating negative attitudes, they also have the potential for bringing people to new levels of empathetic understanding. TV documentaries and biographies of ethnically diverse historical and sports figures, such as *The Jackie Robinson Story*, give viewers new insights. Movies such as *Schindler's List* and *Life Is Beautiful* bring awareness to the plight of Jews during World War II, and *A Beautiful Mind* shows how a brilliant professor coped with schizophrenia.

Merely being exposed to diversity, however, is not effective in changing attitudes over time; children have to be taught nonstereotypic attitudes directly via social experience (Bigler & Liben, 1990). Similarly, even though there are more programs on TV today portraying women in traditionally male-dominated roles, to really influence children's gender-role attitudes, adults have to engage in discussion and provide nonstereotypic models (Dorr & Rabin, 1995).

Books. That books are influential in attitude formation is evidenced by the controversy stirred up by some, resulting in their removal from library shelves (Norton & Norton, 2002). For example, in the 1960s, Garth Williams's *The Rabbit's Wedding* (1982) was criticized because the illustrations showed the marriage of a black rabbit and a white rabbit. In the 1970s, Maurice Sendak's (1970) *In the Night Kitchen* was taken off some library shelves because the child in the story was nude. In the 1980s, Helen Bannerman's *The Story of Little Black Sambo*, which was first published in 1899 and had enjoyed much popularity over the years, was attacked for being offensive to African Americans due to the story line and crudely drawn figures of characters with stereotypic features.

The major controversies in children's books relate to stereotypes (gender, ethnicity, disabilities) and the ways in which sexuality, violence, profanity, and family problems are portrayed (Feldstein, 1989).

That books can be used to influence attitudes is evident in *McGuffey's Reader*, popular in U.S. schools in the early twentieth century. The reader contained stories with moral messages. William Bennett (1993), former U.S. secretary of education, published *The Book of Virtues* for a similar purpose. Spitz (1999) claims that, even when they are not intended to do so, "picture books provide children with some of their earliest takes on morality, taste, and basic cultural knowledge, including messages about gender, race, and class. They supply a stock of images for childen's mental museums" (p. 14). A classic children's book defying gender stereotypes is *The Story of Ferdinand* by Munro Leaf (1936). Ferdinand is a bull who would rather smell the flowers than fight; the message is that it is OK to be oneself rather than conform to cultural role prescriptions.

Community

The community influences attitudes through its customs and traditions. For example, in certain countries, only men are allowed into the teahouses to socialize; women must stay home. Prior to the civil rights movement, in many southern communities, there were signs labeling the bathrooms "White" and "Colored." In many communities today, one finds signs that read, "Adults Only." These examples illustrate attitudes of discrimination according to gender, ethnicity, and/or age. And similar attitudes are acquired by children because they represent the status quo in their environment.

As has been discussed, research shows that positive interactions with people different from oneself tend to foster positive attitudes toward them. Thus, diversity in the community—in terms of ethnicity, economic status, and so on—can help promote tolerance.

A community's attitudes are reflected most obviously in the ways it chooses to spend its tax money. This, in turn, affects the services it provides. A community that provides funding for educational programs, recreation, preventive services, support services, and compensatory services places a high value on children and families. Children are very likely to incorporate their community's attitudes into their own attitudes.

The attitude of the community toward providing support for its families can affect the level of stress and social pathology experienced by some families (Etzioni, 1993; Schorr, 1997). These families, then, may come to feel a diminished ability to control what happens to them (Seligman, 1975). At the same time, several studies have reported that social support received by children is one important resource that protects them against the negative effects of life stressors (Sandler, Miller, Short, & Wolchik, 1989).

Specific social pathologies involving families that have been related to the community's attitude of support (or lack of) are infant death and disease, teenage pregnancy, juvenile delinquency, and child abuse and neglect (Garbarino, 1992). For example, communities that provide prenatal and perinatal support to young, high-risk mothers have lower infant mortality rates (Children's Defense Fund, 2001; Schorr, 1997). One reason for this is that attitudes toward mothering and child health change for the better. Similarly, community attitudes toward providing support and guidance for pregnant teenagers are influential in the teenagers' attitudes toward birth control, education, and occupational goals (Furstenberg, 1976). Community attitudes regarding law enforcement, recreation, youth employment, and curfews can affect the levels of juvenile delinquency (Garbarino, 1992). Finally, the attitudes of the community members toward helping one another can affect the levels of child abuse and neglect in community families by influencing parenting attitudes. Mothers in high-support communities reported that their children were significantly easier to care for than did the mothers in low-support communities (Garbarino & Sherman, 1980).

School

Schools influence attitude formation. In review of various studies, Sadker and Sadker (1994, 2003) traced how gender-role stereotyping is perpetuated in schools. Schools that separate male and female activities, and encourage boys to play in the "block corner" or to take science classes and girls to go to the "housekeeping" area or to take English classes, for example, are teaching children which activities are "gender appropriate." Teachers who project their gender-typed expectations on boys and girls reinforce traditional gender-role behavior. In other words, if a teacher expects boys to be more active and aggressive than girls, the teacher will tend to allow this behavior. Likewise, the teacher who expects girls to be passive and docile will likely encourage girls to conform to this pattern.

Although teachers are generally committed to the idea of ethnic and/or gender equality, biased attitudes in the form of certain classroom practices still emerge, such as the "self-fulfilling prophecy," in which teacher *expectations* of performance influence *actual* performances (Good & Brophy, 1986, 2003). However, classroom organization can be very effective in influencing attitudes toward others. For example, researchers (Johnson & Johnson, 1999; Johnson, Johnson, & Maruyama, 1983) tried to identify conditions in schools that led to positive attitudes regarding ethnically diverse students, as well as students with disabilities. They found that, when members of both heterogeneous and homogeneous groups cooperated instead of competed to achieve a common goal, more positive attitudes resulted among the group members. These positive attitudes included more realistic views of themselves and other group members, higher expectations of success, and increased expectations of favorable future interactions with group members (regardless of how different individuals were).

CHANGING ATTITUDES ABOUT DIVERSITY

According to Aboud (1988), attitudes about diversity, especially prejudice toward various ethnic groups, take different forms in children according to age. Prejudice in children under age 7 is mainly due to cognitive immaturity and lack of social experience. Prejudice is often exhibited because of children's frustrations with authority; they turn on other groups perceived to have less power or status (Van Ausdale & Feagin, 2001).

Katz and Zalk (1978) examined the following techniques to counter the ethnically biased attitudes of Euro-American second- and fifth-graders (as determined by a test). Each method was found to be effective on a short-term basis, and two were effective in the longer term.

- *Increased positive ethnic contact.* Children worked in interethnic teams at an interesting puzzle and were all praised for their work.
- *Vicarious interethnic contact.* Children heard an interesting story about a sympathetic and resourceful African American child.
- *Reinforcement of the color black.* Children were given a marble (which could be traded in for a prize) every time they chose a picture of a black animal.
- *Perceptual differentiation.* Children were shown slides of an African American woman whose appearance varied, depending on whether she was wearing glasses, one of two different hairdos, and a smile or a frown. Each different-appearing face had a name, and the children were tested to see how well they remembered the names.

After 2 weeks, the children's levels of prejudice were measured again. All the groups that had been exposed to any of the four techniques showed less prejudice than did children in the control groups. Four to 6 months after the experiment, a second posttest showed that the children who had learned to perceive differences in the African American faces and those who had heard the stories about African American children had more positive attitudes than did those in the other two groups. Also, younger children showed more gains than older children.

Apparently, prejudicial attitudes can be changed by enabling children to have positive experiences (both real and vicarious) with ethnic minorities. When adults mediate the experience by pointing out individual differences, it is especially effective. Thus, children learn to view people as individuals rather than as representatives of a certain group with certain fixed characteristics.

Another experiment was carried out to help children feel what it is like to experience prejudice, to be discriminated against (Weiner & Wright, 1973). Euro-American third-graders were divided

The friendship between these children is more important than societal attitudes about race.

© Eyewire Collection/Getty Images

into two groups randomly: the Orange people and the Green people. On the first day, the Orange children were "superior"; they were praised by the teacher and given preferential treatment in the day's activities. On this same day, the Green children were "inferior"; they were criticized and denied privileges. On the second day, the positions were reversed: The Green children were favored, and the Orange children were discriminated against. On the third day, and again 2 weeks later, the children's ethnic beliefs were measured. Compared with children who had not had this experience, the experimental group expressed fewer prejudicial beliefs about African Americans and were significantly more likely to want to have a picnic with African American children. Apparently, prejudiced attitudes can be changed by role taking—by experiencing the feelings that discrimination brings.

A similar experiment was carried out in an Iowa third grade class by teacher Jane Elliott using blue and brown eyes as criteria for superiority and inferiority; it was documented in the film *Eye of the Storm* (1971). The experiment was repeated with adult parole officers and documented in the film *A Class Divided* (1992). The children, interviewed as adults, reported a major change in their attitudes toward diversity as a result of the experiment, as did the parole officers.

One of the purposes of the Individuals with Disabilities Education Act of 1990 was to include children with disabilities in public schools. As a result, teachers had to revise prior stereotypic attitudes they might have had and emphasize *abilities* rather than *disabilities* (Heward, 1999)—for example, "Kevin is a third-grader who reads at a fourth-grade level and who needs assistance with physical tasks" rather than "Kevin is wheelchair-bound and requires an aide."

Changing attitudes about diversity involves gender as well as ethnicity and disability. Influences on the development of gender roles are discussed in detail in Chapter 12. One macrosystem influence is Title IX of the Education Code, whose

The participation of individuals with disabilities in athletic events has helped communicate positive attitudes regarding their abilities.

purpose is to provide equal opportunities and funding of activities for girls and boys. Enabling girls to take "shop" classes and boys to take "home economics" classes helped counter popular perceptions about male and female abilities.

Creating an Antibias Classroom Environment

This classroom should include the following:

- Images in abundance of all the children, families, and staff in the program. Photos and other pictures reflecting the varying backgrounds of the children and staff should be displayed attractively
- Images of children and adults from the major racial/ethnic groups in the community and in the larger society
- Images that reflect accurately people's daily lives, both at work and during recreational activities
- A numerical balance among different groups, with people of color *not* represented as "tokens"
- A fair balance of images of women and men, shown doing "jobs in the home" and "jobs outside the home," with both women and men doing blue-collar work (factory worker, repair person), pink-collar work (beautician, salesperson), and white-collar work (teacher, doctor)
- Images of elderly people from varying backgrounds performing different activities
- Images of people with disabilities from varying backgrounds, shown doing work and interacting with their families in recreational activities, and not acting dependent and passive
- Images of diversity in family styles: single mothers or fathers, extended families, gay or lesbian parents (families with two mothers or two fathers), families in which one parent and a grandmother are the parents, interracial and multiethnic families, families of adoptive children, and families with a member who is disabled (either a child or a parent)
- Images of important individuals—past and present—reflecting racial/ethnic, gender, and special needs diversity, and including people who participated in the struggle for social justice
- Artwork—prints, sculptures, and textiles by artists from varying backgrounds that reflect the aesthetic environment and the culture of the families represented in the classroom and the groups in the community and in society.

Source: *Anti-bias Curriculum: Tools for Empowering Young Children* by L. Derman-Sparks and the Anti-bias Task Force. Copyright © 1989 by the National Association for the Education of Young Children. Reprinted by permission.

Motives and Attributes

A **motive** is a need or emotion that causes a person to act. To be motivated is to be moved to do something. An **attribute** is an explanation for one's performance: "Do you attribute an Olympian's athletic ability to training, genetics, or both?"

The theory that people are motivated to act by the inborn urge to be competent, or to achieve, is credited to psychologist Robert White (1959). According to White, people of all ages strive to develop skills that will help them understand and control their environment, whether or not they receive external reinforcement. The motive to explore, understand, and control one's environment is referred to as **mastery motivation** (Mayes & Zigler, 1992). This is illustrated when toddlers open cabinets, empty out drawers, or drop things in the toilet. Whereas mastery motivation is believed to be inborn, **achievement motivation,** the motivation to be competent, is thought to be learned. That is, children learn via socialization what are considered acceptable and unacceptable performance standards in their culture, as well as how to evaluate their behavior accordingly. Achievement motivation expresses itself in the behavior of individuals approaching challenging tasks with the confidence of accomplishment (McClelland, Atkinson, Clark, & Lowell, 1953), such as the child who tries out for the choir saying, "Oh, I know I'll make it."

Ryan and Deci (2000) distinguish between achievement motivation that is *intrinsic* (doing an activity for inherent satisfaction or enjoyment) and *extrinsic* (doing an activity to attain some outcome, obtain a reward, or avoid punishment). Why are some people driven primarily intrinsically, and others extrinsically? Explanations can be categorized in terms of (1) within-person changes (intrinsic) due to cognitive or emotional maturation, such as children becoming more curious as they are able to learn more and becoming more competent as they are able to master more, and (2) socially mediated developmental changes (extrinsic) resulting from contexts children experience as they grow, such as family, school, or peer group, and the accompanying feelings of autonomy or control (Eccles, Wigfield, & Schiefele, 1998). According to Ryan and Deci (2000), home and classroom environments can "facilitate or forestall" intrinsic motivation by "supporting or thwarting" children's needs for competence and autonomy. For example, in a study of parent–child relationships, home learning environments, and school readiness (Lamb, Parker, Boak, Griffin, & Peay, 1999), it was found that children whose parents understood and encouraged their learning through play exhibited independence, curiosity, and creativity in the classroom. In contrast, children whose parents were strict and rule bound over playtime and activities exhibited distractibility and hostility in the classroom. Other studies (Ryan & Deci, 2000) have shown that tangible rewards (money, candy, toys), threats, deadlines, directives, and pressure related to task performance tend to diminish intrinsic motivation because they are experienced as controllers of behavior, whereas choice and the opportunity for self-direction appear to enhance intrinsic motivation because they enable a sense of autonomy.

Motives and attributes are related in that achievement motivation has been linked to locus of control. **Locus of control** refers to how individuals attribute their performance or where they place personal responsibility for success or failure—inside (internal) or outside themselves (external)—for example, "Am I responsible for my grade, or is the teacher?" When individuals believe that they have no control over events, and therefore no responsibility for them, they are no longer motivated to achieve; they have learned helplessness. **Learned helplessness** is a phenomenon exhibited by people who no longer perform effectively in a number of situations (they have learned to be helpless as opposed to competent). The relationship of attributions (explanations for performance) to actual performances is outlined in Figure 11.2.

ACHIEVEMENT MOTIVATION

How do people differ in their motivations to achieve? In a classic study to assess the differences in strengths of people's achievement motives, McClelland and colleagues (1953) developed a projection technique using selected picture cards from the Thematic Apperception Test (TAT). The technique assumes that, when asked to

Figure 11.2

Relationship Between Attribution and Actual Performance

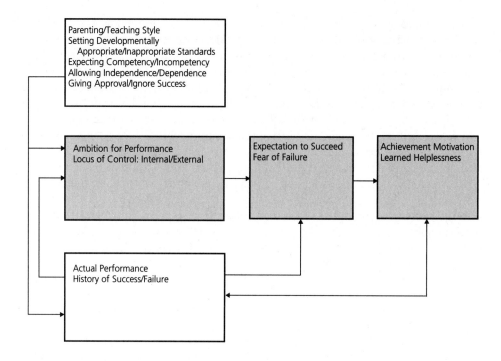

write stories about the pictures, respondees will project their feelings about themselves onto the characters in the pictures.

The pictures show such scenes as two men ("inventors") in a shop working on a machine, a young boy and a violin, or a boy sitting at a desk with an open book in front of him. Subjects are asked to answer the following questions about the pictures:

1. What is happening? Who are the persons?
2. What were the circumstances leading up to the situation in the pictures?
3. What are the characters thinking? What do they want?
4. What will happen? What will be done?

Assessment of the responses involves noting references to achievement goals (concern over reaching a standard of excellence). Subjects who refer to achievement goals are often rated high in achievement motivation; those who rarely or never refer to achievement goals are rated low.

Achievement motivation is often correlated with actual achievement behavior (Camara, 1986). The motivation to achieve, however, may evidence itself only in behavior that children value. For example, a child may be highly motivated to achieve, and this may be exhibited in athletics but not in schoolwork. Thus, different situations have different achievement-attaining values for children (Eccles, Wigfield, & Schiefele, 1998; Harter & Connell, 1984).

Development of Achievement Motivation

How does the motivation to achieve develop? In one study, 1- to 5-year-olds were observed doing objectively measured performance-based tasks, such as hammering pegs in a pegboard, putting puzzle pieces together, building a stack of blocks, and knocking down plastic pins with a bowling ball (Stipek, Recchia, & McClintic, 1992). Some of the tasks were individual, and others involved competition with a peer. The researchers found that children go through three stages in learning to evaluate their achievement against performance standards:

- *Stage 1—joy in mastery.* Children under age 2 approached the given task to master it. If they failed, they tended to move onto another task rather than get upset.
- *Stage 2—approval seeking.* As they approached age 2, toddlers began to recognize the significance of others' reactions to their performance. When they accomplished a task, they tended to smile or say? "I did it," to the nearby adult. When they did not succeed, they tended to turn away.
- *Stage 3—use of standards.* Children age 3 and over showed pride in accomplishments. Some praised themselves; some went on to a more challenging tasks. In most cases, performance was not dependent on others' evaluations. Children age $3\frac{1}{2}$–5 showed happiness when they won a competitive task; losers slowed down or gave up, but did not appear to be upset.

Thus, there seems to be a general developmental progression among children who are learning the cultural value of achievement. But what about individual differences?

The origins of individual differences in achievement motivation (also called "need achievement") have most often been linked to parenting practices. In a classic study (Rosen & D'Andrade, 1959), two groups of 10-year-old boys having similar socioeconomic backgrounds and IQ scores but different levels of achievement need were observed in their homes as their parents watched them do a task. The task was rather difficult. It involved building a tower out of irregularly shaped blocks while blindfolded and restricted to the use of one hand. The parents could say or do anything they pleased, but they could not touch the blocks. They were also told the height of the tower the "average boy" would erect and were asked to predict (confidentially to the researchers) how well their son would do. The parents of the high-need-achievement boys predicted a better level of performance than did the parents of the low-need-achievement boys. This probably reflected the parents' usual behavior of setting higher standards of excellence for their sons to strive for.

While the boys were doing the task, the parents of sons with high-achievement needs were more encouraging and more likely to reward accomplishment with praise. Fathers of the high-need-achievement boys were warm and friendly while their sons were working, but they did not interfere with their sons' decisions regarding how to complete the task, other than giving a hint or two. (They allowed for independence.) The fathers of low-need-achievement boys, in contrast, were more domineering, in that they gave specific directions on how to complete the task, and were more likely to show irritation when things went awry.

Apparently, the parents of the high-need-achievement boys set high standards of excellence for them, but not so high as to discourage the boys. They also allowed the boys to solve problems independently and communicated approval. In contrast, the parents of the low-need-achievement boys set standards that were either too high or not high enough. They also were less likely to permit independence in solving the problem. In short, parenting styles are related to children's development of need achievement in that parents set standards of excellence, expect competence, allow independence, and communicate approval after success—characteristics of the authoritative parenting style. More recent studies also correlate authoritative parenting with achievement in children and adolescents (Baumrind, 1973; Eccles, Wigfield, & Schiefele, 1998; Lamborn, Mounts, Steinberg, & Dornbusch, 1991; Steinberg, Elmen, & Mounts, 1989).

When some investigators (Hermans, Terlaak, & Maes, 1972) questioned teachers, they learned that children with high achievement motivation were viewed as being more interested in striving toward goals, showing a higher degree of personal responsibility for their work, and being more persistent in following through on tasks. Research has demonstrated that achievement motivation is a relatively stable characteristic of personality; longitudinal studies reveal a consistent relationship between levels of achievement motivation in preschool, elementary school, and high school (Deci & Ryan, 1985; Eccles, Wigfield, & Schiefele, 1998; Feld, 1967; Kagan & Moss, 1959).

Achievement Motivation and Parenting Practices/Expectations

A study of the antecedents of achievement motivation was conducted by McClelland and Pilon (1983). They related mothers' reports of child-rearing practices when their children were 5 years old to the children's achievement motivation scores when the children were about age 30. The mothers had been interviewed in 1951 in a study of child-rearing practices. Twenty-five years later, the children were interviewed to assess their achievement motivation.

McClelland and Pilon consistently found a relationship between child-rearing practices emphasizing scheduled feeding and conscientious toilet training (putting the child on the potty at regular times and watching for signs that the child needs to urinate or defecate) and achievement motivation for males and females from lower- and middle-class backgrounds. It is likely that the scheduled feeding and conscientious toilet training were examples of standards of excellence set by the parents. Parental expectations play a significant role in children's motivation to achieve (Ginsberg & Bronstein, 1993; Parsons, Adler, & Kaczala, 1982; Phillips, 1987a).

McClelland and Pilon also found that child-rearing practices emphasizing early independence (by age 5) were *not* significantly related to adult achievement motivation. Perhaps parental expectations for independence by age 5 freed the parents from their role of continually communicating standards to the child. Or perhaps expecting the child to be independent by age 5 was too high a standard. There are indications that, when achievement standards are set at an unrealistic level, the effect is the opposite of what was intended. Thus, children who are expected to do well on tasks with which they are too young to cope exhibit a lower level of achievement motivation. These children, instead of learning to achieve, learn to give up. The desire to achieve, then, is created by optimally challenging children—providing tasks that can be completed with effort (not too easy), so that their accomplishment is meaningful (Burhans & Dweck, 1995; McClelland, 1961). Such tasks are referred to today as "developmentally appropriate."

In sum, the child-rearing environment of children who show high achievement motivation includes developmentally appropriate timing of achievement demands (early but not too early, with continuing encouragement), high confidence in children's abilities, a supportive family environment (orientation toward exploration and investigation, as well as positive feedback), and highly motivated role models (Eccles, Wigfield, & Schiefele, 1998). These research findings provide the rationale for parental involvement in school. Parents who take an active interest in their children's school performance are more likely to have children who achieve in school than are parents who are not interested in their children's school performance.

Achievement Motivation, Child Expectations, and Attributions

Individuals' actual achievement behavior depends not only on their motivation to achieve but also on whether they *expect* to achieve and whether they fear failure.

People are more likely to work hard when they perceive a reasonable chance to succeed than when they perceive a goal to be out of reach (Atkinson, 1964). Children's expectations of success can be measured by asking them to predict a certain grade, indicate how sure they are that they can solve a particular problem, and select the hardest task they think they can do from a collection of tasks varying in difficulty (Phillips, 1987a).

Children with high expectations for success on a task usually persist at it longer and perform better than children with low expectations (Eccles, 1983; Eccles, Wigfield, & Schiefele, 1998). Research (Carr, Borkowski, & Maxwell, 1991) has found that children with high IQs and high expectations of success in school do, in fact, get the highest grades, children with high IQs and low expectations receive lower grades than children with low IQs and high expectations. In addition to child-rearing practices, discussed previously, teaching styles and communication patterns affect children's attributions. When teachers are caring and supportive and emphasize the learning process over the performance outcomes, and when they give feedback, children tend to be motivated to achieve and to expect success (Daniels, Kalkman, & McCombs, 2001).

Individuals' expectation of success is related to (1) their history of success or failure, (2) their perception of how difficult the task is, and (3) the attributions for their performance. Generally, those who have been successful most of the time in the past expect to succeed in the present and future; those who have failed most of the time in the past expect to fail in the present and future.

This girl's achievement is influenced by her sense of personal responsibility to perform and her confidence of success.

In some situations, however, people who usually succeed, fail; conversely, people who usually fail, succeed. A second possible factor, then, in individuals' expectations of success can be how difficult they originally perceived the task to be. Failure on a task perceived to be very easy results in a different self-evaluation than failure on a task perceived to be very difficult.

A third potential factor in individuals' expectations of success involves to what their performance is attributed (Weiner, 1992). People can attribute performance (1) to themselves (their ability or effort), (2) to others (the teacher's opinion of one or the teacher's ability to teach), (3) to the situation (the test too difficult or the room too noisy), or (4) to luck (good or bad). Where people place responsibility for success or failure (inside or outside the self) is referred to as their locus of control.

LOCUS OF CONTROL

Individuals who have strong beliefs that they are in control of their world, that they can cause things to happen if they choose, and that they can command their own rewards have an **internal locus of control** (they are responsible for their own fate). These people attribute their success (or failure) to themselves. Individuals who perceive that others or outside forces have more control over them than they do over themselves have an **external locus of control** (other people or events are responsible for their fate). These people attribute their success (or failure) to things outside themselves.

Regarding control beliefs, Skinner (1995) stressed the importance of perceived relationships between individuals' actions and their success or failure. Achievement is related to whether they think they control the outcome. As children get older, their understanding of causality and explanations for outcomes becomes more differentiated. Specifically, whereas 7- to 8-year-olds tend to consider all possible factors—luck, effort, ability, task difficulty—in explaining performance, 11- and 12-year-olds tend to put more emphasis on external factors such as luck and task difficulty than on internal factors such as ability and effort in attributing locus of control. Moreover, 7- and 8-year-olds think that ability can change with effort, whereas 11- and 12-year-olds perceive ability as relatively stable.

How is locus of control measured? Rotter (1966, 1971) developed a scale that can be used to study the internal/external dimensions of personal responsibility. The scale is constructed so that each item can be scored as internal or external. Some sample items are given in the box titled "Measuring Locus of Control." Subjects are to indicate, in each pair of statements, the more appropriate of the two.

Measuring Locus of Control

I more strongly believe that:

1. a. Promotions are earned through hard work and persistence.
   b. Making a lot of money is largely a matter of getting the "right breaks."

2. a. There is usually a direct connection between how hard I study and the grades I get.
   b. Many times, the grades teachers give seem haphazard to me.

3. a. The number of divorces in our society indicates that more and more people are not trying to make their marriages work.
   b. Marriage is largely a gamble; it's no one's fault if it doesn't work.

4. a. When I am right, I can usually convince others that I am.
   b. It is silly to think that one can really change another person's basic attitudes.

5. a. In our society, earning power is dependent upon ability.
   b. Getting promoted is really a matter of being a little luckier than the next person.

6. a. If one knows how to deal with people, they are really quite easily led.
   b. I have little influence over the way other people behave.

7. a. People can change the course of world affairs if they make themselves heard.
   b. It is only wishful thinking to believe that one can really influence what happens in society at large.

8. a. I am the master of my fate.
   b. A great deal that happens to me is probably a matter of chance.

9. a. Getting along with people is a skill that must be practiced.
   b. It is impossible to figure out how to please some people.

Source: J. B. Rotter (1971). "Who Rules You? External Control and Internal Control." *Psychology Today, 5*, 37–42.

Locus of control is an aspect of personality that interests educators because children with an internal locus of control generally do better academically and are more competent and effective than those with an external locus of control (Nowicki & Segal, 1974; Swick, 1986). For example, in an experiment that required subjects to work on a verbal ability test, children with internal loci of control budgeted the time allotted them in a way that related to the difficulty of each item, whereas children with external loci of control did not (Gozali, Cleary, Walster, & Gozali, 1973). And, in a review of more than 100 studies, Findley and Cooper (1983) found that "internals" earn higher grades and outperform "externals" on standardized achievement tests.

One explanation for the relationship between locus of control and academic achievement is that internals view outcomes as within their control. Therefore, if they succeed, they can figure out what they did correctly and do it again; and if they fail, they believe they can change the outcome in the future by exerting more effort to correct their mistakes (for example, study harder or differently). They develop a mastery-oriented attribution. Externals, in contrast, view outcomes as outside their control. Therefore, if they succeed, they attribute it to good luck; if they fail, they attribute it to bad luck or lack of ability. Because they don't attribute the outcomes of their performance to their own efforts or strategies, they give up quickly. They develop a helpless-oriented attribution (Dweck & Leggett, 1988).

A review of the literature on locus of control (Eccles, Wigfield, & Schiefele, 1998; Young & Shorr, 1986) confirmed that internal locus of control is significantly related to age (older children are more internal), gender (elementary school girls are more internal than are the boys), socioeconomic status (middle- and upper-class children exhibit greater internality than do lower-class children), and achievement. In each case, the diverse socialization experiences of the group likely plays a prominent part.

Development of Locus of Control

How does locus of control develop? Piaget's observations of infants led him to conclude that it is not until about age 6 months that children show any awareness that their own actions can bring about an effect. However, behavior does not become intentional or goal directed until about age 8–12 months. A favorite game of infants this age is "drop and fetch," in which the infant drops a toy from the highchair or playpen and the parent fetches it. Therefore, it is about age 1, according to Piaget, that children begin to distinguish between events caused by their own actions and those that are not (Flavell, Miller, & Miller, 2001). Once children begin to understand that they have an impact on their environment, they begin to experiment with autonomous behaviors—"No, me do it" is commonly heard in the second year.

Children gradually develop a sense of control when things that happen to

This child is given the opportunity to correct a mistake, thereby gaining a feeling of autonomy. Such opportunities enable children to gain a sense of control and lead to self-confidence.

them are contingent upon their actions. As has been discussed in relation to Erikson's (1963) psychosocial theory of personality development, parental responsiveness to children's needs leads to attachment and a sense of trust (first year). When children are allowed to be autonomous, they gain a feeling of control; if not given opportunities to be autonomous, they feel self-doubt (age 2–3). When children are allowed to initiate activities, they feel a sense of control over their environment, rather than guilt over wanting to control it (age 4–5). And when children enter school, their experiences there affect their feelings of industry or inferiority (age 6–12). These are crucial years for the development of self-esteem in that a sense of control and self-determination is related to the perception of self-competence (Beane, 1991).

Thus, locus of control develops through children's actions on the environment and their interactions with others. The outcomes of these actions and interactions influence whether they attribute what happens to them to internal or external causes. The reason children growing up in economically disadvantaged families tend to demonstrate a less internal locus of control than do those from higher income backgrounds may be due to different parenting styles or to different environments (Bain, Holliman, & McCallum, 1989; Stephens & Delys, 1973). Children who are economically disadvantaged have fewer opportunities to develop a sense of being in control or determining life outcomes. For one reason, financially, they have fewer choices, for another, their neighborhoods may be unsafe.

How Parents and Teachers Can Help Children Develop an Internal Locus of Control

1. *Be responsive to children from the moment they are born.* Be affectionate, comforting, and attentive. Children need to know that someone will respond to their actions, or else they will come to believe they have no control over their own actions.
2. *Let children accept consequences for their actions.* If they spill milk, give them something with which to clean it up.
3. *Avoid performing tasks children can do for themselves.* Encourage effort, allow children to make mistakes, and don't expect adult performance.
4. *Give children developmentally appropriate responsibilities.* For example, at age 3, they can put their toys away; at age 5, they can make their beds; at age 7, they can set and/or clear the table.
5. *Give feedback.* Let children know when they have performed well and, if need be, how they can improve.
6. *Be an example of a person who makes things happen.* Don't wait for things to happen and then react.
7. *Encourage children's special interests.* Provide opportunities for children to initiate things themselves by asking questions and stimulating activities.
8. *Set standards and limits for behavior.* Explain the reasons for the rules: "You need to be home by six o'clock so we can all have dinner together."
9. *Show respect for children and for their accomplishments:* "What an interesting painting; can you tell me about it?" rather than, "What is that? It doesn't look like a kitty."
10. *Allow children to make appropriate decisions that affect them:* "You can have six children at your birthday party; whom would you like to invite?" or "Do you want to play soccer this year?"

LEARNED HELPLESSNESS

Martin Seligman presented evidence in his books *Helplessness* (1975) and *Learned Optimism* (1990) that people become passive and lose motivation when placed in situations in which outcomes are unaffected by their behavior. These people believe they are pawns of external circumstances; as a result, they learn to be helpless.

When does helplessness first appear? Research has shown that infants exposed to mobiles that spin independently of their actions do not learn to control new mobiles presented to them that can be activated by turning their heads. In contrast, infants exposed to stationary mobiles and then to mobiles that spin contingent upon their actions (head or arm moving) evidence no difficulty in learning to control the new mobiles. These differences in performance are still present after 6 weeks without any exposure to a mobile (Fincham & Cain, 1986). Thus, certain experiences involving the ability to control outcomes can affect even infants.

Gunnar (1980) demonstrated that the ability to control the on-off button of a potentially frightening toy (such as one that produces loud noise) reduces fear and increases positive-approach responses in 12-month-old infants. Similar findings regarding control have been demonstrated in studies of infant attachment. For example, when a baby cries and the mother responds to his or her needs, the baby experiences a "sense of control" even though he or she is not cognitively aware of it at first. Apparently, this sense of control, or trust that mother will meet his or her needs, enables the baby to develop a secure attachment to the mother (Ainsworth, 1982).

As children grow older and the number of their experiences with objects and people increases, their perceived ability to control outcomes and to understand cause and effect influences when and if they manifest learned helplessness as opposed to achievement motivation (Eccles, Wigfield, & Schiefele, 1998; Fincham & Cain, 1986). (Figure 11.2 summarized the factors involved in attributions for performance and their relationship to actual performance.)

By age 4, some children give up on even developmentally or age-appropriate tasks, such as building a tower out of blocks (Cain & Dweck, 1995). These nonpersistent children tend to believe that they can't do the task and report feeling bad after failures. Children who are persistent, in contrast, tend to believe that they can complete even challenging tasks if they are given more time and if they try harder. Children who are nonpersistent describe their parents as critical or punitive: "Daddy's going to get mad." Children who are persistent describe their parents as supportive and encouraging: "Try it again, you'll do better next time."

Many economically deprived persons and some ethnic minorities have learned that they exert little control over their lives. Due to their experiences, they feel that the external educational, economic, social, and political systems control them. For example, poverty makes higher education a luxury, but without it, people lack the skills, training, and self-assurance to change their condition. Perhaps the lack of motivation often attributed to the lower class is really due to members' lack of control over personal outcomes (National Commission on Children, 1991).

In a series of studies on learned helplessness Carol Dweck and colleagues (Dweck, 1975; Dweck & Bush, 1976; Dweck & Gillard, 1975; Dweck & Reppucci, 1973; Elliot & Dweck, 1991), found that, when children believed their failures to be due to uncontrollable factors in themselves, such as lack of ability (for example, "I failed the math test because I'm dumb in math"), their subsequent task performance deteriorated after failure. In a study of children in grades 4–6 those who had self-critical attributions, or learned helplessness, had little knowledge about effective study techniques to help them succeed at academic tasks (Pomeranz & Saxon, 2001).

Thus, they were not able to link effort or persistence with success. If, however, children are enabled to believe their failure was due to lack of effort, they tend to try harder on subsequent tasks and often show improved performance.

In several studies, Dweck and colleagues found that girls are more likely than boys to demonstrate learned helplessness that comes from attributing lack of ability to themselves. Boys more often tend to believe that when they do not do well it is because they have not worked hard enough. Because boys and girls in the studies scored similarly on achievement tests, it can be inferred that ability was similar but that locus of control was different. The researchers looked to the teachers to see if there was differential feedback to boys and girls relating to failure. They found that when boys submitted poor work they were generally reprimanded for sloppiness, inattention, or lack of effort. In contrast, girls who submitted poor work were generally told, "You didn't do it right even though you tried."

In another study, Dweck and colleagues (1978) set up a classroom experiment. One group of boys and girls who did poorly on an anagram test were told, "You didn't do very well that time; you didn't get it right." Another group was told that they did not do very well and that they did not write the answers neatly enough. This feedback led the boys and girls in the second group to believe that their poor performance was due to lack of effort. When the test was administered again, the boys and girls in the first group gave up more easily after the initial failure, but those in the second group tried harder.

In sum, if parents and teachers praise children for working hard (effort) when they succeed but question their (ability) when they fail, the children are less likely to persist at challenging tasks, thereby developing learned helplessness. Yet, if parents and teachers praise the children's abilities when they succeed and emphasize lack of effort when they fail, the children are more likely to persist at challenging tasks, thereby developing achievement motivation. Thus, if adults treat children as if their mistakes can be remedied by their own actions, the children are likely to reflect this opinion of themselves and to behave accordingly.

How Parents and Teachers Can Help Children Who Have Learned Helplessness

1. *Know the individual abilities (strengths and weaknesses) of the child, and set realistic goals for tasks.* Tasks should be neither too easy nor too hard, but rather challenging enough to make the child work, yet guaranteed to enable the child to succeed.
2. *Provide opportunities to learn by doing.* Experiencing consequences of their actions leads children to develop to a sense of autonomy.
3. *Give feedback as soon as possible for the task performed.* Evaluation leads to insight into successes and failures: "Maybe if you'd wash your brush after using each color, you wouldn't always end up with black."
4. *Give encouragement for trying and for persistence:* "You worked really hard on cutting a straight line; I bet with just a little bit of practice you'll be able to do it."
5. *Let children know it is OK to make mistakes.* Tell them that is how we learn, and ask them how they can correct their mistake next time.
6. *Provide structured opportunities for decision making:* "Do you want to wear the red or the blue sweater?" (rather than "Do you want to wear a sweater?"), or "Do

you want to brush your teeth first or put on your pajamas before bed?" or "You may do your math homework or spelling now."

7. *Explain to children that actions have consequences.* Desirable behavior leads to positive consequences, but undesirable behavior leads to negative consequences. Implementing positive and negative consequences enables children to learn to take responsibility for their actions.

8. *Teach children that they have the power to make changes, and point to things they control:* "Remember when you couldn't pump yourself on the swing? Now look how high you can go!"

9. *Avoid high levels of competition.* Stress cooperation on activities in which every child can make a valued contribution.

10. *Model achievement motivation.* Express pride in accomplishments.

SELF-EFFICACY

Self-efficacy is the belief that one can master a situation and produce positive outcomes. It is related to empowerment (enabling individuals to have control over resources affecting them), as well as to concepts discussed earlier in this chapter, such as personal agency, achievement motivation, internal locus of control, history of and attributions of success/failure, and learned helplessness. Albert Bandura, known for his social cognitive theory (involving learning via observation and modeling), has elaborated on these concepts to formulate a performance-based predictor of students' learning—namely, their perceived capability on specific tasks (Bandura, 1997, 2000). Simply put, self-efficacy is the belief that "I can," and helplessness is the belief that "I can't." Thus, self-efficacy differs from the aforementioned concepts in that it can predict future performance in addition to explaining present performance.

Self-efficacy can be assessed in terms of level, generality, and strength across activities and contexts (Bandura, 1997, 2000). The level of self-efficacy may vary depending on the difficulty of a particular task: "I can read fourth-grade books, but not fifth-grade ones." Generality refers to how self-efficacious beliefs transfer across tasks: "I can figure out a plain geometry problem, but not a solid geometry one." The strength of perceived self-efficacy can be measured by the amount of certainty about performing a given task: "I am not/fairly/quite sure I can accomplish this." Thus, self-efficacy measures try to objectify one's perceived performance capabilities rather than focusing on one's perceived personal qualities, which are considered to be a dimension of self-esteem, discussed later.

Self-efficacy beliefs provide students with a sense of personal agency to motivate their learning through use of such self-regulatory processes as goal setting, self-monitoring, self-evaluation, and strategy use (Zimmerman, 2000). Efficacious students embrace challenging goals. They are better at monitoring their working time, more persistent, less likely to reject correct hypotheses prematurely, and better at solving conceptual problems than are inefficacious students of equal ability. Self-efficacy beliefs affect the self-evaluation standards students use to judge outcomes of their self-monitoring. Self-efficacy beliefs also motivate students' use of learning strategies. Thus, a self-efficacious student might take an advanced placement class and an after-school job. This student might get tutoring to help get a better grade in math or practice free throws until they are automatic. He or she might do extensive research on a project citing different perspectives or enter a science fair with a complicated experiment.

What are some influences on self-efficacy beliefs? The most significant influence is actual experience—successfully performing tasks, solving problems, and making things happen. Next is vicarious experience—observing others execute competent behavior. Also influential are verbal instruction, encouragement, and feedback on performance. Finally, physiological reactions, such as fatigue, stress, or anxiety, may distort an individual's perception of his or her capability at a particular time or during a certain activity. Some examples are "writer's block," an athletic "slump," and math anxiety.

What can be done to support self-efficacious behavior? Self-efficacy measures can be used diagnostically to improve academic motivation (Zimmerman, 2000). For example, the concept of self-efficacy can be applied to various aspects of student achievement, such as a student's choice of activities (Schunk, 2000). Students with low self-efficacy might avoid challenging learning tasks, whereas those with high self-efficacy might expend effort and persist at challenging learning tasks because they believe they will eventually succeed. These teaching strategies can help improve children's self-efficacy (Schunk, 2000; Stipek, 1996):

1. To enable students to focus on a task, provide instruction in specific learning strategies, such as highlighting, summarizing, and outlining.
2. Help students make short- as well as long-term goals, guiding them to evaluate their progress by regularly providing feedback.
3. Make reinforcement contingent on performance of specific tasks, rewarding students for mastering a task rather than merely engaging in one.
4. Give encouragement: "I know you can do this."
5. Provide positive adult and peer role models who demonstrate efficacious behavior—coping with challenging tasks, setting goals, using strategies, monitoring their effectiveness, and evaluating performance.

Self-Esteem

A construct related to self-efficacy is self-concept because it incorporates many forms of self-knowledge and self-evaluative feelings (Zimmerman, 2000). To clarify terms, **self-concept** refers to an individual's idea of her or his identity as distinct from that of others. It includes physical, emotional, psychological, cognitive, social, and behavioral attributes. **Self-esteem** refers to the value the individual places on that identity (Harter, 1998, 1999). Thus, self-esteem can be described as high or low. Some view self-esteem as a global perception of the self, whereas others view it as multidimensional, consisting of (1) scholastic competence, (2) athletic competence, (3) social competence, (4) physical appearance, and (5) behavioral conduct in addition to global self-worth (Harter, 1998, 1999). Occasionally, the terms *positive* or *negative self-concept* are used to describe self-esteem.

To exemplify these opposites, consider the following descriptions of two young girls, Alice and Zelda. Alice displays the characteristics of competent children (discussed in Chapter 4) (Baumrind, 1967). She uses adults as resources after first determining that a job is too difficult. She is capable of expressing affection and mild annoyance, both to peers and to adults. She can lead and follow peers, as well as compete with them. She shows pride in personal accomplishments and can communicate well. She has the ability to anticipate consequences, can deal with abstractions, and can understand other points of view. She can plan and carry out complicated activities. Finally, she is aware of others even while working on her own projects. Zelda, in contrast, displays the characteristics of incompetent children; she is deficient in the aforementioned competencies.

Alice is in kindergarten this year. You notice her immediately because she is so enthusiastic. She is almost always the first to raise her hand when the teacher asks a question. Sometimes she just calls out excitedly, "I know, I know." She doesn't always know, however. Sometimes she makes mistakes and answers incorrectly. When that happens, she shrugs her shoulders and giggles along with her classmates. She approaches her assignments with equal enthusiasm. When one approach fails, she tries another. If her persistence doesn't work, she asks the teacher for help. The other children like her. She is often the leader of the group, but also doesn't seem to mind following. At home she is responsible for dressing herself and keeping her room tidy. She is proud she can tie her shoelaces and make her bed.

Zelda is in first grade this year. Her progress last year in kindergarten was below average. This year it's no better. Zelda's IQ is similar to Alice's, yet Zelda answers most questions with "I don't know." She never raises her hand or volunteers information. She approaches her assignments unenthusiastically and gives up at the first sign of difficulty. She never asks for help, and when the teacher approaches her, she says, "I can't do it." Zelda has few friends and rarely participates in group activities. At home, Zelda is more talkative. She has no responsibilities, and her mother still helps her to dress. She waits for others to do things for her because she "can't" do them for herself. (Chance, 1983, p. 52)

Alice and Zelda, though alike in natural intelligence, are far apart in competence. Alice likes herself and feels comfortable in her environment. She controls her actions and takes responsibility for them. In other words, she decides what she is going to do, does it, and takes pride in doing it. And if she makes a mistake, she owns up to it and tries again. Zelda, however, is full of self-doubt. She thinks her environment is harsh and unfriendly. She feels helpless in controlling what happens to her, so she does not even try. Furthermore, Alice has high self-esteem; she has a sense of trust, autonomy, and initiative. Zelda has low self-esteem; she has a sense of mistrust, self-doubt, and inferiority. Each represents opposite poles in Erikson's (1963) psychosocial stages of development, discussed in Chapter 2. Why have these two young children developed such differing levels of self-esteem?

When Alice was an infant, her mother most likely responded warmly and affectionately to her needs. When she fed Alice, her attention would be focused totally on her. After feeding, Alice's mother cuddled her and talked to her before putting her to bed. Zelda's mother probably was a bit cold and indifferent. She would use Zelda's feeding as a chance to catch up on her reading (she fed Zelda from a bottle). After feeding, Zelda's mother would bathe her and make sure her crib was immaculate, before putting her to bed.

By age 2, Alice was securely attached to her mother. She could be left with a babysitter without too much fuss, yet she was very happy when her mother returned. Zelda, at age 2, was insecurely attached. She would cling to her mother, screaming, when the babysitter came, yet when her mother returned, Zelda would ignore her.

When Alice entered school, she made friends easily. Her eager smile seemed to welcome other children. Even when she put her sweater on inside out and a few children laughed, she just laughed with them. When Zelda entered school, she approached no one. The only friends she made were the two children who sat on either side of her at her table. When Zelda had trouble using her scissors, she just gave up.

DEVELOPMENT OF SELF-ESTEEM

As children grow, they accumulate a set of complex personal evaluations about themselves. They know how they look; they know what they are good at doing and what they are poor at doing. They also know what they would like to look like ("I hope I grow taller than my dad") and what they would like to be doing ("I'm going to be a dancer when I grow up"). And they begin to understand how they are viewed by others. During the process of socialization, children internalize the values and attitudes expressed by significant others and, as a result, come to express them as their own. This holds true for values and attitudes about themselves and about other people, objects, and experiences. Children come to respond to themselves in a way consistent with the way others have responded to them, thereby developing a concept of self. Their self-esteem, emerges from their success or failure at meeting internalized values and attitudes. As was pointed out, Mead (1934) viewed self-esteem as deriving from the reflected appraisal of others. Simplistically, according to Mead, someone who has been treated with concern and approval will have high self-esteem; someone who has been rejected and criticized will have low self-esteem. Thus, Alice's and Zelda's differing levels of self-esteem emerged as a result of cumulative experiences in their young lives with other people, places, and things.

Coopersmith (1967), in a classic investigation, concluded that several factors contribute to the development of self-esteem: "First and foremost is the amount of respectful, accepting, and concerned treatment that an individual receives from the significant others" (p. 37). Alice has a lot; Zelda has little. Second is the individual's "history of successes and the status and position." Alice has had many successes and is popular; Zelda has had few successes and few friends. Third is the individual's "manner of responding to devaluation." Alice is able to minimize or discount the teasing of others; Zelda is sensitive to others' judgments, interpreting them as confirmation of her self-image of helplessness. Recent research concurs with Coopersmith's conclusions (Harter, 1998, 1999).

According to Dorothy Corkille Briggs (1975), author of *Your Child's Self-esteem*, "children value themselves to the degree that they have been valued" (p. 14), "words are less important than the judgments that accompany them" (p. 19), "and a positive identity hinges on positive life experiences" (p. 20). The differences in Alice's and Zelda's early experiences illustrate how self-esteem can be enhanced through messages of acceptance and understanding, and through opportunities for mastery in order to develop feelings of competence.

Coopersmith's classic study involved studying hundreds of fifth- and sixth-grade Euro-American, middle-class, boys. He tested their levels of self-esteem via an inventory, a sample of which is shown below (1967, pp. 265–266):

	Like me	Unlike me
I'm pretty sure of myself.	____	____
I often wish I were someone else.	____	____
I never worry about anything.	____	____
There are lots of things about myself I'd change if I could.	____	____
I can make up my mind without too much trouble.	____	____
I'm doing the best work that I can.	____	____
I give in very easily.	____	____
My parents expect too much of me.	____	____
Kids usually follow my ideas.	____	____

Coopersmith found the boys' self-esteem to be relatively constant, even after retesting them 3 years later. He also asked their teachers to rate them on such behaviors as reactions to failure, self-confidence in new situations, sociability with peers, and need for encouragement and reassurance. He then classified the children on the basis of their scores on the inventory and the teachers' ratings.

The boys were further assessed through clinical tests and observations of their behavior in a variety of situations. For example, they were tested to determine how readily they would yield to group influence in a situation when their own judgment was actually superior. They were also given tasks that were either very difficult or very easy in order to determine whether their interest in working on a task was sharpened or weakened by success or failure. In addition, they were tested for creativity and asked how they usually behaved in real-life situations that called for assertiveness. Finally, their classmates were asked to choose the other children in the class whom they would like to have for friends, and a record was kept of how often each child was chosen.

On the basis of this extensive research, Coopersmith (1967) concluded that there are "significant differences in the experiential worlds and social behaviors of persons who differ in self-esteem":

Persons high in their own estimation approach tasks and persons with the expectation that they will be well received and successful. They have confidence in their perceptions and judgments and believe that they can bring their efforts to a favorable resolution. Their favorable self-attitudes lead them to accept their own opinions and place credence and trust in their reactions and conclusions. This permits them to follow their own judgments when there is a difference of opinion and also permits them to consider novel ideas. The trust in self that accompanies feelings of worthiness is likely to provide the conviction that one is correct and the courage to express those convictions. The attitudes and expectations that lead the individual with high self-esteem to greater social independence and creativity also lead him to more assertive and vigorous social actions. They are more likely to be participants than listeners in group discussions, they report less difficulty in forming friendships, and they will express opinions even when they know these opinions may meet with a hostile reception. Among the factors that underlie and contribute to the actions are their lack of preoccupation with personal problems. Lack of self-consciousness permits them to present their ideas in a full and forthright fashion; lack of self-preoccupation permits them to consider and examine external issues.

The picture of the individual with low self-esteem that emerges from these results is markedly different. These persons lack trust in themselves and are apprehensive about expressing unpopular or unusual ideas. They do not wish to expose themselves, anger others, or perform deeds that would attract attention. They are likely to live in the shadows of a social group, listening rather than participating, and preferring the solitude of withdrawal above the interchange of participation. Among the factors that contribute to the withdrawal of those low in self-esteem are their marked self-consciousness and preoccupation with inner problems. This great awareness of themselves distracts them from attending to other persons and issues and is likely to result in a morbid preoccupation with their difficulties. The effect is to limit their social intercourse and thus decrease the possibilities of friendly and supportive relationships (pp. 70–71; reproduced by special permission of the publisher, Consulting Psychologists Press, Inc., Palo Alto, CA 94306.)

The self-esteem these children feel is influenced by success in their performance.

Coopersmith concluded that self-esteem is based on four criteria:

1. *Significance*—the way one perceives that he or she is loved and cared about by significant others
2. *Competence*—the way one performs tasks she or he considers important
3. *Virtue*—the extent to which one attains moral and ethical standards
4. *Power*—the extent to which one has control or influence over her or his life and that of others

Whereas Coopersmith measured overall self-esteem, Harter (1990, 1998, 1999) measured the five specific areas of competence listed earlier, as well as general feelings of self-worth ("I am happy with myself") in *The Self-Perception Profile for Children.* Harter reported that self-esteem is well established by middle childhood. Children can make global judgments of their worth and distinguish their competencies. For example, a child may perceive him- or herself to be a poor athlete but a good student. Finally, children's perceptions of themselves accurately reflect how others perceive them. Thus, Cooley's, "looking-glass self" and Mead's "generalized other" described in Chapter 2 have found their way into contemporary conceptions of the self.

INFLUENCES ON THE DEVELOPMENT OF SELF-ESTEEM

The significant socializing agents that influence the development of self-esteem are family, school, peers, media, and community.

Family

"There is a growing body of empirical evidence revealing that parental approval is particularly critical in determining the self-esteem of children, supporting the looking-glass self formulation" (Harter, 1998, p. 583).

Coopersmith (1967) investigated children's treatment by significant others, those whose attitudes matter most when children are forming their self-concepts. Specifically, he administered a questionnaire to the children's mothers containing statements having to do with parenting attitudes and practices, and he also interviewed the mothers and children. Coopersmith focused on (1) acceptance of and affection toward the child, (2) the kind and amount of punishment used, (3) the level of achievement demands placed on the child, (4) the strictness and consistency with which rules were enforced, (5) the extent to which the child was allowed to participate in family decision making, (6) the extent to which the child was listened to and consulted when rules were being set and enforced, and (7) the extent to which the child was allowed independence. Interestingly, reviewing the many studies over the past 25 years that examined the relationship between parenting and child and adolescent outcomes, Holmbeck, Paikoff, and Brooks-Gunn (1995) conclude that those children exposed to authoritative parenting, the type described here by Coopersmith, are rated as more competent and higher in self-esteem, moral development, impulse control, and independence feelings than children from other types of parenting environments.

Coopersmith noted some clear relationships between parenting practices and the self-esteem of sons. Parents of boys with high self-esteem were more often characterized as follows:

- *Warm—accepting and affectionate*. They frequently showed affection to their children, took an interest in their affairs, and became acquainted with their friends.
- *Strict, but used noncoercive discipline*. They enforced rules carefully and consistently. They believed that it was important for children to meet high standards. They were firm and decisive in telling the children what they could and could not do. They disciplined their children by withdrawing privileges and by isolation. They tended to discuss the reasons behind the discipline with the children.
- *Democratic*. They allowed the children to participate in making family plans. The children were permitted to express their own opinions even if it involved questioning the parents' point of view.

Baumrind (1967) reported similar findings with regard to the relationship between parenting styles and competent children. The children who were happy, self-reliant, and able to directly meet challenging situations had parents who exercised a good deal of control over their children but who also demanded responsible, independent behavior from them as well. These parents also explained, listened, and provided emotional support. Baumrind's (1991) later research investigating the relationship between authoritarian, authoritative, and permissive parenting styles and the behavior of children approaching adolescence supported her original findings (1971b, 1973, 1977), as discussed in Chapter 4. Studies of competent adolescents found similar connections (Steinberg, 1993).

Why are parental warmth, strictness, and democracy associated with high self-esteem in children? If we view self-esteem in terms of Cooley's (1964) looking-glass self, then parents become children's first mirror, so to speak. If parents are affectionate and accepting, then children will view themselves as worthy of affection and acceptance.

According to various investigators (Baumrind, 1971b; Coopersmith, 1967; Holmbeck, Paikoff, & Brooks-Gunn, 1995), parental strictness helps children develop firm inner controls. When parents give children a clear idea of how to behave, they are providing cues to maximize successful interaction and minimize conflict. Providing standards helps children judge their competence. When children experience a predictable, ordered social environment, it is easier for them to feel in control. Parental strictness combined with warmth demonstrates proof of parental concern for the children's welfare.

A democratic approach leads to confidence in children's ability to express opinions and assert themselves. The opportunity to participate in family discussions enables children to better understand other people's views. Children whose parents respect their opinions and grant them concessions, if warranted, feel like contributing members of the family, and thus significant. And the quality of relationships with their parents continues to influence their self-esteem after the children become adolescents (Harter, 1998, 1999; Walker & Greene, 1986).

School

Keeping in mind that the valued personality type in American culture is responsible, self-reliant, autonomous, and competent, children reared to conform to these traits are likely to have high self-esteem. However, minority group children raised in cultures or ethnic groups that are not dominant in American society do not necessarily have low self-esteem. Studies have shown that children from ethnic minorities generally enter American schools with strong, positive self-concepts, but that failure to conform to the majority group's expectations causes lower scores on measures of self-esteem (Phinney & Rotheram, 1987). More research is needed, especially on specific components of self-esteem; Harter's (1998, 1999) scale of global self-worth, scholastic competence, social acceptance, athletic competence, physical appearance, and behavioral conduct might be useful here.

We probably could predict from the comparison of Alice and Zelda that Alice will go on to succeed in school and that Zelda will continue to fail. It has been found that students with higher self-esteem are more likely to be successful in school and to achieve more than children with low self-esteem (Cole, 1991; Harter, 1998, 1999). This relationship shows up as early as the primary grades and becomes even stronger as the student gets older.

Apparently, then, the more positively children feel about their ability to succeed, the more likely they are to exert effort and to feel a sense of accomplishment when they finish a task. Likewise, the more negatively children evaluate their ability to succeed, the more likely they are to avoid tasks in which there is an uncertainty of success, the less likely they are to exert effort, and the less likely they are to attribute any success or lack of it to themselves ("Oh, it was just luck").

People with low self-esteem tend to have a high fear of failure. This causes them to set either easy goals or unrealistically difficult goals in tasks for which goal setting is required (Bednar, Wells, & Peterson, 1989). For example, in a ring-toss game in which students could toss the rings at the target from any distance they desired, those with low self-esteem stood either right next to the peg or much too far away (Covington & Beery, 1976). Those who stood next to the peg avoided feelings of failure by ensuring success. Those who stood far away ensured failure, but the distance provided an excuse. Students with positive self-esteem were more likely to set goals of intermediate difficulty. Thus, they tended to choose a distance they thought reasonable for success. And if they were given a chance to try the game again, they adjusted the distance according to how they had performed on the first try. Those with low self-esteem did not make use of this information.

So far, the influence of self-esteem on achievement has been discussed, but what about the influence of achievement on self-esteem? According to Bloom (1973),

> successful experiences in school are no guarantee of a generally positive self-concept, but they increase the probabilities that such will be the case. In contrast, unsuccessful experiences guarantee that the individual will develop a negative academic self-concept and increase the probabilities that he will have a generally negative self-concept. (p. 142)

Bloom's observation has been supported by research (Bednar, Wells, & Peterson, 1989). One study, for example, found that preadolescents with high self-concepts were rated by teachers as being more popular, cooperative, and persistent in class; they also showed greater leadership, were lower in anxiety, had more supportive families, and had higher teacher expectations for their future success than students with lower self-concepts (Hay, Ashman, & Vankraayenoord, 1998). Similarly, other studies of school-agers found that achievement in school influenced students' estimations of their competence (Bandura, 2000; Harter, 1998, 1999; Harter & Connell, 1984). This estimation of their competence, or self-efficacy, then, influenced their motivation to achieve.

How Parents and Teachers Can Enhance Children's Self-Esteem

1. *Enable children to feel accepted.* Understand and attend to their needs; be warm; accept their individuality; talk and listen to them.
2. *Enable children to be autonomous.* Provide opportunities for them to do things themselves; give them choices; encourage curiosity; encourage pride in achievement; provide challenges.
3. *Enable children to be successful.* Be an appropriate role model; set clear limits; praise accomplishments and efforts; explain consequences and ways to learn from mistakes.
4. *Enable children to interact with others positively.* Provide opportunities to cooperate with others; enable them to work out differences dealing with feelings and others' perspectives.
5. *Enable children to be responsible.* Encourage participation; provide opportunities for them to care for belongings, help with chores, and help others.

Peers

Children can be quite cruel to one another, as was discussed in Chapter 8. They tease and ostracize children who are different physically, intellectually, linguistically, and/or socially. Peer attitudes about "ideal" size, physique, looks, and physical capabilities can influence children's self-esteem. Harter (1998, 1999) found that perceived physical appearance is consistently most highly correlated with self-esteem, from early childhood through adulthood, with no gender differences.

Historically, it was generally agreed that there were three basic human body types: (1) endomorphic (short, heavy build), (2) mesomorphic (medium, muscular build), and (3) ectomorphic (tall, lean build). Of course, in reality, most people are variations of these basic body types. Body type plays a role in self-esteem in cultures that emphasize a certain ideal type. In the United States, the ideal type for females is slim, well proportioned, and well toned; for males, it is tall and muscular. Thus, pudgy adolescent girls and boys, and skinny adolescent boys are likely to be unhappy with their bodies (O'Dea, & Abraham, 1999; Phelps, Johnston, Jimenez, & Wilczenski, 1993).

Children discriminate among body types and learn the cultural ideal quite early. One study (Johnson & Staffieri, 1971) demonstrated that, by age 8, children distinguished among body types. Most of those children interviewed preferred the mesomorphic type over the other two. They rated endomorphy as socially unfavorable and associated ectomorphy with social submissiveness. It would follow, then, that children who do not conform to the ideal body type of their peers have lower self-esteem. This was found to be true in a study (Tucker, 1983) comparing the relationship between self-esteem and the degree of perceived conformity of individuals' actual physical self to their ideal physical self. The larger the discrepancy, the greater tendency toward low self-esteem.

The rate at which children mature physically compared with their peers affects self-concept. Studies have found that boys who mature early compared to their peers are more likely to have higher self-esteem than boys who are late maturers (Alsaker, 1992; Apter, Galatzer, Beth-Halachmi, & Laron, 1981; Clausen, 1975). Early maturers are better able to excel in sports, are more likely to get attention from girls, and are chosen more often for leadership roles. Girls who mature early (in elementary school), however, are likely to have low self-esteem because they feel awkward and "out of sync" with their peers. By junior high school, though, girls who mature earlier than their peers enjoy higher prestige. Conversely, junior high school and high school girls who mature late develop a more negative self-concept than do their physically developed peers (Rice, 1996). In general, children who differ from their peers, especially in appearance, tend to have lower self-esteem than those who resemble their peers and who conform to their peers' ideal.

Not only does individuals' appearance compared to the perceived ideal of their peers affect self-esteem, so does their perceived status in relation to the rest of the group. Studies have found children's and adolescents' self-esteem to be dependent on their perceived popularity among their peers (Cole, 1991; Harter, 1998, 1999; Walker & Greene, 1986). Another study found that the self-esteem of seventh- to twelfth-graders was related to the status of the peer group to which they belonged at school. Generally, those who belonged to the "in" crowd exhibited higher self-esteem than outsiders (Brown & Lohr, 1987).

Mass Media

Where do children get their attitudes about ideal body and personality types? Advertisements on television and in magazines portray ideal physical stereotypes— handsome, mesomorphic, well-dressed men, and beautiful, trim, well-dressed women. Advertising techniques often lead viewers or readers to believe that the product advertised will produce or perpetuate ideal characteristics. For men, the emphasis is on strength, performance, and skill; for women, it is on attractiveness and desirability (Basow, 1992; Crawford & Unger, 2000; Pipher, 1994; Wolf, 1991). Children's heroes and heroines in the media also serve as models for the ideal type. According to Naomi Wolf (1991), author of *The Beauty Myth*, the self-serving interests of advertisers make the ideal unattainable, thereby actually promoting low self-esteem in order to motivate purchases of their products.

Community

The community may contribute to differences in the self-esteem of males and females. In a longitudinal study of the developmental changes in self-esteem in males and females age 14–23, Block and Robins (1993) noted a tendency for males to increase in self-esteem and for females to decrease. The investigators explained the variation as due to differences in gender-role socialization by society in general. Females are socialized to "get along," to connect and be mutually dependent; males are socialized to "get ahead," to achieve and be self-determinant (Block, 1973; Brown & Gilligan, 1990). Because, as individuals enter adulthood, especially the work world, achievement is rewarded more so than camaraderie, males socialized accordingly gain in self-esteem whereas females not socialized to compete lose in self-esteem. Thus, the discrepancy between the values people are socialized to accept as appropriate and those valued in the "real world" may influence self-esteem. The self-esteem level of previously confident females drops in early adolescence (Rosner & Rierdan, 1994). This may be due to the realization that their socialization of emphasizing relationships rather than competition is not highly valued in American society, or it may be due to lack of encouragement from the school, as discussed previously, or both.

Many adolescent girls wrestle with what it means to be a woman in American society (Basow & Rubin, 1999). Evidence from research suggests that girls are more negatively affected by failure than are boys. This sensitivity tends to limit their willingness to take risks and pursue more challenging opportunities. Also, many young women may still believe that there is an inherent conflict between traditional female goals of interdependence and support and the cultural goals of independence and competition. Belief in this conflict creates ambivalence and anxiety when these young women find themselves in competitive settings (Eccles, Barber, Jozefowicz, Malenchuk, & Vida, 1999). However, females in minority ethnic groups do not generally experience such ambivalence. In fact, African American adult women are respected in their community for being strong, outspoken, and achievement-oriented, as well as for being nurturant and caring, thereby influencing self-esteem. Asian American women subscribing to traditional gender roles were found to have lower self-esteem than those having nontraditional roles (Uba, 1994). For Hispanic American females, a strong ethnic identity and group support contributes to high self-esteem (Phinney & Chavira, 1992).

According to Rosenberg (1975) and others (Harter, 1998, 1999; Martinez & Dukes, 1991), the relation between individuals' social identity (ethnicity, religion, social class) and that of the majority of the people in the neighborhood affects self-esteem. For example, Rosenberg found that Jewish children raised in Jewish neighborhoods were likely to have higher self-esteem than those raised in Catholic neighborhoods. He and others (Martinez & Dukes, 1991) also found that African American students in integrated schools were likely to have lower self-esteem than those in all–African American schools. Children of lower status attending schools in which the majority of children were from higher social statuses also had lower self-esteem than those attending schools in which the majority of children were from lower-status environments. The same was true of upper-status children who were in the minority. Apparently, being socially different affects self-esteem, just as does having a different appearance. Because we all cannot look like the ideal type, and because not everyone belongs to the majority ethnic, racial, or religious group, it's important to enhance the self-esteem of those who are different from the majority.

Individuals with disabilities are examples of those who differ from the majority in appearance. These individuals often have low self-esteem, in part because they do not conform to the ideal body type of society (Koff, Rierdan, & Stubbs, 1990). Another reason is that others often step in to do things for them that they may be capable of doing themselves, if allowed to try. Many individuals with disabilities have developed learned helplessness.

EXAMPLE In a project I directed to train college students with disabilities to work as teacher assistants in various special needs facilities (Berns, 1981), the students with disabilities were given the Tennessee Self-Concept Test upon entering the project (pretest) and a year after participation (posttest). This test measures identity (feelings about who one is), self-satisfaction (feelings about how one acts), physical self (feelings about appearance, skills, and sexuality), moral ethical self (feelings of being a good or bad person), personal self (sense of adequacy as a person), family self (sense of adequacy as a family member), and social self (sense of adequacy in relations with others).

The purpose of measuring the students' levels of self-esteem before and after participation was to find out whether helping others like themselves would contribute to a rise in their self-esteem. A typical example of participation in the project was the student with multiple sclerosis, who relied on a wheelchair for mobility and who chose to work in a school for children with orthopedic impairments and with multidisabilities.

Based on pre- and posttest results, every project participant's total self-esteem score increased. Theoretically, the total self-esteem score reflects the overall level of self-esteem. Persons with high total scores tend to like themselves, feel they are persons of value and worth, have confidence in themselves, and act accordingly. When I asked the students, individually, for an explanation of the positive change in their self-concepts, the most frequent answer was "I realized I could do something worthwhile."

Thus, the community can play a significant role in enhancing self-esteem, especially among community members who feel they are different, by providing opportunities for individuals to do worthwhile and responsible things. Children and youths can help younger children in school or in recreational programs they can be of service to older citizens; they can serve on advisory boards; and they can help with community projects. Older community members can contribute their skills and expertise to younger members. Senior citizens can help in day care facilities, in schools, and in job-training programs; they can also serve on advisory boards and help with community projects. When many different people can have opportunities to work together, they learn that self-esteem comes from feeling proud of one's own contributions, not from being like everyone else.

Epilogue

Adolescence is the time when prior socialization experiences show their influence on the development of self-esteem—the looking-glass self or the generalized other. Anne Frank exhibited an internal locus of control in spite of having to live in such cramped quarters and having to get along with others under dire circumstances. She also was able to maintain a hopeful attitude regarding survival. Unlike Ophelia and Hamlet, Anne's socialization experiences and the continued support of her family enabled her to have high self-esteem and provided her with the coping skills to be resistant to negative developmental outcomes.

Summary

Values are qualities or beliefs that are viewed as desirable or important. As outcomes of socialization, they provide the framework in which individuals think, feel, and act. Children construct and redefine their values as they get older. Some values are basic to all civilized societies; others are basic to a particular society; still others are personal.

An attitude is a tendency to respond positively or negatively to certain persons, objects, or situations. Attitudes are composed of beliefs, feelings, and action tendencies. Attitudes guide behavior.

The development of attitudes is influenced by age, level of cognitive development, and social experiences. Parents and peers have a large impact on children's attitudes through instruction, modeling, reinforcement, and punishment. The media, the community, and the school also have the potential to change prejudicial and stereotypical attitudes toward diversity.

Motives cause people to act. Attributes are explanations of their performance when they do act. Individuals are motivated to develop skills that help them understand and control their environment, whether or not they receive external enforcement. This motivation is exhibited in the need to achieve and the feeling of being in control of the outcomes of their actions. When individuals are no longer motivated to master their environment, overcome obstacles in solving problems, or do their best, they are said to have learned helplessness.

The development of achievement motivation has been linked most often to parenting styles. In general, the child-rearing environment of children who show high achievement motivation includes warmth, developmentally appropriate timing of achievement demands, high confidence in children's abilities, a supportive affective family environment, and highly motivated role models. Achievement is also related to their expectancy for success and fear of failure, as well as their history of success and failure.

Locus of control relates to the sense of personal responsibility. Individuals who believe they are in control of their world have an internal locus of control. Those who perceive that people or events have more control over them than they have over themselves have an external locus of control. External attribution factors include luck and powerful others; internal attribution factors include ability and effort. Those who have an internal locus of control generally are more competent and effective than those with an external locus of control. Locus of control is related to age, gender, socioeconomic status, and performance attributes and outcomes.

When people are placed in situations in which outcomes are unaffected by their behaviors, they become passive and unmotivated. They have learned helplessness. Learned helplessness is influenced by experience and interaction with others, such as the kind of feedback people get for performing tasks.

Self-efficacy refers to individuals' belief that they can master situations and produce positive outcomes. It is a performance-based measure of perceived capability related to achievement motivation, locus of control, and learned helplessness. It involves goal-setting, self-monitoring, self-evaluation, and learning strategies.

Self-esteem, the value individuals place on their self-concept, is derived from the reflected appraisal of others. Simplistically, people who have been treated with concern and approval will have high self-esteem; those who have been rejected and criticized, will have low self-esteem. Specific dimensions of self-esteem include scholastic, athletic, and social competence; physical appearance; behavioral conduct; and global self-worth.

The factors contributing to self-esteem are the amount of respectful, accepting, and concerned treatment individuals receive from significant others; their history of successes and failures; their status among peers; and their manner of responding to devaluation or failure.

Parenting practices contribute to the development of self-esteem. In the dominant U.S. culture, the parenting styles of children with high self-esteem are described as warm, strict, and democratic. Parenting styles in diverse ethnic groups, and children's resulting self-esteem, may differ.

Children with high self-esteem are more likely to be successful in school and are likely to achieve more than children with low self-esteem. Peers influence self-esteem by their reinforcement of "ideal" types. Children who differ from the ideal tend to have lower self-esteem. Peers get their attitudes about ideal types from the media.

The community can contribute to the enhancement of self-esteem of its members by providing worthwhile activities in which to engage.

Activity

PURPOSE *To gain insight into personal values.*

1. The 18 values listed in the box titled "What Values Are Important to You?" are in alphabetical order. Select the value that is most important to you and write a l next to it in column I. Then choose your next most important value and write a 2 beside it in the same column. Continue until you have ranked all eighteen values in column I.
2. Now rank the 18 values as you believe your parents, your spouse, or a close friend would have ranked them. Put these numbers in column II.
3. Finally, rank the 18 values as you believe a person with whom you have not been able to get along would have ranked them. Put these numbers in column III.
4. Compare the rankings of the values in the three columns. How do your values compare with those of the person you are close to? How do they compare with those of the person who is your adversary? Compare your rankings with other people's. What is your relationship with them? Is there any correlation between similarity in values and closeness of relationship?
5. What values are important to you? Because values and morals involve making choices, do the "Forced Choices" exercise that follows.

What Values Are Important to You?

	I	II	III

A COMFORTABLE LIFE ✓
  a prosperous life
EQUALITY
  brotherhood, equal opportunity for all
AN EXCITING LIFE ✓
  a stimulating, active life
FAMILY SECURITY ✓
  taking care of loved ones
FREEDOM
  independence, free choice
HAPPINESS
  contentedness
INNER HARMONY
  freedom from inner conflict
MATURE LOVE
  sexual and spiritual intimacy
NATIONAL SECURITY
  protection from attack
PLEASURE
  an enjoyable, leisurely life
SALVATION
  saved, eternal life
SELF-RESPECT
  self-esteem
A SENSE OF ACCOMPLISHMENT
  lasting contribution
SOCIAL RECOGNITION ✓
  respect, admiration
TRUE FRIENDSHIP ✓
  close companionship
WISDOM ✓
  a mature understanding of life
A WORLD AT PEACE
  free of war and conflict
A WORLD OF BEAUTY
  beauty of nature and the arts

Source: Copyright 1967, 1982 by Milton Rokeach. Halgren Tests, 873 Persimmon Avenue, Sunnyvale, California 94087.

Forced Choices

Instructions: Write your top 10 values from the list in any order. If you had to choose between values 1 and 2, which would you choose. Circle your choice. Between values 1 and 3? Values 1 and 4? and so on. If you had to choose between values 2 and 3, which would you choose? Between values 2 and 4? and so on. Continue making forced choices until you've completed the list. Now rank your values in order.

1. _____
```
1 1 1 1 1 1 1 1
2 3 4 5 6 7 8 9 10
```

2. _____
```
2 2 2 2 2 2 2
3 4 5 6 7 8 9 10
```

3. _____
```
3 3 3 3 3 3
4 5 6 7 8 9 10
```

4. _____
```
4 4 4 4 4
5 6 7 8 9 10
```

5. _____
```
5 5 5 5
6 7 8 9 10
```

6. _____
```
6 6 6 6
7 8 9 10
```

7. _____
```
7 7 7
8 9 10
```

8. _____
```
8 8
9 10
```

9. _____
```
9
10
```

10. _____

☝ Research Terms

Achievement motivation
Attribution theory
Learned helplessness
Locus of control
Prejudice
Self-efficacy
Self-esteem

Related Readings

Aboud, F. (1988). *Children and prejudice*. Cambridge, MA: Basil Blackwell.
Bandura, A. (2000). *Self-efficacy: The exercise of control*. New York: Freeman.
Briggs, D. C. (1975). *Your child's self esteem*. New York: Dolphin.
Harter, S. (1999). *The construction of the self: A developmental perspective*. New York: Guilford.

Lawrence-Lightfoot, S. (1999). *Respect: An exploration.* Boulder, CO: Perseus.

Lewis, H. (1990). *A question of values.* San Francisco: Harper & Row.

McClelland, D. C. (1961). *The achieving society.* New York: Van Nostrand.

McInerney, P. K., & Rainbolt, G. W. (1994). *Ethics.* New York: HarperCollins.

Seligman, M. E. P. (1975). *Helplessness.* San Francisco: Freeman.

Seligman, M. E. P. (1990). *Learned optimism.* New York: Pocket Books.

Simon, S. B., Howe, L., & Kirschenbaum, H. (1972). *Values clarification: A practical handbook of strategies for teachers and students.* New York: Hart.

Tatum, B. D. (1997). *Why are all the Black kids sitting together in the cafeteria?* New York: Basic Books.

Van Ausdale, D., & Feagin, J. R. (2001). *The first R: How children learn race and racism.* Lanham, MD: Rowman & Littlefield.

Chapter 12

Prologue: Then and Now

Self-Regulation/Behavior
  Antisocial Behavior:
    Aggression
  Prosocial Behavior:
    Altruism

Morals
  Development of a Moral
    Code
  Influences on Moral
    Development

Gender Roles
  Development of Gender
    Roles
  Gender-Role Research
  Influences on the
    Development of Gender
    Roles

Epilogue

Summary

Activity

Research Terms

Related Readings

© Tony Freeman/PhotoEdit

Social/Behavioral Socialization Outcomes

All the world's a stage,
And all the men and women merely players:
They have their exits and their entrances;
And one man in his time plays many parts.

—WILLIAM SHAKESPEARE

MORES AND MORALS

THEN The moral values constituting good and bad, right and wrong, form the foundation, or mores, of society because they encompass how people should treat one another. Such values have been immortalized and realized through religion, laws, history, and literature. Moral values are often found in stories read to children. For example, the classic fairy tale *The Goose Girl*, by the Brothers Grimm, is about deception and lying. In the tale, the queen has a daughter who has been promised in marriage to a prince who lives in a distant land. When it comes time for the wedding, the queen provides the princess with her dowry and a maid-in-waiting, who is pledged to look after the princess and deliver her safely to the bridegroom.

However, the servant lies to the queen when she promises to care for the princess and takes advantage of the girl's naiveté and inexperience, depriving her of her royal wardrobe, jewelry, and furnishings—things that would identify her as the bride-to-be.

Upon arrival at the prince's palace, the servant again lies, telling the king that she is the princess and that the girl accompanying her is merely someone she picked up along the way who was looking for work. The king orders the girl (princess) to help look after the geese.

Eventually, the king, suspecting deceit, asks the imposter to propose a punishment for someone who is a fraud. Believing her secret to be safe, she advises that imposters should be placed naked into a cask studded inside with sharp nails and dragged by two horses along the street until dead. The king then tells her that she has pronounced her own fate.

NOW Deception and lies are, unfortunately, common practice in today's society. For example, businesses cut corners, use "bait-and-switch" tactics or deceive customers to increase their profits. Pretense is also prevalent on new technology such as the Internet, where ethical rules are not yet firmly established. Television, and movie, and rock stars; sports heroes; and political leaders—all behave as though possessions, money, power, and prestige are ends that justify lying, ends that are more important than self-respect, honor, and the high regard of others.

Prominent figures who have been caught lying include former President Richard Nixon, who, in the Watergate scandal, spied, stole, and lied to maintain his power; television evangelist Jimmy Swaggart, who was caught with a prostitute; scientists who "adjust" data to obtain grants to fund their research; college basketball stars who "fix" games by missing shots in exchange for money; movie stars who abuse substances and engage in violent behavior; and former President Bill Clinton, who committed adultery and lied about it to maintain his power and avoid censorship.

Although what happens to the servant in *The Goose Girl* represents a concrete punitive consequence, a "built-in check" for wrongdoers, today's famous wrongdoers have alternatives if they get caught—the publicity makes them marketable for talk shows, book deals, and movies. The danger with such alternatives is that the value of deceit is highlighted for children who, due to cognitive immaturity and lack of experience, are especially vulnerable to the influence of powerful role models.

What happened to society's 'built-in check' for moral behavior? According to Sissela Bok (1989), author of *Lying: Moral Choice in Public and Private Life*, certain societal values compete with personal morals:

> The very stress on individualism, on competition, on achieving material success which so marks our society, also generates intense pressures to cut corners. To win an election, to increase one's income, to outsell competitors—such motives impel many to participate in forms of duplicity they might otherwise resist. The more widespread they judge these practices to be, the stronger will be the pressures to join, even compete, in deviousness. (p. 244)

Thus, the social incentives for deceit (to achieve success, recognition for accomplishment, power, or material goods) in our society today have become more compelling than the controls (to be dishonored or shamed).

KEY QUESTIONS

- Why do people's motives for good behavior vary—from fear of getting caught, to "Do unto others as you would have others do unto you," to self-respect?
- How does the pressure for success (achievement, power, wealth) blur the line between right and wrong?
- How can the incentive structure in society for moral behavior be changed—for example, to enable honesty rather than deceit, to be more worthy, or to disable the gains from deception?

Self-Regulation/Behavior

The ability to regulate impulses, behavior, and/or emotions until an appropriate time, place, or object is available for expression is referred to as **self-regulation** (or self-control). As discussed in Chapter 2, self-regulation is one of the aims of socialization. Figure 12.1 shows an ecological model of influences on social and behavioral outcomes such as self-regulation. Self-regulatory behavior involves the ability to delay gratification, to sustain attention to tasks, and to plan and self-monitor goal-directed activities that could apply to social or moral conduct or to academic or athletic achievement (similar to self-efficacy). Self-regulatory skills are significantly related to inhibiting antisocial or aggressive behaviors and to acquiring prosocial or altruistic ones (Lengua, 2002). Children's self-regulatory difficulties may be symptomatic of conduct disorders, attention deficit hyperactivity disorder (ADHD), or depression (Winsler & Wallace, 2002).

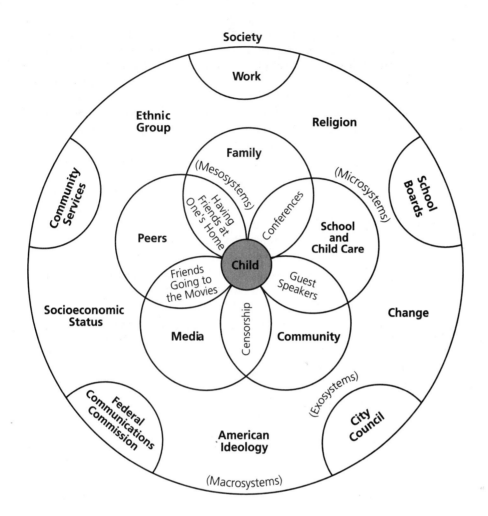

Figure 12.1

An Ecological Model of Human Development

Children's antisocial or prosocial behavior, morals, and gender-role enactment are outcomes of their socialization.

Self-regulation, or control, can be observed in children beginning about age 2 (Berk, 2003) and increasing with age (Logue, 1995). To behave appropriately, children need the cognitive maturity to understand that they are separate, autonomous beings with the ability to control their own actions. They also must have the language development to understand directives, the memory capabilities to store and retrieve caregivers' instructions, and the information-processing strategies to apply them to specific situations. In addition, children need to have some concept of the future, which expands as they get older: "If I don't tease my brother, Mommy says she will take me skating."

According to Vygotsky (1978), children cannot control their behavior until they incorporate adult cultural standards, expressed through communication, into their own speech. This occurs when children transform adult standards (sanctions on behavior, stereotypic roles, ideals for perfection), referred to as "social speech," into private discourse, or "inner speech," to direct their own behavior. An example of an adult standard of behavior communicated to children is resistance to temptation by delaying gratification. The ability to delay gratification involves waiting for an appropriate time to behave to achieve a desired result, instead of succumbing to temptation by acting impulsively, without thought to consequences. Mischel (1996) studied what preschool children say to themselves (inner speech) to promote delay of gratification when faced with tempting situations to gain immediate rewards. The children were given a choice of two rewards: a highly desirable one (such as a toy or candy) that they could have if they waited the prescribed amount of time, or a less desirable one (such as a sticker) that they could have anytime. The preschoolers who had the ability to delay gratification by resisting the temptation of taking the immediate reward used strategies to divert their attention while waiting, such as covering their eyes, singing, and pretending to be asleep.

The development of such self-regulatory ability is partially dependent upon biological factors, such as the child's temperament, and partially due to contextual factors, such as parenting practices (Berk, 2003).

Temperament, as discussed in Chapter 4, consists of genetically based characteristics that determine individuals' sensitivity to various experiences and responsiveness to patterns of social interaction. "Easy" children are more likely to comply with adult standards than those who are slow to warm up or difficult because, physiologically, they are more "relaxed." "Slow-to-warm-up" children may need time, reasoning, repetition, and patience to comply. "Difficult" children need even more of the same because they are more "tense" and, therefore, resistant to change.

Parenting practices influence the development of self-regulation in that the motive for children to internalize adult standards, as discussed in Chapter 2, is attachment. Children are willing to comply with parental demands because they want to please the individuals who love them; they try not to displease them because they fear loss of that love. According to Damon (1988), this is the foundation for respect for authority and social order in society. Authoritative parenting practices, in which there is extensive verbal give-and-take, reasoning, and non-punitive adult control, influence the development of self-control. Self-regulation (self-control) is a continuous process, an outcome of affective, cognitive, and social forces. In the beginning, children respond emotionally to situations instinctively. These biological reactions are responded to accordingly by adults and redefined through social experience. Through continuous instruction, observation, participation, feedback, and interpretation, various levels of self-control are established (Damon, 1988). Children who are maltreated by parents and exposed to domestic violence are less likely to develop self-control and emotional regulatory abilities (Maughan & Cicchetti, 2002).

Because emotional regulation, including the ability to control anger and exhibit empathy, is part of self-control, the focus here is on how these emotions are translated into antisocial and/or prosocial behavior. **Antisocial behavior** includes any behavior that harms other people, such as aggression, violence, and crime. **Prosocial behavior** includes any behavior that benefits other people, such as altruism, sharing, and cooperation.

How do children learn behavior that is pro- rather than antisocial? Whereas antisocial behavior—aggression—has been studied for many years, it is only relatively recently that attention has been given to prosocial behavior—altruism. **Aggression** encompasses unprovoked attacks, fights, or quarrels. Aggression may be *instrumental,* with the goal of obtaining an object, a privilege, or a space; or it may be *hostile,* with the goal of harming another person. (We focus on hostile aggression because instrumental aggression usually declines as children develop language skills to express desires and self-regulatory skills to delay gratification.) **Altruism** encompasses voluntary actions that help or benefit another person or group of people without the actor's anticipation of external rewards. Such actions often entail some cost, self-sacrifice, or risk on the part of the actor (Eisenberg & Fabes, 1998).

ANTISOCIAL BEHAVIOR: AGGRESSION

Aggression in childhood, especially hostile aggression, often forecasts later maladaptive outcomes, such as delinquency and criminality (Coie & Dodge, 1998; Farrington, 1991).

Development of Aggressive Behavior

Theories explaining the causes of aggression fall into several categories: (1) It is biologically influenced, (2) it is learned, (3) it is an information processing impulsive response to frustration, (4) it is a result of social cognitive factors such as peer group pressure or the reduction of restraining socialization forces, or (5) it is socialized by interacting ecological factors.

Biological Theories. Biological influences on behavior include evolution and genetics. "Evolution" refers to the passing on of the survival and adaptive characteristics of the species from one generation to the next; "genetics" refers to the individual characteristics of the parents that are passed on to their children.

Sigmund Freud (1925; Hall, 1954) believed that humans are born with two opposing biological instincts: (1) a life instinct (*Eros*), which causes them to grow and survive, and (2) a death instinct (*Thanatos*), which works toward their self-destruction. According to Freud, the death instinct is often redirected outward, against the external world, in the form of aggression toward others. The energy for the death instinct is constantly generated, and if it cannot be released in small amounts in socially acceptable ways, it will eventually be released in an extreme and socially unacceptable way, such as violence against others or the self. However, if the aggressive instinct can be redirected (crying, punching a doll, hammering nails), then it can be defused.

Lorenz (1966) held that the aggressive instinct is the key factor in the evolution and survival of animals. Such vital functions as protecting one's territory against invasion, defending the young, and engaging in fights to eliminate the weak so that they will not reproduce are basic to the survival of the various species. According to Lorenz, the expression of the aggressive instinct in most humans, especially in Western societies, has been inhibited; consequently, the drive is repressed until it erupts.

The problem with Freud's and Lorenz's theories is that they do not explain the differences in levels of aggressiveness within a society and in various situations.

Some evidence points to a genetic basis for antisocial behavior. Behavioral tendencies that might be influenced genetically include impulse control, frustration tolerance, and activity level (Segal, 1997). There is also a pattern of aggressive and antisocial behavior over the life course (Coie & Dodge, 1998). To exemplify, in a large-scale study of adopted persons, it was found that deviant, criminal behavior was more common in those individuals whose biological parent was a criminal, regardless of the environment in the adoptive family (Mednick, Moffit, Gabrielli, & Hutchings, 1986). For another example, the level of certain hormones present in individuals has been shown to be related to aggressive behavior (Olweus, 1986). In addition, males are more aggressive than females, not only physically but also verbally (Eley, Lichtenstein, & Stevenson, 1999; Maccoby & Jacklin, 1974, 1980).

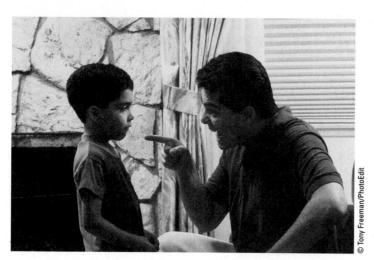

This parent's harsh and punitive child-rearing methods will likely influence this child to have an externally oriented conscience in that the child behaves out of fear of punishment.

In analyzing the research of the relationship of biological factors to aggressive behavior, Coie and Dodge (1998) conclude that aggression occurs indirectly through the interaction of biological processes and environmental events.

Learning Theories. According to Bandura (1973, 1991), children learn through experience when it is appropriate to act aggressively, what forms of aggression are permissible, and to whom they can express aggression without disapproval or punishment. For example, a child cannot hit his or her mother when she takes a toy away because severe socialization consequences ensue. However, the child can hit peers when they take a toy away without experiencing such consequences.

Children identify with role models and imitate behavior. The role models can be peers. For example, a child who has been attending school for a while may come home and display some new behavior never shown before, such as biting when angry. The role models can be parents. For example, parents sometimes respond to aggressive acts by spanking. Of course, punishing aggression with aggression is providing model behavior for the child to imitate.

The role models can also be other adults. In one classic study by Bandura, Ross, and Ross (1963), one group of preschool children watched a film of a woman hitting a Bobo doll (a 5-foot plastic inflated clown), while another group watched a model play with Tinkertoys. After watching the models, the children were left alone with a number of toys, including a Bobo doll and Tinkertoys, and were observed. The children who had watched the aggressive behavior on film acted more aggressively with the Bobo doll than did the other children. They punched, kicked, and hammered the doll, and even made the same aggressive comments the adult had.

Whether models will be imitated depends on their perceived status. For instance, children have been found to imitate high-status dominant models (Bandura, 1989). Characteristics of the observer can also influence the incidence of imitation, such as motivation, ability to remember what is observed, and ability to perform the observed act (Bandura, 1989).

Whether aggressive acts will be imitated by the observer also depends on whether the aggressive model was rewarded or punished. In one experiment (Bandura, 1977), children were exposed to one of three conditions: (1) They viewed a successful, aggressive model on film who was enjoying a victory, (2) they viewed an aggressive model on film who was severely punished by the intended victim, or (3) they did not see any film (this condition was the experimental control). The children who saw the aggressive model rewarded for aggressive behavior exhibited more aggression on subsequent observation than did the children who either saw the model punished or saw no model.

The explanation for these results is that the consequences of the model's behavior served as cues to the kind of behavior that is permissible in a given social context. Responses that are rewarded tend to occur more frequently, because behavior that results in successful outcomes is likely to be repeated (Bandura, 1973, 1991). For example, if a child pushes another in order to get to the swing first and the other child acquiesces (does not resist or retaliate), the aggressor is likely to repeat the aggressive act the next time he or she wants to pursue an activity but is being blocked by someone else.

Responses that are rewarded intermittently resist extinction, or elimination. In other words, responses that are not rewarded every time they occur, but only sometimes, are difficult to "unlearn." Aggressive acts are highly likely to be rewarded intermittently. For instance, they may be tolerated by some children but not by others, and they may be punished by adults when noticed, which may not be every single occurrence.

Given that aggression can be learned through observation of aggressive models, what about the content of television shows and their potential impact on children? As has been discussed, a number of studies (Comstock & Paik, 1991; Huston & Wright, 1998; Perse, 2001) report that both children and adults are exposed to a lot of television violence. Many people believe that watching a lot of aggression on television increases the tendency of viewers, especially children, to behave aggressively. By watching, children may learn that aggression is acceptable and may even learn aggressive techniques. Those who believe that the aggressive instinct is present in all humans suggest that watching aggression is catharsis—a way of releasing pent-up aggressive feelings. It follows that watching aggression on television reduces potential aggressive behavior. Other people believe that televised aggression has little effect on aggressive behavior compared with direct rewards and models for aggression provided by parents, teachers, and friends.

Several factors have been found to moderate the effects of viewing television violence on aggressive behavior (Coie & Dodge, 1998). These include children's repertoire of alternative behaviors, whether they believe the violence on TV is real; whether they identify with the TV characters; whether parents watch and discuss shows with children; and whether the aggressive acts viewed were punished, justified, or rewarded (the aggressor gets something or wins). An alternative behavior might be verbalization. Children who know how to verbalize their frustration ("I don't like it when you take my things"), as opposed to children who do not (when something is taken, the child grabs it back and smacks the transgressor), are less likely to imitate aggressive behavior. Children who, due to cognitive immaturity, believe that what they see on TV is real are more likely to imitate aggression, especially if they identify with the aggressors or if the aggressors are rewarded. Children whose parents mediate TV viewing are less likely to imitate aggression.

There is much documentation on the relationship between parenting practices and childhood aggression (Coie & Dodge, 1998; Kim, Hetherington, & Reiss, 1999; Patterson, 1982; Rubin, Stewart, & Chen, 1995). Coercive, hostile parenting is related to children's aggression. Thus, if parents want to discourage aggressive behavior in their children, they must not model it—for example, by spanking. They must also not reward it, by letting it succeed or go unnoticed. And they must teach alternative acceptable behaviors, such as talking about one's feelings.

Information Processing Theories. Information processing refers to the way individuals attend to, perceive, interpret, remember, and act on events or situations. Those who behave impulsively act without thinking about the consequences. Some people believe impulsivity to be a genetic temperamental trait that affects behavior (Buss & Plomin, 1984; Coie & Dodge, 1998; Kagan, 1994). For example, some researchers have identified a link between low impulsivity and self-control

(Kochanska, DeVet, Goldman, Murray, & Putnam, 1994). Thus, aggressive behavior may be a response to frustrating experiences, especially for impulsive individuals (Staub, 1986). An example would be "road rage," whereby people get involved in verbal or physical fights—or even shoot one another—when cut off in traffic. The strength of the frustrated motive, the degree of interference, and the number of motives blocked determine the intensity of the aggression exhibited (Grusec & Lytton, 1988). If a child's motive is to ride a tricycle during free playtime but the teacher calls everyone in before the child gets a chance, she or he might be frustrated. However, if the child had to wait an especially long time because the other children refused to give up their tricycles and perhaps even teased the waiting child, then the level of frustration is bound to escalate and may be expressed as aggression.

Others (Coie & Dodge, 1998; Dodge, 1986; Dodge & Frame, 1982) suggest that individuals' reaction to frustration depend not so much on the social cues (what *actually* happens) as on how they process the information (their *interpretation* of what happens). Dodge (1986) assumed that children enter each social situation with a memory of past experiences and a goal (making friends, for example). When an event occurs, such as being bumped into, the child must interpret its meaning. The child's past experiences with social interaction, as well as his or her skills in processing information, will influence whether the event is interpreted as "accidental" or "purposeful." Aggressive children tend to interpret ambiguous events as hostile, whereas nonaggressive children tend to view them as benign. Dodge's explanation of how such social information is processed cognitively will be discussed in more detail later.

Social Cognitive Theories. People are influenced by the attitudes, values, and behavior patterns of those around them, particularly significant others. Thus, aggression can be a result of peer group pressure. Studies (Coie & Dodge, 1998; Wall, Power, & Arbona, 1993) have shown that the incidence of violence is much higher in some groups than in others. For example, in some parts of the world and in some subcultures in the United States, violence is the acceptable reaction to personal affronts. The person who wants to be part of the groups that subscribe to this norm must act as expected.

Peers are thought to supply individuals with the attitudes, motivations, and rationalizations to support antisocial behavior, as well as providing opportunities to engage in specific delinquent acts (Coie & Dodge, 1998; Patterson, DeBaryshe, & Ramsey, 1989). A study of children in grades 1–6 found the classroom context to be influential in increasing or reducing aggressive behavior (Kellam, Ling, Merisca, Brown, & Ialongo, 1999). Aggressive first-graders in classrooms with aggressive peers showed an increase in aggressive behavior by sixth grade, whereas aggressive first-graders in classrooms using preventive intervention strategies showed a decrease in aggressive behavior by sixth grade. Whether individuals succumb to group pressure depends on their personalities, the situation, and the number of reference groups to which they belong. If they belong to several groups that accept aggression as a legitimate means for revenge, then the tendency to behave aggressively increases. If, however, they belong to one group that subscribes to this norm but also to other groups that do not, the likelihood of conforming to the aggressive behavior of the one group decreases. Thus, individuals whose peer groups sanction aggression are more likely to exhibit aggressive behavior.

Some people believe that when restraining socialization forces are reduced aggression is more likely. Restraining socialization forces can be external pressures, such as fear of consequences (punishment, criticism, opinion of others), or internal pressures (guilt, shame, moral development level).

Anonymity tends to reduce the restraining forces of external pressures. In other words, when people are anonymous, they are more likely to be aggressive than when not. Anonymity can result when someone is unknown to others (disguised, hidden by darkness) or is "lost in the crowd" (part of a uniformed group, or with too many people to be noticed). When people are anonymous, they cannot be identified by others and so cannot be evaluated, criticized, judged, or punished by them.

When aggressive models are successful, they are likely to be imitated.

Experiments (Baron, 1970; Deax & Wrightsman, 1988) have shown that when, in a laboratory situation, individuals are made to feel anonymous their levels of aggression increase. In a naturalistic study (Diener, Frasier, Beaman, & Kelem, 1976), 1300 children were unobtrusively observed trick-or-treating on Halloween and were also given the opportunity to steal candy and money. When the children were anonymous (identities hidden by costumes), they stole more candy and money than when they had been previously asked to reveal their identities to the adult host.

"Sanctions for evil" (Sanford & Comstock, 1971) provided by the group may reduce internal restraining pressures such as guilt. For example, members of the group may feel that what they are doing is morally required (Duster, 1971). War exemplifies this: In war, loyalty to the group (the army, the regiment, the platoon) obliterates individuality. Soldiers are trained to do as they are ordered; the responsibility for decisions rests with their superiors, not them. Another example of sanctions for evil is the famous Milgram (1963) experiment, in which subjects were told to inflict electric shocks (even though electric shocks were not actually delivered) on other subjects when they gave a wrong answer. Some subjects refused immediately, and others quit the experiment after they heard the other subjects scream; however, 65 percent of the subjects did inflict the maximum level of shock possible when told to do so.

The community usually provides the restraining socialization forces for aggression through its members, its laws, and its police. Community members are a restraining force when they disapprove of aggression by another member. The restraining force is the opinion of the group: "What will the neighbors say if I beat up Fred?" Anonymity or alienation reduces the force of that disapproval: "Why should I care what the neighbors think? They don't know me, so they'll never know who beat up Fred."

The laws of the community spell out what behavior is unacceptable and must be punished. The restraining force of the laws depends on how stringently they are enforced.

The police provide protection for community members. Parents and children living in neighborhoods characterized by high crime rates perceive their environments as unsafe (Fick, Osofsky, & Lewis, 1997). Adaptive behavior can result in fear, social isolation, and/or desensitization to violence.

Ecological Theories. In reviews of the literature, Patterson and colleagues (1989; Reid, Patterson, & Snyder, 2002) have synthesized the findings on aggression in the hypothesis that the route to chronic delinquency is marked by a reliable developmental sequence of ecological experiences. The first experience is ineffective parenting (influenced by such variables as the way the parents themselves were parented, socioeconomic status, ethnicity, neighborhood, and education). The second experience is behavioral conduct disorders that lead to academic failure and peer rejection, which, in turn, lead to increased risk of involvement in a deviant peer group. The third, and final, experience, occurring in early adolescence, is chronic delinquent behavior.

Thus, antisocial behavior appears to be a developmental trait that begins early in life (observable by age 4–5) and often continues into adolescence and adulthood. The socialization for aggression is bidirectional and interactional in several ecological contexts. For instance, it includes poor parenting skills, which affect child behavior, and children's behavior, which affects not only parenting but school performance and peer relationships as well (Snyder & Patterson, 1995). The unintentional coercive training might begin with a parental demand that the child go to bed. When the child refuses, the parent yells, which leads the child to complain about always being picked on. The parent then gives in, thereby reinforcing in the child a coercive method to get his or her way.

Patterson and colleagues (1989; Reid, Patterson, & Snyder, 2002) suggest that prevention of antisocial behavior is feasible if young children who are both antisocial and unskilled in peer interactions can be identified, if they receive social skills training (as discussed in Chapter 8) and academic remediation, and if their parents receive parenting training.

How can children at risk for conduct disorders be identified? A study by Dodge, Petit, and Bates (1994) identified some socialization mediators contributing to risky developmental outcomes. These included harsh parental discipline, lack of maternal warmth, exposure to aggressive adult models, maternal aggressive values, family life stressors, mothers' lack of social support, peer group instability, and lack of cognitive stimulation. The children, who were from the lowest socioeconomic status, were followed from preschool to grade 3. The significance of these mediators as predictors of conduct disorders is that they often accompany socioeconomic stress found in families of low socioeconomic status. Thus, it is not low socioeconomic status or poverty per se that influences aggressive behavior, but the socialization mediators that often accompany such socioeconomic stress (Coie & Dodge, 1998; Huston, McLoyd, & Coll, 1994). Socialization mediators have become the accepted way of studying aggression, as will be discussed next.

Ways of Studying Aggression

The Social Cognitive Model. A social cognitive model for studying aggression has been developed by researchers drawing on earlier studies. Basically, the social cognitive model attempts to identify mediating responses within the individual, such as an internal moral code and an ability to interpret social cues or behavioral responses from others. It also describes how these mediating responses may be predictive, in various situations, of an individual's aggressive behavior (Coie & Dodge, 1998; Parke & Slaby, 1983).

The social cognitive model assumes that developing children make social interpretations about which interactions with others constitute aggressive provocation and require retaliation. As noted previously, according to Dodge (1986), children come to specific social situations with a database (their memory store) and receive social cues as input from the interaction. Children's behavioral responses to those cues are a function of certain cognitive processes: decoding the input, interpreting it, searching for potential responses, coming to a decision, and making a response.

For example, a child who is hit on the back by a peer must decode that action by searching for cues relevant to the peer's intention (Was it on purpose or an accident?) and then focus on those cues. The child must also interpret those cues. (If the hit was intentional, was the peer trying to be friendly or mean?) The child's past experiences (memory store) aid in the interpretation. (If the peer runs away, then the action was intentionally mean; if the peer follows the hit with a comment such as "Let's go," then the action was intentionally friendly.) Once the situation is interpreted, the child has to search for possible behavioral responses (hit back, ignore, verbalize displeasure, and so on). The next step is to decide which response to execute. In choosing a response, the child must first assess the probable consequences of each response he or she has generated ("If I hit back, I may get hit again"). Finally, the child must act out the chosen behavioral response. If, however, the choice is made to respond verbally, the child must possess the necessary language skills to do so.

Dodge and colleagues (1994) generally found that aggressive children were more likely to attribute hostile intentions to their peers than were nonaggressive children. This biased way of thinking, then, increased the likelihood that they would retaliate aggressively, with behavior they thought was justified (although their peers did not).

Other researchers (Perry, Perry, & Rasmussen, 1986) have found that not only do aggressive children often interpret provocation by others erroneously as hostility, they also respond aggressively because they expect their aggressiveness to be successful in eliminating their aversive state or to otherwise improve their plight. This supports Bandura's (1977, 1986) social cognitive theory: Reinforced behavior, even behavior thought to be potentially reinforcing, will be repeated. The reinforcement, in this case, is the reduction of hostile (or perceived hostile) treatment by others.

The Ecological Model. The development of aggression must also be viewed in an ecological context. The complex variables operating in aggressive behavior involve the child (personality, cognitive level, social skills), the family (parenting, interaction), the school (attitudes on handling aggressive behavior), the peer group (modeling, norms, acceptance/rejection), the media (modeling), and the community (socioeconomic stressors, attitudes on handling aggressive behavior, availability of support systems) (Coie & Dodge, 1998; Parke, 1982).

EXAMPLE Robert, age 8, has been referred to the principal's office for the third time in 2 weeks for fighting on the playground. No consequences provided by the teacher seemed to be effective. The principal asked Robert's parents to come to school for a conference. Robert was very angry, insisting, "The other kids always start." He thought to himself, "I'll get them. I'll bring my brother's knife."

For the principal to deal with Robert's aggressiveness, she needs to know that Robert comes from a home in which physical punishment is the means for dealing with misbehavior. Likewise, Robert resorts to physical means when he perceives others treating him badly. She also needs to understand that in Robert's neighborhood gang fights are the primary means of settling disagreements; in fact, Robert's older brother belongs to a gang. Finally, she needs to be aware that Robert has been taught that it is "unmanly" not to fight back when challenged.

Once the principal becomes cognizant of Robert's ecological background, she will be better equipped to try an approach that might reduce his aggressive behavior in school. Robert might need some intensive individual attention from an adult whom he respects and will model. Referring him to a Boys' Club in the community might help. Robert also needs to learn social skills that will enable him to deal with ambiguous and/or confrontational situations without resorting to fighting. And Robert needs help to discover an ability that other children might admire (art, music, drama, or athletics). If the principal can get Robert's parents to support the school's attempts to help their son, there is a better chance the intervention will succeed in changing Robert's antisocial behavior.

The importance of early intervention in antisocial behavior is that aggression can be self-perpetuating. In a review of studies on children who were antisocial, Patterson and colleagues (Patterson, DeBaryshe, & Ramsey, 1989; Snyder & Patterson, 1995) concluded that coercive, or harsh, parenting contributes to the development of children's defiant, aggressive behaviors and hostile interpretations of others' behavior, which, in turn, can cause these children to be rejected by normal peers and to do poorly in school. Moreover, the rejection experienced by aggressive children in early childhood may contribute to their attraction in adolescence to deviant peers who devalue school and engage in antisocial or delinquent acts (Dishion, Patterson, Stoolmiller, & Skinner, 1991). Table 12.1 summarizes the variables contributing to antisocial behavior.

How Parents and Teachers Can Inhibit Aggressiveness in Young Children

1. Organize the environment to minimize conflicts. Minimize crowding. Have plenty of stimulating and engaging developmentally appropriate materials, and enough of them so children can play together with similar materials (bicycles, paint, toys, and so on).

2. Set standards, stick to them, and provide consequences for noncompliance. Let children know that aggression is not sanctioned: "You hit Bobby on the playground; you must sit on the bench now for ten minutes," or "You did not control your temper today. Because you disappointed me, I will have to disappoint you; you cannot stay up late, as you had wanted, to watch that program on television."

3. Stop aggression immediately. If possible, try not to let it escalate to completion. For example, if you see two children struggling over a toy, take the toy and ask both children to tell you their versions of the incident. Then ask them how you should resolve it. If they don't come up with a solution, say, "Well, you both think about it, and meanwhile I'll hold the toy."

4. Give children alternative ways of solving problems. Teach them how to verbalize their feelings and how to listen to others.

CHILD	FAMILY	SCHOOL	PEERS	MEDIA	COMMUNITY
Biological influences (evolution, genetics)	Parenting style (authoritarian, coercive)	Teaching style (authoritarian)	Peer group pressure	Modeling	Modeling
Gender	Interaction	Modeling	Situation	Reinforcement/ punishment of model	Acceptance of and/or sanctions for violence
Hormones	Modeling Reinforcement/ punishment for behavior	Reinforcement/ punishment for behavior Expectations	Aggressive norms Modeling	Mediation by adults	Anonymity/ alienation Safety Socioeconomic stressors
Temperament (impulsivity, frustration tolerance, activity level)	Attitudes		Acceptance/ rejection		Availability of informal/ formal support systems
Ability to delay gratification					
Information processing ability					
Internally/ externally- oriented conscience (guilt vs. fear of punishment)					
Cognitive developmental maturity Social skills					
Moral reasoning/ judgment					

Table 12.1
Variables Contributing to Antisocial Behavior

5. Anticipate possible situations for aggressive behavior to occur in. These might entail children playing together roughly or children complaining that they have nothing to do. Redirect the children into an activity that interests them.

6. Provide opportunities for cooperative activities. Enable children to learn to listen to each other's ideas, to solve problems democratically, to compromise, and to respect each other.

7. Foster helpfulness and cooperation: "Could you help Daniel with that tower he's building?" or "Could you help your sister put on her shoes while I make your lunch?"

8. Be a positive role model. Don't punish aggression with aggression; use alternative disciplinary methods.

9. Discuss rules and the reasons for them. Also discuss violence that children may be exposed to in the media or in their communities. Encourage children to talk about their fears and feelings, and help them develop strategies for feeling protected by adults: "When you are scared, you can tell me," or "Officer Wilson is our friend."

10. Reward prosocial behavior. Give children attention when they share, are helpful or cooperative, or solve problems by discussion; don't allow them to get your attention only by being aggressive.

Sources: (Caldwell and Crary, 1981; Slaby, Roedell, Arezzo, and Hendrix, 1995).

PROSOCIAL BEHAVIOR: ALTRUISM

One of the aims of socialization, as stated previously, is to teach developmental skills, which include getting along with others. To participate in a group, individuals must cooperate, share, and help others when needed. As we all know, some

This child is exhibiting prosocial behavior—altruism—by helping his friend tie his shoe.

© Myrleen F. Cate/PhotoEdit

people exhibit more of these behaviors than others. What is it that motivates some-one to rescue a total stranger from a burning building, to send money to someone whose story has been told in the newspaper, or to volunteer to work in a senior cit-izens center?

Recall that altruism refers to behavior that is kind, considerate, generous, and helpful to others. Like aggression, it shows consistency over time. Altruistic behav-ior begins to appear during the preschool years (in some children, it appears by age 2). Some researchers believe the brain may be "prewired" to be empathetic and to cooperate with others (Hoffman, 2000; Rilling et al., 2002). Children's ability to take the perspective of others increases as they get older, so they become more aware that others' feelings may differ from their own, and thus, they are more capable of experiencing empathy (Eisenberg & Fabes, 1998). Radke-Yarrow and Zahn-Waxler (1986), for example, observed consistent patterns of sharing, helping, and comforting behaviors among 3- to 7-year-olds at play.

Altruistic behaviors in children age 10, 15, and 20 months were examined over a 9-month period (Zahn-Waxler & Radke-Yarrow, 1990; Zahn-Waxler, Radke-Yarrow, Wagner, & Chapman, 1992). The researchers found that between 10 and 12 months of age incidents of emotional distress provoked no significant altruistic responses. Over the next 6 to 8 months, however, concern (exhibited by facial expressions or crying) and positive initiations (exhibited by patting or touching the other person) began to be exhibited in response to the distress of others. Such responses, concerns, and positive interactions became increasingly differentiated and frequent by age 18–24 months. For example, by age 2, children may bring objects to a person in dis-tress, make suggestions about what to do, verbalize sympathy, bring someone else to help, aggressively protect the victim, and/or attempt to evoke a change in the feel-ings of the distressed person. But they may also avoid the encounter, cry, or even behave aggressively. Thus, by age 2, there are many individual differences in the exhibition of behaviors in response to emotional distress.

Prosocial responses, such as cooperating, sharing, giving comfort, and offering to help, become increasingly apparent throughout childhood as children develop cog-nitively and have more social interactions (Eisenberg & Fabes, 1998). For example, toddlers (age 2–3) exhibit some sharing behaviors and demonstrations of sympathy, and often react to others' distress by becoming distressed themselves (Zahn-Waxler et al., 1992). Preschoolers (age 3–6) begin to become less egocentric and exhibit altruistic acts if they also benefit the self ("I'll share so you'll be my friend"). School-agers (age 6–12) who can take the role of others better understand legitimate needs ("I'll help because he can't do it himself"). Adolescents (age 13 and over) under-stand prosocial behavior in terms of more abstract social responsibility and may feel guilty for not acting altruistically when it is needed ("I should participate in the jog-a-thon to raise money for children with cancer") (Eisenberg & Fabes, 1998).

Whether children behave prosocially may depend on the individuals involved, the specific situation, and their interpretation of it. Preschoolers, school-agers, and adolescents assist an individual more if that person has previously helped them (Eisenberg & Fabes, 1998). Children are more likely to help those close to them than those who are unfamiliar (Eisenberg & Fabes, 1998). And children's moods at the time of the incident affects their motivation to be helpful (Carlson, Charlin, & Miller, 1988).

Development of Altruistic Behavior

Similar to theories explaining aggressive behavior, theories of the causes of altruistic behavior are (1) biological (evolution and genetics), (2) learning-based (reinforcement, modeling, and instruction), (3) cognitive-developmental, (4) social-interactional, and (5) cultural.

Biological Theories. Biological drives, such as reproduction (expressed in sexual desire) and survival (expressed in aggression), according to Freud (1938), are seated in the part of the personality that seeks self-gratification. Freud labeled that part the id. Children's experiences with reality cause them to assess the feasibility of satisfying their biological drives. Freud labeled the rational part of the personality the ego, which helps individuals delay gratification. Children also experience pleasant feelings when they comply with parental standards and unpleasant feelings when they don't. Out of fear of parental disapproval or loss of parental love, they develop a superego, or conscience, to regulate their impulses and behave according to internalized parental standards. They may behave prosocially to avoid a feeling of guilt. Thus, according to Freud, children's adoption of prosocial values results from identification with their parents.

Sociobiologists believe that evolution and genes account for certain complex human social behaviors. Children, they contend, are genetically programmed to be kind and considerate as part of human nature. Thus, altruism is behavior that promotes the genetic fitness of others at the expense of their own fitness. Because altruism benefits the group's survival, natural selection favors those members of the species who have this characteristic (even though altruistic members may die in performing altruistic acts). For example, protecting others from harm is considered to be altruistic behavior. In the animal kingdom, the bee that protects the members of its species by stinging an intruder dies. Even though one member of the species dies, its altruistic act enables the other members to live and reproduce. Similarly, in the human species.

> as early human beings bonded together in social groups, perhaps for the purpose of cooperative hunting, selection pressures began to build for those traits that allowed them to adapt to community life. Genes promoting flexibility and conformity, for example, were probably passed on. Aggression had to be harnessed, social structure improvised and forms of communication developed. This acted as a kind of positive feedback loop: better communication led to reduced aggression, and vice versa.
>
> The group, led by a dominant male, benefited each individual and his self-interested genes by providing protection, a ready supply of eligible mates and the ability to surround and bring down larger animals. From these cooperative dealings, sociobiologists say, culture arose: art, ethics, courtship rituals, and the rest. Humans came to reflect a mosaic of traits, each adaptive and not necessarily inherent in their old primate nature. (Nalley, 1983, p. 5)

Hoffman (1981, 1991, 2000) offers evidence supporting the idea that empathy—the vicarious experiencing of another's emotions—is part of human nature in that it is an inherited biological predisposition. Empathy, as well as the internalization of society's moral norms and values, is the motive for altruism. One study (Martin & Clark, 1982) found that newborns became distressed by the cries of other newborns, thus indicating that humans are "wired" from birth to respond to the distress of their peers. Twins (14 months old) were found to react similarly to simulation of distress in others at home and in laboratory settings (Zahn-Waxler, Robinson, & Emde, 1992). Other studies (Eisenberg & Fabes, 1998; Rushton, Fulker, Neal, Nias, & Eysenck, 1986) have found that identical twins (who have identical genes) were more similar to each other on questionnaires designed to assess altruism, empathy, and nurturance than were fraternal twins, who share about half of their genes.

Thus, differences in genetic composition among people have a considerable influence on differences in their tendencies to behave both prosocially and antisocially.

Researchers have identified an area in the front of the brain's cerebral cortex, called the ventromedial area (located behind the bridge of the nose), that processes information regarding both other people's suffering and one's own misdeeds. Apparently, the proper functioning of this area is vital to emotional responsiveness. In one study, adults whose ventromedial areas had been damaged did not react negatively to images of extreme human harm and showed less concern than others for not conforming to social norms for behavior (Damasio, 1994).

In another study, researchers used magnetic resonance imaging (MRI) while subjects played a strategic cooperative/competitive game, based on the classic Prisoners' Dilemma. In this scenario, two suspects are taken into custody by the police, who do not have enough evidence to convict them. The suspects are put in separate rooms to get them to confess, with the one doing so first promised freedom from prosecution. If both confess simultaneously, both get sent to jail for a long time; if neither confesses, the police can jail them only briefly, for a minor offense. Thus, the motive to cooperate is a small consequence rather than a large one for competing to be the first confessor and losing. The researchers found that two areas of the brain significant in dopamine production (pleasure)—the anteroventral stratum in the middle of the brain above the spinal cord and the orbitofrontal cortex in the region above the eyes—were activated when the subjects worked together to share a reward rather than competed, with one getting a reward and the other getting nothing (Rilling et al., 2002). Apparently, the human brain is wired to cooperate and rewards itself for doing so with pleasurable feelings.

Learning Theories. Despite the current uncertainty about how and when altruism begins, it is known that altruism can be encouraged by being directly reinforced or rewarded and by being reinforced after observing someone else engaging in the act (modeling) (Eisenberg & Murphy, 1995). One investigator, for example, found that children age 4 were more likely to share marbles with other children if, after sharing, they were rewarded with bubble gum (Fischer, 1963). However, the effects of giving tangible rewards for prosocial behavior are short-lived. In contrast, social reinforcement, or praise, has been shown to increase altruism in children for longer periods. For example, after having been prompted to share and then praised for doing so, children were found to give more to others (Bar-Tal, Raviv, & Lesser, 1980; Gelfand, Hartman, Cromer, Smith, & Page, 1975).

Although concrete rewards may induce altruism in a given context, the long-term effect of concrete rewards may be negative because they serve to undermine intrinsic motivation (Lepper, 1983; Zimmerman, 2000). And social rewards (praise) may induce altruism in the given context, but not in other contexts (Eisenberg & Fabes, 1998).

The peer group reinforces prosocial behavior, especially when it is directed at peers. Parkhurst and Asher (1992) found that children age 12–14 who were actively rejected by peers were high in antisocial behavior, whereas those who were popular among peers were high in prosocial behavior. As has been well established, peers exert pressure to behave in certain ways. Thus, the desire to maintain friendships may motivate individuals to behave altruistically. For example, people are more willing to donate blood if they believe their peers support such an action (Foss, 1983).

It has been shown repeatedly that observing helpful models encourages observers to be helpful themselves (Bandura, 1986; Eisenberg & Murphy, 1995).

This modeling effect is found whether the model is another child or an adult and whether the model is live or on film. For example, children age 10–11 who observed an adult donating to a charity were more likely themselves to donate than children who did not observe the altruistic model. When the children observed the adult model keeping the money instead of donating it to charity, they also imitated that behavior (Harris, 1970). Media models, as shown on children's TV programs like *Mister Rogers Neighborhood* or *Sesame Street,* who exhibit prosocial behavior are likely to be imitated by their viewers, especially when adults reinforce the shows' messages by discussion (Coates, Pusser, & Goodman, 1976; Huston & Wright, 1998; Perse, 2001; Roberts & Maccoby, 1985).

Modeling altruism has generalizable effects. For example, children who are taught to act helpfully in one situation will also act helpfully in others (Elliot & Vasta, 1970; Radke-Yarrow & Zahn-Waxler, 1986). In another study, after having observed an altruistic model, children were still acting generously 4 months later (Radke-Yarrow & Zahn-Waxler, 1986; Rice & Grusec, 1975).

Children learn from each other; they also model behaviors of admired peers. For example, children who witness the charitable acts of an altruistic peer model are more likely to donate toys or money, even anonymously (Radke-Yarrow, Zahn-Waxler, & Chapman, 1983). Thus, if a child has a group of friends who consistently exhibit prosocial behavior, that child is likely to exhibit it, too (Eisenberg & Fabes, 1998). Children who belong to groups that condone aggressive behavior are likely to exhibit aggression, and those who belong to groups that disapprove of aggressive behavior are less likely to exhibit it.

If altruistic examples are so effective, why not simply instruct children to be kind, considerate, and helpful? Generally, observing adults sharing is more effective than merely telling children to share (Eisenberg & Murphy, 1995). However, in one experiment (Rice & Grusec, 1975), with children who were initially undecided about whether to act altruistically, being told to help was as effective as actually observing adults helping. However, if the child is resistant to sharing, then being told to share is less effective than actual observation. Still, teaching altruism can be as effective as modeling it, especially if the instructions are strongly stated and reasons for sharing are given (Grusec, Saas-Korlsaak, & Simutis, 1978).

The school can train children to be prosocial by using the technique of role-playing (Eisenberg & Mussen, 1989). For example, Staub (1971) worked with pairs of kindergarteners, asking one child to act the part of someone who needed help (carrying something too heavy) and the other child to act the part of a helping person (thinking of ways to help). The children were then asked to change roles. A week after training, "helpfulness" was tested by giving the children a chance to help a crying child in the next room and the chance to share candy with another child. The trained children were compared with a control group, which had not received training. The children who had undergone the reciprocal role training were more likely to be helpful than were the children who had not received this training.

Schools can also assign the responsibility to children to teach others to be helpful or to share (Eisenberg & Murphy, 1995). For example, Staub (1970) explicitly assigned responsibility to kindergarten and first-grade children. When the children were told that they were "in charge" by a departing adult, there was an increase in the probability, especially among the first-graders, that they would go to the aid of another child who was heard crying in the next room. As children get older, the assigned prosocial task is generalized to other situations (Peterson, 1983). For example, children over age 7 who are induced to donate to needy others in one context are more likely to behave similarly in another context several days later (Eisenberg & Murphy, 1995).

Thus, prosocial behavior can be increased in children via real-life experiences. One way is to provide role-playing opportunities for them. When children take the place of a child who needs help, they know what it feels like to be in need; when they take the place of the helper, they learn what to do to be of assistance. Another way is to assign responsibility for a prosocial behavior. The children, then, experience what it is like to be helpful, and they earn adult and peer approval as well.

In sum, parents who instruct children in altruistic acts, practice or model what they teach, and verbally reinforce children's helpful acts will foster prosocial behavior (Deax & Wrightsman, 1988; Eisenberg & Murphy, 1995).

Cognitive-Developmental Theories. Numerous theorists have hypothesized that as children develop cognitively their ability to think about other people increases. Their enhanced sociocognitive skills, particularly perspective taking and moral reasoning, foster prosocial behavior (Eisenberg & Fabes, 1998). When individuals can put themselves in another's place, they are more likely to empathize and give comfort and help.

Kohlberg (1976) viewed prosocial behavior as a component of moral reasoning, which, in turn, is a function of cognitive development. Kohlberg emphasized the contributions of social interactions and cognitions regarding the ability to take others' perspectives and understand consequences of behavior. Whether an individual is self-oriented or other-oriented influences moral reasoning and consequent selfish or altruistic behavior. Emotions such as sympathy and guilt may also play a role in moral judgment and behavior (Eisenberg & Fabes, 1998).

Social Interactional Theories. The bidirectional interactions occurring in social groups influence prosocial behavior. The family provides such a context. A team of researchers (Zahn-Waxler, Radke-Yarrow, & King, 1979) studied young children's altruism by training mothers of a group of 15-month-olds and mothers of a group of 20-month-olds to monitor the children's daily lives. Specifically, the mothers tape-recorded descriptions of every incident in which someone in the child's presence expressed painful feelings (anger, fear, sorrow, pain, and/or fatigue). The mothers also described the events preceding and following each incident, as well as both the child's and their own reactions. Here is one example:

> Today Jerry was kind of cranky; he just started completely bawling and he wouldn't stop. John kept coming over and handing Jerry toys, trying to cheer him up, so to speak. He'd say things like, "Here, Jerry," and I said to John, "Jerry's sad; he doesn't feel good; he had a shot today." John would look at me with his eyebrows kind of wrinkled together like he really understood that Jerry was crying because he was unhappy, not that he was just being a crybaby. He went over and rubbed Jerry's arm and said, "Nice Jerry," and continued to give him toys. (pp. 321–322)

When the researchers found that the number of altruistic reactions varied greatly from child to child, they examined the individual mother's responses. They found that the way the mothers reprimanded their children was clearly related to the children's degree of altruism. The following exemplifies the various responses:

- Moralizing: "Look, you made Susie cry; it's not nice to pull hair."
- Prohibition with an explanation or statement of principle: "You must never poke anyone's eyes! He won't be able to see!"
- Withdrawal of love, physical or verbal: "I can't hug you when you've been mean."
- Neutral: "Russell is crying because you hurt him."

- Prohibitions without explanation: "Don't ever do that!"
- Physical restraint.
- Physical punishment.

Related to a high proportion of observed altruistic behaviors in the children was the mothers' use of moralizing and prohibitions, along with explanations or statements of principle, when antisocial behavior was exhibited. Unexplained verbal prohibitions and physical punishment were associated with low degrees of altruism. Neutral explanations had little effect either way.

What other socializing techniques are related to prosocial behavior in children? A warm, nurturant, affectionate relationship between children and parents, in contrast to a cold, indifferent, distant relationship, seems to contribute to the development of prosocial tendencies (Eisenberg & Murphy, 1995; Staub, 1975).

The manner of execution of parental control—reasonable versus excessive or arbitrary—influences the development of prosocial behavior (Eisenberg & Fabes, 1998). "Control" refers to the setting of certain standards and rules by parents and their insistence on adherence to them when deemed necessary. There is strong evidence that the frequent use of physical punishment by parents results in children's aggression, hostility, and resistance (Aronfreed, 1968; Coie & Dodge, 1998; Eron, Walder, & Lefkowitz, 1971; Patterson, DeBaryshe, & Ramsey, 1989). At the same time, nurturing persons who do not exert control seem to have no effect on prosocial behavior (Radke-Yarrow & Zahn-Waxler, 1986; Rosenhan & White, 1967; Weissbrod, 1976). Baumrind (1967, 1971a), found that firm enforcement of rules, combined with reasoning and warmth (authoritative parenting), was associated with positive and effective social behavior. Thus, when parents are affectionate and have certain firm standards that they explain, children are likely to display prosocial behavior.

Cultural Theories. Anthropological and psychological studies in non-Western cultures have shown that societies vary greatly in the degree to which prosocial and cooperative behaviors are expected (Eisenberg & Fabes, 1998). How does the society people grow up in influence prosocial behavior? It has been documented that some societies provide more opportunities for learning to behave prosocially than do others, particularly by involving older children in the care of younger ones (Graves & Graves, 1983; Triandis, 1995; Whiting & Edwards, 1988). It has also been argued that the value a society places on interdependence, cooperation, and social harmony (collectivistic orientation) versus independence, competition, and individual achievement (individualistic orientation) influences children accordingly (Bronfenbrenner, 1970a; Eisenberg & Fabes, 1998; Garbarino, 1992). For example, Hindu culture emphasizes more duty-based social responsibility than American culture, which emphasizes moral, justice-based social responsibility (Miller & Bersoff, 1993). In other words, Hindus are more likely to respond prosocially out of a sense of duty or obligation, whereas Americans are more likely to do so because "it's the right or fair thing to do."

Cultural variations in children's tendencies to cooperate or compete were investigated in a classic study by Madsen and Shapira (1970), who used various games that can be played cooperatively or competitively (see Figure 12.2).

The game board is 18 inches square and has an eyelet at each corner. A string passes through each of the eyelets and is attached to a metal weight that serves as a holder for a ballpoint pen. A sheet of paper is placed on the game board for each trial so that the movement of the pen as the children pull their strings is recorded automatically.

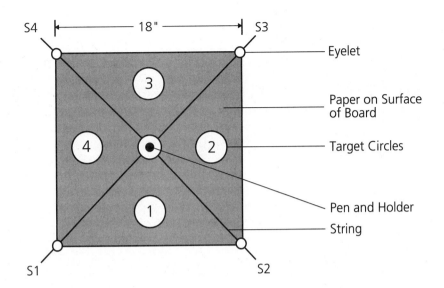

Figure 12.2

Cooperation Game Board
Source: M. C. Madsen &
A. Shapira (1970). Cooperative
and competitive behavior
of urban Afro-American,
Anglo-American, Mexican-
American, and Mexican vil-
lage children. *Developmental
Psychology* 3(1), p. 17.
Copyright © 1970 by the
American Psychological
Association. Reprinted with
permission.

In the cooperative condition, every time the pen crosses all four circles, all the players are rewarded. Thus, the more the children work together, the more they all win. In the competitive condition, each player is rewarded only when the pen crosses his or her circle. In this condition, if the children take turns helping one another, each child can win as often as any other. Some children never figure this out, however, and keep up pulling the pen in their own direction, so no one wins.

Children reared in traditional rural subcultures and small, semi-agricultural, communal settlements cooperated more readily than children reared in modern urban subcultures. For example, schoolchildren in Mexican villages and towns were found to be more cooperative than their urban, middle-class, Mexican, Mexican American, African American, and Euro-American peers (Madsen & Shapira, 1970). Similarly, Israeli children reared on a kibbutz and children from Arab villages were found to be more cooperative than Israeli urban children (Nadler, 1991; Shapira & Lomranz, 1972; Shapira & Madsen, 1974).

In these studies, if cooperation with others on the various test situations was rewarded directly (group rewards to be shared by all), children from all cultures cooperated. If, however, only individual rewards were given for performance, cultural differences showed up. Thus, the Mexican village children and those from Israeli kibbutzim continued to cooperate with each other, even in an individual reward (competitive) situation. "Let's help each other," "Let's take turns," and "Start here—go there—" were typical comments. In contrast, the middle-class and urban African American, Euro-American, Mexican American, and Israeli children tended to compete ineffectively.

Apparently, children raised in traditional rural subcultures and small, semiagricultural communal settlements (collectivistic orientation) have been socialized to have *gemeinschaft* relationships (close personal ties, concern with community members' welfare, reciprocity, readiness to lend a helping hand); children raised in urban subcultures (individualistic orientation) have been socialized to have *gesellschaft* relationships (impersonal ties, competitiveness, obligations based on contracts, behavior for personal advantage). These two types of relationships were discussed in detail in Chapter 10.

© Brian Seed/Getty Images

Children from cultures that give them early responsibility in family functioning tend to exhibit spontaneous altruism.

Cross-cultural comparisons by anthropologists Beatrice and John Whiting (1973, 1975) illustrate in natural settings some of the laboratory findings. Working in small communities in Kenya, India, the Philippines, Okinawa (Japan), Mexico, and the United States, they observed children age 3–10. The children were rated for exhibiting altruistic behavior spontaneously—offering help, which included feeding younger children and assisting in carrying out tasks; offering support, which included giving comfort and reassurance; and acting responsible, which included making helpful suggestions. They were also rated for exhibiting egoistic behavior—seeking help, seeking attention, or dominating another.

The Whitings found that the cultural variable most closely associated with altruistic behavior was the extent to which children in the various cultures were given the responsibility to perform household tasks or chores related to the family's economic security. Most of the children in Kenyan, Mexican, and Philippine cultures ranked well above the median of the total sample in terms of altruism, whereas most of the children in the other three cultures (Okinawan, Indian, and American) scored low in altruism. Presumably, in

> simpler kin-oriented societies, with economies based upon subsistence gardening, altruistic behavior is highly valued and individual egoistic achievement frowned upon. Women must work in the fields, and the children must help in order for the family to subsist. To offer help, to support others, and to be responsible are taught both by precept and practice. Being helplessly dependent, showing off, boasting, and being egoistically dominant are incompatible with such a way of life.
>
> On the other hand, in the more complex societies, where no child knows what he is going to be when he grows up, individual achievement and success must be positively valued. To help a friend sitting next to you in an examination is defined as cheating. To ask for help from specialists such as mechanics, dressmakers, shopkeepers, psychotherapists, priests, or servants is expected and paid for in cash rather than in reciprocal services. (Whiting & Whiting, 1973, p. 64)

CHILD	FAMILY	SCHOOL	PEERS	MEDIA	COMMUNITY
Genetics	Parenting style (authoritative, warm)	Instruction/set standards	Peer group pressure	Mediated discussion by adults	Simple social organization
Temperament	Communication of prosocial/ antisocial instructions	Positive/ negative consequences	Learning by doing	Values cooperation	Traditional rural setting
Age	Reinforcement/ punishment	Reinforcement/ punishment	Collaborative activities	Modeling	Extended family ties
Cognitive maturity	Modeling	Modeling	Modeling		Early assignment of tasks and responsibility to children
Perspective and role-taking ability	Assignment of responsibility	Assignment of responsibility			Individualistic/ collectivistic orientation
Empathy	Opportunities for role-playing	Opportunities for role-playing			Justice-based/ duty-based social responsibility
Moral reasoning/ judgment	Discussion	Discussion			
Situation					

Table 12.2

Variables Contributing to Prosocial Behavior

Thus, "children who . . . perform more domestic chores, help more with economic tasks and spend more time caring for their infant brothers, sisters, and cousins, score high on the altruistic versus egoistic dimension" (1973, p. 63).

Table 12.2 summarizes the variables contributing to prosocial behavior.

How Parents and Teachers Can Foster Prosocial Behavior in Young Children

1. Set an example. Exhibit helping, cooperating, and sharing behavior.
2. Preach prosocial behavior, and give reasons. Take advantage of specific situations to instruct children on how to share, be helpful, and cooperate.
3. Be warm and accepting.
4. Set firm standards of behavior that have consequences when not followed.
5. Provide role-playing opportunities for children in which they can experience others' perspectives.

6. Discuss how children's actions may affect others' feelings.
7. Provide activities that require cooperation, such as group projects.
8. Suggest specific ways in which children can be cooperative and helpful.
9. Assign meaningful responsibilities enabling children to help another person or the group.
10. Praise prosocial behavior.

Sources: Eisenberg and Murphy, 1995; Eisenberg and Mussen, 1989.

Morals

Morals encompass individuals' evaluation of what is right and wrong. They involve acceptance of rules and govern people's behavior toward others. Breaches of morals provoke consequences, as well as judgmental and emotional responses (Damon, 1988; Turiel, 1998).

Morality involves *feeling,* which includes empathy and guilt (Hoffman, 2000). Morality also involves *reasoning,* which includes the ability to understand rules, distinguish right from wrong, and take another person's perspective (Kohlberg, 1976; Piaget, 1965; Selman, 1980). Finally, morality involves *behaving,* which includes prosocial and antisocial acts (Eisenberg, 1986), as well as self-control of impulses.

Children acquire self-control over impulses from family and culture via reinforcement for obedience and sanctions for wrong-doing. They construct moral concepts from social interactions (experience in collaboration and conflict) according to their cognitive and emotional development (Turiel, 1998).

The development of morals has been of concern since the beginning of civilization. Philosophers and theologians have long debated the moral status of the newborn infant: Is the infant inherently good, bad, or neutral? The outcome of this debate has important implications for child rearing. Those who believe that children are morally good tend to be more relaxed and more permissive in their parenting styles. Those who believe that children are morally bad tend to be stricter and more authoritarian in their parenting styles in order to socialize them to be "good." Those who believe that children are morally neutral tend to place more emphasis on the interaction between parent and child because they view morals as developing from experiences of being good and bad and observing right and wrong.

People differ not only in their beliefs about the inherent nature of children but also in their beliefs about what is and what is not acceptable behavior. In other words, people's moral codes differ. Sometimes, moral codes are guided by external rules, such as parental approval, convention, or the law; other times, they are guided by internal rules, such as self-approval or self-condemnation. Moral variability does not stem solely from the influence of family, community, culture, and so on; it reflects the flexible thinking of individuals interpreting aspects of their social worlds (Turiel, 1998).

DEVELOPMENT OF A MORAL CODE

Standards of conduct and morality develop out of the necessity for people to get along with one another. Morality involves obeying society's rules for daily living, such as not stealing, not assaulting others, not maligning another's character, and so on. It also involves personal rules for interacting with others, such as being kind, cooperative, and helpful.

As children develop, their morality changes. Infants and toddlers do not distinguish right from wrong. Thus, when they conform to parental demands, it is usually because they are attached and fear loss of love. Preschoolers and school-agers consider right and wrong to be opposite ends of a spectrum, with nothing in between. They are not capable of factoring "on purpose" or "by mistake" into the judgment of wrongdoing. Adolescents begin to view right and wrong as a matter of degree. They take into account intent in judging an act.

Not only does children's development influence their moral codes, but so do intelligence, motivation, the need for approval, self-control, and the particular situation (Bandura, 1991). Most psychologists (Damon, 1988; Hoffman, 2000; Kohlberg, 1976; Piaget, 1965; Turiel, 1998) believe that children's moral codes develop through social interaction.

Piaget's Theory of Moral Development

Jean Piaget (1965) defined morality as "the understanding of and adherence to rules through one's own volition." Piaget analyzed morality from the perspective of how individuals' social experiences result in the formation of judgments about social relationships, rules, laws, and authority (Turiel, 1998). He approached the question of how individuals develop a moral code by observing and participating in children's games of marbles. He reasoned that games contain complex systems of rules that must be followed in order to play. These rules are handed down from one generation to another and are preserved solely by the respect that is felt for them by the players. Because morality consists of a system of rules, and the essence of all morality can be found in the respect individuals acquire for these rules, one can understand children's developing morality by studying their adherence to game rules.

Piaget worked with a group of Swiss schoolboys age 4–13. He asked them questions about the rules of the game: What are the rules? Where did they come from? Could they be changed? Piaget found that, for the youngest children (age 4–5), the rules were poorly understood and were not binding. For the middle group of children (age 6–9), the rules were regarded as having been made by an authority ("morality of constraint") and were therefore sacred and unchangeable. The rules were followed rigidly; any bending of the rules resulted in cries of "That isn't fair!" For the oldest group (age 10–13), rules were regarded as law emanating from mutual consent ("morality of cooperation"); the rules had to be respected if individuals wanted to be loyal to the group, but they could be changed if the majority of the group agreed.

Generally, children's moral reasoning shifts from the belief that they are subject to another's law, or external control—**heteronomous morality**—to the belief that they are subject to their own law, or internal control—**autonomous morality**. As children develop, they begin to understand that things are not totally right or totally wrong. They gradually come to see things from other perspectives and to consider the intentionality of a given act when deciding whether it is right or wrong.

Piaget examined how children reason about the wrongness of an act in terms of how much damage was done rather than whether the act was purposeful or accidental. Reading pairs of stories like the following, to children of varying ages, he asked which character in the stories was naughtier:

> A little boy who is called John is in his room. He is called to dinner. He goes into the dining room. But behind the door there was a chair, and on the chair there was a tray with fifteen cups on it. John couldn't have known that there was all this behind the door. He goes in, the door knocks against the tray, bang go the fifteen cups, and they all get broken!

> Once there was a little boy whose name was Henry. One day, waiting for a time when his mother was out, he tried to get some jam out of the cupboard. He climbed up on a chair and stretched out his arm. But the jam was too high up and he couldn't reach it and have any. But while he was trying to get it, he knocked over a cup. The cup fell down and broke. (1965, p. 122)

Piaget found that for younger children the goodness or badness of the actors in the story was related solely to the extent of the consequences. That is, they judged John to be naughtier than Henry because John had broken more cups. Older children, however, recognized the role of the intent behind the acts. Thus, they judged Henry to be naughtier than John because Henry had been purposely sneaking something whereas John merely had an accident.

Contemporary researchers have corroborated Piaget's findings when his research methods are replicated (Jose, 1990; Lapsley, 1996; Smetana, 1981). For example, young children in various cultures emphasize consequences more than intent in judging the wrongness of an act.

Kohlberg's Theory of Moral Development

Lawrence Kohlberg (1976), influenced by Piaget's work, developed a theory of moral development after 20 years of interviewing children, adolescents, and adults in different cultures. He proposed that there is no consistent relationship between parental conditions of child rearing and various measures of conscience or internalized values because morality cannot be imposed; rather, it has to be constructed as a consequence of social experiences (Turiel, 1998). Kohlberg presented his subjects with stories involving moral dilemmas and questioned them about the stories. Probably the best known is the following:

> A woman in Europe was near death from cancer. One drug might save her, a form of radium that a druggist in the same town had recently discovered. The druggist was charging $2,000, ten times what the drug cost him to make. The sick woman's husband, Heinz, went to everyone he knew to borrow money, but could get together only about half of what it cost. He told the druggist that his wife was dying and asked him to sell it cheaper or let him pay later. But the druggist said "no." The husband was desperate and broke into the man's store to steal the drug for his wife. Should the husband have done that? Why or why not? (Kohlberg, 1969, p. 379)

Clearly, there is no "right" answer to this story (or the others Kohlberg used). On the one hand, there are the husband's needs; on the other, there are the legal rights of the druggist.

Based on the reasoning behind the responses to the stories (see Table 12.3), Kohlberg concluded that there are six distinct stages, or perspectives, of moral development (see Table 12.4), which are associated with changes in individuals' intellectual development; each perspective is broader, taking into account more variables or aspects of a moral problem (Higgins, 1995). The stages begin at about age 6 and continue to adulthood. It is important to note that children and adults sometimes operate at several different stages simultaneously. Kohlberg's basic findings are as follows (cited in Lickona, 1977):

- The stages of moral reasoning are the same for all persons, regardless of culture.
- Individuals progress from one stage to the next.
- Changes from stage to stage are gradual and result from many social experiences.

	PRO	STAGE 1	CON
I. PRECONVENTIONAL LEVEL [WHAT WILL HAPPEN TO ME?]	If you let your wife die, you will get in trouble. You'll be blamed for not spending the money to save her, and there'll be an investigation of you and the druggist for your wife's death.	Action is motivated by avoidance of punishment, and "conscience" is irrational fear of punishment.	You shouldn't steal the drug: you'll be caught and sent to jail. If you do get away, your conscience will bother you, thinking how the police will catch up with you at any minute.
	PRO	**STAGE 2**	**CON**
	If you do happen to get caught, you could give the drug back, and wouldn't get much of a sentence. It wouldn't bother you much to serve a short jail term, if you have your wife when you get out.	Action motivated by desire for reward or benefit. Possible guilt reactions are ignored and punishment viewed in a pragmatic manner. (Differentiates own fear, pleasure, or pain from punishment—consequences.)	You may not get much of a jail term if you steal the drug, but your wife will probably die before you get out, so it won't do you much good. If your wife dies, you shouldn't blame yourself; it isn't your fault she has cancer.
	PRO	**STAGE 3**	**CON**
II. CONVENTIONAL LEVEL [WHAT WILL OTHERS THINK OF ME?]	No one will think you're bad if you steal the drug, but your family will think you're an inhuman husband if you don't. If you let your wife die, you'll never be able to look anybody in the face again.	Action motivated by anticipation of disapproval of others, actual or imagined-hypothetical (e.g., guilt). (Differentiation of disapproval from punishment, fear, and pain.)	It isn't just the druggist who will think you're a criminal; everyone else will, too. After you steal it, you'll feel bad thinking how you've brought dishonor on your family and yourself; you won't be able to face anyone again.
	PRO	**STAGE 4**	**CON**
	If you have any sense of honor, you won't let your wife die because you're afraid to do the only thing that will save her. You'll always feel guilty that you caused her death if you don't do your duty to her.	Action motivated by anticipation of dishonor; that is, institutionalized blame for failure of duty, and by guilt over concrete harm done to others. (Differentiates formal dishonor from informal disapproval. Differentiates guilt for bad consequences from disapproval.)	You're desperate, and you may not know you're doing wrong when you steal the drug. But you'll know you did wrong after you're punished and sent to jail. You'll always feel guilty for your dishonesty and law-breaking.

Table 12.3

Types of Moral Judgments Made in Heinz's Dilemma

Source: Nicholas J. Anastasiow. *Educational Psychology: A Contemporary View*, p. 131, 1973. CRM Books, Del Mar, California.

	PRO	**STAGE 5**	**CON**
III. POSTCONVENTIONAL LEVEL [WHAT WILL I THINK OF MYSELF?]	You'd lose other people's respect, not gain it, if you don't steal. If you let your wife die, it would be out of fear, not out of reasoning. So you'd just lose self-respect and probably the respect of others, too.	Concern about maintaining respect of equals and of the community (assuming their respect is based on reason rather than emotions). Concern about own self-respect; that is, to avoid judging self as irrational, inconsistent, nonpurposive.	You lose your standing and respect in the community and violate the law. You'd lose respect for yourself if you're carried away by emotion and forget the long-range point of view.
	PRO	**STAGE 6**	**CON**
	If you don't steal the drug and let your wife dies you'd always condemn yourself for it afterward. You wouldn't be blamed and you would have lived up to the outside rule of the law, but you wouldn't have lived up to your own standards of conscience.	Concern about self-condemnation for violating one's own principles. (Differentiates between community respect and self-respect. Differentiates between self-respect for general achieving rationality and self-respect for maintaining moral principles.)	If you stole the drug, you wouldn't be blamed by other people, but you'd condemn yourself because you wouldn't have lived up to your own conscience and standards of honesty.

Table 12.3 *Continued*

- Some individuals move more rapidly than others through the sequence of stages. Some advance further than others—for example, only 25 percent of U.S. adults were found to reason at stage 5 (principled morality).
- Although the particular stage of moral reasoning is not the only factor affecting people's moral conduct, the way they reason does influence how they actually behave in a moral situation.
- Experiences that provide opportunities for role taking (assuming the viewpoints of others, putting oneself in another's place) foster progress through the stages. For example, children who participate in many peer relationships tend to be at more advanced moral stages than children whose peer interaction is low. Within the family, children whose parents encourage them to express their views and participate in family decisions reason at higher moral stages than children whose parents do not encourage these behaviors.

In sum, at the **preconventional level,** the individuals seems to be motivated by the personal consequences of the behavior—How will I be affected? Preconventional moral reasoning focuses on individual results. At the **conventional level,** the individual can look beyond personal consequences and consider others' perspectives—What will they think of me? Conventional moral reasoning focuses on upholding the rules of society. At the **postconventional level,** the individual considers and weighs the values behind various consequences from various points of view—How would I respect myself if I . . . ? Postconventional moral

LEVEL AND STAGE	WHAT IS RIGHT	REASONS FOR DOING RIGHT	SOCIAL PERSPECTIVE OF STAGE
Level I. Preconventional Stage 1: Heteronomous morality	To avoid breaking rules backed by punishment, obedience for its own sake, and avoiding physical damage to persons and property.	Avoidance of punishment, and the superior power of authorities.	Egocentric point of view. Doesn't consider the interests of others or recognize that they differ from the actor's; doesn't relate two points of view. Actions are considered physically rather than in terms of psychological interests of others. Confusion of authority's perspective with one's own.
Stage 2: Individualism, instrumental purpose, and exchange	Following rules only when it is to someone's immediate interest; acting to meet one's own interests and needs and letting others do the same. Right is also what's fair, what's an equal exchange, a deal, an agreement.	To serve one's own needs or interests in a world where you have to recognize that other people have their interests, too.	Concrete individualistic perspective. Aware that everybody has his or her own interest to pursue and that these interests conflict, so that right is relative (in the concrete individualistic sense).
Level II. Conventional Stage 3: Mutual interpersonal expectations, relationships, and interpersonal conformity	Living up to what is expected by people close to you or what people generally expect of your role as son, brother, friend, etc. "Being good" is important and means having good motives, showing concern about others. It also means keeping mutual relationships, such as trust, loyalty, respect, and gratitude.	The need to be a good person in your own eyes and those of others. Your caring for others. Belief in the Golden Rule. Desire to maintain rules and authority, which support stereotypical good behavior.	Perspective of the individual in relationships with other individuals. Aware of shared feelings, agreements, and expectations, which take primacy over individual interests. Relates points of view through the concrete Golden Rule, putting oneself in the other person's shoes. Does not yet consider generalized system perspective.
Stage 4: Social system and conscience	Fulfilling the actual duties to which you have agreed. Laws are to be upheld except in extreme cases where they conflict with other fixed social duties. Right is also contributing to society, the group, or institution.	To keep the institution going as a whole, to avoid the breakdown in the system "if everyone did it," or the imperative of conscience to meet one's defined obligations (easily confused with stage 3 belief in rules and authority).	Differentiates societal point of view from interpersonal agreement or motives. Takes the point of view of the system that defines roles and rules. Considers individual relations in terms of place in the system.

Table 12.4

Stages of Moral Development

Source: "Moral Stages and Moralization," by Lawrence Kohlberg, from *Moral Development and Behavior,* edited by T. Lickona, copyright © 1976 by Holt, Rinehart and Winston, Inc., reprinted by permission of the author and publisher.

LEVEL AND STAGE	WHAT IS RIGHT	REASONS FOR DOING RIGHT	SOCIAL PERSPECTIVE OF STAGE
Level III. Postconventional, or Principled Stage 5: Social contract or utility and individual rights	Being aware that people hold a variety of values and opinions, that most values and rules are relative to your group. These relative rules should usually be upheld, however, in the interest of impartiality and because they are the social contract. Some nonrelative values and rights like *life* and *liberty,* however, must be upheld in any society and regardless of majority opinion.	A sense of obligation to law because of one's social contract to make and abide by laws for the welfare of all and for the protection of all people's rights. A feeling of contractual commitment, freely entered upon, to family, friendship, trust, and work obligations. Concern that laws and duties be based on rational calculation of overall utility, "the greatest good for the greatest number."	*Perspective independent of formal rules.* Perspective of a rational individual aware of values and rights (such as fairness) prior to social attachments and legal contracts. Integrates perspectives by formal mechanisms of agreement, legal contract, objective impartiality, and due process. Considers moral and legal points of view; recognizes that these sometimes conflict and finds it difficult to integrate them.
Stage 6: Universal ethical principles	Following self-chosen ethical principles. Particular laws or social agreements are usually valid because they rest upon such principles. When laws violate these principles, one acts in accordance with the principle. Principles are universal principles of justice: the equality of human rights and respect for the dignity of human beings as individual persons.	The belief as a rational person in the validity of universal moral principles, and a sense of personal commitment to them.	*Perspective of a moral point of view from which social arrangements derive.* Perspective is that of any rational individual recognizing the nature of morality or the fact that persons are ends in themselves and must be treated as such.

Table 12.4 *Continued*

reasoning considers principles that may be more important than upholding society's rules or laws.

For example, a current law in the United States is that all 18- to 25-year-old male citizens and resident male aliens living in the United States must register with the Selective Service. The rationale behind this rule is that, if our country needs men for military service, these men could be called. A postconventional-level individual, who is generally a law-abiding citizen, may choose not to register because it violates his moral code, according to which only volunteers should be called for service; no one should be forced to fight.

Kohlberg (1976, 1986) believed that most children under age 9 are at the preconventional level of moral development (stages 1 and 2). Some preadolescents also score at this level. Most adolescents, and adults, reason at the conventional level (stages 3 and 4) when faced with moral dilemmas. A small percentage of older adolescents may reach the postconventional level (stages 5 and 6). Only a minority of adults are at the postconventional level. Because of the idealistic nature of stage 6 reasoning, it was removed from the Kohlberg moral judgment scoring manual, but it is still considered to be important as a hypothetical construct (Colby & Kohlberg, 1987).

Kohlberg's stage theory of moral development has been criticized by some investigators even though his work has had significant influence on subsequent research (Turiel, 1998). One area of criticism is that the link between moral reasoning and moral behavior is not as strong as Kohlberg's theory would predict (Thoma, Rest, & Davidson, 1991). An individual's moral code consists of both moral reasoning (how one believes one should behave in a certain situation) and moral behavior (how one actually does behave in a certain situation). For some individuals, there is a difference between the two (Hartshorne & May, 1928; Kurtines & Gewirtz, 1991). When people think about real-life moral problems, they tend to rank at a lower stage than they do on hypothetical problems (Turiel, 1998).

Another area of the criticism focuses on Kohlberg's cultural bias toward the Western perspective (individualistic) of morality, justice, or fairness. Studies comparing moral concepts in different cultures (Shweder, Mahapatra, & Miller, 1987) have demonstrated that culture defines morality for children. In collectivistic cultures, what is best or the most "right" may involve putting family obligations or honor above what might be fairer to the individual. For example, Hindu children believe that it is more "wrong" to get a haircut on the day of one's father's funeral than for a husband to beat his wife for going to the movies without permission. Family honor is regarded as morally superior to an individual's painful punishment for disobedience.

Still another area of criticism is gender bias, in that Kohlberg's original sample was all male. According to Gilligan (1982), the differences in the responses of females compared with those of the original male sample shed some doubt on the applicability of Kohlberg's delineated stages of moral reasoning to all human development. Others disagree, citing that in real-life dilemmas, as opposed to hypothetical ones, the moral reasoning of males and females is similar even though females cite relationship and caring issues more often (Turiel, 1998; Walker, 1991).

Gilligan (1982, 1985) also argued that Kohlberg's theory views morality only from the perspective of justice. The **justice moral perspective** (individualistic) emphasizes the rights of the individual. When rights of individuals conflict, equitable rules of justice must prevail. Cultures with an individualistic orientation exhibit just such a moral perspective. According to Gilligan, a perspective of morality that is not given significance by Kohlberg is that of care. The **care moral perspective** (collectivistic) sees people in terms of their connectedness with others. In other words, the welfare of others is intrinsically connected to people's own welfare. People share in each other's fortunes and misfortunes and must accept responsibility for one another's care. Various cultures around the world that have a collective orientation socialize children to have a care moral perspective. For example, children and adolescents growing up in India give priority to interpersonal relationships in moral conflict situations, whereas most children and adolescents growing up in the United States give priority to individual rights (Miller & Bersoff, 1993).

Gilligan (1982) related examples of boys' and girls' reasoning regarding the Heinz dilemma, such as the following:

Jake: For one thing, human life is worth more than money, and if the druggist only makes $1,000 he is still going to live; but if Heinz doesn't steal the drug, his wife is going to die. (Why is life worth more than money?) Because the druggist can get $1,000 later from rich people with cancer, but Heinz can't get his wife again.

Amy: Well, I don't think so. I think there might be other ways besides stealing it, like if he could borrow the money or get a loan or something, but he really shouldn't steal the drug—but his wife shouldn't die either. (Why shouldn't he steal the drug?) If he stole the drug, he might save his wife then, but if he did, he might have to go to jail, and then his wife might get sicker again, and he couldn't get more of the drug, and it might not be good. So, they should really just talk it out and find some other way to make the money. (pp. 26–28)

In these examples, Jake's sense that people sometimes must act on their own, even in opposition to others if they are to do the right thing, is contrasted to Amy's assumption that people can work out their problems by "talking it out." Because Amy sees the social world as a network of relationships, she believes that the solution to the problem lies in making Heinz's wife's condition known to all concerned, especially the druggist. Surely, then, the people will work out a solution that will be responsive to the wife's needs. Jake, however, assumes no such consensus among those involved in the dilemma. Therefore, he believes that Heinz may need to take the law into his own hands if he is to protect his rights. Jake concludes that Heinz's wife is a legitimate part of Heinz's rights by logically calculating the unique value of the wife's life as compared with the money the druggist can get for the drug from others (Damon, 1988).

Despite the criticisms, Kohlberg's model of moral development has stood the test of time. Most psychologists agree that morality, no matter which perspective one takes, is developmental; that is, children universally progress through stages of understanding, and even though the timing of the progression and the highest stage reached are individual, the sequence of the stages is the same. "Debates now center on the roles of emotions and judgments, on the individual and the collectivity, on the contributions of constructions of moral understandings and culturally based meanings, and on how to distinguish between universally applicable and locally based moralties" (Turiel, 1998, p. 868).

INFLUENCES ON MORAL DEVELOPMENT

Situational Contexts

The situation or context an individual is in often influences actual moral behavior. Situational factors include the nature of the relationship between the individual and those involved in the problem, the presence of others, previous experience in similar situations, and the value society places on various responses (Turiel, 1998). For example, killing in self-defense is condoned, whereas killing for revenge is sanctioned.

The relation between moral reasoning and moral behavior is not always clear. People may believe in honesty and feel that individuals who cheat on tests should be punished, yet those same people may cheat on their income tax returns. One classic study (Krebs, 1967) found that in a sample of sixth-graders the behavior of resisting temptation was related to children's stage of moral development, as delineated by Kohlberg. However, another study of a group of 7- to 11-year-olds found no relation between moral reasoning (based on intentionality and justice) and the individual child's behavior when resisting temptation in a laboratory situation (Grinder, 1964).

Turiel (1983, 1998) explains that the inconsistencies exhibited in individuals' moral reasoning are influenced by whether they judge the situation to be a "moral" or a "conventional" situation. According to Turiel, a *moral* situation involves other people's rights or welfare being affected (you cannot hit other people); a *conventional* situation involves rules promoting appropriate behavior in a social group (you must not interrupt when someone else is talking).

Smetana (1981, 1985, 1989) found that even 2½- to 3-year-olds distinguish between moral and conventional rules. Young children view moral transgressions, such as hitting, stealing, and refusing to share, as more serious and deserving of punishment than not saying "please" or forgetting to put away a toy. Thus, young children seem to have a greater understanding of rules in different situations than Piaget originally assumed.

Different cultures define moral and social conventional rules differently, depending on whether the culture has an individualistic or a collectivistic orientation (Shweder, Mahapatra, & Miller, 1987).

Temperament, Self-Control, and Self-Esteem

Moral development may be affected by an individual's temperament (the innate characteristics that determine an individual's sensitivity to various experiences and responsiveness to patterns of social interaction), level of self-control (the ability to regulate one's impulses, behavior, and/or emotions), and self-esteem (one's regard for or opinion of oneself).

Kochanska's (1993, 1995, 1997) studies on children's temperament (inhibited or shy, impulsive or aggressive) and conscience development led him to conclude that children's temperaments can affect parenting methods. For example, maternal reasoning, polite requests, suggestions, and distractions predicted internalized conscience development in inhibited 2- and 3-year-olds, but not in impulsive children. Impulsive children were found to comply with directives when they had a secure attachment; power assertion resulted in anger and defiance. The method, then, to internalize morals for such children is to maintain the affection of the parent.

Additionally, moral development may be related to self-control. Some studies (Mischel, 1974; Mischel, Shoda, & Peake, 1988) have shown that preschool children who exhibit self-control by deferring immediate gratification are also more successful than their more impulsive age mates in resisting the temptation to cheat at experimental games. Also, 10 years later, these self-controlled preschoolers were rated by adults as more competent and socially responsible, because children who can delay gratification can have time to asesses social cues and thus enable positive peer group functioning (Gronau & Waas, 1997).

Finally, moral development may also be influenced by self-esteem—specifically, the extent to which an individual needs approval from others (Hogan & Emler, 1995). For example, a longitudinal study (Dobkin, Tremblay, Masse, & Vitaro, 1995) showed that the need to receive approval from others was negatively correlated with the level of moral behavior. Specifically, the greater the dependency on others for esteem, the more likely a person is to abuse substances and engage in antisocial acts. At the same time, the need for self-approval and feelings of competence was positively correlated with the level of moral behavior and consequent avoidance of drugs.

Age, Intelligence, Social Factors, and Emotions

Kohlberg and his colleagues (Colby, Kohlberg, Gibbs, & Lieberman, 1983) reported data from a 20-year longitudinal study of moral judgment in boys age 10, 13, and 16 when first assessed. The data supported the theory that moral reasoning is significantly linked with age, IQ, education, and socioeconomic status. It also showed that a majority of individuals did not reach stage 4 until early adulthood. In addition, the data indicated no distinction between individuals at stages 5 and 6, using available assessment techniques.

The critical thinking and discussion common in college classes promotes advanced moral reasoning, probably because college provides exposure to diverse views (Mason & Gibbs, 1993).

Several researchers (Walker & Taylor, 1991; Youniss, 1981) believe that moral codes develop through social interaction—through discussion, debate, and emergence of consensus. This may explain why people who grow up in democratic societies, whose existence depends on consensus among the majority, score at Kohlberg's higher levels (Bronfenbrenner & Garbarino, 1976; Miller, 1995).

Kagan (1984) suggested that the morality of most persons is directed more by emotions than by reasoning. Avoidance of unpleasant feelings and achievement of pleasant feelings are the major motivations for morality. Unpleasant feelings include fear of punishment, social disapproval, and failure, as well as guilt and uncertainty. Pleasant feelings include affection, pride, sense of belonging, and contribution.

Family

The family is a social system and so has rules of conduct in order that its members get along. Many of these rules are similar to those of society at large—for example, prohibitions against lying, stealing, aggression, and disorderly conduct. In both family and society, misbehavior is discouraged through sanctions such as disapproval and punishment; good behavior is encouraged through approval. The goal is for children to develop a **conscience**—the "cognitive and affective processes which constitute an internalized moral governor over an individual's conduct" (Aronfreed, 1968).

Although Kohlberg rejected the role of parents in children's construction of morality, Damon (1988) argued that, because parents first introduce children to the laws and logic of a social system, they are a crucial ingredient in the children's moral development. The child-rearing methods that parents implement have an impact on the moral development of children. Several investigations found that parents who discuss various issues with their children, such as the Heinz story, and the values behind such issues, tend to promote more advanced moral thought (Walker & Taylor, 1991).

Other researchers (Eisenberg & Murphy, 1995; Hoffman, 1970, 1983; Hoffman & Saltzstein, 1967) have found that children of parents who are punitive tend to have externally focused consciences (a description that generally corresponds to Kohlberg's stages 1–3). These children are "good" in order to receive praise, avoid punishment, or please others. Children of parents who are warm and affectionate tend to have internally focused consciences (generally corresponding to Kohlberg's stages 4–6). These children are "good" in order to fulfill their duty or conform to their own standards. Internally focused consciences can be conventional (tradition-oriented) and rigid, or humanistic (person-oriented) and flexible. A humanistic conscience develops when parents not only are affectionate but also use induction as a socializing technique—they explain the reasons for their demands and discuss the impact of the children's actions on others.

Hoffman and Saltzstein (1967), in a classic study, identified three kinds of parental discipline techniques that are related to conscience development: power assertion, love withdrawal, and induction. In one study, the researchers asked seventh-graders (matched for intelligence and social class) which method of discipline their parents ordinarily used. They also asked the parents which method of discipline they had used when their child was 5 years old. The children were rated for conscience development along several dimensions: (1) severity of guilt, as expressed in story completions; (2) acceptance of responsibility for wrongdoing, as judged by teachers; (3) tendency to confess misdeeds, as reported by mothers; (4) evaluation of right and wrong independent of rewards and punishment, as reported by mothers; and (5) consideration for other children, as judged by classmates. Results showed that discipline by power assertion was associated with low ratings on conscience development; discipline by induction was associated with high conscience ratings; and discipline by love withdrawal was not significantly associated with conscience development.

More recent studies have also demonstrated the relationship between parental socialization methods and moral development. For example, one study (Kochanska, 1991) found that mothers who deemphasized power strategies when trying to get their toddlers to comply with their rules had children who, when studied 6 years later, had more internally focused consciences. Another study (Kuczynski, Kochanska, Radke-Yarrow, & Girnius-Brown, 1987) found that mothers who used strategies of direct control were associated with children who used strategies of direct defiance, whereas mothers who used negotiations had children more likely to use negotiations. Thus, children seem to model parental socialization methods related to moral development.

It must, however, be kept in mind that moral reasoning is a complicated process involving perceptions, emotions, desires, and judgment. Even though children's earliest social interactions occur in the family, influencing moral development, these biologically influenced cognitive factors are significant (Turiel, 1998).

Peers

Reciprocity is a fundamental ingredient of all human interchange—"Do unto others as you would have them do unto you." Reciprocity is learned by doing through social interaction: I say something, you answer; I smile, you smile back; I grab your toy, you hit me; I share my cookies with you, you play with me.

Kohlberg (1976, 1985) and others (Damon, 1988; Saltzstein, 1976) have suggested that social interaction, especially the opportunities to take the role of another person and to generate rules democratically, can enhance moral development. Children who have more opportunities for participation in the family, peer groups, and social settings may develop faster in terms of moral thought and behavior than children who lack these supports. For example, children who grew up on an Israeli kibbutz—with its intense peer group interaction, opportunities for shared decision making, and cooperative work responsibilities—typically reached stage 4 or 5 in adolescence. In contrast, children who were reared in settings in which there was limited social exchange were often still at stage 1 or 2, even in late adolescence

(Kruger, 1992; Lickona, 1977). Direct training in role taking may even induce people to advance in Kohlberg's developmental stages (Saltzstein, 1975).

Social conflicts between peers are a source of moral development (Killen & Nucci, 1995). Conflicts can stimulate children to take different points of view in order to restore balance in social situations, to consider the rights of others, and to coordinate others' needs with those of the self. Did you ever have to compromise in a disagreement with a friend in order to preserve the friendship?

School

Schools influence moral development through their education programs and their staff (Kohlberg, 1985; Sadker & Sadker, 2003). Because, according to Piaget, moral development begins with the understanding and acceptance of rules, it will be useful to examine the relationship of teaching styles to classroom rules and moral development.

All programs have rules. The purpose of rules in the classroom is to ensure an optimal learning environment. If learning is to take place, students cannot interfere with one another or with the teacher. Students must respect and cooperate with one another when differences arise; they must learn how to compromise.

As has been discussed, traditional programs tend to emphasize rigid adherence to rules regarding behavior, interpersonal relationships, and manners. Teachers who implement traditional programs tend to be authoritarian in that they make the rules and dole out the rewards and consequences. Modern programs also have rules, but they usually are more flexible. Teachers who implement modern programs tend to be authoritative in that they include students in the process of making rules. Damon (1988, 1999) believes that, for teachers to enhance children's moral development, they need to guide children in moral reasoning, provide positive role models, and involve them in group discussions for decision making, social interaction, and perspective taking. For example, one 4-year study (Higgins, 1995) demonstrated that students in a modern, or democratic, high school were more advanced in moral reasoning than students in a traditional, or autocratic, high school. But what do authoritative teachers specifically do to enhance moral development?

Reasoning. Whether the rules emanate from sources external or internal to the individual child, how the teacher communicates the rules, keeping in mind children's cognitive development, can have an impact on their moral development. Consider the teacher who says, "You can't go out to recess until all your materials are put away," versus the teacher who says, "Here, let's put your materials away so that no one will step on them and get hurt." The first teacher is merely parroting a rule, whereas the second teacher is giving the child the reasoning behind the rule. The first teacher may get compliance but will not be fostering moral development; the second teacher will.

Modeling. Teachers create the atmosphere for modeling responses. Research has shown that modeling has a positive effect on moral development (Bandura, 1991, 2000). There is no comparable substitute for a teacher who models compassion, honesty, altruism, and justice. The teacher who encourages children to share yet, when asked for a certain book by another teacher says, "No, I'm sorry; we are going to use it later," and then does not, is not being an effective model. In contrast, the teacher who says, "Let's see this film now (recess time), so Mr. Johnson's class will still have time to see it today, and I'll take you out to recess after the film," is being an effective model for cooperative behavior.

Group Discussions. Certain activities incorporated into classroom programs have been found to foster moral development. For example, research (Higgins, 1995; Kohlberg, 1985; Lickona, 1991, Sadker & Sadker, 2003) has indicated that group discussions on moral issues can raise levels of moral reasoning. Group discussions can deal with various problems in the classroom, such as how certain transgressions (fighting, taking other people's things, tattling) should be handled. Or they can involve planning a group project. Such group projects tend to reduce egocentrism and foster cooperation because an opportunity is provided for everyone to listen to everyone else, and everyone can make a contribution. Many teachers use the team approach for group projects. For example, suppose a group of children on a team has to present an animal project to the class. One child might record the information from books, another illustrate it, another write a poem about it, and another organize and narrate the information to the class. The children choose their jobs and help each other, so the project represents their best team effort.

Still another group discussion technique that enhances moral development is the presentation of moral dilemmas to the class. The following is an example for middle-years children:

> Joe's father promised he could go to camp if he earned the $50 to pay for it, but
> he changed his mind and instead asked Joe to give him the money he had earned.
> Joe lied and said he had only earned $10 (which he gave to his father). He
> then went to camp using the other $40 he had made. Before he went, he told
> his younger brother, Alex, about lying to his father. Should Alex tell their father?
> Why or why not? (Good & Brophy, 1986, p. 121)

The significance for moral development is not in the answers but in the reasoning behind them. Dilemmas should be related to students' levels of cognitive development and interest. Discussions revolving around such dilemmas help students clarify their values, make choices, and understand the consequences of their choices. Hearing what others say also broadens their perspective and increases their alternatives.

As mentioned previously, perspective taking—giving children roles to play and discussing them—has been found to enhance moral development (Gibbs, 1995; Sadker & Sadker, 2003 Staub, 1971). Through role-playing, children learn to view events from a variety of viewpoints. They learn what it feels like to be helpless, to be helped, and to be the helper. For example, how would you feel if you lost your dog? How would you feel if it were returned to you? How would you feel if you returned a lost dog to someone else?

Kohlberg suggests that teachers ask students questions about moral issues and listen to their explanations in order to gain insight into their levels of moral thought. He has found that discussions that are one stage above individuals' present level of moral reasoning are most effective in this regard. Finally, Kohlberg urges teachers to deal with situations posing broad problems and issues, rather than focus too much on discussions involving specific classroom rules and routines, because these specifics cannot be generalized (Kohlberg, 1980, 1985; Lickona, 1977, 1991).

How Teachers Can Promote Moral Growth in the Classroom

1. Build a sense of community in the classroom so that students learn together in an atmosphere of respect and security.
2. Provide opportunities for the children to have a voice in establishing the rules of the classroom and the consequences for not following them.
3. Give reasons for consequences, stressing where possible the effect of the individual child's actions on the group.
4. Discuss the differences between rules for the good order of the school and rules affecting justice and human relations.
5. Provide opportunities for collaborative peer group work.
6. In stories and discussions of everyday experiences, help the children to consider the feelings of other persons, real or fictional.
7. Role-play experiences from events in daily life that lead to disappointments, tensions, fights, and joys in order to provide opportunities for the students to see things from perspectives other than their own.
8. Discuss concepts of fairness and unfairness.
9. Using stories, literature, history, current events and/or films, stimulate discussions that will provoke higher-stage reasoning.
10. Be a role model and point out other role models as they occur in classroom activities.

Sources: Duska and Whelan, 1975; Higgins, 1995.

Mass Media

As has been discussed, television is a significant socializing agent. Does it affect moral behavior? Some critics believe that TV and other popular media have helped create a large number of people who think it's perfectly OK to grab what they want and to do what they want, and the only bad thing is getting caught.

In a study of television and the moral judgment of young children, kindergartners who were heavy TV viewers (based on a television diary kept by their mothers) were found to exhibit less advanced moral reasoning than children who watched little TV (Rosenkoetter, Huston, & Wright, 1990).

Television may contribute to disruption of moral behavior. Specific programs have been followed by antisocial acts modeling the behavior shown on TV (Levin, 1998). Examples include various school shootings following news coverage of the Columbine High School massacre in Littleton, Colorado; or the 5-year-old boy who set fire to his home, killing his 2-year-old sister, following a similar episode on *Beavis and Butt-head;* or the 13-year-old boy and his friend who were acting out the Russian roulette scene from the movie *The Deer Hunter* with a real gun (the boy died instantly).

The National Television Violence Study concluded that not only does violence pervade TV but also involves repeated acts of aggression against victims that go unpunished (Mediascope, 1996). Huesmann (1986) proposed that such repetition results in a cumulative learning process, with specific effects on short- and long-term behavior. One effect is that children learn new ways of aggressing by watching aggressive models. Another is that socialized restraints on aggressive impulses are weakened because many violent acts are performed by heroes and are rationalized in the story context as "good triumphing over evil." The message conveyed, then, is that aggression is an appropriate tool for those who believe they are in the right (Coie & Dodge, 1998). A third effect of viewing violence is **desensitization—** reduced emotional responsiveness. A fourth effect is that the observers' sense of reality is altered. Compared with infrequent ones, frequent viewers believe that real-world violence is more common, that the world is less safe, that group stereotypes are more valid, and that their chances of being victimized are greater (Coie & Dodge, 1998).

Because young children attend primarily to the consequences of acts and not intentions, they are unlikely to understand moral messages of programs, even when these are explicit. When children identify with televised models, they copy the observed behavior and accept the models' attitudes. It has been demonstrated that children's aggressiveness increases after being exposed to an aggressive model and that their altruism increases after being exposed to altruistic models (Perse, 2001). Thus, the particular moral behavior children are exposed to on television is likely to influence their own moral behavior. For example, what are the effects on children of observing rule breaking on television? According to the research literature, observational learning can play a potent role in shaping responses to situations in which breaking an established rule will bring immediate gratifications or benefits to the transgressor. It has been demonstrated that children exposed to a model who breaks an established rule will break rules more often in the absence of an adult than will those who have not been exposed to such an example. At the same time, it has also been established that children who have been exposed to a model who adheres to established rules are more likely to adhere to rules, even when they are highly tempted not to and when their transgression will not be detected (Bandura, 1991; Leibert & Poulos, 1976).

Community

As the writer William Somerset Maugham said, "Conscience is the guardian in the individual of the rules which the community has evolved for its own preservation." Some psychologists (Damon, 1988; Miller & Bersoff, 1993; Shweder, Mehapatra, & Miller, 1987; Turiel, 1998) believe that moral development is influenced by the cultural ideology in the community. For example, as discussed in other chapters, cultural ideology can be oriented toward individualism or collectivism. Individualistic cultures emphasize rights and justice, whereas collectivistic cultures emphasize duties and obligations. These different ideologies influence values and morals in that community members judge behavior accordingly. Individualistic cultures value personal goals; collectivistic cultures value shared goals. Moral concepts in individualistic communities are interpreted in terms of independence, autonomy, self-reliance, and individual rights; in collectivistic communities, they are interpreted in terms of interdependence, conformity, duty, obedience toward authority, tradition, and social harmony. In moral dilemmas, individualistic communities judge whose rights have been violated; collectivistic communities judge what obligations were not fulfilled (Turiel, 1998).

The interaction of the socializing agents in a culture and individuals' levels of intellectual development and motivation determine the levels of moral development. Bronfenbrenner and Garbarino (1976) described three developmental levels of morality that are similar for individuals in all cultures:

- *Level 1: Amoral.* The motivation is basically to seek pleasure and avoid pain. The only moral judgment involved is self-interest. This level of morality is quite normal for very young children, but when it persists into adolescence or adulthood, it is considered to be deviant behavior for the individual and hazardous for the society in which he or she lives (corresponding to Kohlberg's stages 1 and 2).

- *Level 2: System of social agents.* The motivation comes from allegiance to others, either to certain individuals or to groups. The individual behaves in such a way as to gain approval (corresponding to Kohlberg's stages 3 and 4).
- *Level 3: Values and ideas.* The motivation is personal principles. The individual has her or his own system of beliefs and does not depend on other socializing agents for direction (corresponding to Kohlberg's stages 5 and 6).

According to Bronfenbrenner and Garbarino (1976), individuals who attain level 3 have had experiences in which abstract thinking, speculation, and decision making were supported. For these experiences to take place, people need to have some competitive allegiances that create enough tension within themselves to stimulate thought about loyalties and critical behavior. In other words, when people are exposed to a variety of settings and social agents representing different expectations and moral sanctions, inner conflict results. This conflict causes them to look within themselves for moral convictions with which they are comfortable. In contrast, individuals who are exposed to a single setting are exposed to only one set of rules. Because they do not experience conflict, they need not look within themselves for resolution.

Support for Bronfenbrenner's (1970b) theory comes from his findings of differential moral judgments between Russian boarding school students and day school students. The boarding school students, who were exposed to a single socializing agent (school), made moral judgments that were more authority-oriented than those made by the day school students, who were exposed to multiple socializing agents (school, parents, peers). The students were asked to respond to various moral dilemmas, such as the following:

> You and your friends accidentally find a sheet of paper the teacher lost. On this sheet are the questions and answers for a quiz that you are going to have tomorrow. Some of the kids suggest that you do not say anything to the teacher about it, so that all of you can get better marks. What would you really do? Suppose your friends decided to go ahead and keep the paper. Would you go along with them or refuse? (Absolutely certain, fairly certain, I guess so.)

Other moral dilemmas included going to a movie recommended by friends but disapproved of by parents, neglecting homework to be with friends, and accidentally breaking a window and running away.

This moral dilemma test was used by Bronfenbrenner and Garbarino (1976) on groups of 12-year-old boys and girls in 13 different societies, to find out if being exposed to **pluralism**—the existence of more than one belief system—was related to the development of level-3 moral judgment. The 13 societies were ranked on pluralism. Children growing up in the 1970s in countries that ranked high on pluralism, such as the United States and West Germany, were less authority-oriented and had more ideas about moral dilemmas than children growing up in the countries that ranked low on pluralism, such as Poland and Hungary. Thus, cultures that allow individual freedom and in which diversity is common produce children who are likely to have had experiences that stimulate abstract thinking, speculation, and decision making. These experiences occur because of the existence of differing socializing agents competing for individuals' allegiances. They have to make some personal choices, and the process of choosing (values clarification) leads to the development of moral judgment characteristic of level three.

Bronfenbrenner and Garbarino (1976) explained that experiences involving exposure to various socializing agents do not occur in many cultures, and that is why cross-cultural comparisons of levels of moral development show differences among same-aged individuals. Pluralistic societies have many socializing agents with differing values, and so are more likely to produce individuals with level-3 moral judgment. In contrast, monolithic societies have socializing agents with a singular value system and so are less likely to do so. Pluralism per se is no guarantee that individuals will be motivated to attain level-3 moral judgment. There must be integration or a common goal between the individual and the various socializing agents for the conflict over allegiance to occur. For example, a common goal of socializing agents in the United States is achievement. Thus, parents urge children to work hard and do their best, teachers motivate achievement with grades, and teammates cheer the kid who hits a home run.

Occasionally, however, these socializing agents compete for individuals' loyalty—as, for instance, when team practice conflicts with plans to study for a test. Which socializing agent gets loyalty then? When there is no common goal, conflict does not occur. For example, suppose that a child comes home from school, his mother asks him to empty the trash, but he has already promised his friend that he will come over to his house after school to work on a school project. There is no competition between socializing agents for his loyalty because he can easily accomplish both activities.

Other research supports the theory that the more socializing agents individuals are exposed to that have a common goal, yet sometimes compete for allegiance, the more likely they are to have level-3 moral judgment. For example, studies of high school students have found that their stage of moral reasoning is positively related to the quantity and quality of their social participation (school clubs, friendship groups, leadership roles), whether judged by teachers, peers, or themselves (Turiel, 1998). For another example, 14- and 17-year old Finnish adolescents who experienced Western-style individualistic educational practices exhibited more internal moral reasoning than adolescents of the same age who grew up in Estonia during the period of Soviet socialism, with its collectivistic educational practices (Keltikangas-Järvinen, Terav, & Pakaslahti, 1999).

In conclusion, moral development is socially constructed (Davidson & Youniss, 1995). It reflects individuals' schemes of personal and societal values, which include a coordination of emotions, thoughts, and actions (Turiel, 1998). If a person acts exclusively on personal values, he or she may too often overlook the rights and privileges of others in the social environment. To illustrate, in the example discussed in

Stereotyped gender-role behavior is exemplified by these girls playing in the housekeeping corner of a classroom.

Chapter 11, Tammy overlooked her parents' liability if they broke the law and allowed her to have a party with alcohol because she was more concerned with her peers. But if a person acts exclusively on societal values or social convention, contract, or laws, she or he may fail to see how they can unjustly affect a given individual. For example, Tammy's parents did not fully understand her belief that she had to fulfill the expectations of her peers because they were more concerned with their own responsibilities.

Thus, mature moral development—which is influenced by people's capacity to anticipate the future, to predict consequences, and to put themselves in another's place, along with their level of self-esteem—is the ability to make rational decisions that balance their own personal value system with the value system of society.

Gender Roles

The following English nursery rhyme, from the early 1800s, illustrates how gender differences are perceived. Verses like these, in turn, influence how children are socialized to acquire their appropriate gender roles in society (Gould & Gould, 1962):

> *What are little boys made of?*
> *Frogs and snails*
> *And puppy dogs' tails*
> *That's what little boys are made of.*
> *What are little girls made of?*
> *Sugar and spice*
> *And all things nice*
> *That's what little girls are made of.*

A **gender role,** or sex type, refers to the qualities individuals understand to characterize males and females in their culture. It is distinct from sex, which refers to the biological aspects of being male or female. Gender role is more of a psychological construct whereas sex is more of a physical one.

DEVELOPMENT OF GENDER ROLES

Sex typing, or classification into gender roles based on biological sex, begins at birth (Maccoby, 1998, 2000; Ruble & Martin, 1998). The child is given what society considers to be a girl's name or a boy's name. (Woe to those whose names are ambiguous—they will have to cope with that for the rest of their lives. "Toby"—is that a girl's name or a boy's name?) The child is then dressed according to that classification. Certain colors are generally worn by girls, and certain ones by boys. Even though in the United States most children of both sexes wear shirts and pants, those worn by girls are usually decorated differently. And throughout childhood, the child is given certain toys for play usually classified by sex. Girls' toys are generally related to nurturing or home activities (dolls, stuffed animals, dishes); boys' toys are generally related to action or work activities (cars, trucks, tools).

Although various cultures provide a "gender curriculum" (Shaffer, 2000), children play a role in their gender socialization, perhaps driven by biological programming due to being male or female (Maccoby, 2000). For example, my granddaughter, whose mother rarely wears jewelry or make-up, has been fascinated with adorning herself ever since she saw such items in the store. Because of her interest, I polished her nails for her second birthday. Her sister, a year younger, has always been attracted to climbing on everything and loves to take toys apart and throw and kick a ball. For her second birthday, I gave her a riding car.

Theories of Gender-Role Development

There are four main theories explaining how children are socialized to assume gender roles.

Psychoanalytic Theory. This theory deals with how individuals come to *feel* like a male or female. According to Sigmund Freud (cited in Hall, 1954; Freud, 1925), children identify with the same-sex parent out of sexual love for the opposite-sex parent and fear of punishment from the same-sex parent for that love. In other words, a boy identifies with his father because he loves his mother (Oedipus complex) and is fearful that his father, who also loves his mother, will punish him for that love. A girl identifies with her mother because she loves her father (Electra complex) and is fearful that her mother, who also loves her father, will punish her for that love. In identifying with the same-sex parent, children unconsciously take on the characteristics of that parent. Thus, a boy becomes like his father so that his mother will love him as she loves his father, and a girl becomes like her mother so that her father will love her as he loves her mother. The process of gender identification occurs sometime between age 3 and 5, the phallic stage in Freud's sequence of personality development (during which the focus is on the genitals). After age 5 or 6, children enter Freud's latency stage, during which they engage in normal play activities with same-sex peers; sexuality is dormant. At puberty, children enter Freud's genital stage, at which time they normally begin to be sexually attracted to the opposite sex.

Social Learning, or Social Cognitive, Theory. This theory focuses on how individuals come to *behave* as a male or female. According to theorists Walter Mischel (1970) and Albert Bandura (1989), children behave in what are considered to be gender-appropriate ways because they are reinforced or rewarded when they do so, and punished when they do not, by the various agents of socialization. Boys identify with male models (usually their fathers) because they are rewarded for doing so: "You are strong, just like your Dad." Girls identify with female models (usually their mothers) for the same reason: "You look pretty, just like your Mom." Children choose models with whom to identify on the basis of whether the model is perceived to be like themselves, to be warm and affectionate, and to have prestige. When children identify with the same-sex parent, they incorporate that parent's behavior into their own.

Cognitive-Developmental Theory. This theory deals with how individuals come to *think* of themselves as male or female. According to Lawrence Kohlberg (1966), the assumption of gender-role behavior is part of children's total cognitive development. On the basis of their observations and interactions, children accommodate, or reconcile, the differences between the categories of male and female. Once children know and understand the concepts of maleness and femaleness (about age 5 or 6), they then assimilate the appropriate gender behavior that matches their biological sex. In other words, a boy thinks, "I am a boy; therefore, I do boy things," and a girl thinks, "I am a girl; therefore, I do girl things." What children consider to be appropriate gender behavior depends on their experiences in their family, peer group, school, and community, and their observations in the media.

Gender Schema Theory. First proposed by Sandra Bem (1981), as well as by Martin and Halverson (1981, 1987), this theory addresses how individuals come to *perceive* themselves as male or female by processing gender-linked information. A "schema" is a conceptual framework of a person's experiences and understandings. This theory explains how children code new information in terms of gender. The initial basis for coding information is the recognition of males and females as distinct gender categories. Labeling occurs about age 2–3. As children develop, they observe male and female behavior around them form schemas for what males and what females do in their society. These gender schemas influence how new information is processed in that they guide selective attention to and imitation of same-sex models. For example, suppose a girl observes her mother and her grandmother cooking, and observes her father and uncle doing repairs. About age 4–5, she can conceptualize that girls cook and that boys fix things. Because she knows she is a girl, she chooses to engage in cooking activities rather than working with tools at preschool. Thus, she gains information about cooking and rejects information about building or repairing things. By age 7–8, gender behavior is fairly rigid. Gender schema theory helps to explain why gender stereotypes are self-perpetuating and difficult to modify. It is as if children's earliest socialization experiences with gender set the course for later ones. This was demonstrated in a study of 5- to 10-year-olds who were asked to predict feminine or masculine interests of target children with certain characteristics—for example, "I know a child who likes to play with tool kits. How much would this child want to wear a dress?" Older children's responses were more gender stereotypic ("No way!") than those of younger children (Martin, Wood, & Little, 1990).

Gender schema theory also proposes that self-concept is associated with the degree to which children perceive themselves as congruent with their schemas of males or females. If their behavior matches what they interpret as being appropriate to their gender, they feel positive about themselves; if they don't conform to the stereotype, they feel negative about themselves.

GENDER-ROLE RESEARCH

Regardless of which theory or theories seem to best explain gender-role socialization, the fact remains that males and females behave differently. This was documented in a classic review by researchers Eleanor Maccoby and Carol Jacklin (1974), who analyzed over 2000 books and articles on possible psychological differences between males and females. They concluded that males are more aggressive than females, a difference that is apparent in infancy. They also concluded that girls have greater verbal ability than boys and that boys have greater visual-spatial ability than girls. These differences are more apparent in early adolescence. But Maccoby and Jacklin also discovered that some differences traditionally attributed to boys' and girls' behavior are myths. For example, girls are neither more "social" than boys nor more suggestible. Boys do not have higher achievement motivation than girls, they are not more "analytic." More recent reviews of research on gender differences have arrived at similar conclusions (Fagot, 1995; Ruble & Martin, 1998).

Maccoby and Jacklin's (1974) findings have implications for social and educational changes:

> We suggest that societies have the option of minimizing, rather than maximizing, sex differences through their socialization practices. . . . In our view, social institutions and social practices are not merely reflections of the biologically inevitable. A variety of

social institutions are viable within the framework set by biology. It is up to human beings to select those that foster the lifestyles they most value. (p. 374)

Additional research indicates that socialization practices maximize gender differences (Fagot, 1995; Ruble & Martin, 1998; Shaffer, 2000). For example, parents and significant others apply gender stereotypes to children as soon as they are born (or even in utero if the sex is known). As a result, girls and boys are channeled into sex-typed behaviors that do not necessarily reflect their individual abilities or potential (American Association of University Women, [AAUW], 1991).

Block (1984) reviewed the literature on psychological differences between the sexes, focusing on areas such as aggression, activity level, impulsivity, susceptibility to anxiety, achievement-related behaviors, self-concept, and social relationships. She concluded that differences in these areas arise from the different social contexts in which boys and girls grow up. In general, boys are given more opportunities for independent problem solving and exploration, whereas girls are more closely supervised and restricted in their experiences. According to Block, this differential socialization causes boys and girls to think differently about the world around them and to use different strategies in dealing with the world. For example, boys are more curious and competitive; girls seek approval more often and are more affiliated.

By the time children reach preschool, they know which type of behavior is expected of their sex. Several years ago, a little boy in my preschool class who was pretending to iron in the housekeeping corner was told by his friend, "Daddies don't iron!" And as children enter elementary school, their gender roles become even more restrictive (Ruble & Martin, 1998). They play with children of the same sex, thus learning "gender-appropriate" games (the boys tend to play games involving running or throwing a ball at recess; the girls tend to stay close to the teacher, talking or playing games such as jump rope or hopscotch). Because of their cognitive development, they are also becoming more aware of potential models of their sex with whom to identify.

INFLUENCES ON THE DEVELOPMENT OF GENDER ROLES

Family

Mothers and fathers treat sons and daughters differently (Fagot, 1995; Leaper, 2000). Studies have shown that parents describe their newborn sons as stronger, more coordinated, and more alert than daughters, and their newborn daughters as smaller, softer, and more fragile than sons (Huston, 1983; Rubin, Provenzano, & Luria, 1974). Fathers, in particular, engage in more rough-and-tumble play with sons and more cuddly play with daughters (Lamb, 1977; Lytton & Romney, 1991). Parents also buy different toys for their sons and daughters (O'Brien & Huston, 1985; Rheingold & Cook, 1975; Ruble & Martin, 1998). For example, males are given trucks, war toys, and sports equipment, whereas girls are given dolls, dollhouses, and books. Mothers and fathers even communicate differently to sons and daughters, using more directive and supportive language with girls than with boys (Ruble & Martin, 1998).

Throughout childhood, parents encourage males in active, gross-motor, and manipulative play, and encourage females in passive, role taking and fine-motor play, with fathers even more stereotypic than mothers (Huston, 1983; Leaper, 2000). Males are also allowed to take risks (climb trees) and are left unsupervised more often and earlier than females (Basow, 1992; Huston, 1983). Finally, parents exert more achievement and independence demands on males while providing help more readily for females (Basow, 1992; Huston, 1983; Leaper, 2000).

Through observed interactions of fathers and mothers with sons and daughters, it has repeatedly been demonstrated that fathers are the more influential gender-role socialization agent (Caldera, Huston, & O'Brien, 1989; Langlois & Downs, 1980; Ruble & Martin, 1998). For example, fathers' and mothers' reactions to pre-school children's choices of toys, both traditionally feminine (doll furniture, pots and pans) and traditionally masculine (cars, trucks, trains), were observed (Langlois & Downs, 1980; Lytton & Romney, 1991). The researchers found that fathers, more so than mothers, chose different kinds of toys for boys and girls, encouraged play that they considered gender-appropriate, and discouraged play they considered gender-inappropriate. More specifically, the fathers rewarded their children by approving, helping with, and joining in more often for play with gender-appropriate toys than for play with gender-inappropriate toys, and they discouraged play with gender-inappropriate toys more than play with gender-appropriate toys. Mothers encouraged both boys and girls to play with toys traditionally considered appropriate for girls. Mothers also tended to discourage both boys and girls from playing with "masculine" toys. The degree of differences in parental treatment of boys and girls may be influenced by age, socioeconomic status, and ethnicity (Fagot, 1995; Shaffer, 2000).

In addition, fathers engage in more physical play (tickling, wrestling, chasing, playing ball) with both sons and daughters, whereas mothers spend more time in caregiving and nurturing activities (MacDonald & Parke, 1986). Apparently, this differential interaction with children enables mothers to become more, and fathers less, sensitive to the individual needs of children (Lamb, 1986). Further, compared with mothers, fathers give more evaluative feedback of approval and disapproval (Fagot & Leinbach, 1987). Thus, fathers generally appear to be the more playful, less sensitive, more critical parent in terms of gender-role socialization. Regarding relationships within the family, warm, positive father–son and mother–daughter relationships lead to the strongest gender-role identification (Huston, 1983). Sons model their father's behavior, and daughters model their mother's. In this regard, too, studies have found that the father has more influence on gender-role development of both boys and girls (Lamb, 1986).

When mothers are employed outside the home and fathers participate in child care, fathers' nontraditional activities influence their children's attitudes about gender-role stereotypes (Ruble & Martin, 1998). Although mothers employed outside the home still perform most child care and housekeeping chores, husbands of employed wives participate more than husbands of nonemployed wives (Hoffman, 1989). Thus, children whose mothers are employed have less stereotypic role models than those whose fathers are "breadwinners" and mothers are "breadbakers" (Gardner & LeBrecque, 1986). They also receive more independent training, have generally higher career goals, and have somewhat higher achievement motivation. This is particularly true for daughters (Basow, 1992). The most likely explanation is that the mother employed outside the home presents a positive role model for achievement, especially when she is satisfied with her job and gets support for household chores and child care.

The sibling sex constellation (the birth order of sisters and brothers) influence children's gender-role socialization, especially in traditional families (McHale, Crouter, & Tucker, 1999; Rust, Golombok, Hines, Johnson, & Golding, 2000). Not only do sisters and brothers model and reinforce gender-role behavior for their younger siblings, but the differential treatment due to their sex by their parents has an impact on the younger children's gender schemas.

In sum, individual differences in sex typing are influenced by biology, culture, paternal involvement, maternal work status, sex typing of parental roles within the home, and sibling sex constellation (Serbin, Powlishta, & Gulko, 1993; Shaffer, 2000).

Peers

Peers become progressively more influential as gender-role socializing agents as children get older (Leaper, 1994; Schaffer, 2000). Peers begin to exert an influence during preschool and become increasingly important in elementary and high school. For example, peers encourage both boys and girls to play with gender-appropriate toys and actively punish (ridicule and tease) play with toys considered appropriate for the opposite gender, especially among the boys (Fagot, 1977, 1984; Martin, 1989). Children and adolescents try to do what they perceive to be "cool" to gain acceptance and status among their peers. Preadolescent boys gain status on the basis of athletic ability and toughness, whereas girls' status relates to physical appearance and social skills (Basow & Rubin, 1999; Pollack, 1999; Ruble & Martin, 1998).

Sex segregation begins in the preschool years and intensifies during the school years. This can be observed in both boys and girls cross-culturally (Maccoby & Jacklin, 1987; Whiting & Edwards, 1988). Sex-segregated play groups value different behaviors for girls and boys (Maccoby, 1998). Girls tend to enjoy mutual play and to use conflict mitigation strategies, whereas boys tend to play more roughly and competitively, using physical assertion to resolve conflicts.

One of the functions of the peer group, as discussed in Chapter 8, is to socialize children to learn appropriate sociocultural roles. Cognitively, because middle childhood is the time of concrete reasoning, it follows that children of this age have a rigid, rather than flexible, concept of gender roles. Middle-years children are most susceptible to peer influence, which means that they will be likely to adopt via modeling, reinforcement, and punishment the gender roles expected by their peers. For example, boys will be socialized to be active, aggressive, and unemotional; girls will be socialized to be passive, dependent, and compassionate. Children whose activities are regarded as gender-appropriate by the peer group are rewarded by being included in the group. Children whose activities are regarded as gender-inappropriate by the peer group are either teased or left to play alone (Thorne, 1993). "Sissy" and "tomboy" are familiar jeers heard in childhood.

The result of sex segregation is that boys and girls tend to grow up in different peer environments—in other words, different subcultures (Maccoby, 1998; Maccoby & Jacklin, 1987). Sociologists Janet Lever (1978) and Barrie Thorne (1993), in separate studies, found significant differences in the play of boys' and girls' peer groups. Lever observed fifth-grade children, mostly Euro-American and middle class, in three schools. She discovered that boys' play was more complex than girls' play on all of the following dimensions and criteria:

- Size of the group
- Role differentiation
- Player interdependence

Girls usually play in small groups and take turns.

© Myrleen F. Cate/PhotoEdit

- Explicitness of goals
- Number and specificity of rules
- Team formation

Lever (1978) observed that boys typically engage in team sports with 10–25 players, whereas girls typically played tag, jump rope, or hopscotch, usually involving two to six participants. Boys' play often involved multiple roles, whereas girls' play rarely involved role differentiation (they commonly engaged in activities in which they all played the same role, as in skating, or two roles, as in jump rope—the jumper and the turner). Boys' play involved more interdependence, which, in turn, required decision making with regard to strategies. Girls' play tended to require less interdependence, but when it did, the play was of a cooperative nature. Boys' games were found to have more elaborate rules, and interpretations and discussions often ensued. Finally, boys were involved in team play more often.

Thorne (1993), who observed kindergarteners to sixth-graders, found the boys' play to be generally characterized by larger groups, less proximity to adults, more public play, more fighting and physical contact, more dominance attempts, and establishment of a hierarchical "pecking order." Girls' play generally was characterized by smaller and more intimate groups, closer proximity to adults, a strong convention of turn taking, and more mutuality in play and conversation. Such patterns have been observed among both African American children and Euro-American (Coates, 1987).

The significance of peer group play is that it socializes individuals for adult roles in society according to the specific skills that are reinforced. According to Lever (1978), boys' play tends to reinforce the ability to deal with diverse actions simultaneously, coordinate actions in order to foster group cohesiveness and work for collective goals, engage in competition, cope with impersonal rules, and engage in strategic thinking. Girls' play, in contrast, tends to reinforce cooperation, spontaneity, imagination, flexibility, and empathy. What are socialization outcomes resulting from girls' participation in team sports? One study (Miller, Sabo, Farrell, Barnes, & Melnick, 1998) found that athletic participation influenced the status of girls and their relationships with boys. Specifically, girls' athletic participation was associated with later onset of sexual activity, lower frequency of heterosexual intercourse, and fewer partners.

School

> **EXAMPLE** When I attended public school in the 1950s, there were two entrance doors, one marked "Girls" and one marked "Boys." At recess, the girls played jump rope, and the boys either ran around chasing and hitting each other or played ball. When the teacher blew the whistle, everyone lined up, the girls in one line, the boys in another; each line then entered the school building through the appropriate door. Why differentiate? We all knew which sex we were. Surprisingly, many school activities are still sex-segregated.

Schools provide a number of gender-related messages to children, some intentional and some unintentional (Ruble & Martin, 1998). Schools have traditionally treated males and females differently—through portrayals of gender roles in textbooks, through different course requirements (for example, boys took shop and girls took home economics), through treatment by teachers and counselors, and even subtly, through the uneven sex distribution on the staff.

> Men hold a disproportionate number of positions in higher administration, whereas women are more often teachers particularly in the "early" grades. Only in older grades are children likely to have many male teachers, and these are often in classes such as mathematics and science. (Ruble & Martin, 1998, p. 979)

The passage of federal legislation (Title IX Education Amendment) in 1972 outlawed discrimination in education on the basis of sex. As a result, textbooks are reviewed for sexual bias, courses are open to males and females, and teachers and counselors must channel students into higher educational programs or occupations on the basis of individual competencies rather than what traditionally has been viewed as acceptable for the sexes.

One of the effects of Title IX has been the increased participation of girls in sports. In a longitudinal study of sports participation in a sample of public and private American high schools (Women's Sports Foundation, 1989), it was found that both boys and girls who participated had better images of themselves. They were healthier and more energetic, and they had more self-confidence. And following high school, they were more likely to be involved in community groups. This was true of African Americans, Hispanic Americans, and Euro-Americans.

Despite Title IX and the greater awareness of how children develop gender-role attitudes, it will be a while before teachers and school personnel can change any unconscious habitual behavior that interferes with children developing to their full potential. An example of such unconscious behavior is the finding that teachers respond differently to boys and girls. Serbin and her colleagues (Serbin, Powlishta, & Gulko, 1993) found that teachers tend to respond negatively to the aggressive behavior of boys and positively to the proximity-seeking behavior of girls. Research in preschools (Fagot, 1984) confirmed that more teacher attention is given to boys for achievement-related behaviors and to girls for compliance.

Other studies (Sadker, Sadker, & Klein, 1991) revealed some differences in how elementary and high school teachers view male and female students. "Good" male students were described by the teachers as active, adventurous, aggressive, assertive, curious, energetic, enterprising, frank, independent, and inventive. "Good" female students were described as appreciative, calm, conscientious, considerate, cooperative, mannerly, poised, sensitive, dependable, efficient, mature, obliging, and thorough. Such attitudes may influence the way teachers interact with students and may even influence the way the students view their own gender roles. These stereotypic attitudes are similar to those found in Rosenthal and Jacobson's (1968) research on the effect of teachers' expectations on the achievement and behavior of their students (discussed in Chapter 6).

Sadker and Sadker (1994, 2003) report that, from elementary to graduate school, boys are given more teacher attention and encouragement to learn. In their studies, if a girl gave an incorrect answer when asked, the teacher called on someone else; if a boy gave an incorrect response, he was prompted to discover the right answer and then praised. If a girl gave a correct answer when asked, it was accepted with an OK. If a girl called out a correct answer without being asked, she was likely to be reprimanded for talking out of turn; if a boy did the same, his answer was likely to be accepted. Thus, teachers tend to socialize boys to be active, assertive learners, and girls to be quiet, passive learners. Also, boys were more likely to be encouraged to take math and science classes, thereby gaining an advantage in competing for higher-paying jobs; girls were more likely to be encouraged to take business classes, thereby limiting in their career options (AAUW, 1991).

Mass Media

Pictorial Media. The mass media affect gender-role development. Television and movies portray distinct male and female roles, as do books, magazines, and newspapers. For example, not only do males appear with greater frequency on TV than do females, they are also portrayed in a greater variety of occupations than are females and have higher-status jobs (Basow, 1992; Huston & Wright, 1998; Perse, 2001). To illustrate, most of the lawyers, ministers, store owners, and doctors on television are men; women are usually secretaries, nurses, entertainers, teachers, and journalists (Signorielli, 1989, 1993). However, women are shown as experts in ads for food products, laundry soap, and beauty aids (Basow, 1992).

In interactions between men and women on television, the men are ordinarily more dominant, while the women are more passive and less involved in problem solving. For men, the emphasis is on strength, performance, and skill; for women, it is on attractiveness and desirability. That television has the potential for influencing gender-role stereotyping was illustrated by several investigations (Condry, 1989) in which boys and girls were interviewed to determine how often they watched certain television programs and how they felt about males and females having certain occupational roles. Those who frequently watched programs in which women were portrayed in nontraditional female roles more often reported that they felt it was appropriate for women to have such occupations than did those who did not watch such programs very often.

Television has recently become more sensitive to how males and females are portrayed. For example, in several programs that have appeared since the 1980s, women have held difficult and daring jobs (Huston & Wright, 1998; Perse, 2001). However, according to Susan Isaacs (1999), author of *Brave Dames and Wimpettes: What Women Are Really Doing on Page and Screen*, too many "heroines" in movies today are being portrayed as weak or ineffectual because they give in to the stereotypes imposed on them by their gender. For example, in *Thelma and Louise* (1991), the women were dominated and oppressed by men. But they fought back weakly rather than bravely—they were overemotional and ineffectual, going on a shooting spree for revenge and killing themselves rather than face the consequences. Unlike "wimpettes," "brave dames" take responsibility and don't give up; they stand up to injustice and meet challenges. Examples are Marge in *Fargo* (1996) and Erin in *Erin Brockovich* (2000). Marge is police chief in the town of Fargo, and though very pregnant, she does her job with dignity, respect, and a sense of humor. Erin is a single mother who, while working for a lawyer to support her family, uncovers serious violations of the Environmental Protection Act. She courageously fights business interests to win settlements for the families suffering the devastating consequences of the careless disposal of toxic wastes.

Although TV and movies have some influence, children's prior attitudes about gender roles influence the impact of what they attend to. Children with highly stereotyped attitudes focus on traditional role portrayals, whereas children with more flexible attitudes attend equally well to both traditional and nontraditional role portrayals (List, Collins, & Westby, 1983; Signorielli, 1993).

That television impacts gender attitudes was demonstrated in Canada, where television was introduced into several towns that had previously been unable to receive TV signals. Children in one town (Notel) had less traditional gender attitudes prior to TV introduction than children from a comparable town with access to multiple TV channels. After a couple years of television exposure, the children from Notel showed sharp increases in traditional gender attitudes (Kimball, 1986).

Print Media. Gender-role stereotypes also appear in the print media. A research study by sociologist Janet Chafetz (1974) examined the Christmas toy catalogs of the two largest mail-order companies in the United States. Both of the catalogs had boys' and girls' sections. The boys' section featured athletic items and sports figure dolls, building and technological toys (tractors, spaceships, cars), and war toys. The girls' section featured dolls, household items (dishes, appliances), and beauty aids. In my informal review of mail catalogs for toys from stores, I find this still generally holds true.

Studies of the Caldecott Medal picture books for preschool children, one focusing on books from 1979 to 1982 (Collins, Ingoldsby, & Dellman, 1984), and another on books from 1989 to 1992 (Dellman-Jenkins, Florjancic, & Swadener, 1993), show an improvement in the representation of females as active, central characters. Males still dominate the world of picture books, however, and are generally presented in more independent, varied, productive, and exciting roles, whereas females are generally presented in more domostic, dependent, helping, and pleasing roles (Turner-Bowker, 1996).

Popular Music. Stereotypes about men's and women's behavior are visible in rock music videos (Hansen & Hansen, 1988). Males are depicted as sexually aggressive, rational, demanding, and adventuresome, whereas females are portrayed as emotional, deceitful, illogical, frivolous, dependent, and passive. Rock music videos also show violence against women and treat women as sex objects (Basow, 1992; Huston & Wright, 1998).

Interactive Media. Most of the action-packed interactive media software is male-dominated and attractive to boys. One study (Dietz, 1998) found that nearly 80 percent of video games included aggression or violence as part of the strategy or object. In 28 percent of the games, women were portrayed as sex objects. Females are in stereotypically dependent roles and often are portrayed as sexual objects (Provenzo, 1991).

In sum, children learn much from the media about what is culturally expected of males and females.

Community

The community influences gender-role development through its attitudes regarding what is appropriate behavior for males and females and through the gender-role models it provides with whom children can identify. The community's attitudes on gender roles affect what behaviors it reinforces and punishes in children. Comments like "That's unladylike" or "Go and stick up for yourself like a man" make a big impression on children. Sometimes community attitudes are expressed by the language used to describe males and females. Are females described by their appearance and men by their actions? Are occupational roles gender-free ("mail carrier," "salesperson")?

If the community has stereotypical attitudes—that women are nurturant and that men are problem solvers, for example—the assignment of occupations to one or the other gender will be affected. One study (Arvey & Chapman, 1982) found that, when identical applicants were compared, women received higher ratings for jobs as grocery clerks or telephone operators, whereas men were rated more favorably for auto parts or hardware clerk positions. Today, women still dominate occupations that involve providing service, nurturing, or teaching; men dominate such occupations as engineering, architecture, law, and medicine, which all involve problem solving (U.S. Bureau of the Census, 2000). Such attitudes, together with the social visibility of men and women in their jobs, affect children's perceptions of and expectations for themselves. The U.S. government has enacted and enforced equal opportunity laws, thereby opening up previously restricted fields to women; now, perhaps, gender stereotypes in the world of work will gradually diminish.

Ethnicity influences children's perceptions and expectations for their gender, as does religion. For example, Asian American females are expected to marry, assume domestic duties, and bear children even if they work (Sue, 1989). Mexican American women are traditionally subordinant to men. However, as women increasingly work outside the home, they will have more equality in family decisions (Espin, 1993). Religious orientation has also been found to play an influential role in career choices of high school seniors in that those attending religious schools indicated a greater preference for traditional gender occupations than those attending public schools (Rich & Golan, 1992).

Not all communities differentiate male and female roles in the ways commonly seen in the United States. Anthropologists Beatrice Whiting and Carolyn Edwards (1988) studied the interaction patterns of 2- to 10-year-olds in 12 communities around the world to clarify how children were socialized for their respective gender roles. Although they found that in most of the societies boys were dominant and aggressive, and girls were dependent, compliant, and nurturant, there were cross-cultural differences in the tasks assigned to each gender. For example, in Nyansongo, an agricultural community in Kenya, as in many other East African communities, boys are categorized with girls and women until they reach puberty. Then the pubescent males are assigned "masculine" activities that, when accomplished, become part of the initiation rites into "manhood." Until that time, however, boys participate in caring for their younger siblings and help with domestic chores as needed. Girls, then, have some free time to play during those times when the boys assume their chores. Nyansongo men spend much of the day away from their families, and so fathers have little impact on their children's development. Compared with children from other cultures, Nyansongo children display less stereotypic gender roles.

In the United States, there are cultural variations in the gender-role expectations and gender stereotypes of individuals with diverse racial, ethnic, socioeconomic, and sexual orientations (Basow & Rubin, 1999; Shaffer, 2000). For example, in a study of sex typing and gender-role attitudes, it was found that African American women were twice as likely as Euro-American women to describe themselves as androgynous—having both active-instrumental and nurturant-expressive traits (Binion, 1990). In another study (Vasquez-Nutall, Romero-Garcia, & DeLeon, 1987), Hispanic American women were found to be more submissive and dependent than Euro-American women. Similar findings held true for Asian American women (Uba, 1994).

In conclusion, to the extent that children grow up in a *restrictive* gendered world with strong pressures toward conformity, they will likely place importance on behaving accordingly. In contrast, to the extent that children grow up in a *flexible* gendered world emphasizing individual choice, they will be less likely to conform to stereotypic gender behavior (Eccles & Bryan, 1994; Shaffer, 2000). New measures

This adolescent boy exhibits nonstereotyped gender-role behavior by reading to a group of preschoolers.

are currently being developed to assess both children's and adult's attitudes about sex typing in regard to multiple domains (traits, activities, occupations). Some questions being researched are how attitudes of others guide the sex-role typing of the self, and how self-attitudes about gender guide behavior (Liben & Bigler, 2002).

Points to Ponder

Plasticity is the biological construct of the brain having the capacity to change and to be shaped by experience. It is evidenced by the increased connections in neurons in infancy and toddlerhood, when the developing child is exposed to many stimulating experiences. Plasticity continues to occur, but at a lesser rate, throughout development, and potential connections not used are lost. Based on your experience, how does the principle of plasticity relate to socialization in general and to self regulation, morals, and gender roles in particular?

How to Determine the Type of Gender-Role Models Provided by the Community

- In general, do mothers and fathers in the community stay home to raise their families, or are they employed outside the home?
- In what activities do most mothers and fathers in the community engage?
- Do children have an opportunity to observe people in their occupations?
- Do men and women who have various occupations come to school and talk to the children?

- Who occupies the positions of leadership in the community (government, church, service organizations, political organizations)?
- In what kinds of activities do boys and girls participate in the community outside of school?
- How are community jobs labeled?

Epilogue

Moral values are the cornerstone of society. Without concepts of "good" and "bad," people could not live with one another. Cultural values, such as individualism and collectivism, influence ethical behavior. For example, according to Bok (1989), pressure for success (achievement, power, wealth) as defined by individualistic societies can blur the line between "right" and "wrong." In the fairy tale, *The Goose Girl*, the woman lied to better her life situation; in real life, Richard Nixon, Jimmy Swaggart, and Bill Clinton all lied to maintain theirs. In collectivistic societies, pressure to be loyal to family or peer group and/or to "save face" may be a motive to lie or to not reveal the truth. Even in the United States, recognizing the cohesiveness of family loyalties, spouses may not testify against each other in court. How values, attitudes, motives, attributes, and morals develop and are supported is influenced by significant others and by factors inherent in the individual. When microsystems work together and their efforts are supported by the macrosystem, positive outcomes for ethical standards and prosocial behavior in children can occur.

Summary

The ability to regulate one's impulses, behavior, and/or emotions until an appropriate time, place, or object is available for expression is referred to as self-regulation, or self-control. Self-regulatory behavior includes the ability to delay gratification, sustain attention to a task, and plan and self-monitor a goal-directed activity. Self-regulatory skills are significantly related to inhibiting antisocial behaviors and to acquiring prosocial ones. Antisocial behavior includes any behavior that harms other people, such as aggression, violence, and crime. Prosocial behavior includes any behavior that benefits other people, such as altruism, sharing, and cooperation.

The theories explaining the causes of aggression are that it is biologically influenced; it is learned; it is an information processing impulsive response to frustration; it is a result of social cognitive factors, such as peer group pressure, or the reduction of restraining socialization forces; and it is socialized by ecological interacting factors.

Aggression can be studied from a social cognitive perspective (behavior is influenced by how one interprets social cues) and from an ecological perspective (behavior is influenced by the contexts of family, school, peer group, media, and community). Aggression can be inhibited by organizing the environment, establishing standards of and consequences for behavior, providing alternative ways of solving problems, offering positive role models, and encouraging discussion and communication.

The theories explaining the causes of altruism are biological (evolution and genetics) learning (reinforcement, modeling, and instruction), cognitive developmental, social interactional, and cultural.

The family influences altruistic behavior. An authoritative parenting style (characterized by warmth, firm control, and reasoning) seems to encourage altruistic behavior, whereas an authoritarian parenting style (characterized by coldness and physical punishment) seems to foster aggressive behavior. Moralizing and prohibitions, with explanations as to why antisocial behavior is unacceptable, increase prosocial behavior, as do role-taking opportunities.

The media provide role models for behavior and can influence altruism. Schools can train children to be prosocial through discussion and role-playing activities. Peer groups provide real experiences in prosocial behavior (learning by doing) and reinforcement for behaving in certain ways.

The community influences prosocial behavior through cultural values of cooperation and social harmony. Children from traditional, rural cultures who are given the responsibility to perform various household tasks related to the family's economic security exhibit more altruism than children from modern, urban cultures, who tend to be more competitive and achievement-oriented.

Morals encompass individuals' evaluations of what is right and wrong. They involve acceptance of rules and govern behavior toward others. Morality involves feeling, reasoning, and behavior. Children's moral code develop through social interaction and reflect their level of intellectual development and their attitudes. The process involves an awareness of alternatives, the ability to take another's perspective and to make judgments, and awareness of feelings about conformity and autonomy.

As children develop, their morality changes. Infants and toddlers do not distinguish right from wrong. Preschoolers and school-agers consider only the act, and not the intent. Adolescents consider both intent and situation. Important developmental theory include Piaget's (heteronomous and autonomous morality), Kohlberg's (preconventional, conventional, postconventional morality) and Gilligan's (morality of care versus morality of justice). In general, at the lower moral development levels, people act out of concern for personal consequences; at the middle levels, they act out of concern for what others think; at the higher levels, they act to avoid self-condemnation.

Influences on moral development include cultural perspective, age, intelligence, social factors, situational contexts, temperament, self-control, emotions, and self-esteem. Also, parenting methods such as reasoning and modeling, peer experiences in social interaction and role taking, opportunities to democratically make rules, school group discussions on moral dilemmas, media portrayals of moral behavior, and community factors such as ideology, are influential.

Cultural ideology influencing moral development involves the degree of pluralism in a society. According to Bronfenbrenner and Garbarino, individuals who are exposed to many socializing agents are more likely to achieve a higher level of moral reasoning than are those exposed to few socializing agents. Whether the culture stresses individualism or collectivism is also influential in internal or external moral orientations.

An individual's moral development is socially constructed and represents his or her scheme of personal and societal values, which include a coordination of emotions, thoughts, and actions.

A gender role, or sex type, refers to the qualities that individuals understand as characterizing males and females in their culture. The four main theories of gender-role development are psychoanalytic (feelings), social learning, or social cognitive (behaving), cognitive developmental (thinking), and gender schema (information processing).

Males and females behave differently. Research confirms that males tend to be more aggressive and to exhibit greater visual-spatial ability, and that females tend to exhibit greater verbal ability. Additional research indicates that socialization practices maximize gender differences. As a result, girls and boys are channeled into sex-typed behaviors valued by their culture.

Warm, positive father–son and mother–daughter relationships lead to the strongest gender-role identification. Parenting practices influence the gender-role development of both boys and girls. Sibling sex constellation is another factor.

Peers exert strong pressure to conform to traditionally stereotypical gender roles via modeling, reinforcement, punishment, and sex-segregated activities. The school, by its differential treatment of males and females, maximizes gender differences. This results from teachers' responses to boys and girls and from gender-role models in textbooks. And the media still tend toward stereotypic portrayals of gender roles. The community's attitudes regarding gender roles and the models provided influence children's sex typing.

Activity

PURPOSE *To analyze changes in children's social behavior over time.*

1. Separately observe a group (more than two) of preschoolers (age 3–5) and a group of school-agers (age 6–12) in a "free play" activity.
2. Record and compare incidents of prosocial (at least one) and antisocial activity (at least one) for the children in each group—antecedents, behavior, consequences.
   a. What event, item, or interaction preceded the prosocial or antisocial activity (antecedent)?
   b. How did the children involved act (behavior)? Describe physical and verbal behavior.
   c. What were the outcomes to all involved (consequences)?
3. Analyze similarities and differences in how preschoolers and school-agers interact with one another in a "free play" setting.
4. What factors, other than age, do you think influenced their behavior?

Research Terms

Aggressive behavior
Androgyny
Altruistic behavior
Ethics
Gender-role stereotyping
Moral behavior
Self-regulatory behavior

Related Readings

Basow, S. A. (1992). *Gender stereotypes and roles* (3rd ed.). Pacific Grove, CA: Brooks/Cole.

Best, R. (1983). *We've all got scars: What boys and girls learn in elementary school.* Bloomington: Indiana University Press.

Bok, S. (1989). *Lying: Moral choice in public and private life.* New York: Vintage.

Damon, W. (1988). *The moral child: Nurturing children's natural moral growth.* New York: Free Press.

Dunn, J. (1988). *The beginnings of social understanding.* Cambridge, MA: Harvard University Press.

Ekman, P. (1989). *Why kids lie: How parents can encourage truthfulness.* New York: Penguin Books.

Gilligan, C. (1982). *In a different voice: Psychological theory and women's development.* Cambridge, MA: Harvard University Press.

Isaacs, S. (1999). *Brave dames and wimpettes: What women are really doing on page and screen.* New York: Ballantine.

Levine, M. (2002). *A mind at a time.* New York: Simon & Schuster.

Maccoby, E. E. (1998). *The two sexes: Growing up apart, coming together.* Cambridge, MA: Harvard University Press.

Mussen, P. H., & Eisenberg-Berg, N. (1977). *Roots of caring, sharing, and helping: The development of prosocial behavior in children.* San Francisco: Freeman.

Olweus, D. (1993). *Bullying at school: What we know and what we can do.* Cambridge, MA: Blackwell.

Osofsky, J. D. (1997). *Children in a violent society.* York, PA: Guilford Press.

Pipher, M. (1994). *Reviving Ophelia: Saving the selves of adolescent girls.* New York: Ballantine Books.

Pollack, W. S. (1999). *Real boys: Rescuing our sons from the myths of boyhood.* New York: Henry Holt.

Slaby, R. G., et al. (1995). *Early violence prevention: Tools for teachers of young children.* Washington, DC: National Association for the Education of Young Children.

Staub, E. (1975). *The development of prosocial behavior in children.* Morristown, NJ: General Learning Press.

Thorne, B. (1993). *Gender play: Girls and boys in school.* New Brunswick, NJ: Rutgers University Press.

Appendix A Developmental Tasks in Ten Categories of Behavior of the Individual from Birth to Death

	INFANCY (BIRTH TO 1 OR 2)	EARLY CHILDHOOD (2–3 TO 5–6–7)	MIDDLE CHILDHOOD (5–6–7 TO PUBESCENCE)
I. Achieving an appropriate dependence/independence pattern	1. Establishing oneself as very dependent being 2. Beginning the establishment of self-awareness	1. Adjusting to less private attention; becoming independent physically (while remaining strongly dependent emotionally)	1. Freeing oneself from primary identification with adults
II. Achieving an appropriate giving–receiving pattern of affection	1. Developing a feeling for affection	1. Developing the ability to give affection 2. Learning to share affection	1. Learning to give as much love as one receives; forming friendships with peers
III. Relating to changing social groups	1. Becoming aware of the alive as against the inanimate, and the familiar against the unfamiliar 2. Developing rudimentary social interaction	1. Beginning to develop the ability to interact with age mates 2. Adjusting in the family to expectations it has for the child as a member of the social unit	1. Clarifying the adult world as distinguished from the child's world 2. Establishing peer groups and learning to belong
IV. Developing a conscience	1. Beginning to adjust to the expectations of others	1. Developing the ability to take directions and to be in the obedient presence of authority 2. Developing the ability to be obedient in the absence of authority where conscience substitutes for authority	1. Learning more about rules and developing true morality

538

EARLY ADOLESCENCE (PUBESCENCE TO PUBERTY)	LATE ADOLESCENCE (PUBERTY TO EARLY MATURITY)	MATURITY (EARLY TO MIDDLE ADULTHOOD)	LATE ADULTHOOD (BEYOND FULL POWERS OF ADULTHOOD TO SENESENCE)
1. Establishing one's independence from adults in all areas of behavior	1. Establishing oneself as an independent individual in an adult manner	1. Learning to be interdependent—now learning on, now succoring others, as need arises. 2. Assisting one's children to become gradually independent and autonomous beings	1. Accepting graciously and comfortably the help needed from others as powers fail and dependence becomes necessary
1. Accepting oneself as a worthwhile person really worthy of love	1. Building a strong mutual affectional bond with a (possible) marriage partner	1. Building and maintaining a strong and mutually satisfying marriage relationship 2. Establishing a wholesome affectional bonds with one's children and grandchildren 3. Meeting wisely the new needs for affection of one's own aging parents 4. Cultivating meaningfully warm friendships with members of one's own generation	1. Facing loss of one's spouse and finding some satisfactory sources of affection previously received from mate 2. Learning new affectional roles with own children, now mature adults 3. Establishing ongoing satisfying affectional patterns with grandchildren and other members of the extended family 4. Finding and preserving mutually satisfying friendships outside the family circle
1. Behaving according to a shifting peer code	1. Adopting an adult-patterned set of social values by learning a new peer code	1. Keeping in reasonable balance activities in the various social service, political, and community groups and causes that make demands on adults 2. Establishing and maintaining mutually satisfactory relationships with the in-law families of spouse and married children	1. Choosing and maintaining ongoing social activities and functions appropriate to health, energy, and interests
	1. Learning to verbalize contradictions in moral codes, as well as discrepancies between principle and practice, and resolving these problems in a responsible manner	1. Coming to terms with the violations of moral codes in the larger as well as in the more intimate social scene, and developing some constructive philosophy and method of operation 2. Helping children to adjust to the expectations of others and to conform to the moral demands of the culture	1. Maintaining a sense of moral integrity in the face of disappointments and disillusionments in life's hopes and dreams

(continued)

	INFANCY (BIRTH TO 1 OR 2)	EARLY CHILDHOOD (2–3 TO 5–6–7)	MIDDLE CHILDHOOD (5–6–7 TO PUBESCENCE)
V. Learning one's psychosociobiological gender role		1. Learning to identify with male adult and female adult roles	1. Beginning to identify with one's social contemporaries of the same gender
VI. Accepting and adjusting to a changing body	1. Adjusting to adult feeding demands 2. Adjusting to adult cleanliness demands 3. Adjusting to adult attitudes toward genital manipulation	1. Adjusting to expectations resulting from one's improving muscular abilities 2. Developing sexual modesty	
VII. Managing a changing body and learning new motor patterns	1. Developing a physiological equilibrium 2. Developing eye–hand coordination 3. Establishing satisfactory rhythms of rest and activity	1. Developing large muscle control 2. Learning to coordinate large muscles and small muscles	1. Refining and elaborating skill in the use of small muscles
VIII. Learning to understand and control the physical world	1. Exploring the physical world	1. Meeting adult expectations for restrictive exploration and manipulation of an expanding environment	1. Learning more realistic ways of studying and controlling the physical world
IX. Developing an appropriate symbol system and conceptual abilities	1. Developing preverbal communication 2. Developing verbal communication 3. Rudimentary concept formation	1. Improving one's use of the symbol system 2. Enormous elaboration of the concept pattern	1. Learning to use language actually to exchange ideas or to influence one's hearers 2. Beginning understanding of real causal relations 3. Making finer conceptual distinctions and thinking reflectively
X. Relating oneself to the cosmos		1. Developing a genuine, though uncritical, notion about one's place in the cosmos	1. Developing a scientific approach

EARLY ADOLESCENCE (PUBESCENCE TO PUBERTY)	LATE ADOLESCENCE (PUBERTY TO EARLY MATURITY)	MATURITY (EARLY TO MIDDLE ADULTHOOD)	LATE ADULTHOOD (BEYOND FULL POWERS OF ADULTHOOD TO SENESENCE)
1. Strong identification with one's own gender mates 2. Learning one's role in heterosexual relationships	1. Exploring the possibilities for a future mate and acquiring "desirability" 2. Choosing an occupation 3. Preparing to accept one's future role in manhood or womanhood as a responsible citizen of the larger community	1. Learning to be a competent husband or wife, and building a good marriage 2. Carrying a socially adequate role as a citizen and worker in the community 3. Becoming a good parent and grandparent as children arrive and develop	1. Learning to live on a retirement income 2. Being a good companion to an aging spouse 3. Meeting bereavement of spouse adequately
1. Reorganizing one's thoughts and feelings about oneself in the face of significant bodily changes and their concomitants 2. Accepting the reality of one's appearance 3. Controlling and using a "new" body	1. Learning appropriate outlets for sexual drives	1. Making a good sex adjustment within marriage 2. Establishing healthful routines of eating, resting, working, playing within the pressures of the adult world	1. Making a good adjustment to failing powers as aging diminishes strengths and abilities
		1. Learning the new motor skills involved in housekeeping, gardening, sports, and other activities expected of adults in the community	1. Adapting interests and activities to reserves of vitality and energy of an aging body
		1. Gaining intelligent understanding of new horizons of medicine and science sufficient for personal well-being and social competence	1. Mastering new awareness and methods of dealing with physical surroundings as an individual with occasional or permanent disabilities
1. Using language to express and to clarify more complex concepts 2. Moving from the concrete to the abstract and applying general principles to the particular	1. Achieving the level of reasoning of which one is capable	1. Mastering technical symbol systems involved in income tax, Social Security, complex financial dealings, and other contexts familiar to Western culture	1. Keeping mentally alert and effective as long as is possible through the later years
	1. Formulating a workable belief and value system	1. Formulating and implementing a rational philosophy of life on the basis of adult experience 2. Cultivating a satisfactory religious climate in the home as the spiritual soil for development of family members	1. Preparing for eventual and inevitable cessation of life by building a set of beliefs that one can live and die with in peace

Appendix B Basic Parenting Styles

Permissive

The *permissive* parent attempts to behave in a nonpunitive, acceptable, and affirmative manner toward the child's impulses, desires, and actions. He or she consults with him/her about policy decisions and gives explanations for family rules. He or she makes few demands for household responsibility and orderly behavior. He or she presents himself/herself to the child as a resource for him/her to use as he/she wishes, not as an active agent responsible for shaping or altering his/her ongoing or future behavior. He or she allows the child to regulate his/her own activities as much as possible, avoids the exercise of control, and does not encourage him/her to obey externally defined standards. He or she attempts to use reason but not overt power to accomplish his/her ends (Baumrind, 1968, p. 256).

Authoritarian

The *authoritarian* parent attempts to shape, control, and evaluate the behavior and attitudes of the child in accordance with a set standard of conduct, usually an absolute standard, theologically motivated and formulated by a higher authority. He or she values obedience as a virtue and favors punitive, forceful measures to curb self-will at points where the child's actions or beliefs conflict with what he or she thinks is right conduct. He or she believes in inculcating such instrumental values as respect for authority, respect for work, and respect for the preservation of order and traditional structure. He or she does not encourage verbal give and take, believing that the child should accept his/her word for what is right (Baumrind, 1968, p. 261).

Authoritative

The *authoritative* parent attempts to direct the child's activities but in a rational, issue-oriented manner. He or she encourages verbal give and take, and shares with the child the reasoning behind his/her policy. He or she values both expressive and instrumental attributes, both autonomous self-will and disciplined conformity. Therefore, he or she exerts firm control at points of parent–child divergence, but does not hem the child in with restrictions. He or she recognizes his/her own special rights as an adult, but also the child's individual interests and special ways. The authoritative parent affirms the child's present qualities, but also sets standards for future conduct. He or she uses reason as well as power to achieve his/her objectives. He or she does not base decisions on group consensus or the individual child's desires, but also does not regard himself/herself as infallible or divinely inspired (Baumrind, 1968, p. 261).

Appendix C How to Choose a Good Early Childhood Program*

A good early childhood program can benefit your child, your family, and your community. Your child's educational, physical, personal, and social development will be nurtured in a well-planned program. As a parent, you will feel more confident when your child is enrolled in a suitable program, and the time your family spends together will be more satisfying as a result. Early childhood education plays an important role in supporting families, and strong families are the basis of a thriving community.

If you are thinking about enrolling your child in an early childhood program, you probably have already decided upon some of your basic priorities, such as location, number of hours, cost, and type of care that best suits your child. If you feel that a group program is appropriate, you can obtain a list of licensed programs for young children from your local licensing agency. Then you can call several programs for further information, and arrange to visit the programs that seem best for you and your child so you can talk with teachers, directors, and other parents.

What should you look for in a good early childhood program? Professionals in early childhood education and child development have found several indicators of good quality care for preschool children. You will especially want to meet the adults who will care for your child—they are responsible for every aspect of the program's operation.

Who Will Care for Your Child?

1. The adults enjoy and understand how young children learn and grow.
   - Are the staff members friendly and considerate to each child?
   - Do adult expectations vary appropriately for children of differing ages and interests?
   - Do the staff members consider themselves to be professionals? Do they read or attend meetings to continue to learn more about how young children grow and develop?
   - Does the staff work toward improving the quality of the program, obtaining better equipment, and making better use of the space?
2. The staff view themselves positively and therefore can continually foster children's emotional and social development.
   - Does the staff help children feel good about themselves, their activities, and other people?
   - Do the adults listen to children and talk with them?
   - Are the adults gentle while being firm, consistent and yet flexible in their guidance of children?

- Do the staff members help children learn gradually how to consider others' rights and feelings, to take turns and share, yet also to stand up for personal rights when necessary?
- When children are angry or fearful, are they helped to deal with their feelings constructively?

3. There are enough adults to work with a group and to care for the individual needs of children.
   - Are infants in groups of no more than eight children with at least two adults?
   - Are two- and three-year-old children in groups of no more than fourteen children with at least two adults?
   - Are four- and five-year-olds in groups of no more than twenty children with at least two adults?

4. All staff members work together cooperatively.
   - Does the staff meet regularly to plan and evaluate the program?
   - Are they willing to adjust the daily activities for children's individual needs and interests?

5. Staff observe and record each child's progress and development.
   - Does the staff stress children's strengths and show pride in their accomplishments?
   - Are records used to help parents and staff better understand the child?
   - Are the staff responsible to parents' concerns about their child's development?

What Program Activities and Equipment Are Offered?

1. The environment fosters the growth and development of young children working and playing together.
   - Does the staff have realistic goals for children?
   - Are activities balanced between vigorous outdoor play and quiet indoor play? Are children given opportunities to select activities of interest to them?
   - Are children encouraged to work alone as well as in small groups?
   - Are self-help skills such as dressing, toileting, resting, washing, and eating encouraged as children are ready?
   - Are transition times approached as pleasant learning opportunities?

2. A good center provides appropriate and sufficient equipment and play materials and makes them readily available.
   - Is there large climbing equipment? Is there an ample supply of blocks of all sizes, wheel toys, balls, and dramatic play props to foster physical development as well as imaginative play?
   - Are there ample tools and hands-on materials such as sand, clay, water, wood, and paint to stimulate creativity?
   - Is there a variety of sturdy puzzles, construction sets, and other small manipulative items available to children?
   - Are children's picture books age-appropriate, attractive, and of good literary quality?
   - Are there plants, animals, or other natural science objects for children to care for or observe?
   - Are there opportunities for music and movement experiences?

3. Children are helped to increase their language skills and to expand their understanding of the world.
   - Do the children freely talk with one another and with the adults?
   - Do the adults provide positive language models in describing objects, feelings, and experiences?
   - Does the staff plan for visitors or trips to broaden children's understanding through first-hand contacts with people and places?
   - Are the children encouraged to solve their own problems, to think independently, and to respond to open-ended questions?

How Do the Staff Relate to Your Family and the Community?

1. A good program considers and supports the needs of the entire family.
   - Are parents welcome to observe, discuss policies, make suggestions, and participate in the work of the center?
   - Do the staff members share with parents the highlights of their child's experiences?
   - Are the staff alert to matters affecting any member of the family that may also affect the child?
   - Does the staff respect families from varying cultures or backgrounds?
   - Does the center have written policies about fees, hours, holidays, illness, and other considerations?
2. Staff in a good center are aware of and contribute to community resources.
   - Does the staff share information about community recreational and learning opportunities with families?
   - Does the staff refer family members to a suitable agency when the need arises?
   - Are volunteers from the community encouraged to participate in the center's activities?
   - Does the center collaborate with other professional groups to provide the best care possible for children in the community?

Are the Facility and Program Designed to Meet the Varied Demands of Young Children, Their Families, and the Staff?

1. The health of children, staff, and parents is protected and promoted.
   - Are the staff alert to the health and safety of each child and of themselves?
   - Are meals and snacks nutritious, varied, attractive, and served at appropriate times?
   - Does the staff wash hands with soap and water before handling food and after changing diapers? Are children's hands washed before eating and after toileting?
   - Are surfaces, equipment, and toys cleaned daily? Are they in good repair?
   - Does each child have an individual cot, mat, or crib?
   - Are current medical records and emergency information maintained for each child and staff member? Is adequate sick leave provided for staff so they can remain at home when they are ill?

- Is at least one staff member trained in first aid? Does the center have a health consultant?
- Is the building comfortably warm in cold weather? Are the rooms ventilated with fresh air daily?

2. The facility is safe for children and adults.
   - Are the building and grounds well-lighted and free of hazards?
   - Are furnishings, sinks, and toilets safely accessible to children?
   - Are toxic materials stored in a locked cabinet?
   - Are smoke detectors installed in appropriate locations?
   - Are indoor and outdoor surfaces cushioned with materials such as carpet or wood chips in areas with climbers, slides, or swings?
   - Does every staff member know what to do in an emergency? Are emergency numbers posted by the telephone?

3. The environment is spacious enough to accommodate a variety of activities and equipment.
   - Are there at least 35 square feet of usable playroom floor space indoors per child and 75 square feet of play space outdoors per child?
   - Is there a place for each child's personal belongings such as a change of clothes?
   - Is there enough space so that adults can walk between sleeping children's cots?

Appendix D Teaching Strategies for Young Children Who Have Specific Disabilities[*]

Visual Disability

ARTS AND CRAFTS

1. Mark paint cans and brushes with some tactile code—for example, circle = red, triangle = yellow, and so on.
2. Use variety of textures in paint—for example, raw oatmeal.
3. Praise efforts of child to overcome distaste for touching wet or sticky substances.
4. Have child help make play dough from dry ingredients. It will help child accept the final product.

MUSIC AND MOVEMENT

1. Let child explore each instrument.
2. Use one-handed instruments first (maracas, clappers, bells, tambourine).
3. Use two-handed instruments later (sand blocks, sticks, drums, triangle).
4. Physically guide child in handling instruments.
5. Use peer as partner by having blind child place hand on partner's upper arm or shoulder.

GROUP OR CIRCLE TIME

1. Have assigned places to help child learn classmates' voices and names.
2. At beginning of year, ask other children to identify themselves before speaking.

GENERAL SUGGESTIONS

1. Keep furniture stationary until child is familiar with room.
2. Warn child when changes are made.
3. When child loses toy, allow child time to retrieve; assist with verbal guidance.
4. Identify coat hook with some other object—for example, "next to the door."
5. Water play is usually a favorite; provide it often.
6. Cut out tactile shapes and attach to shelves for block storage.

DO

1. Provide many activities that use senses other than hearing.
2. Use short films in which story may be understood without seeing the action.

[*]Source: J. A. Schickedanz, M. E. York, I. S. Stewart, & D. A. White (1990). *Strategies for Teaching Young Children* (3rd ed.) pp. 108–111. Reprinted by permission of Prentice-Hall, Inc., Englewood Cliffs, N.J.

AVOID

1. Long films.
2. Activities that are primarily visual in nature.

Physical Impairment

ARTS AND CRAFTS

1. Substitute large-handled brushes and large crayons or felt markers for small crayons.
2. Use training scissors if necessary.
3. Tilt surface for better visibility.
4. Outline fingerpaint paper with tape to help child with severe involuntary movements.

MUSIC AND MOVEMENT

1. Substitute "hands on knees" for walking and "hands on high" for running.
2. Stabilize instruments: tape or tie to hand or wrist or place between child's knees.
3. Substitute hand and arm circling for body turning.
4. When singing a "who's missing" song, move child instead of sending out of room.
5. Be creative! Think what you can substitute for actions a child cannot do.

GROUP OR CIRCLE TIME

1. Use "sitting box" to replace wheelchair. Cut a box to simulate a seat. Cut holes for knit ties at hip level, and place a pillow between the knees.

GENERAL SUGGESTIONS

1. Use tray or shallow box to hold small objects; make back higher, front lower.
2. Use nonslip mat—for example, a towel under items to prevent slipping.
3. In listening center, pair with nonhandicapped child to turn pages of book while both use earphones.

DO

1. Put child's feet on a small stool when placing child at a table.
2. Move child to proximity of ongoing activities.
3. Place child with balancing difficulties behind others in a line.

AVOID

1. Allowing nonhandicapped children to push wheelchair when in line. (Child may feel loss of control and become upset.)
2. Long periods of keeping child in same position (more than 20–30 minutes).

Hearing Disability

ARTS AND CRAFTS

1. Provide multisensory experiences.
2. Provide vocabulary appropriate to activity.
3. Avoid complex verbal directions.
4. Demonstrate, if necessary.

MUSIC AND MOVEMENT

1. Have other children demonstrate movement or action.
2. Use items and individual flannel boards to illustrate songs. As children sing, have them hold up appropriate items or flannel cut-outs.

GROUP OR CIRCLE TIME

1. Translate to group what child says, when possible.
2. Seat for best vision of teacher and other children.
3. Talk in natural tone of voice; avoid exaggerated or loud voice.

GENERAL SUGGESTIONS

1. Provide names of objects with which child is working.
2. Draw picture of fire drill and children in line; practice drill.
3. Practice use of commonly understood sign for "wait" and "stop" before field trips.
4. Pair child with a hearing child for field trips.

DO

1. Let child choose another activity when telling a story with no visual interest.
2. Encourage total communication–that is, lip-reading, signing, and pantomime.

AVOID

1. Playback equipment that requires removal of hearing aids.
2. Films with long dialogue not closely related to action.

Developmental Delay

ARTS AND CRAFTS

1. Use one-skill activities in the beginning.
2. Define edges of paper: use white glue or fold up edges.
3. Complete first two of a three-step activity others can do.
4. Send home written explanation of child's craft work.
5. Encourage independence: avoid doing for child.

MUSIC AND MOVEMENT

1. Use simple songs with strong rhythms.
2. Alternate quiet with active.
3. Use recordings that have a slower than normal tempo.
4. Pace speed of songs to children.
5. Provide many activities for walking, running, jumping, and so on.
6. Use wall or back of chair for support in activity.

GROUP OR CIRCLE TIME

1. Keep group small when possible.
2. Give praise for sitting and attending several times during session.
3. Make realistic expectations for attention span.
4. If sharing time is part of your program, ask parents to provide items from home (for example, kitchen utensils).

GENERAL SUGGESTIONS

1. If necessary, teach and use consistent verbal clues or signals for bathroom.
2. Have extra set of clothes available and plastic bag for soiled clothes.
3. Use velcro instead of buttons and snaps.
4. Model appropriate play.

DO

1. Pair child with a capable child who likes to help.
2. Be aware of length of time child has been present at an activity.

AVOID

1. Long films: 8–10 minutes are enough, especially at the beginning of the year.
2. Long periods of keeping the child in the same position (more than 20–30 minutes).

Appendix E Teacher Observation Form for Identifying Preschool Children Who May Require Additional Services

Child's Name _____ Birth Date _____

Date _____ Teacher's Name _____

LANGUAGE	YES	NO	SOMETIMES
1. Does the child use two- and three-word phrases to ask for what he or she wants?			
2. Does the child use complete sentences to tell you what happened?			
3. When the child is asked to describe something, does he or she use at least two or more sentences to talk about it?*			
4. Does the child ask questions?			
5. Does the child seem to have difficulty following directions?			
6. Does the child respond to questions with the right answers?			
7. Does the child seem to talk too softly or too loudly?			
8. Are you able to understand the child?			

LEARNING	YES	NO	SOMETIMES
9. Does the child seem to take at least twice as long as the other children to learn pre-academic concepts?			
10. Does the child seem to take half the time needed by other children to learn pre-academic concepts?			
11. Does the child have difficulty attending to group activities for more than five minutes at a time?			
12. Does the child appear extremely shy in group activities—for instance, not volunteering answers or answering questions he or she is asked, even though you think he or she knows the answers?			

MOTOR	YES	NO	SOMETIMES
13. Does the child continuously switch a crayon back and forth from one hand to the other when he or she is coloring?			
14. Do the child's hands appear clumsy or shaky when he or she is using them?			
15. When the child is coloring with a crayon, does the hand that he or she is not using appear tense (for instance, clenched into a fist)?			
16. When the child walks or runs, does one side of his or her body seem to move differently from the other side? For instance, does the child seem to have better control of the leg and arm on one side than on the other?			

*Question applies if child is four years or older.

	YES	NO	SOMETIMES
17. Does the child seem to fear or not be able to use stairs, climbing equipment, or tricycles?			
18. Does the child stumble often or appear awkward when he or she moves?			
19. Is the child capable of dressing himself or herself except for tying his or her shoes?*			

SOCIAL	**YES**	**NO**	**SOMETIMES**
20. Does the child engage in at least two disruptive behaviors a day (tantrums, fighting, screaming, etc.)?			
21. Does the child appear withdrawn from the outside world (fiddling with pieces of string, staring into space, rocking his or her body, banging his or her head, talking to himself, etc.)?			
22. Does the child play alone and seldom talk to the other children?			
23. Does the child spend most of the time trying to get attention from adults?			
24. Does the child have toileting problems at least once a week (wet or soiled)?			

VISUAL OR HEARING	**YES**	**NO**	**SOMETIMES**
25. Do the child's eye movements appear jerky or not coordinated?			
26. Does the child seem to have difficulty seeing objects? For instance, does he or she: tilt his or her head to look at things? hold objects close to his or her eyes? squint? show sensitivity to bright lights? have uncontrolled eye-rolling? complain that his or her eyes hurt?			
27. Does the child appear awkward in tasks requiring eye–hand coordination such as pegs, puzzles, or coloring?			
28. Does the child seem to have difficulty hearing? For instance, does he or she: consistently favor one ear by turning the same side of his or her head in the direction of the sound? ignore, confuse, or not follow directions? complain of head noises or dizziness? have very high or very low monotonous tone of voice?			

GENERAL HEALTH	YES	NO	SOMETIMES
29. Does the child seem to have an excessive number of colds?			
30. Does he or she have frequent absences because of illness?			
31. Do his or her eyes water?			
32. Does he or she have discharge from: his or her eyes? his or her ears?			
33. Does the child have sores on his or her body or head?			
34. Does the child have periods of unusual movements (like rapid eye blinking) or "blank spells" that seem to appear and disappear without relationship to the social situation?			
35. Does he or she have hives or rashes? Does he or she wheeze?			
36. Does he or she have a persistent cough?			
37. Is he or she excessively thirsty? Ravenously hungry?			
38. Have you noticed any of the following conditions: constant fatigue? irritability? restlessness? feverish cheeks or forehead?			
39. Is the child overweight?			
40. Is he or she physically or mentally lethargic?			
41. Has he or she lost weight without being on a diet?			

Source: Model Preschool Center for Children with Disabilities, Seattle, Washington.

Glossary

Abuse Maltreatment, including physical, sexual, psychological, and/or emotional abuse.

Accommodation Piagetian term for mental adaptation to one's environment by reconciling differences of experiences.

Achieved status Status, class, rank, or position determined by education, occupation, income, and place of residence.

Achievement motivation The motivation to be competent and the tendency to approach challenging tasks with confidence of accomplishment.

Active listening Involves trying to understand what is being said and what is really meant by listening and checking on the accuracy of comprehension of the message received.

Adoption The legal process of taking a child into one's own family and treating him or her as one's own.

Advocacy The process of supporting a person, group, or cause.

Affective Having to do with feelings or emotions.

Aggression Unprovoked attacks, fights, or quarrels.

Alcoholism A chronic, progressive, and potentially fatal disease characterized by tolerance and physical dependence or pathologic organ changes, or both—all the direct or indirect consequences of the alcohol ingested.

Alternative education Involves a learner-centered curriculum rather than one that is arbitrarily imposed by a school district or teacher.

Altruism Voluntary actions that help or benefit another person or group of people without the actor's anticipation of external rewards. Such actions often entail some cost, self-sacrifice, or risk on the part of the actor.

Americanization Assimilation of cultural minority groups into the U.S. majority culture.

Antisocial behavior Any behavior that harms other people, such as aggression, violence, and crime.

Apprenticeship Process in which a novice is guided to participate in and master tasks by an expert.

Ascribed status Status, class, rank, or position determined by family lineage, gender, birth order, or skin color.

Assessment An evaluation according to certain specified criteria.

Assimilation Piagetian term for mental adaptation to one's environment by incorporating experiences.

Assumptive realities Assumptions about situations and people that one believes are real and true.

Attachment An affectional tie that one person forms to another person, binding them together in space and enduring over time.

Attitude The tendency to respond positively (favorably) or negatively (unfavorably) to certain persons, objects, or situations.

Attributes Explanations for one's performance.

Authentic assessment An evaluation of performance on an actual task.

Authoritarian A style of parent-centered parenting characterized by the belief in and enforcement of unquestioning obedience to authority.

Authoritative A style of democratic parenting characterized by the belief in authority that is based on competence or expertise.

Autism A severe behavior disorder usually characterized by extreme withdrawal and lack of language and communication skills.

Autocracy A society in which one person has unlimited power over others.

Autonomous morality Piaget's stage of moral development at which children realize that rules are arbitrary agreements that can be changed by those who have to follow them.

Behavior What one does or how one acts in response to a stimulus.

Behaviorism The doctrine that observed behavior, rather than what exists in the mind, provides the only valid data for psychology.

Bilingual/multicultural education Education in the student's native language, as well as in English, to enhance self-concept.

Binuclear family Situation in which children are part of two family homes and two family groups.

Caldecott Medal Award given yearly for the most distinguished picture book for children.

Care moral perspective Sees people in terms of their connectedness with others; other's welfare is intrinsically connected to one's own welfare.

Catharsis The relief of fears, conflicts, aggressive feelings, and problems by bringing them into consciousness.

Charter School A private or community-run school, funded by the school district, that reflects a shared educational philosophy.

Child care The same as day care.

Chronosystem Temporal changes in ecological systems producing new conditions that affect development.

Classism The differential treatment of people because of their class background and the reinforcing of these differences through values and practices of societal institutions.

Cliques Friends who view themselves as mutually connected and do things together.

Cognitive Having to do with the process of knowing or perceiving.

Cognitive conceit Elkind's term for children in Piaget's stage of concrete operations who put too much faith in their reasoning ability and cleverness.

Cognitively oriented curriculum Curriculum that attempts to blend the virtues of purposeful teaching with open-ended, child-initiated activities.

Collectivism Emphasizes interdependent relations, social responsibilities, and the well-being of the group.

Community A group of people living in the same geographic area (neighborhood, town, or city) under common laws; also, a group of people having fellowship, a friendly association, a mutual sharing, and common interests.

Community ecology Comprises the psychological and practical relationships between humans and their social and physical environments.

Competence Involves behavior that is socially responsible, independent, friendly, cooperative, dominant, achievement-oriented, and purposeful.

Competitive goal structure Situation in which students work against each other to achieve goals that only a few students can attain.

Concrete operations Piaget's third stage of cognitive development, applying to children age 7–11, characterized by the ability to apply logical, systematic principles to specific experiences, but the inability to distinguish between assumptions or hypotheses and facts or reality.

Conformity The condition of being similar to or in agreement with others; action in accordance with the rules or customs of a group.

Conscience The internal structure of one's socially learned standards of right and wrong by which an individual judges his or her behavior.

Contagion The phenomenon whereby an individual exposed to a suggestion acts on it.

Conventional level Kohlberg's term to describe moral reasoning wherein the individual can look beyond personal consequences and consider other's perspectives.

Cooperative goal structure Situation in which students work together to accomplish shared goals.

Cottage industry One in which work takes place in the home.

Crowds Loosely organized reference groups or cliques.

Cultural pluralism Mutual appreciation and understanding of various cultures in society; cooperation of diverse groups; coexistence of different languages, religious beliefs, and lifestyles; autonomy for each group to work out its own social purposes and future without interfering with the rights of other groups.

Culture The knowledge, beliefs, art, morals, law, customs, and traditions acquired by humans as members of society.

Curriculum Includes the goals and objections of the school program, the teacher's role, the equipment and materials, the space arrangement, the kinds of activities, and the way they are scheduled.

Day care The care given to children by persons other than parents during the parts of the day that parents are absent.

Deductive reasoning Reasoning from a known principle to an unknown, from the general to the specific, or from a premise to a logical conclusion.

Delinquency Failure to do what the law requires; a misdeed.

Democracy Society in which those ruled have equal power to that of those who rule.

Democratic Characterized by the acceptance and practice of the principles of equality of rights, opportunity, and treatment.

Desensitization The gradual reduction in response to a stimulus due to repeated exposure.

Developmental appropriateness Involves knowledge of children's normal growth patterns and individual differences.

Developmental interaction curriculum Curriculum that is individualized in relation to each child's stage of development while providing many opportunities for children to interact and become involved with peers and adults.

Developmental task A task that lies between an individual need and a societal demand.

Direct instruction curriculum Curriculum based on behaviorist principles.

Disability Reduction in the functioning of a particular body part or organ, or its absence.

Discipline Involves punishment, correction, and training that develops self-control.

Discrimination Perception of distinctions; difference or favoritism in treatment of others.

Eclectic Gathered from various sources, systems, theories, and so on.

Ecology The distribution of human groups with reference to material resources, and the consequent social and cultural patterns.

Economics The production, distribution, and consumption of goods and services.

Egalitarian Extended family in which both sides are relatively equal.

Egocentric The cognitive inability to take another's point of view, and the consequent belief that everyone else looks at things the way one does.

Emancipation Being set free from servitude or slavery.

Empowerment When individuals gain control over resources affecting them.

Equalitarian (egalitarian) family Family in which the father and mother have equal authority and dominance.

Equilibrium Piagetian term for the state of balance between assimilation and accommodation, thereby allowing knowledge to be incorporated.

Ethnicity An attribute of membership in a group in which members continue to identify themselves by national origin, culture, language, race, or religion.

Ethnographic study A systematic recording of the distribution and characteristics of different cultures for the purpose of comparison.

Etiology The cause(s) of a condition or disease, including genetic, physiological, and psychological or environmental factors.

Exosystem A setting in which children do not actually participate, but which affects them in one of their microsystems (for example, parents' jobs, the school board, the city council).

Extended day care Care provided for children by persons other than their parents, before or after school hours or during vacations.

Extended family A family consisting of kin related to the nuclear family who live nearby and are economically and emotionally dependent on each other.

External locus of control Perception that people or events are responsible for one's fate.

Extinction The gradual disappearance of a learned behavior, due to the removal of the reinforcement.

Fable A fictitious story meant to teach a moral lesson. The characters are usually animals.

Family Any two or more related people living in one household.

Family of orientation The family into which one is born.

Family of procreation The family that develops when one marries and has children.

Feedback Valuative information about one's behavior.

Fixation Freudian term referring to arrested development.

Folktale A legendary or mythical story originating and handed down among the common people.

Formal operations Piaget's fourth stage of cognitive development, applying to children over the age of 11, characterized by the ability to think logically about abstract ideas and hypotheses as well as concrete facts.

Foster care Parental care afforded someone not related by blood.

Gangs Group of people who form an alliance for a common purpose and engage in unlawful or criminal activity.

Gemeinschaft Communal, cooperative, close, intimate, informal interpersonal relationships.

Gender role The qualities an individual understands to characterize males and females in his or her culture.

Generativity Interest in establishing and guiding the next generation.

Gesellschaft Associative, practical, objective, formal interpersonal relationships.

Goodness-of-fit Accomodation of parenting styles to children's temperaments.

Group pressure A socialization method that involves information to certain group norms.

Guidance Involves direction, demonstration, supervision, and influence.

Handicap Something that hampers a person; a disadvantage, a hindrance.

Handicapism Assumptions and practices that promote the deferential and unequal treatment of people because they are different physically, mentally, or behaviorally.

Head Start Federally funded comprehensive preschool program providing educational, health, and social services for qualified families in order to compensate for the effects of poverty, ethnic minority status, and/or disability, and intended to enable children to enter school ready to learn.

Heterogenous Composed of unrelated or unlike elements or parts.

Heteronomous morality Piaget's stage of moral development at which children think of rules as moral absolutes that cannot be changed.

High-context macrosystem Culture generally characterized by intuitiveness, emotionality, cooperation, group identity, and tradition.

Home Start Federally funded program that extended the support services of Head Start by sending trained visitors to the homes of qualified families to teach parents how to work with their children.

Homogeneous Composed of similar or identical elements or parts.

Humanism A system of beliefs concerned with the interests and ideals of humans rather than those of the natural or spiritual world.

Ideology Involves concepts about human life and behavior.

Imaginary audience The beliefs that others are as concerned with one's behavior and appearance as one is oneself.

Impairment Physical damage or deterioration.

Incest Sexual relations between persons closely related.

Inclusion The educational philosophy of being part of the whole; the idea that all children are entitled to fully participate in their school and community.

Individualism An emphasis on individual fulfillment and choice.

Individualized Educational Program (IEP) A form of communication between school and family, developed by the group of people responsible for a handicapped child's education (teachers, parents, and other involved personnel).

Individualized goal structure Reflects the idea that one student's achievement of the goal is unrelated to other students' achievement of that goal.

Inductive reasoning Reasoning from particular facts or individual cases to a general conclusion.

Information processing Refers to the way an individual attends to, perceives, interprets, remembers, and acts on events or situations.

Inner-directed person One whose guidance comes from within.

Integration The organization of various minority groups into one harmonious group.

Internalization The process by which externally controlled behavior shifts to internally, or self-controlled, behavior.

Internal locus of control The perception that one is responsible for one's own fate.

Intervention The process of mediating as an influencing or protecting force.

Justice moral perspective Emphasizes the rights of the individual; equitable rules of justice must prevail.

Kibbutz Israeli collective, where work and profits are shared.

Kinesthetic Sensations from nerve endings resulting from touch or movement.

Laissez-faire The policy of letting people do as they please.

Latchkey children Children who carry their own keys and let themselves into their homes.

Learned helplessness A condition exhibited by people who no longer perform effectively in a number of situations, because they have learned to be helpless, as opposed to competent. This occurs when they feel their actions no longer provide them with control over outcomes.

Learner-directed curriculum Curriculum in which the learning activities emerge from individual interests and teacher guidance.

Learning style A consistent pattern of behavior and performance by which an individual approaches educational experiences; results from the interaction of biological and contextual influences.

Literacy Refers to the ability to communicate via reading and writing.

Locus of control One's attribution of performance or perception of responsibility for one's actions; may be internal or external.

Logical consequence Natural outcome of misbehavior in which parents do not interfere.

Low-context microsystem Culture generally characterized by rationality, practicality, competition, individuality, and progress.

Macrosystem The society and ideology in which one grows up (for example, the United States, the middle class, Spanish ancestry, the Roman Catholic church).

Mainstreaming A system for integrating students with disabilities into regular classes.

Maltreatment Intentional harm to or endangerment of a child.

Marriage A legal contract with certain rights and obligations.

Mass media Newspapers, magazines, books, radio, television, videos, and other means of communication that reach large audiences via an impersonal medium between sender and receiver.

Mastery motivation The inborn motive to explore, understand, and control one's environment.

Matriarchal family Family in which the mother has formal authority and dominance.

Mediate To interpose, come between, or intervene.

Melting pot The philosophy that society should socialize diverse groups to blend into a common culture.

Mesosystem Interrelationships between two or more of a person's microsystems (for example, home and school, or school and community).

Microsystem One's immediate setting at a particular time (for example, the family, school, or neighborhood).

Modeling A form of imitative learning that occurs by observing the behavior of another person (the model).

Modern or **open schools** Child-, or learner-, centered schools, in which the curriculum emerges from each child's interests, with support from the teacher, and value developing from the whole child.

Modern society One that looks to the present for ways to behave, thereby being responsive to change.

Montessori curriculum Curriculum involving different-aged children with materials designed for exercises in daily living, sensory development, and academic development; the teacher facilitates individual learning via observation and encouragement.

Morality of constraint Consists of behavior based on respect for persons in authority.

Morality of cooperation Consists of behavior based on mutual understanding between equals.

Morals An individual's evaluation of what is right and wrong. Morals involve one's acceptance of rules and govern one's behavior toward others.

Motives Needs or emotions that cause a person to act.

Multicultural education Education that maintains respect for students' culture and ethnicity to enhance self-concept.

Myth A traditional story of unknown authorship, usually explaining some phenomenon of nature, the origin of humankind, or the customs, institutions, or religious rites of a people.

Negative reinforcement The termination of an unpleasant condition following a desired response.

Neglect Maltreatment involving abandonment, lack of supervision, improper feeding, lack of adequate medical or dental care, inappropriate dress, uncleanliness, or lack of safety.

Neighborhood A community composed of people living near one another and having friendly relations.

Networking A system of parallel involvement or communication connections that foster operation as a unit.

Newbery Medal Award given for the most distinguished contribution to American literature for children.

Norms Rules, patterns, or standards that express cultural values and reflect how individuals are supposed to behave.

Nuclear family Family consisting of a husband and a wife and their children.

On-task Doing what one is supposed to do.

Operant Producing an effect.

Other-directed person One who cues his or her behavior from others.

Parenting The implementation of a series of decisions about the socialization of children.

Passive listening Listening without interrupting.

Patriarchal family Family in which the father has formal authority and dominance.

Pedophilia An adult's preference for or addiction to sexual relationships with children.

Peers Individuals who are of approximately the same gender, age, and social status and who share interests.

Permissive A style of child-centered parenting characterized by a lack of contraints on behavior.

Personal agency The realization that one's actions cause outcomes.

Physical abuse Maltreatment involving deliberate harm to the child's body.

Play Behavior enjoyed for its own sake.

Pluralism The existence of more than one belief system.

Political ideology Refers to theories pertaining to government.

Positive reinforcement Reward, or pleasant consequence, given for desired behavior.

Postconventional level Kohlberg's term to describe moral reasoning wherein the individual considers and weighs the values behind various consequences of behavior from different points of view.

Preconventional level Kohlberg's term to describe moral reasoning wherein the individual considers and weighs the personal consequences of behavior.

Prejudice An attitude involving prejudgment; the application of a previously formed judgment to some person, object, or situation.

Preoperational Piaget's second stage of cognitive development, applying to children about age 2–7, characterized by the use of symbols to represent objects, by judgment based on how things look, and by the belief that everyone has the same viewpoint.

Preventive services Those that attempt to lessen the stresses and strains of life resulting from social and technological changes and to avert problems.

Primogeniture The right of the eldest son to inherit his father's estate.

Professional One who is engaged in an occupation requiring advanced training, usually involving intellectual work.

Project Follow Through Federally funded program that extended the support services of Head Start to third grade.

Prosocial behavior Behavior that benefits other people, such as altruism, sharing, and cooperation.

Protestant ethic Refers to the belief in individualism, thrift, self-sacrifice, efficiency, personal responsibility, and productivity.

Psychological or **emotional abuse** Maltreatment involving a destructive pattern of continual attack by an adult on a child's self-esteem and social competence, taking the forms of rejecting, isolating, terrorizing, ignoring, and/or corrupting.

Punishment Physical or psychologically painful stimuli, or the temporary withdrawal of pleasant stimuli, when undesirable behavior occurs.

Pygmalion In Greek legend, a king of Cyprus and a sculptor who fell in love with his statue of a maiden, Galatea. He prayed to Aphrodite to have his statue brought to life.

Reality testing Testing assumptions against facts.

Reasoning Giving explanations, or causes, for an act.

Rehabilitation Restoration to a state of physical, mental, or moral health through treatment and training.

Rehabilitative services Those that enable or restore one's ability to participate in the community.

Reinforcement An object or event that is presented following a behavior, serving to increase the likelihood that it will occur again. Reinforcement can be positive or negative.

Religion A unified system of beliefs and practices relative to sacred things.

Resilience Refers to the ability to recover from or adjust to misfortune or change.

Rite A ceremonious act.

Rites of passage Rituals that signify changes in individuals' status as they move through life.

Ritual A set form or system; a ceremonial observation of a prescribed rule or custom.

Routines Repetitious acts or established procedures.

Segregation Separation of minority groups from the majority group.

Selective attention Choosing stimuli from one's environment to notice, observe, and consider.

Self-concept An individual's perception of his or her identity as distinct from others.

Self-control The ability to regulate one's impulses, behavior, and/or emotions until an appropriate time, place, or object is available for expression (self-regulation).

Self-efficacy The belief that one can master a situation and produce positive outcomes.

Self-esteem The value one places on his or her identity.

Self-regulation The process of bringing one's emotions, thoughts, and/or behavior under control.

Sensorimotor Piaget's first stage of cognitive development, applying to children from birth to about age 1½ or 2, characterized by the use of one's senses and motor abilities to interact with the environment and achieve an understanding of the here and now.

Sex typing Classification into gender roles based on biological sex.

Sexual abuse Maltreatment such that a person forces, tricks, or threatens a child in order to have sexual contact with him or her.

Shaping The systematic immediate reinforcement of successive approximations of the desired behavior until the desired behavior occurs and is maintained.

Social cognition Refers to conceptions and reasoning about people, oneself, relations between people, social groups' roles and rules, and the relation of such conceptions to social behavior.

Social competence Involves behavior influenced by the understanding of others' feelings and intentions, the ability to respond appropriately, and the knowledge of consequences of one's actions.

Socialization The processes by which individuals acquire the knowledge, skills, and dispositions that enable them to participate as more or less effective members of groups and society.

Social support Refers to the resources (tangible, intellectual, social, emotional) provided by others, usually in times of need.

Sociocentrism The ability to understand and relate to the views and perspectives of others.

Socioeconomic status Rank or position within a society, based on social and economic factors.

Sociogram A diagram showing preferences among group members for each other.

Sociometry Techniques to measure patterns of acceptance, neglect, and rejection among members of a group.

Sociotherapy An intervention to enable children who have trouble making and keeping friends to learn to relate to others.

Standard A level or grade of excellence regarded as a goal or measure of adequacy.

Standardized tests Tests in which an individual is compared to a norm on scientifically selected items.

Stereotype An oversimplified, fixed attitude or set of beliefs about members of a particular group.

Stress Results from demands that exceed a person's ability to cope.

Supportive services Those that promote the health, education, and welfare of society.

Symbols Acts or objects that have come to be generally accepted as standing for something else.

Tabula rasa Refers to the mind before impressions are recorded on it by experience; blank slate.

Teacher-directed curriculum One in which the learning activities are planned by the teacher for all the children.

Temperament The innate characteristics that determine an individual's sensitivity to various experiences and responsiveness to patterns of social interaction.

Therapy The process of healing or curing.

Tradition Customs, stories, beliefs, and so on, handed down from generation to generation.

Traditional school Teacher-centered school in that the curriculum is predetermined by the teacher and evaluation is based on success in mastering the learning objectives, which emphasize factual knowledge, and preserving American cultural heritage.

Tradition-directed person One who looks to tradition or the past for guidance and models of behavior.

Traditional society One that relies on customs handed down from past generations as ways to behave.

Transductive reasoning Reasoning from one particular fact or case to another, similar fact or case.

Values Qualities or beliefs that are viewed as desirable or important.

Uninvolved A style of insensitive parenting, with few demands or rules.

Values clarification The process of discovering what things are most important or valuable to one.

Violence The overt expression of physical force against one's will, under threat of being hurt or killed.

Voucher A coupon in the amount the school district would normally spend on a child's education that the child's family can "spend" at whatever school they choose, public or private.

Zone of proximal development (ZPD) Vygotsky's term for the space between what one is capable of learning independently and that which one can learn by participating with more capable others.

References

Aaronson, L. S., & MacNee, C. L. (1989). Tobacco, alcohol and caffeine use during pregnancy. *Journal of Obstetrics, Gynecology and Neonatal Nursing, 18,* 279–287.

Aboud, F. (1988). *Children and prejudice.* Cambridge, MA: Basil Blackwell.

Abramovitch, R., & Grusec, J. E. (1978). Peer interaction in a natural setting. *Child Development, 49,* 60–65.

Adams, G. R., & Crane, P. (1980). Assessment of parents' and teachers' expectations of preschool children's social preferences for attractive or unattractive children and adults. *Child Development, 51,* 224–231.

Adams, G. R., Gullotta, T. P., & Markstrom-Adams, C. (1994). *Adolescent life experiences* (3rd ed.). Pacific Grove, CA: Brooks/Cole.

Adler, P. A., & Adler, P. (1998). *Peer power: Preadolescent culture and identity.* New Brunswick, NJ: Rutgers University Press.

Agne, K. J. (1992). Caring: The expert teacher's edge. *Educational Horizons, 70*(3), 120–124.

Ainsworth, M. D. S. (1973). The development of infant–mother attachment. In B. M. Caldwell & H. N. Ricciuti (Eds.), *Review of child development research* (Vol. 3). Chicago: University of Chicago Press.

———. (1979). Infant-mother attachment. *American Psychologist, 34,* 932–937.

———. (1982). Attachment: Retrospect and prospect. In C. M. Parkes & J. Stevenson-Hinde (Eds.), *The place of attachment in human behavior.* New York: Basic Books.

Ainsworth, M. D. S., & Bell, S. M. (1970). Attachment, exploration, and separation: Illustrated by the behavior of one-year-olds in a strange situation. *Child Development, 41,* 49–67.

Ainsworth, M. D. S., Bell, S. M., & Stayton, D. J. (1971). Individual differences in strange-situation behavior of one-year-olds. In H. R. Shaffer (Ed.), *The origins of human social relations.* London: Academic Press.

Ainsworth, M. D. S., Blehar, M., Waters, E., & Wall, S. (1978). *Patterns of attachment: A psychological adjustment: A psychological study of the strange situation.* Hillsdale, NJ: Lawrence Erlbaum.

Alexander, J. E., & Tate, M. A. (1999). *Web wisdom.* Mahwah, NJ: Lawrence Erlbaum.

Alsaker, F. D. (1992). Pubertal timing, overweight, and psychological adjustment. *Journal of Early Adolescence, 12,* 396–419.

Amato, P. (1998). More than money? Men's contributions to their children's lives. In A. Booth & A. C. Crouter (Eds.), *Men in families. When do they get involved? What difference does it make?* Mahwah, NJ: Lawrence Erlbaum.

American Academy of Child and Adolescent Psychiatry (AACAP). (1997). *Facts for families: Children of alcoholics.* www.aacap.org

———. (1997). *Facts for families: The influence of music and rock videos.* www.aacap.org

———. (1999). *Facts for families: The adopted child.* www.aacap.org

American Academy of Pediatrics (AAP). (1995). The role of schools in combating substance abuse. *Pediatrics, 95*(5), 784–785.

———. (1996). The impact of music lyrics and music videos on children and youth. Policy Statement. *Pediatrics, 98*(6), 1219–1221.

———. (2002). *Peer groups and cliques.* www.aap.org

American Association of University Women. (AAUW). (1991). *How schools shortchange girls.* Washington, DC: AAUW Educational Foundation.

American Bar Association (1996). *Guide to family law: The complete and easy guide to the laws of marriage, parenthood, separation, and divorce.* New York: Times Books.

Anastasiow, N. J. (1973). *Educational psychology: A contemporary view.* New York: Random House.

Anderson, D. R., Huston, A. C., Schmitt, K. L., Linebarger, D. L., & Wright, J. C. (2001). Early childhood television viewing and adolescent behavior: The recontact study. *Monographs of the Society for Research in Child Development, 66* (1).

Andreasen, M. (2001). Evolution in the family's use of television: An overview. In J. Bryant & J. A. Bryant (Eds.). *Television and the American family* (2nd ed.). Mahwah, NJ: Lawrence Erlbaum.

Apter, A., Galatzer, A., Beth-Halachmi, N., & Laron, Z. (1981). Self-image in adolescents with delayed puberty and growth retardation. *Journal of Youth and Adolescence, 10,* 501–505.

Arensberg, C. M., & Niehoff, A. H. (1975). American cultural values. In J. P. Spradley & M. A. Rynkiewich (Eds.), *The Nacirema: Readings on American culture.* Boston: Little, Brown.

Aries, P. (1962). *Centuries of childhood: A social history of family life.* New York: Knopf.

Arnett, J. (1991). Adolescents and heavy metal music: From the mouths of metal heads. *Youth and Society, 33*(1), 76–98.

Aronfreed, J. (1968). *Conduct and conscience.* New York: Academic Press.

Aronson, E., & Patenoe, S. (1996). *The jigsaw classroom: Building cooperation in the classroom.* Reading, MA: Addison-Wesley.

Arvey, R. D., & Chapman, J. E. (1982). The employment interview. *Personnel Psychology, 25,* 281–290.

Asch, S. E. (1958). Effects of group pressure upon the modification and distortion of judgments. In E. E. Maccoby, T. M. Newcomb, & E. L. Hartley (Eds.), *Readings in social psychology.* New York: Holt, Rinehart & Winston.

Asendorpf, J. B., & Baudoniere, P. (1993). Self-awareness and other-awareness: Mirror self-recognition and synchronic imitation among unfamiliar peers. *Developmental Psychology, 29,* 88–95.

Asher, S. R. (1982). Some kids are nobody's best friend. *Today's Education, 71*(1), 23.

Asher, S. R., & Coie, J. D. (1990). *Peer rejection in childhood.* New York: Cambridge University Press.

Asher, S. R., Gottman, J. M., & Oden, S. L. (1977). Children's friendships in school settings. In E. M. Hetherington & R. D. Parke (Eds.), *Contemporary readings in child psychology.* New York: McGraw-Hill.

Atkin, C., & Gibson, W. (1978). *Children's nutrition learning from television advertising.* Unpublished manuscript, Michigan State University.

Atkinson, A. H., & Green, V. P. (1990). Cooperative learning: The teacher's role. *Childhood Education, 67*(1), 8–11.

Atkinson, J. W. (1964). *An introduction to motivation.* Princeton, NJ: Van Nostrand.

Ausubel, D. P. (1957). *Theory and problems of child development.* New York: Grune & Stratton.

Avery, C. D. (1971). A psychologist looks at the issue of public versus residential school placement for the blind. In R. L. Jones (Ed.), *Problems and issues in the education of exceptional children.* Boston: Houghton Mifflin.

Bagwell, C. L., Coie, J. D., Terry, R. A., & Lochman, J. E. (2000). Peer clique participation and social status in preadolescence. *Merrill-Palmer Quarterly, 46*(2), 280–305.

Bagwell, C. L., Newcomb, A. F., & Bukowski, W. M. (2000). Preadolescent friendship and peer rejection as predictors of adult adjustment. In W. Craig (Ed.), *Childhood social development.* Malden, MA: Blackwell.

Bain, S., Holliman, B., & McCallum, R. S. (1989). Children's self-predictions and teachers' predictions of basic concept mastery: Effects of socioeconomic status, locus of control, and achievement. *Journal of Psychoeducational Assessment, 7,* 235–245.

Baker, A. K., Barthelemy, K. J., & Kurdek, L. A. (1993). The relation between fifth and sixth graders' peer-rated classroom social status and their perceptions of family and neighborhood factors. *Journal of Applied Developmental Psychology, 14,* 547–556.

Baker, C. H., & Young, P. (1960). Feedback during training and retention of motor skills. *Canadian Journal of Psychology, 14,* 257–264.

Balk, D. E. (1995). *Adolescent development.* Pacific Grove, CA: Brooks/Cole.

Ball, S. J., & Bogatz, G. (1970). *The first year of Sesame Street: An evaluation.* Princeton, NJ: Educational Testing Service.

Bandura, A. (1965). Influence of models' reinforcement contingencies on the acquisition of imitative responses. *Journal of Personality and Social Psychology, 1,* 589–595.

———. (1973). *Aggression: A social learning analysis.* Englewood Cliffs, NJ: Prentice-Hall.

———. (1974). Behavior theory and the models of man. *American Psychologist, 29,* 859–869.

———. (1977). *Social learning theory.* Englewood Cliffs, NJ: Prentice-Hall.

———. (1986). *Social foundations of thought and action: A social cognitive theory.* Englewood Cliffs, NJ: Prentice-Hall.

———. (1989). Social cognitive theory. In R. Vasta (Ed.), *Annals of child development. Vol. 6. Six theories of child development: Revised formulations and current issues.* Greenwich, CT: JAI Press.

———. (1991). Social cognitive theory of moral thought and action. In W. M. Kurtines & J. L. Gewirtz (Eds.), *Handbook of moral behavior and development* (Vol. 1). Hillsdale, NJ: Lawrence Erlbaum.

———. (1997). *Self-efficacy: The exercise of control.* New York: Freeman.

———. (2000). Self-efficacy. In A. Kazdin (Ed.), *Encyclopedia of Mental Health* (Vol. 3). San Diego: Academic Press.

Bandura, A., Ross, D., & Ross, S. (1963). Imitation of film-mediated aggressive models. *Journal of Abnormal and Social Psychology, 66,* 3–11.

———. (1965). A comparative test of status, envy, social power, and secondary reinforcement theories of identificatory learning. *Journal of Abnormal and Social Psychology, 67,* 527–534.

Bandura, A., & Walters, R. H. (1963). *Social learning and personality development.* New York: Holt, Rinehart & Winston.

Bangert-Drowns, R. L., Kulik, C. C., Kulik, J. A., & Morgan, M. (1991). The instructional effect of feedback in test-like events. *Review of Educational Research, 61,* 213–238.

Banks, J. A. (2002). *Introduction to multicultural education* (3rd ed.). Needham Heights, MA: Allyn & Bacon.

Bannerman, A. (1899). *The story of little black Sambo.* Philadelphia: Lippincott.

Barber, B. R. (1996). *Jihad vs. McWorld: How globalism and tribalism are reshaping the world.* New York: Ballantine Books.

Barclay, K., Benelli, C., & Curtis, A. (1995). Literacy begins at birth: What caregivers can learn from parents of children who read early. *Young Children, 50*(4), 24–28.

Barker, R. G., & Gump, P. G. (1964). *Big school, small school: High school size and student behavior.* Stanford, CA: Stanford University Press.

Barnett, D., Manley, J., & Cicchetti, D. (1993). Defining child maltreatment: The interface between policy and research. In D. Cicchetti & S. Toth (Eds.), *Child abuse, child development, and social policy.* Norwood, NJ: Ablex.

Barnett, R. C., & Hyde, J. S. (2001). Women, men, and family: An expansionist theory. *American Psychologist, 56*(10), 781–796.

Baron, R. (1970). *Anonymity, deindividuation and aggression.* Unpublished Ph.D. dissertation, University of Minnesota.

Barry, F., & Garbarino, J. (2001). Children and the community. In R. T. Ammerman & M. Hersen (Eds.), *Handbook of prevention and treatment with children and adolescents: Interventions in the real world context.* New York: Wiley.

Barry, H., Child, I. L., & Bacon, M. K. (1957). Relation of child training to subsistence economy. *American Anthropologist, 61,* 51–63.

Bar-Tal, D., Raviv, A., & Lesser, T. (1980). The development of altruistic behavior: Empirical evidence. *Developmental Psychology, 16,* 516–524.

Basow, S. A. (1992). *Gender stereotypes and roles* (3rd ed.). Pacific Grove, CA: Brooks/Cole.

Basow, S. A., & Rubin, L. R. (1999). Gender influence on adolescent development. In N. G. Johnson, M. C. Roberts, & J. Worell (Eds.), *Beyond appearance: A new look at adolescent girls.* Washington, DC: American Psychological Association.

Baumrind, D. (1966). Effects of authoritative parental control on child behavior. *Child Development, 37,* 887–907.

———. (1967). Child care practices anteceding three patterns of preschool behavior. *Genetic Psychology Monographs, 74,* 43–88.

———. (1971a). Current patterns of parental authority. *Developmental Psychology, 4,* 1–101.

———. (1971b). Current patterns of parental authority. *Developmental Psychology Monographs, 4*(1) (Part 2).

———. (1973). The development of instrumental competence through socialization. In A. Pick (Ed.), *Minnesota symposium on child psychology* (Vol. 7). Minneapolis: University of Minnesota Press.

———. (1977, April). *Socialization determinants of personal agency.* Paper presented at the biennial meeting of the Society for Research in Child Development, New Orleans.

———. (1989). Rearing competent children. In W. Damon (Ed.), *Child development today and tomorrow.* San Francisco: Jossey-Bass.

———. (1991). Effective parenting during the early adolescent transition. In P. A. Cowan & E. M. Hetherington (Eds.), *Family transitions.* Hillsdale, NJ: Lawrence Erlbaum.

Bauserman, R. (2002). Child adjustment in joint custody versus sole custody arrangements. A meta-analytic review. *Journal of Family Psychology, 16*(1), 91–102.

Baydar, N., & Brooks-Gunn, J. (1991). Effects of maternal employment and child care arrangements on preschoolers' cognitive and behavioral outcomes. Evidence from the children of the National Longitudinal Survey of Youth. *Developmental Psychology, 27*(6), 932–945.

Beane, J. A. (1991). Sorting out the self-esteem controversy. *Educational Leadership, 49*(1), 25–30.

Bednar, R. L., Wells, M. G., & Peterson, S. R. (1989). *Self-esteem.* Washington, DC: American Psychological Association.

Beez, W. V. (1968). Influence of biased psychological reports on teacher behavior and pupil performance. *Proceedings of the 75th APA Annual Convention.* Washington, DC: American Psychological Association.

Begley, S. (1997, Spring/Summer). How to build a baby's brain. *Newsweek,* 28–32.

Behrman, R. E. (Ed.). (1997a). Executive summary: Welfare to work. *The Future of Children, 7*(1).

———. (Ed.). (1997b). Executive summary: Children and poverty. *The Future of Children, 7*(2).

———. (Ed.). (1999). Executive summary: When school is out. *The Future of Children, 7*(1).

———. (Ed.). (2002). Children and welfare reform: Analysis and recommendations. *The Future of Children, 12*(1), 5–25.

Bell, P. A., Greene, T. C., Fisher, J. D., & Baum, A. (2000). *Environmental psychology* (5th ed.). Belmont, CA: Wadsworth.

Belle, D. (1989). Studying children's social networks and social supports. In D. Belle (Ed.), *Children's social networks and social supports.* New York: Wiley.

Belle, D. (1999). *The after-school lives of children: Alone and with others while parents work.* Mahwah, NJ: Lawrence Erlbaum.

Belsky, J. (1988). The "effects" of infant day care reconsidered. *Early Childhood Research Quarterly, 3,* 235–272.

———. (1992). Consequences of child care for children's development: A deconstructionist view. In A. Booth (Ed.), *Childcare in the 1990s: Trends and consequences.* Hillsdale, NJ: Lawrence Erlbaum.

———. (1993). Etiology of child maltreatment: A developmental-ecological analysis. *Psychological Bulletin, 114,* 413–434.

Belsky, J., & Rovine, M. (1988). Nonmaternal care in the first year of life and infant–parent attachment security. *Child Development, 59,* 157–167.

Bem, S. L. (1981). Gender schema theory: A cognitive account of sex-typing. *Psychological Review, 88,* 354–364.

Bengston, V. L. (2001). Beyond the nuclear family: The increasing importance of multigenerational bonds. *Journal of Marriage and Family, 63,* 1–16.

Bennett, C. I. (2003). *Comprehensive multicultural education: Theory and practice* (5th ed.). Needham Heights, MA: Allyn & Bacon.

Bennett, W. J. (1993). *The book of virtues: A treasury of great moral stories.* New York: Simon & Schuster.

Bereiter, C., & Engelmann, S. (1966). *Teaching disadvantaged children in the preschool.* Englewood Cliffs, NJ: Prentice-Hall.

Berenda, R. (1950). *The influence of the group on the judgment of children.* New York: King's Crown Press.

Berger, E. H. (1995). *Parents as partners in education: Families and schools working together* (4th ed.). Columbus, OH: Merrill.

Berk, L. E. (2003). *Child development* (6th ed.). Needham Heights, MA: Allyn & Bacon.

Berk, L. E., & Winsler, A. (1995). *Scaffolding children's learning: Vygotsky and early childhood education.* Washington, DC: National Association for the Education of Young Children.

Berndt, T. J. (1979). Developmental changes in conformity to peers and parents. *Developmental Psychology, 15,* 608–616.

———. (1983). Correlates and causes of sociometric status in childhood: A commentary on six current studies of popular, rejected and neglected children. *Merrill-Palmer Quarterly, 29,* 439–448.

Berndt, T. J., & Ladd, G. W. (1989). *Peer relationships in child development.* New York: Wiley.

Bernhard, J. K., Lefebvre, M. L., Kilbride, K. M., Chud, G., & Lange, R. (1998). Troubled relationships in early childhood education: Parent–teacher interactions in ethnoculturally diverse childcare settings. *Early Education and Development, 9,* 5–28.

Berns, R. (1981). *When handicaps come in handy.* Washington, DC: Department of Health, Education, and Welfare, National Institute of Education, Educational Resources Information Center. (ED 208621).

Bernstein, A. (1984, September). *Parents,* 40–44, 48–49.

Bernstein, B. (1961). Social class and linguistic development: A theory of social learning. In A. H. Halsey, J. Floud, & C. A. Anderson (Eds.), *Education, economy and society.* New York: Free Press.

Best, R. (1983). *We've all got scars: What boys and girls learn in elementary school.* Bloomington: Indiana University Press.

Bettelheim, B. (1976). *The uses of enchantment. The meaning and importance of fairy tales.* New York: Random House.

Bhavnagri, N. P. (1997). The cultural context of caregiving. *Childhood Education, 74*(1), 2–7.

Bigler, R. S., Brown, C. S., & Markell, M. (2001). When groups are not created equal: Effects of group status on the formation of intergroup attitudes in children. *Child Development, 72,* 1151–1162.

Bigler, R. S., & Liben, L. S. (1990). The role of attitudes and interventions in gender-schematic processing. *Child Development, 61,* 1440–1452.

Bigner, J. (1979). *Parent–child relations.* New York: Macmillan.

Biklen, D., & Bogdan, R. (1977). Media portrayals of disabled people: A study in stereotypes. *Interracial Books for Children Bulletin, 6, 7, 8,* 4–9.

Biller, H. B. (1993). *Fathers and families: Paternal factors in child development.* Westport, CT: Auburn House.

Binion, V. J. (1990). Psychological androgyny: A black female perspective. *Sex roles, 22,* 487–507.

Biskind, P. (1983). *Seeing is believing. How Hollywood taught us to stop worrying and love the fifties.* New York: Pantheon Books.

Bjorklund, D. F. (1994). *Children's thinking* (2nd ed.). Pacific Grove, CA: Brooks/Cole.

Black, C. (1991). *It will never happen to me!* (reissue ed.). Denver: M.A.C.

Blake, J. (1989). *Family size and achievement.* Berkeley: University of California Press.

Blas, A. (1990). Kohlberg's theory and moral development. In D. Schrader (Ed.), *New directions for child development* (No. 47). San Francisco: Jossey-Bass.

Block, J. H. (1973). Conceptions of sex role: Some cross-cultural and longitudinal perspectives. *American Psychologist, 28,* 512.

———. (1984). The influence of differential socialization on the personality development of males and females. In A. Pines & C. Maslach (Eds.), *Experiencing social psychology* (2nd ed.). New York: Knopf.

Block, J. H., & Robins, R. W. (1993). A longitudinal study of consistency and change in self-esteem from early adolescence to early adulthood. *Child Development, 64,* 909–923.

Bloom, B. S. (1973). Individual differences in achievement. In L. J. Rubin (Ed.), *Facts and feelings in the classroom.* New York: Viking Press.

———. (1982). *Human characteristics and school learning.* New York: McGraw-Hill.

Blume, J. (1970). *Are you there, God? It's me, Margaret.* New York: Dell.

———. (1974). *Blubber.* New York: Dell.

Bogenschneider, K., Wu, M., Raffaeli, M., & Tsay, J. C. (1998). Parental influences on adolescent peer orientation and substance use: The interface of parenting practices and values. *Child Development, 69,* 1672–1688.

Bok, S. (1989). *Lying: Moral choice in public and private life.* New York: Vintage Books.

Bolger, K. E., & Patterson, C. J. (2001). Developmental pathways from child maltreatment to peer rejection. *Child Development, 72,* 549–568.

Bornstein, M. H. (1995). Parenting infants. In M. H. Bornstein (Ed.), *Handbook of parenting* (Vol. 1). Hillsdale, NJ: Lawrence Erlbaum.

Bossard, J. H. S., & Boll, E. S. (1954). The status of children in society. In J. H. S. Bossard & E. S. Boll (Eds.), *The society of child development*. New York: Harper & Row.

———. (1956). *The large family system*. Philadelphia: University of Pennsylvania Press.

Boswell, D. A., & Williams, J. E. (1975). Correlates of race and color bias among preschool children. *Psychological Reports, 36*, 147–154.

Bowlby, J. (1966). *Maternal care and mental health* (2nd ed.). New York: Schocken Books. (Original work published by the World Health Organization of the United Nations, Geneva, 1952.)

———. (1969). *Attachment* (Vol. 1). New York: Basic Books.

———. (1973). *Loss* (Vol. 2). New York: Basic Books.

———. (1988). *A secure base: Parent–child attachment and healthy human development*. New York: Basic Books.

Bowman, H. E., & Ahrons, C. R. (1985). Impact of legal custody status on fathers' parenting postdivorce. *Journal of Marriage and the Family, 47*, 481–488.

Boyd, B. J. (1997). Teacher response to superhero play: To ban or not to ban? *Childhood Education, 74*(1), 23–28.

Boyer, E. L. (1991). *Ready to learn: A mandate for the nation*. Princeton, NJ: Carnegie Foundation for the Advancement of Technology.

Boyer, P. J. (1983, March 15). TV grants kids a short shrift. *Los Angeles Times* (Part VI), p. 1.

Bradley, R. H. Caldwell, B. M., & Rock, S. L. (1990). Home environment classification system: A model for assessing the home environments of developing children. *Early Education and Development, 1*, 237–265.

Brady, M. (2000). The standards juggernaut. *Phi Delta Kappan, 81* (9), 649–651.

Bray, S. H. (1988). Children's development during early remarriage. In E. M. Hetherington & J. D. Arasteh (Eds.), *Impact of divorce, single parenting and stepparenting on children*. Hillsdale, NJ: Lawrence Erlbaum.

Brazelton, T. B. (1984). Working parents. *Newsweek, 15*, (5), 66–70.

Bredekamp, S. (Ed.). (1986). *Developmentally appropriate practice*. Washington, DC: National Association for the Education of Young Children.

———. (Ed.). (1993). *Developmentally appropriate practice in early childhood programs serving children from birth through age eight*. Washington, DC: National Association for the Education of Young Children.

Bredekamp, S., & Copple, C. (Eds.). (1997). *Developmentally appropriate practice in early childhood programs* (rev. ed.). Washington, DC: National Association for the Education of Young Children.

Brenner, J., & Von Moschzisker, M. (1971). *The school without walls*. New York: Holt, Rinehart & Winston.

Bria, G. (1998). *The art of family*. New York: Dell.

Bridges, K. B. (1933). A study of social development in early infancy. *Child Development, 4*, 36–49.

Briggs, D. C. (1975). *Your child's self-esteem*. New York: Dolphin.

Brim, O. G. (1966). Socialization through the life cycle. In O. G. Brim & S. Wheeler (Eds.), *Socialization after childhood: Two essays*. New York: Wiley.

Britton, G., & Limpkin, M. (1983). Basal readers: Paltry progress pervades. *Interracial Books for Children Bulletin, 14*(6), 4–7.

Brody, G. H., & Flor, D. L. (1998). Maternal resources, parenting practices, and child competence in rural, single-parent African American families. *Child Development, 69*, 803–816.

Bromer, J. (1999). Cultural variations in child care: Values and action. *Young Children, 54*(6), 72–75.

Bronfenbrenner, U. (1970a). *Two worlds of childhood: U.S. and U.S.S.R.* New York: Russell Sage.

———. (1970b). Reaction to social pressure from adults versus peers of Soviet day-school and boarding-school pupils in the perspective of an American sample. *Journal of Personality and Social Psychology, 15*, 179–189.

———. (1970c, November). *Who cares for American's children?* Address presented at the National Association of Educators of Young Children Conference, Boston.

———. (1977). Is early intervention effective? In S. Cohen & T. J. Comiskey (Eds.), *Child development: Contemporary perspectives*. Itasca, IL: Peacock.

———. (1979). *The ecology of human development*. Cambridge, MA: Harvard University Press.

———. (1980). Reunification with our children. In P. Mussen, J. Conger, & J. Kagan (Eds.), *Readings in child and adolescent psychology: Contemporary perspectives*. New York: Harper & Row.

———. (1989). Ecological systems theory. In R. Vasta (Ed.), *Annals of child development* (Vol. 6). Greenwich, CT: JAI Press.

———. (1995). Developmental ecology through space and time: A future perspective. In P. Moen, G. H. Elder, Jr., & K. Luscher (Eds.), *Examining lives in context: Perspectives on the ecology of human development*. Washington, DC: American Psychological Association.

Bronfenbrenner, U., & Crouter, A. (1982). Work and family through time and space. In S. B. Kammerman & C. D. Hayes (Eds.), *Families that work: Children in a changing world*. Washington, DC: National Academy Press.

Bronfenbrenner, U., & Garbarino, J. (1976). The socialization of moral judgment and behavior in cross-cultural perspective. In T. Lickona (Ed.), *Moral development and behavior*. New York: Holt, Rinehart & Winston.

Bronfenbrenner, U., & Morris, P. A. (1998). The ecology of developmental process. In W. Damon (Ed.), *Handbook of child psychology* (5th ed., Vol. 1). New York: Wiley.

Bronson, M. B. (2000). *Self-regulation in early childhood: Nature and nurture.* New York: Guilford Press.

Brook, J. S., & Cohen, P. (1990). The psychological etiology of adolescent drug use: A family interactional approach. *Genetic Psychology Monographs, 116*(2).

Brooks-Gunn, J., & Furstenberg, F. F., Jr. (1989). Adolescent sexual behavior. *American Psychologist, 44*(2), 249–257.

Brophy, B. (1989, August 7). Spock had it right: Studies suggest that kids thrive when parents set firm limits. *U.S. News & World Report,* 49–51.

Brophy, J. E. (1986). Teacher influences on student achievement. *American Psychologist, 41,* 1069–1077.

———. (1992). Probing the subtleties of subject matter teaching. *Educational Leadership, 49*(7), 4–8.

Brophy, J. E., & Good, T. L. (1986). Teacher behavior and student achievement. In M. Wittrock (Ed.), *Handbook of research on teaching* (3rd ed.). New York: Macmillan.

Brown, B. B., Clasen, D. R., & Eicher, S. A. (1986). Perceptions of peer pressure, peer conformity dispositions and self-reported behavior among adolescents. *Developmental Psychology, 22,* 521–530.

Brown, B. B., & Lohr, M. J. (1987). Peer group affiliation, adolescent self-esteem, and integration of ego-identity and symbolic-interaction theories. *Journal of Personality and Social Psychology, 52*(1), 47–57.

Brown, J. D. (1998). *The self.* New York: McGraw-Hill.

Brown, J., & Cantor, J. (2000). An agenda for research on youth and the media. *Journal of Adolescent Health, 278,* 2–7.

Brown, L. M., & Gilligan, C. (1990, March). *The psychology of women and the development of girls.* Paper presented at the meeting of the Society for Research on Adolescence, Atlanta.

Brown, L. S., & Zimmer, D. (1986). An introduction to therapy issues of lesbian and gay male couples. In N. S. Jacobson & A. S. Gurman (Eds.), *Clinical handbook of marital therapy.* New York: Guilford Press.

Brown, M. W. (1947). *Goodnight moon.* New York: Harper & Row.

Bruner, J. (1981). The art of discovery. In M. Kaplan-Sangoff & R. Y. Magid (Eds.), *Exploring early childhood.* New York: Macmillan.

Bryant, J., & Rockwell, S. C. (1994). Effects of massive exposure to sexually oriented prime-time television programming on adolescents' moral judgment. In D. Zillman, J. Bryant, & A. C. Huston (Eds.), *Media, children, and the family: Social, scientific, psychodynamic, and clinical perspectives.* Hillsdale, NJ: Lawrence Erlbaum.

Bugental, D. B., & Goodenow, J. J. (1998). Socialization processes. In W. Damon (Ed.), *Handbook of child psychology* (5th ed., Vol. 3). New York: Wiley.

Bullock, J. R. (1992, Winter). Children without friends: Who are they and how can teachers help? *Childhood Education,* 92–96.

Burchinal, M. R., Peisner-Feinberg, E., Bryant, D. M., & Clifford, R. (2000). Children's social and cognitive development and child-care quality: Testing for differential associations related to poverty, gender, or ethnicity. *Applied Developmental Science, 4*(3), 149–165.

Burhans, K. K., & Dweck, C. S. (1995). Helplessness in early childhood. The role of contingent worth. *Child Development, 66,* 1719–1738.

Burton, C. B. (1986). Children's peer relationships. *ERIC Digest.* (ED 265936).

Buss, A. H., & Plomin, R. (1984). *Temperament: Early developing personality traits.* Hillsdale, NJ: Lawrence Erlbaum.

Cain, K. M., & Dweck, C. J. (1995). The relation between motivational patterns and achievement cognitions through the elementary school years. *Merrill-Palmer Quarterly, 41,* 25–52.

Caldera, Y. M., Huston, A. C., & O'Brien, M. (1989). Social interactions and play patterns of parents and toddlers with feminine, masculine, and neutral toys. *Child Development, 60,* 70–76.

Caldwell, B. M. (1986). Education of families for parenting. In M. W. Yogman & T. B. Brazelton (Eds.), *In support of families.* Cambridge, MA: Harvard University Press.

Caldwell, B. M., & Bradley, R. H. (1984). *Manual for the home observation for measurement of the environment.* Little Rock: University of Arkansas Press.

Caldwell, B. M., & Crary, D. (1981). Why are kids so darned aggressive? *Parents, 56*(2), 52–56.

Camara, K. A. (1986). Family adaptation to divorce. In M. W. Yogman and T. B. Brazelton (Eds.), *In support of families.* Cambridge, MA: Harvard University Press.

Campbell, J. J., Lamb, M. E., & Hwang, C. P. (2000). Early child-care experiences and children's social competence between $1\frac{1}{2}$ and 15 years of age. *Applied and Developmental Science, 4*(3), 166–175.

Cantor, J. (1998). *"Mommy, I'm scared": How TV and movies frighten children and what we can do to protect them.* San Diego: Harcourt Brace.

Carle, E. (1986). *The very hungry caterpillar.* New York: Putnam.

Carlsen, G. R. (1980). *Books and the teenage reader.* New York: Harper & Row.

Carlson, M., Charlin, V., & Miller, N. (1988). Positive mood and helping behavior: A test of six hypotheses. *Psychological Bulletin, 55,* 211–229.

Carpenter, C. J. (1983). Activity, structure, and play: Implications for socialization. In M. B. Liss (Ed.),

Social and cognitive skills: Sex roles and children's play. New York: Academic Press.

Carpenter, C. J., Huston, A. C., & Hart, W. (1986). Modification of preschool sex-typed behaviors by participation in adult-structured activities. *Sex Roles, 4,* 603–615.

Carr, M., Borkowski, J. G., & Maxwell, S. E. (1991). Motivational components of underachievement. *Developmental Psychology, 27*(1), 108–118.

Cashdan, S. (1999). *The witch must die: How fairy tales shape our lives.* New York: Basic Books.

Caudill, W. (1988). Tiny dramas: Vocal communication between mother and infant in Japanese and American families. In G. Handel (Ed.), *Childhood socialization.* New York: Aldine de Gruyter.

Center for Communication and Social Policy. (1998). *National television violence study 3.* Thousand Oaks, CA: Sage.

Center for Media Education. (1997). *The deceiving web of online advertising.* www.cme.org

———. (1997). *Commercials.* www.cme.org

Center for Media and Public Affairs. (1999). *I'm okay, you're dead! TV and movies suggest violence is harmless.* www.cmpa.com/pressrel

Centers for Disease Control and Prevention. (1994). *Preventing tobacco use among young people: A report of the Surgeon General.* Atlanta: U.S. Department of Health and Human Services.

Cesarone, B. (1994, January). Video games and children. *ERIC Digest.* (ED-PS-94-3).

Chafel, J. A. (1997). Schooling, the hidden curriculum, and children's conceptions of poverty. Social Policy Report. *Society for Research in Child Development, 11*(1).

Chafetz, J. S. (1974). *Masculine/feminine or human? An overview of the sociology of sex roles.* Itasca, IL: Peacock.

Chall, J. (2000). *The academic achievement challenge: What really works in the classroom.* New York: Guilford Press.

Chance, P. (1983). Your child's self-esteem. In H. E. Fitzgerald & T. H. Carr (Eds.), *Annual editions, Human development 83/84.* Guilford, CT: Dushkin.

Chao, R. (1994). Beyond parent control and authoritarian parenting style: Understanding Chinese parenting through the culture notion of training. *Child Development, 65,* 1111–1119.

Char, C. A., & Meringoff, L. K. (1981, January). The role of story illustrations: Children's story comprehension in three different media. *Harvard Project Zero Technical Report* (No. 22).

Chase-Lansdale, P. L., & Hetherington, E. M. (1990). The impact of divorce on life-span development: Short and long-term effects. In D. Featherman & R. M. Lerner (Eds.), *Lifespan development and behavior* (Vol. 6). Orlando, FL: Academic Press.

Cherian, V. I. (1989). Academic achievement of children of divorced parents. *Psychological Reports, 64,* 355–358.

Chess, S., & Thomas, A. (1987). *Know your child.* New York: Basic Books.

Child Welfare League of America. (2002). *Fact sheet.* www.cwla.org

Children Now. (May, 1998). *A different world: Children's perceptions of race and class in media.* Oakland, CA: Author.

Children's Defense Fund (CDF). (1990). *Children, 1990: A report briefing book and activity primer.* Washington, DC: Author.

———. (1994). *The state of America's children: Yearbook 1994.* Washington, DC: Author.

———. (2001). *The state of America's children: Yearbook 2001.* Washington, DC: Author.

Chomsky, N. (1972). Stages in language development and reading exposure. *Harvard Educational Review, 42,* 1–33.

Chmielewski, C. (1997, September). Sexual harassment meet Title IX. *NEA Today, 16*(2), 24–25.

Christenson, P. G., & Roberts, D. F. (1998). *It's not only rock & roll: Popular music in the lives of adolescents.* Cresskill, NJ: Hampton Press.

Cicchetti, D., & Lynch, M. (1993). Toward an ecological transactional model of community violence and child maltreatment: Consequences for children's development. *Psychiatry, 56,* 96–118.

Cillesen, A. H. N., & Bukowski, W. M. (2000). *Recent advances in the measurement of acceptance and rejection in the peer system.* San Francisco: Jossey-Bass.

Clarke-Stewart, K. A. (1987). Predicting child development from day care forms and features: The Chicago study. In D. A. Phillips (Ed.), *Quality in childcare. What does research tell us? Research Monographs of the National Association for the Education of Young Children* (Vol. 1). Washington, DC: National Association for the Education of Young Children.

———. (1988). The "effects" of infant day care reconsidered: Risks for parents, children, and researchers. *Early Childhood Research Quarterly, 3,* 293–318.

———. (1989). Infant day care: Maligned or malignant? *American Psychologist, 44*(2), 266–273.

———. (1992). Consequences of child care for children's development. In A. Booth (Ed.), *Childcare in the 1990s: Trends and consequences.* Hillsdale, NJ: Lawrence Erlbaum.

———. (1993). *Daycare* (rev. ed.). Cambridge, MA: Harvard University Press.

Clarke-Stewart, K. A., Allhusen, V. D., & Clements, D. C. (1995). Nonparenting caregiving. In M. H. Bornstein (Ed.), *Handbook of parenting* (Vol. 3). Mahwah, NJ: Lawrence Erlbaum.

Clausen, J. A. (1975). The social meaning of differential physical and sexual maturation. In S. E. Dragastin & G. H. Elder (Eds.), *Adolescence in the life cycle.* New York: Wiley.

Coates, B., Pusser, H. E., & Goodman, I. (1976). The influence of "Sesame Street" and "Mister Rogers' Neighborhood" on children's social behavior in the preschool. *Child Development, 47*, 138–144.

Coates, D. L. (1987). Gender differences in the structure and support characteristics of black adolescents' social networks. *Sex Roles, 17*, 719–736.

Cochran, M. (1993). Parenting and personal social networks. In T. Luster & L. Okagaki (Eds.), *Parenting: An ecological perspective*. Hillsdale, NJ: Lawrence Erlbaum.

Cochran, M., & Henderson, C. R. Jr. (1986). *Family matters: Evaluation of the parental empowerment program*. Ithaca, NY: Cornell University. (ED 262862).

Cocks, J. (1985, September 30). Rock is a four-letter word. *Time*, 70–71.

Cohen, D., Pettigrew, T., & Riley, R. (1972). Race and the outcoming of schooling. In R. Mosteller & D. P. Moynihan (Eds.), *On equality of educational opportunity*. New York: Random House.

Cohen, R., Bornstein, R., & Sherman, R. C. (1973). Conformity behavior of children as a function of group make-up and task ambiguity. *Developmental Psychology, 9*, 124–131.

Cohen, S., Glass, D. C., & Singer, J. E. (1973). Apartment noise, auditory discrimination, and reading ability in children. *Journal of Experimental Social Psychology, 9*, 407–422.

Coie, J. D., & Cillesen, A. (1993). Peer rejection: Origins and effects on children's development. *Current Directions in Psychological Science, 2*, 89–92.

Coie, J. D., & Dodge, K. A. (1998). Aggression and antisocial behavior. In N. E. Eisenberg (Ed.), *Handbook of childhood psychology* (5th ed.). New York: Wiley.

Coie, J. D., Dodge, K. A., & Kupersmidt, J. B. (1990). Peer group behavior and social status. In S. R. Asher & J. D. Coie (Eds.), *Peer rejection in childhood*. New York: Cambridge University Press.

Colby, A., & Kohlberg, L. (1987). *The measurement of moral judgement: Vol. 1. Theoretical foundations and research validation*. Cambridge: Cambridge University Press.

Colby, A., Kohlberg, L., Gibbs, J., & Lieberman, M. A. (1983). A longitudinal study of moral judgment. *Monographs of the Society for Research in Child Development, 48*(1–2), (Serial No. 200).

Cole, D. A. (1991). Change in self-perceived competence as a function of peer and teacher evaluation. *Developmental Psychology, 27*, 682–688.

Cole, E., & Duva, J. (1990). *Family preservation: An orientation for administrators and practitioners*. Washington, DC: Child Welfare League of America.

Coleman, J. (1961). *The adolescent society*. New York: Macmillan.

———. (1966). *Equality of educational opportunity*. Washington, DC: U.S. Government Printing Office.

Coleman, J. S. (1990). *Foundations of social theory*. Englewood Cliffs, NJ: Prentice-Hall.

Collins, L. J., Ingoldsby, B. B., & Dellman, M. M. (1984). Sex-role stereotyping in children's literature: A change from the past. *Childhood Education, 60*(4), 278–285.

Collins, W. A., Harris, M. L., & Susman, A. (1995). Parenting during middle childhood. In M. H. Bornstein (Ed.), *Handbook of parenting* (Vol. 1). Mahwah, NJ: Lawrence Erlbaum.

Collins, W. A., Maccoby, E. E., Steinberg, L., Hetherington, E. M., & Bornstein, M. H. (2000). Contemporary research on parenting: The case for nature and nurture. *American Psychologist, 55*(2), 218–232.

Collodi, C. (1972). Pinocchio. In *The new Walt Disney treasury*. New York: Garden Press.

Comer, I. P. (1988). Educating poor minority children. *Scientific American, 259*(5), 42–48.

Comstock, G., & Paik, H. (1991). *Television and the American child*. San Diego: Academic Press.

Comstock, G., & Sharrer, E. (1999). *Television: What's on, who's watching and what it means*. San Diego: Academic Press.

———. (2001). The use of television and other film-related media. In D. G. Singer & J. L. Singer (Eds.), *Handbook of children and the media*. Thousand Oaks, CA: Sage.

Condry, J. (1989). *The psychology of television*. Hillsdale, NJ: Lawrence Erlbaum.

Condry, J. C., & Simon, M. L. (1974). Characteristics of peer- and adult-oriented children. *Journal of Marriage and the Family, 36*, 543–546.

Condry, J., Bence, P., & Scheibe, C. (1988). Nonprogram content of children's television. *Journal of Broadcasting and Electronic Media, 32*(3), 255–270.

Connors, L. J., & Epstein, J. L. (1995). Parent and school partnerships. In M. H. Bornstein (Ed.), *Handbook of parenting* (Vol. 4). Mahwah, NJ: Lawrence Erlbaum.

Cooley, C. (1964). *Human nature and the social order*. New York: Schocken Books. (Original work published 1909.)

Coontz, S. (1997). *The way we really are: Coming to terms with America's changing families*. New York: Basic Books.

Cooper, J., & Mackie, D. (1986). Video games and aggression in children. *Journal of Applied Social Psychology, 16*, 726–744.

Coopersmith, S. (1967). *The antecedents of self-esteem*. San Francisco: Freeman.

Corcoran, M. E., & Chandry, A. (1997). The dynamics of childhood poverty. *The Future of Children, 7*(2), 40–54.

Corsaro, W. A. (1981). Friendship in the nursery school: Social organization in a peer environment. In S. R. Asher & J. M. Gottman (Eds.), *The development of children's friendships*. Cambridge: Cambridge University Press.

Cost, Quality, and Child Outcomes Study (CQO) (1995). *Cost, quality, and child outcomes in child care centers, executive summary* (2nd ed.). Denver: Economics Department, University of Colorado.

———. (1999). *The children of the cost, quality, and outcomes study go to school.* Denver: Economics Department, University of Colorado.

Council of Better Business Bureaus. (2000). *The children's advertising review unit. Self-regulatory guidelines for children's advertising.* www.bbb.org/advertising/caruguid.asp

Covington, M. V., & Beery, R. G. (1976). *Self-worth and school learning.* New York: Holt, Rinehart & Winston.

Cowan, P. A., Powell, D., & Cowan, C. P. (1998). In W. Damon (Ed.), *Handbook of child psychology* (5th ed., Vol. 4). New York: Wiley.

Cox, M. J., Owen, M. T., Henderson, V. K., & Margand, N. A. (1992). Prediction of infant–father and infant–mother attachment. *Developmental Psychology, 28*(3), 474–483.

Crawford, M. T., & Unger, R. (2000). *Women and gender: A feminist psychology* (3rd ed.). New York: McGraw-Hill.

Crespo, C. J., Smit, E., Troiano, R. P., Bartlett, S. J., Macera, C. A., & Anderson, R. E. (2001). Television watching, energy intake, and obesity in U.S. children. *Archives of Pediatric and Adolescent Medicine, 155,* 360–365.

Crick, N. R., Casas, J. F., & Ku, Hyon-Chin. (1999). Relation of physical forms of peer victimization in preschool. *Developmental Psychology, 35,* 376–385.

Crime Prevention Center. (1988). *Child abuse prevention handbook.* Sacramento: California Department of Justice.

Crnic, K., & Acevedo, M. (1995). Everyday stress and parenting. In M. H. Bornstein (Ed.), *Handbook of parenting* (Vol. 4). Mahwah, NJ: Lawrence Earlbaum.

Crook, C. (1992). Cultural artifacts in social development: The case of computers. In H. McGurk (Ed.), *Childhood social development: Contemporary perspectives.* Hove, England: Lawrence Erlbaum.

Crouter, A. C., Bumpus, M. F., Maguire, M. C., & McHale, S. M. (1999). Linking parents' work pressure and adolescent's well-being: Insights into dynamics in dual-earner families. *Developmental Psychology, 35,* 1453–1461.

Crouter, A. C., & McHale, S. M. (1993). The long arm of the job: Influences of parental work on child-rearing. In T. Luster & L. Okagaki (Eds.), *Parenting: An ecological perspective.* Hillsdale, NJ: Lawrence Erlbaum.

Cubberley, E. P. (1919). *Public education in the United States.* Boston: Houghton Mifflin.

Curran, D. (1985). *Stress and the healthy family.* Minneapolis: Winston Press.

Dahl, R. (1964). *Charlie and the chocolate factory.* New York: Knopf.

Daiute, C. (1983). Writing, creativity and change. *Childhood Education, 59*(4), 227–231.

Damasio, A. R. (1994). *Descartes' error: Emotion, reason, and the human brain.* New York: Putnam.

Damon, W. (1988). *The moral child: Nurturing children's natural moral growth.* New York: Free Press.

Damon, W. D. (1999). The moral development of children. *Scientific American, 281*(2), 72–78.

Daniels, D. H., Kalkman, D. L., & McCombs, B. L. (2001). Young children's perspectives on learning and teacher practices in different classroom contexts: Implications for motivation. *Early Education and Development, 12,* 253–273.

Davidson, E., & Schniederwind, N. (1992). Class differences: Economic inequality in the classroom. In D. A. Byrnes & G. Kiger (Eds.), *Common bonds: Anti-bias teaching in a diverse society.* Wheaton, MD: Association for Childhood International.

Davidson, P., & Youniss, J. (1995). Moral development and social construction. In W. M. Kurtines & J. L. Gewirtz (Eds.), *Moral development: An introduction.* Boston: Allyn & Bacon.

Dean, C. (1984). Parental empowerment through family resource programs. *Human Ecology Forum, 14*(1), 17–22.

Deax, K., & Wrightsman, L. J. (1988). *Social psychology* (5th ed.). Pacific Grove, CA: Brooks/Cole.

Deci, E. L., & Ryan, R. M. (1985). *Intrinsic motivation and self-determination in human behavior.* New York: Plenum.

Decker, L. E., & Decker, V. A. (2001). *Engaging families & communities: Pathways to educational success.* Fairfax, VA: National Community Education Association.

Dellman-Jenkins, M., Florjancic, L., & Swadener, E. B. (1993). Sex roles and cultural diversity in recent award-winning picture books for young children. *Journal of Research in Childhood Education, 7*(2), 74–82.

Dennison, B. A., Erb, T. A., & Jenkins, P. L. (2002). Television viewing and television in bedroom associated with overweight risk among low-income preschool children. *Pediatrics, 109,* 1028–1035.

Depanfilis, D., Holder, W., Corey, M., & Olson, E. (1986). *Child-at-risk field training manual.* Charlotte, NC: ACTION for Child Protection.

Department of Health and Human Services (2002). *HHS invests in America's children.* Washington, DC: Author.

Derman-Sparks, L. (1989). *Anti-bias curriculum: Tools for empowering young children.* Washington, DC: National Association for the Education of Young Children.

Desmond, R. J., Singer, J. L., & Singer, D. G. (1990). Family mediation: Parental communication patterns and the influences of television on children. In J. Bryant (Ed.), *Television and the American family.* Hillsdale, NJ: Lawrence Erlbaum.

DeToledo, S., & Brown, D. E. (1994). *Grandparents as parents*. New York: Guilford Press.

Devereaux, E. C. (1970). The role of peer group experience in moral development. In J. P. Hill (Ed.), *Minnesota Symposia on Child Psychology* (Vol. 4). Minneapolis: University of Minnesota Press.

Dewey, J. (1944). *Democracy and education*. New York: Macmillan.

DeWolff, M. S., & van IJzendoorn, M. H. (1997). Sensitivity and attachment: A meta-analysis on parental antecedents of infant attachment. *Child Development, 67*, 3071–3085.

Diener, E., Frasier, S. C., Beaman, A. L., & Kelem, R. T. (1976). Effects of deindividuation variables on stealing among Halloween trick-or-treaters. *Journal of Personality and Social Psychology, 33*, 178–183.

Dietz, T. L. (1998). An examination of violence and gender-role portrayals in video games: Implications for gender socialization and aggressive behavior. *Sex Roles, 38*, 425–442.

Dishion, T. J., McCord, J., & Poulin, F. (1999). When interventions harm: Peer groups and problem behavior. *American Psychologist, 54*(8), 755–764.

Dishion, T. J., Patterson, G. R., Stoolmiller, M., & Skinner, M. L. (1991). Family, school, and behavioral antecedents to early adolescent involvement with antisocial peers. *Developmental Psychology, 27*, 172–180.

Dobkin, P. L., Tremblay, R. E., Masse, L. C., & Vitaro, F. (1995). Individual and peer characteristics in predicting boys' early onset of substance abuse: A seven-year longitudinal study. *Child Development, 66*, 1198–1214.

Dodge, K. A. (1983). Behavioral antecedents of peer social status. *Child Development, 54*, 1386–1399.

———. (1986). A social information processing model of social competence in children. In M. Perlmutter (Ed.), *Minnesota symposia on child psychology* (Vol. 18). Hillsdale, NJ: Lawrence Erlbaum.

Dodge, K. A., Bates, J. E., & Petit, G. S. (1990). Mechanisms in the cycle of violence. *Science, 250*, 1678–1683.

Dodge, K. A., & Frame, C. L. (1982). Social cognitive biases and deficits in aggressive boys. *Child Development, 53*, 620–635.

Dodge, K. A., Petit, G. S., & Bates, J. E. (1994). Socialization mediators of the relation between socioeconomic status and child conduct problems. *Child Development, 65*, 649–665.

Doherty, W. J. (1999). *The intentional family: Simple rituals to strengthen family ties*. New York: Avon Books.

Doherty, W. J., Kouneski, E. F., & Erickson, M. F. (1998). Responsible fathering: An overview and conceptual framework. *Journal of Marriage and the Family, 60*, 277–292.

Dorr, A. (1982). Television and the socialization of the minority child. In G. L. Berry & C. Mitchell-Kerman (Eds.), *Television and the socialization of the minority child*. New York: Academic Press.

Dorr, A. (1986). *Television and children: A special medium for a special audience*. Beverly Hills, CA: Sage.

Dorr, A., & Rabin, B. E. (1995). Parents, children, and television. In M. H. Bornstein (Ed.), *Handbook of parenting* (Vol. 4). Mahwah, NJ: Lawrence Erlbaum.

Dougherty, W. H., & Engle, R. E. (1987). An 80's look for sex equality in Caldecott winners and Honor books. *Reading Teacher, 40*(4), 394–398.

Downey, D. B., & Powell, B. (1993). Do children in single-parent households fare better with same-sex parents? *Journal of Marriage and the Family, 55*, 55–76.

Dreikurs, R., & Grey, L. (1968). *A new approach to discipline: Logical consequences*. New York: Hawthorn.

Dresser, N. (1996). *Multicultural manners: New rules of etiquette for a changing society*. New York: Wiley.

Duncan, G. J., & Raudenbush, S. W. (2001). Neighborhoods and adolescent development: How can we determine the links? In A. Booth & A. C. Crouter (Eds.), *Does it take a village?* Mahwah, NJ: Lawrence Erlbaum.

Dunlop, K. H. (1977). Mainstreaming: Valuing diversity in children. *Young Children, 32*(4), 26–32.

Dunn, J. (1988). *The beginnings of social understanding*. Cambridge, MA: Harvard University Press.

———. (1992). Siblings and development. *Current Directions in Psychological Science, 1*(1), 6–9.

———. (1993). *Young children's close relationship: Beyond attachment*. Newbury Park, CA: Sage.

Dunn, J., Davies, L. C., O'Connor, T. G., & Sturgess, W. (2000). Parents' and partners' life course and family experiences: Links with parent–child relationships in different family settings. *Journal of Child Psychology and Psychiatry and Allied Disciplines, 41*, 955–968.

Dunn, L. M. (1968). Special education for the mildly retarded—Is much of it justified? *Exceptional Children, 35*(24), 5–22.

Durkheim, E. (1947). *The elementary forms of the religious life*. Glencoe, IL: Free Press.

Duska, R., & Whelan, M. (1975). *Moral development: A guide to Piaget and Kohlberg*. New York: Paulist Press.

Duster, T. (1971). Conditions for guilt-free massacre. In N. Sanford & C. Comstock (Eds.), *Sanctions for evil*. San Francisco: Jossey-Bass.

Duvall, E. M., & Miller, B. C. (1985). *Marriage and family development* (6th ed.). New York: Harper & Row.

Dweck, C. S. (1975). The role of expectations and attributions in the alleviation of learned helplessness. *Journal of Personality and Social Psychology, 31*, 674–685.

———. (1981). Social-cognitive processes in children's friendships. In S. R. Asher & J. M. Gottman (Eds.), *The development of children's friendships*. Cambridge: Cambridge University Press.

———. (1990). Self-theories and goals: Their roles in motivation, personality, and development. In R. Dienstbier (Ed.), *Nebraska Symposium on Motivation* (Vol. 36). Lincoln: University of Nebraska Press.

Dweck, C. S., & Bush, E. S. (1976). Sex differences in learned helplessness: I. Differential debilitation with peer and adult evaluators. *Journal of Personality and Social Psychology, 12,* 147–156.

Dweck, C. S., Davidson, W., Nelson, S., & Enna, B. (1978). Sex differences in learned helplessness: II. The contingencies of evaluative feedback in the classroom: III. An experimental analysis. *Developmental Psychology, 14,* 268–276.

Dweck, C. S., & Gillard, D. (1975). Expectancy statements as determinants of reactions to failure: Sex differences in persistence and expectancy change. *Journal of Personality and Social Psychology, 32,* 1077–1084.

Dweck, C. S., & Leggett, E. L. (1988). A social-cognitive approach to motivation and personality. *Psychological Review, 95,* 256–273.

Dweck, C. S., & Reppucci, N. D. (1973). Learned helplessness and reinforcement responsibility in children. *Journal of Personality and Social Psychology, 25,* 109–116.

Eccles, J. (1983). Expectancies, values, and academic behaviors. In J. T. Spence (Ed.), *Achievement and achievement motives: Psychological and sociological approaches.* San Francisco: Freeman.

Eccles, J. S., Barber, B., Jozefowicz, D., Malenchuk, O., & Vida, M. (1999). Self-evaluation of competence, task values, and self-esteem. In N. G. Johnson, M. C. Roberts, & J. Worell (Eds.), *Beyond appearance: A new look at adolescent girls.* Washington, DC: American Psychological Association.

Eccles, J. S., & Bryan, J. (1994). Adolescence and gender-role transcendence. In M. Stevenson (Ed.), *Gender roles across the life span.* Muncie, IN: Ball State University Press.

Eccles, J. S., Wigfield, A., & Schiefele, U. (1998). Motivation to succeed. In W. Damon (Ed.), *Handbook of child psychology* (5th ed., Vol. 3). New York: Wiley.

Eder, D. (1995). *School talk. Gender and adolescent school culture.* New Brunswick, NJ: Rutgers University Press.

Eisenberg, N. (1986). *Altruistic emotion, cognition and behavior.* Hillsdale, NJ: Lawrence Erlbaum.

———. (1998). Introduction. In W. Damon (Ed.), *Handbook of child psychology* (5th ed., Vol. 3). New York: Wiley.

Eisenberg, N., & Fabes, R. A. (1998). Prosocial development. In W. Damon (Ed.), *Handbook of child psychology* (5th ed., Vol. 4). New York: Wiley.

Eisenberg, N., Martin, C. L., & Fabes, R. A. (1996). Gender development and gender effects. In D. C. Berliner & R. C. Calfee (Eds.), *Handbook of educational psychology.* New York: Macmillan.

Eisenberg, N., & Murphy, B. (1995). Parenting and children's moral development. In M. H. Bornstein (Ed.), *Handbook of parenting* (Vol. 4). Mahwah, NJ: Lawrence Erlbaum.

Eisenberg, N., & Mussen, P. (1989). *The roots of prosocial behavior in children.* Cambridge: Cambridge University Press.

Elder, G. H., Jr. (1963). Parental power legitimation and its effect on the adolescent. *Sociometry, 26,* 50–65.

———. (1974). *Children of the Great Depression: Social change in life experience.* Chicago: University of Chicago Press.

———. (1979). Historical change in life patterns and personality. In P. Baltes & O. Brim (Eds.), *Life-span development and behavior* (Vol. 2). New York: Academic Press.

———. (1998). The life course and human development. In W. Damon (Ed.), *Handbook of child psychology* (5th ed., Vol. 1). New York: Wiley.

Elder, G. H., Jr., & Bowerman, C. E. (1963). Family structure and child-rearing patterns: The effect of family size and sex composition. *American Sociological Review, 30,* 81–96.

Elder, G. H., Jr., & Hareven, T. K. (1993). Rising above life's disadvantage: From the Great Depression to war. In G. H. Elder, Jr., J. Modell, & R. D. Parke (Eds.), *Children in time and space: Development and historical insights.* New York: Cambridge University Press.

Elder, G. H., Jr., Van Nguyen, T. V., & Casper, A. (1985). Linking family hardship to children's lives. *Child Development, 56,* 361–375.

Elders, J. (1994). Violence as a public health issue for children. *Childhood Education, 70*(5), 260–262.

Eldridge, S. (1999). *Twenty things adopted kids wish their adoptive parents knew.* New York: Dell.

Eley, T. C., Lichtenstein, P., & Stevenson, J. (1999). Sex differences in the etiology of aggressive and nonaggressive antisocial behavior: Results from two twin studies. *Child Development, 70,* 155–168.

Elkin, F., & Handel, G. (1989). *The child and society* (5th ed.). New York: Random House.

Elkind, D. (1981a). Egocentrism in children and adolescents. In D. Elkind (Ed.), *Children and adolescents: Interpretive essays on Jean Piaget* (3rd ed.). New York: Oxford University Press.

———. (1981b). How grown-ups help children learn. *Education Digest, 80*(3), 20–24.

———. (1984). *All grown up and no place to go: Teenagers in crisis.* Reading, MA: Addison-Wesley.

———. (1988). *The hurried child: Growing up too fast too soon* (rev. ed.). Reading, MA: Addison-Wesley.

———. (1994). *Ties that stress: The new family imbalance.* Cambridge, MA: Harvard University Press.

Elliot, E. S., & Dweck, C. S. (1988). Goals: An approach to motivation and achievement. *Journal of Personality and Social Psychology, 54,* 5–12.

Elliot, R., & Vasta, P. (1970). The modeling of sharing: Effects associated with vicarious reinforcement, symbolization, age, and generalization. *Journal of Experimental Child Psychology, 10,* 8–15.

Ellis, J. B. (1994). Children's sex-role development: Implications for working mothers. *Social Behavior and Personality, 22,* 131–136.

Ellis, S., Rogoff, B., & Cromer, C. C. (1981). Age segregation in children's social interactions. *Developmental Psychology, 17,* 399–407.

Emery, R. E. (1988). *Marriage, divorce, and children's adjustment.* Newbury Park, CA: Sage.

———. (1989). Family violence. *American Psychologist, 44,* 321–332.

Epps, S., & Jackson, B. J. (2000). *Empowered families, successful children.* Washingon, DC: American Psychological Association.

Epstein, J. L. (1983). Longitudinal effects of family–school–person interactions on student outcomes. In J. L. Epstein (Ed.), *Research in sociology of education and socialization* (Vol. 4). Greenwich, CT: JAI Press.

———. (1995). School/family/community partnerships. *Phi Delta Kappan, 76*(9), 701–712.

Epstein, J. L., & Dauber, S. L. (1991). School programs and teacher practices of parent involvement in inner-city elementary and middle schools. *The Elementary School Journal, 91*(3), 288–305.

Erikson, E. H. (1963). *Childhood and society.* New York: Norton.

———. (1980). *Identity and the life cycle.* New York: Norton.

Eron, L., Walder, L. O., & Lefkowitz, M. M. (1971). *Learning of aggression in children.* Boston: Little, Brown.

Escobedo, T. H., & Huggans, J. H. (1983). Field dependence-independence: A theoretical framework for Mexican American cultural variables? In T. H. Escobedo (Ed.), *Early childhood bilingual education: A Hispanic perspective.* New York: Teachers College Press.

Espin, O. M. (1993). Psychological impact of migration on Latinos. In D. R. Atkinson, G. Morten, & D. W. Sue (Eds.), *Counseling American minorities* (4th ed.). Dubuque, IA: Brown & Benchmark.

Estes, E. (1944). *The hundred dresses.* New York: Harcourt Brace Jovanovich.

Etzioni, A. (1993). *The spirit of community: The reinvention of American Society.* New York: Touchstone.

Evans, E. D., & McCandless, B. R. (1978). *Children and youth: Psychosocial development.* New York: Holt, Rinehart & Winston.

Evans, E. D., Rutberg, J., Sather, C., & Turner, C. (1991). Content analysis of contemporary teen magazines for adolescent females. *Youth Society, 23*(1), 99–120.

Evans, G. W., Hygges, S., & Bullinger, M. (1993). *Psychology and the environment.* Unpublished manuscript, Cornell University.

Evans, G. W., Palsane, M. N., Lepore, S. J., & Martin, J. (1989). Residential density and psychological wealth: The mediating effects of social support. *Journal of Personality and Social Psychology, 57*(6), 994–999.

Fagan, J. (1993). Drug selling and illicit income in distressed neighborhoods. The economic lives of street-level drug users and dealers. In G. Peterson & A. H. Washington (Eds.), *Drugs, crime, and social isolation.* Washington, DC: Urban Institute Press.

Fagot, B. I. (1977). Consequences of moderate cross-gender behavior in preschool children. *Child Development, 48,* 902–907.

———. (1984). Teacher and peer reactions to boys' and girls' play styles. *Sex Roles, 11,* 691–702.

———. (1985). Beyond the reinforcement principle: Another step toward understanding sex-role development. *Developmental Psychology, 21,* 1097–1104.

———. (1995). Parenting boys and girls. In M. H. Bornstein (Ed.), *Handbook of parenting* (Vol. 1). Mahwah, NJ: Lawrence Erlbaum.

Fagot, B. I., & Leinbach, M. D. (1987). Socialization of sex roles within the family. In B. Carter (Ed.), *Current conceptions of sex roles and sex typing: Theory and research.* New York: Praeger.

Falbo, T., & Polit, D. (1986). A quantitative review of the only child literature: Research evidence and theory development. *Psychological Bulletin, 100,* 176–189.

Fantz, R. L. (1965). Visual perception from birth as shown by pattern selectivity. *Annals of the New York Academy of Sciences, 118,* 793–814.

Farmer, S. (1989). *Adult children of abusive parents.* New York: Ballantine Books.

Farrington, D. P. (1991). Childhood aggression and adult violence: Early precursors and later life outcomes. In D. J. Pepler & K. H. Rubin (Eds.), *The development and treatment of childhood aggression.* Hillsdale, NJ: Lawrence Erlbaum.

Farrington, D. P. & Loeber, R. (2000). Epidemiology of juvenile violence. *Juvenile Violence, 9,* 733–748.

Federal Interagency Forum on Child and Family Statistics. (2001). *America's children: Key national indicators of well-being, 2001.* Washington, DC: Author.

Feld, S. C. (1967). Longitudinal study of the origins of achievement strivings. *Journal of Personality and Social Psychology, 7,* 408–414.

Feldman, F. L., & Scherz, F. (1987). *Family social welfare.* New York: Atherton Press.

Feldstein, B. (1989). Selection as a means of diffusing censorship. In M. K. Rudman (Ed.), *Children's literature: Resources for the classroom.* Norwood, MA: Christopher Gordon.

Feurstein, R. (1980). *Instrumental enrichment.* Baltimore: University Park Press.

Fick, A. L., Osofsky, J. D., & Lewis, M. L. (1997). Perceptions of violence: Children, parents, and police officers. In J. D. Osofsky (Ed.), *Children in a violent society.* New York: Guilford Press.

Field, T., Masi, W., Goldstein, S., & Perry, S. (1988). Infant day care facilitates preschool social behavior. *Early Childhood Research Quarterly, 3,* 341–359.

Fiese, B. H., Sameroff, A. J., Grotevant, H. D., Wamboldt, F. S., Dickenstein, S., & Fravel, D. H. (1999). The stories that families tell: Narrative coherence, narrative interaction, and relationship beliefs. *Monographs of the Society for Research in Child Development, 64*(2) (Serial No. 257).

Fincham, F. D., & Cain, K. (1986). Learned helplessness in humans: A developmental analysis. *Developmental Review, 6,* 301–333.

Findley, M. S., & Cooper, H. N. (1983). Locus of control and academic achievement: A literature review. *Journal of Personality and Social Psychology, 44,* 419–427.

Finkelhor, D. (1984). *Child sexual abuse: New theory and research.* New York: Free Press.

Finn, J. D., & Achilles, C. M. (1990). Answers and questions about class size: A statewide experiment. *American Association Research Journal, 27*(3), 557–577.

Fischer, W. (1963). Sharing in preschool children as a function of amount and type of reinforcements. *Genetic Psychological Monographs, 68,* 215–245.

Fiske, E. B. (1980). School vs. television. *Parents, 55*(1), 54–59.

———. (1992). *Smart schools, smart kids.* New York: Touchstone.

Flavell, J. (1986). The development of children's knowledge about the appearance–reality distinction. *American Psychologist, 41,* 418–425.

Flavell, J. H., Miller, P. H., & Miller, S. A. (2001). *Cognitive development* (4th ed.). Englewood Cliffs, NJ: Prentice-Hall.

Fletcher, A. C., Darling, N. E., Steinberg, L., & Dornbusch, S. M. (1995). The company they keep: Relation of adolescents' adjustment and behavior to their friends' perceptions of authoritative parenting in the social network. *Developmental Psychology, 31,* 300–310.

Fontana, D. J. (1992). *Save the family, save the child; What we can do to help children at risk.* New York: Dutton.

Forman, D. R., & Kochanska, G. (2001). Viewing imitation and child responsiveness: A link between teaching and discipline domains of socialization. *Developmental Psychology, 37,* 198–200.

Foss, R. D. (1983). Community norms and blood donation. *Journal of Applied Social Psychology, 13,* 281–290.

Foster-Clark, F. S., & Blyth, D. A. (1991). Peer relations and influences. In R. M. Lerner, A. C. Petersen, & J. Brooks-Gunn (Eds.), *Encyclopedia of adolescence* (Vol. 2). New York: Garland.

Fox, R. F. (2000). *Harvesting minds: How TV commercials control kids.* Westport, CT: Praeger.

Fragin, S. (2000, November). Who cares for kids? *Working Mother,* 57–75.

Fraiberg, S. (1977). *Every child's birthright: In defense of mothering.* New York: Basic Books.

Francke, L. B. (1983). *Growing up divorced.* New York: Fawcett/Crest.

Frank, A. (1993). *Anne Frank: The diary of a young girl* (B. M. Mooyaart, Trans.). New York: Bantam. (Original work published 1947.)

Frede, E. C. (1995). The role of program quality in producing early childhood program benefits. *The Future of Children, 5*(3), 115–132.

Freud, A. (1968). *The psychoanalytical treatment of children.* New York: International Universities Press.

Freud, S. (1925). Some psychical consequences of the anatomical distinction between the sexes. In J. Strachey (Ed. and Trans.), *The standard edition of the complete psychological works of Sigmund Freud.* London: Hogarth Press.

———. (1938). *The basic writings of Sigmund Freud.* New York: Random House.

Freud, S. (1999). The social construction of normality. *Families in Society: The Journal of Contemporary Human Services, 80*(4), 333–337.

Friedrich, L. K., & Stein, S. H. (1973). Aggressive and prosocial television programs and the national behavior of preschool children. *Monographs of the Society for Research in Child Development, 38* (Serial No. 151).

Fuligni, A. J., & Eccles, J. S. (1993). Perceived parent–child relationships and early adolescents' orientation toward peers. *Developmental Psychology, 29,* 622–632.

Fuligni, A. J., Tseng, V., & Lam, M. (1999). Attitudes toward family obligations among American adolescents with Asian, Latin American, and European backgrounds. *Child Development, 70,* 1030–1044.

Fulton, L. (1994). Peer education partners: A program for learning and working together. *Teaching Exceptional Children, 26*(4), 6–8, 10–11.

Funkhouser, J. E., & Gonzales, M. R. (1997). *Family involvement in children's education: Successful local approaches.* Washington, DC: U.S. Department of Education.

Furman, W. (1995). Parenting siblings. In M. H. Bornstein (Ed.), *Handbook of parenting* (Vol. 1). Mahwah, NJ: Lawrence Erlbaum.

Furman, W., & Masters, J. C. (1980). Affective consequences of social reinforcement, punishment, and neutral behavior. *Developmental Psychology, 16,* 100–104.

Furstenberg, F. (1976). *Unplanned parenthood: The social consequences of teenage childbearing.* New York: Free Press.

Furstenburg, F. F., & Cherlin, A. J. (1991). *Divided families: What happens to children when parents part.* Cambridge, MA: Harvard University Press.

Galinsky, E. (1981). *Between generations: The six stages of parenthood.* New York: Times Books.

———. (1992). The impact of child care on parents. In A. Booth (Ed.), *Childcare in the 1990s: Trends and consequences.* Hillsdale, NJ: Lawrence Erlbaum.

Gallay, L. S., & Flanagan, C. A. (2001). The well-being of children in a changing economy: Time for a new social contract in America. In R. D. Taylor & M. C. Wang (Eds.), *Resilience across contexts: Family, work, culture, and community.* Mahwah, NJ: Lawrence Erlbaum.

Galston, W. A. (1999). Does the Internet strengthen community? *Report from the Institute for Philosophy and Public Policy, 19*(4).

Galton, L. (1980). *Your child in sports.* New York: Watts.

Gandini, L. (1993). Fundamentals of the Reggio Emilia approach to early childhood education. *Young Children, 49*(1), 4–8.

Garbarino, J. (1977). The human ecology of child maltreatment: A conceptual model for research. *Journal of Marriage and the Family, 39*, 721–736.

———. (1985). Habitats for children: An ecological perspective. In J. F. Wohlwill & W. Van Vliet (Eds.), *Habitats for children: The impact of density.* Hillsdale, NJ: Lawrence Erlbaum.

———. (1986). Can American families afford the luxury of childhood? *Child Welfare, 65*(2), 119–128.

———. (1992). *Children and families in the social environment* (2nd ed.). New York: Aldine de Gruyter.

———. (1995a). *Raising children in a socially toxic society.* San Francisco: Jossey-Bass.

———. (1995b). *Building a socially nourishing environment with children.* San Francisco: Jossey-Bass.

Garbarino, J., & Eckenrode, J. (1997). *Understanding abusive families: An ecological approach to theory and practice.* New York: Jossey-Bass.

Garbarino, J., & Gilliam, G. (1980). *Understanding abusive families.* Lexington, MA: Heath.

Garbarino, J., Guttman, E., & Seely, J. W. (1986). *The psychologically battered child: Strategies for identification, assessment and intervention.* San Francisco: Jossey-Bass.

Garbarino, J., & Sherman, D. (1980). High-risk neighborhoods and high-risk families: The human ecology of child maltreatment. *Child Development, 51*, 188–198.

Garcia, R. L. (1998). *Teaching for diversity.* Bloomington, IN: Phi Delta Kappa Educational Foundation.

Garcia-Coll, C. T., Meyer, E. C., & Britton, L. (1995). Ethnic and minority parenting. In M. H. Bornstein (Ed.), *Handbook of parenting* (Vol. 2). Mahwah, NJ: Lawrence Erlbaum.

Gardner, H. (1999). *Intelligence reframed: Multiple intelligences for the 21st century.* New York: Basic Books.

Gardner, K. E., & LaBrecque, S. V. (1986). Effects of maternal employment on sex-role orientation of adolescents. *Adolescence, 21*(84), 875–885.

Gargiulo, R. M., & Graves, J. B. (1991). Parental feelings. *Childhood Education, 67*(3), 176–178.

Gatz, I. L. (1975). On children and television. *Elementary School Journal, 75*(7), 415–418.

Gay, L. (1998). *The history of rock music.* orpheus. la.utk.edu/music

Geen, R. G. (1994). Television and aggression: Recent development in research and theory. In D. Zillman, J. Bryant, & A. C. Huston (Eds.), *Media, children and the family: Social scientific, psychodynamic and clinical perspectives.* Hillsdale, NJ: Lawrence Erlbaum.

Gelfand, D., Hartman, D. P., Cromer, C. C., Smith, C. L., & Page, B. C. (1975). The effects of instructional prompts and praise on children's donation rates. *Child Development, 46*, 980–983.

Gellene, D. (1996, August 7). Scaring up lots of young readers. *Los Angeles Times*, pp. A1, A18–19.

Gerbner, G., Gross, L., Jackson-Beck, N., Jeffries-Fox, S., & Signorielli, N. (1978). *Violence profile* (No. 9). Philadelphia: University of Pennsylvania Press.

Gesell, A., & Ilg, F. (1943). *Infant and child in the culture of today.* New York: Harper & Row.

Ghazvini, A., & Mullis, R. L. (2002). Center-based care for young children: Examining predictors of quality. *Journal of Genetic Psychology, 163*, 112–126.

Gibbs, J. C. (1995). The cognitive developmental perspective. In W. M. Kurtines & J. L. Gewirtz (Eds.), *Moral development: An introduction.* Boston: Allyn & Bacon.

Gilkeson, E. C., & Bowman, G. W. (1976). *The focus is on children.* New York: Bank Street Publications.

Ginsberg, G. S., & Bronstein, D. (1993). Family factors related to children's intrinsic/extrinsic motivational orientation and academic performance. *Child Development, 64*, 1461–1474.

Goff, B. G., & Goddard, H. W. (1999). Terminal core values with adolescent problem behaviors. *Adolescence, 34*, 47–60.

Goffin, S. G., & Lombardi, J. (1988). *Speaking out: Early childhood advocacy.* Washington, DC: National Association for the Education of Young Children.

Golden, H. (1962). *You're entitled.* New York: Crest.

Golding, W. (1954). *Lord of the flies.* New York: Putnam.

Goldman, J. (1994, January 23). Rose Kennedy, 104, dies; matriarch of a dynasty. *Los Angeles Times*, pp. A1, A20.

Goldstein, A. P. (1991). *Delinquent gangs: A psychological perspective.* Champaign, IL: Research Press.

Goleman, D. (1995). *Emotional intelligence.* New York: Bantam Books.

Gollnick, D. M., & Chinn, P. C. (2002). *Multicultural education in a pluralistic society* (6th ed.). Upper Saddle River, NJ: Merrill/Prentice-Hall.

Good, T. C., & Brophy, J. E. (1986). *Educational psychology* (3rd ed.). New York: Longman.

———. (2003). *Looking in classrooms* (9th ed.). New York: Allyn & Bacon.

Goode, W. J. (1982). *The family* (2nd ed.). Englewood Cliffs, NJ: Prentice-Hall.

Goodlad, J. I. (1984). *A place called school: Prospects for the future.* New York: McGraw-Hill.

Goodman, G. S., Emery, R. E., & Haugaard, J. F. (1998). Developmental psychology and law: Divorce, child maltreatment, foster care, and adoption. In W. Damon (Ed.), *Handbook of child psychology* (5th ed., Vol. 4). New York: Wiley.

Goodman, M. E. (1964). *Race awareness in young children* (rev. ed.). New York: Collier Books.

Gordon, I. J. (1971). *Parental involvement in compensatory education.* Urbana, IL: Research Press.

Gore, T. (1987). *Raising PG kids in an X-rated society.* Nashville, TN: Abington Press.

Gorn, G. J., & Goldberg, M. E. (1982). Behavioral evidence of the effect of televised food message on children. *Journal of Consumer Research, 9,* 200–205.

Gorsuch, R. L. (1976). Religion as a major prediction of significant human behavior. In W. J. Donaldson, Jr. (Ed.), *Research in mental health and religious behavior.* Atlanta: Psychological Studies Institute.

Gottman, J., Gonso, J., & Rasmussen, B. (1975). Social interaction, social competence, and friendship in children. *Child Development, 46,* 709–718.

Gould, W. S., & Gould, C. B. (1962). *Annotated Mother Goose.* New York: Clarkson N. Potter.

Gozali, H., Cleary, T. A., Walster, G. W., & Gozali, J. (1973). Relationship between the internal-external control construct and achievement. *Journal of Educational Psychology, 64,* 9–14.

Graves, N. B., & Graves, T. O. (1983). The cultural context of prosocial development: An ecological model. In D. L. Bridgeman (Ed.), *The nature of prosocial development: Interdisciplinary theories and strategies.* New York: Academic Press.

Greely, A. M. (2001, March/April). The future of religion in America. *Society,* 32–37.

Green, F. (1990, June 13). Officials say schools aren't prepared for first wave of crack babies. *San Diego Union,* pp. A1, A14, A15.

Greenberg, B. S. (1994). Content trends in media sex. In D. Zillman, J. Bryant, & A. C. Huston (Eds.), *Media, children and the family: Social scientific, psychodynamic, and clinical perspectives.* Hillsdale, NJ: Lawrence Erlbaum.

Greenberger, E., & Chen, C. (1996). Perceived family relationships and depressed mood in early and late adolescence. A comparison of European and Asian Americans. *Developmental Psychology, 32,* 707–717.

Greenberger, E., & Goldberg, W. A. (1989). Work, parenting, and the socialization of children. *Developmental Psychology, 25*(1), 22–35.

Greenberger, E., O'Neil, R., & Nagel, S. K. (1994). Linking workplace and homeplace; Relations between the nature of adults' work and their parenting behaviors. *Developmental Psychology, 30,* 990–1002.

Greenfield, L. A. (Ed.). (1998, March). *Violence by intimates: Analysis of data on crimes by current or former spouses, boyfriends, and girlfriends.* Washington, DC: U.S. Department of Justice.

Greenfield, P. M. (1984). *Mind and media: The effects of television, video games and computers.* Cambridge, MA: Harvard University Press.

Greenfield, P. M., & Juvonen, J. (1999). A developmental look at Columbine. *APA Monitor Online, 30*(7).

Greenfield, P. M., & Suzuki, L. K. (1998). Culture and human development: Implications for parenting, education, pediatrics, and mental health. In W. Damon (Ed.), *Handbook of child psychology* (5th ed., Vol. 4). New York: Wiley.

Griffiths, M. D. (1991). Amusement machine playing in childhood and adolescence: A comparative analysis of video games and food machines. *Journal of Adolescence, 14,* 53–74.

Grinder, R. E. (1964). Relations between behavior and cognitive dimensions of conscience in middle childhood. *Child Development, 34,* 881–891.

Grolnick, W. S., & Ryan, R. M. (1989). Parents' styles associated with children's self-regulation and competence in school. *Journal of Educational Psychology, 81,* 143–154.

Gronau, R. C., & Waas, G. A. (1997). Delay of gratification and cue utilization: An examination of children's social information processing. *Merrill-Palmer Quarterly, 43,* 305–322.

Groos, K. (1901). *The play of man.* New York: Appleton.

Grotevant, H. D. (1998). Adolescent development in family contexts. In W. Damon (Ed.), *Handbook of child psychology* (5th ed., Vol. 3). New York: Wiley.

Grusec, J. E., & Lytton, H. (1988). *Social development: History, theory, and research.* New York: Springer-Verlag.

Grusec, J. E., Saas-Korlsaak, P., & Simutis, Z. M. (1978). The role of example and moral exhortation in the training of altruism. *Child Development, 49,* 920–923.

Gunnar, M. R. (1980). Contingent stimulation: A review of its role in early development. In S. Levine & H. Ursin (Eds.), *Coping and health.* New York: Plenum.

Haefner, M. J., & Wartella, E. A. (1987). Effects of sibling coviewing on children's interpretations of television programs. *Journal of Broadcasting and Electronic Media, 31,* 153–168.

Haith, M. M. (1966). The response of the human newborn to visual movement. *Journal of Experimental Child Psychology, 3*, 235–243.

Hale, J. (1991). The transmission of cultural values to young African American children. *Young Children, 46*(6), 7–15.

———. (1994). *Unbank the fire.* Baltimore: Johns Hopkins University Press.

Haley, G. E. (1989). Cited in J. Trelease, *The new read-aloud handbook.* New York: Penguin Books.

Hall, C. S. (1954). *A primer of Freudian psychology.* New York: New American Library.

Hall, E. T. (1964). *The silent language.* New York: Doubleday.

———. (1966). *The hidden dimension.* New York: Doubleday.

———. (1976). *Beyond culture.* New York: Doubleday.

Hallahan, D. P., & Kauffman, J. M. (2002). *Exceptional children: Introduction to special education* (9th ed.). Needham Heights, MA: Allyn & Bacon.

Hamm, N. H., & Hoving, K. L. (1969). Conformity of children in an ambiguous perceptual situation. *Child Development, 40*, 773–784.

Han, W. J., Waldfogel, J., & Brooks-Gunn, J. (2001). The effects of early maternal employment on later cognitive and behavioral outcomes. *Journal of Marriage and Family, 63*, 336–354.

Hansen, C. H., & Hansen, R. D. (1988). How rock music videos can change what is seen when boy meets girl: Priming stereotypic appraisal of social interactions. *Sex Roles, 19*, 287–316.

Hardman, M., Drew, C. J., & Egan, M. W. (1999). *Human exceptionality: Society, school, and family* (6th ed.). Boston: Allyn & Bacon.

Hareven, T. K. (1989). Historical changes in children: Networks in the family and community. In D. Belle (Ed.), *Children's social networks and social support.* New York: Wiley.

Harms, T., & Clifford, R. M. (1980). *Early childhood environment rating scale.* New York: Teachers College Press.

Harris, J. R. (1998). *The nurture assumption: Why children turn out the way they do.* New York: Free Press.

Harris, M. (1970). Reciprocity and generosity: Some determinants of sharing in children. *Child Development, 41*, 313–328.

Harris, M. B., & Turner, P. (1986). Gay and lesbian parents. *Journal of Homosexuality, 12*, 101–113.

Harris, R. (1999). *A cognitive psychology of mass communication* (3rd ed.). Mahwah, NJ: Lawrence Erlbaum.

Harrison, A., Serafica, F., & McAdoo, H. (1984). Ethnic families of color. In R. D. Parke (Ed.), *Review of child development research: Vol. 7. The family.* Chicago: University of Chicago Press.

Harrison, A. O., Wilson, M. N., Pine, C. J., Chan, S., & Buriel, R. (1990). Family ecologies of ethnic minority children. *Child Development, 61*, 347–362.

Hart, B., & Risley, T. R. (1995). *Meaningful differences in the everyday experiences of young American children.* Baltimore: Brookes.

Hart, C. H., DeWolf, D. M., & Burts, D. C. (1992). Linkages among preschoolers' playground behavior, outcome expectations, and parental disciplinary strategies. *Early Education and Development, 3*, 265–283.

Harter, S. (1990). Issues in the assessment of the self-concept of children and adolescents. In A. M. LaGreco (Ed.), *Through the eyes of the child: Obtaining self-reports from children and adolescents.* Boston: Allyn & Bacon.

———. (1998). The development of self-representations. In W. Damon (Ed.), *Handbook of child psychology* (5th ed., Vol. 3). New York: Wiley.

———. (1999). *The construction of the self: A developmental perspective.* New York: Guilford Press.

Harter, S., & Connell, J. P. (1984). A model of children's achievement and related self-perceptions of competence, control, and motivational orientations. In J. Nicholls (Ed.), *The development of achievement-related cognition and behavior.* Greenwich, CT: JAI Press.

Hartshorne, H., & May, M. (1978). *Studies in the nature of character: Vol. I. Studies in deceit.* New York: Macmillan.

Hartup, W. W. (1964). Friendship status and the effectiveness of peers as reinforcing agents. *Journal of Experimental Child Psychology, 1*, 154–162.

———. (1983). Peer relations. In P. H. Mussen (Ed.), *Handbook of child psychology* (4th ed., Vol. 4). New York: Wiley.

———. (1989). Social relationships and their developmental significance. *American Psychologist, 44*(2), 120–126.

———. (1996). The company they keep: Friendships and their developmental significance. *Child Development, 67*, 1–13.

Hartup, W. W., & Coates, B. (1967). Imitation of a peer group and rewardingness of the model. *Child Development, 38*, 1003–1016.

Hassett, J. (1981). But that would be wrong. *Psychology Today, 15*(11), 34.

Hatcher, B., & Beck, S. S. (1997). *Learning opportunities beyond the school* (2nd ed.). Olney, MD: Association for Childhood Education International.

Haugland, S. W., & Wright, J. L. (1997). *Young children and technology.* Boston: Allyn & Bacon.

Hauser-Cram, P., Warfield, M. E., Shokoff, J. P., & Krauss, M. W. (2001). Children with disabilities: A longitudinal study of child development and parent well-being. *Monographs of the Society for Research in Child Development, 66*(3) (Serial No. 266).

Havighurst, R. (1972). *Human development and education* (3rd ed.). New York: McKay.

Hay, D. F. (1985). Learning to form relationships in infancy: Parallel attainments with parents and peers. *Developmental Review, 5,* 122–161.

Hay, I., Ashman, A. F., & Van Kraayenoord, C. E. (1998). Educational characteristics of students with high or low self-concepts. *Psychology in the Schools, 35,* 391–400.

Hayes, J. W., & Lipset, S. M. (1993/1994, Winter). Individualism: A double-edged sword. *The Responsive Community,* 69–80.

Hayton, J. C., George, G., & Zahra, S. A. (2002). National culture and entrepreneurship: A review of behavioral research. *Entrepreneurship: Theory and Practice, 26*(4), 33–53.

Hayward, D. G., Rothenberg, M., & Beasley, R. R. (1974). Children's play in urban playground environments: A comparison of traditional, contemporary, and adventure playground types. *Environment and Behavior, 6*(2), 131–168.

Healy, J. (1991). *Endangered minds: Why children don't think and what to do about it.* New York: Touchstone Books.

———. *Failure to connect: How computers affect our children's minds and what we can do about it.* New York: Touchstone Books.

Heath, S. B. (1983). *Ways with words: Language, life and work in communities and classrooms.* Cambridge, MA: Harvard University Press.

———. (1989). Oral and literate traditions among black Americans living in poverty. *American Psychologist, 44*(2), 367–373.

Helburn, S. W., & Howes, C. (1996). Child care cost and quality. *The Future of Children, 6*(2), 62–82.

Helfer, R., & Kempe, C. H. (1989). *The battered child* (4th ed.). Chicago: University of Chicago Press.

Henderson, A. T., & Berla, N. (Eds.). (1994). *A new generation of evidence: The family is critical to student achievement.* Washington, DC: National Committee for Citizens in Education.

Henderson, Z. P. (1990, Summer). Short reports. *Human Ecology Forum, 18*(4), 37.

Hermans, H. J. M., Terlaak, J. J. F., & Maes, P. C. J. M. (1972). Achievement and fear of failure in family and school. *Developmental Psychology, 6,* 520–528.

Hess, R. D. (1986). Family influences on school readiness and achievement in Japan and the United States: An overview of a longitudinal study. In H. Stevenson, H. Azuma, & K. Hakuta (Eds.), *Child development and education in Japan.* New York: Freeman.

Hess, R. D., & Holloway, S. D. (1984). Family and school as educational institutions. In R. D. Parke (Ed.), *Review of child development research: Vol. 7. The Family.* Chicago: University of Chicago Press.

Hetherington, E. M. (1972). The effects of father absence on personality development in adolescent daughters. *Developmental Psychology, 7,* 313–326.

———. (1988). Parents, children, and siblings six years after divorce. In R. A. Hinde & J. Stevenson-Hinde (Eds.), *Relationships within families.* Oxford: Oxford University Press.

———. (1989). Coping with family transitions: Winners, losers, and survivors. *Child Development, 60,* 1–4.

———. (1993). A review of the Virginia longitudinal study of divorce and remarriage: A focus on early adolescence. *Journal of Family Psychology, 7,* 39–56.

Hetherington, E. M., Bridges, M., & Insabella, G. M. (1998). What matters? What does not? Five perspectives on the association between marital transitions and children's adjustment. *American Psychologist, 53,*(2), 167–184.

Hetherington, E. M., & Camara, K. A. (1984). Families in tradition: The processes of dissolution and reconstitution. In R. D. Parke (Ed.), *Review of child development research: Vol. 7. The family.* Chicago: University of Chicago Press.

Hetherington, E. M., & Clingempeel, W. G. (1992). Coping with marital transitions. *Monographs of the Society for Research in Child Development, 57*(2–3) (Serial No. 227).

Hetherington, E. M., Cox, M., & Cox, R. (1982). Effects of divorce on parents and children. In M. Lamb (Ed.), *Nontraditional families.* Hillsdale, NJ: Lawrence Erlbaum.

Hetherington, E. M., Stanley-Hagan, M., & Anderson, E. R. (1989). Marital transitions. *American Psychologist, 44*(2), 303–312.

Heward, W. L. (1999). *Exceptional children: An introduction to special education* (6th ed.). Englewood Cliffs, NJ: Prentice-Hall.

Heward, W. L., & Orlansky, M. D. (1994). *Exceptional children: An introductory survey of special education* (4th ed.). Columbus, OH: Merrill.

Hewitt, J. P. (1994). *Self and society: A symbolic interactionist social psychology.* Boston: Allyn & Bacon.

Hewlett, S. A., & West, C. (1998). *The war against parents.* Boston: Houghton Mifflin.

Higgins, A. (1995). Educating for justice and community: Lawrence Kohlberg's vision of moral education. In W. M. Kurtines & J. L. Gewirtz (Eds.), *Moral development: An introduction.* Boston: Allyn & Bacon.

Hill, J., & Radimer, K. A. (1997). A content analysis of food advertisement in television for Australian children. *Australian Journal of Nutrition and Dietetics, 54*(4), 174–180.

Hilliard, A. (1992, Summer). Behavioral style, culture, and teaching and learning. *Journal of Negro Education, 61*(3), 370–371.

Hirschfield, L. (1997). The conceptual politics of race: Lessons from our children. *Ethos: Journal of the Society for Psychological Anthropology, 25,* 63–92.

Hochschild, A. R. (1989). *The second shift.* New York: Avon Books.

———. (1997). *The time bind.* New York: Metropolitan Books.

Hofferth, S. (1992). The demand for and supply of child care in the 1990s. In A. Booth (Ed.), *Child care in the 1990s: Trends and consequences.* Hillsdale, NJ: Lawrence Erlbaum.

———. (1996). Child care in the United States today. *The Future of Children, 6*(2), 41–61.

Hoffman, L. W. (1989). Effects of maternal employment in the two-parent family. *American Psychologist, 44*(2), 283–292.

Hoffman, M. L. (1970). Moral development. In P. H. Mussen (Ed.), *Carmichael's manual of child psychology* (Vol. 2). New York: Wiley.

———. (1981). Is altruism part of human nature? *Journal of Personality and Social Psychology, 70,* 237–241.

———. (1983). Affective and cognitive processes in moral internalization. In E. T. Higgins, D. N. Ruble, & W. W. Hartup (Eds.), *Social cognition and social development.* Cambridge: Cambridge University Press.

———. (1991). Empathy, social cognition, and moral actions. In W. M. Kurtines & J. L. Gewirtz (Eds.), *Handbook of moral behavior and development: Vol. 1. Theory.* Hillsdale, NJ: Lawrence Erlbaum.

———. (2000). *Empathy and moral development.* New York: Cambridge University Press.

Hoffman, M. L., & Saltzstein, H. D. (1967). Parent discipline and the child's moral development. *Journal of Personality and Social Psychology, 5,* 45–57.

Hofstede, G. (1991). *Organizations and cultures: Software of the mind.* New York: McGraw-Hill.

Hogan, R., & Emler, N. (1995). Personality and moral development. In W. M. Kurtines & J. L. Gewirtz (Eds.), *Moral development: An introduction.* Boston: Allyn & Bacon.

Hohmann, M., & Weikart, D. P. (1995). *Educating young children: Active learning practices for preschool educators and child care programs.* Ypsilanti, MI: High/ScopePress.

Holmbeck, G. N., Paikoff, R. L., & Brooks-Gunn, J. (1995). Parenting adolescents. In M. H. Bornstein (Ed.), *Handbook of parenting* (Vol. 1). Mahwah, NJ: Lawrence Erlbaum.

Honig, A. S. (1986). Stress and coping in children (Part I). *Young Children, 41*(4), 50–63.

———. (1993). Mental health for babies: What do theory and research teach us? *Young Children, 48*(3), 69–76.

———. (1995). Choosing child care for young children. In M. H. Bornstein (Ed.), *Handbook of parenting* (Vol. 4). Mahwah, NJ: Lawrence Erlbaum.

Hopkins, H. R., & Klein, H. A. (1994). Multidimension self-perception: Linkages to parental nurturance. *The Journal of Genetic Psychology, 154,* 465–473.

Horowitz, F. D., & Paden, L. Y. (1973). The effectiveness of environmental intervention programs. In B. M. Caldwell & H. N. Riccuiti (Eds.), *Review of child development research* (Vol. 3). Chicago: University of Chicago Press.

Horowitz, R. (1979). Psychological effects of the " open classroom." *Review of Educational Research, 49,* 71–86.

Howes, C. (1988). Peer interaction of young children. *Monographs of the Society for Research in Child Development, 43*(1) (Serial No. 217).

Howes, C., & Matheson, C. C. (1992). Sequences in the development of competent play with peers; Social and social pretend play. *Developmental Psychology, 28,* 961–974.

Howes, C., Matheson, C. C., & Hamilton, C. E. (1994). Maternal, teacher, and child care history correlates of children's relationships with peers. *Child Development, 65,* 264–273.

Huck, C. S., & Helper, S. (Eds.). (1996). *Children's literature in the elementary school* (6th ed.). New York: WCB/McGraw-Hill.

Huesmann, L. R. (1986). Psychological processes promoting the relation between exposure to media violence and aggressive behavior by the viewer. *Journal of Social Issues, 42,* 125–139.

Huesmann, L. R., Eron, L. D., Klein, R., Brice, P., & Fisher, P. (1983). Mitigating the imitation of aggressive behavior by changing children's attitudes about media violence. *Journal of Personality and Social Psychology, 44,* 899–910.

Hughes, F. P. (1998). *Children, play, and development* (3rd ed.). Boston: Allyn & Bacon.

Humphrey, J. H. (1993). *Sports for children: A guide for adults.* Springfield, IL: Thomas.

Hunt, J. McV. (1961). *Intelligence and experience.* New York: Ronald Press.

Hurd, T. L., Lerner, R. M., & Barton, C. E. (1999). Integrated services. Expanding partnerships to meet the needs of today's children and families. *Young Children, 54*(2), 74–80.

Huston, A. C. (1983). Sex-typing. In P. H. Mussen (Ed.), *Handbook of child psychology* (4th ed., Vol. 4). New York: Wiley.

Huston, A. C., Carpenter, C. J., Atwater, J. B., & Johnson, L. M. (1986). Gender, adult structuring of activities, and social behavior in middle childhood. *Child Development, 57,* 200–209.

Huston, A. C., Duncan, G. J., Granger, R., Bos, J., McLoyd, V., Mistry, R., Crosby, D., Gibson, C., Magnuson, K., Romich, J., & Ventua, A. (2001). Work-based antipoverty programs for parents can enhance the school performance and social behavior of children. *Child Development, 72,* 318–336.

Huston, A. C., McLoyd, V. C., & Coll, C. G. (1994). Children and poverty: Issues in contemporary research. *Child Development, 65,* 275–282.

Huston, A. C., Watkins, B. A., & Kunkel, D. (1989). Public policy and children's television. *American Psychologist, 44*(2), 424–433.

Huston, A. C., & Wright, J. C. (1998). Mass media and children's development. In W. Damon (Ed.), *Handbook of child psychology* (5th ed., Vol. 4). New York: Wiley.

Huston, A. C., Zillman, D., & Bryant, J. (1994). Media influence, public policy, and the family. In D. Zillman, J. Bryant, & A. C. Huston (Eds.), *Media, children, and the family: Social scientific, psychodynamic, and clinical perspectives.* Hillsdale, NJ: Lawrence Erlbaum.

Hutchison, R. (1987). Ethnicity and urban recreation: Whites, blacks and Hispanics in Chicago's public parks. *Journal of Leisure Research, 19,* 205–222.

Hymel, S., Bowker, A., & Woody, E. (1993). Aggressive versus withdrawn unpopular children: Variations in peer and self-perceptions in multiple domains. *Child Development, 64,* 879–896.

Inhelder, B., & Piaget, J. (1958). *The growth of logical thinking from childhood to adolescence.* New York: Basic Books.

Inkeles, A. (1969). Social structure and socialization. In D. A. Goslin (Ed.), *Handbook of socialization theory and research.* Chicago: Rand McNally.

Isaacs, S. (1999). *Brave dames and wimpettes: What women are really doing on page and screen.* New York: Ballantine Books.

Iverson, T. J., & Segal, M. (1990). *Child abuse and neglect: An information and reference guide.* New York: Garland.

Jackson, R. K., & McBride, W. D. (1985). *Understanding street gangs.* Sacramento: Custom.

Jacobs, J. S., & Tunnell, M. O. (1996). *Children's literature, briefly.* Englewood Cliffs, NJ: Prentice-Hall.

Jacobson, J. L., & Wille, D. E. (1986). The influence of attachment pattern on developmental changes in peer interaction from the toddler to the preschool period. *Child Development, 57,* 338–347.

Jaffe, M. L. (1998). *Adolescence.* New York: Wiley.

James, M., & Jongeward, D. (1971). *Born to win.* Reading, MA: Addison-Wesley.

Jensen, A. R. (1969). How much can we boost IQ and scholastic achievement? *Harvard Educational Review, 39,* 1–123.

———. Speed of information processing and population differences. In S. H. Irvine & J. W. Berry (Eds.), *Human abilities in cultural context.* New York: Cambridge University Press.

Johnson, D. W., & Johnson, R. T. (1999). *Learning together and alone: Cooperative, competitive, and individualistic learning* (5th ed.). Boston: Allyn & Bacon.

Johnson, D. W., Johnson, R. T., & Maruyama, G. (1983). Interdependence and interpersonal attraction among heterogeneous and homogeneous individuals: A theoretical formulation and a meta-analysis of the research. *Review of Education Research, 53,* 5–54.

Johnson, J. A., Dupuis, V. L., Musial, D., & Hall, G. E. (2003). *Foundations of American education: The essential edition* (12th ed.). Needham Heights, MA: Allyn & Bacon.

Johnson, P. A., & Staffieri, J. R. (1971). Stereotype affective properties of personal names and somatotypes in children. *Developmental Psychology, 5*(1), 176.

Johnson, R. (2002, July 24). Obituary: Chaim Potok. *Los Angeles Times,* p. B13.

Johnson, W. B., & Packer, A. E. (Eds.). (1987). *Work force 2000.* Indianapolis, IN: Hudson Institute.

Johnston, J. R., Kline, M., & Tschann, J. M. (1989). Ongoing post-divorce conflict: Effects on children of joint custody and frequent access. *Journal of Orthopsychiatry, 59*(4), 576–592.

Johnston, J., & Ettema, J. S. (1982). *Positive images: Breaking stereotypes with children's television.* Newbury Park, CA: Sage.

Jones, K. L., Smith, D. W., Ulleland, C. L., & Streissguth, P. (1973). Patterns of malformation in offspring of chronic alcoholic mothers. *Lancet, 1,* 1267–1271.

Jose, P. E. (1990). Just world reasoning in children's immanent justice judgments. *Child Development, 61,* 1024–1033.

Jung, C. G. (1938). *Psychology and religion.* New Haven, CT: Yale University Press.

Kagan, J. (1971). *Personality development.* New York: Harcourt Brace Jovanovich.

———. (1984). *The nature of the child.* New York: Basic Books.

———. (1994). *Galen's prophecy: Temperament in human nature.* New York: Basic Books.

Kagan, J., & Moss, H. (1959). Stability and validity of achievement fantasy. *Journal of Abnormal and Social Psychology, 58,* 357–364.

Kagan, J., Reznick, S., Davies, J., Smith, J., Sigal, H., & Miyake, K. (1986). Selective memory and belief: A methodological suggestion. *International Journal of Behavioral Development, 9,* 205–218.

Kagan, J., Reznick, J. S., & Gibbons, J. (1989). Inhibited and uninhibited types of children. *Child Development, 60,* 838–845.

Kagicibasi, C. (1996). *Family and human development across cultures: A view from the other side.* Mahwah, NJ: Lawrence Erlbaum.

Kaiser Family Foundation. (1999). *Kids and media and the new millennium.* Menlo Park, CA: Author.

Kalichman, S. C. (1999). *Mandated reporting of suspected child abuse: Ethics, law, and policy* (2nd ed.) Washington, DC: American Psychological Association.

Kallen, H. M. (1956). *Cultural pluralism and the American ideal.* Philadelphia: University of Pennsylvania Press.

Kantrowitz, B. (1996). Gay families come out. *Newsweek, 128*(19), 50–57.

Kantrowitz, B., & Wingert, P. (1990). Step by step. *Newsweek, 94*(27), 24–34.

———. (1998). Learning at home: Does it pass the final test? *Newsweek, 132*(14), 64–71.

———. (2001). Unmarried with children. *Newsweek, 14*(11), 46–54.

Kaplan, K. (2002, April 18). Going mobile. *Los Angeles Times*, pp. S1, S4.

Karoly, L. A. (Ed.) (1998). *Investing in our children: What we know and don't know about the costs and benefits of early childhood interventions.* Santa Monica, CA: Rand.

Kaslow, F. W. (2001). Families and family psychology at the millenium: Intersecting crossroads. *American Psychologist, 56*(1), 37–46.

Katchadourian, H. (1990). Sexuality. In S. S. Feldman & G. R. Elliot (Eds.), *At the threshold: The developing adolescent.* Cambridge, MA: Harvard University Press.

Katz, L. B. (1984). *More talks with teachers.* Urbana, IL: Elementary and Early Childhood Education.

Katz, P., & Zalk, S. (1978). Modification of children's racial attitudes. *Developmental Psychology, 14*(5), 447–461.

Katz, P. A. (Ed.). (1975). *Toward the elimination of racism.* New York: Pergamon Press.

Kaufman, J. (1989). The regular education policy. A trickle-down theory of education of the hard to teach. *Journal of Special Education, 23*, 256–278.

Kearny, M. (1999). The role of teachers in helping children of domestic violence. *Childhood Education, 75*(5), 290–296.

Keats, E. J. (1967). *Peter's chair.* New York: Harper & Row.

Kellam, S. G., Ling, X., Merisca, R., Brown, C. H., & Ialongo, N. (1999). The effect of the level of aggression in the 1st grade classroom on the course and malleability of aggressive behavior into middle school. *Development and Psychopathology, 10*, 165–185.

Kelly, J. B. (2000). Children's adjustment in conflicted marriage and divorce: A decade's review of research. *Journal of the American Academy of Child and Adolescent Psychiatry, 39*, 963–973.

Kelley-Vance, L., & Schreck, D. (2002). The impact of collaborative family/school reading programs on student reading rate. *Journal of Research in Reading, 25*(1), 43–53.

Keltikangas-Järvinen, L., Terav, T., & Pakaslahti, L. (1999). Moral reasoning among Estonian and Finnish adolescents: A comparison of collectivist and individual settings. *Journal of Cross-Cultural Psychology, 30*, 257–290.

Kempe, R. S., & Kempe, C. H. (1978). *Child abuse.* Cambridge, MA: Harvard University Press.

Kemple, K. M. (1991). Research in review: Preschool children's peer acceptance and social interaction. *Young Children, 46*(5), 47–54.

Keniston, K. (1977). *All our children: The American family under pressure.* New York: Harcourt Brace Jovanovich.

Kennell, J., Voos, D., & Klaus, M. (1976). Parent-infant bonding. In R. Helfer & C. H. Kempe (Eds.), *Child abuse and neglect: The family and the community.* Cambridge, MA: Ballinger.

Killen, M., & Nucci, L. P. (1995). Morality, autonomy, and social conflict. In M. Killen & D. Hart (Eds.), *Morality in everyday life: Developmental perspectives.* Cambridge: Cambridge University Press.

Kim, J. E., Hetherington, E. M., & Reiss, D. (1999). Associations among family relationships, antisocial peers, and adolescents' externalizing behaviors: Gender and family type differences. *Child Development, 70*, 1209–1230.

Kimball, M. M. (1986). Television and sex-role attitudes. In T. M. Williams (Ed.), *The impact of television: A natural experiment in three communities.* Orlando, FL: Academic Press.

Kindermann, T. (1998). Children's development within peer groups: Using composite social maps to identify peer networks and study their influences. In W. M. Bukowski & A. H. Cillesen (Eds.), *New directions for child development* (No. 80). San Francisco: Jossey-Bass.

Kinman, J. R., & Henderson, D. L. (1985). An analysis of sexism in Newbery Medal award books from 1977 to 1984. *The Reading Teacher, 38*(9), 885–889.

Kinney, D. A. (1993). From nerds to normals. *Sociology of Education, 66*(1), 21–40.

Kirk, S., Gallagher, J. J., & Anastasiow, N. J. (2000). *Educating exceptional children* (9th ed.). Boston: Houghton Mifflin.

Kluckhohn, F. (1961). Dominant and variant value orientation. In C. Kluckhohn & H. Murray (Eds.), *Personality in nature and society.* New York: Knopf.

Kluckhohn, F., & Strodbeck, F. (1961). *Variations in value orientations.* Evanston, IL: Row Peterson.

Kluger, J., & Park, A. (2001). The quest for a super kid. *Time, 157*(7), 50–55.

Koblinsky, S., & Behana, N. (1984). Child sexual abuse: The educator's role in prevention, detection, and intervention. *Young Children, 39*(6), 3–15.

Kochanska, G. (1993). Toward a synthesis of parental socialization and child temperament in early development of conscience. *Child Development, 64*, 325–347.

———. (1995). Children's temperament, mothers' discipline, and security of attachment: Multiple pathways to emerging internalization. *Child Development, 66*, 597–615.

———. (1997). Multiple pathways to conscience for children with different temperaments: From toddlerhood to age 5. *Developmental Psychology, 33,* 228–240.

Kochanska, G., DeVet, K., Goldman, M., Murray, K., & Putnam, S. P. (1994). Maternal reports of conscience development and temperament in young children. *Child Development, 65,* 852–868.

Koff, E., Rierdan, J., & Stubbs, M. L. (1990). Gender, body image, and self-concept in early adolescence. *Journal of Early Adolescence, 10,* 56–68.

Kohl, H. (1967). *36 children.* New York: New American Library.

———. *Growing minds: On becoming a teacher.* New York: Harper & Row.

Kohlberg, L. (1976). Moral stages and moralization. In T. Lickona (Ed.), *Moral development and behavior.* New York: Holt, Rinehart & Winston.

———. (1980). *Recent research in moral development.* New York: Holt, Rinehart & Winston.

———. *Essays on moral development: Vol. 2. The psychology of moral development.* San Francisco: Harper & Row.

———. The just community approach to moral education in theory and practice. In M. W. Berkowitz & F. Oser (Eds.), *Moral education: Theory and application.* Hillsdale, NJ: Lawrence Erlbaum.

———. (1986). A current statement on some theoretical issues. In S. Modgil & C. Modgil (Eds.), *Lawrence Kohlberg.* Philadelphia: Folmer.

Kohn, M. L. (1977). *Class and conformity: A study in values* (2nd ed.). Chicago: University of Chicago Press.

Kohn, M. L., Naoi, A., Schoenbach, V., Schooler, C., & Slomczynski, K. M. (1990). Position in the class structure and psychological functioning in the United States, Japan, and Poland. *American Journal of Sociology, 95*(4), 864–1008.

Kostelnik, M. J., Whiren, A. P., & Stein, L. C. (1986). Living with He-Man. *Young Children, 41*(4), 3–9.

Kounin, J. (1970). *Discipline and group management in the classroom.* New York: Holt, Rinehart & Winston.

Kozol, J. (1991). *Savage inequalities: Children in America's schools.* New York: Crown.

Krebs, R. (1967). *Some relations between moral judgment, attention and resistance to temptation.* Unpublished Ph.D. dissertation, University of Chicago.

Krononberger, L. (1966). Uncivilized and uncivilizing. *TV Guide, 14*(9), 15.

Kruger, A. C. (1992). The effect of peer and adult–child transductive discussions on moral reasoning. *Merrill-Palmer Quarterly, 38,* 191–211.

Kuczen, B. (1987). *Childhood stress.* New York: Dell.

Kuczynski, L., Kochanska, G., Radke-Yarrow, M., & Girnius-Brown, O. (1987). A developmental interpretation of young children's noncompliance. *Developmental Psychology, 23,* 799–806.

Kunkel, D., & Roberts, D. (1991). Young minds and marketplace values: Issues in children's television advertising. *Journal of Social Issues, 47,* 57–72.

Kupersmidt, J. B., Coie, J. D., & Dodge, K. A. (1990). The role of poor peer relationships in the development of disorder. In S. R. Asher & J. D. Coie (Eds.), *Peer rejection in childhood.* New York: Cambridge University Press.

Kurtines, W. M., & Gewirtz, J. (Eds.). (1991). *Handbook of moral behavior and development.* Hillsdale, NJ: Lawrence Erlbaum.

Ladd, G. W. (1990). Having friends, keeping friends, making friends, and being liked by peers in the classroom: Predictions of children's early school adjustment. *Child Development, 61,* 1081–1100.

———. (1999). Peer relationships and social competence during early and middle childhood. *Annual Review of Psychology,* 333–344.

Ladd, G. W., & LeSieur, K. D. (1995). Parents and peer relationships. In M. H. Bornstein (Ed.), *Handbook of parenting* (Vol. 4). Mahwah, NJ: Lawrence Erlbaum.

Ladd, G. W., & Pettit, G. S. (2002). Parenting and the development of children's peer relationships. In M. Bornstein (Ed.), *Handbook of parenting* (2nd ed.). Mahwah, NJ: Lawrence Erlbaum.

Laible, D. J., & Thompson, R. A. (2000). Mother–child discourse, attachment security, shared positive affect, and early conscience development. *Child Development, 71,* 1424–1446.

Lamb, M. E. (1977). The development of mother–infant and father–infant attachment in the second year of life. *Developmental Psychology, 13*(6), 637–648.

———. (1981). Fathers and child development: An integrated overview. In M. E. Lamb (Ed.), *The father's role in child development.* New York: Wiley.

———. (1986). The changing roles of fathers. In M. E. Lamb (Ed.), *The father's role: Applied perspectives.* New York: Wiley.

———. (1997). *The role of the father in child development* (3rd ed.). New York: Wiley.

———. (1998). Nonparental child care: Context, quality, correlates, and consequences. In W. Damon (Ed.), *Handbook of Child Psychology* (5th ed., Vol. 4). New York: Wiley.

———. (2000). The effects of quality of care on child development. *Applied Developmental Science, 4*(3), 112–115.

Lamb, M. E., Hwang, C. P., Ketterlinus, R. D., & Fracasso, M. F. (1999). Parent–child relationships: Development in the context of the family. In M. H. Bornstein & M. E. Lamb (Eds.), *Developmental psychology: An advanced textbook* (4th ed.) Mahwah, NJ: Lawrence Erlbaum.

Lamb, M. E., Parker, F., Boak, A. Y., Griffin, K. W., & Peax, L. (1999). Parent–child relationship, home learning environment, and school readiness. *School Psychology Review, 28,* 413–425.

Lamborn, S. D. , Mounts, N. S., Steinberg, L., & Dornbusch, S. (1991). Patterns of competence and adjustment among adolescents from authoritative, authoritarian, indulgent, and neglectful families. *Child Development, 62,* 1049–1065.

Landre, R., Miller, M., & Porter, D. (1997). *Gangs: A handbook for community awareness.* New York: Facts on File.

Langlois, J. H. (1986). From the eye of the beholder to behavioral reality: Development of social behavior and social relations as a function of physical attractiveness. In C. P. Herman, M. P. Zanna, & E. T. Higgins (Eds.). *Physical behavior: The Ontario Symposium* (Vol. 3). Hillsdale, NJ: Lawrence Erlbaum.

Langlois, J. H., & Downs, A. C. (1980). Mothers, fathers, and peers as socialization agents of sex-typed behaviors in young children. *Child Development, 51,* 1217–1247.

Lapsley, D. K. (1996). *Moral psychology.* Boulder, CO: Westview Press.

Larrick, N. (1975). Children of television. *Teacher Magazine, 93,* 75–77.

Larson, R. (1995). Secrets in the bedroom: Adolescents' private use of media. *Journal of Youth and Adolescence, 24*(5), 535–550.

Larson, R., Kubey, R., & Colletti, J. (1989). Changing channels: Early adolescent media choices and shifting investments in family and friends. *Journal of Youth and Adolescence, 18*(16), 583–599.

Larson, T. (1992). Understanding stepfamilies. *American Demographics, 14,* 360.

Lasker, J. (1972). *Mothers can do anything.* Chicago: Albert Whitman.

Lazar, I. (1977). The persistence of preschool effects: A long-term follow-up on fourteen infant and preschool experiments. *Final report to the administration on children, youth and families.* Washington, DC: Office of Human Services, U.S. Department of Health, Education, and Welfare.

Lazar, I., & Darlington, R. B. (1982). Lasting effect of early education: A report from the consortium for longitudinal studies. *Monographs of the Society for Research in Child Development, 47*(2–3) (Serial No. 195).

Leach, P. (1994). *Children first.* New York: Knopf.

Leaf, M. (1936). *The story of Ferdinand.* New York: Viking Press/Penguin Books.

Leaper, C. (1994). Exploring the correlates and consequences of gender segregation: Social relationships in childhood, adolescence, and adulthood. In C. Leaper (Ed.), *New directions for child development* (No. 65). San Francisco: Jossey-Bass.

———. (2000). Gender, affiliation, assertion, and the interactive context of parent–child play. *Developmental Psychology, 36,* 381–393.

Leershen, C., & Namuth, T. (1988). *Alcohol and the family, 111*(3), 62–68.

Leibert, R. M., Neil, M., & Davidson, E. S. (1973). *The early window: Effects of television on children and youth.* New York: Pergamon Press.

Leibert, R. M., & Poulos, R. W. (1976). Television as a moral teacher. In T. Lickona (Ed.), *Moral development and behavior.* New York: Holt, Rinehart & Winston.

Leibert, R. M., & Sprafkin, J. (1988). *The early window: Effects of television on children and youth* (3rd ed.). New York: Pergamon Press.

LeMasters, E. E. (1988). Blue-collar aristocrats and their children. In G. Handel (Ed.), *Childhood socialization.* New York: Aldine de Gruyer.

Lengua, L. (2002). The contribution of emotionality and self-regulation to the understanding of children's response to multiple risk. *Child Development, 73,* 144–161.

Lepper, M. R. (1983). Social-control processes and the internalization of social values: An attributional perspective. In E. T. Higgins, D. N. Ruble, & W. W. Hartup (Eds.), *Social cognition and social development: A sociocultural perspective.* Cambridge: Cambridge University Press.

Lerner, J., Mardell-Czudnowski, C., & Goldberg, G. (1987). *Special education for the early childhood years* (2nd ed.). Englewood Cliffs, NJ: Prentice-Hall.

Lerner, J. V. (1993). The influence of child temperamental characteristics on parent behaviors. In T. Luster & L. Okagaki (Eds.), *Parenting: An ecological perspective.* Hillsdale, NJ: Lawrence Erlbaum.

Lerner, R. M. (1998). Theories of human development: Contemporary perspectives. In W. Damon (Ed.), *Handbook of child psychology* (5th ed., Vol. 1). New York: Wiley.

Lever, J. (1976). Sex differences in the games children play. *Social Problems, 23,* 478–487.

———. (1978). Sex differences in the complexity of children's play. *American Sociological Review, 43,* 471–482.

Levin, D. E. (1998). *Remote control childhood? Combating the hazards of media culture.* Washington, DC: National Association for the Education of Young Children.

Levin, D. E., & Carlsson-Paige, N. (1995). The Mighty Morphin Power Rangers: Teachers voice concern. *Young Children, 50*(6), 67–72.

Levine, D. U., & Levine, R. F. (1996). *Society and education* (9th ed.). Needham Heights, MA: Allyn & Bacon.

Lewin, K., Lippitt, R., & White, R. (1939). Patterns of aggressive behavior in experimentally created social climates. *Journal of Social Psychology, 10,* 271–299.

Lewit, E. M., & Baker, L. S. (1995). School readiness. *Critical Issues for Children and Youths: The Future of Children 5*(2), 128–139.

Liben, L. S., & Bigler, R. S. (2002). The developmental course of gender differentiation: Conceptualizing, measuring, and evaluating constructs and pathways. *Monographs of the Society for Research in Child Development, 67* (2) (Serial No. 269).

Lickona, T. (1977). How to encourage moral development. *Learning, 5*(7), 36–43.

———. (1991). *Educating for character.* New York: Bantam Books.

Limber, S. P., & Nation, M. A. (1998). Violence within the neighborhood and community. In P. K. Trickett & C. J. Schellenbach (Eds.), *Violence against children in the family and the community.* Washington, DC: American Psychological Association.

Linney, J. A., & Seidman, E. (1989). The future of schooling. *American Psychologist, 44*(2), 336–340.

Lionni, L. (1968). *The biggest house in the world.* New York: Pantheon Books.

Lippitt, R., & White, R. K. (1943). The social climate of children's groups. In R. G. Barker, J. S. Korinen, & H. F. Wright (Eds.), *Child behavior and development.* New York: McGraw-Hill.

List, J. A., Collins, W. A., & Westby, S. D. (1983). Comprehension and inferences from traditional and nontraditional sex-role portrayals on television. *Child Development, 54,* 1579–1587.

Logue, A. W. (1995). *Self-control: Waiting until tomorrow for what you want today.* Englewood Cliffs, NJ: Prentice-Hall.

Lohr, J. M., & Staats, A. (1973). Attitude conditioning in Sino-Tibetan languages. *Journal of Personality and Social Psychology, 26,* 196–200.

Lonigan, C. J., Burgess, S. R., & Anthony, J. L. (2000). Development of emergent literacy and early reading skills in preschool children: Evidence from a latent-variable longitudinal study. *Developmental Psychology, 36,* 596–613.

Long, L., & Long, T. (1982). The unspoken fears of latchkey kids. *Working Mother, 5*(76), 88–90.

———. (1983). *The handbook for latchkey children and their parents.* New York: Arbor House.

Lorenz, K. (1966). *On aggression.* New York: Harcourt, Brace & World.

Love, J. M., Schochet, P. Z., & Meckstroth, A. L. (1996). Are they in any real danger? What research doesn't tell us about child care quality and children's well-being. Child Care and Research Policy Papers. *ERIC Digest* (ED415030).

Lowenthal, B. (1999). Effects of maltreatment and ways to promote children's resiliency. *Childhood Education, 75*(4), 204–209.

Lull, J. (1980). The social uses of television. *Human Communication Research, 6,* 197–209.

Luster, T., & Okagaki, L. (1993). Multiple influences on parenting: Ecological and life-course perspectives. In T. Luster & L. Okagaki (Eds.), *Parenting: An ecological perspective.* Hillsdale, NJ: Lawrence Erlbaum.

Lustig, M. & Koester, J. (1999). *Intercultural competence: Interpersonal communication across cultures.* New York: Longman.

Luthar, S. S., & Becker, B. E. (2002). Privileged but pressured? A study of affluent youth. *Child Development, 73,* 1593–1610.

Lytton, H., & Romney, D. M. (1991). Parents' differential socialization of boys and girls: A meta-analysis. *Psychological Bulletin, 109,* 267–296.

Maccoby, E. E. (1990). Gender and relationships: A developmental account. *American Psychologist, 45,* 513–520.

———. (1998). *The two sexes: Growing up apart, coming together.* Cambridge, MA: Harvard University Press.

———. (2000). Perspectives on gender development. *International Journal of Behavioral Development, 24,* 398–406.

Maccoby, E. E., & Jacklin, C. N. (1974). *The psychology of sex differences.* Stanford, CA: Stanford University Press.

———. (1980). Sex differences in aggression: A rejoinder and reprise. *Child Development, 51,* 964–980.

———. (1987). Gender segregation in childhood. *Advances in Child Development and Behavior, 20,* 239–287.

Maccoby, E. E., & Martin, J. (1983). Socialization in the context of family: Parent–child interaction. In P. H. Mussen (Ed.), *Handbook of child psychology* (4th ed., Vol. 4). New York: Wiley.

MacDonald, K., & Parke, R. D. (1986). Parent–child physical play: The effects of sex and age of children and parents. *Sex Roles, 15*(7–8), 367–378.

MacLeod, A. S. (1994). *American childhood.* Athens: University of Georgia Press.

Madon, S., Jussim, L., & Eccles, J. (1997). In search of the powerful self-fulfilling prophecy. *Journal of Personality and Social Psychology, 72,* 791–809.

Madsen, M. C., & Shapira, A. (1970). Cooperative and competitive behavior of urban Afro-American, Anglo-American, and Mexican-American and Mexican village children. *Developmental Psychology, 3,* 16–20.

Maehr, M. L. (1974). *Sociocultural origins of achievement.* Monterey, CA: Brooks/Cole.

Maidman, F. (Ed.). (1984). *Child welfare: A sourcebook of knowledge and practice.* New York: Child Welfare League of America.

Main, M., & Solomon, J. (1990). Procedures for identifying infants as disorganized/disoriented during the Ainsworth Strange Situation. In M. T. Greenberg, D. Cicchetti, & E. M. Cummings (Eds.), *Attachment in the preschool years: Theory, research, and intervention.* Chicago: University of Chicago Press.

Mann, J. (1982). What is TV doing to America? *U.S. News & World Report, 93*(5), 27–30.

Marcossen, M., & Fleming, V. (Eds.) (1978, November). *The children's political checklist.* Washington, DC: Coalition for Children and Youth.

Margolin, G. (1998). Effects of domestic violence on children. In P. K. Trickett & C. J. Schellenbach (Eds.), *Violence against children in the family and the community.* Washington, DC: American Psychological Association.

Margolis, C. (1971). The black student in political strife. *Proceedings of the 79th Annual Convention of the American Psychological Association, 10,* 395–396.

Marshall, P. L. (2002). *Cultural diversity in our schools.* Belmont, CA: Wadsworth.

Martin, C. L. (1989). Children's use of gender-related information in making social judgments. *Developmental Psychology, 25,* 80–88.

Martin, C. L., & Halverson, C. F. (1981). A schematic processing model of sex-typing and stereotyping in children. *Child Development, 52,* 1119–1134.

———. (1987). The roles of cognition in sex-roles and sex-typing. In D. B. Carter (Ed.), *Current conceptions of sex roles and sex-typing: Theory and research.* New York: Praeger.

Martin, C. L., Wood, C. H., & Little, J. K. (1990). The development of gender stereotype components. *Child Development, 61,* 1891–1904.

Martin, G., & Pear, J. (1996). *Behavior modification: What it is and how to do it* (5th ed.). Upper Saddle River, NJ: Prentice-Hall.

Martin, G. B., & Clark, R. D. (1982). Distress crying in neonates: Species and peer specificity. *Developmental Psychology, 18,* 3–9.

Martinez, R., & Dukes, R. L. (1991). Ethnic and gender differences and self-esteem. *Youth and Society, 3,* 318–338.

Mason, K. O., & Duberstein, L. (1992). Consequences of child-care practices and arrangements for the well-being of parents and providers. In A. Booth (Ed.), *Child care in the 1990s: Trends and consequences.* Hillsdale, NJ: Lawrence Erlbaum.

Mason, M. G., & Gibbs, J. C. (1993). Social perspective taking and moral judgment among college students. *Journal of Adolescent Research, 8,* 109–123.

Maughan, A., & Cicchetti, D. (2002). Impact of child maltreatment and inter adult violence on children's emotion-regulation abilities and socioemotional adjustment. *Child Development, 73,* 1525–1542.

Mayes, L. C. & Zigler, E. (1992). An observational study of the affective concomitants of mastery in infants. *Journal of Psychology and Psychiatry, 4,* 659–667.

McCartney, K., & Galanopoulos, A. (1988). Child care and attachment: A new frontier the second time around. *American Journal of Orthopsychiatry, 58*(1), 16–24.

McClelland, D. C. (1961). *The achieving society.* New York: Van Nostrand.

McClelland, D. C., Atkinson, J. W., Clark, R. A., & Lowell, E. L. (1953). *The achievement motive.* New York: Appleton-Century-Crofts.

McClelland, D. C., & Pilon, D. A. (1983). Sources of adult motives in patterns of parent behavior in early childhood. *Journal of Personality and Social Psychology, 44,* 564–574.

McCloskey, R. (1948). *Blueberries for Sal.* New York: Viking Press.

McCormick, L., & Holden, R. (1992). Homeless children: A special challenge. *Young Children, 47*(6), 61–67.

McGoldrick, M., Giordano, J., Pearse, J. K., & Giordano, J. (1996). *Ethnicity and family therapy* (2nd ed.) New York: Guilford Press.

McGuire, W. J. (1985). Attitudes and attitude change. In G. Lindzey & E. Aronson (Eds.), *Handbook of social psychology* (3rd ed., Vol. 2). New York: Random House.

McHale, J. P. (1995). Coparenting and triadic interactions during infancy: The roles of marital distress and child gender. *Developmental Psychology, 31,* 985–996.

McHale, S. M., Crouter, A. C., & Tucker, C. J. (1999). Family context and gender-role socialization in middle childhood: Comparing girls to boys and sisters to brothers. *Child Development, 70,* 990–1004.

McHale, S. M., Updegraff, K. A., Helms-Erikson, H., & Crouter, A. C. (2001). Sibling influences on gender development in middle childhood and early adolescence: A longitudinal study. *Developmental Psychology, 37,* 115–125.

McHale, S. M., Updegraff, K. A., Jackson-Newsom, J., Tucker, C. J., & Crouter, A. C. (2000). When does parents' differential treatment have negative implications for siblings? *Social Development, 9,* 149–172.

McLanahan, S. S., & Carlson, M. J. (2002). Welfare reform, fertility, and father involvement. *Children and Welfare Reform: The Future of Children, 12*(1), 147–165.

McLane, J. B., & McNamee, G. D. (1990). *Early literacy.* Cambridge, MA: Harvard University Press.

McLoyd, V. C. (1990). The impact of economic hardship on black families and children. Psychological distress, parenting, and socioemotional development. *Child Development, 61,* 311–346.

———. (1998). Socioeconomic disadvantage and child development. *American Psychologist, 53,* 185–204.

———. (1998). Children in poverty: Development, public policy, and practice. In W. Damon (Ed.), *Handbook of child psychology* (5th ed., Vol. 4). New York: Wiley.

McLuhan, M. (1964). *Understanding media: The extension of man.* New York: McGraw-Hill.

———. A McLuhan mosaic. In G. Sanderson & F. Macdonald (Eds.), *Marshall McLuhan: The man and his message.* Golden, CO: Fulcrum.

McNally, L., Eisenberg, J., & Harris, J. D. (1991). Consistency and change in maternal child-rearing practices and values: A longitudinal study. *Child Development, 62*, 190–198.

McNeal, J. (1987). *Children as consumers.* Lexington, MA: Lexington Books.

McNeely, C. A., Nonnemaker, J. M., & Blum, R. (2002). Promoting student connectedness to school: Evidence from the National Longitudinal Study of Adolescent Health. *Journal of School Health, 72*(4).

Mead, G. H. (1934). *Mind, self, and society.* Chicago: University of Chicago Press.

Meadow-Orlans, K. P. (1995). Parenting with a sensory or physical disability. In M. H. Bornstein (Ed.), *Handbook of parenting* (Vol. 4). Mahwah, NJ: Lawrence Erlbaum.

Mediascope Inc. (1996). *National television violence study.* Studio City, CA: Author.

Mednick, S. A., Moffit, M., Gabrielli, W., Jr., & Hutchings, B. (1986). Genetic factors in criminal behavior: A review. In D. Olweus, J. Block, & M. Radke-Yarrow (Eds.), *Development of antisocial and prosocial behavior: Research, theories, and issues.* Orlando, FL: Academic Press.

Medrich, E. A., Roizen, J., Rubin, V., & Buckley, S. (1981). *The serious business of growing up: A study of children's lives outside of school.* Berkeley: University of California Press.

Meisels, S. J., & Wasik, B. A. (1990). Who should be served? Identifying children in need of early intervention. In S. J. Meisels & J. P. Shonkoff (Eds.), *Handbook of early childhood intervention.* New York: Cambridge University Press.

Mercer, J. (1973). *Labeling the mentally retarded: Clinical and social system perspectives on mental retardation.* Berkeley: University of California Press.

Meringoff, L. K. (1980). Influence of the medium on children's story comprehension. *Journal of Educational Psychology, 72*, 240–249.

Meyers, J., & Kyle, J. E. (1998). The makings of a family-friendly city and municipal government's role. *Nation's Cities Weekly, 21*(28), 9–16.

Milgram, S. (1963). Behavioral study of obedience. *Journal of Abnormal and Social Psychology, 67*, 371–378.

Miller, B. C., Christopherson, C. R., & King, P. K. (1993). Sexual behavior in adolescence. In T. P. Gullotta, G. R. Adams, & R. Montemayor (Eds.), *Adolescent sexuality.* Newbury Park, CA: Sage.

Miller, D. F. (1989). *First steps toward cultural differences: Socialization in infant/toddler day care.* Washington, DC: Child Welfare League of America.

Miller, D. R., & Swanson, G. E. (1958). *The changing American parent.* New York: Wiley.

Miller, J. G. (1995, March). *Culture, context, and personal agency: The cultural grounding of self and morality.* Paper presented at the biennial meeting of the Society for Research in Child Development, Indianapolis, IN.

Miller, J. G., & Bersoff, D. M. (1992). Culture and moral judgment: Resolved? *Journal of Personality and Social Psychology, 62*, 541–554.

Miller, J. G., & Bersoff, D. M. (1993, March). *Culture and affective closeness in the morality of caring.* Paper presented at the biennial meeting of the Society for Research in Child Development, New Orleans.

Miller, K. S., Forehand, R., & Kotchick, B. A. (1999). Adolescent behavior in two ethnic minority samples: The role of family variables. *Journal of Marriage and the Family, 61*, 85–98.

Miller, L. B., & Dyer, J. L. (1975). Four preschool programs: Their dimensions and effects. *Monographs of the Society for Research in Child Development, 40*(5–6) (Serial No. 162).

Minkler, M., & Roe, K. (1993). *Grandmothers as caregivers.* Newbury Park, CA: Sage.

Mintz, S. (1998). From patriarchy to androgeny and other myths. Placing men's family roles in historical perspectives. In A. Booth & A. C. Crouter (Eds.), *Men in families.* Mahwah, NJ: Lawrence Erlbaum.

Minuchin, P. M. (1977). *The middle years of childhood.* Monterey, CA: Brooks/Cole.

Minuchin, P. M., & Shapiro, E. K. (1983). The school as a context for social development. In P. H. Mussen (Ed.), *Handbook of Child Psychology* (4th ed., Vol. 4). New York: Wiley.

Mischel, W. (1970). Sex typing and socialization. In P. H. Mussen (Ed.), *Carmichael's manual of child psychology* (Vol. 1). New York: Wiley.

———. (1974). Processes in the delay of gratification. In L. Berkowitz (Ed.), *Advances in experimental social psychology* (Vol. 7). Orlando, FL: Academic Press.

———. (1996). From good intentions to will power. In P. M. Gollwitzer & J. A. Bargh (Eds.), *The psychology of action.* New York: Guilford Press.

Mischel, W., Shoda, Y., & Peake, P. K. (1988). The nature of adolescent competencies predicted by preschool delay of gratification. *Journal of Personality and Social Psychology, 54*, 687–696.

Mistry, R. S., Vandewater, E. A., Huston, A. C., & McLoyd, V. C. (2002). Economic well-being and children's social adjustment: The role of family process in an ethnically diverse low-income sample. *Child Development, 73*, 935–951.

Mize, J., & Ladd, G. W. (1990). A cognitive social learning approach to social skill training with low-status preschool children. *Developmental Psychology, 26*, 388–397.

Mize, J., & Pettit, G. S. (1997). Mothers' social coaching, mother-child relationships, style, and children's peer competence: Is the medium the message? *Child Development, 68*, 312–332.

Montessori, M. (1967). *The absorbent mind.* New York: Holt, Rinehart & Winston.

Montgomery, K. C. (2000). Children's media culture in the new millenium: Mapping the digital landscape. *Children and Computer Technology: The Future of Children, 10*(2), 145–167.

Moore, S. G., & Bulbulian, K. N. (1976). The effects of contrasting styles of adult–children interaction on children's curiosity. *Developmental Psychology, 12*(2), 171–172.

Murdock, G. P. (1962). Structures and functions of the family. In R. F. Winch, R. M. McGinnis, & H. R. Barringer (Eds.), *Selected studies in marriage and the family.* New York: Holt, Rinehart & Winston.

Murphy, S. (1999). *The cheers and the tears: A healthy alternative to the dark side of youth sports today.* San Francisco: Jossey-Bass.

Nadler, A. (1991). Help-seeking behavior. Psychological costs and instrumental benefits. In M. S. Clark (Ed.), *Prosocial behavior.* Newbury Park, CA: Sage.

Naisbitt, J. (1994). *Global paradox.* New York: Avon Books.

Naisbitt, J., & Aberdene, P. (1990). *Megatrends 2000.* New York: William Morrison.

Nalley, R. (1983). Sociobiology: A new view of human nature. In H. E. Fitzgerald & T. H. Carr (Eds.), *Human development 83/84.* Guilford, CT: Dushkin.

National Association for the Education of Young Children (NAEYC). (1984). *Accreditation criteria and procedures of the national academy of early childhood programs.* Washington, DC: Author.

———. (1986). Position statement on developmentally appropriate practice in early childhood programs serving children from birth through age 8. *Young Children, 41*(6), 3–19.

———. (1996a). NAEYC position statement: Responding to linguistic and cultural diversity—recommendations for effective early childhood education. *Young Children, 51*(2), 4–12.

———. (1996b). Public policy report: Be a children's champion. *Young Children, 51*(2), 58–60.

National Center for Education Statistics. (2000). Washington, DC: U.S. Department of Education. nces.ed.gov

National Center for Health Statistics (NCHS). (2000). U.S. Department of Health and Human Services. www.cdc.gov/nchs

———. (2001). Births to teenagers in the United States, 1940–2000. U.S. Department of Health and Human Services. *NVSR, 49*(10).

National Clearinghouse on Child Abuse and Neglect. (2002). www.calib.com/nccanch

National Coalition Against Domestic Violence. (1999). The Violence Against Women Act of 1999.

National Commission on Children. (1991). *Beyond rhetoric: A new American agenda for children and families.* Washington, DC: U.S. Government Printing Office.

National Commission on Drug-Free Schools. (1990). *Toward a drug-free generation: A nation's responsibility.* Washington, DC: U.S. Government Printing Office.

National Commission on Excellence in Education (NCEE). (1983). *A nation at risk: The imperative for educational reform.* Washington, DC: U.S. Government Printing Office.

National Education Association. (2001, June). *Hate crime prevention.* Legislative Action Center. www.nea.org

National Education Goals Panel. (1999). *The national education goals report: Building a nation of learners 1999.* Washington, DC: U.S. Government Printing Office.

National Institute of Child Health and Human Development (NICHD). (1996). Characteristics of infant child care: Factors contributing to positive caregiving. Early Child Care Research Network. *Early Childhood Research Quarterly, 11,* 269–306.

———. (1997). The effects of infant child care on infant–mother attachment security: Results of the NICHD study of early child care. Early Child Care Research Network. *Child Development, 68,* 860–879.

———. (1998). Early child care and self-control, compliance, and problem behavior at twenty-four and thirty-six months. Early Child Care Research Network. *Child Development, 69,* 1145–1170.

———. (2000). Characteristics and quality of child care for toddlers and preschoolers. *Applied Developmental Science, 4,* 116–135.

———. (2002). *Adventures in parenting.* Washington, DC: U.S. Government Printing Office.

National Institute on Media and the Family (2001). *Fact sheet: Effects of video playing on children.* www.mediaandthefamily.org

National Research Council. (1993). *Losing generations: Adolescents in high-risk settings.* Washington, DC: National Academy Press.

National Science Foundation. (1994). *Investing in human resources: A strategic plan for the human capital initiative: Executive summary.* Washington, DC: Author.

Nazario, T. A. (1988). *In defense of children: Understanding the rights, needs, and interests of the child.* New York: Scribner.

Nettles, S. M. (1990). *Community involvement and disadvantaged students: A review.* Baltimore: Johns Hopkins Center for Research on Effective Schooling for Disadvantaged Students.

Neuman, S. G. (1991). *Literacy in the television age: The myth of the TV effect.* Norwood, NJ: Ablex.

Nielson, A. C. (2000). *Nielson media research.* New York: Author.

Niles, F. S. (1981). The youth culture controversy: An evaluation. *Journal of Early Adolescence, 1*(3), 265–271.

Norton, D. E., & Norton, S. E. (2002). *Through the eyes of a child: An introduction to children's literature* (6th ed.). Upper Saddle River, NJ: Prentice-Hall.

Nowicki, S., & Segal, W. (1974). Perceived parental characteristics, locus of control orientation, and behavioral correlates of locus of control. *Developmental Psychology, 10,* 33–37.

O'Brien, M., & Huston, A. C. (1985). Activity level and sex-stereotyped toy choice in toddler boys and girls. *Journal of Genetic Psychology, 146,* 527–534.

O'Brien, S. (1984). *Child abuse and neglect: Everyone's problem.* Wheaton, MD: Association for Education International.

O'Dea, J. A., & Abraham, S. (1999). Association between self-concept and body weight, gender, and pubertal development among male and female adolescents. *Adolescence, 34,* 64–79.

Oden, S., & Asher, S. (1977). Coaching children in social skills for friendship making. *Child Development, 48,* 495–506.

Ogbu, J. U. (1994). From cultural differences to cultural frames of reference. In P. M. Greenfield & R. R. Cocking (Eds.), *Cross-cultural roots of minority child development.* Hillsdale, NJ: Lawrence Erlbaum.

Olweus, D. (1986). Aggression and hormones: Behavioral relationship with testosterone and adrenaline. In D. Olweus, J. Block, & M. Radke-Yarrow (Eds.), *Development of antisocial and prosocial behavior: Research, theories, and issues.* Orlando, FL: Academic Press.

Olweus, D. (1993). *Bullying at school: What we know and what we can do.* Cambridge, MA: Blackwell.

O'Neil, R., & Parke, R. D. (1997, March). Objective and subjective features of children's neighborhoods: Relations to positive regulatory strategies and children's social competence. Paper presented at the biennial meeting of the Society for Research in Child Development, Washington, DC.

Oppenheimer, T. (1997). The computer delusion. *The Atlantic Monthly, 280*(1), 45–48, 50–56, 61–62.

Ornstein, A. C., & Levine, D. U. (1982). Multicultural education: Trends and issues. *Childhood Education, 58*(4), 245.

———. (1989, September/October). Social class, race and school achievement: Problems and prospects. *Journal of Teacher Education, 40*(4), 17–23.

Orwell, G. (1946). *Animal farm.* New York: Harcourt Brace.

Osler, S. F., & Kofsky, E. (1965). Stimulus uncertainty as a variable in the development of conceptual ability. *Journal of Experimental Child Psychology, 2,* 264–279.

Osofsky, J. D. (1997). Children and youth violence: An overview of the issue. In J. Osofsky (Ed.), *Children in a violent society.* New York: Guilford Press.

Pagano, A. I. (1997). Community service groups enhance learning. In B. Hatcher & S. S. Beck (Eds.), *Learning opportunities beyond the school* (2nd ed.). Olney, MD: Association for Childhood Education International.

Pagelow, M. D. (1982). Children in violent families. Direct and indirect victims. In S. B. Hill & B. J. Barnes (Eds.), *Young children and their families.* Lexington, MA: Heath.

Paik, H., & Comstock, G. (1994). The effects of television violence on antisocial behavior: A meta-analysis. *Communication Research, 21,* 516–546.

Palladino, G. (1996). *Teenagers: An American history.* New York: Basic Books.

Papert, S. (1993). *The children's machine: Rethinking school in the age of the computer.* New York: Basic Books.

———. (1999). *Mindstorms: Children, computers, and powerful ideas* (2nd ed.). New York: Basic Books.

Park, K. A., & Waters, E. (1989). Security of attachment and preschool friendships. *Child Development, 60,* 1076–1080.

Park, L. S. (2001). *A single shard.* Boston: Clarion/ Houghton Mifflin.

Parke, R. D. (1982). On prediction of child abuse: Theoretical considerations. In R. Starr (Ed.), *Prediction of abuse: Policy implications.* Philadelphia: Ballinger.

———. (1990, Fall). Family–peer systems: In search of a linking process. *Newsletter: Developmental Psychology.* Washington, DC: American Psychological Association (Division 7).

———. (1995). Fathers and families. In M. H. Bornstein (Ed.), *Handbook of parenting* (Vol. 3). Mahwah, NJ: Lawrence Erlbaum.

Parke, R. D., & Buriel, R. (1998). Socialization in the family: Ethnic and ecological perspectives. In W. Damon (Ed.), *Handbook of child psychology* (5th ed., Vol. 3). New York: Wiley.

Parke, R. D., & Lewis, N. G. (1981). The family in context: A multilevel interactional analysis of child abuse. In R. Henderson (Ed.), *Parent–child interaction.* New York: Academic Press.

Parke, R. D., & Slaby, R. B. (1983). The development of aggression. In P. H. Mussen (Ed.), *Handbook of child psychology* (4th ed., Vol. 4). New York: Wiley.

Parker, J. G., & Asher, S. R. (1987). Peer relations and later adjustment: Are low-accepted children "at risk"? *Psychological Bulletin, 102,* 357–389.

Parker, J. G., & Gottman, I. M. (1989). Social and emotional development in a relational context: Friendship interaction from early childhood to adolescence. In T. J. Berndt & G. W. Ladd (Eds.), *Peer relations in child development.* New York: Wiley.

Parkhurst, J. T., & Asher, S. R. (1992). Peer rejection in middle school: Subgroup differences in behavior, loneliness, and interpersonal concerns. *Developmental Psychology, 28,* 231–241.

Parsons, J. E., Adler, T. F., & Kaczala, C. M. (1982). Socialization of achievement attitudes and beliefs: Parental influences. *Child Development, 53,* 310–321.

Parten, M. (1932). Social play among preschool children. *Journal of Abnormal and Social Psychology, 27,* 243–269.

Pate-Bain, H., Achilles, C. M., Boyd-Zaharias, J., & McKenna, B. (1992). Class size does make a difference. *Phi Delta Kappan, 74*(30), 253–256.

Patterson, C. J., Kupersmidt, J. B., & Vaden, N. A. (1990). Income level, gender, ethnicity, and household composition as predictors of children's school-based competence. *Child Development, 61,* 485–494.

Patterson, G. R. (1982). *Coercive family processes.* Eugene, OR: Castilia Press.

Patterson, G. R., & Capaldi, D. (1991). Antisocial parents: Unskilled and vulnerable. In P. A. Cowan & M. E. Hetherington (Eds.), *Family transitions: Advances in family research* (Vol. 2). Hillsdale, NJ: Lawrence Erlbaum.

Patterson, G. R., DeBaryshe, D., & Ramsey, E. (1989). A developmental perspective on antisocial behavior. *American Psychologist, 44*(2), 329–335.

Patterson, G. R., & Dishion, T. J. (1988). Multilevel family process models: Traits, interactions, and relationships. In R. A. Hinde & J. Hinde-Stevenson (Eds.), *Relationships within families.* Oxford: Oxford University Press.

Patterson, G. R., Littman, R. A., & Bricker, W. (1976). Assertive behavior in children: A step toward a theory of aggression. *Monographs of the Society for Research in Child Development, 32* (Whole No. 113).

Patterson, G. R., Reid, J. B., & Dishion, T. J. (1992). *Antisocial boys.* Eugene, OR: Castilia Press.

Pavao, J. M. (1999). *The family of adoption.* Boston: Beacon Press.

Pearl, D. (Ed.). (1982). *Television and behavior: Ten years of scientific progress and implications for the eighties: Vol. 1. Summary report.* Washington, DC: U.S. Government Printing Office.

———. (1984). Violence and aggression. *Society, 21*(6), 17–22.

Perry, D. G., Perry, L. C., & Rasmussen, P. (1986). Cognitive social learning mediators of aggression. *Child Development, 57,* 700–711.

Perse, E. M. (2001). *Media effects and society.* Mahwah, NJ: Lawrence Erlbaum.

Pettit, G. S., & Mize, J. (1993). Substance and style: Understanding the ways in which parents teach children about social relationships. In S. Duck (Ed.), *Learning about relationships.* Newbury Park, CA: Sage.

Pham, A. (2002, November 9). A single-minded focus on multiple threads. *Los Angeles Times,* pp. C1, C3.

Phelps, L. A., Johnston, L. S., Jimenez, D. P., & Wilczenski, F. L. (1993). Figure preference, body dissatisfaction, and body distortion in adolescence. *Journal of Adolescent Research, 28,* 297–310.

Phillips, D. A. (1987a). Socialization of perceived academic competence among highly competent children. *Child Development, 58,* 1308–1320.

———. (1992). Child care and parental well-being: Bringing quality of care into the picture. In A. Booth (Ed.), *Child care in the 1990s: Trends and consequences.* Hillsdale, NJ: Lawrence Erlbaum.

Phillips, D. A., & Howes, C. (1987). Indicators of quality in child care: Review of research. In D. A. Phillips (Ed.), *Quality in child care. What does research tell us?* Washington, DC: National Association for the Education of Young Children.

Phillips, M. (Ed.). (1981). *Statement on child advocacy.* New York: Child Welfare League of America.

Phinney, J. S., & Chavira, V. (1992). Ethnic identity and self-esteem: An exploratory longitudinal study. *Journal of Adolescence 13,* 171–183.

Phinney, J. S., & Rotheram, M. J. (Eds.). (1987). *Children's ethnic socialization: Pluralism and development.* Newbury Park, CA: Sage.

Piaget, J. (1952). *The origins of intelligence in children* (M. Cook, Trans.). New York: New American Library.

———. (1965). *The moral judgment of the child* (M. Gabain, Trans.). New York: Free Press.

———. (1974). *The language and thought of the child* (M. Gabain, Trans.). New York: New American Library.

Pinderhughes, E. E., Dodge, K. A., Bates, J. E., Petit, G. S., & Zelli, A. (2000). Discipline responses influences of parents' socioeconomic status, ethnicity, beliefs about parenting, stress, and cognitive emotional processes. *Journal of Family Psychology, 14*(3), 380–400.

Pipher, M. (1994). *Reviving Ophelia: Saving the selves of adolescent girls.* New York: Ballantine Books.

Pitcher, E. G., & Schultz, L. H. (1983). *Boys and girls at play: The development of sex roles.* New York: Bergin & Garvey.

Poinsett, A. (1997, March). *The role of sports in youth development.* New York: Carnegie Corporation.

Pollack, W. S. (1999). *Real boys: Rescuing our sons from the myths of boyhood.* New York: Henry Holt.

Pomerantz, E. M., & Saxon, J. L. (2001). Conceptions of ability as stable and self-evaluative processes: A longitudinal examination. *Child Development, 72,* 152–173.

Postman, N. (1985). The disappearance of childhood. *Childhood Education, 61*(4), 288–293.

———. (1986). *Amusing ourselves to death.* New York: Penguin Books.

———. (1992). *Technopoly: The surrender of culture to technology.* New York: Vintage Books.

———. (1994). *The disappearance of childhood* (rev. ed.). New York: Vintage Books.

Power, T. G. (1987). Parents as socializers: Maternal and paternal views. *Journal of Youth and Adolescence, 18,* 203–220.

Powlista, K. K., Serbin, L. A., & Moller, L. C. (1993). The stability of individual differences in gender typing: Implications for understanding gender segregation. *Sex Roles, 239*(11–12), 723–737.

Prinsky, L. E., & Rosenbaum, J. L. (1987). Leerics or lyrics? *Youth and Society, 18,* 384–394.

Proctor, P. C. (1984). Teacher expectations: A model for school improvement. *Elementary School Journal, 84*(4), 469–481.

Provenzo, E. F. (1991). *Video kids: Making sense of Nintendo.* Cambridge, MA: Harvard University Press.

Putnam, L. (1986). Reading program decisions: The connection between philosophy and practice. *Childhood Education, 62*(5), 330–336.

Putnam, P. C. (1983, February). *A descriptive study of two philosophically different approaches to reading readiness, as they were used in six inner-city kindergartens.* Washington, DC: George Washington University. (ERIC Document Reproduction Service. ED 220 807/808).

Radke-Yarrow, M., & Zahn-Waxler, C. (1970). Dimension and correlates of prosocial behavior in young children. *Child Development, 47,* 118–125.

———. (1986). The role of familial factors in the development of prosocial behavior: Research findings and questions. In D. Olweus, J. Block, & M. Radke-Yarrow (Eds.), *Development of antisocial and prosocial behavior: Research, theories, and issues.* Orlando, FL: Academic Press.

Radke-Yarrow, M., Zahn-Waxler, C., & Chapman, H. (1983). Prosocial dispositions and behavior. In P. H. Mussen (Ed.), *Handbook of child psychology* (4th ed., Vol. 4). New York: Wiley.

Ramirez, M., & Castaneda, A. (1974). *A cultural democracy, bicognitive development and education.* New York: Academic Press.

Ramsey, P. (1998). *Teaching and learning in a diverse world: Multicultural education for young children* (2nd ed.). New York: Teachers' College Press.

Rawlings, M. K. (1938). *The yearling.* New York: Scribner.

Reed, S., & Sautter, R. C. (1990). Children of poverty. *Phi Delta Kappan, 71*(10) 1–12.

Reid, J. B., Patterson, G. R., & Snyder, J. (2002). *Antisocial behavior in children and adolescents: A developmental analysis and model for intervention.* Washington, DC: American Psychological Association.

Rheingold, H. L., & Cook, K. V. (1975). The content of boys' and girls' rooms as an index of parent behavior. *Child Development, 46,* 459–463.

Rice, F. P. (2001). *The adolescent: Development, relationships, and culture* (10th ed.). Needham Heights, MA: Allyn & Bacon.

Rice, M. L., Huston, A. C., Truglio, R., & Wright, J. C. (1990). Words from "Sesame Street": Learning vocabulary while viewing. *Developmental Psychology, 26,* 421–428.

Rice, M., & Grusec, J. (1975). Saying and doing: Effects on observer performance. *Journal of Personality and Social Psychology, 32,* 584–593.

Rich, D. (1992). *Megaskills* (rev. ed.). Boston: Houghton Mifflin.

Rich, M., Woods, E. R., Goodman, E., Emans, S. J., & DuRant, R. H. (1998). Aggressors or victims: Gender and race in music video violence. *Pediatrics, 101*(4), 669–674.

Rich, Y., & Golan, R. (1992). Career plans for male-dominated occupations and female seniors in religious and secular high schools. *Adolescence, 27,* 73–86.

Richman, A. L., LeVine, R. A., New, R. S., & Howrigan, G. A. (1988). Maternal behavior to infants in five cultures. In R. A. Levine, P. M. Miller, & M. M. West (Eds.), *Parental behavior in diverse societies.* San Francisco: Jossey-Bass.

Rice, F. P. (1996). *Development, relationships, and culture* (8th ed.). Needham Heights, MA: Allyn & Bacon.

Rickel, A. U., & Becker, E. (1997). *Keeping children from harm's way: How national policy affects psychological development.* Washington. DC: American Psychological Association.

Rilling, J. K., Gutman, D. A., Zeh, T. R., Pagnoni, G., Berns, G. S., & Kilts, C. D. (2002). A neural basis for social cooperation. *Neuron, 35,* 377–405.

Ritts, V., Patterson, M. L., & Tubbs, M. E. (1992). Expectations, impressions, and judgments of physically attractive students: A review. *Review of Educational Research, 62,* 413–426.

Rivkin, M. S. (1995). *The great outdoors: Restoring children's right to play outside.* Washington, DC: National Association for the Education of Young Children.

Roberts, D. F., & Christenson, P. G. (2001). Popular music in childhood and adolescence. In D. G. Singer & J. L. Singer (Eds.), *Handbook of children and the media.* Thousand Oaks, CA: Sage.

Roberts, D. E., & Maccoby, E. E. (1985). Effects of mass communication. In G. Lindsey & E. Aronson (Eds.), *Handbook of social psychology* (3rd ed., Vol. 2). New York: Random House.

Rodin, J. (1976). Crowding, perceived choice and response to controllable and uncontrollable outcomes. *Journal of Experimental Social Psychology, 12,* 564–578.

Rogoff, B. (1990). *Apprenticeship in thinking: Cognitive development in social context.* New York: Oxford University Press.

———. (2003). *The cultural nature of human development.* New York: Oxford University Press.

Rogosch, F. A., Cicchetti, D., Shields, A., & Toth, S. L. (1995). Parenting dysfunction in child maltreatment. In M. H. Bornstein (Ed.), *Handbook of parenting* (Vol. 4). Mahwah, NJ: Lawrence Erlbaum.

Rose, A. (1986, May 20). Breaking down cultural barriers. *Los Angeles Times*, pp. 1, 6 (Orange County Edition, Part II).

Rosen, B. C., & D'Andrade, R. G. (1959). The psychosocial origins of achievement motivation. *Sociometry, 22,* 185–218.

Rosenberg, M. (1975). The dissonant context and the adolescent self-concept. In S. E. Dragastin & G. H. Elder, Jr. (Eds.), *Adolescence in the life cycle: Psychological change and social context.* New York: Wiley.

Rosenfeld, A. H. (1985). Music, the beautiful disturber. *Psychology Today, 19*(12), 48–56.

Rosenhan, D., & White, G. (1967). Observation and rehearsal as determinants of prosocial behavior. *Journal of Personality and Social Psychology, 5,* 424–431.

Rosenkoetter, L. I., Huston, A. C., & Wright, J. C. (1990). Television and the moral judgment of the young child. *Journal of Applied Developmental Psychology, 11,* 123–127.

Rosenthal, R., & Jacobson, L. (1968). *Pygmalion in the classroom.* New York: Holt, Rinehart & Winston.

Rosner, B. A., & Rierdan, J. (1994, February). *Adolescent girls' self-esteem: Variations in developmental trajectories.* Paper presented at the meeting of the Society for Research on Adolescence, San Diego.

Ross, H., & Sawhill, I. (1975). *Time of transition: The growth of families headed by women.* Washington, DC: Urban Institute.

Ross, J. L. (1988). Challenging boundaries: An adolescent in a homosexual family. *Journal of Family Psychology, 2*(2), 227–240.

Ross, R. P., Campbell, T., Wright, J. C., Huston, A. C., Rice, M. L., & Turk, P. (1984). When celebrities talk, children listen: An experimental analysis of children's responses to TV ads with celebrity endorsement. *Journal of Applied Developmental Psychology, 5,* 185–202.

Rotherdam, M. J., & Phinney, J. S. (1987). Ethnic behavior patterns as an aspect of identity. In J. S. Phinney, & M. J. Rotherdam (Eds.), *Children's ethnic socialization: Pluralism and development.* Newbury Park, CA: Sage.

Rotter, J. B. (1966). Generalized expectancies for internal versus external control of reinforcement. *Psychological Monographs, 80* (Whole No. 609).

———. (1971). Who rules you? External control and internal control. *Psychology Today, 5,* 37–42.

Rovenger, J. (2000). Fostering emotional intelligence. *School Library Journal, 46*(2), 40–43.

Rubenstein, E. A. (1988). Television and the young viewer. *American Scientist, 65*(6), 685–693.

Rubenstein, J., & Howes, C. (1976). The effects of peers on toddler interaction with mothers and toys. *Child Development, 47,* 597–605.

Rubin, J. Z., Provenzano, F. J., & Luria, A. (1974). The eye of the beholder: Parents' views on the sex of newborns. *American Journal of Orthopsychiatry, 43,* 720–731.

Rubin, K. H., Bukowski, W., and Parker, J. G. (1998). Peer interactions, relationships, and groups. In W. Damon (Ed.), *Handbook of child psychology* (5th ed., Vol. 3). New York: Wiley.

Rubin, K. H., & Coplan, R. J. (1992). Peer relationships in childhood. In M. H. Bornstein & M. E. Lamb (Eds.), *Developmental psychology: An advanced textbook* (3rd ed.). Hillsdale, NJ: Lawrence Erlbaum.

Rubin, K. H., Stewart, S. L., & Chen, X. (1995). Parents of aggressive and withdrawn children. In M. H. Bornstein (Ed.), *Handbook of parenting* (Vol. 1). Mahwah, NJ: Lawrence Erlbaum.

Ruble, D., & Martin, C. L. (1998). Gender development. In W. Damon (Ed.), *Handbook of child psychology* (5th ed., Vol. 3). New York: Wiley.

Ruopp, R., Travers, J., Glantz, F., & Codlen, G. (1974). *Children at the center: Final results of the national day care study.* Cambridge, MA: Abt Associates.

Rushton, J. P., Fulker, D. W., Neal, M. C., Nias, D. K. B., & Eysenck, H. J. (1986). Altruism and aggression: The heritability of individual differences. *Journal of Personality and Social Psychology, 50,* 1192–1198.

Rust, J., Golombok, S., Hines, M., Johnson, K., & Golding, J. (2000). The role of brothers and sisters in the gender development of preschool children. *Journal of Experimental Child Psychology, 77,* 292–303.

Rutter, M. (1971). Parent–child separation: Psychological effects on the children. *Journal of Child Psychology and Psychiatry, 12,* 233–256.

Rutter, M., Giller, H., & Hagell, A. (1998). *Antisocial behavior by young people.* Cambridge: Cambridge University Press.

Rutter, V. (1994, May/June). Lessons from step families. *Psychology Today, 27,* 30–33, 60, 62, 64, 66, 68–69.

Ryan, R. M., & Deci, E. L. (2000). Intrinsic and extrinsic motivations: Classic definitions and new directions. *Contemporary Educational Psychology, 1,* 54–67.

Saarni, C., Mumme, D. L., & Campos, J. J. (1998). Emotional development: Action, communication, and understanding. In W. Damon (Ed.), *Handbook of child psychology* (5th ed., Vol. 3). New York: Wiley.

Sadker, D. M. P., & Sadker, D. M. (2003). *Teachers, schools, and society* (6th ed.). New York: McGraw-Hill.

Sadker, M., & Sadker, D. (1994). *Failing at fairness: How America's schools cheat girls.* New York: Scribner.

Sadker, M., Sadker, D., & Klein, S. (1991). The issue of gender in elementary and secondary education. *Review of Research in Education, 17,* 269–334.

Saltzstein, H. D. (1975, April). Role taking as a method of facilitating moral development. Symposium on Role-Taking and Moral Development. Paper presented at the meeting of the Eastern Psychological Association, New York.

————. (1976). Social influence and moral development: A perspective on the role of parents and peers. In T. Lickona (Ed.), *Moral development and behavior.* New York: Holt, Rinehart & Winston.

Sameroff, A. J. (1983). Developmental systems: Contexts and evolution. In P. H. Mussen (Ed.), *Handbook of child psychology* (4th ed., Vol. 4). New York: Wiley.

————. (1987). The social content of development. In N. Eisenberg (Ed.), *Contemporary topics in developmental psychology.* New York: Wiley.

————. (1994). Developmental systems and family functioning. In R. D. Parke & S. G. Kellan (Eds.), *Exploring family relationships with other social contexts.* Hillsdale, NJ: Lawrence Erlbaum.

Sampson, R. J. (1983). Structural density and criminal victimization. *Criminology, 21,* 276–293.

Sampson, R. J., & Laub, J. H. (1994). Urban poverty and the family context of delinquency: A new look at structure and process in a classic study. *Child Development, 65,* 523–540.

Sandler, I. N., Miller, P., Short, J., & Wolchik, S. A. (1989). Social support as a protective factor for children in stress. In D. Belle (Ed.), *Children's social networks and social supports.* New York: Wiley.

Sandler, I. N., Tein, J. Y., & West, S. G. (1994). Coping, stress, and the psychological symptoms of children of divorce: A cross-sectional and longitudinal study. *Child Development, 64,* 1744–1763.

Sandstrom, M. J., & Coie, J. D. (1999). A developmental perspective on peer rejection: Mechanisms of stability and change. *Child Development, 70,* 955–966.

Sanford, N., & Comstock, C. (Eds.). (1971). *Sanctions for evil.* San Francisco: Jossey-Bass.

Santrock, J. W., & Sitterle, K. A. (1987). Parent–child relationships: Stepmother families. In K. Pasley & M. Ihinger-Tallman (Eds.), *Remarriage and stepparenting: Current research and theory.* New York: Guilford Press.

Santrock, J. W., & Warshak, R. A. (1979). Father custody and social development in boys and girls. *Journal of Social Issues, 35,* 112–125.

Santrock, J. W., Warshak, R. A., & Eliot, G. (1982). Social development and parent–child interaction in father-custody and stepmother families. In M. E. Lamb (Ed.), *Nontraditional families.* Hillsdale, NJ: Lawrence Erlbaum.

Savage, D. G. (1983, February 15). Freeway noise linked to poorer test scores. *Los Angeles Times,* p. 1 (Part I).

Scarr, S. (1984). *Mother care/other care.* New York: Basic Books.

————. (1992). Theories for the 1990s: Developmental and individual differences. *Child Development, 63,* 1–19.

Schaefer, E. S. (1991). Goals for parent and future-parent education. *The Elementary School Journal, 91*(3), 239–247.

Scheibe, C. (1989). Character portrayal and values in network TV commercials. Unpublished M.A. thesis, Cornell University. Cited in J. Condry, *The psychology of television.* Hillsdale, NJ: Lawrence Erlbaum.

Schickedanz, J. (1986). *More than the ABCs: The early stages of reading and writing.* Washington, DC: National Association for the Education of Young Children.

————. (1990). Preschoolers and academics: Some thoughts. *Young Children, 46*(1), 4–13.

Schneider, B. H., Atkinson, L., & Tardif, C. (2001). Child–parent attachment and children's peer relations. A quantitative review. *Developmental Psychology, 37,* 86–100.

Schorr, L. B. (1997). *Common purpose: Strengthening families and neighborhoods to rebuild America.* New York: Anchor Books.

Schorr, L. B., Both, D., & Copple, C. (Eds.). (1991). *Effective services for young children: Report of a workshop.* Washington, DC: National Academy Press.

Schorr, L. B., with D. Schorr (1988). *Within our reach: Breaking the cycle of disadvantage.* New York: Doubleday/Anchor Press.

Schramm, W., Lyle, J., & Parker, E. (1961). *Television in the lives of our children.* Stanford, CA: Stanford University Press.

Schunk, D. H. (2000). *Theories of learning* (3rd ed.). Upper Saddle River, NJ: Prentice-Hall.

Schweinhart, L. J., & Weikart, D. P. (1993). Success by empowerment: The High/Scope Perry Preschool study through age 27. *Young Children, 49*(1), 54–58.

————. (1998). Why curriculum matters in early childhood education. *Educational Leadership, 55*(6), 57–60.

Schweinhart, L. J., Weikart, D. P., & Larner, M. B. (1986a). Child-initiated activities in early childhood programs may help prevent delinquency. *Early Childhood Research Quarterly, 1*(3), 303–312.

————. (1986b). Consequences of three preschool curriculum models through age 15. *Early Childhood Research Quarterly, 1*(1), 15–45.

Sebald, H. (1986). Adolescents' shifting orientation toward parents and peers: A curvilinear trend over recent decades. *Journal of Marriage and the Family, 48,* 5–13.

————. (1989). Adolescent peer orientation: Changes in the support system during the last three decades. *Adolescence, 24,* 937–945.

————. (1992). *Adolescence: A social psychological analysis* (4th ed.). Englewood Cliffs, NJ: Prentice-Hall.

Segal, N. L. (1997). Genetic bases of behavior: Contributions to psychological research. In N. L. Segal, G. E. Weisfeld, & C. C. Weisfeld (Eds.), *Uniting psychology and biology.* Washington, DC: American Psychological Association.

Seligman, M. E. P. (1975). *Helplessness.* San Francisco: Freeman.

———. (1990). *Learned optimism*. New York: Pocket Books.

Selman, R. L. (1980). *The growth of interpersonal understanding*. New York: Academic Press.

Selman, R. L., & Selman, A. P. (1979). Children's ideas about friendship: A new theory. *Psychology Today, 12*(4), 71–80.

Sendak, M. (1963). *Where the wild things are*. New York: Harper & Row.

———. (1970). *In the night kitchen*. New York: Harper & Row.

Serbin, L. A., O'Leary, K. D., Kent, R. N., & Tonick, I. J.(1973). A comparison of teacher response to the preacademic and problem behavior of boys and girls. *Child Development, 44*, 796–804.

Serbin, L. A., Powlishta, K. K., & Gulko, J. (1993). The development of sex typing in middle childhood. *Monographs of the Society for Research in Child Development, 58*(2), (Serial No. 232).

Sexton, D., Snyder, P., Sharpton, W. R., & Strickin, S. (1993). Infants and toddlers with special needs and their families. *Childhood Education, 69*(5), 278–286.

Seyle, H. (1956). *The stress of life*. New York: McGraw-Hill.

Shaffer, D. R. (2000). *Social and personality development*. Belmont, CA: Wadsworth.

Shantz, C. U. (1983). Social cognition. In P. H. Mussen (Eds.), *Handbook of child psychology* (4th ed., Vol. 3). New York: Wiley.

Shapira, A., & Lomranz, J. (1972). Cooperative and competitive behavior of rural Arab children in Israel. *Journal of Cross-Cultural Psychology, 3*, 353–359.

Shapira, A., & Madsen, M. C. (1974). Between- and within-group cooperation and competition among kibbutz and non-kibbutz children. *Developmental Psychology, 10*, 140–145.

Sherif, M. (1956). Experiments in group conflict. *Scientific American, 195*(2), 54–58.

Sherif, M., Harvey, O. J., White, B. J., Hood, W. R., & Sherif, C. W. (1961). *Intergroup conflict and cooperation: The robber's cave experiment*. Norman: Institute of Group Relations, University of Oklahoma.

Shields, M. A., & Behrman, R. E. (2000). Children and computer technology: Analysis and recommendations. *The Future of Children, 10*(2), 4–30.

Shonk, S. M., & Cicchetti, D. (2001). Maltreatment, competency, deficits, and risk for academic and behavioral maladjustment. *Developmental Psychology, 37*, 3–17.

Shweder, R. A., Mahapatra, M., & Miller, J. G. (1987). Culture and moral development. In J. Kagan & S. Lamb (Eds.), *The emergence of morality in young children*. Chicago: University of Chicago Press.

Sigman, M., Neumann, C., Carter, E., & Cattle, D. J. (1988). Home interactions and the development of Embu toddlers in Kenya. *Child Development, 57*, 1251–1261.

Signorella, M. L., Bigler, R. S., & Liben, L. S. (1993). Developmental differences in children's gender schemata about others: A meta-analytic review. *Developmental Review, 13*, 147–183.

Signorielli, N. (1989). Television and conceptions about sex roles: Maintaining conventionality and the status quo. *Sex Roles, 21*(5–6), 341–360.

———. (1993). Television, the portrayal of women and children's attitudes. In C. L. Berry & J. K. Samen (Eds.), *Children and television: Images in a changing sociocultural world*. Newbury Park, CA: Sage.

Silverstein, L. B., & Auerbach, C. F. (2001). The myth of the "normal" family. Society for the Advancement of Education. In K. R. Gilbert (Ed.), *Annual Editions 02/03: The Family*. Guilford, CT: McGraw-Hill/Dushkin.

Simeonsson, R. J., & Bailey, D. B. (1986). Siblings of the handicapped child. In J. J. Gallager & W. Vietze (Eds.), *Families of handicapped persons*. Baltimore: Brookes.

Singer, D. G., & Singer, J. L. (1976). Family television viewing habits and the spontaneous play of preschool children. *American Journal of Orthopsychiatry, 46*, 496–502.

———. (1990). *House of make-believe*. Cambridge, MA: Harvard University Press.

Singer, D. G., Singer, J. L., & Zuckerman, D. M. (1990). *The parent's guide: Use TV to your child's advantage*. Reston, VA: Acropolis Books.

Skalka, P. (1983). Take control of your TV. *Friendly Exchange, 3*(1), 26–27.

Sklaroff, S. (2002). One nation under a groove. *U.S. News & World Report, 133*(2), 20–21.

Skeels, H. M. (1966). Adult status of children with contrasting early life experiences. *Monographs of the Society for Research in Child Development, 31*(3) (Whole No. 105).

Skinner, B. F. (1948). *Walden two*. New York: Macmillan.

———. (1954). The science of learning and the art of teaching. *Harvard Educational Review, 25*, 86–97.

Skinner, E. A. (1995). *Perceived control, motivation, and coping*. Thousand Oaks, CA: Sage.

Skolnick, A. (1987). *The intimate environment: Exploring marriage and the family* (4th ed.). Boston: Little, Brown.

Slaby, R. G., Roedell, W. C., Arezzo, D., & Hendrix, K. (1995). *Early violence prevention: Tools for teachers of young children*. Washington, DC: National Association for the Education of Young Children.

Slavin, R. E. (1991). Synthesis of research on cooperative learning. *Educational Leadership, 48*(5), 71–82.

Slavin, R. E., Devries, D. L., & Hutten, B. H. (1975). *Individual vs. team competition: The interpersonal consequences of academic performance.* Baltimore: Johns Hopkins University Center for Social Organization of Schools. (Report No. 188).

Sleek, S. (1998). Isolation increases with internet use. *APA Monitor, 29*(9), 1, 30–31.

Small, J. (Ed.). (1987). *Children of alcoholics: A special report.* Washington, DC: National Institute on Alcohol Abuse and Alcoholism.

Small, S., & Luster, T. (1994). Adolescent sexual activity: An ecological risk-factor approach. *Journal of Marriage and the Family, 56,* 181–192.

Small, S., & Supple, A. (2001). Communities as systems: Is a community more than the sum of its parts? In A. Booth & A. C. Crouter (Eds.), *Does it take a village?* Mahwah, NJ: Lawrence Erlbaum.

Smetana, J. (1981). Preschool children's conceptions of moral and social rules. *Child Development, 52,* 1333–1336.

———. (1985). Preschool children's conceptions of transgressions: Effects of varying moral and conventional domain-related attributes. *Developmental Psychology, 21,* 18–29.

———. (1989). Toddlers' social interactions in the context of moral and conventional transgressions in the home. *Developmental Psychology, 25,* 499–508.

Smith, A. B., Dannison, L. L., & Vach-Hasse, T. (1998, Fall). When "grandma" is "mom." *Childhood Education, 75*(1), 12–16.

Smith, D. D., & Bassett, D. (1991). The REI debate: A time for a systematic research agenda. In J. Lloyd, A. C. Repp, & N. N. Sing (Eds.), *Perspectives on integration of atypical learners in regular education settings.* Sycamore, IL: Sycamore Press.

Smith, P. K., & Dutton, S. (1979). Play and training indirect and innovative problem solving. *Child Development, 60,* 830–836.

Snow, M. E., Jacklin, C. N., & Maccoby, E. E. (1981). Birth order differences in peer sociability at thirty-three months. *Child Development, 52,* 589–596.

Snyder, J. J., & Patterson, G. R. (1995). Individual differences in social aggression: A test of a reinforcement model of socialization in the natural environment. *Behavior Therapy, 26,* 371–391.

Soldier, L. L. (1985). To soar with the eagles: Enculturation and acculturation of Indian children. *Childhood Education, 61*(3), 185–191.

Solomon, C. (1999, October 2). The Gen-P gold mine. *Los Angeles Times,* pp. F1, F18.

Spencer, M. B. (2001). Resiliency and fragility factors associated with the contextual experiences of low resource urban African American male youth and families. In A. Booth & A. C. Crouter (Eds.), *Does it take a village?* Mahwah, NJ: Lawrence Erlbaum.

Spitz, E. H. (1999). *Inside picture books.* New Haven, CT: Yale University Press.

Spitz, H. R. (1992). Early childhood intervention. In T. G. Sticht, M. J. Beeler, & B. A. McDonald (Eds.), *The intergenerational transfer of cognitive skills.* Norwood, NJ: Ablex.

Spitz, R. (1946). Hospitalism: An inquiry into the genesis of psychiatric conditioning in early childhood. In A. Freud (Ed.), *Psychoanalytic studies of the child* (Vol. 1). New York: International Universities Press.

Spock, B. (1946). *The common sense book of baby and child care.* New York: Duell Sloan Pearce.

———. (1957). *The pocket book of baby and child care.* New York: Pocket Books.

———. (1968). *Baby and child care.* New York: Pocket Books.

———. (1985). *Raising children in a difficult time* (2nd ed.). New York: Pocket Books.

Sprafkin, J. M., Leibert, R. M., & Poulos, R. W. (1975). Effects of a prosocial example on children's helping. *Journal of Experimental Child Psychology, 20,* 119–126.

Sroufe, L. (1978). Attachment and the roots of competence. *Human Nature, 1,* 50–57.

———. (1996). *Emotional development.* Cambridge: Cambridge University Press.

St. Peters, M., Marguerite, F., Huston, A. C., Wright, J. C., & Eakins, D. J. (1991). Television and families: What do young children watch with their parents? *Child Development, 62,* 1409–1413.

Stabiner, K. (1993, August). Get 'em while they're young. *Los Angeles Times Magazine,* pp. 12, 14, 15, 16, 38.

Stallings, J. (1974). *Follow through classroom observation evaluation, 1972–1973: Executive summary.* Menlo Park, CA: Stanford Research Institute.

Starr, R. H. Jr. (1990, June). The lasting effects of child maltreatment. *The Word and I,* 484–499.

Staub, E. (1970). A child in distress: The effect of focusing responsibility on children on their attempts to help. *Developmental Psychology, 2,* 152–153.

———. (1971). The use of role playing and induction in children's learning of helping and sharing behavior. *Child Development, 42,* 805–816.

———. (1975). *The development of prosocial behavior in children.* Morristown, NJ: General Learning Press.

———. (1986). A conception of the determinants and development of altruism and aggression: Motives, the self, and the environment. In C. Zahn-Waxler, E. M. Cummings, & R. Iannotti (Eds.), *Altruism and aggression: Biological and social origins.* Cambridge: Cambridge University Press.

Stein, L. C., & Kostelnick, M. J. (1984). A practical problem-solving model for conflict resolution in the classroom. *Childcare Quarterly, 13,* 5–20.

Steinberg, L. (1986). Latchkey children and susceptibility to peer pressure: An ecological analysis. *Developmental Psychology, 22,* 433–439.

———. (1987). Single parents, step parents, and the susceptibility of adolescents to antisocial peer pressure. *Child Development, 58,* 269–275.

———. (1993). *Adolescence.* New York: McGraw-Hill.

———. (1996). *Beyond the classroom: Why school reform has failed and what parents need to do.* New York: Touchstone.

Steinberg, L., Elmen, J. D., & Mounts, N. S. (1989). Authoritative parenting, psychosocial maturity, and academic success among adolescents. *Child Development, 60,* 1424–1436.

Steinberg, L., Lamborn, S. D., Darling, N., Mounts, N., & Dornbusch, S. M. (1994). Over-time changes in adjustment and competence among adolescents from authoritative, authoritarian, indulgent, and neglectful families. *Child Development, 65,* 754–770.

Steinberg, L., & Morris, A. S. (2001). Adolescent development. *Annual Review of Psychology, 52,* 83–110.

Steinberg, L., Mounts, N. S., Lambourn, S. D., & Dornbusch, S. M. (1991). Authoritative parenting and adolescent adjustment across various ecological niches. *Journal of Research on Adolescence, 1,* 19–36.

Steinman, S. B., Zimmelman, S. E., & Knoblauch, T. M. (1985). A study of parents who sought joint custody following divorce. Who reaches agreement and sustains joint custody and who returns to court. *Journal of the American Academy of Child Psychiatry, 24,* 554–563.

Stendler, C. B. (1950). Sixty years of child training practices. *Journal of Pediatrics, 36,* 122–134.

Stepfamily Association of America. (2000). www.saafamilies.org

Stephens, M. W., & Delys, P. (1973). External control expectancies among disadvantaged children at preschool age. *Child Development, 44,* 670–674.

Stevenson, H., Stigler, J. W., Lee, S., Kitamura, S., & Kato, T. (1986). Achievement in mathematics. In H. Stevenson, H. Azuma, & K. Hakuta (Eds.), *Child development and education in Japan.* New York: Freeman.

Stevenson, H. W. (1972). *Children's learning.* New York: Appleton-Century-Crofts.

Stevenson, H. W., & Lee, S. Y. (1990). Contents of achievement: A study of American, Chinese, and Japanese children. *Monographs of the Society for Research in Child Development, 55*(1–2) (Serial No. 221).

Stewart, E. C., & Bennett, M. J. (1991). *American cultural patterns: A cross-cultural perspective* (rev. ed.). Yarmouth, ME: Intercultural Press.

Stinnett, N., & Birdsong, C. W. (1978). *The family and alternate life styles.* Chicago: Nelson Hall.

Stinnett, N., & Defrain, J. (1985). *Secrets of strong families.* Boston: Little, Brown.

Stipek, D. J. (1996). Motivation and instruction. In D. C. Berliner & R. C. Calfee (Eds.), *Handbook of educational psychology.* New York: Macmillan.

Stipek, D., Recchia, A., & McClintic, S. (1992). Self-evaluation in young children. *Monographs of the Society for Research in Child Development, 57*(1) (Serial No. 226).

Stomfay-Stitz, A. M. (1994). Pathways to safer schools. *Childhood Education, 70*(5), 279–282.

Strasburger, V. C., & Hendren, R. L. (1995). Rock music and music videos. *Pediatric Annals, 24,* 103.

Straus, M. A. (1992). Children as witness to marital violence: A risk factor for lifelong problems among a nationally representative sample of American men and women. In D. F. Schwarz (Ed.), *Children and violence: Report of the twenty-third Ross Roundtable on Critical Approaches to Common Pediatric Problems.* Columbus, OH: Ross Laboratories.

Streitmatter, J. (1994). *Toward gender equity in the classroom: Everyday teachers' beliefs and practices.* New York: State University of New York Press.

Strouse, J. S., Buerkel-Rothfuss, N., & Long, E. C. J. (1995). Gender and family as moderators of the relationship between music video exposure and adolescent sexual permissiveness, *Adolescence, 30*(119), 505–522.

Subrahmanyam, K., Kraut, R. E., Greenfield, P. M., & Gross, E. F. (2001). New forms of electronic media. In D. G. Singer & J. L. Singer (Eds.), *Handbook of children and the media.* Thousand Oaks, CA: Sage.

Sue, D. W. (1989). Ethnic identity: The impact of two cultures on the psychological development of Asians in America. In D. R. Atkinson, G. Morten, & D. W. Sue (Eds.), *Counseling American minorities* (3rd ed.). Dubuque, IA: Brown.

Sutton-Smith, B. (1971). Children at play. *Natural History, 80,* 54–59.

———. (1972). *The folkgames of children.* Austin: University of Texas Press.

———. (1982). Birth order and sibling status effects. In M. E. Lamb (Ed.), *Sibling relationships: Their nature and significance over the lifespan.* Hillsdale, NJ: Lawrence Erlbaum.

Swick, K. J. (1986). Locus of control and interpersonal support as related to parenting. *Childhood Education, 62,* 41–50.

———. (1997). Learning about work; Extending learning through an ecological approach. In B. Hatcher & S. S. Beck (Eds.), *Learning opportunities beyond the school* (2nd ed.). Olney, MD: Association for Childhood Education International.

Taishido Study Group. (1984/1985). Generations of play in Taishido. *Childrens' Environment Quarterly, 1*(4), 19–28.

Tamis-LeMonda, C. S., & Cabrera, N. (1999). Perspectives on father involvement: Research and policy. *Society for Research in Child Development, 12*(2).

Teale, W. H. (1984). Reading to young children: Its significance for literary development. In H. Coleman,

A. Oberg, & F. Smith (Eds.), *Awakening and literacy.* Portsmouth, NH: Heinemann.

Teasley, S. D., & Parker, J. G. (1995, March). *The effects of gender, friendship, and popularity on the targets and topics of adolescent gossip.* Paper presented at the Bienniel Meeting of the Society for Research in Child Development, Indianapolis, IN.

Tharp, R. G. (1989). Psychocultural variables and constraints: Effects on teaching and learning in schools. *American Psychologist, 44*(2), 349–359.

Thiederman, S. (1991). *Bridging cultural barriers for success: How to manage the cultural work force.* New York: Lexington Books.

Thoma, S. J., Rest, J. R., & Davidson, M. L. (1991). Describing and testing a moderator of the moral judgment and action relationship. *Journal of Personality and Social Psychology, 61,* 659–669.

Thomas, A., & Chess, S. (1977). *Temperament and development.* New York: Brunner/Mazel.

———. (1980). *The dynamics of psychological development.* New York: Brunner/Mazel.

Thomas, A., Chess, S., & Birch, H. S. (1970). The origin of personality. *Scientific American, 223,* 102–109.

Thompson, M., Cohen, L. J., & Grace, C. O. (2002). *Best friends, worst enemies: Understanding the social lives of children.* New York: Ballantine Books.

Thompson, R. A. (1994). Social support and the prevention of child maltreatment. In G. B. Melton & F. Barry (Eds.), *Safe neighborhoods: Foundations for a new national strategy on child abuse and neglect.* New York: Guilford Press.

Thompson, R. L., & Larson, R. (1995). Social context and the subjective experience of different types of rock music. *Journal of Youth and Adolescence, 24*(6), 731–744.

Thompson, R. S. (1998). Early sociopersonality development. In W. Damon (Ed.), *Handbook of child psycholgy* (5th ed., Vol. 3). New York: Wiley.

Thompson, S. H. (1998). Working with children of substance-abusing parents. *Young Children, 53*(1), 34–37.

Thompson, W. E., & Dodder, R. A. (1986). Containment theory and juvenile delinquency: A reevaluation through factor analysis. *Adolescence, 21,* 365–376.

Thornburg, H. D. (1981). The amount of sex information learning obtained during early adolescence. *Journal of Early Adolescence, 1,* 171–183.

Thorne, B. (1993). *Gender play: Girls and boys in school.* New Brunswick, NJ: Rutgers University Press.

Thuy, V. G. (1983). The Indochinese in America: Who are they and how are they doing? In D. T. Nakanishi & M. Huano-Nakanishi (Eds.), *The education of Asian and Pacific Americans: Historical perspectives and prescriptions for the future.* Phoenix: Oryx Press.

Tizard, J., Schofield, W. N., & Hewison, J. (1982). Collaboration between teachers and parents in assisting children's reading. *British Journal of Education, 52,* 1–15.

Tobin, J. J., Wu, D. Y. H., & Davidson, D. H. (1989, April). How three key countries shape their children. *World Monitor, 36*–45.

Toch, T. (1996, October 7). Schools that work. *U.S. News & World Report, 66,* 58–64.

Toffler, A. (1990). *Powershift.* New York: Bantam Books.

Tonnies, F. (1957). *Community and society* (Gemeinshaft und Geseillshaft) (C. P. Loomis, Trans.). East Lansing: Michigan State University.

Took, K. J., & Weiss, D. S. (1994). The relationship between heavy metal and rap music and adolescent turmoil. Real or abstract? *Adolescence, 29*(115), 613–623.

Toufexis, A. (1991). Innocent victims. *Time, 137*(19), 56–60.

Tozer, S. E., Violas, P. C., & Senese, G. (2002). *School and society: Historical and contemporary perspectives* (4th ed.). New York: McGraw-Hill.

Trelease, J. (2001). *The read-aloud handbook* (5th ed.). New York: Viking Press.

Triandis, H. C. (1994). *Culture and social behavior.* New York: McGraw-Hill.

———. (1995). *Individualism and collectivism.* Boulder, CO: Westview Press.

Troy, M., & Sroufe, L. A. (1987). Victimization among preschoolers: Role of attachment relationship history. *Journal of the American Academy of Child and Adolescent Psychiatry, 26,* 166–172.

Trumbull, E., Rothstein-Fisch, C., Greenfield, P. M., & Quiroz, B. (2001). *Bridging cultures between home and school.* Mahwah, NJ: Lawrence Erlbaum.

Tubman, J. G. (1993). Family risk factors, parental alcohol use, and problem behaviors among school-age children. *Family Relations, 42,* 81–86.

Tucker, L. A. (1983). Self-concept: A function of self-perceived somatotype. *Journal of Psychology, 14,* 123–133.

Turiel, E. (1966). An experimental test of the sequentiality of developmental stages in the child's moral judgments. *Journal of Personality and Social Psychology, 3,* 611–618.

———. (1983). *The development of social knowledge: Morality and convention.* Cambridge: Cambridge University Press.

———. (1998). The development of morality. In W. Damon (Ed.), *Handbook of child psychology* (5th ed., Vol. 3). New York: Wiley.

Turnbull, A. P., & Turnbull, H. R., III. (1997). *Families, professionals, and exceptionality* (3rd ed.). Columbus, OH: Merrill.

Turner-Bowker, D. M. (1996). Gender stereotyped descriptors in children's picture books: Does "Curious Jane" exist in the literature? *Sex Roles, 35,* 461–488.

Tushscherer, P. (1988). *TV interactive toys: The new high tech threat to children.* Bend, OR: Pinnaroo.

Tyler, R. (1992). Prenatal drug exposure: An overview of associated problems and intervention strategies. *Phi Delta Kappan, 73*(9), 705–708.

Uba, L. (1999). *Asian Americans: Personality patterns, identity, and mental health.* New York: Guilford Press.

Ungar, M. T. (2000). The myth of peer pressure. *Adolescence, 35*(137), 167–171.

U.S. Bureau of the Census. (2000). *Statistical Abstract of the United States* (120th ed.). Washington, DC: U.S. Government Printing Office.

U.S. Department of Education (USDE). (1989). *What works: Schools without drugs.* Washington, DC: U.S. Government Printing Office.

———. (1991a). *America 2000: An education strategy.* Washington, DC: U.S. Government Printing Office.

———. (1991b). *Preparing children for success: Guideposts for achieving our first national goal.* Washington, DC: U.S. Government Printing Office.

———. (1994). *Strong families, strong schools: Building community partnerships for learning.* Washington, DC: U.S. Government Printing Office.

U.S. Department of Health and Human Services (USDHHS). (1991). *Healthy people 2000: National health promotion and disease prevention objectives.* Washington, DC: U.S. Government Printing Office.

———. (1992). Project No. OE1 09-91-0065. Washington, DC: U.S. Government Printing Office.

U.S. Department of Justice. (2000, August). Youth gangs in school. *Juvenile Justice Bulletin.* Washington, DC: U.S. Government Printing Office.

Van Ausdale, D. & Feagin, J. R. (2001). *The first R: How children learn race and racism.* Lanham, MD: Rowman & Littlefield.

Vandell, D. L., & Mueller, E. C. (1995). Peer play and friendship during the play years. In H. C. Foot, A. J. Chapman, & J. R. Smith (Eds.), *Friendship and social relations in children.* New Brunswick, NJ: Transaction Books.

Vandell, D. L., & Su, Hsiu-Chih. (1999). Child care and school-age children. *Young Children, 54*(6), 62–71.

Vanderslice, V. J. (1984). Empowerment: A definition of process. *Human Ecology Forum, 14*(1), 2–3.

Van der Voort, T. H. A., & Valkenburg, P. M. (1994). Television's impact on fantasy play: A review of research. *Developmental Review, 14,* 27–51.

Vander Zanden, J. W. (1995). *Sociology: The core* (3rd ed.). New York: McGraw-Hill.

Vasquez, J. A. (1990). Teaching to the distinctive traits of minority students. *The Clearing House, 63,* 299–304.

Vasquez-Nutall, E., Romers-Garcia, I., & DeLeon, B. (1987). Sex roles and perceptions of femininity and masculinity of Hispanic women: A review of the literature. *Psychology of Women Quarterly, 11,* 409–425.

Vaughn, S., Bos, C. S., & Schumm, J. S. (1997). *Teaching mainstreamed, diverse, and at-risk students in the general education classroom.* Boston: Allyn & Bacon.

Verdugo, R., Kuttner, A., Seidel, S., Wallace, C., Sosa, M., & Faber, M. (1990). *Safe schools manual: A resource on making schools, communities, and families safe for children.* Washington, DC: National Education Association.

Vigil, J. D. (1980). *From Indians to Chicanos: The dynamics of Mexican-American culture.* Prospect Heights, IL: Wavel and Press.

Vincze, M. (1971). The social contacts of infants and young children reared together. *Early Child Development and Care, 1,* 99–109.

Vorrath, H. H., & Brendtro, L. K. (1985). *Positive peer culture* (2nd ed.). New York: Aldine.

Vosler, N. R., & Robertson, J. G. (1998). Nonmarital co-parenting: Knowledge-building for practice. *Families in Society: The Journal of Contemporary Human Services, 79*(2), 149–157.

Vygotsky, L. S. (1978). *Mind and society: The development of higher psychological processes* (M. Cole, V. John-Steiner, S. Scribner, & E. Souberman, Eds.). Cambridge, MA: Harvard University Press.

Walker, L. J. (1991). Sex differences in moral development. In W. M. Kurtines & J. Gewirtz (Eds.), *Handbook of moral behavior and development* (Vol. 2). Hillsdale, NJ: Lawrence Erlbaum.

Walker, L. J., & Taylor, J. H. (1991). Family interaction and the development of moral reasoning. *Child Development, 62,* 264–283.

Walker, L. S., & Greene, J. W. (1986). The social context of adolescent self-esteem. *Journal of Youth and Adolescence, 15*(4), 315–323.

Wall, J. A., Power, T. G., & Arbona, C. (1993). Susceptibility to antisocial peer pressure and its relation to acculturation in Mexican-American adolescents. *Journal of Adolescent Research, 8,* 403–418.

Wallach, L. B. (1993). Helping children cope with violence. *Young Children, 48*(4), 4–11.

Wallerstein, J. S., & Kelly, J. B. (1996). *Surviving the breakup. How parents and children cope with divorce.* New York: Basic Books.

Wallerstein, J. S., Corbin, S. B., & Lewis, J. H. (1988). Children of divorce: A ten-year study. In E. M. Hetherington & J. D. Arasteh (Eds.), *Impact of divorce, single parenting and stepparenting on children.* Hillsdale, NJ: Lawrence Erlbaum.

Wang, A. Y. (1994). Pride and prejudice in high school gang members. *Adolescence, 29,* 279–291.

Wang, J., & Wildman, L. (1995). The effects of family commitment in education on student achievement in seventh grade mathematics. *Education, 115,* 317–319.

Wang, M. C. (2000). Preface. In R. D. Taylor & M. C. Wang (Eds.), *Resilience across contexts: Family, work, culture, and community.* Mahwah, NJ: Lawrence Erlbaum.

Ward, C. (1978). *The child in the city.* New York: Pantheon Books.

Warren, R. (1983). The community in America. In R. L. Warren & L. Lyon (Eds.), *New perspectives on the American community.* Homewood, IL: Dorsey Press.

Wartella, E. A., & Jennings, N. (2000). Children and computers: New technology—old concerns. *The Future of Children, 10*(2), 31–43.

Waters, E., Posada, G., Crowell, J., & Keng-ling, L. (1993). Is attachment theory ready to contribute to our understanding of disruptive behavior problems? *Development and Psychopathology, 5,* 215–224.

Weber, M. (1930). *The Protestant ethic and the spirit of capitalism.* London: Allen.

Weiner, B. (1992). *Human motivation: Metaphors, theories, and research.* Newbury Park, CA: Sage.

Weiner, M., & Wright, F. (1973). Effects of undergoing arbitrary discrimination upon subsequent attitudes toward a minority group. *Journal of Applied Social Psychology, 3,* 94–102.

Weinstein, C. S. (1991). The classroom as a social context for learning. *Annual Review of Psychology, 42,* 493–525.

Weisner, D. (2001). *The three pigs.* Boston: Clarion/ Houghton Mifflin.

Weiss, L. H., & Schwarz, J. C. (1996). The relationship between parenting types and older adolescents' personality, academic achievement, adjustment and substance use. *Child Development, 67,* 2101–2114.

Weiss, M. F. (1994). Children's attitudes toward the mentally ill: An eight-year longitudinal follow-up. *Psychological Reports, 74,* 51–56.

Weissbourd, R. (1996). *The vulnerable child: What really hurts America's children and what we can do about it.* Reading, MA: Addison-Wesley.

Weissbrod, C. (1976). Noncontingent warmth, induction, cognitive style, and children's imitative donation and rescue effort behaviors. *Journal of Personality and Social Psychology, 34,* 274–281.

Weitzman, L. J. (1972). Sex-role socialization in picture books for preschool children. *American Journal of Sociology, 77,* 1125–1150.

———. (1985). *The divorce revolution.* New York: Free Press.

Wentzel, K. A., & Erdley, C. A. (1993). Strategies for making friends: Relations to social behavior and peer acceptance in early adolescence. *Developmental Psychology, 29,* 819–826.

Werner, E. E. (1993). Risk, resilience, and recovery: Perspectives from the Kauai longitudinal study. *Development and Psychopathology, 5,* 503–515.

Werner, E. E., & Smith, R. S. (1992). *Overcoming the odds: High risk children from birth to adulthood.* Ithaca, NY: Cornell University Press.

West, M. M. (1988). Parental values and behavior in the outer Fiji Islands. In R. A. Levine, P. M. Miller, & M. M. West (Eds.), *Parental behavior in diverse societies.* San Francisco: Jossey-Bass.

White, B. L. (1971, October). *Fundamental early environmental influences on the development of competence.* Paper presented at Third Western Symposium on Learning: Cognitive Learning, Western Washington State College, Bellingham.

———. (1995). *The new first three years of life.* New York: Simon & Schuster.

White, B. L., & Watts, J. C. (1973). *Experience and environment: Major influences on the development of the young child* (Vol. 1). Englewood Cliffs, NJ: Prentice-Hall.

White, L. (1960). Symbol, the basis of language and culture. In W. Goldschmidt (Ed.), *Exploring the ways of mankind.* New York: Holt, Rinehart & Winston.

White, R. W. (1959). Motivation reconsidered: The concept of competence. *Psychology Review, 66,* 297–333.

White, S., & Tharp, R. G. (1988, April). *Questioning and wait-time: A cross-cultural analysis.* Paper presented at the annual meeting of the American Educational Research Association, New Orleans.

Whitebook, M., Howes, C., & Phillips, D. (1989). *Who cares? Child care teachers and the quality of care in America: Final report, National Child Care Staffing Study.* Oakland, CA: Child Care Employee Project.

Whitehead, B. F. (1998). *The divorce culture: Rethinking our commitment to marriage and family.* New York: Vintage Books.

Whitehurst, G. J., & Lonigan, C. J. (1998). Child development and emergent literacy. *Child Development, 69,* 848–872.

Whiting, B. B., & Edwards, C. P. (1988). *Children of different worlds: The formation of social behavior.* Cambridge, MA: Harvard University Press.

Whiting, B. B., & Whiting, J. W. M. (1973). Altruistic and egoistic behavior in six cultures. In L. Nader & T. W. Maretski (Eds.), *Cultural illness and health: Essays in human adaptation.* Washington, DC: American Anthropological Association.

———. (1975). *Children of six cultures: A psychoanalysis.* Cambridge, MA: Harvard University Press.

Whittaker, J. K. (1983). Social support networks in child welfare. In J. K. Whittaker & J. Garbarino (Eds.), *Social support networks: Informal helping in the human services.* New York: Aldine.

Willer, B., Hofferth, S. L., Kisker, E. E., Divine-Hawkins, P., Farquhar, E., & Glantz, F. B. (1991). *The demand and supply of child care in 1990.* Washington,

DC: National Association for the Education of Young Children.

Williams, G. (1982). *The rabbit's wedding*. New York: HarperCollins.

Williams, R. M. (1960a). *American society: A sociological interpretation*. New York: Knopf.

———. (1960b). Generic American values. In W. Goldschmidt (Ed.), *Exploring the ways of mankind*. New York: Holt, Rinehart & Winston.

Wilson, B. J., & Gottman, J. M. (1995). Marital interaction and parenting. In M. H. Bornstein (Ed.), *Handbook of parenting* (Vol. 4). Hillsdale, NJ: Lawrence Erlbaum.

Wilson, B. J., & Weiss, A. J. (1993). The effects of sibling coviewing on preschoolers' reactions to a suspenseful movie scene. *Communication Research, 20*, 214–248.

Wilson, S., & Mishra, R. (1999, April 28). In high school, groups provide identity. *Washington Post*, p. A1.

Wilson, W. J. (1987). *The truly disadvantaged: The underclass and public policy*. Chicago: University of Chicago Press.

———. (1995). Jobless ghettos and the social outcome of youngsters. In P. Moen, G. H. Elder, & K. Luscher (Eds.), *Examining lives in context: Perspectives on the ecology of human development*. Washington, DC: American Psychological Association.

Winn, M. (1977). *The plug-in drug*. New York: Bantam.

Winsler, A. & Wallace, G. L. (2002). Behavior problems and social skills in preschool children: Parent-teacher agreement and relations with classroom observations. *Early Education and Development, 13*, 41–58.

Woititz, J. G. (1990). *Adult children of alcoholics: Common characteristics* (expanded ed.). Hollywood, FL: Heath Communications.

Wolery, M., & Wilbers, J. S. (1994). Introduction to the inclusion of young children with special needs in early childhood programs. In M. Wolery & J. S. Wilbers (Eds.), *Including children with special needs in early childhood programs*. Washington, DC: National Association for the Education of Young Children.

Wolf, N. (1991). *The beauty myth: How images of beauty are used against women*. New York: Anchor.

Wolfe, D. A. (1994). The role of intervention and treatment services in the prevention of child abuse and neglect. In G. B. Melton & F. Barry (Eds.), *Safe neighborhoods: Foundations for a new national strategy on child abuse and neglect*. New York: Guilford Press.

Wolfenstein, M. (1953). Trends in infant care. *American Journal of Orthopsychiatry, 23*, 120–130.

Women's Sports Foundation. (1989). *Minorities in sports*. New York: Author.

Wright, J. C., Huston, A. C., Reitz, A. L., & Piemymat, S. (1994). Young children's perceptions of television reality: Determinants and developmental differences. *Developmental Psychology, 30*(2), 229–239.

Wright, J. C., St. Peters, M., & Huston, A. C. (1990). Family television use and its relation to children's cognitive skills and social behavior. In J. Bryant (Ed.), *Television and the American family*. Hillsdale, NJ: Lawrence Erlbaum.

Yafai, S. (1992). *Individualism vs. collectivism: What to do?* Unpublished paper. University of California at Los Angeles, Department of Psychology.

Yogman, M. W., & Brazelton, T. B. (1986). The family: Stressed yet protected. In M. W. Yogman & T. B. Brazelton (Eds.), *In support of families*. Cambridge, MA: Harvard University Press.

York, S. (1991). *Roots and wings: Affirming culture in early childhood programs*. St. Paul, MN: Toys 'n' Things Press.

Young, B. A., & Smith, T. M. (1997). *The condition of education, 1997*. Washington, DC: U.S. Department of Education.

Young, E. (1992). *Seven blind mice*. New York: Putnam.

Young, K. T. (1994). *Starting points*. New York: Carnegie Corporation.

Young, T. W., & Shorr, D. N. (1986). Factors affecting locus of control in school children. *Genetic, Social, and General Psychology Monographs, 112*(4).

Youniss, J. (1981). Moral development through a theory of social construction: An analysis. *Merrill-Palmer Quarterly, 27*, 385–403.

Youniss, J., & Volpe, J. (1978). A relational analysis of children's friendship. In W. Damon (Ed.), *Social cognition*. San Francisco: Jossey-Bass.

Zahn-Waxler, C., & Radke-Yarrow, M. (1990). The origin of empathetic concern. *Motivation and Emotion, 14*, 107–130.

Zahn-Waxler, C., Radke-Yarrow, M., & King, R. A. (1979). Child-rearing and children's prosocial initiations toward victims of distress. *Child Development, 50*, 319–330.

Zahn-Waxler, C., Radke-Yarrow, M., Wagner, E., & Chapman, M. (1992). Development of concern for others. *Developmental Psychology, 28*, 126–136.

Zahn-Waxler, C., Robinson, J., & Emde, R. (1992). The development of empathy in twins. *Developmental Psychology, 28*, 1038–1047.

Zajonc, R. B. (1976). Family configuration and intelligence. *Science, 912*, 227–236.

Zarbatany, L., Hartmann, D. P., & Rankin, D. B. (1990). The psychological functions of preadolescent peer activities. *Child Development, 61*, 1067–1080.

Zaslow, M., Tout, K., Smith, S., & Moore, K. (1998). Implications of the 1996 welfare legislation for children: A research perspective. Society for Research in Child Development. *Social Policy Report, 12*(3).

Zill, N., & Schoenbom, C. (1990). *Developmental, learning, and emotional problems: Advance data.* National Center for Health Statistics (No. 190). Washington, DC: U.S. Department of Health and Human Services.

Zion, G. (1956). *Harry the dirty dog.* New York: Harper & Row.

Zimmerman, B. J. (2000). Self-efficacy: An essential motive to learn. *Contemporary Educational Psychology, 23,* 82–91.

Zussman, J. U. (1980). Situational determinants of parental behavior: Effects of competing cognitive activity. *Child Development, 51,* 792–800.

Photo Credits

p. 1 (top)   Hulton Archive/Getty Images

p. 1 (bottom)   © Bob Daemmrich/Getty Images

p. 7   © Tony Freeman/PhotoEdit

p. 11   Lewis Wickes Hine/© CORBIS

p. 17 (left)   © Jeremy Walker/Getty Images

p. 17 (right)   © Bonnie Kamin/PhotoEdit

p. 24   © David Young-Wolff/Getty Images

p. 25   © Mark Richards/PhotoEdit

p. 27   © Michael Newman/PhotoEdit

p. 32   Four by Five/Superstock

p. 38   © Superstock

p. 40   Niyati Reeve/Getty Images

p. 45   © Michael Newman/PhotoEdit

p. 53   © Laura Dwight/PhotoEdit

p. 55   © Elizabeth Crews

p. 60   Superstock

p. 66   © Tom McCarthy/PhotoEdit

p. 76   © Jose Carrillo/PhotoEdit

p. 83   Library of Congress

p. 91   © Robert E. Daemmrich/Getty Images

p. 101   © Myrleen F. Cate/PhotoEdit

p. 105   © Tony Freeman/PhotoEdit

p. 112   © Alan Oddie/PhotoEdit

p. 116   © Bushnell-Soiffer/Getty Images

p. 121   © Myrleen F. Cate/PhotoEdit

p. 130   © Sanna Lindberg/Getty Images

p. 133   © Robert E. Daemmrich/Getty Images

p. 146   © Jose Carrillo/PhotoEdit

p. 151 (top)   © Ziigy Kaluany/Getty Images

p. 151 (bottom)   © Rhoda Sidney/PhotoEdit

p. 158   © Myrleen F. Cate/PhotoEdit

p. 171   © Elizabeth Crews

p. 176   © Wadsworth/Thomson Learning

p. 183   © David Young-Wolff/PhotoEdit/PictureQuest

p. 185   © Myrleen F. Cate/PhotoEdit

p. 195   © Robert E. Daemmrich/Getty Images

p. 201   © Wadsworth/Thomson Learning

p. 202   © Superstock

p. 210   © Robert E. Daemmrich/Getty Images

p. 215   © Peter Cade/Getty Images

p. 226   © Wadsworth/Thomson Learning

p. 232   © Wadsworth/Thomson Learning

p. 233   © Michael Newman/PhotoEdit

p. 240   © Guy Cali/Stock Connection/PictureQuest

p. 243   AP/Wide World Photos

p. 244   © Davis Barber/PhotoEdit

p. 249   © Will Hart/PhotoEdit/PictureQuest

p. 253   © Wadsworth/Thomson Learning

p. 260   © SW Productions/Index Stock Imagery/PictureQuest

p. 263   © Dick Luria/Getty Images

p. 269   © Wadsworth/Thomson Learning

p. 277   © Spencer Grant/PhotoEdit

p. 280   © Wadsworth/Thomson Learning

p. 289   © David Young-Wolff/PhotoEdit

p. 293   © Myrleen F. Cate/PhotoEdit

p. 302   © Elizabeth Crews

p. 308   © Tony Freeman/PhotoEdit

p. 313   © Photo Network/PictureQuest

p. 315   © Jim Pickerell/Stock Connection/PictureQuest

p. 318   © John Neubauer/PhotoEdit

p. 327   © Richard Hutchings/PhotoEdit

p. 339   © Michael Newman/PhotoEdit

p. 353   Network Productions/Index Stock Imagery

p. 357   AP/Wide World Photos

p. 359 (both)   © Michael Newman/PhotoEdit

p. 366   Jerome Tigne/Getty Images

p. 372   PhotoDisc Collection/Getty Images

p. 380   Stephen Mallon/Getty Images

p. 384   Holos/Getty Images

p. 389   © Michael Newman/PhotoEdit

p. 395   © Tony Freeman/PhotoEdit

p. 399   © Robert Brennner/PhotoEdit

p. 401   © Mark Richards/PhotoEdit

Index

A

Abstractions, 64
Abuse, 161
    physical, 161, 203
    possible indications of, 203–205
    protecting children from, 202–206, 426–429
    psychological/emotional, 162–163, 204–205
    sexual, 161–162, 204
Academic achievement, 363
Academic goals, 213
Academic preschool, 194
Accommodation, 193
Achieved status, 101–102, 136
Achievement motivation, 70, 151, 453–464
    assessment of, 453–454
    attributions and, 453, 457
    development of, 454–456
    empowerment of, 39–40
    expectations of success and, 456–457
    individualism/collectivism and, 262
    learned helplessness and, 461–463
    locus of control and, 457–460
    parenting styles and, 156, 456
    self-efficacy and, 463–464
    socialization and, 70
Action for Children's Television (ACT), 368
Active coping style, 45
Adaptation, 9
Adolescents
    activities engaged by, 317–319
    belonging needs of, 294
    divorce and, 86
    friendships among, 320–321
    personal identity of, 295–297
    preventing problem behavior in, 142–143
    psychosocial development of, 38
    self-concept of, 295–297
    sexual behavior of, 311–312
    social interactions of, 294
    See also Children
Adopted children, 95–96
Adoption Assistance Program, 421
Adoption process, 410
Adult Children of Alcoholics (Woititz), 274
Adulthood
    friendship development and, 320–321
    psychosocial development in, 38–39
Adult leadership styles, 332–333
Adult-mediated group interaction, 331–332
Advertising

Children's Television Act and, 347
    susceptibility of children to, 50, 356–358, 359
Advocacy, 51, 268, 412, 425–426
Advocacy groups, 425–426
Aesop's fables, 340
Affective/cognitive socialization outcomes, 436–479
    attitudes, 443–452
    attributes, 457–464
    motives, 452–457
    readings related to, 478–479
    self-esteem, 464–474
    summary of, 475–476
    values, 438–443, 477–478
Affective mechanisms, 52
Affective socialization methods, 52–54
African Americans
    authority roles and, 133
    communication patterns of, 134
    discipline/guidance of children by, 135
    emotional displays and, 134
    ethnic attitudes and, 450
    self-esteem and, 473
    skills emphasis of, 136
Agents of socialization. See Socialization agents
Aggression, 484, 485–494
    biological theories of, 485–486
    causes of, 485–490
    ecological theories of, 490
    information processing theories of, 487–488
    inhibiting in children, 492, 494
    learning theories of, 486–487
    models for studying, 490–492
    social cognitive theories of, 488–491
    television violence and, 487
    variables contributing to, 493
    See also Antisocial behavior
AIDS, 418
Alcoholism, 273–275
Alcohol use/abuse
    at-risk children and, 273–275
    prenatal exposure to, 274
    See also Substance use/abuse
All Our Children: The American Family Under Pressure
    (Carnegie Council on Children), 412
Alternative education, 403
Altruism, 63, 484–485, 494–504
    biological theories of, 496–497
    cognitive-developmental theories of, 499
    cultural theories of, 500–503
    development of, 495–503
    fostering in children, 503–504

learning theories of, 497–499
social interactional theories of, 499–500
variables contributing to, 503
See also Prosocial behavior
American Academy of Child and Adolescent Psychiatry
(AACAP), 95, 273, 380, 382, 383
American Academy of Pediatrics (AAP), 234
American Association of University Women (AAUW),
257, 525
American Psychiatric Association (APA), 440
Americans with Disabilities Act (ADA), 226, 270
America's Children: Key Indicators of Well-Being, 2001
(Federal Interagency Forum), 27
Amorality, 519–520
Analytical cognitive style, 264
Anderson, Hans Christian, 48
Anecdotal records, 267
Anglo Americans. *See* Euro-Americans
Animal Farm (Orwell), 390
Anne Frank: The Diary of a Young Girl, 437
Anonymity, 489
Antisocial behavior, 484, 485–494
definition of, 484
developmental theories of, 485–490
inhibiting in children, 492, 494
models for studying, 490–492
variables contributing to, 493
See also Aggression
Antivalues, 359
Apprenticeship methods, 68–69
in peer groups, 305–306
Appropriate parenting practices, 158–159
Are You There, God? It's Me, Margaret (Blume), 62
Aristotle, 289
Arousal, 306, 356
Ascribed status, 101–102, 136
Asian Americans
authority roles and, 133
communication patterns of, 134
discipline/guidance of children by, 135, 137
emotional displays and, 134, 137
gender roles and, 532
learning styles of, 265
parenting by, 109
Assessment
achievement motivation, 453–454
authentic, 285
disability, 267–269
personal values, 477–478
Assimilation, 193, 217
Associative play, 314
Assumptive realities, 299
Attachment, 52, 150
child care and, 183
parenting behavior and, 151–152

socialization and, 52–54
types of, 152
Attention deficit hyperactivity disorder (ADHD), 482
Attitudes, 69, 443–452
community influences on, 448–449
definition of, 69, 443
development of, 443–445
ethnic, 444
family influences on, 445–447
mass media influences on, 355–356, 447–448
peer influences on, 447
prejudicial, 444–445, 450–452
school influences on, 449–450
Attributions, 69–70, 457–464
definition of, 69, 452
learned helplessness and, 461–463
locus of control and, 453, 457–460
motives related to, 453, 457
performance related to, 453, 454
self-efficacy and, 463–464
Authentic assessment, 285
Authoritarian-aggressive behavior, 127–128
Authoritarian leadership, 254, 332–333
Authoritarian parents, 64, 151, 153–154, 294, 296, 542
Authoritative parents, 64, 151, 153, 154, 294, 296, 542
Authority
attitudes toward, 46
collective orientation and, 133
family patterns of, 97–98
individualistic orientation and, 136–138
Autocracy, 125
Autonomous morality, 308, 505
Autonomy vs. shame and doubt stage, 36–37
Avoidant attachment, 152

B

Babies. *See* Infants
Bandura, Albert, 59, 71, 251, 463, 486, 523
Bank Street Curriculum, 196
Bannerman, Helen, 448
Barney & Friends (TV show), 243
Bayley Scales of Infant Development, 156
Beautiful Mind, A (film), 448
Beauty Myth, The (Wolf), 472
Beavis and Butt-head (TV show), 518
Behavior, 70
antisocial, 484, 485–494
ethnic patterns of, 45–47
observation of, 267–268, 551–553
prosocial, 150, 484–485, 494–504
self-regulation of, 39, 70–71
sociocultural characteristics and, 127–129
television viewing and, 359–360
Behavioral learning theory, 71, 250

Behavioral modification methods, 58
Behavior indicators, 27
Behaviorism, 139–140, 194
Belief systems
    gang formation and, 329
    religious orientation and, 111–113
    See also Values
Belonging needs, 291–294
Bem, Sandra, 524
Bennett, William, 371, 448
Bereiter, Carl, 194–195
Bettelheim, Bruno, 375
Beverly Hills, 90210 (TV show), 304
Beyond Rhetoric: A New American Agenda for Children and Families (NCC), 413
Bible stories, 77
Biggest House in the World, The (Lionni), 379
Bilingual education, 222–223
Binuclear family, 89
Biological theories
    of aggression, 485–486
    of altruism, 496–497
Biotechnology, 23
Black, Claudia, 274
Blubber (Blume), 322
Blueberries for Sal (McCloskey), 378
Blume, Judy, 62, 322
Bodily-kinesthetic intelligence, 265
Body types, 471–472
Bok, Sissela, 482
Book of Virtues, The, (Bennett), 371, 448
Books, 371–379
    attitudes influenced by, 448
    childhood development and, 373–374
    contemporary concerns about, 374–377
    developmental levels and, 378–379
    fantasy vs. reality in, 374–376
    gender roles portrayed in, 376–378, 531
    literacy and reading of, 371–372
    socialization process and, 49–50, 372–374
    stereotypes in, 376–378
    violence in, 376
    See also Magazines; Print media
Bowlby, John, 182
Boy Code, 438
"Boy Who Cried Wolf, The" (Aesop), 340
Brave Dames and Wimpettes: What Women Are Really Doing on Page and Screen (Isaacs), 530
Briggs, Dorothy Corkille, 466
Bronfenbrenner, Urie, 14, 350, 401
Brook, Judith, 142
Brookline Early Education Program (BEEP), 423
Bruner, Jerome, 59
Buddhism, 112
Bullying, 303, 327–328

Bureaucratic occupations, 130
Bush, George W., 179
Businesses
    child care and, 190–191
    schools and, 233, 245

C

Cable television, 367
Caldecott Medal, 373, 376
Care moral perspective, 511
Carle, Eric, 373
Carnegie Council on Children, 412
Cashdan, Sheldon, 376
Catharsis, 376
Census Bureau, 82, 188, 398
Center-based child care, 186, 191, 192
Center for Media and Public Affairs (CMPA), 354
Center for Media Education (CME), 368, 383
Centers for Disease Control (CDC), 418
Chafetz, Janet, 531
Change
    concept of childhood and, 10–12
    consequences of, 26–28
    societal, 8–10, 23–28
Channel One news program, 243–244
Charles, Ray, 224
Charlie and the Chocolate Factory (Dahl), 340–341
Charren, Peggy, 368
Charter schools, 216
Checklists, 267
Child abuse and neglect. *See* Maltreatment of children
Child Abuse Prevention and Treatment Act (CAPTA), 202, 422, 429
Child advocacy, 412, 425–426
Child and Adolescent Service System Program, 419
Child and Family Resource Program (CFRP), 186
Child at Risk Field (CARF), 158
Child care, 171–209
    accreditation of, 177
    basics of, 174
    businesses and, 190–191
    child protection and, 202–206, 421–422
    chronosystem influences on, 179–181
    cognitive development and, 184–186
    collaborative caregiving and, 200–202
    communities and, 188–189, 409–410, 421–422
    cultural frameworks and, 200–202
    curriculum models for, 191, 193–197
    definition of, 172
    government and, 189–190
    guidelines for evaluating, 543–546
    historical trends in, 179–181
    ideologies of, 197–199
    influences on outcomes of, 187

macrosystem influences on, 178–179
maltreatment indicators and, 203–205
mesosystem influences on, 186–191
prevalence of, 172–173
psychological development and, 181–184
quality of, 174–177
readings related to, 208–209
schools and, 188
social development and, 184
socialization process and, 48, 191–199
special needs for, 421–422
summary of, 206–208
types of, 173–174, 191, 192
Child-centeredness, 10, 140–141
Child development
    peer groups and, 291–297
    socialization process and, 3–8
Childhood, concept of, 10–12
Child Nutrition Services, 414, 418
Child protective laws, 202
Child rearing. *See* Parenting
Children
    adopted, 95–96
    belonging needs of, 292–294
    custody arrangements and, 87–91
    disabled, 145–147, 224–228, 266–270
    divorce and, 85–87
    domestic violence and, 275–276
    family dynamics and, 141–147
    friendships among, 319–320
    guidance and discipline of, 159, 160
    improving social skills in, 324–325
    latchkey, 188, 420
    maltreatment of, 160–167, 426–429
    personal identity of, 294–295
    physical abuse of, 161
    play activities of, 317–319
    protecting from maltreatment, 202–206, 421–422
    psychological/emotional abuse of, 162–163
    psychosocial development of, 36–38
    self-care by, 419–420
    self-concept of, 294–295
    sexual abuse of, 161–162
    social interactions of, 292–294
    social role of, 97
    societal change and, 8–10
    stepfamilies and, 91–93
    stress on, 9, 113–114
    temperament of, 143–145
    violence prevention in, 234
    See also Adolescents; Infants
Children as Consumers (McNeal), 358
Children's Bureau, 404
Children's Defense Fund (CDF), 398, 412, 425
Children's Health Insurance Program (CHIP), 417

Children's Television Act (1990), 347, 368
Children with disabilities. *See* Disabled children
Child Welfare League of America (CWLA), 405, 425
Child welfare services, 408–409, 419
Chronosystem, 19–23
    child care influenced by, 179–181
    community services influenced by, 404–405
    families influenced by, 113–115
    mass media influenced by, 345–346
    parents influenced by, 138–150
    peer groups influenced by, 314–319
    schools influenced by, 228–236
    teachers influenced by, 276–282
Church groups, 51
Cities
    family-friendly, 50, 394–395
    interaction patterns in, 402
    noise levels in, 396–397
    population density of, 395–396
Civic goals, 213
Civil Rights Act (1964), 98, 125, 219, 222
Class Divided, A (film), 451
Classism, 221–222
Classrooms
    antibiased environment in, 452
    class size and, 244–245
    management of, 255, 281
    promoting moral growth in, 518
    See also Schools; Teachers
Clinton, Bill, 481
Cliques, 304
Cocaine abuse, 273
Cognitive conceit, 299
Cognitive development
    child care and, 184–186
    peer groups and, 299–301
    Piaget's theory of, 191, 193
    print media and, 373
Cognitive-developmental theory, 71
    gender-role development and, 523
    prosocial behavior and, 499
Cognitively oriented curriculum, 191, 193–194
Cognitive socialization methods, 61–64
    instruction, 61–62
    reasoning, 63–64
    standard setting, 62–63
Cohesiveness, 117
Coleman, James, 219, 305
Coleman Report, 219–220
Collaborative caregiving, 200–202
Collectivism, 45, 132–136
    authority roles and, 133
    communication patterns and, 133–134
    discipline/guidance of children and, 135
    emotional displays and, 134

moral development and, 519
skills emphasis and, 135–136
teachers and, 261–263
Collodi, Carlo, 33
Colonial Americans, 139
Columbine High School, 232, 305, 321, 518
Comer, James, 238
Commercialism, 358
Common Purpose (Schorr), 107, 425
Common Sense Book of Baby and Child Care, The (Spock), 140
Communication
collectivism and, 133–134
enabling in children, 325
individualism and, 136
styles of, 46
Communicativeness, 117
Communities, 50, 389–435
advocacy groups in, 425–426
attitudes influenced by, 448–449
child care and, 188–189, 409–410, 421–422
children's development in, 423–424
definition of, 391
economic factors in, 398–399
family services and, 418–422
gender roles and, 531–534
health care and, 417–418
homelessness in, 415–417
interaction patterns in, 401–402
learning environment of, 403–404
maltreatment of children in, 166–167, 426–429
media linked to, 366–368
moral development and, 519–522
parenting styles and, 157–158
physical factors in, 395–398
poverty in, 413–415
protecting children in, 426–429
readings related to, 435
schools linked to, 244–245
self-esteem influenced by, 473–474
social and personal factors in, 399–402
socialization process and, 50–51, 394–402
structure and functions of, 391–393
summary of, 430–431
support systems of, 404–412
Community ecology, 391
Community services, 404–412
case studies on, 431–434
child advocacy and, 412–413
chronosystem influences on, 404–405
effectiveness of, 423
federal assistance programs and, 412–422
macrosystem influences on, 404–405
mesosystem influences on, 422–424
preventative, 405–407
reasons for necessity of, 404

rehabilitative, 410–411
supportive, 407–410
types of, 412
Compensation, 185
Competence, 150
parenting styles and, 154–155
social, 297
Competitive goal structures, 280, 281, 282
Competitive/independent orientation, 136–138
See also Individualism
Complex societies, 127
Comprehensive Child Development Program (CCDP), 186
Compromise, 325
Computers
educational use of, 231–232
experiential learning on, 59, 383
Internet and, 382–384
multimedia experiences on, 343, 384
socialization process and, 49–50
video games on, 384
Concrete operations stage, 193, 299, 379
Conflict
peer, 329, 516
resolution of, 309
Conformity, 297–298, 300
Conscience, 514
Constructivism, 59, 278
Contagion, 381
Conventional moral reasoning, 507, 508, 509
Cooley, Charles Horton, 36
Cooperation, 500–502
Cooperative Extension Service, 406
Cooperative goal structures, 280, 281, 282
Cooperative/interdependent orientation, 133–136
See also Collectivism
Cooperative learning, 266–267
Cooperative play, 314
Coping styles, 45–46
Corporal punishment, 166–167
Correctional services, 410–411
Counseling
family, 407–408
peer, 330
Crevecoeur, Hector Saint-John de, 218
Crowds, 304
Cubberley, Elwood P., 217
Cultural pluralism, 218
Cultural theories of altruism, 500–503
Culture, 64, 126
child care and, 200–202
educational goals and, 213
family and, 44
gender roles and, 532
mass media and, 343
moral development and, 519–520

parenting and, 126–129
socialization methods and, 64–68
teachers and, 258–263
Curriculum, 191
adapted to learning styles, 266
cognitively oriented, 191, 193–194
developmental-interaction, 196–197
direct-instruction, 194–195
gender, 522–523
Montessori, 195–196
preschool, 191, 193–197
teacher- vs. learner-directed, 191
Custody arrangements, 87–91
joint custody, 89–90
kin custody, 90–91
single-parent custody, 87–89
Custody Wars (Mason), 89

D

Daedalus myth, 2
Dahl, Roald, 340
D'Amato, Alfonse, 322–323
Day care. *See* Child care
Day nurseries, 178, 179
Death instinct, 485
Deductive reasoning, 63
Deer Hunter, The (film), 518
Delay of gratification, 483–484
Democracy, 125
Democratic leadership, 254, 332, 333
Desensitization, 356, 519
Developmental appropriateness
child care and, 176, 200
parenting practices and, 159
Developmental delay, 549–550
Developmental-interaction curriculum, 196–197
Developmental tasks, 40–42
summary chart of, 538–541
Dewey, John, 140, 196, 229, 278–279
Diagnostic and Statistical Manual, 440
Difficult children, 144
Direct-instruction curriculum, 194–195
Disability, 224
Disabled children
changing attitudes about, 451
family involvement with, 268–269
history of dealing with, 225–226
identification and assessment of, 267–269
inclusion concept and, 227–228, 269–270
legislation related to, 226–227
maltreatment of, 166
parenting of, 145–147
prejudice towards, 444–445
rehabilitative services for, 411

schools and, 224–228
self-esteem of, 473–474
strategies for teaching, 547–550
teachers and, 266–270
Discipline/guidance
collective orientation and, 135
individualistic orientation and, 137
parenting practices and, 159, 160
Dishabituation, 214
Disorganized/disoriented attachment, 152
Distance education, 232
Divorce, 82–93
children and, 85–87
custody arrangements and, 87–91
family functioning and, 83–85
laws pertaining to, 83–84
remarriage and, 91–93
stepfamilies and, 91–93
Domestic responsibilities, 84, 85
Domestic violence, 275–276
Donne, John, 391
Drug use/abuse
drug testing and, 235
prenatal exposure to, 273
See also Substance use/abuse
Dual-earner families, 98–100
Dubroff, Jessica, 2, 28–29
Dunn, Lloyd, 225–226
DVD players, 367–368

E

Earl v. Board of Education of Tecumseh, Oklahoma Public School District (2002), 235
Early Childhood Environment Rating Scale, 174
Early childhood programs
guidelines for evaluating, 543–546
See also Preschool programs
Easy children, 144
Ecological model of human development, 14
Ecological systems, 14–23
chronosystem and, 19–23
exosystems, 16–17
macrosystems, 17–19
mesosystems, 16
microsystems, 15–16
Ecological theories of aggression, 490, 491–492
Ecology, 3, 14
Economic Opportunity Act (1964), 178, 229
Economics, 127
communities and, 398–399
family functioning and, 98, 114–115
federal indicators of, 27
parenting culture and, 127–129
school programs and, 235

supportive services and, 407, 414–415
See also Socioeconomic status
Education
    accountability in, 282
    alternative, 403
    bilingual, 222–223
    community services and, 406–407
    contemporary reforms in, 229–230
    decision factors in, 214–215
    disabled children and, 224–228
    families and, 82, 84, 96, 237–242, 283–284
    inclusion concept in, 227–228
    individualized programs for, 227
    learning styles and, 236–237
    multicultural, 222–223
    philosophies of, 277–279
    purposes of, 213
    special, 225–226, 227
    standardization of, 282
    See also Schools; Teachers
Educational Excellence for All Children Act (1999), 230
Educational television (ECT), 368–369
Education Amendments Act (1972), 217
Education for All Handicapped Children Act (1975),
    226, 229, 404
Education indicators, 27
Edwards, Carolyn, 532
Egalitarian attitude, 46
Egalitarian families, 80
Egocentrism, 48, 63
Elder, Glen, 20–21, 399
Elderly people
    psychosocial development and, 39
    supportive services for, 408
Electra complex, 523
Elementary and Secondary Education Act (ESEA), 216,
    229, 282
Elliott, Jane, 451
Emile (Rousseau), 211, 278
Emotional abuse, 162–163
    indicators of, 204–205
Emotional deprivation, 205
Emotional intelligence, 39
Emotional regulation, 39, 234, 484
Emotional support, 82, 84, 100
Emotions
    collective orientation and, 134
    individualistic orientation and, 136–137
    moral development and, 514
Empathy, 234, 496
"Emperor's New Clothes, The" (Anderson), 48
Employer-sponsored day care, 190
Empowerment, 117
Engelmann, Siegfried, 194–195
English as a second language (ESL), 222

Entrepreneurial occupations, 130
Environmental risk factors, 270
Equal Educational Opportunity Act (1974), 222
Equilibrium, 193
Erikson, Erik, 36, 37, 300–301, 460
Erin Brokovich (film), 530
Esperanto, 218
Estes, Eleanor, 374
Ethnicity, 17, 131
    attitudes and, 444, 450–451
    behavior patterns and, 45–47
    families and, 108–111
    gender roles and, 532
    media stereotypes and, 361, 376, 377–378
    norms/values and, 110–111
    parenting and, 109, 131–138
    prejudice and, 444, 450–451
    schools and, 217–222
    self-esteem and, 473
    sexual activity and, 312
    socialization patterns and, 110
    teachers and, 258–263
E.T. the Extra-terrestrial (film), 33–34
Euro-Americans
    communication patterns of, 136
    discipline/guidance of children by, 137
    ethnic attitudes and, 450–452
    family cohesiveness and, 117
    parenting by, 109
    skills emphasis of, 137–138
Exosystems, 16–17
Experiential learning, 59–60
Exploratory play, 315
Extended day care, 172
Extended family, 80–81
External locus of control, 457
Extinction, 56, 58
Eye of the Storm (film), 451

F

Fairy tales, 376
Families, 76–120
    adopted children in, 95–96
    attitudes influenced by, 445–447
    binuclear, 89
    changes in, 82–100
    chronosystem influences on, 113–115
    contemporary challenges for, 116–117
    custody arrangements in, 87–91
    definitions of, 78–79
    disabled children and, 268–269
    divorce and, 82–93
    dual-earner, 98–100
    economic changes and, 114–115

egalitarian, 80
empowerment of, 117
ethnic orientation and, 45–47, 108–111
extended, 80–81
functions of, 81–82, 96–100
gangs and, 329
gender roles and, 525–527
government programs for, 418–422
homosexual, 94–95
macrosystem influences on, 101–113
maltreatment of children in, 164–166, 426–429
mass media and, 350–351, 365–366, 369–370
matriarchal, 80
moral development and, 514–515
nuclear, 79–80
parenting styles and, 141–150
patriarchal, 80
portrayed on television, 77
readings related to, 120
religion and, 111–113
schools linked to, 237–242
self-esteem influenced by, 468–470
sibling effects in, 147–148
single-parent, 87–89
size factors in, 147
socialization and, 44–47, 82, 84, 96
social roles in, 82, 84, 96–98
social support provided by, 80–81
socioeconomic status and, 101–108
sociopolitical changes and, 114
stepfamilies and, 91–93
stress and, 113–114, 117
structures of, 79–81, 82–96
student learning and, 283–284
substance abuse in, 273–275
summary of, 118–119
support provided by, 80–81
technological changes and, 115
television viewing and, 350–351, 365–366, 369–370
unmarried parents and, 93–95
Family and Medical Leave Act (FMLA), 177
Family day care, 173, 191, 192
Family-friendly cities, 50
Family of orientation, 79
Family of procreation, 79
Family Preservation and Support Services Program, 408
Family services, 407–408, 418–422
Family support programs, 186
Family systems' theory, 78
Family ties, 82–83
Family Violence Prevention and Services Program, 422
Fantasy vs. reality
    in books and magazines, 374–376
    in interactive media, 384
    in television and movies, 351–353

Fargo (film), 530
Fathers
    gender roles and, 525–526
    single, 88–89
    social role of, 97
    stepfamilies and, 91–93
    unmarried, 94–95
    See also Parents
Federal Communications Commission (FCC), 346, 356
Federal Economic Recovery Act (1933), 180
Federal Interagency Forum, 27
Federal Trade Commission (FTC), 383
Feedback, 58–59
Fetal alcohol syndrome (FAS), 274
Field-dependent learning, 264
Films. *See* Movies
Fixations, 140
Folktales, 378
Formal operations stage, 193, 299, 379
Foster care services, 410
4-H clubs, 406–407
Fraiberg, Selma, 182
Frank, Anne, 437
Freed, Alan, 380
Freestyle (TV show), 361
Freud, Anna, 314
Freud, Sigmund, 70, 139–140, 196, 485, 496, 523
Freud, Sophie, 439
Friendships, 319–321

G

Galinsky, Ellen, 148
Games, 317–318
    team sports, 333–334, 528
    video, 384, 531
    See also Play
Gandhi, Mahatma, 23
Gangs, 328–329
Garbarino, James, 27–28
Gardner, Howard, 237, 265
Gay parents, 94–95
Gemeinschaft relationships, 132, 402, 502
Gender, 72
Gender issues
    children of divorce and, 86
    media stereotypes and, 361, 376–378
    schools and, 217
    self-esteem and, 473
    sex segregation and, 527–530
    teachers and, 257–258
Gender roles, 72, 522–534
    acquisition of, 40
    changing attitudes about, 451–452
    community influences on, 531–534

definition of, 72, 522
developmental theories of, 523–524
family influences on, 525–527
mass media influences on, 361, 376–378, 530–531
parenting styles and, 145
peer influences on, 311–312, 527–528
research on, 524–525
school influences on, 528–530
sex typing and, 522
Gender schema theory, 524
Generalized other, 36, 70, 468
Generativity, 38
Generativity vs. self-absorption stage, 38–39
Genetics
aggressive behavior and, 485
altruistic behavior and, 496–497
risk factors and, 270
Gesell, Arnold, 140
Gesellschaft relationships, 132, 402, 502
Gibran, Kahlil, 121
Gilkeson, Elizabeth, 196
Globalization, 24
Global village, 344
Goals 2000 initiative, 282, 403
Goal structures, 280–282
Golding, William, 290
Goode, William, 102
Goodlad, John, 47, 213
Goodness-of-fit, 144
Goodnight Moon (Brown), 372
Goosebumps books, 375
Goose Girl, The (Brothers Grimm), 481
Government
child care and, 189–190
community services and, 404–405
school violence and, 233
values and policies of, 442–443
Grandparents, children raised by, 90–91
Great Depression, 20, 398
Group discussions, 517
Group pressure, 65–66
Guidance of children, 135, 137, 159, 160
See also Discipline/guidance
Gusii people, 126

H

Habituation, 214
Hall, Edward T., 17
Hall, G. Stanley, 139
Hamlet (Shakespeare), 437, 438
Hammarskjold, Dag, 436
Handicap, 224, 225
Handicapism, 225
Hard rock, 381

Hardy Boys books, 375
Harris, Eric, 305
Harry Potter books, 375
Harry the Dirty Dog (Zion), 378
Hate crimes, 233
Havighurst, Robert, 40
Head Start program, 81, 106, 178, 185, 404, 423
Health care, 417–418
Health indicators, 27
Hearing disabilities, 549
Helplessness (Seligman), 461
Heterogenous neighborhoods, 396
Heteronomous morality, 308, 505
Hewlett, Sylvia Ann, 28
High-context macrosystems, 18–19
Hispanic Americans
authority roles and, 133
discipline/guidance of children by, 135
emotional displays and, 137
gender roles and, 410, 532
learning styles of, 264
skills emphasis of, 136
Historical trends
in child care, 179–181
in parenting, 138–141
HIV infection, 418
Homelessness, 415–417
Home schooling, 211
Homogenous neighborhoods, 396
Homosexual parents, 94–95
Housing arrangements, 397
Huck, Charlotte, 376
Human Capital Initiative, 442
Human development
ecological model of, 14
See also Child development
Humanism, 139
Hundred Dresses, The (Estes), 374

I

Icarus myth, 2
Identity vs. identity diffusion stage, 38
Ideologies, 197
child care, 197–199
school, 235
Imaginary audience, 299–300
Imaginative play, 353–354
Imitative learning, 60–61
peer groups and, 302–303
television and, 355
Imitative play, 315
Impairment, 224
Inappropriate parenting practices, 159–167
Incest, 162

Inclusion, 227–228
Individualism, 45, 132–133, 136–138
    authority roles and, 136
    communication patterns and, 136
    discipline/guidance of children and, 137
    emotional displays and, 136–137
    moral development and, 519
    skills emphasis and, 137–138
    teachers and, 261–263
Individualized Education Program (IEP), 227, 266–267
Individualized Family Service Plan (IFSP), 267
Individualized goal structures, 280, 281, 282
Individuals with Disabilities Education Act (IDEA),
    226–227, 266, 451
Induction, 515
Inductive reasoning, 63
Industrial Revolution, 11
Industry vs. inferiority stage, 37–38
Infants
    attachment and socialization of, 52–54, 152
    effects of child care on, 181–184
    personal identity of, 294
    play activities of, 316–317
    psychosocial development of, 36
    social interactions of, 292–293
    temperament of, 143–145
    See also Children; Toddlers
Information intermediaries, 24–25
Information processing, 362, 487–488
In-home child care, 191, 192
Initiative vs. guilt stage, 37
Insecure attachment, 152, 183
Inside Picture Books (Spitz), 372
Instruction, 61–62, 446
Integrity vs. despair stage, 39
Intellectual development, 362–363
Intelligence
    child care and, 184–186
    moral development and, 514
    multiple intelligences theory, 237, 265–266
    peer group acceptance and, 321
    socioeconomic status and, 105
    television viewing and, 362–363
Intentional socialization, 7, 13
Interactions. *See* Social interactions
Interactive media, 382–384
    access of children to, 382–383
    gender roles portrayed in, 531
    safety rules for, 383–384
    television toys and, 358
    video games and, 384
Internalization, 4
Internal locus of control, 457, 460
International Nanny Association (INA), 177
Internet, 382–384
    access of children to, 382–383

educational use of, 231, 232
    problem issues related to, 382
    safety rules for, 383–384
    socialization process and, 49–50
Interpersonal intelligence, 266
Interpretation, 325, 488
Intervention programs, 185–186
In the Night Kitchen (Sendak), 448
Intimacy vs. isolation stage, 38
Intrapersonal intelligence, 266
Isaacs, Susan, 530
It Will Never Happen to Me (Black), 274

J

Jackie Robinson Story, The (film), 448
Jacklin, Carol, 524
Japanese Americans. *See* Asian Americans
Jefferson, Thomas, 214
Jigsaw-puzzle method, 282
Jihad vs. McWorld (Barber), 24
Job Opportunities and Basic Skills Training (JOBS), 409
Johnson, Lyndon, 106, 178, 219, 404
Joint custody, 89–90
Judaism, 112, 137–138
Jung, Carl, 113
Justice moral perspective, 511
Juvenile justice system, 411

K

Kaiser Family Foundation, 349
Karr, Alphonse, 1
Keats, Ezra Jack, 379
Keller, Helen, 172
Keniston, Kenneth, 412
Kennedy, Rose, 39
Kids and Media and the New Millennium (Kaiser Family
    Foundation), 349
Kin custody, 90–91
King, Rodney, 65
Klebold, Dylan, 305
Kluckhohn, Florence, 110
Kohl, Herbert, 254
Kohlberg, Lawrence, 506–512, 523
Kohn, Melvin, 130–131
Kozol, Jonathon, 254, 272

L

Laissez-faire leadership, 254, 332, 333
Language development, 373
Lantham Act (1942), 180
Lasker, Joe, 374
Lassie (TV show), 360
Latchkey children, 188, 420

Lau v. Nichols (1974), 222
Lawrence, D. H., 76
Leadership styles
    peer group dynamics and, 332–333
    teacher effectiveness and, 253–254
Leaf, Munro, 448
Learned helplessness, 233, 272, 395–396, 453, 461–463
Learned Optimism (Seligman), 461
Learner-directed education, 191, 195, 197, 277–279
Learning
    attachment and, 53–54
    communities and, 403–404
    cooperative, 266–267
    experiential, 59–60
    family involvement in, 283–284
    imitative, 60–61, 355
    observational, 60–61, 355
    philosophies of, 277–279
    readiness for, 241–242
    See also Education
Learning by doing, 59–60
Learning styles, 236–237
    curriculum adapted to, 266
    teachers and, 263–266
Learning theories
    of aggression, 486–487
    of altruism, 497–499
Least restrictive environment (LRE), 227
Lesbian parents, 94–95
Life instinct, 485
Life Is Beautiful (film), 448
Lincoln, Abraham, 101, 214
Linguistic intelligence, 265
Lionni, Leo, 379
Literacy, 371–372
Literature. *See* Books
Locke, John, 111, 139
Locus of control, 453, 457–460
    development of, 459–460
    internal vs. external, 457
    measurement of, 458
Logical consequences, 57
Logical-mathematical intelligence, 265
LOGO software, 231–232
Looking-glass self, 36, 70, 468
Lord of the Flies (Golding), 290
Love withdrawal, 515
Low-context macrosystems, 18–19
Lower-class families, 104, 105–106, 107, 131
Lying: The Moral Choice in Public and Private Life (Bok), 482

M

Maccoby, Eleanor, 524
Macroculture, 259–260
Macrosystems, 17–19

    child care influenced by, 178–179
    community services influenced by, 404–405
    families influenced by, 101–113
    low- vs. high-context, 18–19
    mass media influenced by, 346–349
    parents influenced by, 124–128
    peer groups influenced by, 306–313
    schools influenced by, 214–228
    teachers influenced by, 276–282
Magazines, 371–379
    contemporary concerns about, 374–378
    gender stereotypes in, 378
    literacy development and, 371–372
    socialization process and, 372–374
    See also Books; Print media
Maltreatment of children, 160–167
    child protection and, 202–206, 426–429
    community and, 166–167
    correlates and consequences of, 163–167
    family issues and, 164–166, 428–429
    indications of, 203–205
    intervention programs for, 427–428
    neglect as, 161, 163, 204
    physical abuse as, 161, 202, 203
    prevention of, 429
    psychological or emotional abuse as, 162–163, 204–205
    risk and resilient factors in, 163, 164
    sexual abuse as, 161–162, 204
    treatment programs and, 428–429
    victims of, 166
Marriage, 93
    divorce and, 83–87
    parenting and quality of, 149
    stepfamilies and, 91–93
    See also Families
Martin, Ricky, 381
Mary Poppins (Shepard and Travers), 172
Mason, Mary Ann, 89
Mass media, 339–388
    advertising and, 356–358, 359
    aggressive behavior and, 487
    altruistic behavior and, 498
    attitudes influenced by, 447–448
    books and, 371–379
    chronosystem influences on, 345–346
    communities and, 366–368
    computers and, 382–384
    culture and, 343
    definition of, 342
    families and, 350–351, 369–370
    fantasy vs. reality and, 351–353, 374–376
    gender roles and, 530–531
    imaginative play and, 353–354
    Internet and, 382–384
    macrosystem influences on, 346–349
    magazines and, 371–379

moral development and, 518–519
movies and, 349–370
multimedia and, 345–346, 382–384
music and, 379–382
parental mediation and, 365–366
print media and, 371–379
readings related to, 388
schools and, 243–244, 368–369
selective attention and, 363–365
self-esteem influenced by, 472
socialization and, 49–50, 344, 363–366, 372–374
sound media and, 379–382
stereotypes and, 360–361, 376–378
summary of, 385–386
television and, 349–370
values and, 359–361
violence and, 354–356
Mastery motivation, 70
Maternal and Child Health Services, 418
Matriarchal families, 80
Maugham, William Somerset, 519
McCloskey, Robert, 378
McGuffey's Reader, 448
McLuhan, Marshall, 339, 342, 344, 345
McNeal, James, 358
Mead, George, 4
Mead, Margaret, 425
Measurements of behavior, 268
Media. *See* Mass media
Mediating structures, 54
Mediation, 234
Medicaid, 418
Medical assessment, 268
Melting-pot concept, 218
Mental health services, 411
Mercer, Jane, 226
Mesosystems, 16
child care influenced by, 186–191
community services influenced by, 422–424
mass media influenced by, 366–370
parents influenced by, 156–158
peer groups influenced by, 330–334
schools influenced by, 236–245
teachers influenced by, 282–285
Methods of socialization. *See* Socialization methods
Microcultures, 261
Microsystems, 15–16
parents influenced by, 150–156
peer groups as, 326
Midas myth, 122
Middle-class families, 104, 106, 107, 131
Milton, John, 32
Minority groups, 218–219
Mischel, Walter, 523
Mister Rogers' Neighborhood (TV show), 360, 498

Mobile technology, 23–24
Model-building play, 315
Modeling, 60–61, 302
altruism, 498
attitudes, 445
morality, 516–517
peer group, 302–303
Modern societies, 102
Montessori, Maria, 195
Montessori curriculum, 195–196
Moral development, 504–522
age and, 514
community influences on, 519–522
emotions and, 514
family influences on, 514–515
intelligence and, 514
Kohlberg's theory of, 506–512
mass media influences on, 518–519
peer influences on, 307–309, 515–516
Piaget's theory of, 308, 505–506
school influences on, 516–518
self-control and, 513
self-esteem and, 513–514
situational factors and, 512–513
social factors and, 514
temperament and, 513
Morality of constraint, 308
Morality of cooperation, 308
Morals/morality, 71–72, 307, 504–522
autonomous, 308, 505
definition of, 71, 504
development of, 504–512
heteronomous, 308, 505
Mother Care/Other Care (Scarr), 183
Mothers
gender roles and, 525–526
single, 87–88
social role of, 96–97
stepfamilies and, 91–93
unmarried, 94–95
working, 98–99
See also Parents
Mothers Can Do Anything (Lasker), 374
Motivation
achievement, 39–40, 70, 151, 453–464
intrinsic vs. extrinsic, 453
mastery, 70, 453
Motives, 69–70, 452–457
attributions related to, 453, 457
definition of, 69, 452
Movies, 349–370
attitudes influenced by, 447–448
contemporary concerns about, 350–363
gender roles portrayed in, 530
mesosystem influences on, 366–370

rating system for, 348–349
sexuality portrayed in, 360
socialization process and, 49–50
violence in, 354–356
See also Mass media; Television
MTV (Music Television), 381
Multicultural education, 222–223
Multimedia, 343, 345, 382–384
See also Interactive media
Multiple intelligences theory, 237, 265–266
Multitasking, 115
Murdock, George, 78
Music, 379–382, 531
Musical intelligence, 265
Music videos, 381
Muslims, 112

N

Naisbitt, John, 25
Nancy Drew books, 375
National and Community Service Act (1990), 403
National Association for Family Child Care
(NAFCC), 177
National Association for the Education of Young Chil-
dren (NAEYC), 175–176, 177, 259, 285
National Center for Education Statistics, 173
National Center for Health Statistics, 82, 85, 312
National Center on Child Abuse and Neglect, 421
National Citizens' Committee for Broadcasting
(NCCB), 368
National Clearinghouse on Child Abuse and Neglect,
426
National Commission on Children (NCC), 398,
412–413
National Commission on Excellence in Education
(NCEE), 229–230, 362
National Congress of Parents and Teachers, 426
National Day-Care Study, 174
National Educational Goals Panel, 230
National Education Association (NEA), 233
National Institute of Child Health and Human Develop-
ment (NICHD), 158, 174
National Institute on Media and the Family, 384
Nationalism, 24
National League of Cities, 50, 394
National Park Service, 406
National Recreation Association, 406
National Science Foundation, 442
National Television Violence Study (NTVS), 354, 518
Nation at Risk: The Imperative for Educational Reform, A
(NCEE), 229–230
Native Americans
authority roles and, 133
communication patterns of, 134, 136

discipline/guidance of children by, 135, 137
emotional displays and, 134
learning styles of, 264–265
skills emphasis of, 136
Naturalist intelligence, 266
Need achievement. *See* Achievement motivation
Negative reinforcement, 54, 58
Neglect, 161, 163, 204
Neighborhoods
economic stratification of, 51
geographic settings for, 399–400
homogenous vs. heterogenous, 396
socialization process in, 394
See also Communities
Newberry Medal, 374, 377
Nixon, Richard, 481
No Child Left Behind Act (2001), 216, 272, 282
No-fault divorce laws, 84
Noise, 396–397
Normality, 439–440
Norms, 110, 331
Nuclear family, 79–80
Nursery schools, 178
Nurturance, 82, 84, 100
Nyansongo people, 532

O

Observational learning, 60–61, 355
Observing behavior, 267–268
form used for, 551–553
Obsolescence, 115
Occupations of parents, 130–131
Oedipus complex, 523
Older adults. *See* Elderly people
Onlooker play, 314
Only-children, 148
Operant socialization methods, 54–60
extinction, 56
feedback, 58–59
learning by doing, 59–60
punishment, 56–57
reinforcement, 54–56
Oral stories, 340
Orwell, George, 390–391
Osofsky, Joy, 28
Outcomes of socialization, 69–72, 436–537
affective/cognitive, 436–479
antisocial behavior, 484, 485–494
attitudes, 69, 443–452
attributes, 69–70, 457–464
gender roles, 72, 522–534
morals, 71–72, 504–522
motives, 69–70, 452–457
prosocial behavior, 484–485, 494–504

self-esteem, 70, 464–474
self-regulation, 70–71, 482–484
social/behavioral, 480–537
values, 69, 438–443

P

Parallel play, 314
Parallel thinking, 231
Parenting, 121–170
    achievement motivation and, 456
    adolescents and, 142–143
    age of children and, 141–142
    aggressive behavior and, 487
    altruistic behavior and, 499–500
    appropriate practices in, 158–159
    attachment and, 151–152
    attitudes influenced by, 445–447
    authoritarian style of, 151, 153–154
    authoritative style of, 151, 153, 154
    child maltreatment and, 160–167
    chronosystem influences on, 138–150
    collective orientation and, 133–136
    culture and, 126–129
    custody arrangements and, 87–91
    disabled children and, 145–147
    ethnicity and, 109, 131–138
    family dynamics and, 141–150
    gender roles and, 145, 525–527
    grandparents and, 90–91
    historical trends in, 138–141
    inappropriate practices in, 159–167
    individualistic orientation and, 136–138
    macrosystem influences on, 124–138
    marital quality and, 149
    mesosystem influences on, 156–158
    microsystem influences on, 150–156
    moral development and, 514–515
    permissive style of, 151, 153–154
    political ideology and, 125–126
    readings related to, 169–170
    religion and, 131
    school involvement and, 238–241
    self-esteem influenced by, 468–470
    sibling effects and, 147–148
    size of families and, 147
    societal change and, 8–10
    socioeconomic status and, 129–131
    stages of changes in, 148
    stepfamilies and, 91–93
    stress factors and, 149–150
    styles of, 150–158, 294, 296, 442, 542
    summary of, 167–169
    teacher partnerships and, 271
    television mediation and, 365–366, 369–370
    temperament and, 143–145
    uninvolved style of, 151, 153, 159
    values and, 442
Parents
    abusive, 161–163, 205
    adoptive, 95–96
    alcoholic, 273–275
    divorce of, 83–87
    drug-addicted, 273
    homosexual, 94–95
    neglectful, 161, 163
    occupations of, 130–131
    single, 87–89
    unmarried, 93–95
    See also Fathers; Mothers
Parents and Teachers Association (PTA), 368
Parents Anonymous, 428–429
Parents' Music Resource Center (PMRC), 381
Park, Linda Sue, 374
Parks, 405–407
Passive coping style, 45
Paternalistic policies, 23
Patriarchal families, 80
Peer counseling, 330
Peer groups, 289–338
    acceptance by, 321–323
    adult-mediated interactions in, 331–333
    apprenticeship methods in, 305–306
    attitudes influenced by, 447
    belonging needs and, 291–294
    bullies and victims in, 327–328
    chronosystem influences on, 314–319
    cognitive development and, 299–301
    collaboration in, 329–330
    developmental significance of, 291–297, 306–313
    dynamics and hierarchies of, 326–330
    family problems and, 323
    friendship development in, 319–321
    gangs and, 328–329
    gender roles and, 311–312, 527–528
    getting along with others in, 306–307
    inclusion and exclusion from, 326–327
    leadership styles and, 332–333
    macrosystem influences on, 306–313
    mesosystem influences on, 330–334
    modeling in, 302–303
    moral development and, 307–309, 515–516
    neglect or rejection by, 321–323
    personal identity and, 294–297, 312–313
    play activities and, 314–319
    psychological development and, 297
    punishment in, 303–305
    readings related to, 338
    reinforcement in, 301–302
    schools linked to, 242–243
    self-concept and, 294–297
    self-esteem influenced by, 471–472

sex education through, 311–312
    social development and, 297–298
    socialization process and, 48–49, 291–306
    social support provided by, 312–313
    sociocultural roles and, 309–312
    sociotherapy and, 323–325
    summary of, 335–336
    team sports and, 333–334
    values and, 307–309
Peers, 291
Peer tutoring, 266, 267, 329–330
Performance
    achievement evaluated against, 455
    attributions related to, 453, 454
Perinatal risk factors, 270
Permissive parents, 64, 151, 153–154, 294, 296, 542
Personal agency, 437
Personal goals, 213
Personal identity, 6, 294–297
Personality development, 36
Personal Responsibility and Work Opportunity Reconcil-
    iation Act (1996), 409
Personal video recorders (PVRs), 345–346
Pestalozzi, Johann, 139
Peter's Chair (Keats), 378–379
Physical abuse, 161
    indicators of, 203
Physical disabilities, 548
Physical stressors, 113
Piaget, Jean, 59, 63, 71, 140, 191, 193, 229, 299, 308,
    314, 329, 351–352, 353, 459, 505–506
Pinocchio story, 33
Pipher, Mary, 437–438
PL 99-457 legislation, 267
Plasticity, 533
Plato, 210, 277, 390–391
Plautus, Titus Maccius, 389
Play, 314–319
    activity types and, 315
    adolescents and, 319
    children and, 317–319
    infants/toddlers and, 316–317
    neighborhood settings for, 397–398
    sex segregation and, 527–528
    stages or forms of, 314
Playgrounds, 397–398
Plug in Drug, The (Winn), 350
Pluralism, 520–521
Political ideology
    parenting and, 125–126
    schools and, 235
Pollack, William, 438
Population density, 395–396
Positive peer culture (PPC), 330
Positive reinforcement, 54, 58
Postconventional moral reasoning, 508, 510

Postman, Neil, 358, 383
Potok, Chaim, 224
Poverty
    class stratification and, 104
    economic assistance and, 413–415
    homelessness and, 415–417
    school violence and, 233
    teachers and, 271–272
Power assertion, 515
Power structures, 25–26
Preconventional moral reasoning, 507, 508, 509
Prejudice, 443
    attitude change and, 450–452
    development of, 444–445
Prenatal risk factors, 270, 273, 274
Preoperational stage, 193, 378–379
Preschool programs, 178
    benefits of, 189–190
    curriculum models for, 191, 193–197
    guidelines for evaluating, 543–546
    sociocultural roles and, 309–311
    See also Child care
Preventative services, 405–407
Print media, 371–379
    childhood development and, 373–374
    contemporary concerns about, 374–378
    developmental levels and, 378–379
    fantasy vs. reality in, 374–376
    gender roles portrayed in, 376–378, 531
    literacy and, 371–372
    socialization process and, 372–374, 378–379
    stereotypes in, 376–378
    See also Books; Magazines
Prisoners' Dilemma, 497
Problem solving, 234
Prosocial behavior, 150, 484–485, 494–504
    definition of, 484
    developmental theories of, 495–503
    fostering in children, 503–504
    parenting styles and, 152–154
    peer group acceptance and, 321
    variables contributing to, 503
    See also Altruism
Protective services, 409
Protestant ethic, 112, 138, 259
Psychoanalytic theory, 70–71, 523
Psychological abuse, 162–163
    indicators of, 204–205
Psychological assessment, 268
Psychological development
    child care and, 181–184
    peer groups and, 297
Psychological stressors, 113
Psychology of Television, The (Condry), 365
Psychosocial development
    print media and, 374

stages of, 36–39, 300–301
Public Broadcasting Service (PBS), 243, 367
Public interest groups, 368
Punishment, 56–57, 58
    in families, 446–447
    in peer groups, 303–305
Pygmalion in the Classroom (Rosenthal and Jacobson), 255

R

Rabbit's Wedding, The (Williams), 448
Racism
    gang formation and, 329
    prejudicial attitudes and, 444, 450–451
    See also Prejudice
Raising Children in a Socially Toxic Environment (Garbarino), 27
Ramsey, Jon Benet, 123
Rating scales, 267
Rawlings, Marjorie, 379
Read-Aloud Handbook, The (Trelease), 372
Reading Rainbow (TV show), 362
Reading skills, 362–363, 373
Real Boys: Rescuing Our Sons from the Myths of Boyhood (Pollack), 438
Reality testing, 299
Reasoning, 63–64
    moral, 506–510, 516
    types of, 63
Reciprocity, 515
Recreational services, 405–407
Rehabilitation, 411
Rehabilitative services, 410–411
Reinforcement, 54–56, 58
    in families, 446–447
    in peer groups, 301–302
Relational cognitive style, 264
Religion, 111, 131
    families and, 111–113
    functions of, 112–113
    parenting and, 131
    schools and, 223–224
Remarriage, 91–93
Renaissance, 10
Reproduction, 82, 96
Republic, The (Plato), 277, 390
Resilience, 270
Resilient factors
    in child maltreatment, 163, 164
    in school children, 270–271
Resistant attachment, 152
Reviving Ophelia: Saving the Selves of Adolescent Girls (Pipher), 437
Risk factors
    in child maltreatment, 163, 164
    in school children, 270

Rites of passage, 67
Rituals, 67, 350–351
Robber's Cave experiment, 13
Rock music, 380
Rogers, Carl, 229
Rogers, Fred, 360
Role-playing, 498
Role reversal, 165
Roles. *See* Gender roles; Social roles
Roman Catholics, 111
Roosevelt, Franklin, 180
Rough-and-tumble play, 316
Rousseau, Jean-Jacques, 111, 139, 211, 278
Routines, 68
Rowlings, J. K., 375
Rules, 307
Ruskin, John, 171

S

Sadker, Myra and David, 377
Sanctions for evil, 489
Satellite television, 367
Savage Inequalities (Kozol), 254, 272
Scarr, Sandra, 182–183
Schindler's List (film), 448
Schools, 210–248
    attitudes influenced by, 449–450
    bilingual/multicultural education in, 222–223
    businesses supportive of, 233, 245
    characteristics of effective, 245
    child care and, 188
    chronosystem influences on, 228–236
    class size in, 244–245
    communities linked to, 244–245
    contemporary reforms for, 229–230
    disabled children and, 224–228
    educational decisions and, 214–215
    ethnic diversity and, 217–222
    families linked to, 237–242
    gender roles and, 217, 528–530
    goals for, 213, 230
    inclusion concept and, 227–228
    learning styles and, 236–237
    macrosystem influences on, 214–228
    media linked to, 243–244, 368–369
    mesosystem influences on, 236–245
    moral development and, 516–518
    parenting styles and, 157
    peer groups linked to, 242–243
    readiness concept and, 285
    readings related to, 248
    religion and, 223–224
    school choice policies and, 216
    self-esteem influenced by, 470–471
    socialization process and, 47–48, 212–213

special education in, 225–226, 227
substance use/abuse in, 234–235
summary of, 246–247
technology used in, 231–232
violence in, 232–234
See also Education; Teachers
Schorr, Lisbeth, 107, 425
Scout groups, 51, 407
Secure attachment, 152, 183
Segregation
ethnic, 221
sex, 527
Selective attention, 363–365
Self-concept, 34–39, 294–297, 464
Self-efficacy, 59, 463–464
Self-esteem, 70, 464–474
community influences on, 473–474
criteria for, 468
development of, 466–468
enhancing in children, 471
family influences on, 468–470
gang members and, 329
mass media influences on, 472
moral development and, 513–514
peer influences on, 471–472
school influences on, 470–471
self-concept and, 34, 36, 464
Self-fulfilling prophecy, 449
Self-Perception Profile for Children, The (Harter), 468
Self-regulation, 39, 70–71, 150, 482–484
moral development and, 513
parenting styles and, 152–153
socialization and, 70–71
Seligman, Martin, 461
Sendak, Maurice, 373, 375, 448
Senescence, 39
Senior citizens, 408
Sensorimotor stage, 193
Sequential thinking, 231
Sesame Street (TV show), 365, 498
Seven Blind Mice (Young), 444
Seventeen magazine, 378
Sex, 72, 522
Sex education
peer groups and, 311–312
television and, 360
Sexism, 377
Sex segregation, 527
Sex typing, 522
Sexual abuse, 161–162
indicators of, 204
Sexual activity, 311–312
Seyle, Hans, 113
Shakespeare, William, 437, 480
Shaping, 54
Shepard, Mary, 172

Shy children, 291
Siblings
disabled children and, 146–147
gender-role socialization by, 526
socialization effects of, 147–148
Simple societies, 127
Single parents, 87–89
Single Shard, A (Park), 374
Situational factors, 512–513
Skeels, Harold, 182
Skeezer (Yates), 369
Skills emphasis
collective orientation and, 135–136
individualistic orientation and, 137–138
Skinner, B. F., 12, 71, 229, 250
Slow-to-warm-up children, 144
Small towns, 50, 401–402
Sociable-intimate behavior, 127–128
Social/behavioral socialization outcomes, 480–537
antisocial behavior, 484, 485–494
gender roles, 72, 522–534
morals, 71–72, 504–522
prosocial behavior, 484–485, 494–504
readings related to, 537
self-regulation, 70–71, 482–484
summary of, 534–536
Social classes
descriptions of, 103–104
U.S. percentages of, 103
See also Socioeconomic status
Social cognition, 299
Social cognitive theory, 71
of aggression, 488–491
of gender-role development, 523
Social competence, 297
Social control, 402
Social development
child care and, 184
peer groups and, 297–298
Social goals, 213
Social interactional theories of altruism, 499–500
Social interactions
communities and, 401–402
families and, 44
moral development and, 514
peer groups and, 291–294
temperament and, 43
Socialization, 3, 12, 32–75
agents of, 42–51
aims of, 34–42
child care programs and, 48, 191–199
child development and, 3–8
communities and, 50–51, 394–402
disabled people and, 225–226
ecological context for, 14–19
ethnic orientation and, 108–111

families and, 44–47, 82, 84, 96
input and output of, 12–13
intentional, 7, 13
mass media and, 49–50, 344, 363–366, 372–374
methods of, 52–69
outcomes of, 42, 69–72, 436–537
peer groups and, 48–49, 291–306
process of, 42
religion and, 111–113
schools and, 47–48, 212–213
societal change and, 8–10
socioeconomic status and, 105–107
teachers and, 250–252, 279–282
temperament and, 5–6, 43
unintentional, 7–8
Socialization agents, 42–51
    child care, 48
    community, 50–51
    families, 44–47
    mass media, 49–50
    peers, 48–49
    schools, 47–48
Socialization methods
    affective methods, 52–54
    apprenticeship methods, 68–69
    cognitive methods, 61–64
    observational methods, 60–61
    operant methods, 54–60
    sociocultural methods, 64–68
Socialization outcomes, 42, 69–72
Social learning theory, 523
Social roles, 40
    families and, 82, 84, 96–98
    individualism/collectivism and, 262–263
    peer groups and, 309–312
    See also Gender roles
Social Security Act (1935), 409
Social Security benefits, 414
Social Services Block Grant, 419
Social skills, 324–325
Social space, 28
Social support, 51
    communities and, 404–412
    families and, 80–81
    peer groups and, 312–313
Societal change
    consequences of, 26–28
    contemporary trends and, 23–26
    educational reform and, 229–230
    parenting methods and, 138–141
    socialization and, 8–10
Societal trends, 23–26
Sociocentrism, 63
Sociocultural roles, 309–312
Sociocultural socialization methods, 64–68
    group pressure, 65–66

rituals and routines, 67–68
    symbols, 68
    tradition, 66–67
Sociocultural stressors, 113
Socioeconomic status
    ascribed vs. achieved, 101–102
    class descriptions and, 103–104
    communities and, 51, 398–399
    families and, 44, 101–108
    gang formation and, 329
    parenting and, 129–131
    professionals and, 108
    socialization and, 105–107
    teen sexual activity and, 312
Sociometry, 323
Sociopolitical changes, 114
Sociotherapy, 323–325
Socrates, 250
Socratic method, 250
Solitary play, 314
Sophocles, 249
Sound media, 379–382
Spatial intelligence, 266
Special education, 225–226, 227
Spitz, Ellen, 372
Spitz, Rene, 181–182
Spock, Benjamin, 140–141
Sports, 333–334, 528
Standardized tests, 285
Standards, 62–63, 117
Stepfamilies, 91–93
Stepfamily Association of America, 91
Stereotypes, 360, 443
    books and, 376–378
    television and, 360–361
Stine, R. L., 375
Story of Ferdinand, The (Leaf), 448
Story of Little Black Sambo, The (Bannerman), 448
Strange Situation experiment, 152
Stratemeyer, Edward, 375
Stress, 113
    families and, 113–114, 117
    parenting quality and, 149–150
Submissive attitude, 46
Substance use/abuse
    adolescent behavior and, 142–143
    alcoholism and, 273–275
    drug testing and, 235
    prenatal exposure to, 273, 274
    schools and, 234–235
    teachers and, 272–275
Sullivan, Anne, 172
Superhero/heroine play, 316
Supplemental Security Income (SSI), 414
Supportive services, 407–410
    See also Social support

Survival instinct, 393
Survivor (TV show), 290
Swaggart, Jimmy, 481
Symbols, 68

T

Tabula rasa, 139
Teacher-directed education, 191, 197, 277, 278, 279
Teacher observation form, 268, 551–553
Teachers, 249–288
  at-risk children and, 270–276
  characteristics of, 252–257
  chronosystem influences on, 276–282
  classroom management by, 255
  cultural issues and, 258–263
  disabled children and, 266–270
  domestic violence issues and, 275–276
  educational accountability and, 282
  effectiveness of, 252
  ethnic issues and, 258–263
  expectations of, 255–257
  family involvement and, 271, 283–284
  gender issues and, 257–258
  impoverished children and, 271–272
  individualism/collectivism and, 261–263
  leadership styles of, 253–254
  learning styles and, 263–266
  macrosystem influences on, 276–282
  mesosystem influences on, 282–285
  moral development and, 518
  observation of behavior by, 267–268, 551–553
  parent partnerships with, 271
  philosophies of education and, 277–279
  readiness concept and, 285
  readings related to, 288
  socialization and, 250–252, 279–282
  student empowerment by, 283–285
  substance abuse issues and, 272–275
  summary of, 285–287
  See also Education; Schools
Team games tournament (TGT), 332
Team sports, 333–334, 528
Technology
  families and, 115
  schools and, 231–232, 236
  See also Computers
Technopoly: The Surrender of Culture to Technology (Postman), 383
Teenagers. *See* Adolescents
Television, 349–370
  academic achievement and, 363
  advertising on, 356–358, 359
  aggressive behavior and, 487
  altruistic behavior and, 498
  arousal theories and, 356

attitudes influenced by, 355–356, 447–448
community linkages to, 366–368
contemporary concerns about, 350–363
desensitization and, 356
family involvement and, 350–351, 365–366, 369–370
fantasy vs. reality on, 351–353
federal regulations and, 346–347
gender roles portrayed on, 530–531
imaginative play and, 353–354
intellectual development and, 362–363
mesosystem influences on, 366–370
moral behavior and, 518–519
music videos on, 381
observational learning and, 61, 355
parental mediation and, 365–366
pervasive influence of, 344
physical activity and, 351
portrayal of families on, 77
rating system for, 347–348
school linkages to, 368–369
selective attention and, 363–365
sexuality portrayed on, 360
socialization process and, 49–50, 363–366
stereotypes on, 360–361
values perpetuated through, 359–361
viewing patterns of children, 349
violence on, 354–356, 487, 518–519
See also Mass media; Movies
Temperament, 5
  characteristics of, 143
  interactions and, 43
  moral development and, 513
  parenting styles and, 143–145, 484
  self-regulation and, 484
  socialization and, 5–6, 43
Temporary Assistance for Needy Families (TANF), 104, 179, 409, 414
Testing play, 315
Textbooks. *See* Books
Thelma and Louise (film), 530
Thematic Apperception Test (TAT), 453–454
36 Children (Kohl), 254
Three Pigs, The (Weisner), 373
Time-out, 56
Time samples, 268
Title IX, Education Amendments Act (1972), 217, 529
Toddlers
  friendship patterns of, 319
  play activities of, 316–317
  social interactions of, 292–293
  See also Children; Infants
Toffler, Alvin, 25
Tonnies, Ferdinand, 132, 402
Tradition, 66–67
Traditional societies, 102
Transductive reasoning, 63

Travers, Pamela, 172
Trelease, Jim, 372
Trust vs. mistrust stage, 36
Turnbull, Ann, 146
Turnbull, H. Rutherford, 146
Tutoring, peer, 266, 267, 329–330
TV Guide, 344

U

Underclass families, 104
Unemployment, 398–399
Unemployment compensation, 414
Uniform Parentage Act, 87
Unintentional socialization, 7–8
Uninvolved parents, 151, 153, 159, 294, 296
Unmarried parents, 93–95
Upper-class families, 103–104, 106–107
Urban environments. *See* Cities
Utilitarian community, 390
Utopian community, 390

V

Values, 69, 359, 438–443
    decisions, consequences and, 441–443
    definition of, 69, 439
    ethnic orientation and, 110–111
    functional families and, 117
    governmental policies and, 442–443
    mass media and, 359–361
    parenting styles and, 442
    peer groups and, 307–309
    self-assessment of, 477–478
Values clarification, 441–442
V-chips, 347
Very Hungry Caterpillar, The (Carle), 373
Veterans' benefits, 414
Victimization, 303, 327–328
Videocassette recorders, 367–368
Video games, 384, 531
Violence, 232, 354
    domestic, 275–276
    preventing, 233–234
    school, 232–234, 236
    storybook, 376
    television, 354–356, 487, 518–519
    video game, 384

Virtual field trips, 232
Visual disabilities, 547–548
Vocational goals, 213
Vocational Rehabilitation Act (1973), 269–270
Voucher system, 216
Vygotskian theory, 71
Vygotsky, Lev, 71, 229, 254, 305–306, 314, 329, 483

W

Walden Two (Skinner), 12, 13
War Against Parents, The (Hewlett and West), 28
War on Poverty, 106, 219, 442
Watson, John B., 139–140
Weikart, David, 191
Weisner, David, 373
Welfare reforms, 179
West, Cornel, 28
Where the Wild Things Are (Sendak), 372–373, 375
White, Leslie, 68
White, Robert, 452
Whiting, Beatrice, 127, 532
Whiting, John, 127
Williams, Garth, 448
Winn, Marie, 350
Witch Must Die, The (Cashdan), 376
Woititz, Janet Geringer, 274
Wolf, Naomi, 472
Working mothers, 98–99
Works Progress Administration (WPA), 180
World Wide Web. *See* Internet

Y

Yates, Elizabeth, 369
Yearling, The (Rawlings), 379
Young, Ed, 444
Your Child's Self-esteem (Briggs), 466
Youth Build program, 107

Z

Ziferstein, Isidore, 359
Zigler, Edward, 188
Zion, Gene, 378
Zone of proximal development (ZPD), 254, 306, 329